Vernacular Knowledge

# Vernacular Knowledge
*Contesting Authority, Expressing Beliefs*

Edited by
Ülo Valk and Marion Bowman

SHEFFIELD UK   BRISTOL CT

Published by Equinox Publishing Ltd.
UK:   Office 415, The Workstation, 15 Paternoster Row, Sheffield,
      South Yorkshire S1 2BX
USA:  ISD, 70 Enterprise Drive, Bristol, CT 06010

www.equinoxpub.com

First published 2022
© Ülo Valk, Marion Bowman and contributors 2022

All rights reserved. No part of this publication may be reproduced or transmitted in any form or by any means, electronic or mechanical, including photocopying, recording or any information storage or retrieval system, without prior permission in writing from the publishers.

British Library Cataloguing-in-Publication Data
A catalogue record for this book is available from the British Library.

ISBN-13  978 1 78179 236 0   (hardback)
         978 1 78179 237 7   (paperback)
         978 1 80050 214 7   (ePDF)
         978 1 80050 254 3   (ePub)

Library of Congress Cataloging-in-Publication Data
Names: Valk, Ülo, 1962- editor. | Bowman, Marion, 1955- editor.
Title: Vernacular knowledge : contesting authority, expressing beliefs / edited by Ülo Valk and Marion Bowman.
Description: Sheffield, South Yorkshire ; Bristol, CT : Equinox Publishing Ltd, 2022. | Includes bibliographical references and index. | Summary: "This volume presents vernacular knowledge as a realm of discourses and beliefs that challenge institutional authorities and official truths"-- Provided by publisher.
Identifiers: LCCN 2022008392 (print) | LCCN 2022008393 (ebook) | ISBN 9781781792360 (hardback) | ISBN 9781781792377 (paperback) | ISBN 9781800502147 (epdf) | ISBN 9781800502543 (epub)
Subjects: LCSH: Knowledge, Theory of. | Authority. | Belief and doubt.
Classification: LCC BD161 .V47 2022 (print) | LCC BD161 (ebook) | DDC 121--dc23/eng/20220801
LC record available at https://lccn.loc.gov/2022008392
LC ebook record available at https://lccn.loc.gov/2022008393

Typeset by S.J.I. Services, New Delhi, India

This volume is dedicated to our dear friend and extraordinary scholar,
Leonard Norman Primiano (1957–2021)

*Photograph courtesy of Dawnielle Marie Phil*

# Contents

Acknowledgements ix

An Introduction to Vernacular Knowledge 1
*Ülo Valk*

**Part 1: Politics and Vernacular Strategies of Resistance**

1 In Quest of Lost Heritage, Ethnic Identity, and Democracy:
The Belarusian Case 25
*Anastasiya Astapova*

2 Humour and Resistance in Russia's Ecological Utopia:
A Look at the Anastasia Movement 47
*Irina Sadovina*

3 Visual Media and the Reconfiguration of Divinity in
Moldovan Radical Religion 70
*James A. Kapaló*

**Part 2: Narrating and Creating the Past**

4 Blessings beyond Time and Place: The Fluid Nature of
Narrative Tradition in Contemporary Hinduism 101
*Martin Wood*

5 Truth, Variation and the Legendry: The Case of Saint
Madhavadeva's Birthplace in Assam 117
*Ülo Valk*

6 Unearthing the Narratives of the Róngkups of Sikkim:
From Vernacular Alternatives to Institutionalized Beliefs 140
*Reep Pandi Lepcha*

**Part 3: Renegotiating Tradition and Authority**

7 When a Cosmic Shift Fails: The Power of Vernacular
Authority in a New Age Internet Forum 165
*Robert Glenn Howard*

| 8 | Making Sense: The Body as a Medium to Supernatural Reality<br>*Kristel Kivari* | 189 |
|---|---|---|
| 9 | Seeking as a Late Modern Tradition: Three Vernacular Biographies<br>*Steven J. Sutcliffe* | 214 |
| 10 | Practices of *Niggunim*: Contemporary Jewish Song in a Vernacular Religion Perspective<br>*Ruth Illman* | 237 |

## Part 4: Vernacular Knowledge and Christianity

| 11 | Feminist Folk, Christian Folk and Black Madonnas<br>*Melanie Landman* | 263 |
|---|---|---|
| 12 | Negotiating Vernacular Authority, Legitimacy and Power: Creativity, Ambiguity and Materiality in Devotion to Gauchito Gil<br>*Marion Bowman* | 284 |
| 13 | The Upper Room: Domestic Space, Vernacular Religion, and the Observant University Catholic<br>*Leonard Norman Primiano* | 309 |

## Part 5: Afterlife and Afterdeath

| 14 | Dealing with the Dead: Vernacular Belief Negotiations among the Khasi of Northeastern India<br>*Margaret Lyngdoh* | 339 |
|---|---|---|
| 15 | An Immured Soul: Contested Ritual Traditions and Demonological Narratives in Contemporary Mongolia<br>*Alevtina Solovyeva* | 361 |
| 16 | Ghosts in Belief, Practice and Metaphor<br>*Paul Cowdell* | 385 |
|  | Afterword: 25 Years of Vernacular Religion Scholarship<br>*Marion Bowman* | 405 |
|  | Index | 419 |

# Acknowledgements

The editors of this volume thank the authors for their valuable contributions, and for their patience and cooperation during the editorial process. We are greatly indebted to Helen Kästik for her commitment, professionalism and continuous optimism in the final, most challenging phase of editing the book. Likewise, we thank Daniel E. Allen for his careful work on the English language editing. We also acknowledge, and express our gratitude for, the forbearance of our spouses, Maarja and Leslie, during this process.

Numerous colleagues and friends over recent years have been involved in discussions related or leading to the content of this volume, provided useful references, and given feedback on particular articles; we thank everybody who has had a positive impact on the process.

We are also grateful to Janet Joyce and Valerie Hall at Equinox for their patience, support and friendly consent in accepting a manuscript which in some respects looks rather different from the one that we initially envisioned, and to Sarah Norman for her meticulous editorial work.

Finally, we acknowledge the supportive role of the University of Tartu in bringing this project to fruition, and the financial support of the Estonian Research Council (grant projects IUT2-43 and PRG670) and of the EEA Financial Mechanism 2014–2021 Baltic Research Program in Estonia (grant project EMP340).

# An Introduction to Vernacular Knowledge

*Ülo Valk**

Knowledge, belief and authority are entangled concepts that all imply human agency. Knowledge belongs to somebody, to individuals, groups or institutions, and empowers them with authority and the skills necessary for action. Authority indicates the power to judge what qualifies as valid knowledge and both to control and exercise it. Belief implies trust in that which upholds knowledge and authority; it shapes values, standpoints and worldviews. Understanding social realities can hardly be possible without considering power relations between individuals and communities and the mechanisms of maintaining hierarchies and order, which are often sanctioned not only by law and traditions but also by religious institutions.

Don Yoder distinguished between 'high' or 'official' religion and folk religion and claimed that they co-exist in tension with each other. His discussion of the 'religious dimension of folk-culture' (Yoder 1974: 11, 14) was a step away from former studies that trivialized folk beliefs as superstitions and considered them obsolete 'survivals' in the age of modernity. Today we bear witness to the fact that folk beliefs have not disappeared; instead they thrive in multiple forms and circulate both in old and new channels of communication, including social media. Whereas Bruno Latour (1993) showed that in spite of all its advancements in sciences the Western world has never become modern, Jason Ā. Josephson-Storm

---

* **Ülo Valk** is Professor of Estonian and Comparative Folklore at the University of Tartu. His publications include the monograph *The Black Gentleman: Manifestations of the Devil in Estonian Folk Religion* (Academia Scientiarum Fennica, 2001), *Vernacular Religion in Everyday Life: Expressions of Belief* (co-edited with Marion Bowman; Equinox, 2012), and *Storied and Supernatural Places: Studies in Spatial and Social Dimensions of Folklore and Sagas* (co-edited with Daniel Sävborg; Finnish Literature Society, 2018). He is the editor of *Numen: International Review for the History of Religions* (Brill).

in his *Myth of Disenchantment* (2017) has shown that we have never become disenchanted, because magic, divination and the supernatural have not faded away but appear in new contexts. The grand project of the Enlightenment that has been implemented for centuries has only had a limited effect. Vernacular beliefs and related practices abound today even in the most secular societies and appear both in religious and non-religious contexts. Leonard N. Primiano (1995), who advocated 'vernacular religion' as a paradigm and a new methodology, aimed at a more comprehensive understanding of religion, not narrowing down its domain but considering a new perspective, that of (all) religious people and their experiences. As vernacular religion is not a dialectic counterpart of some other concept, such as 'official' or 'institutional' religion, it is less straightforward than 'folk religion' and carries ambiguity and even conflicting meanings. As Primiano (2012: 387) notes, 'vernacular religiosity has the potential to manifest dimensions of both confirmation and contestation, of legitimization of the hegemonic as well as resistance to such societal and cultural manifestations of power'. Vernacular does not refer to a definite kind of religious act or a univocal expression but to relationality and openness to other lived forms of expression, knowledge and authority.

Vernacular has become one of the key words in contemporary folkloristics and a useful tool in studying several areas of culture, such as narrative and local knowledge (see Goldstein 2015). Vernacular religion as a concept and method also emerged within the disciplinary frames of folklore studies, where beliefs have been documented, studied and theorized for centuries (see Anttonen 2004; Bowman and Valk 2012; Magliocco 2012; Mullen 2000). There is a long path from collecting superstitions as weird reminiscences or survivals from the past or expressions of mental backwardness to conceptualizing belief as an integral part of human life. Beliefs today are seen not so much as building blocks of worldviews; rather, when we talk about belief we refer to the ties, connections and correlations that keep the worldview together and position us in the related world. Similar semantic changes have occurred in thinking about folklore. In the early phase of the discipline it was conceptualized as a set of oral artefacts and cultural survivals of social and ethnic Others, such as the uneducated peasantry in Europe or the uncivilized peoples in remote corners of colonial empires. Today folklore is theorized as a realm of culture that involves active individual participation and creative expressivity that tends to elude institutional control. Folklore can be distinguished from professional and elite culture, as it is informal, embedded in traditions and transmitted by unofficial means (McNeill 2013: 1-19). Folklore remains 'outside authorship' and can hardly be regulated by intellectual property legislation (Hafstein 2014). It can barely be singled out or compartmentalized as it appears 'in myriad forms and interactions'—expressed both by individuals and their communities (Blank 2014: 13). Simon Bronner has defined folklore as *'traditional knowledge, put into, and drawing from, practice'* (Bronner 2017: 46, italics in original). Hence, there is an obvious discrepancy between the common meaning of folklore in vernacular and academic discourses. Popular usage of the word often implies something trivial and senseless, clearly distinct from prestigious forms of culture and legitimate forms of knowledge. Folklore can also refer to something antiquated, dusty and outmoded but maintained as heritage, echoing scholarly views from the past and certain ideologies, such as romantic nationalism, which applied folklore for certain political purposes. In contemporary scholarship, folklore rather indicates the personal dimension of culture—as a part of the everyday life of each and every human being. Rather than being simply reproductive, folklore is formative, producing worldviews, preparing our positions in social interaction and preferences in the multi-dimensional realm of media, both off- and online. Instead of taking persistent forms, folklore is often ephemeral as it emerges in direct response to recent events, the breaking news of the day, acute social issues and political tensions. Even though its roots are in the past, folklore points to the future where its effects and uses become visible. The expressive, outward orientation of folklore indicates its constant movement from the level of individuals and small groups towards shared, communal culture, from intimate and local towards regional and global. On the other hand, the global also has echoes, and becomes personalized as it is emotionally and mentally processed by individuals involved in the co-production of folklore as an inherently human enterprise. It also empowers us with knowledge and confidence as we recognize ourselves as members of groups, communities and networks that share certain values, attitudes and beliefs, and dissent from others. As a tool of building identities and relationships, folklore is related to social differentiation, contradistinctions, oppositions and conflict zones (see Bauman 1972; Briggs 2012). It is an arena for voicing different opinions and disagreements, but also for echoing outspoken views and sentiments—all these discursive practices that distinguish social actors, setting them apart. As Dorothy Noyes (2016: 327-328) notes, 'folk' as a sociocultural category carries 'a heavy evaluative charge, positive or negative depending on the user's position', and contrastive significance, implying an Other or Others. Hence, in order to understand folklore, we have to consider the surrounding social space and the power relations that folklore always involves.

Power is one of those instrumental words, the usage of which extends from vernacular to analytic, scientific and philosophical discourses. We can talk about sacred locations in the landscape as places of power, but also of power as a category in physics, power of will and mind, and power as social rule and dominance. Power can be invisible, but infuses both material and intangible worlds in a complex web of relationships, shaping social realities in a world that is in constant making. It is filled with actors with different socio-ontological statuses, such as living humans—both powerful and powerless—but also the dead, deities and spirits, as close kin to humans; animals, birds, fish and insects; stones, trees and other plants; man-made and imaginary objects, such as books, works of art or technological equipment. All these human and other-than-human entities are in interaction and co-exist in the entangled realm of connections, co-forming the social 'not as a special domain, a specific realm, or a particular sort of thing, but only as a very peculiar movement of re-association and reassembling', as Latour (2005: 7) characterized it. This constantly emergent social world comes into being through the never-ending cognitive work that we are involved in as individuals and social beings. Cognitive modalities, such as belief, disbelief, doubt, imagination and knowledge, help us to orient ourselves and take stands in this world in the making.

## Vernacular Knowledge and Belief

In his influential book *Belief, Language, and Experience* (1972) Rodney Needham called for jettisoning belief as an analytical category in anthropology and the study of religion because of the methodological troubles involved. He argued that discerning belief as an inner state of mind is not possible and the meaning of the word in English is ambiguous. Another problem of belief lies in its association with knowledge. The two have often been juxtaposed as a pair of binary oppositions, accrediting knowledge as a source of authority and discrediting belief as counter-factual and therefore inferior—as a delusion or ignorance. According to Byron Good (1994: 20), belief as an analytic category in anthropology carries negative connotations, which refer to the 'so-called folk sciences' and 'cultural accounts either of the unknowable or of mistaken understandings of the "natural world"'. He concludes that (ibid.: 21):

> it was fateful for anthropology when belief emerged as a central category for the analysis of culture. This formation of anthropological discourse was linked to the philosophical climate within which anthropology emerged, a climate in which empiricist theories and sharp conflicts between the natural sciences and religion were prominent.

Benjamin Gatling (2020: 309) has criticized the usage of belief as a reified idea that is abstracted from social action and is erroneously considered as explanation for behaviour. Belief as an analytic category has its roots in Christianity, in particular in the Protestant tradition with its emphasis on the individual relationship with God. Approaching other religious traditions, where practices and rituals prevail, through the concept of belief can be misleading. However, in spite of serious criticism of the analytic value of belief from different angles, it has remained a valid and useful category in the study of religion and anthropology (see Bae 2016; 2017; Bivins 2016; Blum 2020; Lindholm 2012, etc.). As a concept and a word it extends from scholarship to vernacular discourses and instead of becoming a technical term, it has remarkable flexibility and semantic range. In vernacular epistemology belief can indicate faith in God and attachment to certain values, but it can also refer to opinions and sentiments regarding everyday life. Ethan H. Shagan, who has studied the history of belief in Western culture, has defined modern belief as 'private judgement' and hence, modernity has not brought the decline of belief but rather its 'boundless proliferation' (2018: 6, 29). Because of the idiosyncrasy, differentiation and multiplicity involved in believing and in belief, it is grounded to use the word not only in the singular but also in plural.

In the current volume the concept of belief is not loaded with the semantic burden of the Enlightenment that questions its truthfulness. Rather, following the traditions of Western epistemology we see knowledge and belief as related concepts, considering knowledge as an 'epistemically rational belief' or 'justified belief' (Foley 2014: 37). However, the strategies of justification of beliefs—the 'epistemic folkways' (Goldman 2000) or 'emic epistemologies' (Hammer 2004)—are different from philosophical epistemology and knowledge production in the sciences. The goal of this volume is not to assess vernacular knowledge as regards its veracity or inaccuracy, rationality or irrationality, but to offer a set of case studies that highlight how vernacular knowledge is made, what techniques are involved, how it is related to vernacular religion and how it might interact/intersect with institutionally approved truths. According to Fredrik Barth, the fruitful approach in studying the varieties of human knowledge is not to 'dismiss most of them for faulty method' but to ask 'how these varieties are variously produced, represented, transmitted and applied' (2002: 10). This kind of affirmative research agenda enables one to see vernacular knowledge as a ground for successful social action, maintaining traditions, constructing identities, building ties between individuals and groups, and ascertaining shared values and beliefs.

Whereas 'belief' has often been scientifically discredited because it implies religious ontologies and existence of the supernatural, in the present book 'belief' has even broader meaning, as it encompasses secular viewpoints and mundane assumptions. This kind of extended understanding correlates to the work of André Droogers, who has theorized the concept of worldview, 'as a human capacity to raise and answer life's ultimate questions' and involving 'the variety of answers given, in religions, secular worldviews, ideologies and spiritualities' (2014: 23). Following the work of Ninian Smart, Droogers prefers 'worldview' as a general category to other notions, such as 'religion' or 'ideology', because it brings together the secular and the religious and highlights the similarities between these outlooks. The current book seeks to overcome the dichotomy between religious and non-religious meaning-making, as implied in the terms belief and knowledge. Yet we assume that it is analytically useful to distinguish different kinds of knowledge, such as vernacular, religious and scientific knowledge—all grounded in some kind of belief. According to Linda Zagzebski (2014: 400) the distinctive trait of religious knowledge is that it depends 'heavily on trust in authorities and exemplars of wisdom', and yet in other ways it 'is just like any other knowledge'. As regards scientific knowledge, Paul Hoyningen-Huene (2016: 14), a philosopher of science, claims that it 'differs from other kinds of knowledge, in particular from everyday knowledge, primarily by being more systematic'. Everyday knowledge appears as 'much more unordered, less disciplined, less circumspect, or, in a word, less systematic' (ibid.: 71). Hoyningen-Huene (ibid.: 61) also writes about assumptions that we rely on in everyday life as certain kinds of vernacular theory:

> As their scientific counterparts, these theories are hypothetical, and often involve unobservable entities in order to explain the course of events ... These [non-scientific] theories include religious and pseudo-religious convictions (whatever their precise difference) as well as

superstition of all sorts and conspiracy theories. Whatever the cognitive or existential merits or other of these theories are, they certainly differ from the sort of theories discussed above [i.e. scientific theories] by their looseness. Their explanations are often vague, sketchy, certainly not quantitative, and stand more often than not on dubious epistemic grounds. In a word, they are much less systematic than the theoretical explanations supplied by various sciences.

In the above discussion it is important to note that the difference between the two forms of knowledge and theorizing is far from being absolute; rather the distinction lies in the scope and measure of creating order. The strategies of argumentation, representation and transmission of knowledge are different, but knowledge production is an inherent part of everyday life, not confined to scientific discourses and educational institutions. The 'looseness' and lack of systematicity can also be interpreted as signs of the flexibility, adaptability and resilience of vernacular knowledge.

Nowadays, where sciences have gained prestige and authority, the two forms of knowledge are strongly interrelated. Claiming scientific justification and verifiability of beliefs and practices is a strategy in many religions today ranging from Christianity, Judaism and Islam to Hinduism, Buddhism, Spiritism, Scientology, Transcendental Meditation and other traditions (see Lewis and Hammer 2011). Reliance on scientific methods, terminology and theories also appears in the validation of vernacular beliefs (see Kitta 2019: 50; Valk 2011). On the other hand, vernacular beliefs and theories are a useful target to fortify the legitimate status of sciences in society. Fighting and debunking pseudo-scientific phenomena and defending the monopoly of scientific truth in public media is currently the mission of sceptical activists (Uibu 2012). The entanglement of vernacular and institutional forms of knowledge is a topic that is addressed by many scholars. Clare Birchall (2006: 21–22), who has studied conspiracy theories and gossip, writes about 'popular knowledge' as a discursive form of popular culture that does not require specialist training and retains 'an ambivalent relationship to more legitimated ways of knowing'. The concept of popular knowledge in her work derives from Michel Foucault, who characterized it as subjugated, disqualified as inadequate to its task or insufficiently elaborated: naïve, located low down on the hierarchy. In contrast to the institutionally grounded, organized scientific discourse, Foucault (1980: 82) described it as 'particular, local, regional knowledge, a differential knowledge incapable of unanimity'. Tim Ingold too has portrayed traditional knowledge as something lived, localized, and related to places. As he wrote, knowledgeability consists in the capacity to situate information, to 'understand its meaning, within the context of a direct perceptual engagement with our environments' (Ingold 2000: 21). In this changing world, for many of us today the primary environment is not the natural setting or home-bound social surroundings but the digital world. Andrew Peck has studied the memetic culture on the internet and found that if memes are appropriated by institutions, these uses are often challenged and confronted by vernacular expressivity. In the context of folkloric creativity on the internet, Peck (2020: 98–101) writes about the performances of 'vernacular knowledge'.

In the discussion above we have noted a variety of terms to denote the kinds of knowledge that exist alongside its legitimate institutional forms, such as scientific and religious knowledge. Different scholars have written about 'folk sciences', 'subjugated knowledge', 'everyday knowledge', 'traditional knowledge', 'subaltern knowledge, 'popular knowledge', 'local knowledge' and 'vernacular knowledge'. Why do we prefer the vernacular? The concept proceeds from 'vernacular religion' and blends into the related methodological and theoretical discussions both in folkloristics (e.g. Goldstein 2015; Goldstein and Shuman 2016; Howard 2011, 2013; Mullins 2019) and the study of religion (e.g. Bowman 2014; Illman and Czimbalmos 2020). Vernacular knowledge wipes out the dichotomy between secular and religious, extends the religious connotations of belief and covers its secular forms, which equally shape our understanding of reality. In addition, the notion of vernacular is strongly associated with the institutional as its alternative counterpart, referring to social establishments related to power (see Howard 2011), an aspect that is essential in research. This juxtaposition and entanglement of the two discourses and perspectives—acquisition of authority by contesting and relocating it—appears central in vernacular discourses, including debates and argumentation on the internet. Robert Glenn Howard has theorized these disputes and discussions as expressions of vernacular authority. He writes,

> vernacular authority emerges when an individual makes appeals that rely on trust specifically because they are not institutional. Trust is justified by the assertion because the claim does not rely on any authority arising from formally instituted social formations like a church, a newspaper company, or an academic journal. (Howard 2013: 81)

Likewise, vernacular knowledge is in dialogue with the institutional, which does not mean that it is inferior, subdued and marginalized—a kind of 'little tradition' in opposition to the 'great tradition' of institutionally controlled culture (cf. Redfield 1955). Any efforts to subjugate it by the institutional expressions of knowledge lead to its empowerment, which is mainly due to the flexibility and resilience of the vernacular to use multiple conduits and take new forms that cannot eventually be controlled by institutional powers. As its main medium is language, not in official, authorized or literarily refined forms, but vernacular language, it eludes regulation and supervision.

Vernacular knowledge is not a systematic and consistent doctrine but rather an expressive strategy and its never-finalized product, which appears in manifold forms, both verbal and non-verbal. It can be expressed in oral, written and printed genres but also acted out in visual art, symbols, music, rituals and behaviour. It can be finalized in writing or works of art but more often it occurs in private and public interaction. Communication partners can be members of small communities, although today this exchange has extended to the World Wide Web and engaged global networks. Vernacular knowledge is in perpetual fluctuation, remaking and variation. It is 'incipient' (see Bronner 2018), constantly taking new forms that oscillate from informal communication to the channels of institutionally controlled media. Among recent examples are the boom in fake news (Mould 2018), rumours about surveillance (Astapova 2017), conspiracy theories (cf. Astapova, Bergmann et al. 2021; Astapova, Pintilescu et al. 2021; Dyrendal, Robertson and Asprem 2018); Internet memes and YouTube videos. While being informational, vernacular knowledge can be serious or even cautionary, but it also takes humorous, ironic and playful modes (see Birchall 2006: 23). Without aiming at unity and coherence, it can be inconsistent, controversial and fragmentary. Its argumentation tends to be bolstered with factuality and personal experience narratives. Yet, even if 'true stories' are perceived as narratives from the traditional folk repertoire, it does not mean that they lose their veracity—quite the contrary. Certain traditional genres, such as legends, carry strong epistemic weight, even if they contradict rationality and factual evidence. The storyrealm can be conceptualized both as domain of imagination and as socio-physical reality—the tangible world of live experience. Vernacular knowledge does not limit reality by fixing it within definite frames but leaves its existential horizons open. Tanya M. Luhrmann in her work on ritual magic in England has characterized its techniques through the power of rhetoric, which is imaginative, ambiguous and fiction-laden. A magician acquires a state of knowledge that 'is not committed to an ordinary truth-status assertion about its claims, and understands the crucial terms through experiential involvement, not clear definition' (Luhrmann 1989: 219). The oscillation of genre boundaries between factuality and fiction evokes a specific kind of outlook as the supernatural becomes plausible, even conceivable, and yet its presence is not unquestionably certain, depending on the point of view. As the supernatural world is co-produced by belief and disbelief as two complementary vernacular modalities its ontological status is liminal. The realm of spirits, ghosts, magic and extra-terrestrial powers keeps haunting modernity and the scientific worldview as its problematic Other, which abounds with 'accounts of extraordinary and mystical experiences and alternative, sometimes subversive truth claims' (Jöhncke and Steffen 2015: 10). Whereas religious or scientific knowledge can hardly accommodate this lore without discrediting and dispelling it as a residual 'fantasy', vernacular knowledge can easily accommodate it, even though its status between the storyrealm, psychological and physical reality remains uncertain. Belief does not suspend or exclude knowledge, but validates it, and 'we can examine the process of believing as a way of knowing' (Motz 1998: 340).

## Findings and Conclusions of this Volume

Whereas producing scientific knowledge relies on rigorous methods and verified factual evidence, vernacular knowledge is a domain of liberty and disagreement. It often goes far beyond the scientific episteme, contradicts and questions it, and undermines institutional authority. Vernacular beliefs, rumours and narratives can thus become a political force of resistance, eroding the position of those who hold the power and institutional control. Part 1 of the book begins with **Anastasiya Astapova**'s chapter on political folklore in contemporary Belarus. Astapova has studied beliefs about relics of great cultural value such as the book manuscript by the twentieth-century writer Uladzimir Karatkevich and the holy cross made in 1161 on the order of Saint Euphrosyne. According to rumours, Karatkevich's work was stolen by the KGB and is still in their archives, and the sacred cross might have been taken by the Moscow secret services during World War II. Such narratives function as powerful tools in the struggle for democracy and the consolidation of national identity in a Belarus that is distinguishing itself from Russia. Yet, as Astapova shows, the legends involved do not conflict directly with the political order but are entangled with official discourses, manifesting 'a vernacular blend of various patterns of reasoning'. **Irina Sadovina** in her chapter on the

Anastasia movement—a countercultural movement of ecological spirituality in contemporary Russia—examines vernacular responses to its doctrinal foundations. The movement relies on the books of Vladimir Megre, although the reception of these writings among community members often takes humorous forms, such as jokes and parodies. It appears that committed Anastasia followers and other spiritual seekers often apply humour, both critically and self-reflexively, as they negotiate their positions within the communities and embrace spiritual truths. **James A. Kapaló** in his chapter has studied Inochentism and Archangelism, religious movements in Moldova that resisted political oppression, formed secretive underground networks, and were persecuted both by Romanian and Soviet authorities. Kapaló has examined the power of visual media and the related narrative traditions in contesting dominant religious doctrines, the Orthodox Church and the state. Inochentists creatively used photomontage techniques and mass-produced photo icons that transgressed the ideas of Orthodox sainthood and iconographical models. Religious life in Moldovan villages emerges as a realm of hidden resistance and vernacular creativity that is rooted in Orthodoxy while confronting its institutions.

Part 2 of the book addresses belief narrative traditions in South Asia. **Martin Wood** has studied the hagiography of the Gujarati Hindu saint Jalaram Bapa, who passed away in 1881. However, he still appears in contemporary stories of healings and other miracles where he actively intervenes in the lives of his followers. In addition to oral storytelling, Jalaram Bapa continues his saintly afterlife in multiple forms, such as book, film, theatre, devotional singing and ritual practice. As new additions are made to the hagiography, the chain of memory about him appears fluid. However, the life story of the saint is also a contested realm because of disagreements among the devotees and religious authorities. **Ülo Valk** has studied another case of contestation regarding Madhavadeva, a neo-Vaishnava saint who lived in the sixteenth century and has become one of the cultural icons of Assam. His birthplace remained unknown until it was miraculously discovered in the twentieth century due to some supernatural events and dreams. Soon, two competing shrines emerged within a short distance of each other, sustained by different religious institutions that are competing for the status of true birthplace of the saint. Both shrines are surrounded by narrative cycles of oral history and supernatural legends that share common motifs and provide evidence in relation to the dispute. The chapter concludes with a discussion on folkloric storytelling in its double function of being a mechanism for producing truth and epistemological uncertainty. **Reep Pandi Lepcha**'s chapter takes the reader into the state of Sikkim in the eastern Himalayas, highlighting the narrative traditions among the Róngkups, the indigenous people of the region. Several cycles of oral narratives reflect their mythic history and its turning points, such as the Róngkups' encounter with Buddhism as a new faith. Narratives also discuss relationships with other ethnic communities, such as the Bhutia, who formed the social elite of the country. The chapter shows that whereas shared stories can be powerful tools in building social and ethnic identity, they can also be used as instruments of power in holding institutional control and shaping socio-political realities.

Part 3 of the book starts with **Robert Glenn Howard**'s chapter on New Age folk beliefs as they are discussed on the internet in webs of vernacular communication that bring like-minded people together. Howard has used computational methods to map an online forum focusing on the prophecy about 'cosmic shift', related to the fears of the Mayan calendar ending on December 21, 2012. He has studied how digital networks amplify the vernacular authority that everyday communication holds in resisting institutional dominance. **Kristel Kivari** has participated in the work of the Estonian Geopathic Association and explored dowsing practices, where the human body becomes the instrument of clairvoyance. Dowsing manifests non-verbal vernacular knowledge, based on intuitive feeling and sensing of places, as the natural and supernatural worlds are woven together. In these practices beliefs do not form articulated and coherent systems but are 'echoed and articulated in actions, decisions, and the web of verbal hints and accounts'. **Steven J. Sutcliffe** in his chapter offers a comprehensive discussion of seekership as a strategy of narrativization of one's life, which is recognized as one of the core practices of New Spirituality. He finds the roots of seekership deep in culture and thinking, appearing already in the quest in fairytales. According to Vladimir Propp's structural model, these narratives begin with an initial state of 'lack', leading finally to a positive outcome. Sutcliffe conceptualizes late modern seekership as 'a practical response to symbolic "lack"'. He has examined three vernacular seekership narratives from post-war biographies and shows that they appear as variations on a shared repertoire of thought and behaviour, and as guidebooks for learning the seeker's role. **Ruth Illman** has done fieldwork in London to study contemporary Jewish spirituality, expressed in the mystical practices of *niggunim*, generally wordless singing stemming from the religious traditions of Hasidic Jews. She approaches the problem of 'authenticity' from the perspective of practitioners but also as seen by some scholars, who question the continuity of *niggunim* and see it as commodification of heritage and vulgarization of the original chanting, the goal of which was to elevate the soul to God. Illman draws attention to the vernacular understanding of authenticity as 'a shared search for meaning and community, rather than a historically essential or purely individual existential striving'. Thus, in *niggunim* the source of authenticity is not the 'correct' practice but the communal experience of singing and bodily sensations of knowledge being mediated to mind and heart.

Part 4 of the book addresses vernacular Christianity and its current reinterpretations. **Melanie Landman** in her chapter discusses the image of the black Madonna in feminist spirituality, where she appears as a figure of sexual, political and spiritual liberation from the repressive patriarchal power of the Church. The chapter examines the creative strategies of the feminist and Christian 'folk' in developing the interpretations of black Madonnas, and in bringing together strands and elements of religious practices, such as pilgrimages, devotions, private and public rituals, production of written texts, websites and art. Based on her fieldwork in an Anglican black Madonna shrine, Landman highlights the usefulness of vernacular religion as a lens in relation to how her Anglican informants processed and prioritized different sorts of historical knowledge, the significance of their personal experience, and their ability 'to act as their own religious authority yet at the same time being part of a wider congregation under the supervision of the Church of England'. **Marion Bowman**'s chapter focuses on the material culture relating to Gauchito Gil, an immensely popular but officially unrecognized devotional figure in Argentina. She explores the pragmatic role of devotional artefacts and items sold at his shrine, which bolster his status through linking him with other saints and sacred images, and argues that the operational strategies that appear to empower Gauchito Gil and enhance his status can be conceptualized as proximity, approximation and appropriation. As the devotion is rooted in the context of Argentine vernacular Catholicism, the chapter explores the complex vernacular negotiations of religious legitimacy, relationality and authority not simply as a contestation between the Church and the people, but within the Church amongst its own functionaries, thus further highlighting how oversimplistic the polarized paradigm of 'folk' versus 'official' religion can be. **Leonard Norman Primiano** begins his chapter with a reflective and analytical discussion of vernacular religion as a concept and methodology, and its difference from approaches that 'call attention to status differences between those individuals who practice religion *and* those individuals who administer religious institutions as well as practice it'. In his case study he has analysed the idiosyncratic and 'unicultural' religious life and residential space of an American university undergraduate. His dormitory room emerges as a unique and meaningful configuration of material culture, an artistic environment where the sacred and the secular co-exist as part of his culturally inflected Catholic lifeworld, in relation but in some respects in contrast to the social realities of everyday student life.

The final section of the book addresses the relationship between the living and the dead, and cultures of death in their diversity. **Margaret Lyngdoh**'s fieldwork has taken her to remote corners of northeastern India to study the religious life of the Khasi, one of the indigenous ethnic communities whose culture has never become a part of the Hinduized world. Lyngdoh has studied the afterlife beliefs and related death customs of different Khasi clans, which manifest considerable diversity. The impact of Christianity has affected the death culture of the Khasi but it has not eradicated the indigenous belief world. Resistance to the authoritarian doctrines of Christianity has kept the Khasi afterlife in a restless state of continuous transition. **Alevtina Solovyeva** has undertaken research on demonological beliefs, narratives and the related ritual practices in the rural settings of contemporary Mongolia. She has studied restless places, locations of persistent supernatural activity as part of local landscape mythology. Solovyeva shows that Mongolian society is going through a period of intense change, including re-traditionalization, westernization, rethinking of the Socialist past and globalization. These processes are also reflected in the afterlife beliefs and the repertoire of demonological narratives. In the final chapter **Paul Cowdell** sheds light on the discussions and disputes of ghost beliefs, ghostly experiences and the related terminology and its varieties in England today. His main focus is on interviews with the members of the Spiritualists' National Union (SNU) and their interpretations. Cowdell has also critically examined the metaphoric rhetoric of ghosts in hauntology as a current trend in the social sciences. He concludes that the metaphoric approach has 'led to disregarding the very people whose beliefs and practices we should be considering'. Such a call for the necessities of doing fieldwork, of generating new sources and reflecting upon the existing vernacular knowledge, instead of replacing it with theoretical discussions detached from live culture, expresses the ethos of the whole book.

## Authority, Tradition and Experience

Many chapters in this volume discuss vernacular beliefs, narratives, theories and practices that are socially and discursively marginalized and neglected in the existing scholarship. The term vernacular itself carries 'the possibility of stigma' (Goldstein and Shuman 2016: 4), which implies deprivation, subordination and inferiority. However, vernacular expressivity involves communicative powers and argumentative mechanisms that constantly erode the dominant and the authoritarian. By undermining the authority of the mainstream they advocate alternative positions and proclaim the primacy of vernacular knowledge. According to Richard Bauman (2004: 150), authorization—'the process of rendering discourse authoritative'—happens in communication. Authority is not an inherent textual quality, not something that is pre-given, but a product of mediational performances, involving the replication of a prior discourse. The mediator in this process takes a lower position if compared with the source of the text, which is attributed to somebody whose position excels 'on the basis of social rank, artistic skill, spiritual power, or political power' (ibid.: 151). Imbuing text with authority thus implies a discursive submission—'the subordination of present discourse to discourse that emanates from the past' (ibid.: 153). Authorization of vernacular knowledge relies on similar strategies of employing existing knowledge. The epistemic weight of arguments grows if they are not original and inventive but instead derive from a well-established discursive tradition that has been accepted as true. Building up vernacular knowledge is a process of crafting tradition, making it anonymous, and claiming objectivity—representing things as they are. Evoking this tradition can happen in the form of storytelling—circulating familiar narrative plots, sharing personal experiences that are framed with traditional interpretations, or references to factual evidence that confirm shared beliefs—as shown in several chapters in the current book. Vernacular knowledge is not autonomous but imbued with elements from institutional knowledge and yet contradistinguished from the latter, as its rival in competing for truth. As an alternative discourse it can challenge, confront and outweigh institutional doctrines by employing traditional genres such as legend and personal experience narrative, which shape worldviews with arguments that might not always be rational but are forcefully compelling, as they are bolstered with evidence that carries weight. Attempts by institutional authorities to eradicate vernacular knowledge can hardly succeed.

Instead, public attacks empower it with resilience and inspire the production of counter-evidence that supports alternative standpoints.

Finally, let us ask about the basic strategies of providing evidence for belief justification in the production of vernacular knowledge. As already noted, explicit or implicit references to traditional knowledge always work. In contrast to scientific knowledge, which aims at innovation, vernacular knowledge is not new; in contrast to religious knowledge it does not rely on scriptural and clerical authority. However, there is something salient in vernacular knowledge, which seemingly contradicts its appeal to tradition as the source of ultimate authority. Primiano has accentuated individual creativity as one of the distinctive features of vernacular religion, which he has outlined as 'the study of the religion of the individual inside and outside of religious institutions' (Primiano, this volume). Likewise, vernacular knowledge includes a strong element of subjectivity, as its authorization does not rely on tradition only, but depends heavily on somebody's personal experience. Eyewitnessing something, testifying to an event, going through a unique bodily or emotional experience, can become powerful arguments to verify existing beliefs and formulating 'narratives of experience' (Hammer 2004).

Whether it is a confrontation with demonic powers, acts of bewitchment or divination, encounter with aliens or angels, channelling divine wisdom, detecting surveillance, suffering from vaccination or radiation, witnessing miraculous healing, feelings of peace and tranquillity in sacred locations or feeling fear and terror in cursed places—all these experiences provide compelling evidence for something bigger than a single case. Each event testifies to the realness of former experiences and hidden aspects of the world. The witness can also be another individual whose testimony is shared in storytelling. There are multiple channels and modes of communication today to transmit experiences and accumulate them, building on the existing knowledge. In order to become an experienced individual, it is not enough to learn from one's own life but to learn from and incorporate the experience of others. Likewise, taking a critical stand towards experience narratives is part of the process, as multiple beliefs, doctrines and frames of interpretation co-exist. Personal experience is always assessed within the context of former experiences, shared interpretative frameworks, and traditional 'belief narratives'— diverse stories that address both mundane and supernatural topics and shape our perception of reality (see Valk 2021).

Knowledge does not grow from experiences; rather we need knowledge in order to explain what we perceive (see Scott 2012). These two complementary determinants—tradition and individual experience—form the basic tools and resources of knowing and orienting oneself in the world; they co-authorize vernacular knowledge and provide it with veracity. Experience produces evidence, and evidence is used in communicative practices to generate discursive authority (see Kuipers 2013). Building up and maintaining vernacular knowledge becomes possible in the close interaction of people—and in this process individual creativity merges with tradition. Whereas creativity can dominate in single acts of communication and in narrating subjective experiences, tradition as 'cultural reproduction' (Oring 2012) overshadows the individual element if we study vernacular knowledge as a historical process. The dynamic flow, heterogeneity and incongruity of the traditions of vernacular knowledge do not allow us to theorize it as something systematic or comprehensive. Let us remember the words of Hoyningen-Huene about its looseness and Primiano's emphasis on creativity in discussing the vernacular. Without forming a coherent discourse or a system of beliefs, vernacular knowledge is embodied in multiple disconnected and often contradictory discourses and practices. Vernacular knowledge cannot be studied on its own but can be approached through its formative manifestations—certain cases that cannot be detached from their communicative, social and historical contexts. Bearing these preliminary observations in mind, let us delve into the following chapters that represent and discuss the varieties of vernacular knowledge.

## Acknowledgements

I am grateful to Marion Bowman and to Leonard N. Primiano for many years of co-operation and friendship, for their pioneering work in the study of religion and folkloristics, and for countless inspiring conversations.

This article has been supported by the Estonian Research Council (grant project PRG670).

## References

Anttonen, Veikko. 2004. 'Theory and Method in the Study of "Folk Religion"'. *Temenos: Nordic Journal of Comparative Religion* 39–40 (2003–2004): 73–79.
https://doi.org/10.33356/temenos.4818

Astapova, Anastasiya. 2017. 'In Search for Truth: Surveillance Rumors and Vernacular Panopticon in Belarus'. *Journal of American Folklore* 130 (517): 276–304. https://doi.org/10.5406/jamerfolk.130.517.0276

Astapova, Anastasiya, Eirikur Bergmann, Asbjørn Dyrendal, Annika Rabo, Kasper Grotle Rasmussen, Hulda Thórisdóttir and Andreas Önnerfors. 2021. *Conspiracy Theories and the Nordic Countries*. New York: Routledge.

Astapova, Anastasiya, Onoriu Colăcel, Corneliu Pintilescu and Tamás Scheibner, eds. 2021. *Conspiracy Theories in Eastern Europe: Tropes and Trends*. London; New York: Routledge. https://doi.org/10.4324/9780429326073

Bae, Bosco B. 2016. 'Believing Selves and Cognitive Dissonance: Connecting Individual and Society via "Belief"'. *Religions* 7 (7): 1–14. https://doi.org/10.3390/rel7070086

Bae, Bosco B. 2017. 'Belief and Acceptance for the Study of Religion'. *Method & Theory in the Study of Religion* 29 (1): 57–87. https://doi.org/10.1163/15700682-12341374

Barth, Fredrik. 2002. 'An Anthropology of Knowledge'. *Current Anthropology* 43 (1): 1–18. https://doi.org/10.1086/324131

Bauman, Richard. 1972. 'Differential Identity and the Social Base of Folklore'. In *Toward New Perspectives in Folklore*, edited by Américo Paredes and Richard Bauman, 31–41. Austin; London: University of Texas Press.

Bauman, Richard. 2004. *A World of Others' Words: Cross-Cultural Perspectives on Intertextuality*. Malden, MA: Blackwell.

Birchall, Clare. 2006. *Knowledge Goes Pop: From Conspiracy Theory to Gossip*. Oxford; New York: Berg. https://doi.org/10.26530/OAPEN_390769

Bivins, Jason C. 2016. 'Belief'. In *The Oxford Handbook of the Study of Religion*, edited by Michael Stausberg and Steven Engler, 495–509. Oxford: Oxford University Press. https://doi.org/10.1093/oxfordhb/9780198729570.013.35

Blank, Trevor J. 2014. *Toward a Conceptual Framework for the Study of Folklore and the Internet*. Boulder: University Press of Colorado. https://doi.org/10.2307/j.ctt6wrr8p

Blum, Jason N. 2020. 'Belief: Problems and Pseudo-Problems'. *Journal of the American Academy of Religion* 86 (3): 642–664. https://doi.org/10.1093/jaarel/lfy001

Bowman, Marion. 2014. 'Vernacular Religion, Contemporary Spirituality and Emergent Identities: Lessons from Lauri Honko'. *Approaching Religion* 4 (1): 101–113. https://doi.org/10.30664/ar.67542

Bowman, Marion, and Ülo Valk. 2012. 'Introduction: Vernacular Religion, Generic Expressions and the Dynamics of Belief'. In *Vernacular Religion in Everyday Life: Expressions of Belief*, edited by Marion Bowman and Ülo Valk, 1–19. Sheffield; Bristol, CT: Equinox.

Briggs, Charles L. 2012. 'What We Should Have Learned from Américo Paredes: The Politics of Communicability and the Making of Folkloristics'. *Journal of American Folklore* 125 (495): 91–110. https://doi.org/10.5406/jamerfolk.125.495.0091

Bronner, Simon J. 2017. *Folklore: The Basics*. London; New York: Routledge. https://doi.org/10.4324/9781315688381

Bronner, Simon J. 2018. 'The Challenge of American Folklore to the Humanities'. *Humanities* 7 (1): 1–31. https://doi.org/10.3390/h7010017

Droogers, André. 2014. 'The World of Worldviews'. In *Methods for the Study of Religious Change: From Religious Studies to Worldview Studies*, edited by André Droogers and Anton van Harskamp, 17–42. Sheffield; Bristol: Equinox.

Dyrendal, Asbjørn, David G. Robertson and Egil Asprem, eds. 2018. *Handbook of Conspiracy Theory and Contemporary Religion*. Leiden; Boston: Brill. https://doi.org/10.1163/9789004382022

Foley, Richard. 2014. 'Epistemic Rationality'. In *The Routledge Companion to Epistemology*, edited by Sven Bernecker, and Duncan Pritchard, 37–46. New York: Routledge.

Foucault, Michel. 1980. *Power/Knowledge: Selected Interviews and Other Writings 1972-1977*, edited by Colin Gordon. New York: Pantheon Books.

Gatling, Benjamin. 2020. 'There Isn't Belief, Just Believing: Rethinking Belief as a Keyword of Folklore Studies'. *Journal of American Folklore* 133 (529): 307–328. https://doi.org/10.5406/jamerfolk.133.529.0307

Goldman, Alvin I. 2000. 'Epistemic Folkways and Scientific Epistemology'. In *Epistemology: An Anthology*, edited by Ernest Sosa and Jaegwon Kim with the assistance of Matthew McGrath, 438–444. Malden, MA; Oxford: Blackwell.

Goldstein, Diane. 2015. 'Vernacular Turns: Narrative, Local Knowledge, and the Changed Context of Folklore'. *Journal of American Folklore* 128 (508): 125–145. https://doi.org/10.5406/jamerfolk.128.508.0125

Goldstein, Diane E., and Amy Shuman. 2016. 'Introduction: The Stigmatized Vernacular: Where Reflexivity Meets Untellability'. In *The Stigmatized Vernacular: Where Reflexivity Meets Untellability*, edited by Diane E. Goldstein and Amy Shuman, 1–13. Bloomington; Indianapolis: Indiana University Press. https://doi.org/10.2979/stigmatizedvernacular.0.0.01

Good, Byron. 1994. *Medicine, Rationality and Experience: An Anthropological Perspective*. Cambridge: Cambridge University Press. https://doi.org/10.1017/CBO9780511811029

Hafstein, Valdimar. 2014. 'The Constant Muse: Copyright and Creative Agency'. *Narrative Culture* 1 (1): 9–47. https://doi.org/10.13110/narrcult.1.1.0009

Hammer, Olav. 2004. *Claiming Knowledge: Strategies of Epistemology from Theosophy to New Age*. Leiden; Boston: Brill. https://doi.org/10.1163/9789047403371

Howard, Robert Glenn. 2011. 'Vernacular'. In *Folklore: An Encyclopedia of Beliefs, Customs, Tales, Music, and Art*, vol. 3, 2nd revised edn, edited by Charlie T. McCormick and Kim Kennedy White, 1240–1246. Santa Barbara, CA: ABC-Clio.

Howard, Robert Glenn. 2013. 'Vernacular Authority: Critically Engaging "Tradition"'. In *Tradition in the Twenty-First Century: Locating the Role of the Past in the Present*, edited by Trevor J. Blank and Robert Glenn Howard, 72–99. Logan: Utah State University Press. https://doi.org/10.7330/9780874218992.c03

Hoyningen-Huene, Paul. 2016. *Systematicity: The Nature of Science*. Oxford; New York: Oxford University Press.

Illman, Ruth, and Mercédesz Czimbalmos. 2020. 'Knowing, Being, and Doing Religion: Introducing an Analytical Model for Researching Vernacular Religion'. *Temenos: Nordic Journal of Comparative Religion* 56 (2): 171–199. https://doi.org/10.33356/temenos.97275

Ingold, Tim. 2000. *The Perception of the Environment: Essays on Livelihood, Dwelling and Skill*. London; New York: Routledge.

Jöhncke, Steffen, and Vibeke Steffen. 2015. 'Introduction: Ethnographies on the Limits of Reason'. In *Between Magic and Rationality: On the Limits of Reason in the Modern World*, edited by Vibeke Steffen, Steffen Jöhncke and Kirsten Marie Raahauge, 9–39. Copenhagen: Museum Tusculanum Press.

Josephson-Storm, Jason Ā. 2017. *The Myth of Disenchantment: Magic, Modernity, and the Birth of the Human Sciences*. Chicago; London: University of Chicago Press. https://doi.org/10.7208/chicago/9780226403533.001.0001

Kitta, Andrea. 2019. *The Kiss of Death: Contagion, Contamination, and Folklore*. Logan: Utah State University Press. https://doi.org/10.7330/9781607329275

Kuipers, Joel. 2013. 'Evidence and Authority in Ethnographic and Linguistic Perspective'. *Annual Review of Anthropology* 42: 399–413.
https://doi.org/10.1146/annurev-anthro-081309-145615

Latour, Bruno. 1993. *We Have Never Been Modern*. Cambridge, MA: Harvard University Press.

Latour, Bruno. 2005. *Reassembling the Social: An Introduction to Actor-Network-Theory*. Oxford: Oxford University Press.

Lewis, James R., and Olav Hammer, eds. 2011. *Handbook of Religion and the Authority of Science*. Brill Handbooks on Contemporary Religion 3. Leiden; Boston: Brill Academic.

Lindholm, Charles. 2012. '"What is Bread?" The Anthropology of Belief'. *Ethos* (Special Issue: *The Dynamics of Belief and Experience: Cultural and Psychological Responses across Religious Traditions*) 40 (3): 341–357.
https://doi.org/10.1111/j.1548-1352.2012.01261.x

Luhrmann, Tanya M. 1989. *Persuasions of the Witch's Craft: Ritual Magic in Contemporary England*. Cambridge, MA: Harvard University Press.

Magliocco, Sabina. 2012. 'Religious Practice'. In *A Companion to Folklore*, edited by Regina F. Bendix and Galit Hasan-Rokem, 136–153. Malden; Oxford; Chichester: Wiley-Blackwell. https://doi.org/10.1002/9781118379936.ch7

McNeill, Lynne S. 2013. *Folklore Rules: A Fun, Quick, and Useful Introduction to the Field of Academic Folklore Studies*. Logan: Utah State University Press.
https://doi.org/10.7330/9780874219067

Motz, Marilyn. 1998. 'The Practice of Belief'. *Journal of American Folklore* 111 (441): 339–355. https://doi.org/10.2307/541314

Mould, Tom. 2018. 'Introduction to the Special Issue on Fake News: Definitions and Approaches'. *Journal of American Folklore* 131 (522): 371–378.
https://doi.org/10.5406/jamerfolk.131.522.0371

Mullen, Patrick B. 2000. 'Belief and the American Folk'. *Journal of American Folklore* 113 (448): 119–143. https://doi.org/10.2307/541285

Mullins, Willow G. 2019. 'Our Lady of Authenticity: Folklore's Articles of Faith'. In *Implied Nowhere: Absence in Folklore Studies*, edited by Shelley Ingram, Willow G. Mullins and Todd Richardson, 19–37. Jackson: University Press of Mississippi. https://doi.org/10.14325/mississippi/9781496822956.003.0002

Needham, Rodney. 1972. *Belief, Language, and Experience*. Chicago: University of Chicago Press.

Noyes, Dorothy. 2016. *Humble Theory: Folklore's Grasp on Social Life*. Bloomington; Indianapolis: Indiana University Press. https://doi.org/10.2307/j.ctt1zxz0bs

Oring, Elliott. 2012. 'Thinking through Tradition'. In Elliott Oring, *Just Folklore: Analysis, Interpretation, Critique*, 220-239. Los Angeles: Cantilever Press.

Peck, Andrew. 2020. 'The Death of Doge: Institutional Appropriations of Internet Memes'. In *Folklore and Social Media*, edited by Andrew Peck and Trevor J. Blank, 83–107. Logan: Utah State University Press. https://doi.org/10.7330/9781646420599.c004

Primiano, Leonard N. 1995. 'Vernacular Religion and the Search for Method in Religious Folklife'. *Western Folklore* (Special Issue: *Reflexivity and the Study of Belief*) 54 (1): 37-56. https://doi.org/10.2307/1499910

Primiano, Leonard N. 2012. 'Afterword: Manifestations of the Religious Vernacular: Ambiguity, Power, and Creativity'. In *Vernacular Religion in Everyday Life: Expressions of Belief*, edited by Marion Bowman and Ülo Valk, 382-394. Sheffield; Bristol, CT: Equinox.

Redfield, Robert. 1955. 'The Social Organization of Tradition'. *The Far Eastern Quarterly* 15 (1): 13-21. https://doi.org/10.2307/2942099

Scott, Joan Wallach. 2012. 'The Evidence of Experience'. In *Religious Experience: A Reader*, edited by Craig Martin and Russell T. McCutcheon with Leslie Dorrough Smith, 151-173. Sheffield: Equinox.

Shagan, Ethan H. 2018. *The Birth of Modern Belief: Faith and Judgment from the Middle Ages to the Enlightenment*. Princeton, NJ: Princeton University Press. https://doi.org/10.2307/j.ctv39x5gv

Uibu, Marko. 2012. 'Võitlus teaduse nimel: Skeptilise aktivismi kujunemine, retoorilised võtted ning eesmärgid'. [The Battle for Science: The Formation, Rhetorical Tools, and Aims of Skeptical Activism]. *Ajalooline Ajakiri/The Estonian Historical Journal* 3 (4): 337-357.

Valk, Ülo. 2011. 'Folklore and Discourse: The Authority of Scientific Rhetoric, from State Atheism to New Spirituality'. In *Handbook of Religion and the Authority of Science*, edited by James R. Lewis and Olav Hammer, 847-866. Brill Handbooks on Contemporary Religion 3. Leiden; Boston, MA: Brill Academic.

Valk, Ülo. 2021. 'What are Belief Narratives? An Introduction'. *Narrative Culture* 8 (2): 175-186. https://doi.org/10.13110/narrcult.8.2.0175

Yoder, Don. 1974. 'Toward a Definition of Folk Religion'. *Western Folklore: Symposium on Folk Religion* 33 (1): 2-15. https://doi.org/10.2307/1498248

Zagzebski, Linda. 2014. 'Religious Knowledge'. In *The Routledge Companion to Epistemology*, edited by Sven Bernecker and Duncan Pritchard, 393-400. New York: Routledge.

Part 1

# Politics and Vernacular Strategies of Resistance

# Chapter 1

# In Quest of Lost Heritage, Ethnic Identity, and Democracy: The Belarusian Case

*Anastasiya Astapova*[*]

## The Missing Book

Throughout its history, the territory of current Belarus was a part of Kyivan Rus', the Great Duchy of Lithuania and the Polish-Lithuanian Commonwealth. Yet today the country is mainly associated with Russia, due to its long history within the Russian Empire (1795–1918) and the USSR (1919–1990), when Belarus became a window display and an exemplary republic within the socialist union (Eke and Kuzio 2000: 537). The resemblance of two East Slavic languages—Russian and Belarusian—became another reason for the almost complete lack of symbolic borders between Belarusians and Russians. In addition, after World War II, the Belarusians acquired their own stable myth of the Partisan Republic within the cult of the Great Victory and Soviet Union as the people who gloriously fought against the Nazis (Lewis 2013: 200). The kinship with Russia as the big brother was promoted at the level of state ideology. In this context, however, some ideas about Belarusian ethnic, linguistic and historical distinctiveness other than 'Partisan Republic' or 'younger brother' emerged.

---

[*] **Anastasiya Astapova** is an Associate Professor of Folkloristics at the University of Tartu (Estonia) and a member of the Estonian Young Academy of Science. In addition to her interest in migration and the Russophone population in the Baltic States, Astapova has been doing research on Belarus (which culminated in her monograph *Humor and Rumor in the Post-Soviet Authoritarian State*, Rowman and Littlefield, 2021) as well as on conspiracy theories (see, for instance, the co-edited volume *Conspiracy Theories in Eastern Europe: Tropes and Trends*, Routledge, 2021, and the co-authored volume *Conspiracy Theories and the Nordic Countries*, Routledge, 2021).

26   *Vernacular Knowledge*

In 1965, at the end of the Khruschev Thaw—the era famous for the denunciation of Stalin's personality cult and the weakening of repressions—the Belarusian writer Uladzimir Karatkevich (1930–1984; see Figure 1.1) published *Kalasy pad Syarpom Tvaim* ('The Ears of Rye Under Thy Sickle'), perhaps the first historical novel in the Belarusian language (Karatkevich 1965). The book described the 1863–1864 January Uprising in the Polish-Lithuanian Commonwealth, which called for a confrontation of the Russian Empire's oppression and the granting of land to peasants. Polish, imperial Russian and Soviet history has generally recognized the central role of the Poles in the Uprising (Savchenko 2009: 42–44; Maldzis 1990: 42–43). *The Ears of Rye Under Thy Sickle*, however, contradicted the conventional historiography regarding the ethnic make-up of the protesters. Karatkevich acknowledged the part played by the Poles in the leadership of the insurrection, but also insisted on the significance of the *shlyakhta*, the Belarusian privileged noble class (conventionally regarded as Polish otherwise), who, according to Karatkevich, were conscious of and proud of their Belarusian origins.

Initially, Karatkevich planned to write his novel in three volumes: (1) the preparation for the Uprising, (2) the Uprising *per se*, and (3) its defeat (Vyerabyei 1997: 131). Nevertheless, only the first book, *The Ears of Rye Under Thy Sickle*, was published, focusing on the fictional character of the Belarusian *shlyakhtich* (nobleman) Ales' Zahorski, not only highborn and educated, but also in close touch with the peasantry. Among the first of the *shlyakhta* to recognize his true Belarusian belonging, he meets Kastuś Kalinowski, the other major protagonist and a future (real-life) leader of the January Uprising. Seeking the well-being of their people, both enter an illegal organization preparing for the insurgence. With this, the first book ends, with expectations for the second and third volumes which would have described the most interesting events for the historical novel—the Uprising itself.

The publication of *The Ears of Rye Under Thy Sickle* became a matter of controversy. First, the genre of historical prose was rather new for Belarusian literature, which caused multiple criticisms of those pieces that did not exactly correspond to historical reality. Second, many thought the description of the *shlyakhta* in the novel was too vivid, depriving the peasantry of enough attention (while the Soviet principles called for attributing the central social role to the working class and peasantry) (Kisyalew 2005: 221; Shchadryna 2005: 428). Most importantly, Karatkevich stressed the role of the Belarusians in the Uprising, while before they had been barely considered to have exhibited national consciousness in the nineteenth century. Karatkevich's protagonists are not ashamed to speak the Belarusian language; they are well aware of their ethnic distinctiveness and their right to freedom from oppressors. The novel questioned the stereotype of the poor, oppressed and suffering Belarusian which had been established by the literature of the early twentieth century (Bekus 2010: 60), and instead promoted the image of a strong, talented, brave, smart and noble people (Syamyonava 2005: 286). Because of this, Karatkevich was often unofficially labelled a nationalist, a status that was not appropriate for a Soviet writer (Shchadryna 2005: 427).

**Figure 1.1**. A photo of Uladzimir Karatkevich taken after he graduated from Kyiv University (after 1954) (Arkhivy Belarusi n.d.)

In the meantime, the defenders of Karatkevich were enchanted by the different Belarus presented in the novel: 'It turns out that we were not only wearing bast shoes [shoes made from linden or birch bark and traditionally associated with poor peasants], but also had educated noble families, wonderful castles, and princely hunts', wrote the artist Arlyen Kashkuryevich (2005: 462), admiringly. Another artist, Feliks Yanushkyevich (2005: 504), recounts that his school class was so fascinated by the publication of the novel that even a pupil with Russian origins claimed that 'this is a masterpiece', and 'together with others started to fill in his school diary and speak only in Belarusian'. 'More and more young people became attached to Belarusian literature due to Karatkevich', the folklorist and literary critic Arsyen' Lis (1994: 403) remembers.

No matter how controversial, the success of the first book gave way to excitement about its possible continuation. Two other volumes (thus making a trilogy) were planned by Karatkevich: sequels about the Uprising *per se* and its defeat. However, these parts were never published. Literature scholars suggest many reasons for this: the criticism Karatkevich received for the first volume, his unwillingness to have his protagonists killed (which would have been the logical end for a book about the defeated Uprising), other writings taking up his time, and his health problems (followed by his death in 1984). Some consider that Karatkevich's short stories about the January Uprising, *Zbroya* ('Weapons') and *Sinyaya-sinyaya* ('Blue-blue'), published later became a form of the continuation. In this uncertainty, the long-awaited sequel to Karatkevich's epic work attracted lots of speculation and rumour, which became public as soon as the possibility arose.

In 1990, during perestroika and glasnost,[1] the literary critic and friend of Karatkevich, Adam Maldzis, published *Life and Ascension of Uladzimir Karatkevich* which revealed many facts about the writer's personal and professional life. In the book, Maldzis insisted that Karatkevich had written the continuation to *The Ears of Rye Under Thy Sickle*, claiming that the first draft had disappeared in 1982 when Karatkevich and his wife had been on holiday and their flat had been robbed. It was not the loss of gold, silver and cut glassware items that most distressed the writer. Maldzis (1990: 81) quotes Karatkevich's lament: 'They knew what to steal! They punched me in the guts!' In addition, Maldzis asserts that although 'the best Minsk Sherlock Holmeses' took part in the search for the thieves, they failed because 'the best specialists' must have been involved in the robbery. In his book and interviews, Maldzis (ibid.) expresses the hope that 'the villainy of the century' will one day be revealed. Although not all of the researchers agreed that the book had even existed, Maldzis's belief in the villainy engendered multiple discussions in literature circles (Vyerabyei 1997: 167–173).

It is not by chance that Maldzis's book and the debate coincided with the late 1980s–early 1990s freedom of speech, the Soviet Union's collapse, and the 1991 independence of Belarus. The full three-part version of *The Ears of Rye Under Thy Sickle* was to prove that once, before the Belarusians came under Russian influence, they had been a nation conscious of their distinctiveness, able to resist the oppressors. Thus, the full book could have become one of the major Belarusian works of arts to refer to the development of national identity. The legend of the Missing Book was in line with the pro-European inclination that dominated in early independent Belarus, appealing to the original sense of European belonging, emphasizing the significance of pre-Russian history and challenging both Russian imperialism and communism. This went in line with the early Belarusian independence development in the early 1990s, when the leading Belarusian National Front political party, headed by Zianon Pazniak, managed to implement a significant pro-European and anti-Russian cultural agenda at state policy level (Leshchenko 2004: 335). They stimulated the replacement of Russian with Belarusian language and hastily promoted the nationalist version of history.

However, the nationalistic inclination in the development of the new Belarus in the early 1990s was challenged by a new political actor, Alyaksandr Lukashenka, who immediately attracted people by promoting well-known communist patriotic values and ideological tenets. He promised familiar stability—a matter much more important to the people who had experienced the uncertainty and confusion of transitional post-Soviet years than a vague promise of sovereignty and European belonging. Having thwarted the radical nationalist Pazniak at the 1994 presidential election, Lukashenka served two consecutive terms as president. Then he changed the constitution through a referendum, so he was able to run yet again, and was elected to another six terms (at the time of writing this chapter). His continuous presidency, however, is opposed by dissidents arguing against what has been labelled 'the last dictatorship of Europe'. They also insist that Lukashenka's regime is of an anti-Belarusian nature since it destroys Belarusian national identity by endorsing neo-Soviet ideology and having close ties with Russia. The tension gains special strength after every election when the protests, mainly held in Minsk, are violently suppressed by the state. Little wonder that when open protest becomes dangerous, alternative forms of contesting authority are used. The legend of the Missing Book, which seemed to have been dormant for a while in the 1990s, has reawakened.

## *The Ears of Rye Under Thy Sickle* Today

In 2011 in Tallinn, I recorded an interview with a Belarusian dissident living in one of the European Union countries. Deeply interested in Belarusian culture, a Belarusian speaker Pyotr[2] was the first to tell me about the Missing Book legend, which was the start of this whole research:

> **P:** The novel *The Ears of Rye Under Thy Sickle* is an unfinished work of literature. There is a legend [*legenda*] stating that the draft of its sequel

was stolen by the KGB [Committee for State Security] while Karatkevich was away from his apartment for a holiday. It seems that the legend was born from the interviews of Adam Maldzis, even though some critics insist that it is *Weapons* or *Blue-Blue* that became the real sequels. But I am sure, no, I want to believe that the manuscript exists somewhere in the KGB archives either in Minsk or in Moscow—this cult work of art may become a bomb for the revival of the national self-consciousness. The description of how the Uprising was being prepared from the first book is one thing, but the Uprising itself with these bloody scenes of hangings and other persecutions by Russians is totally different ... The idea of looking for the stolen book of Karatkevich could unite the cultural forces of Belarus and the Belarusian diasporas.

**A**: But aren't the KGB archives closed?

**P**: Yes! But if the representatives of the diaspora and the scholarly world initiate, demand the investigation, it could become an idea similar to the one around which the Estonian nation formed. Estonians were engaged in choral art, and here at least we can unravel some documents from the archives ... Of course, since the KGB was involved, people who did it are probably still alive, maybe still on service. They are interested not to reveal this crime against the Belarusian culture. But we can create many legends, many technologies on the basis of it and promote it, forming the Belarusian idea around it. We struggle to retrieve something we used to have. This turns into the legend: since people respond to it, it is not some archival or critics' information any more. (Recorded in Tallinn in September 2011)

Compared to the ideas expressed by Maldzis in the early 1990s, Pyotr adds the motif of the KGB—the main security agency for the Soviet Union from 1954 until its collapse in 1991—involved in the crime. It should be said that Belarus is the only country in the former Soviet Union that retained this name for the Committee for State Security, which logically presupposes continuity between the two agencies. It is not surprising then that the rumours about two KGBs also become continuous, since their aims allegedly remain similar—to suppress Belarusian culture (within the anti-Belarusian regime of Lukashenka too). It also explains Maldzis's earlier claim that the best specialists were involved in the robbery: perhaps the critic did not want to arouse his suspicion of KGB involvement in the published source, just giving a hint of it.

Pyotr recognizes the potential power of the legend, which can become instrumental in many ways: from uniting various cultural and political forces to opening the KGB archives for the general public, something that certainly means democratization. Rather than blindly searching for the sequel, he recognizes that the story of the Missing Book is a legend (which does not prevent him from believing it) around which, applying folklore to reality, it is possible to build national identity.

My further exploration showed that Karatkevich's legend and his whole image has recently become the means for the construction of Belarusian identity without openly resisting the current ideology. The renewal of the discussions about the legend from the 1990s presumably owes a debt to a young writer Dzyanis Martsinovich, his multiple publications on Karatkevich's biography, and his aim to popularize the writer. For instance, *The Don Juan List of Karatkevich* strives to attract those who are not interested in Karatkevich's writings but might be interested in the juicy details of the legendary writer's life (Martsinovich 2012). In spite of the catchy title, which aims to attract more readers, the book preserves a decent image of Karatkevich, aiming to show how respectful he was towards women. In no way contradicting the doctrines of the current Belarusian state, the book promotes state-approved Belarusian heritage 'for dummies' in order to use this heritage to propagate something more. The legend of the Missing Book has a similar function and is also campaigned for by Martsinovich.

In his article 'The Continuation of *The Ears of Rye Under Thy Sickle*: Myth or Reality?', relying on the arguments on the topic in the 1990s, Martsinovich, who lives and works in Belarus, does not accuse the KGB or any other particular actor of villainy (Martsinovich 2005; 2010). Even though his attempts to make the loss of the book the concern of contemporary Belarusian society do not seem to be widely known, these attempts sometimes elicit feedback confirming his view. For instance, when he published his article about the sequel on his blog, it received the following anonymous comment:

> The thing is that my granny was a friend of Karatkevich, and literally a month before his death his flat was robbed. He was not feeling well even without it, as his wife had just died. So when he and my granny were talking, Karatkevich said that the manuscript of his main work had been stolen and there was no sense in living further. When my granny asked whether he was speaking about *The Ears of Rye Under Thy Sickle*, his answer was fuzzy, but it became absolutely clear that the final part had been finished but stolen by some freaks along with some other manuscripts. This in particular 'finished him off'. (Martsinovich 2010)

The idea of the Missing Book is promoted not only by Martsinovich and some of his followers. In 2009, an essay dedicated to *The Ears of Rye Under Thy Sickle* and its lost sequel was submitted to the school Olympiad (a high school academic competition) held in one of the Belarusian cities.[3] The pupil referenced the biographies of Karatkevich and, additionally, offered an explanation about why the book had been stolen:

> The author of the book wanted to show the truth about the 1863–1864 Uprising led by Kastuś Kalinowski without the lies which were so widespread at that time. The leaders of the Soviet party did not like this freethinking. They needed the books to be published in accordance with Soviet history. But Karatkevich did not agree to this rule. That is why his book was stolen.[4]

In a private interview, the author of the essay claimed that he was unaware that Martsinovich's article existed. If this is true, his essay and Martsinovich's work on this topic appeared independently in the 2000s.

Here I should mention that for research purposes I have also been systematically holding impromptu and arranged interviews on the issues of political and ethnic identity with Belarusians living in Belarus and abroad since 2011. I pay constant attention to the idea of the Missing Book, always asking about it in the interviews; however, even though many know and admire *The Ears of Rye Under Thy Sickle*, the idea of a sequel and the necessity of revealing it mainly belongs to a narrow circle of intellectuals working, for instance, for literary or Belarusian-language journals. However, those who did not know about it—whether supporters of Lukashenka or dissidents—after hearing the story from me, agreed that it could have been true. Many of them introduced new information supporting the legend. For instance, one of the interlocutors, Syarhyei, recounted that he heard this story, justifying belief in it by adding that Karatkevich had not died a natural death: 'There were the rumours also that it was not accidental that his heart attack happened when there were no doctors around' (recorded in Minsk in December 2012). In other words, Karatkevich had some enemies interested in the extermination of his heritage and himself.

In the biographies and interviews, Karatkevich appeared to be the hero of multiple anecdotes depicting him as a trickster and in a way making him more human, with his own personal life and failings. Many know that Karatkevich was an alcoholic, but his drinking problem is often rationalized:

> At that time an intelligent person, a person who did not have the possibility to express himself the way he wanted, needed to have something in order not to blow up from the inside; so everyone found this 'something', not because of the good living ... In the Soviet times, a teacher said to my friend: 'With your dissident ideas you should either find an independent job or end up as an alcoholic'. A person had to find a niche

in order to remain sane. Many people drank a lot. This is not negative, to my mind. (Recorded in Minsk in January 2013)

Similarly, Nancy Ries, an anthropologist who concentrated on late Soviet and early post-Soviet transformations, argues that alcoholism was not only a social and medical problem. In addition, it was a behavioural and narrative phenomenon giving countless possibilities to the sophisticated and ironic resistance and opposition to the regime discipline (Ries 2005: 130).

The legendary image of an author worthy of writing a nationally important book is curiously ambiguous in many other ways. It is exemplary of the phenomenon well described by Alexei Yurchak (2006: 283) who acknowledges that in Soviet times, 'reproducing the system and participating in its continuous internal displacement were mutually constitutive processes'. On the one hand, Karatkevich indeed was a part of the Soviet system, as he generally approved of socialism and belonged to the state-controlled Writers' Union (Maldzis 1990: 88). On the other hand, he challenged the system in many ways: his family came from the rich and educated class with several dissidents among his ancestors (Vyerabyei 1997: 257; Maldzis 1990: 17), he is known to have celebrated the day when Stalin died (Vyerabyei 1997: 11) and to have failed his PhD exam being unable to answer the questions about the Soviet politician Lavrentiy Beria (Maldzis 1990: 19). After all, he wrote several books defying the Soviet conventions. Two dichotomies—being amenable and simultaneously defiant to the socialist system—paradoxically coexisted in his case.

## The Genre of the Missing Book Story

The idea about the Missing Book resembles the plot of the Saviour and the Redeemer that was recurrent in tsarist Russia in the seventeenth century. It evolved around Dmitriy, the son of Ivan the Terrible. Dmitriy died in infancy, but the legend stated that he did not die, that he grew up in imprisonment and, if released, would escape, occupy the throne and make the country prosper. The belief was so active that several impostors, false Dmitriys, claimed the throne. The motifs of this legend are similar to the ones in the Missing Book story: the Saviour is taken/stolen; kept in prison/closed archives; escapes/resurfaces, and redeems his/its people. In this type of legend, characterized by Kirill Chistov as utopian, the future prosperous period is never described, as the 'prehistory' of the ideal life instead becomes the focus. Utopian legends become the form of protest, reflecting historical optimism and appearing in the circumstances of social instability and concentration of expectations (Chistov 2003: 474).

In a similar vein, the utopian legend about the sequel has arisen twice. The first peak coincided with the early 1990s when the country was at the crossroads of independence and had to choose the political direction of its development. Similar processes were taking place during the 1990s transition in other countries. Ries noticed the popularity of the image of the redeemer—'a human or some other entity capable of acting as an equalizing reconciliatory force, erasing the contradictions, reviving the long-awaited unity and destroying the hierarchies'—in neighboring Russia. Occultist, UFO and New Age beliefs popular there in the 1990s (Ries 2005: 203–204) are functionally similar to the legend of *The Ears of Rye Under Thy Sickle*, promising rescue from chaos and crisis.

The second peak of belief in the Missing Book in Belarus started in the middle of the 2000s when Lukashenka changed the constitution and became the president of the country for the third time, leaving little hope for change. Following James Scott (1990: 81), who suggests that utopian beliefs can be understood as negation within an existing pattern of exploitation, I consider that the legends about lost national heritage might constitute a peaceful and oblique undermining of Lukashenka's supposedly anti-national regime.

Along with the term 'utopian legend', one may analyse the story through the prism of the conspiracy theory, which pivots on an indistinct and rather depersonalized indication of an antagonist responsible for a crime. As with other conspiracy theories, the idea of the lost book is nurtured by the existence of historical precedents, such as the opening of the archives in various formerly socialist countries, which uncovered substantial crimes against their peoples. Moreover, as David Aaronovitch (2010: 11) suggests, the idea of conspiracy also makes one a part of the genuinely elite heroic group who can see past the official version. This is exactly what has happened in Belarus with those educated and intelligent people who promote the idea of cultivating identity-related knowledge among the less-aware and uninterested strata of society. At the same time, generating the discourse alternative to the official one allows its promoters to underline their fundamental mismatch with the existing recalcitrant system (Sloterdijk 1988: 40).

The story of the Missing Book has many parallels and connections alluding, for instance, to the concept of a black book of secret knowledge or to the myth of creative forces of nature falling asleep and later reviving. The motif of the powerful Missing Book is incorporated into the panoply of other plots, including *The Name of the Rose* by Umberto Eco (1983) and the story of the missing legendary book of Nostradamus. The latter book *Nostradamus Vatinicia Code* signed by Michel de Notredame was found in 1994 and is considered by some as a compilation of prophecies for the future (*The Lost Book of Nostradamus* 2007).

The idea of rediscovering lost heritage or a masterpiece is known in many nationalist ideologies and is often successful. For instance, the 1809 unification of Finland with Russia caused a small group of Finnish patriotic intellectuals, who were afraid of forced Russification, to turn to their past to strengthen the future. They argued that strength may be rediscovered if Finns collected their folk poems and worked them into an organized whole so that 'the exalted Finnish nationality, in the luster and glory ... would arouse the admiration of the present and of the future' (Wilson 1973: 831). In 1835 a Finn, Elias Lönnrot, fulfilled this prophecy with the publication of the famous epic *Kalevala.* Similarly, Ray Cashman observes the Irish case of the Lough Derg pilgrimage site, where in the early 1890s a group of local Protestants destroyed the original Drumawark cross. For a century, the notion of autochthonous power was undermined by the significant absence of a cross, until its replica was erected in 1999 (Cashman 2008: 377–378).

Such cases of heritage lost and searched for often relate to the rediscovery of forgotten tragedies against the ethnic (or religious) group to strengthen this group's identity by projecting the image of the common enemy. Another example from Ireland is that of the Archbishop of Dublin who has recently called on the Irish government to establish a fully-fledged independent inquiry into secret graveyards for the infants and mothers consigned to nursing homes run by the Roman Catholic church in the last century (McElroy 2014). Like Ireland, Belarus has its own cross and graveyards to rediscover very much in line with the missing manuscript narrative.

## The Cross of Saint Euphrosyne and Kurapaty

Pazniak, the major right-wing opponent of the current president Lukashenka, published the book *New Age* (2002) dedicated to Belarusian cultural and political issues, in which he examines several other examples of the missing Belarusian heritage. One of the articles in the book concentrates on the Cross of Saint Euphrosyne (see Figure 1.2), an Orthodox relic made in 1161 on the order of Saint Euphrosyne of Polotsk, one of the 15 patron saints of Belarus. Pazniak (2002: 98–99) claims that the Cross, mysteriously lost early in World War II, was actually stolen by Moscow secret services and is still kept in Moscow, not for the sake of its cultural or material value, but to deprive Belarus of its Holy Grail, a symbol that could mobilize the nation. The idea of the lost cross and the potential it has to unify the nation has been developed by many other activists, including the aforementioned Maldzis (*Vk.com* 2015).

**Figure 1.2.** Reproduction of the cross of Saint Euphrosyne of Polotsk (Batyushkov 1890: 25)

Pazniak was also the first to initiate the case of Kurapaty (see Figure 1.3), claiming to have discovered a mass grave of victims executed between 1937 and 1941 during the Great Purge (a Soviet campaign of repressions and mass executions) in the Kurapaty area near Minsk (Pazniak et al. 1994). This discovery coincided with the declaration of independence in Belarus and added impetus to the nationalist anti-Russian movement, since the mass killings were perpetrated by the Soviets and, according to many experts, it was the best representatives of Belarusian intelligentsia who had been shot. The story of the lost cross and the mass grave are supplemented by other efforts undertaken by Pazniak to uncover the crimes of Russians who, as he argues, have been purposefully destroying

Belarusians since the seventeenth century through wars, purges and the Chernobyl catastrophe. 'Any friendship with Russia was and will be dangerous and ruining for Belarusians', he concludes (Pazniak 2002: 50).

Kurapaty has gained unique importance for constructing the Belarusian identity. Since the remains of many victims have not been excavated, their names are mostly unknown too. Yet, some of the relatives and descendants who assume that their loved ones must have been killed here put the names of the victims on crosses. Since it remains unknown where many Soviet purges victims were buried, for many, Kurapaty became a symbolic graveyard where the families come to commemorate their members. Recently, several crosses were decorated with Polish symbols and Polish nameboards (see Figure 1.4): some Polish families, knowing that their ancestors were shot in the purges in this region, assumed that this could be the ancestors' graveyard and decided to commemorate them similarly to Belarusians. The crosses with Polish signifiers, however, were damaged several times with the nameboards destroyed. Some observers assume this happened because the vandals thought that the place is to constitute an exclusively Belarusian identity-related narrative of suffering. It is not to be intruded upon and confused with some other ethnicities' tragedies.

**Figure 1.3.** Kurapaty graveyard. Photograph by Anastasiya Astapova

38  *Vernacular Knowledge*

**Figure 1.4.** A polish cross at Kurapaty. Photograph by Anastasiya Astapova

Three stories—the Missing book, the Cross, and Kurapaty—illustrate the same grand narrative of victimization, an ambiguous case when history, ideology and legendry get blurred. One of the leading post-Soviet anthropologists, Serguei Oushakine, calls such narratives, in particular the Kurapaty story, 'the lament of self-victimization'. He defines this term, offered as a retrospective attempt to represent imperial history, in colonial terms, which constantly rethink and reinterpret the Soviet past (Oushakine 2011: 212). This process, according to Oushakine, involves escapism—trying to turn to better times and treating worse times as an unfortunate mistake. He argues that the utopian desire of the Belarusians to uncover the sources of 'national authenticity' behind those which were imposed by the occupation, rather than overcoming the colonial experience today, has resulted in a series of dead ends, polarizing society. According to Oushakine (ibid.: 232), these attempts to revive the past, which could have succeeded but never did, perpetuate historically available forms of subjectivity. Similarly, Maksim Zhbankov (2008: 147) suggests that the absence of fresh ideas and original cultural texts in Belarus formed a space of multivalent and conflicting signs which results in the expanded manufacture of competing myths, total mythologization of cultural space, and cultural trash.

Even leaving aside the question of what an original cultural text might be, I strongly disagree with the ideas of cumbersome mythological trash and the potencies of the vague 'historical forms' that Oushakine discusses. Actual fieldwork in Belarus helps us to understand that the existing narratives of Kurapaty, the Cross of Saint Euphrosyne, or Karatkevich's book are, perhaps, among the few forms of creativity and political involvement available in the context of existing ideology. The condemnation of these belief narratives ignores the phenomena one encounters from the first interviews: common knowledge about violent suppression of the protests, rumours about general surveillance and unfair punishments in Belarus ('a country designed to watch', as one of my interlocutors noted), or gossip about people being fired even after telling a joke about the president. In a system erected to neutralize, if not completely suppress, any kind of novel activity or creativity, the number of forms of 'historical subjectivities' is very limited.

Among the intellectuals promoting the narratives described, many used to be active dissidents, but the violent suppression of the protests, as well as the indifference of the majority of their co-citizens, caused the erection of alternative realities and other strategies for the country's development. The younger generation of these intellectuals has conceivably learnt from the mistakes of the older and turned directly to alternative tools, legends among them. Moreover, such a way of thinking is, perhaps, the only way a young creative person may afford to live and work in Belarus in spite of disagreeing with its policies. For instance, as I showed, the idea about the Missing Book is mostly promoted by the intelligentsia: employed in the state organizations and staying away from open protest, they still search for democratic changes through soft measures that can be fostered by the publication of a famous novel, rather than revolution.

Again, according to the fieldwork, these narratives do not polarize society, as Oushakine thinks. Indeed, the polarization, which reached a height of tension after the country's independence, may seem to split society into the majority (according to the number of those who vote for Lukashenka), who see the Golden Age in the Soviet Union, and the minority, who appeal for revival based on Belarusian literature and art. Yet, to my mind, the gap between the two groups is not as crucial, given that many people fall out of the classification by embracing both Lukashenka's ideology and nationalist sentiments.

Often, two positions do not represent separate and opposite realms, but rather become partners in a symbiotic relationship of vernacular discourse with a multitude of subjective and individual dimensions (Bowman and Valk 2012; Primiano 1995). Every Belarusian I interviewed has his or her personal set of beliefs nurtured by both official and alternative doctrines, with remaining space for new ones. Even though the three legends are mainly embraced by a seemingly negligible minority of intellectuals, it became obvious from the interviews that the legend of the Missing Book, for instance, is readily accepted by those who have never heard about it. There were no cases when someone, whether one of Lukashenka's supporters or a dissident, expressed adamant disbelief. The significance of Karatkevich as a writer is widely recognized and many, regardless of their political values, are interested in reading the sequel. Moreover, the official ideology allows the presence of Karatkevich's writings (including *The Ears of Rye Under Thy Sickle*) in the school programme and sanctions the opening of museums and erection of monuments to honour him.

In 2013, trying to pin down the attitude of contemporary Belarusian state ideology towards the Missing Book narrative, I visited the museum of Karatkevich in his hometown, Orsha. The exhibitions lacked any hints about the Missing Book, and when I asked the museum assistant about it, she confirmed that Karatkevich had started to write it, but the manuscript was stolen from his flat. Any other question of mine on the topic encountered a dead end, as the museum attendant claimed that her elder colleague responsible for giving more information was on leave that day. Thus, even though the Missing Book has much less significance for the representatives of the official discourse than for those who actively promote it, it is an ideologically sanctioned story open for discussion from both sides.

Little wonder that the alternative discourse tries to build upon the existing and approved knowledge accepted by the majority and not contradict officialdom. Dissidents try to establish their own coherent complex of mythical narratives, otherwise limited by the threats to safety. In circumstances in which it is not possible to freely discuss these problems, intellectuals concentrate on alternative ways of restoring the Belarusian nation as they see it. This allows them to express the need for change without harming their current professional activities and personal lives.

In the same way, in the Soviet Union those who wanted to promote Belarusian national development could do it through the state or not at all: Belarusian nationalism was not only compatible with Soviet power structures, but existed within them in a kind of institutional symbiosis (Savchenko 2009: 89). The contemporary Belarusian political regime, often compared to late Soviet socialism, enables the same strategies.

The narratives about Karatkevich, the Cross, and Kurapaty also result from the belatedness of the Belarusian nationalist development. As Yelena Gapova (2008: 42) writes, at the end of the 1980s, almost every Soviet republic put forward 'a pack of claims' against the Soviet oppression of ethnic groups: the Soviet occupation in the Baltic states, the Chernobyl catastrophe in Ukraine, the exhaustion of national resources in Kazakhstan, and Stalin's crimes against peoples and their cultures everywhere. The ideology of many of the post-Soviet countries came not only through factual but also symbolic liberation from Soviet influence— the acknowledgement and articulation of the cost of the Soviet period and building new identities on the basis of this acknowledgement. For instance, Uzbek post-Soviet history portrays Uzbeks as 'pristine' victims of Russian and Soviet exploitation, which focused on the extermination of intellectuals (Adams 2010: 33). As Oushakine himself recognizes, following Caroline Humphrey (2002), the stories about the lost national culture cannot only be reduced to the search for a scapegoat or the mobilizing of the nation. In addition, 'these traumatic narratives should be construed as a painful practice of "unmaking" the Soviet way of life' (Oushakine 2009: 114). Having chosen Lukashenka at the first election, Belarus never had a chance to vocalize its claims, which were, perhaps, essential for the young independent state.

Finally, the colonization and impoverishment of Belarus may be seen as continuous and ongoing: the current decline of the Belarusian language, the dependency of Belarus on Russian resources, and multiple legends about Lukashenka's power being bolstered by the Kremlin (as an occasionally useful puppet ruler for the neighbouring semi-colony) maintain the image of Belarus as subaltern and colonial. In such a situation, ideas about uncovering the malevolent deeds of the Soviets, Russians, or anti-national Lukashenka regime, all of them seen as targeted against Belarusian independence, culture and well-being, become the logical development of the desire for democratization and the retrieval of national uniqueness which are inextricably connected with it.

## Conclusion

Unlike many post-Soviet countries that are immersed in open memory wars, Belarus had only a short period of ideological 'instability' in the early 1990s. However, the production of alternative knowledge about Belarus during this brief period of democratization was so intense that this knowledge still re-emerges every time there is a need for it. As the need for Karatkevich's book proliferates again when it becomes clear that Lukashenka is non-dismissible, so do the narratives of Euphrosyne's Cross or the Kurapaty graveyard. A seemingly irrecoverable past resurges in order to satisfy the quest for national sentiment and liberalization.

Logically, this quest goes in an anti-Russian direction. If the Belarusian nation needs to be distinctive, it first and foremost searches for distinctiveness from Russia, with whom it is so often confused and on whom it used to be dependent. The current continuation of this dependency, in spite of Belarusian formal autonomy, compares Lukashenka's regime with the Soviet or Russian regime in its anti-Belarusianness, adding a hidden layer to circulating legends that, at first sight, do not seem to be anti-Lukashenka. Charging Russians or Soviets (which seem to be equated in this case) with crimes against Belarusian culture also helps to justify the country's backwardness, whether in the search for identity or any other sphere of life. The negotiation happening through legends is a part of a process characteristic of post-Soviet countries, which takes longer in Belarus because of the limits, restrictions and censorship of divergent opinions. Finally, the hunt for the Missing Book, which is presumed to be the Rosetta stone of Belarusian history, allows an unconventional reading of this history.

Yet, in spite of their novel understanding of history, the Belarusian legends presented above do not contradict the existing ideology. Both

Euphrosyne and Karatkevich are recognized as the leading Belarusian cultural figures by the current state, and the idea of Kurapaty has never been openly denounced by it either. The belief narratives presented in this chapter are based on generally accepted truth, promoting nationalist history without conflicting with the current official script and letting the promoters live and work safely in Belarus. Realizing that the attitude of their society towards the political situation and Belarusianness is not just black and white, but a vernacular blend of various patterns of reasoning for each individual, the advocates of the legends propagate their own values in an attempt to trigger a folk response and, based on this thinking, to mobilize popular support for alternative thinking. Multiple successful examples of national identity evolving out of utopian legends in other countries show that this is possible. As a Belarusian political refugee wrote on his Facebook page, 'Belarusians will find the Cross [of Saint Euphrosyne] and bring it back to Polotsk, and I will see it. No matter where it is now ... Precisely when they become a unified nation—'the' nation, then the Cross will reappear...'

Needless to say that these items of national heritage acquired additional meaning during the Belarusian protests against Lukashenka's regime in 2020–2021. Karatkevich's novel alone became a symbol of the Belarusian reawakening. In 2020, *The Ears of Rye Under Thy Sickle* became the top book borrowed from Belarusian libraries (NNV 2021). The title of the book was also used as the title of the anti-regime Telegram channel reporting on the cracks in the Belarusian political system and human rights violations (*Telegram* 2021). One of the main opponents of Lukashenka, an imprisoned candidate from the opposition Viktar Babaryka party, sent reports of favourite reading in prison, with *The Ears of Rye Under the Sickle* being top of the list (*Salidarnasts'* 2021). The usefulness of the novel in nation-building, as envisioned long ago by its fans, has been proven now that it is needed.

## Acknowledgements

This research was supported by the European Social Fund's Doctoral Studies and Internationalisation Programme DoRa; the Estonian Research Council (Institutional Research Project IUT2–43) and by the European Union through the European Regional Development Fund (Centre of Excellence, CECT). I would like to thank Marion Bowman, Irina Sadovina and Ülo Valk for their comments and help.

## Notes

1 Perestroika (restructuring) and glasnost (openness) were the political movements launched by the last Soviet leader Mikhail Gorbachev to relax bureaucracy and censorship and transform the rigid Soviet regime into a more modern social democracy.
2 Here and hereafter, I use pseudonyms for the interviewees' names.
3 Ethical reasons prevent me from mentioning the names of the city, event or author.
4 From the privately shared draft of the work.

## References

Aaronovitch, David. 2010. *Voodoo Histories: The Role of the Conspiracy Theory in Shaping Modern History*. New York: Riverhead.
Adams, Laura L. 2010. *The Spectacular State: Culture and National Identity in Uzbekistan*. Durham, NC; London: Duke University Press. https://doi.org/10.2307/j.ctv11318c6
Arkhivy Belarusi. n.d. *Uladzimir Karatkevich*. http://archives.gov.by/index.php?id=896482 (accessed August 25, 2019).
Batyushkov, Pompey. 1890. *Belorussiya i Litva*. Saint-Petersburg: Obshchestvennaya Pol'za.
Bekus, Nelly. 2010. *Struggle over Identity: The Official and the Alternative 'Belarusianness'*. Budapest: Central European University Press.
https://doi.org/10.7829/9789639776685Bekus
Bowman, Marion, and Ülo Valk, eds. 2012. *Vernacular Religion in Everyday Life: Expressions of Belief*. Sheffield; Bristol, CT: Equinox.
Cashman, Ray. 2008. 'Visions of Irish Nationalism'. *Journal of Folklore Research* 45 (3): 361–381. https://doi.org/10.2979/JFR.2008.45.3.361
Chistov, Kirill. 2003. *Russkaya narodnaya utopiya (genezis i funktsii sotsial'no-utopicheskikh legend)*. Saint-Petersburg: 'Dmitriy Bulanin'.
Eco, Umberto. 1983. *The Name of the Rose*. New York: Harcourt.
Eke, Steven, and Taras Kuzio. 2000. 'Sultanism in Eastern Europe: The Socio-political Roots of Authoritarian Populism in Belarus'. *Europe-Asian Studies* 52 (3): 523–547. https://doi.org/10.1080/713663061
Gapova, Yelena. 2008. 'O politicheskoy ekonomii "Natsional'nogo yazyka" v Belarusi'. In *Belorusskiy format: nevidimaya real'nost'*, edited by Al'mira Usmanova, 30–70. Vilnius: EHU. https://doi.org/10.33899/tanra.2008.161770
Humphrey, Caroline. 2002. *The Unmaking of Soviet Life: Everyday Economies after Socialism*. Ithaca, NY: Cornell University Press. https://doi.org/10.7591/9781501725722
Karatkevich, Uladzimir. 1965. 'Kalasy pad Syarpom Tvaim'. *Polymya* 2–6.
Kashkuryevich, Arlyen. 2005. 'Ya Ubachu Inshuyu Belarus'. In *Uladzimir Karatkevich. Byw, Yosts'. Budu: uspaminy, intyerv'yu, esse*, edited by G. V. Shablinskaya, 461–467. Minsk: Mastatskaya litaratura.
Kisyalew, Hennadz'. 2005. 'Yon Daryw Syabrowstva'. In *Uladzimir Karatkevich. Byw, Yosts'. Budu: uspaminy, intyerv'yu, esse*, edited by G. V. Shablinskaya, 218–244. Minsk: Mastatskaya litaratura.

Leshchenko, Natalia. 2004. 'A Fine Instrument: Two Nation-Building Strategies in Post-Soviet Belarus'. *Nations and Nationalism* 10 (3): 333–352. https://doi.org/10.1111/j.1354-5078.2004.00170.x

Lewis, Simon. 2013. 'Toward Cosmopolitan Mourning: Belarusian Literature between History and Politics'. In *Memory and Theory in Eastern Europe*, edited by Uilleam Blacker, Alexander Etkind and Julie Fedor, 195–216. New York: Palgrave Macmillan. https://doi.org/10.1057/9781137322067_10

Lis, Arsyen'. 1994. *Tsyazhkaya Daroha Svabody. Artykuly, Etsyudy, Partryety*. Minsk: Mastatskaya litaratura.

*The Lost Book of Nostradamus*. 2007. History Channel Movie. http://topdocumentaryfilms.com/the-lost-book-of-nostradamus/ (accessed September 3, 2015).

Maldzis, Adam. 1990. *Zhytstsyo I Uznyasyennye Uladzimira Karatkevicha*. Minsk: Mastatskaya litaratura.

Martsinovich, Dzyanis. 2005. 'Pratsyag Kalasow—Mif tsi Realnasts'? Rozdum pra Isnavanne Pratsyagu ramana Uladzimira Karatkevicha'. *Rodnaye Slova* 9: 96–98.

Martsinovich, Dzyanis. 2010. 'Pratsyag Kalasow—Mif abo Realnasts'?' *Blog Dzyanisa Martsinovicha*, October 30, 2010. http://martsinovich.of.by/archives/69 (accessed March 24, 2022).

Martsinovich, Dzyanis. 2012. *Donzhuanski Spis Karatkevicha*. Minsk: Chyetyrye Chyetvyertsi.

McElroy, Damien. 2014. 'More Irish Mass Graves Likely to be Found, Warns Archbishop of Dublin'. *Telegraph*, June 8, 2014. http://www.telegraph.co.uk/news/worldnews/europe/ireland/10885038/More-Irish-mass-graves-likely-to-be-found-warns-Archbishop-of-Dublin.html (accessed August 25, 2019).

NNV. 2021. 'Aleksiyevich, Korotkevich i Sinsero: chto chitali zhiteli Vitebshchiny vo vremya epidemii Covid-19'. *Narodnyya naviny Vitsyebska*, September 2, 2021. https://vitebsk.cc/2021/02/09/aleksievich-korotkevich-i-sinsero-chto-chitali-zhiteli-vitebshhiny-vo-vremya-epidemii-covid-19/ (accessed April 22, 2021).

Oushakine, Serguei. 2009. *The Patriotism of Despair: Nation, War and Loss in Russia*. Ithaca, NY; London: Cornell University Press.

Oushakine, Serguei. 2011. 'V poiskakh mesta mezhdu Stalinym i Gitlerom: O postkolonial'nykh istoriyakh sotsializma'. *Ab Imperio* 1: 209–233.

Pazniak, Zianon. 2002. *Novaye Stahoddzye*. Warsaw: Byelaruskiya Vyedamastsi.

Pazniak, Zianon, Yauheniy Shmygalew, Mikalai Kryvaltsevich and Alyeh Iov. 1994. *Kurapaty*. Minsk: Tyehnalohiya.

Primiano, Leonard Norman. 1995. 'Vernacular Religion and the Search for Method in Religious Folklife'. *Western Folklore* (Special Issue: *Reflexivity and the Study of Belief*) 54 (1): 37–56. https://doi.org/10.2307/1499910

Ries, Nancy. 2005. *Russkiye razgovory: Kul'tura i rechevaya povsednevnost' epokhi perestroyki*. Moscow: Novoye Literaturnoye Obozreniye.

*Salidarnasts'*. 2021. 'Babariko iz "Amerikanki" porekomendoval 5 knig, kotorye sleduyet prochest' belorusam'. *Salidarnasts'*, January 14, 2021. https://gazetaby.com/post/babariko-iz-amerikanki-porekomendoval-5-knig-kotor/173435 (accessed April 22, 2021).

Savchenko, Andrew. 2009. *Belarus—A Perpetual Border*. Leiden; Boston, MA: Brill. https://doi.org/10.1163/ej.9789004174481.i-239

Scott, James C. 1990. *Domination and the Arts of Resistance: Hidden Transcripts*. New Haven, CT; London: Yale University Press.

Shchadryna, Valyantsina. 2005. 'Yak u Maskve vuyshli "Kalasy pad Syarpom Tvaim"'. In *Uladzimir Karatkevich. Byw, Yosts'. Budu: uspaminy, intyerv'yu, esse*, edited by G. V. Shablinskaya, 426-430. Minsk: Mastatskaya litaratura.

Sloterdijk, Peter. 1988. *Critique of Cynical Reason*. Minneapolis: University of Minnesota Press.

Syamyonava, Ala. 2005. 'Rytsar Sonyechnay Stsihii'. In *Uladzimir Karatkevich. Byw, Yosts'. Budu: uspaminy, intyerv'yu, esse*, edited by G. V. Shablinskaya, 279-286. Minsk: Mastatskaya litaratura.

*Telegram*. 2021. 'Kalasy pad syarpom tvaim'. *Telegram*. https://t.me/kalasypad/25 (accessed April 22, 2021).

Vk.com. 2015. 'Sledy Ukradennogo Zaŝitnika Belorusov, Kresta Efrosin'i Polotskoj, Vedut v Moskvu'. *Vk.com*, January 26, 2015. https://vk.com/wall-103070859?offset=100 (accessed March 24, 2022).

Vyerabyei, Anatol'. 1997. *Abudzhanaya Pamyats': Narys Zhytstsya i Tvorchastsi Uladzimira Karatkevicha*. Minsk: Mastatskaya litaratura.

Wilson, William. 1973. 'Herder, Folklore and Romantic Nationalism'. *Journal of Popular Culture* 6 (4): 819-835. https://doi.org/10.1111/j.0022-3840.1973.00819.x

Yanushkyevich, Feliks. 2005. 'Ars Longa'. In *Uladzimir Karatkevich. Byw, Yosts'. Budu: uspaminy, interv'yu, esse*, edited by G. V. Shablinskaya, 503-511. Minsk: Mastatskaya litaratura.

Yurchak, Alexei. 2006. *Everything Was Forever, until it Was No More: The Last Soviet Generation*. Princeton, NJ: Princeton University Press.

Zhbankov, Maksim. 2008. 'Belorusskaya kul'tura: Vremya nol''. In *Belorusskiy format: nevidimaya real'nost'*, edited by Al'mira Usmanova, 141-165. Vilnius: EHU.

Chapter 2

# Humour and Resistance in Russia's Ecological Utopia: A Look at the Anastasia Movement

*Irina Sadovina**

## Introduction

Intentional communities, with their aspirations to build an alternative world here and now, as well as their relative independence from larger economic structures, are among the strongest embodiments of the counterculture. At the same time, as the emergence of authoritarian enclaves of Jonestown-style alternative thinking drives home, countercultural movements inevitably develop authority structures of their own as they attempt to organize people into action based on assertions of greater truth. Noting this tendency towards hierarchy and authority in institutionalized spiritual movements, Paul Heelas suggests that it forms one of the core challenges of the New Age, which he defines as the ethic of an autonomous spiritual Self. On an individual level, listening to the inner voice may seem a logical and sustainable strategy. However, in order to function socially, an individual inevitably enters into a relationship with the outside world and its voices of authority (Heelas 1996: 213). To hold together the ethic of the independent Self and the demands of living in a community calls for a careful balancing act (ibid.: 216).

This chapter explores the role of jokes and parody in constructing and contesting authority in intentional communities animated by the ethic of Self-spirituality. It focuses specifically on back-to-the-land settlements

* **Irina Sadovina** is a scholar of comparative cultural studies. She received a PhD in comparative literature from the University of Toronto in 2018, and another in folkloristics from the University of Tartu in 2020. She has taught at the University of Missouri, the Volga State University of Technology, and the School of Advanced Studies at the University of Tyumen.

inspired by a Russian book series *The Ringing Cedars of Russia*. These books, written by former businessman Vladimir Megre, promote the idea that the degradation of human civilization can be stopped in its tracks if all people return to the Earth and embrace a lifestyle of self-sufficiency and spirituality. Bestsellers of the New Age book market in Russia, and translated into many languages, the books have inspired a movement of ecological spirituality known as the Anastasia movement (cf. Megre 1996, 2003, 2008a, 2008b).

In the following pages, I will briefly situate the movement in the history of European and Russian ecospirituality and in the post-Soviet context in which it developed. I will then explain how the question of authority poses a problem for the movement in the practical application of Anastasia's ideas. Discussing the jokes and parodies created in Anastasia communities, I will show that humour provides their members with the means of supporting, challenging or creatively negotiating structures of authority within the communities and the ideology that engendered them.

## The Anastasia Movement

Vladimir Megre, author of *The Ringing Cedars of Russia* series, wrote the books as an account of his encounters with an unusual young woman who lived in the Siberian forests. The first book of the series, *Anastasia*, came out in 1996, and the last one, *Anasta*, in 2010. Altogether Megre has written ten books, which have sold 11 million copies and have been translated into 23 languages (Biography 2019). He has also established the Anastasia Foundation for the Support of Culture and Creativity. Megre maintains an official website[1] and speaks extensively at readers' conferences.

The books' ideas are anchored in the figure of Anastasia. She is described as a perfect human who, like generations of her ancestors, grew up in the forest, outside the Weberian 'iron cage' of modern civilization. This unusual upbringing allowed her to preserve her extraordinary spiritual insight and abilities that could be seen as paranormal, but which the books claim to be consistent with primordial human nature. Anastasia shares with Megre her ideas about humanity's history and future (and, incidentally, confesses her love for him and bears him two children). The movement's critics strongly doubt Anastasia's existence, citing the books' more fantastical episodes and Megre's supposed acknowledgement of Anastasia's fictional nature (see, for example, 'Sekta Vladimira Megre

"Anastasiya'" [Vladimir Megre's Cult 'Anastasia'] on the Russian Orthodox portal *K Istine* [*K Istine* 2016]). Megre's own evasive responses, exemplified in Anastasia's motto 'I exist for those for whom I exist', actively sustain the ambiguity (Megre 1996).

According to Anastasia, human history started with a Golden Age, a Vedic or Vedrussian earthly paradise in which people lived in harmony and participated in the creation of the world together with God. Civilization, with its ignorance and violence, culminating in contemporary technocracy, has hindered the progression of Vedrussian civilization, plunging people into misery and hastening an apocalypse. This pessimistic vision, however, is not inevitable, as Anastasia brings words of hope. The end of the world may be prevented, and humanity's innate abilities to co-create the world as God's partners can be recovered, provided people restore the earth to harmony and commit to a radically different and profoundly spiritual way of life.

The way towards planetary spiritual recovery, in Anastasia's vision, is the Kin's Domain, a hectare of land where a family could build a new life of higher consciousness. This new ecological and spiritual lifestyle would hasten the return of the Vedrussian Golden Age of wisdom, power and love, extensively described in the books. The movement's name, *The Ringing Cedars of Russia*, comes from the important role that cedars play in Anastasia's philosophy: they possess healing powers and can transmit wisdom and positive energy to humans.

Many Anastasia followers have indeed chosen to radically change their lifestyles in order to bring about the Golden Age (Pranskevičiūtė 2015). According to the movement's official website, as of August 2, 2022, there were 390 registered Kin's Settlements (ecovillages with Kin's Domains) in Russia alone (*Anastasiya* 2022). The books also gave impetus to much creative output among its readers, inspiring other books, magazines, art and music. Singer-songwriters who celebrate Anastasia's ideas in their songs are called the Bards of the Sun. Many of these musicians frequently go on tours, seeking to inspire and uplift their audiences. Several festivals, both official and grassroots, are associated with *The Ringing Cedars of Russia*. In addition to regular festivals and concerts, the movement has a strong commercial component, with sales of cedar products, handmade items, books and other related merchandise. In 2013, it also officially registered a political party (*Anastasiya* 2013). How-to videos on sustainable living and documentaries about life in a Kin's Settlement have also been produced. A notable example is the film series called *Kin's Domains of the Earth*. In the trailer for one film in the series, Andrey Shadrov's 2012 feature *Slavnoye 2: New Dawn*, the voiceover, accompanied by a dramatic action movie soundtrack, describes life in the Slavnoye Kin's Settlement as an ecospiritual dream come true:

> Ten years ago it was their dream, but today it's already reality. They live in their dream, they build their future themselves, they turn abandoned fields into blossoming gardens and enchanted forests. They restore rivers and villages. They give birth to healthy children, grow ecologically pure vegetables. They revive forgotten holidays, folk traditions, lead a healthy lifestyle. People of the new civilization. Builders of Kin's Domains. Creators of beauty on the planet. The secret to a happy life has been discovered! (Shadrov 2012, my translation from Russian)

## Ecological Spirituality

The secret to a happy life revealed in Kin's Domains is not entirely unexpected. The ideals of self-sufficiency and deep ecology that underlie Anastasia's project have a long history in Russia and indeed the world. This chapter cannot, for obvious reasons, provide a comprehensive account of this phenomenon, but it will nevertheless introduce several points of reference that will ground Kin's Domains in a larger historical context.

The emphasis on individual responsibility and rediscovering untapped human potential situates the Anastasia books firmly in the field of Self-spirituality, which Heelas identifies as the defining characteristic of the New Age. What distinguishes *The Ringing Cedars of Russia* from scores of spiritual self-development groups and teachings in contemporary Russia is the central emphasis on a radically environmentalist lifestyle, a sort of rural utopianism. The back-to-the-land ideal has its own respectable genealogy: in *The Re-Enchantment of the West*, Christopher Partridge (2005: 42) remarks on the 'significant greening of the Western consciousness'. Green lifestyles and holistic practices are staple topics in mainstream publishing. Environmental issues play a prominent role in national and international politics and, perhaps even more tellingly, in marketing campaigns and corporate business practices. Despite their ubiquity in these secular discourses, ecological concerns, as Partridge (ibid.: 43) argues, have 'a strong sacralising bias' because of the affinity they have with a holistic vision of the unity of all beings and the Self's responsibility towards them.

The particular brand of ecological spirituality represented by *The Ringing Cedars* movement can be located in a specific historical moment.

Scholars and ecology advocates explain that the initial loss of enchantment with nature in Western culture was caused by the technological leaps of the Industrial Revolution and the radical changes in social structures brought about by modernity (ibid.: 44). This narrative is useful but rather broadly sketched out, and far be it from researchers of vernacular belief to posit uniform rises and falls in enchantment. The concept of vernacular belief, developed by Leonard Primiano (1995), emphasizes the innumerable pockets of counter-discourses and counter-practices that exist at any given moment alongside the more visible and dominant strands of social life. Nevertheless, the notion of the loss of enchantment, regardless of its sociohistorical verifiability, remains influential and relevant. It is this perception of a crisis that animates various turns 'back to nature', in their Romantic, post-Romantic, neo-Romantic, New Age and other guises.

It is difficult, if not impossible, to speak of either Romanticism or New Age in terms of definable characteristics. Instead, it seems instructive to start with specific figures and projects associated with back-to-the-land spirituality, such as the fin-de-siècle 'centres of life' described by Martin Green (2000). Green defines 'centres of life' as places where people gather in an attempt to resist the dominant course of humanity's development, by sharing the pursuit of simple living and an interest in folk knowledge. Two of the communities mentioned by Green are particularly helpful in contextualizing *The Ringing Cedars of Russia* in a larger history of ecospirituality.

Count Leo Tolstoy's philosophy of simple life and social-justice-minded Christianity gave rise to several intentional communities in the Russian Empire and beyond, inspiring Gandhi's farm communities and the Whiteway agricultural colony in England (Green 2000: 52). Tolstoy's teaching championed nonviolence, anarchism and simplicity. It idealized the peasantry and promoted personal moral responsibility. We can certainly draw a link between Tolstoy's philosophy and the marriage of agrarian and moral ideals in *The Ringing Cedars of Russia*. Quasi-Tolstoyan ideas appear in Anastasia's teaching, expressed in a melodic prose that seems to rise directly from traditional peasant songs or folk tales.

Around the same time as Tolstoyans attempted to build new Christian communities of justice and equality, the Mountain of Truth, in Ascona, Switzerland, was attracting European intellectuals keen to liberate themselves from the oppressive grasp of urban civilization. Despite its rather different demographic makeup and ideological underpinnings, Ascona has a literary connection with the Anastasia movement. In the 1918 novel

*The Heretic of Soana* by Gerhart Hauptmann, a writer connected with the Ascona community, we encounter the figure of a female hermit, unspoiled by civilization, who leads the male protagonist (a priest) away from the church to the worship of Eros (Hauptmann 2020). The woman is depicted as exceptional: wise, beautiful, infinitely enchanting—in fact, irresistible. Compare this character with Megre's descriptions of Anastasia:

> I was facing a very young woman with long golden hair and a splendid shape. Her beauty was extraordinary. She was an exceptional model. It was hard to imagine anybody who could possibly compete with her among the winners of the most prestigious beauty contests. Also, as it was revealed later on, her intellect was extremely sharp, too. Absolutely everything was appealing about her and she was full of charm. (Megre 1996)

Anastasia has another, more immediate, predecessor: the female protagonist of Alexander Kuprin's 1898 novel *Olesya* (Kuprin 1956). A fin-de-siècle Russian classic and a staple of the high school curriculum, Kuprin's novel tells the story of a young woman living in the woods, gifted with a deep connection with nature, irresistible charm, higher wisdom and seemingly supernatural abilities. Encountering Olesya and winning her love, the male protagonist feels inwardly transformed yet is unable to protect her from the rage of the villagers, who turn against her, accusing her of being a witch. The Anastasia books contain several scenes of confrontation between the wise woman of the forest and the fallen, uncomprehending representatives of civilization: in *The Space of Love*, Anastasia successfully resists being captured by researchers, while in *Who Are We?*, she even confronts the world of local organized crime. Unlike her literary counterpart, Olesya, Anastasia emerges victorious, successfully expanding the consciousness of both antagonistic groups and bringing them to see the error of their ways.

## The Post-Soviet Religious Landscape

The examples of Tolstoy and Kuprin show that environmental ideas and ecospirituality in particular have long been a part of Russian intellectual life. In the twentieth century, however, their development into full-scale intentional communities and alternative movements was curbed by the state's tight control of the ideological landscape of the country. Nevertheless, the roots of many contemporary alternative movements in Russia can be traced to late Soviet underground publications and holistic health groups (Honey 2006: 199). After the breakup of the Soviet Union, there was a blossoming of alternative ideas and religious practices, previously suppressed by an officially atheist state. The influx of foreign influences and Western missionaries also served to diversify and enliven the country's alternative spiritual scene. At the same time, the religious discourse in Russia is currently dominated by the significant and growing social power of the Orthodox Church, which attempts to influence the government in the repression of alternative religious movements. The anti-cult movement supported by the church (Shterin 2001) succeeded in discrediting many religious groups, and a cautious attitude towards these groups has become commonplace.

Nevertheless, the types and activities of 'alternative' religions remain complex and dynamic, and delimiting a research object can be tricky. Ideas develop, diverge or merge, and people constantly alter their practices or adopt new ones. In her study of the Russian Native Faith *Rodnoverie*, Kaarina Aitamurto (2016) discusses this very difficulty: despite several common traits within Russia's Neo-Pagan discourse, it is difficult to pin down its defining characteristics. In my own fieldwork in St Petersburg I was similarly struck both by the interconnectedness of many alternative religious groups and by the seeming paradoxes in the expressed and practiced beliefs of people I met. Having had personal connections to people involved in the Anastasia movement and other alternative spiritual pursuits for many years, I started fieldwork in 2012, conducting interviews and participant observation in St Petersburg, Yoshkar-Ola and the Pskov region. In the course of my research I attended or volunteered at festivals, conferences, workshops and spontaneous gatherings. While my fieldwork took place mainly in the summer, friendships with some of my informants developed on a more permanent and continuous basis.

The conversations and events in which I participated did not easily fit the clear-cut categories of Neo-Pagan or New Age. My research therefore needed to be structured not around predetermined categories, but around the interconnected, mutable processes of belief going on in the milieu I had entered. In his conceptualization of vernacular belief, Primiano (1995: 44) defines the 'process of religious belief' as 'the complex linkage of acquisition and formation of beliefs which is always accomplished by the conscious and unconscious negotiations of and between believers'. In this chapter, I explore the role of humour in these negotiations, and it is in an instance of such humour that I found a concept in which to anchor my research.

This concept is the term 'sectarians'. It was used by the media and the Russian Orthodox Church as a derogatory description of followers of New Religious Movements (*sekta* in contemporary use is the Russian equivalent of the English 'cult'). However, the term has been adopted and used ironically by the followers of these movements themselves. In summer 2012, I was present at a conversation where a young woman, Liza, who has been involved with alternative spirituality for over three years, presented a typology of sectarians to a girl who was new to the whole scene.[2] Even in everyday conversations, I heard the term sectarians very often as people used it to position themselves and others in the loose, organic network of Russian alternative religions. This appropriation of a derogatory term, akin to the adoption of the term queer by the LGBTQ community, serves to indicate the awareness of a label imposed from the outside, the recognition of its inappropriateness, and a decision to forcefully reclaim it as a sign of the community's invincibility in response to discursive violence.[3]

## *The Ringing Cedars* and Authority Structures Within and Without

Anastasia's followers, like many others who pursue alternative spirituality in Russia, have good reason to joke about being sectarians. In contrast to the positive self-representation of Anastasia's movement, the Russian Orthodox Church labels it a totalitarian sect. The figure of Anastasia has inspired intense devotion in many followers, which allows Orthodox sources to define the movement as the 'cult of Anastasia', the members of which 'worship' the 'holy woman' of the taiga (the Siberian boreal forest).

*The Ringing Cedars* movement has been condemned in the influential anti-cult writings of Aleksandr Dvorkin (2002), a former clergyman working with the blessing of the Russian Orthodox Church. The movement's reputation has also suffered from negative and sensationalist representations in mainstream media,[4] although Anastasia's followers have been encouraged by Prime Minister Dmitriy Medvedev's support of the idea of Kin's Domains (*Poseleniya* 2012).

To be classified as a 'totalitarian sect', however, *The Ringing Cedars of Russia* must be proven to possess a strong centralized authority and a hostile attitude to the world outside the community. As a countercultural movement, *Ringing Cedars* is necessarily opposed to the mainstream. The drastic lifestyle changes that the books' readers make naturally give rise to accusations of fanaticism, intolerance and even brainwashing. Moreover, arguably Megre could be seen as a strong charismatic leader who maintains the movement's momentum, clarifying its main ideas and to a certain extent directing its development. While in his books Megre insists that the Anastasia movement's ideas are compatible with any religion, the books have clearly defined ideas about God, the world, and human nature. They are often overtly critical of the Orthodox Church, and contain elements of conspiracy theory, positing the existence of a secret priesthood, a sort of world government that has orchestrated humanity's gradual decline.

*The Ringing Cedars of Russia*, therefore, can certainly be seen as having a leadership and even some dogmatic elements. Nevertheless, closer engagement through ethnographic studies, such as Yuliya Andreyeva's (2017), Rasa Pranskevičiūtė's (2015) and my own (Sadovina 2017), reveals that individuals who identify with the movement embrace active, self-conscious, at times ironic attitudes to its ideas and values. Given the democratic nature of Anastasia's vision and its emphasis on Self-spirituality, the discursive space opened up by the books created as much opportunity for contesting authority as it did for asserting it.

As more Kin's Settlements were established, an even greater variety of approaches to the books and their ideas emerged. A Kin's Settlement dweller I met in the Pskov region described the books' early popularity as 'the brightest years for Anastasia followers'. Combining a hint of nostalgia for a time of greater commitment with a critique of the more entrepreneurial activities within the movement, such as the current proliferation of both cedar products and *Ringing Cedar* paraphernalia, he continued: 'Now you can buy cedars on every street corner, but back then…' (Interview, August 12, 2012, Pskov region). The rapid expansion of the movement has attracted the attention of the Orthodox Church and the media, which has produced sensationalist or demonizing—and therefore, uniform and simplistic—representations of it. In addition to greater visibility, however, this expansion also meant that centralized control over the movement's ideas and practices has become increasingly impossible, even if such attempts were made. This relative freedom within a movement naturally gives rise to explicit conflicts over which groups or persons have the power to decide how the books' central ideas should be interpreted or implemented.

## Theories of Humour

The connection between humour and power is a principal theme that seems to unite diverse pockets of humour research in the disciplines of folklore studies, anthropology, sociology, literary studies and linguistics. The sheer multiplicity and disjointed nature of research into humour, highlighted in Victor Raskin's *Primer of Humor Research* (2008), encourages me to adopt the straightforward three-part model proposed by John Morreall (2008: 211) in his overview of philosophical and religious approaches to humour. Morreall distinguishes three concepts that underlie theories of humour: incongruity, superiority and relief. Incongruity—or, in Elliott Oring's (2003: 2) more precise definition, the perception of 'appropriate incongruity'—refers to the double structure of a joke, which combines logical and 'normal' statements with elements that make no sense either in the closed universe of the joke or in a larger social context. Understood in the light of appropriate incongruity, jokes transgress the limits of what is logical and what is thinkable, which means that jokes always contradict the authority of common sense, if not more concrete examples of authority, such as political regimes. In contrast, Morreall's second concept, superiority, emphasizes more direct assertions of power through humour: jokes about the culture's others, who are seen as stupid, greedy, promiscuous, or in other ways unsuccessful, would fall into this category. Finally, the third concept, relief, presents humour as a roundabout, indirect way of asserting power: jokes serve to express hostility, aggression, or a critique of the social order that cannot be expressed in other ways. This last approach draws on works like James Scott's *Domination and the Arts of Resistance: Hidden Transcripts* (1990), which explore the way oppressed groups claim power. Relief theories are developed in more detail by Oring. In *Risky Business*, Oring (2004: 216–226) describes five potential views of the function of political jokes: they might provide a way to express repressed opinions, release pent-up aggression, enable revolutionary acts, sustain a sceptical coexistence with the ruling ideological regime, or help assert an identity independent from the regime.

This model, of course, does not account for the subtlety and variety of scholarship on humour, but it provides a good road map. Indeed, it seems that most theories of humour prioritize one of these three features, either exclusively or in combination with others. In addition to forming around one of these three main ideas, different explanations of humour are also determined by the nature of the theoretical impulse that animates them. Salvatore Attardo (1994: 1) distinguishes three types of theories of humour: essentialist (which seeks to pin down what humour is), teleological (which is interested in the goals and functions of humour) and substantialist (which derives the meaning of humour from its content).

An inquiry into the relationship between humour and authority, which this chapter attempts, gravitates naturally, though not exclusively, towards a teleological paradigm. My aim is neither to give a decisive definition of Anastasian humour nor to explain its nature. Rather, what do irreverent jokes in a spiritual community of the *Ringing Cedars* do in relation to the movement's authority structures? To follow Morreall's taxonomy, do these jokes aim to disturb the norm through appropriate incongruity, to openly express superiority over other members of community or outsiders, or to offer a half-acknowledged release of pent-up resentment?

In the material I gathered, there is evidence in support of all three explanations. What I am interested in, however, is not determining the primary function of humour, but discovering the specific ways in which it works in the context of post-Soviet alternative spirituality and the specific paradoxes of authority that it creates. As Christie Davies points out, 'It is *impossible* to infer anything about purpose, function or emotion from the mere text of a joke' (2008: 160; original emphasis). A thorough knowledge of context is important, then, to 'infer anything' about humour. Larry Danielson (1986: 47), writing on religious folklore, echoes this demand for contextualization: the nuances of religious folklore and religious humour in particular are fully visible only to those who belong to the community itself. Acknowledging my ambivalent status as a sympathetic outsider within the Anastasia community, I nevertheless venture to elucidate those nuances of meaning that have been perceptible to me.

## Humour and Authority

Despite the multiplicity of its potential functions, when it comes to its relationship to authority, humour has been discussed as either opposing or supporting the social order. Discussing sociological approaches to humour, Giselinde Kuipers writes:

> Humor obviously fulfills important social functions, but more recent studies tend to stress the multiple functions of humor, which can be a threat as well as a contribution to the social order: cohesion, control, relief, but also the expression of conflict, inciting resistance, insulting, ridiculing or satirizing others. (Kuipers 2008: 367)

Harking back to Alfred Radcliffe-Brown's (1940) study of 'joking relationships' between relatives, jokes, even and especially transgressive ones, could be seen as reinforcing the *status quo* (Oring 2008: 185). On the other hand, humour's potential to challenge power relations has often been emphasized in the studies of ritual humour (see Douglas 1968; Oring 2008: 187). Naturally, this dichotomy gives birth to a combined approach to humour as both upholding and resisting the hegemonic order, an approach of which Bakhtinian studies of festivals as overlaps of signification systems are a notable example.

When it comes to instances of humour in the Anastasia community, there is no shortage of examples that seem to either uphold the movement's ideals or explicitly challenge them. In the next sections, I will discuss several examples of such humour and suggest that the conservative/oppositional dichotomy limits the way we can talk about the role of humour in relation to authority. I will then propose an alternative reading of such humour as a component of spiritual search in the context of post-Soviet alternative spirituality.

### Spontaneous Critique of Fanaticism: 'Spitters' and 'Egovillages'

The tongue-in-cheek use of the term sectarian points to a self-reflexive attitude among the Anastasia followers who employ it. One conversation I recorded between Liza and two other young women, Anna and Lena, exemplifies a critical and even mocking approach. Anna had just purchased land in a Kin's Settlement and started building her own Kin's Domain. She had recently planted cedars on her plot of land then left for the city. The rest were curious to know whether Anna followed Anastasia's planting instructions, which include holding the seed in one's mouth to pass on the information about the body's needs through one's saliva.

> **Lena**: All you need is to talk to [the seeds] over long distances.
> **Liza**: So, are you sending them good vibes?
> **Anna**: Well, I left ... But when I planted them, I sent them some [vibes]. 'Grow!' I said and left, haven't been back yet.
> **Lena**: Did you spit? On the seeds? ... Did you lick the roots all over?
> [Everyone laughs]
> **Anna**: No.
> **Liza**: How will [the seeds] know what sorts of cedars they need to grow into?
> **Anna**: I'm gonna replant them later. That's when I'll spit.
> [Laughter]

**Anna**: It's difficult to spit.
**Liza**: Why?
**Anna**: You stand there thinking 'what an idiot'.
[Laughter]
**Liza**: Was there anyone else there?
**Anna**: Well, the neighbours are around constantly. They're watching, after all.
**Lena**: But they're just the same!
**Anna**: Nobody spits.
**Lena**: They probably spit in secret.
**Liza**: They're all spitters. (August 7, 2012, St Petersburg)

This private conversation provided a stage for spontaneous joking expression of disapproval of Anastasia 'fanatics' and Anna's uneasiness about being perceived as such. By jokingly pretending to ensure that Anna followed the procedure, these women showed that they actually perceived an excessively public and literal application of Anastasia's rules to be absurd. In doing so, they showed both their mastery of the Anastasia discourse and distanced themselves from the attitude of blind conformity.

Another striking example of such humorous creativity is a video made by a Belarusian ethno-folk band called Khortitsa. The band is associated with the Bards of the Sun and is very much part of the Anastasia scene. Their homemade video, *Egovillage Khortitsa: The Rugged North of White Russia* (see Shemendyuk 2011), is a parody of life in a Kin's Settlement, which suggests that, far from being a shortcut to spiritual bliss, ecovillages are faced with problems caused by their residents' egos. By specifically referencing promotional films like the *Kin's Domains of the Earth* series, Khortitsa pokes fun at rigid, idealized visions of ecovillage life, showing these to be absurd when taken too seriously. In the words of one Khortitsa member, the video was made 'so that people don't think that Anastasia followers make nice and cloyingly sweet movies'.

The video follows the imaginary life of Dem'yan, 'a gentleman of the Kin's Estate'. Dem'yan and the occasional operator of the video, Konstantin, exchange witty remarks in a hilarious running commentary that parodies the tropes of Anastasia discourse. In one scene, Konstantin shows the main 'house' to the visitors, performing naïve reverence for nature and illustrating a general lack of practicality:

**Konstantin**: Okay, let's go into the house. But be careful. It's just that we read that we should not kill any plants, so we don't mow or weed. So try to walk through these thorns as carefully as you can.
**Dem'yan**: For the sake of the thorns.

The video's characters live in a complete wreck of a house but see it through the rose-coloured glasses of ecospiritual ideals.

> Here is our Space of Love. Of course, it's not ready yet, but it's already cozy. This is our neighbour. The neighbour is a bit crazy. This is our nuptial bed. We haven't really cleaned up, we didn't know you were coming...

In another part of the video, the image of Anastasia fanatics is developed further. As we follow Dem'yan into a roofless 'guesthouse', we are introduced to a young woman who is supposedly visiting the Kin's Domain: 'This girl, who only yesterday was locked up in a mental institution, is now ready to work in Dem'yan's garden'. The girl looks up with a vacant gaze and says: 'Yes, I am ready to work for Dem'yan'. Another 'guest' interrupts: 'Guys, she's acting this way because she has only just finished reading the Anastasia books for the first time'. The girl is represented as a recent convert to the Anastasia 'sect', but, as Konstantin reassures us, 'it's only in the beginning that she looks so fanatical'.

Khortitsa also makes fun of self-assured dogmatism within the *Ringing Cedars* movement. In one scene, a man pretending to be drunk staggers into the room, and the 'ecovillagers' welcome him as a fresh Anastasia convert. They encourage him to find his soul mate and build a Space of Love, but issue a warning as well: 'Hey, be careful! We have pure thoughts here, and censorship!' Elsewhere, Dem'yan explains that the guesthouse was built solely for the purposes of conducting seminars: 'We just think that we have enough wisdom to teach people to lead a right life. A *right* life, not this ignorant life that they lead, but a right, harmonious, beautiful life'. By exaggerating the stereotypical language of Anastasia followers and juxtaposing it with incongruous images of abandoned houses and overgrown shrubs, Khortitsa ridicule the sense of spiritual superiority within the movement.

## For or Against? *Ringing Cactuses of Rus'* and Minstrels of the Moon

In addition to spontaneous conversational humour and playful improvised videos, the Anastasia movement produced a more formalized, even institutionalized, type of humour. One notable example is the website called the *Ringing Cactuses of Rus'*, created and copyrighted in 2007 by the 'readers of V. Megre's books'. The introduction to the Ringing Cactuses explains that the website was created as an antidote to the writings of readers who treated Anastasia's ideas as a new religion or a replacement for communist ideology (*Byt' Dobru* 2007).[5] The Ringing Cactuses website is currently listed as under reconstruction. Only a limited number of materials is available: as of June 9, 2021, it only hosts 25 song files (each downloaded a couple of thousand times on average) and a few articles posted by users, most of which are preoccupied with debunking secret government plots and revealing hidden secrets in history. Some jokes originally posted on the website can still be found elsewhere on Anastasia websites, and some have been told to me in conversations. Anna, in her account of the Ringing Cactuses website and its fate, told me the following joke: 'After the local power station shut off the illegal power line, the Svetorus'ye ("Light-Rus"') Settlement was separated into two parts: Temnorus'ye ("Dark-Rus"') and Svetovorus'ye ("Light-Thievery")' (October 11, 2012, St Petersburg).

Anna herself was registered on the Ringing Cactuses website and contributed some jokes. She describes the emergence of this humorous website as follows:

> when I first entered this whole scene of Light, even then there already started to appear the first people who noticed that something was off. Too much Light, not enough real action. And the Bards of Light, the Bards of the Sun, wander around the world, move into the houses of benevolent welcoming parties, wreak havoc there, throw their socks around, and respond to all mishaps like this: 'well, we are the Bards of the Sun, we do all this for some profound reasons'. So many people began to laugh at this a little bit. And even jokes began to appear. Different ones. And anecdotes. In general, many people started teasing those who talked a lot and didn't do anything. (October 11, 2012, St Petersburg)

According to Anna, the impetus behind the *Ringing Cactuses of Rus'* also gave rise to the Minstrels of the Moon, a group of musicians who positioned themselves as an alternative to the unfailingly positive and patriotic songs of Anastasia's Bards of the Sun. As Anna explains:

> These were guys who wrote beautiful songs, but didn't fit the canon that everyone else had to fit. Me, I fell victim to the regime. [Laughs.] I rejected negative songs [laughs] and poems. That's it. I stopped writing them. But there were people who did not fall under the power of the regime. And they wanted to write, but they wanted to be part of the scene. And [Anastasia's] ideas had entered their consciousness, so they created … the Moon Minstrels group. It's the same people, I think, who created the *Ringing Cactuses of Rus'*. (October 11, 2012, St Petersburg)

These transgressive heroes never directly opposed the movement's values, but they often approached the discourse in a satirical, light-hearted way. Their online group on vk.com, for example, has a photo album called 'Naked Truth)))' [sic], where they post pictures (often of themselves) with humorous captions, poking fun at their friends, at the seriousness of the Bards of the Sun, and the ignorant ways of the uninitiated.

Even though Ringing Cactuses and Minstrels of the Moon oppose themselves to the Anastasia mainstream, their jokes never aim to seriously challenge the authority of Megre's books. There is nothing about humour that binds it necessarily to a transgressive function: jokes do not only contest authority, but can very well serve to reinforce it. The Anastasia books, after all, are themselves not at all devoid of humour: Megre's clueless blunders often contrast comically with Anastasia's wisdom and grace, while she has a strong playful side and readily recognizes the humorous in their generally serious discussions. In *Co-creation*, Megre's fourth book, for example, Anastasia tells Megre of an extinct animal called the *prentozavr* (or, in John Woodsworth's translation, 'brontosaurus'). The *prentozavr*, according to Anastasia's account, was able to breathe fire with the flammable gas escaping from his stomach. Human bodies produce the same gas, explains Anastasia, encouraging the sceptical Megre to test her words on his own. When Megre fails to understand that she is talking about passing wind, and asks for details, Anastasia laughs and avoids a straight answer: 'What are you, a little child? Think for yourself—it is a private experience' (Megre 2008a: 20).

In *The Book of Kin*, Anastasia even stresses the importance of satirical humour in the Golden Age civilization of ancient VedRussia:

> Every other person living in Rus' at that time was a poet and a wit. And there were bards in Rus'—they were called *bayans* back then. And this is how it all took place in those times. For decades the priest's foot soldiers waged a propaganda campaign to the effect that God had to be bowed down to. And here and there people began to listen and reflect on the message. Upon seeing this, the bayan would simply laugh and make up a parable, which he would then sing. And the parable would quickly spread throughout Rus'. And over the next ten years or so Rus' would have a good laugh at the priests' sermons. (Megre 2008b: 167–168)

The Anastasia books do not, therefore, promote a grave and humourless spirituality, but instead celebrate the role of humour as an effective strategy of exposing deviations from the truth and maintaining the right social order without explicit ideological warfare. The humour of

Khortitsa and the Minstrels of the Moon, as well as the jokes originally posted on *Ringing Cactuses of Rus'*, clearly have a place in the mainstream of the movement. It may offer insider criticism or poke some gentle fun at excessive fanaticism, but this serves to highlight the sustainability and vitality of the movement itself. Retold in casual situations, these jokes can confirm the rightness and righteousness of the Anastasia path, even as they create the pleasure of transgression and independent critical thinking. Ultimately, the humour of Anastasia followers enables a kind of ironic identification with the movement. One can recognize the parodic undertones of a Soviet-style poster with Anastasia's face superimposed onto communist Mother Russia and at the same time identify with the call issued by the VedRussian Motherland.

## Humour, Authority and Spiritual Seeking

Humour within the Anastasia movement can also be understood in terms outside of the dichotomous relationship with authority that I initially posited. For an alternative view, let us turn to Anna's explanation of why the oppositional impulse of projects like Ringing Cactuses is ultimately ineffective. The biting humour directed at the 'regime' relied on a strong identification with it and could result in interminable ideological fights. Anna suggests a different strategy: to move on, relinquish attachment, and enjoy what the movement has to offer in a personal way.

> When you let go, you give freedom, you understand that the train moves on its own, and you don't even want to be there. Being on the train, you thought that you are responsible for this train … You were a patriot of this train! Until you travelled abroad. Now you look at it and, of course, you have much that connects you with it … But what's the point of branching off into an opposition nearby, so that you're kind of part of it, but in your own comfortable … opposition. There is no point, and I am increasingly ready to just go there and be in the mainstream, but be myself, enjoy it in my own way. The need for opposition falls away. (October 11, 2012, St Petersburg)

The individualist strategy described by Anna can illuminate the following critique of Anastasia's ideas. One young woman I met, Masha, judged the movement rather harshly: 'the VedRussian thing is already rotten' (July 2012, Leningrad Oblast). Despite this strong expression of disapproval, Masha was committed to many of Anastasia's ideals: she lived in a Kin's Domain, attended Anastasia festivals and went on tours with the Bards of the Sun. Similarly, in her taxonomy of 'sectarians', Liza described the distinction between 'orthodox Anastasia followers who are fanatical' and 'sensible' ones. Like Masha, Liza is not opposed to the movement itself, loves Megre's books and confesses that they moved her significantly. Many of her friends live in Kin's Settlements, and, at the time of our conversation, she and her husband were planning to move to a non-denominational and Anastasia-friendly ecovillage. Despite her identification with and support of the Anastasia movement, Liza described its faithful adherents with biting humour: 'The Orthodox Anastasia followers are characterized by pure thoughts, clear eyes and a determination to make friends with all the little squirrels of the forest!' (August 9, 2012, St Petersburg). In this remark, Liza both distanced herself from a particular type of behaviour and belief, while not disavowing the importance of the movement to her personal choices.

To Liza, Masha and many other 'sectarians' that I met, the movement is a dynamic thing that is now growing out of its initial idealistic stage, which allows its members to engage with the ideas enthusiastically, critically or humorously, while pursuing their personal spiritual and practical goals.

Another notable example of such a pragmatic attitude comes from my conversation with Anna about the Kin's Domain she recently purchased in a village called Kshoty. As a young woman with no experience of construction work, she needed help to build a house on her patch of land. She was therefore concerned with attracting some male friends to help her with the construction. She had also become interested in the history of the area where her plot was located and did some research in local archives. What she discovered gave her an unconventional idea of how to attract robust Anastasia followers for construction work.

> **Anna**: So I was digging through 15th century census records ... Kshoty used to be called Kshety, and there was a military settlement here ... And so I realized that ... I began to look for the Sanskrit word ... I somehow remembered the word *Kshatriya*, and I found that ... *Kshat* means to hurt, *Kshatriya* is a warrior, *Kshatrinya* is the warrior's wife. *Kshetra* is a field ... So, I am thinking something along the lines of ancient Aryan warriors ... Yeah, let it be about roots! Kshoty is an ancient Aryan village. It has to be the Rus' people, Aryans! Blue-eyed, tall, handsome.
> **Irina**: Why?
> **Anna**: Because it's not trendy to say that we originate from Indians, but if Indians came from us ... that's all the rage right now. And so Slavophiles will trickle in...
> **Irina**: Why do we need them?

**Anna:** Well they ... I mean ... It's the inflow of people. Fresh blood ... and flesh. Fresh labour. There is so much to build. And how do we force the likes of them to build things? Through ideas alone. (February 28, 2013, Tartu, Estonia)

What makes Anna's story so funny is her thorough knowledge and understanding of the Anastasia community, as well as her ability to be ironic about her own role as a spokesperson for this ethno-ecological utopia. A popular blogger about spirituality and sustainable life on the land, a founder of a women's craft organization, a former organizer of a holistic living festival, and an occasional performer with the Bards of the Sun, Anna lends her voice to the discursive space of Vedic Russian spirituality. Her Kshoty story makes no attempt to hide a blatantly opportunistic treatment of linguistic evidence to concoct a theory about the village's Aryan origins. The funniest thing about it, of course, is that it is actually quite believable, being a skilful parody of Aryan origin theories that proliferate in the Russian book market and especially in esoteric circles (Shnirelman 2014). Anna's joking shows that she understands very well how this ideology works, and how it can be used to motivate people. In a way, her joke is also self-parody, since her success as a blogger and seminar leader depends greatly on her ability to persuade and inspire. In her writing and teaching, Anna tells stories and invokes ancient wisdom to promote many of Anastasia's values, yet her jokes also show that she is self-aware and even self-critical.

These examples of humour as a primarily individualist rather than directly oppositionist or ideologically conservative approach highlight the main difference between the humour of the Anastasia movement and the political anecdotes of Soviet dissidents. As Alexei Yurchak (1997: 162) explains, humour directed against the authority of the state's totalizing ideology was the product of a particular late Soviet subjectivity, which perceived the hegemonic order as both false and inevitable. The Anastasia movement, like the Soviet state, can function as a closed ideological system that tautologically explains everything with reference to a few central concepts, but there is a significant difference between the two systems. For Yurchak's Soviet subjects, the available strategies for relating to authority were limited to ambiguous compliance ('pretence misrecognition'), dissident-style rebellion and full-on support of the regime (ibid.: 169). Anastasia followers, as we have seen, have another option: neither accepting, enthusiastically or cynically, the status quo, nor forming a sustained 'opposition' as described by Anna. Additionally, they can also use humour to negotiate their personal relationships to the authority of Anastasia's words and the institutional structures of the movement. Humour, in this case, helps people stage and execute their own 'spiritual journey', navigating discourses of authority and determining for themselves what they find useful in them and what they regard as laughable.

## Conclusion

This article highlights the role of jokes in the way that people relate to authority structures in alternative spirituality movements and the authoritative discourses associated with them. In a movement like *The Ringing of Cedars of Russia*, positioned on the margins of the larger public sphere yet confronting its own internal challenges of organization and institutionalization, individuals use humour to establish and experience their relationship with authority in various ways. As we have seen, humour can reinforce a sense of community by confirming 'orthodox' values or by enabling criticism of certain aspects of it.

As the examples in this article have shown, there is a third way in which humour can structure individuals' relationships to authority in countercultural spiritual movements like *The Ringing Cedars of Russia*. Humour creates multiple discursive pathways through which people negotiate their personal spiritual journeys, understand the distribution of authority in social settings and exercise the 'independent thinking' so prized in the Anastasia movement and in New Age in general (Heelas 1996: 23). Anastasia's followers and other self-consciously 'sectarian' spiritual seekers use humour actively, critically and self-reflexively as they wrestle with important questions of how to relate to the truth they choose to embrace, how to coexist with others who may or may not share their vision of this truth, and how to make this truth a part of their personal lives.

## Acknowledgements

This research was supported by the European Social Fund's Doctoral Studies and Internationalisation Programme DoRa; the Estonian Research Council (Institutional Research Project IUT2–43), and by the European Union through the European Regional Development Fund (Centre of Excellence, CECT). The research was made possible thanks to the participation of Anna and other individuals who shared with me their jokes and insights.

## Notes

1 https://anastasia.ru/ (accessed July 19, 2019).
2 All names have been changed, unless otherwise requested by the individual interviewed. All interviews were conducted in Russian; the translations are mine.
3 See Elliott Oring's 'Self-Degrading Jokes and Tales' in *Jokes and Their Relations* on different functions of self-degrading humour (2010: 122–134).
4 See, for example, Alesya Lonskaya's article on raw diet in ecovillages for the magazine *Russian Reporter* (2011).
5 This introduction, along with many other materials, is available on the website of the *Byt' Dobru* newspaper (the title, *Good Shall Prevail*, is taken from a chapter in Megre's fifth book, *Who Are We?*). This Russian-language newspaper is dedicated to promoting an environmentally conscious lifestyle and life in Kin's Domains.

## References

Aitamurto, Kaarina. 2016. *Paganism, Traditionalism, Nationalism: Narratives of Russian Rodnoverie*. London; New York: Routledge. https://doi.org/10.4324/9781315599304

Anastasiya. 2013. 'Rodnaya Partiya zaregistrirovana! Pozdravlyayem!' *Fond Anastasiya*. http://anastasia.ru/news/detail/10184 (accessed July 19, 2019).

Anastasiya. 2022. 'Spisok poseleniy, sostoyashchikh iz Rodovykh Pomestiy'. *Fond Anastasiya*. www.anastasia.ru/static/patrimony_list.php (accessed August 2, 2022).

Andreyeva, Yuliya. 2017. 'Proyekty preobrazovaniya mira v novom religioznom dvizhenii "Anastasiya": antropologicheskiye aspekty religii N'yu-Ėydzh v sovremennoy Rossii'. PhD diss., Peter the Great's Museum of Anthropology and Ethnography (Kunstkamera) of the Russian Academy of Sciences.

Attardo, Salvatore. 1994. *Linguistic Theories of Humor*. Berlin; New York: Mouton de Gruyter.

Biography. 2019. 'Biografiya'. *Vladimir Megre: ofitsial'nyy sayt*. https://vmegre.com/biography (accessed July 18, 2019).

Byt' Dobru. 2007. 'Yumor s sayta 'Zvenyashchiye Kaktusy Rusi''. *Byt' Dobru* 11. http://gazeta.bytdobru.info/statya/1341-yumor-s-saita-zvenyashchie-kaktusy-rusi (accessed June 9, 2021).

Danielson, Larry. 1986. 'Religious Folklore'. In *Folk Groups and Folklore Genres: An Introduction*, edited by Elliott Oring, 45–69. Logan: Utah State University Press.

Davies, Christie. 2008. 'Undertaking the Comparative Study of Humor'. In *The Primer of Humor Research*, edited by Victor Raskin, 157–182. Berlin; New York: Mouton de Gruyter. https://doi.org/10.1515/9783110198492.157

Douglas, Mary. 1968. 'The Social Control of Cognition: Some Factors in Joke Perception'. *Man* 3 (3): 361–376. https://doi.org/10.2307/2798875

Dvorkin, Aleksandr. 2002. 'Kul't "Anastasii"'. In *Sektovedeniye: Totalitarnyye sekty. Opyt sistematicheskogo issledovaniya*. Nizhniy Novgorod: Izdatel'stvo bratstva vo imya svyatogo knyazya Aleksandra Nevskogoi. https://azbyka.ru/otechnik/sekty/sektovedenie-totalitarnye-sekty/7_21 (accessed July 19, 2019).

Green, Martin. 2000. 'New Centres of Life'. In *Beyond New Age: Exploring Alternative Spirituality*, edited by Steven Sutcliffe and Marion Bowman, 51-64. Edinburgh: Edinburgh University Press.

Hauptmann, Gerhart. 2020. *The Heretic of Soana*, translated by Bayard Quincy Morgan. London: Alma Books.

Heelas, Paul. 1996. *The New Age Movement: The Celebration of the Self and the Sacralization of Modernity*. Oxford; Cambridge, MA: Blackwell.

Honey, Larisa. 2006. 'Transforming Selves and Society: Women, Spiritual Health and Pluralism in Post-Soviet Moscow'. PhD diss., City University of New York.

K Istine. 2016. 'Sekta Vladimira Megre "Anastasiya"'. *Missionersko-apologeticheskiy proyekt K Istine*. http://www.k-istine.ru/sects/anastasia/anastasia_about.htm (accessed July 19, 2019).

Kuipers, Giselinde. 2008. 'The Sociology of Humor'. In *The Primer of Humor Research*, edited by Victor Raskin, 361-398. Berlin; New York: Mouton de Gruyter. https://doi.org/10.1515/9783110198492.361

Kuprin, Alexander. 1956. *The Garnet Bracelet, and Other Stories*, translated by Stepan Apresyan. Moscow: Foreign Languages Publishing House.

Lonskaya, Alesya. 2011. 'Golodnyy obraz zhizni'. *Russkiy Reportër*, December 26, 2011. https://expert.ru/russian_reporter/2011/51/golodnyij-obraz-zhizni/ (accessed July 19, 2019).

Megre, Vladimir. 1996. *Anastasia*, translated by Larisa Malgosheva-Bartone. http://loveforlife.com.au/files/7743129-ANASTASIA-Vladimir-Megre.pdf (accessed July 19, 2019).

Megre, Vladimir. 2003. *Kto zhe my?* [*Who Are We?*]. Moscow: Dilya.

Megre, Vladimir. 2008a. *Co-creation*, translated by John Woodsworth. Stateline, NV: Ringing Cedars Press.

Megre, Vladimir. 2008b. *Book of Kin*, translated by John Woodsworth. Stateline, NV: Ringing Cedars Press.

Morreall, John. 2008. 'Philosophy and Religion'. In *The Primer of Humor Research*, edited by Victor Raskin, 211-242. Berlin; New York: Mouton de Gruyter. https://doi.org/10.1515/9783110198492.211

Oring, Elliott. 2003. *Engaging Humor*. Urbana; Chicago: University of Illinois Press.

Oring, Elliott. 2004. 'Risky Business: Political Jokes under Repressive Regimes'. *Western Folklore* 63 (3): 209-236.

Oring, Elliott. 2008. 'Humor in Anthropology and Folklore'. In *The Primer of Humor Research*, edited by Victor Raskin, 183-210. Berlin; New York: Mouton de Gruyter. https://doi.org/10.1515/9783110198492.183

Oring, Elliott. 2010. *Jokes and Their Relations*. New Brunswick, NJ: Transaction Publishers.

Partridge, Christopher. 2005. *The Re-Enchantment of the West*, vol. 2. *Alternative Spiritualities, Sacralization, Popular Culture, and Occulture*. London; New York: T&T Clark.

Poseleniya. 2012. 'O proyekte'. *Poseleniya*. http://poselenia.ru/about (accessed August 23, 2019).

Pranskevičiūtė, Rasa. 2015. 'Communal Utopias within Nature-Based Spiritualities in the Post-Soviet Region: The Visions of an Ideal World among Vissarionites and Anastasians'. In *The Borders of Subculture: Resistance and the Mainstream*, edited by Alexander Dhoest, Steven Malliet, Barbara Segaert and Jacques Haers, 183–200. New York: Routledge. https://doi.org/10.4324/9781315722733-12

Primiano, Leonard Norman. 1995. 'Vernacular Religion and the Search for Method in Religious Folklife'. *Western Folklore* (Special Issue: *Reflexivity and the Study of Belief*) 54 (1): 37–56. https://doi.org/10.2307/1499910

Radcliffe-Brown, Alfred R. 1940. 'On Joking Relationships'. *Africa: Journal of the International African Institute* 13 (3): 195–210. https://doi.org/10.2307/1156093

Raskin, Victor, ed. 2008. *The Primer of Humor Research*. Berlin; New York: Mouton de Gruyter. https://doi.org/10.1515/9783110198492

*Ringing Cactuses of Rus' = Zvenyashchiye Kaktusy Rusi*. http://kaktusy.at.ua/ (accessed June 9, 2014).

Sadovina, Irina. 2017. 'The New Age Paradox: Spiritual Consumerism and Traditional Authority at the Child of Nature Festival in Russia'. *Journal of Contemporary Religion* 32 (1): 83–103. https://doi.org/10.1080/13537903.2016.1256653

Scott, James C. 1990. *Domination and the Arts of Resistance: Hidden Transcripts*. New Haven, CT: Yale University Press.

Shadrov, Andrey. 2012. 'Sekret schastlivoy zhizni raskryt!' *YouTube*. The trailer of *Slavnoye: Novyy Rassvet* [Slavnoye: The New Dawn]. https://www.youtube.com/watch?feature=player_embedded&v=shi5WrNEnxg (accessed August 19, 2019).

Shemendyuk, Aleksei. 2011. 'EGOposeleniye Khortitsa:)))' [The Khortitsa Egovillage]. Video posted at vk.com. https://vk.com/video/@arhkedr?z=video-7245786_159292413%2Fclub7245786%2Fpl_-7245786_-2 (accessed May 31, 2021).

Shnirelman, Victor. 2014. 'Hyperborea: The Arctic Myth of Contemporary Russian Radical Nationalists'. *Journal of Ethnology and Folkloristics* 8 (2): 121–138. https://www.jef.ee/index.php/journal/article/view/158 (accessed August 18, 2019).

Shterin, Marat. 2001. 'New Religions in the New Russia'. *Nova Religio: The Journal of Alternative and Emergent Religions* 4 (2): 310–321. https://doi.org/10.1525/nr.2001.4.2.310

Yurchak, Alexei. 1997. 'The Cynical Reason of Late Socialism: Power, Pretense, and the Anekdot'. *Public Culture* 9 (2): 161–188. https://doi.org/10.1215/08992363-9-2-161

Chapter 3

# Visual Media and the Reconfiguration of Divinity in Moldovan Radical Religion

James A. Kapaló*

## Introduction

In twentieth-century Moldova, religious movements arose that were led by men and women considered to be the physical embodiment or incarnation of divine, angelic and saintly persons. The corporeal 'living' manifestations of Christ, the Holy Spirit, Mary, the Archangel Michael, the Prophet Elijah and John the Baptist walking the Moldovan countryside represented 'embodied' acts of resistance to the totalitarian political regimes and hegemonic religious institutions of the time that sought total control of the religious field and of spiritual life. Visual media, in the form of vernacular icons, photographs and photomontages, played a central role in contesting dominant religious beliefs and doctrines and reimagining and reconfiguring divine–human relations.

The homes of members of the movements discussed in this chapter are often full of icons, and in this they resemble the homes of their devout Orthodox Christian neighbours. Inochentist icons, however, differ in significant ways; they challenge canonical norms and radically re-imagine the relationship between divinity and humanity. For Orthodox believers,

* **James A. Kapaló** is Senior Lecturer in the Study of Religions at University College Cork, Ireland. He is the author of two monographs, *Text, Context and Performance: Gagauz Folk Religion in Discourse and Practice* (Brill, 2011) and *Inochentism and Orthodox Christianity: Religious Dissent in the Russian and Romanian Borderlands* (Routledge, 2019). He was Principal Investigator of the European Research Council project Creative Agency and Religious Minorities: Hidden Galleries in the Secret Police Archives and Central and Eastern Europe (project no. 677355), from 2016 to 2021. His research interests include Orthodox Christianity in the modern world, the securitization of religion in twentieth-century Eastern Europe, and folk religion and vernacular knowledge systems.

icons and the special 'icon corner' (found in the eastern or south-eastern corner of the kitchen or living room) play an important role as aids to and the site of rituals, prayers and personal devotions. During the long decades of persecution and oppression at the hands of the state that the 'illegal sects' (discussed below) suffered, often encouraged and supported by the Orthodox Church, groups employed new media and visual techniques to represent their changed relationship with divine and heavenly agents. In so doing they transformed their visual and material 'lifeworld', radically altering their religious worldview. In this chapter, I highlight how the vernacular imagination put images to work in creating new forms of embodied divinity (Morgan 2005: 40–46).

The movements discussed here are often grouped together under the term 'Inochentism' as they look back to the life and teaching of the Orthodox monk Inochentie of Balta as a defining moment heralding in the End of Days (see Kapaló 2019). Inochentie began life as Ioan Levizor, a boy from a poor peasant family from the village of Cosăuți in the western Russian province of Bessarabia, today's Republic of Moldova, which during Soviet times constituted the Moldavian Soviet Socialist Republic (MSSR). He led a religious revival that was initially centred on the cult and relicts of a local holy man called Feodosie Levitzki (Teodosie Levițchi in Romanian), creating what one early commentator referred to as a 'Moldavian Lourdes' at the monastery in Balta, a small provincial town today located in Ukraine (Upson-Clark 1927: 108). Increasingly, however, the pilgrims focused on the apocalyptic preaching and charismatic healing ministry of Inochentie himself. Much controversy surrounded the few short years of Inochentie's revival starting from May 1909 when, according to Inochentite tradition, he was promoted to the priesthood to preside over the reburial of Levitzki's remains, to his death on December 30, 1917 at the subterranean utopian community *Grădină raiului*, the Garden of Paradise, that his followers had founded during his years in exile. Soon after Inochentie's death, in the face of sanctions from the Orthodox Church and persecution at the hands of the Bolsheviks, various groups of his original followers formed distinct underground networks and communities all over Bessarabia and in parts of Ukraine, numbering in the several thousands. These groups kept alive key aspects of Inochentie's teachings on the impending Last Judgment, sin and demonology, and important practices that distinguished them from their Orthodox neighbours, such as extreme fasting, celibacy and pacifism. These communities transmitted the key narratives of the miraculous deeds, prophecies, persecution and ultimate heavenly ascension of Inochentie through texts, songs and images.

The persecution of Inochentists reached its apogee in 1940s Romania (which then included the territory of today's Republic of Moldova) when, as part of a general cleansing of undesirables from wartime Romania, 2,000 Inochentists were scheduled for deportation, alongside Jews and Roma, to concentration camps on the territory of Romanian occupied Transnistria.[1] In the Soviet Union, from the 1920s through to the 1970s, there were intermittent campaigns waged against Inochentism that resulted in deportations, trials and imprisonments of many followers.

'Inochentism' and 'Inochentist' are problematic terms. Inochentie never preached something called 'Inochentism' in the same sense that Jesus never preached 'Christianity' in first-century Palestine. Inochentie was a charismatic Orthodox monk who attracted a large following of peasants and, with the resources he gathered from this devout following he was able to establish a utopian community organized along monastic lines. He pushed the boundaries of Orthodox Christianity, was difficult for the authorities to control and exceeded his mandate, according to his superiors. Very early on in the movement, however, commentators began to refer to his followers as *sectanți* (sectants), *inochentiști* or *inochenteni* (inochentists) and the movement as Inochentism (see Kapaló 2019: 11–12). Over the past century the various currents and networks that look back to Inochentie hold differing views about the use of the term 'Inochentist'; some regard this a pejorative term as they consider themselves *the* true Orthodox whilst others prefer the term *inochentari* (which could be rendered as Inochentarian in English), as this expression was said to have been handed down in the community since the time of Inochentie. Some later groups were given their own names derived from the titles of their leaders; followers of the Archangel Michael became *arhangheliști* (Archangelists), and followers of the John the Father became *tătuniști* ('those of the Father'). One of the principal characteristics of Inochentite tradition is the practice of outward discursive dissimulation, a result of their persecution at the hands of the authorities and representatives of the Orthodox Church. Followers of Inochentie portray their movement as a revival of 'pure Orthodoxy'; they stress the monastic origins of the movement, practise celibacy and follow strict fasting rules similar to those of Orthodox monasteries. However, the 'hidden transcript', to borrow James Scott's term (1990), of the Inochentite tradition critiques the official Church and challenges Orthodox theology and cosmology, using powerful religious and political symbols and narratives. These 'hidden transcripts' are revealed through the hagiography of Inochentie and through the iconographic tradition that illustrates his *vita* narrative whilst also presenting Inochentie in various heavenly offices.

This chapter is based on three distinct sets of sources. Since 2006, I have met with members of various Inochentist groups, many of whom have invited me into their homes. For almost a century these groups have formed extremely secretive clandestine networks. Although overt surveillance and oppression by the state ended with the collapse of the Soviet Union and the end of communism in Romania, these groups continue to face societal prejudice, largely based on propaganda published during Soviet times that continues to be used against them by the Orthodox Church. Access to these groups is very difficult as they remain extremely suspicious of outsiders. My conversations with Inochentists have focused on aspects of belief and practice as well as their life narratives and experiences of state repression. Access to the homes of contemporary Inochentists has also been critical in understanding the centrality of religious material and visual culture for these groups.

A second major set of sources for this chapter are the secret police archives in Romania and the Republic of Moldova. Inochentists were banned from practising their beliefs during certain periods in Greater Romania (1919–1941, 1942–1944) as well as under communism in both Soviet Moldavia and communist Romania. They were frequently placed under strict surveillance and subject to arrest and imprisonment; this is all recorded in the secret police archives as well as in the archives of other civil authorities and the law courts. The opening of the secret police archives across post-communist Eastern Europe, which began in the 1990s following the end of communism, initially took place as part of a broad movement for transitional justice aimed at overcoming the legacy of repressive regimes and working towards justice and reconciliation in society (Verdery 2014). This included using the archives to vet individuals to prove they had not been informers or collaborators with the regime, a process referred to as 'lustration', and giving citizens the opportunity to view their individual files as 'information compensation'. These moves were highly problematic and led to political manipulation and blackmail. The failure of policies and practices of transitional justice revealed that the archives contained fabricated crimes, false testimonies, made-up conversations, and silences about excessive punishments and torture. This in turn has provoked intense debates about the 'truth value' of the contents of the archives. However, alongside the interrogation reports, informers' statements and arrest warrants, the kind of documents that thus far have been the focus of research in the archives, the files pertaining to the religious groups discussed here, also contain a wide range of visual and devotional materials in the form of mass-produced photo icons, photomontages and pamphlets as well as hand-written hymns, prayers and letters, confiscated by the authoritarian regimes of the time. My research makes use of this material, which in many cases has not been preserved anywhere else. The Romanian archives hold materials from both the Securitate, the Romanian national security agency from the communist era, and the Siguranța, the state security service of the inter-war and wartime periods up to 1944. In the Republic of Moldova, I had access to Siguranța files from the period when the territory of Moldova was within Greater Romania, and records of military courts as well as limited access to some KGB files from Soviet Moldavia.

My third set of sources comprise print media, state anti-sect propaganda publications, and Church missionary and heresiological materials. These are in many ways as problematic in terms of their 'truth value' as the secret police archives. It will come as no surprise that these sources contain numerous errors, intentional slurs, gross exaggerations and fabrications supported with false evidence. Nevertheless, they sometimes record examples of visual materials. The state-controlled media in Soviet Moldavia, for example, recognized the centrality of the material dimension of the Inochentist worldview and published examples of this material. The images presented in these publications are an important supplement to the collections in the archives and the materials I was able to photograph in Inochentist homes. The Orthodox Church missionary manuals also contain valuable information pertaining to Inochentist material culture and in a couple of instances the Orthodox Church published examples of non-canonical Inochentist icons (see, for example, Nica 1943). Inochentism is also the subject of a rare, and hence little-read, but invaluable monograph-length study published in 1926 by a church historian and theologian, Nicolae Popovschi, who discusses the origins and impact of the movement in a remarkably even-handed way for his time (Popovschi 1926).

Following an account of the origins of Inochentism, in this chapter I explore the relationship between the Inochentist ideas of holy and divine personhood and their representation in icons, photographs and photomontages, beginning with Inochentie himself and then going on to explore one of the related 'successor' movements, Archangelism, which has proved the most enduring and active of the many iterations of Inochentism.

## Inochentie's Revival

Understanding Inochentie's revival is complicated by the fact that it took place in a border region that was both ethnically mixed and politically contested by Russia and Romania.[2] This has led some to view the movement in primarily ethnic or national terms (see Clay 1998; Bâtcă 1999). Inochentie was an ethnic Moldovan, a Romanian speaker from Bessarabia, and his followers were also largely drawn from his ethnic kin. The Russian Orthodox Church to which they belonged had for several decades been engaged in a process of slavicization of the liturgy and Russification of Church life (Nistor 1991: 233-234; Păcurariu 1993; Dima 1994: 182-184). In this context, Inochentie's spirited preaching in the local Romanian dialect and his later disregard for Church authority have been read as ethnically motivated or inspired. This is, however, far from the full picture.

Concern over the activities of Inochentie were first raised by bishop Dimitrie of Kherson, who in 1910 reported to the Holy Synod that the hieromonk Inochentie had a 'harmful influence' on the pilgrims visiting the monastery in Balta (Popovschi 1926: 23). On the basis of this report the Holy Synod, in October of that year, instructed Serafim, the Bishop of Podolia, to remove Inochentie from the monastery and keep him under supervision while conducting a thorough investigation into the claims made against Inochentie (ibid.). Meanwhile, the Church in Bessarabia, headed by Bishop Serafim (Chichagov) of Chişinău, who was outspoken in his anti-Moldovan sentiments (Clay 1998: 257-259), also instigated its own investigation that reported to the Holy Synod on November 5, 1910 and advised that Inochentie be immediately removed to one of the monastery-prisons in the Russian far north (Popovschi 1926: 24).[3]

Inochentie, however, was not without powerful supporters. Bishop Serafim of Podolia, on whose territory Inochentie and the Balta pilgrims were located and under whose custody the Holy Synod had placed him, delayed fulfilling the Holy Synod's instructions to investigate Inochentie's activities and in his own report on the Balta phenomenon refuted the Bishop of Bessarabia's (Serafim Chichagov) accusations, claiming on the contrary that Inochentie 'is godly, modest, selfless and quite ordinary, he is a monk who enthusiastically serves his neighbour and is not able to deceive or to tell untruths' (Popovschi 1926: 25). He also intervened with the Holy Synod requesting that Inochentie be placed in a monastery in the diocese of Podolia where he could be placed under a skilful spiritual father for guidance, rather than be sent into exile in the Russian north (ibid.).

The various reports on Inochentie's activities highlight the influence that Inochentie had over the simple Moldovan peasants and suggest that he was using this to exploit them for personal financial gain (Serafim 1913). It is likely that behind these claims there lay some envy on the part of the bishops of Bassarabia and Kherson, who stood to lose financially from the continued exodus of pilgrims to the neighbouring diocese of Podolia. Indeed, Serafim (Chichagov) publicly blamed the 'spiritual leaders' of the diocese of Podolia for allowing the monastery at Balta to amass considerable wealth from the Moldovan peasants (Serafim 1913: 2). Another report, this time by the Directorate of the Chief Medical Inspector commissioned by the Bishop of Kherson and the governor of the province, from January 28, 1911 describes an 'epidemic of nervous illness amongst the Moldovan pilgrims' (Popovschi 1926: 26). The findings of this report, which were later published in the Russian journal *Sovremennaya psikhiatriya*, describe how the pilgrims 'trembled uncontrollably, jerked their limbs, groaned, hiccupped, beat themselves, fell to the floor, and spoke ecstatically' (Clay 1998: 255) which the psychiatrist V. S. Yakovenko pathologized as the combined result of

> the abuse of liquor and poor food, spiritual darkness and low level of intellectual and moral development, taken together, produce a weakening of the organism, an exaggerated irritability of the nervous system, and such instability that when powerful new exciting factors operate, there arises a nervous disease. (Upson-Clark 1927: 109)

Despite the campaign of the two neighbouring bishops, the Holy Synod, in decision no. 2567 of March 22–April 26, 1911, found Inochentie not guilty of crimes that would warrant his removal to the far north and instead entrusted him to the Bishop of Podolia instructing that he be removed from Balta and placed in another monastery sufficiently far away. The official reports, taken together, portray the whole movement as simply the product of a gullible, illiterate and psychologically vulnerable peasantry that had fallen prey to a charlatan monk who aimed to exploit them for personal gain. However, the substance of Inochentie's message, according to the reports gathered from pilgrims, and certainly by 1913 when the campaign of repression of the movement was fully underway, had become increasingly apocalyptic and it is this eschatological aspect of Inochentie's message that began to define the identity of Inochentie and transform the worldview of his followers.

## Inochentie as Elijah and Enoch

The exile of Inochentie, which was finally ordered on February 1912 when the Holy Synod of Russia commanded his removal to the monastery of Murom (Murmansk), a prison monastery for opponents of the Russian church and state in Olonets district in the Russian far north (Popovschi 1926: 31), precipitated a mass exodus of many hundreds of followers to be close to their spiritual father. Inochentie remained there for almost a year surrounded by some of his closest followers, including his brother Simion Levizor, his sister Domnica Ursu and his mother Csenia Levizor (ibid.: 42). Eventually, however, when it came to light that Inochentie was subject to a very lenient regime at the monastery and following a fall out with the spiritual father of the monastery, Miercurie, Inochentie absconded on February 5, 1913 together with at least 500 pilgrims, managing to avoid capture for 11 days in the harsh Russian winter. He was re-arrested on February 16 while making his way to the town of Cargopol and soon after this, the Ministry of Justice served notice that Inochentie should be imprisoned until trial. A judgement was reached on June 6, 1913 at the Court of Appeal in St. Petersburg, sentencing him to six months in the prison of Petrozavodsk (ibid.: 38–43). Thereafter, despite repenting and signing a confession on June 30, 1913 (Serafim 1913), and because of his continued preaching, he spent the following four years in various prisons, including the infamous Solovetky monastery, known for the severity of torture and punishment practised there (Popovschi 1926: 49). Meanwhile, the Orthodox Church instigated a mission to the Balta region to combat the ideas of Inochentie and to convince the people to return to their previous lives.

Under these conditions of persecution by the Church and the state, Inochentie's followers back home in Bessarabia, Podolia and Kherson began to sell all their worldly possessions, take up celibacy and construct, or rather dig, an underground monastic complex, New Jerusalem, next to which they founded a community known as *Grădină raiului* ('the Garden of Paradise') or *Raiul pământului* ('Heaven on Earth') to await the End of Days. *Raiu* ('paradise'), as it was commonly referred to, was founded on the site of a miraculous well near the village of Lipețcoe (Popovschi 1926: 229) in Ananiev district, just over the provincial border inside Kherson province, about 30 kilometres from Balta. Followers of Inochentie told visitors to the site that, 'this is the only well in which water will remain at the Second Coming' (ibid.: 232).

Except for a number of letters attributed to Inochentie[4] that he sent from the various prisons in which he was confined between 1911 and 1917, Inochentie left behind no writings. The only contemporary sources of his ideas and beliefs are his confession, referred to above and published by Bishop Serafim of Bessarabia (1913), which was no doubt extracted under duress, and a missionary manual prepared by the diocese of Bessarabia to assist priests sent to combat the emerging movement (Chirica and Skvoznikov 1916 [1913]). From these sources plus some contemporary accounts of pilgrims and followers of Inochentie, Popovschi made the first attempt to understand the Inochentists' worldview. Even in the years immediately following the emergence of the movement, however, he complained that the beliefs and ideas of Inochentists are difficult to piece together and that reliable sources are sparse and often contradictory. He affirmed with some certainty, however, that

> the fundamental idea of Inochentie's thinking was that the time of the antichrist has arrived, the end time has come, when on any day or at any hour we must be ready for the end of the world and the terrible judgement. (Popovschi 1926: 65)

This intense expectation was strengthened by the outbreak of war in 1914. Whereas initially followers of Inochentie spoke of him as a teacher and a holy man endowed with special gifts of healing and prophecy (ibid.: 142), as the persecution of Inochentie and his followers intensified and their apocalyptic expectations reached new levels, Inochentie was said to embody important characters in the scriptural and vernacular narratives of the End of Days, most notably the prophets Elijah and Enoch, the person of the 'Spirit of Truth' revealed in the Gospel of John and the Holy Spirit, the third person of the Trinity.

One of the most important sources of the Inochentite religious imaginary derives from Romanian popular apocrypha and folk cosmology, which in turn had been inherited from charismatic Judaism, the current that runs through Judaism parallel to the priestly Torah- and Temple-based forms of worship (Vermes 2013: 1–3). This tradition is revealed in both biblical and post-biblical literature and was expanded on in later Christian apocrypha. Of the wonder-working 'Men of God' of charismatic Judaism who heal, produce rain and multiply food, Elijah and Enoch stand out as they were carried up bodily into heaven without dying. Their unique status as 'undying' prophets explains their association in the Romanian tradition with the passage in Revelation in which 'two witnesses', described as prophets, will prophesy for 1,260 days before being killed by the Beast from the Abyss and, after three days, rise up on a cloud to heaven (Revelation 11:3-12). In Romanian apocryphal literature, Elijah and Enoch will herald in the end times by unveiling Satan's attempt to destroy the world and battling with him until they are killed (Gaster n.d.: 162).

The fact that by at least 1913, Inochentists associated this episode with the appearance of Inochentie is attested in Inochentie's confession (Serafim 1913: ix) and the missionary manual (Chirica and Skvoznikov 1916 [1913]: 8-10, 19-20). Popovschi, in his collection of contemporary accounts, quotes one follower as saying, 'the prophet Elijah did not die on Earth as usually happens like any other holy man, but was taken up to heaven alive. Inochentie is the prophet Elijah, who was killed and will be raised up like Jesus Christ' (Popovschi 1926: 144). Even during Inochentie's lifetime he began to be portrayed in icons and photographs as a variety of saintly or holy personalities, including the prophet Elijah. Inochentie's identity as Elijah and/or Enoch was just one of a wide variety of views amongst Inochentie's followers as to his status or person (ibid.: 145). More outrageous still, from the perspective of the Orthodox Church, was the belief that Inochentie was the embodiment on Earth of the Holy Spirit, or of *Duhul adevărului*, the Spirit of Truth, revealed in the Gospel of John, or that they were both somehow combined in the figure of Inochentie.

## Inochentie as the Holy Spirit

Popovschi gives several examples collected by missionary priests dating back to 1912 of Inochentist preachers claiming that Inochentie in some way or other embodies or manifests the Holy Spirit. He asserts that 'the harder Inochentie was pursued by the authorities the more his followers amplified their opinions on his personality. Ideas such as Inochentie is the Holy Spirit first arose when he was sent to Murom' (Popovschi 1926: 143). Beliefs, however, remained diverse:

> some amongst the Inochentists, in 1913, believed that Inochentie is the Holy Spirit embodied, the third Person of the Holy Trinity, others named him the Spirit of the Truth, drawing a distinction between the Holy Spirit [*Duhul Sfînt*] and the Spirit of the Truth [*Duhul adevărului*]. (Ibid.: 144)

The missionary manual dedicates particular attention to this very problem, refuting the Inochentist claim that Inochentie is the Spirit of the Truth. Pointing to three passages from the Gospel of John (John 14:26,

15:26 and 16:13), which all speak about the 'Spirit of the Truth' who will follow after Jesus, the manual highlights the errors of Inochentist scriptural interpretation:

> The Holy Spirit, they say, will come to Earth appearing in human form, he will teach you all the truth and will prophesy the future, and what we saw at *părinţelu* [the father, referring to Inochentie], and we have heard from him about the future. This profound error of the Inochentists is drawn, as is shown, from an incorrect interpretation by Inochentists of scripture. (Chirica and Skvoznikov 1916 [1913]: 3)

Numerous variations of the belief in Inochentie's relationship to the Holy Spirit existed at the time, and these currents continue to exist today. It is, however, very difficult to ascertain whether any of these ideas were actually taught by Inochentie himself. As the pressure on Inochentie's followers mounted, Popovschi realized, they became less willing to openly discuss their beliefs:

> And here you have to keep in mind that Inochentists reluctantly confided Innocent's teaching. From this fact, some researchers conclude that Inochentie suggested to his followers that they should not confide and say much in front of the parish priests. (Popovschi 1926: 63–64)

As the Church authorities progressively silenced Inochentists through their missionary campaigns, it was noticed that an iconographic tradition was emerging which represented visually the ideas that the Church was condemning as heretical and which couldn't be openly spoken by his followers.

> In keeping with these ideas, Inochentists used icons with the image of Inochentie. So, in 1913, in some villages in Bessarabia, an 'extraordinary envoy' of Inochentie, whose identity remains unknown, showed a photograph to the Moldovans in which are pictured God the Father, God the Son, and in the place of the Holy Spirit, the monk Inochentie with an image of a dove at his breast. (Popovschi 1926: 151)

Such images (see Figure 3.1) were widespread and exist in multiple variants in the homes of Inochentists today. Archimandrite Antim Nica, who was sent as a Romanian Orthodox missionary to the area around Balta when it was occupied by Romania during World War II,[5] observed that 'the image of Inochentie, in painted or photograph form, can be seen in Transnistria in many Moldovan families, placed between icons in the East corner of the house' (Nica 1943: 41), adding later that 'More clearly than in their pious writings, the beliefs of Inochentists are reflected in their iconography' (ibid.: 47).

Kapaló  *Visual Media and the Reconfiguration of Divinity*  81

**Figure 3.1.** Photograph of a mass-produced lithograph icon with Inochentie enthroned in heaven next to Christ with a dove at his breast symbolizing the Holy Spirit taken in the home of an Inochentist in Lipețcoe, Ukraine. Photograph by James A. Kapaló, 2012

When Inochentie was finally released from exile in the spring of 1917 following an appeal to the Holy Synod on the part of his followers and aided by the events of the February Revolution, he returned to *Raiu*, arriving in June of that year where, according to his hagiography, he began once again to preach the Gospel of Christ, do great miracles and heal the sick. He died soon after on December 30, 1917 (Popovschi 1926: 54). He was buried on New Year's Day 1918 in a catacomb next to a small chapel in the underground complex that had been especially prepared to receive his remains. Many pilgrims continued to visit the site until *Grădină raiului* was destroyed by the Bolsheviks in September 1920. The hagiography *The Life and Deeds of Father Inochentie of Balta 1909–1917* (*În scurt viața* 1924), penned by Inochentie's followers between 1913 and 1924, tells how many of Inochentie's close followers and family were killed and how several others were imprisoned in Odesa. One final miraculous episode is recounted in later versions of his *Life and Deeds*; on October 2, 1920 the Bolsheviks are said to have removed Inochentie's remains from his tomb only to find his body, after almost three years, entirely intact as if he were alive and giving off an unearthly aroma of spices.

When the commissar of the Bolshevik troops tried to rip the priestly cross from around Inochentie's throat he rose up from his coffin. The commissar fled in panic. Inochentie's body was taken that evening to the hospital in Ananiev, a local town, and when the doctor was about to cut into Inochentie with his scalpel, Inochentie began to breathe and his face was 'pink, pink like a rose…' (*Pre scurt viața* 2010: 70). In panic, the soldiers resealed the coffin and locked the room placing two men on guard whilst they called a senior doctor in Odesa. In the middle of the night, after being knocked senseless by a loud sound like thunder and lightning, the soldiers came round to witness a cloud resting above the hospital in which a great light shone. From the light came a great pillar of fire from the ground up to the sky. The body of Inochentie rose out of the coffin and into the pillar of fire and up to heaven in great glory (ibid.).

By the time of Inochentie's death, a rich iconographic tradition had emerged that contravened canonical norms by portraying Inochentie as a divine person seated in heaven next to Christ and variously described as the Holy Spirit embodied, the Spirit of the Truth and even one of God's two Sons (Nica 1943: 48). At the same time, followers of Inochentie had learned to be wary of what they said with regard to Inochentie's preaching and his identity. As the mass pilgrimages were halted by the Church and Inochentie himself was silenced, visual representations of Inochentie became increasingly important as a means of transmitting the message of a changed reality in which the third person of the Trinity was walking the Earth and heralding in the End of Days.

### A New Lifeworld

Following the death, and resurrection, of Inochentie, his followers were scattered and divided between two states. Those from Podolia and Kherson provinces became citizens of the Soviet Union whilst the majority of his Moldovan followers were now in the territory of Greater Romania. Divided between two hostile states and having witnessed the destruction of *Raiu*, the sacred centre of the movement, by the Bolsheviks, followers of Inochentie found themselves in a radically new context.

Despite the strongly ethnic Moldovan and Romanian-speaking character of the movement, which had led some early commentators to consider it a kind of 'grassroots' ethnic mobilization against Russian rule, Inochentism also came to be considered dangerous by the Romanian State. In Greater Romania, as it was known in its enlarged post-Trianon form, the Romanian Orthodox Church played a central role in the national project of creating a unitary state from the diverse territories that Romania had acquired. Alongside efforts to disempower and disperse the large national minorities in the new territories, including more than two million Hungarians in Transylvania and large numbers of Jews and Russian speakers who dominated the urban centres of Bessarabia (see Livezeanu 1995: 90), the new state also wished to stamp out any sign of religious dissent. By 1925, Romania had effectively outlawed proselytism and banned Inochentism alongside most of the other new and 'foreign' religious groups and movements (Dobrincu 2007: 586–587). By the mid-1930s, the repression of Inochentists had become more and more severe and brutal, including at least one fatal incident involving the shooting of Inochentist 'rebels' by gendarmes (ANIC-MJDJ, 69/1932).

In the neighbouring regions of the Soviet Union, 'just as the Romanians were attempting to integrate the Bessarabians into Greater Romania, the Soviets worked to pull them in the opposite direction' (King 2000: 51). One aspect of this was to create a new Moldavian Autonomous Soviet Socialist Republic (MASSR) just over the river Dniester, which marked the border between the two states, in districts with a significant Romanian speaking minority. This new political entity included the town of Balta as its capital, the initial Inochentist pilgrimage site, as well as Lypets'ke, the site of the *Raiu* utopian community which had recently been destroyed by the Bolsheviks. In place of the Inochentist community, the Soviet authorities created a collective farm named 'From Darkness to Light' (Dembo 1930; King 2000: 51) in an attempt to prevent it functioning as a religious centre for the local community. During the early years of Soviet power, policies towards religion were not as overtly oppressive as they would become later and were directed at separating Church and state. The Separation Decree of 1918 seemed to level the religious field by granting equal legal recognition for citizens to profess any faith or none (Wanner 2007: 36) and this was followed by moves to reduce the economic power of the Orthodox Church and its control over education. These moves fed the belief on the part of the Romanian authorities that the Soviet Union was somehow empowering sectarians, such as the Inochentists. By 1923, however, the Communist Party of Ukraine had noticed that controlling sectarians was significantly more difficult than controlling the Orthodox Church and following the 13th Party Congress in 1924 antireligious policy changed in favour of propaganda as its main tool to counter religious belief of all shades (ibid.: 39). The newspaper *Bezbozhnik* ('Godless'), which was published from 1922 to 1941 by the League of Militant Atheists, published numerous anti-sect articles including regular reference to Inochentism (see, for example, Dembo 1930). After 1929, a 'threefold secularization process' (Wanner 2007: 52) was in place aimed at eliminating the role of religion in social, moral and political life. This included dismantling the Orthodox Church and its authority, removing religion from the public sphere and the propagation of an alternative Marxist materialist ideology.

In addition to persecution at the hands of the state authorities in both territories, Inochentists were also the subject of severe condemnation preached from the altar (Popovschi 1926: 154). Inochentie had been a member of the clergy, representing the monastic tradition of Orthodoxy and during his ministry he had attracted a large following of sympathetic monks from monasteries in the region. His followers, at least initially, were not anti-clerical; they recognized the clergy's authority and remained members of the Orthodox Church. In the decades that followed his death, however, many Inochentists developed a marked ambivalence towards the Church and suspicion towards the clergy, and fiercely criticized their failings. In this context, the practices associated with Inochentism moved to domestic and clandestine spaces, in both the Soviet Union, where all forms of religion were eventually oppressed and pushed from the public sphere, and in Greater Romania, where the state was intent on creating a homogenous nation based on the majority Romanian Orthodox identity. Generally speaking, in the Orthodox regions of the Soviet Union the home setting therefore took on additional significance with the icons and icon corners (or home altars) remaining an important sacred space (Kononenko 2006: 48). In Romania, where Inochentist communities began to construct for themselves alternative religious spaces, secret 'hideouts' dug under their homes and gardens also transformed the material environment of religious practice.

Vera Shevzov (2007: 62) defines the Orthodox liturgy as the basis of the community's 'lifeworld', highlighting its distinct role in bringing 'ecclesial narratives and the Church's visual culture' together in transformative ways. The narrative performance of liturgy transforms the viewer's relationship to the icons presented during the ritual drama, giving them new meaning and power. Inochentism emerged out of this Orthodox lifeworld but over time remoulded it significantly in response to the changing social and political context. The uses and meaning of icons, and visual material culture more broadly, changed for Inochentists as they created new visual tools to animate a new central narrative, the life, passion, death and resurrection of Inochentie. Through the production of narrative icons of

Inochentie's life, that became widespread and were reproduced in multiple variants and forms, as postcards, wall hangings and illustrated books (see Figure 3.2), these changes became integral to a re-imagined and re-embodied cosmological order no longer focused on the liturgy performed in and by the Orthodox Church but now defined by the subterranean hideouts excavated under homes and the new mission to spread the narrative of Inochentie and his teachings on the impending End of Days.

**Figure 3.2.** Photograph of large narrative icon of the life of Inochentie taken in the home of an Inochentist in Lypets'ke, Ukraine. Photograph by James A. Kapaló, 2012

The production of icons and hagiographies is of course a traditional means within Orthodoxy of establishing the saintly status of spiritual or political figures. As Per-Arne Bodin (2009) suggests, there are established rules for the production of such a 'canonical identity' for 'holy' or 'saintly' figures. The interplay between this process and the historical and political reality they represent can give us important insights into 'the shaping of sacred discourse and its confrontation with the discourses of history and politics' (ibid.: 88). One means by which events and characters from the present or recent past are 'institutionalized' is through their 'typologization' in relation to the figures and events from the Bible and sacred history. In this move 'history is levelled or annihilated, and temporality itself is abolished. History merges with the eternal' (ibid.: 89).

In the case of the Inochentist movement, the history of persecution at the hands of the Russian Church and Tsarist authorities became central to a vernacular theology of 'redemptive suffering' (Clay 1998: 261) and the core narrative was utilized by indexing analogous events in the biblical narrative. Thus Moses and the Exodus narrative are mirrored in Inochentie's 'exodus' from Russian captivity; Jesus' feeding of the 5,000 is mirrored in Inochentie's feeding of 3,000 during his epic escape from captivity in Solovetsky (see Figure 3.2); Jesus' trial before the Sanhedrin and Pontius Pilot by Inochentie's trial before the Holy Synod and the Tsar Nicholas; Jesus' 'passion' by the torments Inochentie suffered during imprisonment and, finally, Jesus' resurrection is mirrored by Inochentie's own bodily ascension to heaven (see Figure 3.2). In the narrative iconographic tradition, Inochentie's life is presented in terms of a whole range of parallels from biblical narrative.

As part of the effective communication of their message, Inochentists employed the new media of photomontage and mass-produced photo postcard images and texts. These were carried from village to village across the Bessarabian countryside, easily concealed about their person. There are reports of them being sold on markets from suitcases. Hidden under officially sanctioned religious icons and booklets, they were sold to knowing customers 'on-request' for the price of 10 lei (ANIC-IGJ, 154/1941, 22). The Holy Synod took very seriously the danger posed by the subversive and heretical images and texts being produced by all religious dissenters, but especially Inochentists, whose materials so closely resembled Orthodox images and publications that they passed a ruling in 1936, to be enforced by the Ministry of Internal Affairs through the gendarmerie, requiring all religious icons, crosses and religious publications to be approved by the Church (ANIC-IGJ, 22/1941, 82). Arrests were frequently made based on the possession of illegal icons and Inochentists were, by the 1940s, routinely sent to the military courts (ANIC-IGJ 22/1941, 43) where they received anything between a small fine to six months in a labour camp. Moise Olteanu and Ion Nasulea from the village of Roşu, in Cahul county were each sentenced to six months in a labour camp on February 18, 1943 by the 3rd Army Military Court for possession of Inochentist icons, standing accused of conducting Inochentist propaganda (ANRM-TMC3A 738-2-164, 50).

The new images now being produced by Inochentists became socially embedded in a different way to traditional icons, and the 'social apparatus' through which they were created and deployed (Morgan 2005: 32) had also radically changed. Through a new juxtaposition of narrative and image the Inochentist 'brothers' and 'sisters', as they referred to one another, produced new ways of seeing by employing visual techniques and means of production. Inochentists were overwhelmingly rural and of peasant background, as were the majority of recent converts to other so-called sects such as the Adventists and the Jehovah's Witnesses. As well as sharing an intense apocalyptic sensibility with these groups, Inochentists may well have learned new means of presenting their ideas from their co-villagers and from their co-inmates of the Romanian prisons and labour camps of the time.

Figure 3.3 illustrates one way that text and image were configured in a relationship designed to establish a parallel between Inochentie's sacrifice and that of Jesus Christ. Here an image of Inochentie under arrest, surrounded by Tsarist militia, is juxtaposed with extracts from the New Testament on the reverse, opening with an abridged and slightly altered version of Jesus' discourse on the Good Shepherd from John 10:14-16:

> Here is the good shepherd, the good shepherd lays down his life for his sheep, he recognises his sheep and his sheep recognise His voice and follow Him. But the one who is not the shepherd when he sees the wolf leaves the sheep and flees because they do not belong to him and he does not care for the sheep and the wolf comes and scatters and attacks them.

In this way, scripture is used to support the association between Inochentie and Jesus. In the section of the text that follows, this is taken one step further with the torments suffered by Inochentie being equated to Christ's suffering.

88  Vernacular Knowledge

 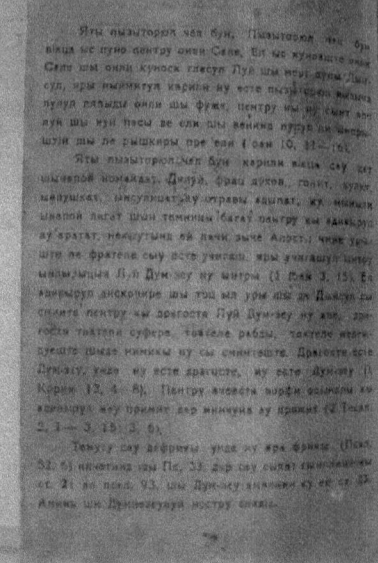

**Figure 3.3**. A printed double-sided postcard with Inochentie in captivity on one side and the discourse on the Good Shepherd on the reverse. This postcard was confiscated from followers of Inochentie arrested close to the site of the Garden of Paradise in 1942 (ANIC-IGJ 120/1942, 25). Source: © National Historical Archives of Romania

> Here is the good shepherd whose life was given and is not given back. By his spiritual brothers, chased, cursed, shot [with a gun], insulted, given poison to drink, with hands tied behind his back, put in prison because he revealed the truth, not heeding what the Apostle says: Whoever hates his brother is a murderer, and the murderer will not enter the Kingdom of God. (1 John 3:15)

From the numerous records in the archives of the police, gendarmerie and the secret police in Romania it is evident that the new materials, both visual and textual, produced by the movement were important vehicles for spreading the message of Inochentie and were part of a decentring of religious monopolies through the suggestion and materialization of alternative modes of divine and worldly reality.

## 'And the Archangel Michael Looked Just Like Me'

In the final section of this chapter, I explore the juxtaposition of sacred image and sacred place in one of the successor movements that grew out of the Inochentist milieu. Archangelism emerged as a distinct current in the 1920s and went on to constitute the most widespread and, from the perspective of the authorities, the most troubling branch of Inochentism. The founders were young peasant boys, Alexandru, Grigore and Ion Culeac, from the village of Todirești in the north of Bessarabia, as Moldova was then known. They were initially followers of Inochentie who later became visionaries and leaders in their own right. Alexandru's visionary career began in 1920, when he claimed he was just 19 years old (police records show him to have been 10 years older!). His vision was published in a 36-page booklet in 1924 under the title *A Vision that Appeared in the Year 1920* (Culeac 1924). Grigore, his younger brother by one year, also had visions that were published under the title *The Visions of Grigore Culeac and His Sufferings for the Confession of the Second Coming of Jesus Christ* (Culeac n.d.). Alexandru, Ion and Grigore drew on the capital associated with their forerunners, Inochentie and Feodosie, whom they claim had prophesied their coming. Alexandru's vision opens with a preamble that sets the stage for the appearance of the Archangel Michael on Earth.

> The sound of the trumpet of the Last Judgement. So is it said that the Archangel Michael will come to wage war with the Antichrist, and this he has done now and this is the witness of the 2 [the two prophets]. Thus it was told 10 years ago by Father Inochentie and Saint Feodosie, and so is it now happening in Bessarabia. It is said that the Holy Trinity in three persons, two of them were the father and the son and the third the Spirit of the Holy Archangel Michael. (Culeac 1924: 5)

And to ensure there was no doubt who the Archangel Michael on Earth is, he adds,

> and these two great and powerful prophets, Father Inochentie and Saint Feodosie, prophesied and said that there will come in Bessarabia young and old, great and small. They said there will come a youngster of 17 years after him [Inochentie]. (Ibid.: 6)

Grigore too, after introducing his own visions as 'heavenly [visions] of the second coming of Jesus Christ on Earth in the flesh', refers to his forerunners, imploring Christians to have faith in Inochentie as Elijah and Feodosie as Enoch, the two great and powerful prophets who 'prophesied and found the path to judgement' (Culeac n.d.). Taking on various divine or saintly identities, the brothers initiated parallel networks and, according to later Soviet reports, they divided up the territory of Bessarabia between them with Alexandru claiming the region between Chișinău and

Bălți (Karpunina and Sibiriakov 1959: 27). Alexandru's followers became known as Archangelists, and Ion's, who was revered as John the Baptist, as *Tătuniștii*, or followers of the Father. The closing passage of Alexandru's vision of 1920 establishes three principal persons of the new movement, himself as Archangel Michael coterminous with the Holy Spirit, his brother Ion as John the Baptist and his wife as the Mother of God:

> the whole mystery of all the beloved of the Lord of Hosts and our Lord Jesus Christ and the Holy Spirit Archangel Michael. The Consubstantial Trinity undivided which is working today on Earth in the flesh, and John the Baptist and the Mother of God. (Culeac 1924: 36)

The evolution of the related but distinct groups the Culeacs founded is difficult to piece together but following the death of Ion in 1945, the Archangelists and Tătunists appear to have merged into one network under Alexandru and Ion's wife Ecaterina Stechi (Shvedov 1959: 3).

Already in 1924, Alexandru had grasped the power of the image, and of photomontage in particular, to convey his message of divine election and embodiment. In the image that appears in the frontispiece to his *Vision that Appeared in the Year 1920* (see Figure 3.4) he is pictured as the Archangel Michael endowed with symbolic attributes, including a dove at his heart to indicate the composite character of *sfântului Duh arhangelul Mihail*, The Holy Spirit Archangel Michael (Culeac 1924: 26). The importance to the Archangelist movement of representations of the Archangel Michael is also evident from Soviet media sources. Media reports and propaganda publications often drew attention to the significance of the production and distribution of religious images for the success of the Archangelist sect, whilst also ridiculing the crudity of their production. In 1959, readers of the newspaper *Sovetskaya Kultura* ('Soviet Culture') are shown how Archangelists produced their crude icons: 'on a picture torn from a Church book is pasted a photograph of Alexander Culeac, thus we obtain the "Archangel Michael"' (Shvedov 1959: 3). By the time this image was published in 1959, Alexandru Culeac had twice been arrested and sentenced. The first time he was sentenced in 1945 by a Special Session of the NKVD (as the Soviet state security police was called at the time) to five years' exile in Kazakhstan from where he managed to escape and return to Moldavia (ASISRM-KGB 022997, vol. 2: 209–10). He was arrested again on September 27, 1947 together with nine members of his community and was charged with 'anti-Soviet agitation, encouraging the people not to enter the *kolkhoz*, not to pay taxes and not to serve in the Soviet Army' (ASISRM-KGB 022997, vol. 1: 7). On January 23, 1948, he was sentenced by the Supreme Court of the Moldavian Soviet Socialist Republic to 10 years' imprisonment (ASISRM-KGB 022997, vol. 2: 209–210). He was released in 1958 as part of a general amnesty and was allowed to return home (Țopa and Sibiriac 1958: 2). In an account Alexandru gave of his career following his release, which was published in a manual for teachers of Atheism under the title 'Repentance of a Sinner' (Karpunina and Sibiriakov 1959) and which in all probability was given under duress, he explains how the production of the icon that 'looked just like me' at the beginning of his career was instrumental in the promotion of his divine status and the success of the movement.

**Figure 3.4.** Photomontage icon of Alexandru Culeac, the 'Archangel Michael', from the frontispiece of the 1924 edition of *A Vision that Appeared in the Year 1920* (ANRM-TMC3A 738-1-6846, 19). © National Archives of the Republic of Moldova

> I decided then to make an icon with my image. I commissioned it from a painter who painted the *Day of Judgement* and the *Ascension of the Archangel Michael*, as well as my ascension to heaven. The Icon was a success. And the Archangel Michael looked just like me. I declared this icon to be holy. And it started here. People threw themselves down on their knees in front of the Icon. They kissed it and prayed to it to heal them from illness. I don't know if the icon cured anyone but in exchange we received a handsome income. They brought us cereals, money, carpets and cattle. (Karpunina and Sibiriakov 1959: 28)

Despite having been forced to publicly confess and renounce his status as the Archangel Michael to his followers by the Soviet authorities, Archangelism and the veneration of the Culeac brothers continued secretly until today. From the 1920s until the end of the Soviet system in Moldova in 1991, Archangelists maintained a secret network of safehouses and subterranean chapels. The movement attracted many young people who took on the role of wandering apostles or 'saints', spending their lives in hiding, living underground and travelling between villages at night so as not to be detected by the authorities. The subterranean hide-outs became the new sacred spaces of Archangelist belief and were modelled on the Garden of Paradise, the first Inochentist underground utopian project. Crime-scene photographs taken by the KGB record the spaces and material world of the underground that was hidden from public view and revealed only occasionally for dramatic effect in the Soviet press and propaganda materials. Having moved away radically from the old reality of the Orthodox liturgical lifeworld, Archangelists awaited the End of Days sheltered from the outside world in a new material reality of their own creation, peopled by their brothers and sisters and shepherded by a God on Earth: 'Today God wants to take revenge on us for being unbelievers. He came to Earth for a second time to gather his children and to separate believers from atheists. Atheists will go into the fire...' (ASISRM-KGB 020193, 191).

In the post-Soviet era, Archangelist imagery has moved above ground and images of the Archangel Michael can be seen openly on display in homes (see Figure 3.5). The accusations made against the movement, which included ritual murder of babies, suicide pacts, sabotage of state farms and sexual promiscuity, were either invented or exaggerated by the Soviet propaganda machine. Recently declassified case files contain details of the 'rehabilitation' and cancelation of convictions against Archangelists by the Special Plenary of the Supreme Court of the Republic of Moldova in the years following the end of Soviet power. However, in contemporary Moldova, Inochentists and Archangelists continue to be condemned by the Orthodox priesthood and are the subject of societal prejudice and stigma based on the Soviet-era image of them created in the press. The practice of outward dissimulation continues to be characteristic of Archangelist discourse.

> The only difference is we don't go to Church, at home we have the same songs, the same Gospels, we have all the same things, we just don't go to Church, there is nothing that could be called a 'new religion', we are just more strict, like in the monasteries, like in the olden times. (Archangelist woman, southern Moldova, August 13, 2011)

The message of the return to Earth of the Holy Spirit embodied as Inochentie or of the Archangel Michael returning to battle Satan in the final conflict before the End of Days is today projected visually in ways that are still not spoken openly. Inochentist images are the principal tool through which the relationship between earthly and heavenly reality are represented and reconfigured.

**Figure 3.5.** Photo of an icon corner in an Archangelist home with a photo icon of Archangel Michael (aka Alexandru Culeac) on the right-hand side. Photograph by James A. Kapaló, 2011

## Conclusion

The Inochentist movement presented a problem to successive states and regimes. During the Tsarist period, the movement was considered a danger because of its location on a disputed ethnic borderland and its power to undermine the Russian Church hierarchy's ability to control the spiritual life of Moldovans. Later, the Romanian state considered Inochentism an impediment to the full incorporation of Bessarabia into a unitary nation-state free of religious and ethnic diversity. Inochentism was also viewed as a threat to the 'body' of the ethnic nation because of believers' refusal to marry, reproduce or take up arms against the enemies of the state. For the Soviet Union, in the general struggle against religion the so-called sectarian groups proved the most difficult to control as they had more fluid forms of organization and could function with only limited material resources. Because of the frequent changes of border and state jurisdiction, many Inochentist communities experienced persecution at the hands of both the Romanian and the Soviet authorities (with the earlier generations of Inochentists also having lived through Tsarist repression). Inochentism represented resistance on two fronts, against the 'worldly' Orthodox Church and whichever state or political system they found themselves in.

The idea that Christ or other divine or saintly persons have returned to Earth and walk amongst us in a new guise was not an Inochentist innovation. Amongst radical and mystical Russian sects, starting with the *Khristovshchina* or Christ Faith in the seventeenth century, the bodily reincarnation of successive Christs and of the Holy Spirit, in both male and female form, was at the heart of their radical beliefs (Zhuk 2004: 15). The belief in human incarnations of divine persons is condemned in Russian Orthodoxy as the heresy of *chelovekoobozhaniye*, 'worshiping man' (Engelstein 1999: 51) and Inochentism came to be associated with this current of Russian mysticism (see Leu Botoşăneanu 1929). What is distinctive about Inochentism, however, is the central role that visual representations came to play in generating and embodying divinity and transforming beliefs at a time when the Orthodox Church and state authorities were silencing Inochentie and his followers. Inochentists continue to practise outward discursive dissimulation in contrast to their use of powerful visual imagery and symbolism that challenges both the Orthodox Church and the state. For this reason, visual sources are essential for understanding how Inochentists have re-imagined the cosmological order.

Inochentist images do important work in changing the way that divinity is perceived and the way that reality is viewed. The new ordering of society, the result of the changed political and social context of persecution, generated new spaces for domestic or 'subterranean' ritual, alternative material 'lifeworlds' in which new creative practices and new visual and textual communities could take shape. Mass production techniques allowed these new images to be disseminated quickly and cheaply making them accessible as 'evidence' of the divine nature of Inochentie and his successors. The production of photo-icons and the use of photomontage techniques allowed Inochentists to transgress canonical rules for the production of holiness and sainthood. The images they produced broke with the Orthodox icon tradition by representing the *living* with divine attributes. These new material visual representations of embodied divinity, which utilized the latest photographic techniques, *looked like* and *accompanied* the very men and women who were claiming to embody divinity. Inochentist iconography, therefore, despite its Orthodox roots and visual style, represents a distinct new ordering of the 'being, reality and value' of the cosmos (Margaret Miles cited in Shevzov 2007: 61) in a rapidly changing social world.

## Acknowledgements

The research for this article received funding from the European Research Council (ERC) under the European Union's Horizon 2020 research and innovation programme No. 677355. The author also acknowledges the generous support of the Royal Irish Academy, which funded initial archival research in the secret police archives in Romania. Special thanks go to Dr Igor Cașu for assistance with archival materials in Moldova and to Dumitru Lăpușneanu for his invaluable advice regarding Inochentist belief and practice.

## Archival Sources

ANIC-IGJ – *Archiva Naționale Istorice Centrale* – fond. *Inspectoratul General al Jandarmeriei* (Romania) [Central National Historical Archive – General Inspectorate of the Gendarmerie], dosar. 22/1941, 154/1941 and 120/1942.

ANIC-MJDJ – *Archiva Naționale Istorice Centrale* – fond. *Ministerul Justiției Judicare* [Central National Historical Archive – Ministry of Judicial Justice], dosar. 69/1932.

ANRM-TMC3A *Archiva Națională a Republicii Moldova* – fond. *Tribunalul militar al Corpului III armată, Chișinău* [National Archive of the Republic of Moldova – Military Tribunal of the 3rd Army Corps, Chișinău], dosar. 738-2-164; 738-1-6846.

ASISRM-KGB – *Archiva Serviciului de Informații și Securitate a Republicii Moldova, fostul KGB* [Archive of the Information and Security Service of the Republic of Moldova, the ex-KGB], personal file 020193; 022997.

## Notes

1. Marshall Antonescu, Romania's wartime dictator, ordered the deportation and internment of circa 2,000 Inochentists in Transnistria in August 1942 (Achim 2013: 542–544). The archival record in Romania and Moldova, however, is incomplete and it has not been possible to substantiate whether this order was actually carried out (see Kapaló 2019: 205–210).
2. Balta, the original pilgrimage site around which Inochentie's career evolved, and *Gradină raiului*, the subterranean monastic community founded by Inochentie's followers, were located in the Russian province of Podolia close to the provinces of Bessarabia (roughly corresponding to today's Republic of Moldova) and Kherson.
3. In Imperial Russia, Orthodox clergy were often sentenced to serve public penance in monasteries for breaches of church law or for disobeying their superiors. Secular courts too could incarcerate individuals in monasteries for causing social disturbances or in order to control individuals with mental disorders. The penal system was characterized by 'blurred boundaries between sin and crime' (Demoskoff 2014: 44) and legitimate authority of Church and state. Solovetsky monastery was one of two monasteries, however, that was used to hold prisoners of greater political importance and was notorious for the harsh conditions and treatment meted out to prisoners supplying the model for the Soviet Gulag system (Applebaum 2004).
4. The author's copy of 'The Letters of Father Inochentie Sent from the Island of Solovetsky and from Other Prisons to His Followers at the Garden of Paradise' (*Scrisorile Părintelui Inochentie trimise din ostrovul Solovețki și de prin alte închisori următorilor Săi dela Grădina Raiului*) (1911–1917) is a word-processed and edited version sourced from a contemporary follower of Inochentie who claims they were passed down in manuscript form to the present.
5. During World War II, the region between the river Dniester and the river Bug was administered by Romania as the Transnistria Governorate. This multi-ethnic region included the whole territory of the former Soviet Moldavian ASSR, which

existed from 1924 to 1940, with Balta, the site of Inochentie's original monastery, and Lipets'ke, the location of the Garden of Paradise both within its borders.

## References

Achim, Viorel, ed. 2013. *Politica Regimului Antonescu față de Cultele Neoprotestante: Documente*. Bucharest: Editura Institutului Național pentru Studierea Holocaustului din România 'Elie Wiesel'; Polirom.
Applebaum, Anne. 2004. *Gulag: A History of the Soviet Camps*. London: Penguin.
Bâtcă, V. 1999. 'Biserică Ortodoxă și Spiritualitatea Românească în Basarabia Interbelică'. *Luminătorul* 4 (43): 14–21.
Bodin, Per-Arne. 2009. *Language, Canonization and Holy Foolishness: Studies in Postsoviet Russian Culture and the Orthodox Tradition*. Stockholm: Stockholm University Press.
Chirica, Feodosie, and Alecsandru Skvoznikov. 1916 [1913]. *Conspecte pentru cursuri missionere norodnice de înfruntarea învățăturii cei minciunoase a lui ieromonahul Innochentie, alcătuite de missioneri-propoveduitori a eparhiei-protoiereul Feodosie Chirica și Alecsandru Timofevici Skvoznikov* [Syllabus for popular missionary course to counter the false teachings of hieromonk Inochentie, composed by the missionary preachers of the diocese – archpriest Feodosie Chirica and Alecsandru Timofevici Skvoznikov]. Kishinev: Eparhialnaya Tipografia.
Clay, Eugene C. 1998. 'Apocalypticism in the Russian Borderlands: Inochentie Levizor and his Moldovan Followers'. *Religion, State and Society* 26 (3–4): 251–260. https://doi.org/10.1080/09637499808431829
Culeac, Alexandru. 1924. *O vedenie ce s'a arătat în anul 1920* [A Vision that Appeared in the Year 1920]. Iași: Institutul de Arta Grafice 'Versuri și Proză'.
Culeac, Grigore. n.d. *Vedeniile lui Grigore Culeac și pătimirile lui pentru mărturisirea venirii a doua a domnului Isus Hristos* [The Visions of Grigore Culeac and His Sufferings for the Confession of the Second Coming of Jesus Christ]. Iași: Viața Românească S.C.
Dembo, V. 1930. 'Innokentievtsina'. *Bezbozhnik*, October 7, 1930.
Demoskoff, A. Joy. 2014. 'Monastic Incarceration in Imperial Russia'. In *Orthodox Christianity in Imperial Russia: A Source Book on Lived Religion*, edited by Heather J. Coleman, 43–57. Bloomington; Indianapolis: Indiana University Press.
Dima, Nicholas. 1994. 'Politics and Religion in Moldova: A Case Study'. *The Mankind Quarterly* 34 (3): 175–194. https://doi.org/10.46469/mq.1994.34.3.3
Dobrincu, Dorin. 2007. 'Religie și Putere în România – Politica statului față de confesiunile (neo)protestante: 1919-1944'. *Romanian Political Science Review* 7 (3): 583–673.
Engelstein, Laura. 1999. *Castration and the Heavenly Kingdom: A Russian Folktale*. Ithaca, NY; London: Cornell University Press.
Gaster, Mozes. n.d. *Studii de Folclor Comparat*. București: Editura Saeculum I.O.
În scurt viața... 1924. *În scurt viața și faptele Părintelui Inochentie de la Balta*. Bârlad: Tip. Const. D. Lupașcu.
Kapaló, James A. 2019. *Inochentism and Orthodox Christianity: Religious Dissent in the Russian and Romanian Borderlands*. London; New York: Routledge. https://doi.org/10.4324/9781315588698

Karpunina, I. B., and I. Sibiriakov. 1959. 'Pocăința unui păcătos'. In *Materiale în Ajutorul Lectorului Ateist*, 27–30. Chişinău: Societatea pentru Răspîndirea Conoștințelor Politice și Științifice a R.S.S. Moldoveneşti.

King, Charles. 2000. *The Moldovans: Romania, Russia, and the Politics of Culture*. Stanford, CA: Hoover Institution Press.

Kononenko, Natalie. 2006. 'Folk Orthodoxy: Popular Religion in Contemporary Ukraine'. In *Letters from Heaven: Popular Religion in Russia and Ukraine*, edited by John-Paul Himka and Andriy Zayarnyuk, 46–75. Toronto; Buffalo, NY; London: University of Toronto Press. https://doi.org/10.3138/9781442676640-005

Leu Botoșăneanu, Grigoriu (Arhiereul). 1929. *Confesiuni și Secte: Studiu Istoric-Misionar*. București: Tipografia Cărților Bisericești.

Livezeanu, Irina. 1995. *Cultural Politics in Greater Romania: Regionalism, Nation Building and Ethnic Struggle, 1918-1930*. Ithaca, NY; London: Cornell University Press.

Morgan, David. 2005. *The Sacred Gaze: Religious Visual Culture in Theory and Practice*. Berkeley, LA; London: University of California Press.

Nica, Antim [Archimandrite]. 1943. 'Viața religioasă în Transnistria'. *Transnistria Creștină* 2 (January–June): 9–55.

Nistor, Ion. 1991. *Istoria Basarabiei*. București: Humanitas.

Păcurariu, Mircea. 1993. *Basarabia: Aspecte din Istoria Bisericii și a Neamului Românesc*. Iași: Editura Mitroploiei Moldovei și Bucovinei.

Popovschi, Nicolae. 1926. *Mișcarea de la Balta său Inochentizmul în Basarabia*. Chișinău: Tipografia Eparhială 'Cartea Românească'.

*Pre scurt viața...* 2010. *Pre scurt viața și faptele Sfântului Părintelui Inochentie de la Balta sau Evanghelia Dreptății*. Chișinău: Trei Crai dela Răsărit.

Scott, James C. 1990. *Domination and the Art of Resistance: Hidden Transcripts*. New Haven, CT; London: Yale University Press.

Serafim [Archbishop of Chișinău and Hoțin]. 1913. *Atărnarea Arhiepiscopului Serafim către Eparhie*.

Shevzov, Vera. 2007. 'Scripting the Gaze: Liturgy, Homilies, and the Kazan Icon of the Mother of God in Late Imperial Russia'. In *Sacred Stories: Religion and Spirituality in Modern Russia*, edited by Mark D. Steinberg and Heather J. Coleman, 61–92. Bloomington; Indianapolis: Indiana University Press.

Shvedov, I. 1959. 'Karera arhangela Mikhaila'. *Sovetskaya Kultura*, April 4, 1959: 3.

Țopa, F., and A. Sibiriac. 1958. 'Oameni vii cu suflete'. *Tinerea Moldovei*, March 9, 1958: 2.

Upson-Clark, Charles. 1927. *Bessarabia, Russia and Roumania on the Black Sea*. New York: Dodd, Mead, & Co.

Verdery, Katherine. 2014. *Secrets and Truths: Ethnography in the Archive of Romania's Secret Police*. Budapest; New York: CEU Press.

Vermes, Geza. 2013. *Christian Beginnings: From Nazareth to Nicaea, AD 30-325*. London: Penguin.

Wanner, Catherine. 2007. *Communities of the Converted: Ukrainians and Global Evangelism*. Ithaca, NY; London: Cornell University Press.

Zhuk, Sergei I. 2004. *Russia's Lost Reformation: Peasants, Millennialism, and Radical Sects in Southern Russia and Ukraine, 1830–1917*. Washington DC: Woodrow Wilson Center Press.

**Part 2**

# Narrating and Creating the Past

Chapter 4

# Blessings beyond Time and Place: The Fluid Nature of Narrative Tradition in Contemporary Hinduism

*Martin Wood*[*]

Although he physically passed away in 1881, many devotees of the Gujarati Hindu saint Jalaram Bapa speak of having direct, personal experiences of his presence in the here and now. There is, however, no one alive today who could speak of having any kind of direct recollection or memory of him or his wife Virbai Ma. This does not mean that Jalaram's life, miracles, healings and teachings have been forgotten—and since his death the Jalaram tradition has developed into a substantial expression of globalized Hinduism in the contemporary world. In the 135 years since his passing, memories of Jalaram and the ways in which they have been preserved and transmitted have multiplied and undergone a number of transformations, passing from the individual memories and memorates of those who had encountered him when he was alive to what some scholars might consider to be 'popular' and 'collective' memory today (see Johnson et al. 1982; Halbwachs 1992).

This is not to say that there is nothing that could be considered a core, authoritative source of memory, but in the Jalaram tradition that authoritative source has been expanded and stretched, added to, interpreted, translated, reformatted and re-contextualized, culturally, socially, geographically and materially. Far from remaining a fixed, 'snap-frozen'

---

[*] **Martin Wood** is currently senior lecturer in the department of Religion, Philosophy and Ethics at the University of Gloucestershire, UK. Since 2003 he has worked closely with numerous Hindu traditions in the UK, New Zealand and India and specifically with the Jalaram Bapa tradition since 2010. His current research examines the experience of the presence of the Gujarati Saint Jalaram Bapa and how this informs the lived experience of his devotees in the contemporary UK context.

source, the narrative of Jalaram Bapa has taken numerous forms that have been carried from his home village of Virpur in Gujarat to East Africa, back to India and out into multiple diasporic contexts simultaneously, all of which are forms of memory that cement the relationship between the past and the present. As we shall also see, however, the memory of Jalaram, or at least the manner in which that memory is preserved and transmitted, is as contested as it is diverse.

**Memory**

As Christian L. Novetzke (2007: 230) suggests, scholarly interest in the social and cultural study of memory in the Western context has, in recent years, 'enjoyed a bonanza of theoretical and critical' attention (see Assmann 2006 [2000]; Halbwachs 1992; Johnson et al. 1982; Rampley 2000). When it comes to the discussion concerning Hinduism and memory, however, the conversation has often turned to the question of whether Western social and cultural theory can be fruitfully applied (Sharma 2003; Thapar 1990).

Despite this, a sizeable body of work considering the ways that memory is transmitted in and among Indic traditions has developed, much of which has focused on the hagiographies and accounts of the lives and events of saints, gurus and religious personalities. Kirin Narayan (1989) discusses the way that folk narrative and story have been employed by Hindu religious teachers as a means of passing on important religious beliefs and practices, and raises some important theoretical issues about the performance of narrative as a means of instruction. Robin Rinehart considers the use of hagiography as a 'mediator' of the sacred (1999: 12) and he also provides a stimulating chapter concerning orality, literacy and memory in relation to textual and vernacular Hinduisms (2004). Heidi Pauwels (2010) discusses the links between religious community formation and hagiography, offering an important insight into the way different communities employ narrative when it comes to laying claim to religious personalities, whilst James Hegarty (2012) discusses the role of Sikh hagiography and Guru Nanak, suggesting that it provides an insight into, 'Sikh ways of "comprehending and representing things"' (2012: 133). Recently Rico G. Monge, Kerry P. C. San Chirico and Rachel J. Smith (2016) have provided another important contribution to the study of hagiography in the Dharmic traditions which covers several ways in which hagiography functions in relation to religious truth.

When it comes to untangling the context from which Jalaram's teachings emerged, I acknowledge the methodological concerns raised by both Hegarty and Pauwels when I suggest that we should see 'hagiographical accounts of Jalaram's life as narratives within a particular social, religious and political agenda' (Wood 2015: 119). In this chapter, however, I would like to remove myself from discussions that concern themselves exclusively with history and hagiography in Indic traditions and examine the fluid role of memory and hagiography in the material life of Jalaram devotees today.

In this respect, like Oren B. Stier (2015: 146), I take Danièle Hervieu-Léger's cue when she speaks of religion as a 'chain of memory'. Here, the stuff of religion is transmitted through generations and 'memory takes shape in relics, monuments, and other materialisations, along with ritual practices designed to bring the body to bear on the religious relationship to the past in the present' (Stier 2015: 146). My suggestion is that the hagiography concerning the life, miracles and teachings of Jalaram Bapa has developed its own evolving chain of memory, one that documents, preserves, transmits and underpins the religious materiality of this contemporary Hindu tradition in a number of geographical, cultural and religious contexts.

Furthermore, the themes that permeate the Jalaram narrative are as multiple as the forms in which they are remembered and transmitted. I intend to consider the role of memory through the lens of devotees' continued experience of the saint's miracles and presence, examining the ways in which such experiences cross religious thresholds. Here, I will examine how this ongoing, evolving narrative draws on the collective memory and shapes the individual experience of ordinary devotees whilst at the same time creating new collective narratives that facilitate the evolution of a distinctive religious identity. I would like, therefore, to consider the role of miracle and apparition in the development of this hagiographical chain of memory, particularly in regard to miraculous healings, not only of those who might refer to themselves as Hindus but also those who practise Islam in one form or another.

## Presence and Healing

I have dealt elsewhere with the narratives that tell of the life, ethical teachings and miraculous blessings (*parcha*) of Jalaram (see Wood 2010; 2017) but here I would like to refer again to one particular event that will

104  *Vernacular Knowledge*

serve to practically underpin the theoretical considerations forwarded by this chapter. This particular event, related in the saint's first printed hagiography *Bhakta Shree Jalaram*, written by Saubhagyachand Rajdev and published in 1958, concerns the miraculous healing of a local Muslim boy suffering from a seemingly incurable and fatal condition.[1] A short summary of the story is as follows:

> In Virpur, the son of Jamal Ghanchi[2] aged 10 years fell sick ... [and] Jamal lost all hopes for his son's life ... One day he was going to the Bazar for medicine. On the way, Harji tailor met him. Harji asked Jamal about his son's health and enquired as to why he looked so sad. Jamal replied that he had lost all hope for his son's life ... Harji consoled Jamal and advised him to approach Jalaram for his blessing. Jamal took the vow on the spot ... 'If he will open his eyes and look towards me, I shall give 40 maps of corn for your ashram'.

> A miracle happened and the same night, Jamal's son opened his eyes and asked for something to eat ... He [Jamal] went straight to Jalaram's ashram [and] prostrated himself before Jalaram and began to weep ... It needs no mention that Jamal's son survived and enjoyed a long life. (Rajdev 1966: 18–19)

Significantly, such miraculous blessings did not cease to occur with the saint's death in 1881 and accounts of Jalaram's *parcha*s did not cease with the publication of Rajdev's hagiography in the late 1950s. The narrative of Jalaram Bapa continues to cross rigid historical, cosmological and religious thresholds, and events bearing striking similarity to the one briefly described above, along with a variety of other blessings, have regularly occurred since his death. Devotees believe that Jalaram has been ever present as they migrated from India to East Africa and eventually settled in the UK.[3] I would now like to highlight two particular examples of the replication and communication of the Jamal Ghanchi miracle.

The first event took place at the Shree Jalaram Prathana *mandir* (temple) in Leicester in the late 1990s.[4] The parents of a young Ismaili Muslim boy of Gujarati descent, suffering from a life-threatening condition, prayed to Jalaram Bapa urging him to help them raise the substantial funds needed for a lifesaving operation. The family almost instantaneously received more than enough money to achieve their goal and the boy recovered speedily from his operation. This event was spoken of widely by devotees in the *mandir* community and no doubt the local Ismaili community (both of which maintain Lohana[5] heritage), although at the time it was not communicated by any other means.

More recently in 2015 another very similar event occurred at the Shree Jalaram *mandir* in Greenford, West London. The account of this miracle was published in the *mandir*'s fifteenth anniversary souvenir magazine, an abridged version of which follows:⁶

> T ... an Albanian [Muslim] from Macedonia ... is a good friend of P who comes to the temple off and on with our regular devotee Kalpesh. P introduced T to Pujya Bapa based on his own divine experiences earlier and had been sending Bapas blessings in the form of wristbands received from priests. T's ... [eight-year-old] son was born with ... [a condition] ... that led to many complications including a kidney failure ... and his general condition seemed to be worsening. Prayers were offered to Jalaram Bapa and Kalpesh took the blessed wristbands for T and [his son]. According to T, 'No sooner they got the band the situation started to turn around...'
>
> He recalls ... 'We were advised that the waiting time for the operation would be ... months ... Soon after the band was tied on my son's hand, we learnt that the operation had been brought forward to the very next Tuesday ... The operation was a major success and the post operation recovery, too, was nothing short of a miracle ... even the doctors treating him confirmed this ... as for me I truly experienced Pujya Jalaram's presence ... and could see him in white traditional clothes all around me! I knew for sure that he was present at the time [of the operation] ... I have made a vow to Pujya Bapa to donate 10% of all my earnings ... I feel a blissful contentment when I make the donations'. (Rajani 2015: 87)

The account finishes with a comment from the writer: 'no wonder [this has] strengthened T's belief that he has experienced Bapa's *parcho* ... He has, in fact, given us permission to dramatise this event and present it as a one act play for the *mandir*'s 15th Anniversary Celebration' (ibid.: 15).

Beyond the obvious joy, relief and the belief in Jalaram's presence and blessings, what is important here is the manner in which the story of this blessing was communicated to the wider community. As above, a full written account of the event was published in the *mandir* celebrations' souvenir magazine and distributed to devotees nationally and internationally. Then, as promised, in November 2015, during the *mandir*'s fifteenth anniversary celebrations, a fully dramatized version of the events described was indeed performed in Greenford Town Hall, in front of 500 specially invited guests. The Leicester and Greenford events are just two examples of how the narrative of Jalaram Bapa has moved well beyond the confines of nineteenth-century Gujarat, historically and geographically. This hagiographical development is not, however, a purely contemporary feature of the chain of memory that devotees have engaged with since the saint's death. To illustrate this, I have attempted to provide a theoretical and descriptive framework that follows the trajectory of the tradition's evolving narrative. This framework presents us with eight characteristic links, each of which will be unpacked and illustrated with relevant examples. I have either been provided with these examples directly by devotees during fieldwork, or through various other sources directly related to the tradition. These links are as follows: oral, written, expanded, translated, transplanted, materialized, performed, and importantly for this chapter, contested.

## Links in the Chain of Memory

### *Oral*

As Rinehart (2004: 67) has suggested, there has been a long tradition of drawing upon a vast array of oral and, with reference to the second link, written sources when it has come to creating 'the many varieties of contemporary Hinduism in practice throughout India and Hindu diaspora communities abroad'. This foundational link in the chain of memory concerning Jalaram refers to the localized collections of individual memories transmitted orally during and immediately after the saint's life and focus exclusively on Jalaram.

According to devotees, Jalaram's philosophy and ethical position focused almost exclusively on feeding people in the Virpur region of Gujarat. From 1820 he and his wife Virbai were entirely consumed with the task of establishing, running and maintaining a *sadavrat annakshetra*, or charitable kitchen. At this time, neither the saint nor the growing number of local devotees committed any of his teachings or accounts of his miracles to paper, and consequently the original narratives of Jalaram remained entirely oral and were transmitted orally to subsequent generations.

This reliance upon localized memory challenges the strict historiography and contests the Western authoritative view that concerns itself with proof, accuracy and historical validity. Here we find what Chakrabarty describes as the hegemony of Feuerbach and Durkheim when it comes to Western academic discourse on such phenomena: 'Gods, spirits and apparitions *can* be said to exist, but only as the by-product of a society's effervescence' (Chakrabarty 2000: 16). In Indic traditions, and in particular devotional vernacular traditions, the need for such verification is rejected in the process of transmitting that which is remembered. The oral is placed in a position of primacy over the written and the read, perhaps because, as Novetzke suggests, memory tends to refuse 'disciplinary, formal or literary boundaries' (2007: 241). One might suggest that rather like the great epics, the *Mahabharata* for example and its innumerable oral versions (Doniger 2015: 50), the Jalaram narrative in its oral form is characterized by a fluidity that facilitates constant expansion and development. Indeed, whilst the core hagiography has remained largely consistent whilst at the same time confounding Western academic paradigms, for the Jalaram tradition the oral tradition continues to interact with and inform consequent links in the chain of memory and continues to provide hundreds of contributions to its ongoing evolution.

## Written

It is not until 1958 that we witness the first pivotal shift from a purely localized oral/memory tradition to one in which the regional, diasporic and cross-religious collective memories become consolidated in a written, published form. Rajdev's *Bhakta Shree Jalaram* is now widely considered to be the single authoritative, written source of the key events that characterize the Jalaram narrative. According to one devotee these are the authentic recollections from later generations of the saint's family and people from the Virpur region who knew him. *Bhakta Shree Jalaram* is, therefore, a retrospective record of the memories of those who encountered Jalaram when he was alive, memories that have been passed down orally through successive generations and were communicated to Rajdev. The publication expands upon the experience of Jalaram's miracles when he was alive but also makes considerable mention of devotees' experiences of Jalaram's blessings and presence after his death. Many of these post-mortem experiences were sent to Rajdev by first- and second-generation migrants living in colonial East Africa, South Africa and Fiji. Such accounts also shine a light on the evolving universalist Jalaram ethic, especially as a large number of these accounts of miracles are from Europeans, non-Gujarati Indians and non-Hindus. Thus we see not only a consolidation of Jalaram's life in written form, but also substantial reference to the ongoing experiences of devotees.

Whilst on one level, *Bhakta Shree Jalaram* is the literary cornerstone of the tradition, it has over time taken on a variety of significant meanings for many devotees. Some informants with whom I have spoken in the UK, for example, view the book as a historical account of the saint's life and refer to it as Itihasa, or a traditional history. Others, however, see the book as more than just a straight historical account, suggesting that it has Puranic[7] as well as Itihasic qualities although they stop short of comparing it to the *Ramayana*, the Bible or the Qur'an. For others, however, both the book in its material form and its contents are entirely sacred, and devotees, especially those with whom I have spoken in Gujarat, treat it with the utmost respect, keeping it covered; some even consider it to have talismanic and protective qualities.

## *Expanded, Translated and Transplanted*

The next three links in the chain of memory take the story of Jalaram out of the localized context. These links characterize the rapid development of the tradition as it finds itself located beyond the confines of Gujarat. Each link is forged in quick succession as we witness the narrative becoming expanded, translated and transplanted.

Whilst the core content of the hagiography, both oral and written, has itself remained largely consistent, even in successive editions, the later experiences of Jalaram's blessings have become so numerous that the tradition of collecting them and publishing them has continued with a monthly publication called *Jalaram Jyoti*. First published in 1960, *Jalaram Jyoti* publishes accounts of hundreds of miraculous experiences sent by devotees and non-devotees throughout Gujarat and the diaspora, and according to its current website, 'Pujya Jalaram Bapa gave the ideal of keeping all human beings alike, apart from the difference of caste, ideal for keeping love for everyone, and Jalaram Jyoti Magazine presented these same ideals in front of the society as a matter of fact' (*Jalaram Jyoti* n.d.); also included on the website is a comprehensive list of contemporary *parcha*s (*Jalaram parcha* n.d.).

The core narrative and hagiography has up to this stage been transmitted and written in Gujarati only, but in 1966 the first abridged version of *Bhakta Shree Jalaram* translated into English was published by Rajdev himself. This version contains brief accounts of the key blessings, events of the saint's life and some accounts of more contemporary miracles. There is also an interesting account of Virpur, the saint's home village, taken from the Census of India of 1961, which includes a reference to Jalaram's universal appeal: 'Besides thousands of followers of Jalaram all over the state there is a large number in other parts of India and Africa. The devotees include not only Hindus but also Jains, Parsis, Khojas,[8] etc' (Trivedi, Doctor and Vankani 1965). As devotees of the tradition found their situation in East Africa becoming increasingly tenuous (see Mattausch 1998), the late 1960s saw many leave their long-term homes in Uganda, Kenya and Tanzania. Many of these economic refugees consequently found themselves in the UK, where centres of the Lohana and more specifically the Jalaram tradition community became established in Leicester and West London. At this time both the devotees and the narrative of Jalaram found themselves transplanted into the Western diasporic context. Many younger devotees found themselves in an English-speaking education system and socio-cultural environment and demand increased for accessible translations of Jalaram's narrative. This demand was met first in 1984 with Ramanlal Soni's *Jalaram Bapa* and later with Rekhaben Shah's *Shri Jalaram Vandana* (2000), both of which are widely available in the UK, North America and Australasia.

## Materialization

The establishment of autonomous *mandirs* and *mandir* communities throughout East Africa and the West is illustrative of an increased material manifestation of the Jalaram narrative that focuses on his continued blessings and ethical position in relation to food and feeding those in need. Here, the materialization link in the chain of memory has evolved from the narrative concerning the establishment of the charitable kitchen in Virpur, augmented by the miracle that conferred its storeroom with the capacity to 'remain inexhaustible' (Rajdev 1966: 72; Soni 1984: 64). The theme of the ever-full *sadavrat* (charitable kitchen) storeroom is also intertwined with Jalaram's ability to multiply food miraculously in times of need. The perfect example of the Jalaram narrative becoming material is the *sadavrat* kitchen at the Greenford *mandir*. Many devotees speak of the storeroom at the *mandir* being always full of food sometimes donated anonymously and often by individuals who are non-Indian or non-devotee. In some cases it is believed that Jalaram himself has appeared personally to leave parcels of food at the *mandir*, food that consequently becomes highly prized as *prasadam*, sacred food, and as a sign that he is ever present.

## Performance

Performances or re-enactments of Jalaram's narrative were rare occurrences in the years just after his death; however, theatrical performances of his life and miracles have become more common in recent years, as instanced by the Greenford *mandir* community and their *JalaramTV*

YouTube channel. As well as broadcasting numerous important ceremonies or *pujas* and *chalissas* in the Jalaram calendar, devotional singing or *bhajan* sessions and recitations of Hindu epics, there have also been re-enactments of events and miracles in Jalaram's life.

Three such re-enactments, taken directly from Rajdev's original hagiography, were posted on the YouTube channel in 2012 and in January 2017 narration and re-enactment met in the staging of the *Shree Jalaram Jeevan Charita Katha*, which was hosted by the North London Lohana Community and held in the Dhamecha Lohana community centre in Harrow. A *Katha* was described to me as a telling of a religious story by a religious expert who adds context and interpretation to the narrative. Another described it as a seminar from which devotees might draw spiritual guidance and ethical inspiration. In this case the priest from the Jalaram *mandir* in Greenford was the narrator and the lavish event was sponsored by a number of prominent families in the community.

## Contestation

In this last section I will evaluate the way in which the links in the chain of memory have come together and laid the foundations for the contestation over ownership of the life story of the saint. In particular I will pay attention to the issues concerning the right for any person to play the role of Jalaram in a commercial film production. The problem of producing a film that depicts the life of the saint has been brought into sharp focus over the last two decades and certain proposals concerning re-enactments or broadcasts of the Jalaram narrative have found themselves the subject of legal action in the state of Gujarat. In what has become a regionally famous episode in the development of the story of Jalaram, Raghuram Jaishukram Chandrani, adopted descendant of the saint, custodian of the tradition's most sacred shrine and Jalaram's original house in Virpur, went to court in 2006 to obtain a permanent injunction to prevent an Indian film company (represented by Kirtibhai Mansukhbhai Raval) from

> making, releasing, publishing, exhibiting ... promoting or advertising or entering into any film festivals or in any manner producing in any format, film, drama, serial or any other literary or artistic expression in respect of the life of Shri Jalaram Bapa and/or his family members ... without the consent of the plaintiff. (Shah 2010: 1)

Interestingly, this is not the first time that prominent members of the local Jalaram community have contested proposals to depict Jalaram's life in a dramatic fashion. Raghuram's grandfather, the late Girdharram Bapa Chandrani, actively contested attempts to stage a production of Jalaram's life some years before. Furthermore, he also objected to the making of a film about the life and events of the saint called Sant Shiromani in 1963. The film was eventually released on the grounds that no one physically played the part of Jalaram and only pictures of him were used in the production. However, in the 2006 *Chandrani vs Raval* case two specific issues arose: the right to the privacy of the Chandrani family and the right to publicly depict the figure and image of Jalaram.

The first issue concerns the legal right not to be associated in any way with the proposed film as it could lead to an infringement of the personal and private lives of the saint's family. Chandrani's relationship with the saint was, however, contested in this respect. Jalaram and Virbai had never raised their own children and there was no way to provide contemporary legal evidence that Jalaram had adopted a son. The question of this relationship was resolved and it was decided that, based upon the evidence offered, Mr Chandrani was indeed a descendant of the saint by adoption and therefore very much a member of the saint's family.

The second issue, that which concerns rights over publicity, also raises the question of authenticity. The film, it was proposed, would be based entirely on Rajdev's book *Bhakta Shree Jalaram* (1958). Although the content of that book, that no one in the Virpur community objected to, has been spoken of by devotees as the definitive source of his life, and considered by other devotees as a sacred text, the writing of the book was undertaken by Rajdev according to his own initiative. The question of authenticity arises when we consider the nature of the miraculous events that coloured the saint's life. No one has suggested that the story of Jalaram, a well-known, devout and charitable man, referred to as a saint, is not authentic. The question of authenticity of the stories of miracles and healings mentioned throughout are, however, somewhat beyond the realms of legal verification. Again, we encounter the issue of the Western historiographical hegemony mentioned earlier, only this time it is placed in a litigation context. How do you prove in a court of law that the events and miracles that characterized Jalaram's life actually happened?

It would appear that in this example of contestation the success and evolution of the Jalaram story, as demonstrated by the chain of memory outlined, has evidently raised special problems for the custodians of the Virpur shrine and the descendants of the saint. This is brought into sharp focus when we consider the degree of autonomy within the tradition in relation to the vast amount of material that relates directly to Jalaram's life. On the one hand, relatives of the saint in Virpur may object to a film being made that portrays the life of Jalaram according to Rajdev's account. On the other hand, as pointed out in the trial notes, the Chandrani case had not considered the voluminous material relating to the life of Bapa such as in the form of the magazine *Jalaram Jyot*, Rajdev's publication *Bhakta Shree Jalaram* and the photographs of paintings of the life sketch of Jalaram on the walls and roof of Dharamashala at Virpur (Shah 2010: 21).

So, why would there be any contestation over the making of the film in this context? After all, one film has already been made and there are any number of other films concerning the Hindu divine and significant religious persons. One need only do a brief survey to find cinematic dramatizations of the Hindu epics, many of them made in India, such as the *Mahabharata*, *The Bhagavad Gita* and *The Ramayana*; more localized deities are also depicted (for example, Santoshi Ma), and the likes of Gandhi have not escaped the attention of the world of cinema. There are sensitivities concerning film and religion in India, however, and as Steve Derné points out when discussing Hindi films in particular, their 'wide reach makes censors believe that nothing in them should offend any religious, communal, or regional group, so censorship policies give voice to vocal, conservative Hindus' (in Babb and Wadley 1995: 196). This is not to say that Raval's film would locate the story of Jalaram in the 'Bollywood' mode of cinema. Devotees with whom I have spoken, however, tend to agree with the Chandranis and have raised concerns based on the grounds that the kind of film that Raval was proposing, where the actual person of Jalaram is played by someone, would compromise the deep spiritual nature of the narrative. Furthermore, devotees also feared that the narrative would be taken out of the hands of the tradition and represented in ways that some devotees considered to be inappropriate in relation to its moral and social ethical message.

Despite the concerns of the Chandranis in Virpur this legal contestation over Jalaram's narrative has formed yet another chapter in the constantly evolving Jalaram story. It also highlights the nature of regional and *mandir*-specific autonomy and authority in the global Jalaram community. This is interesting as, whilst Virpur will always represent the heart of the Jalaram narrative and remains the most important location for the tradition, differing temple communities, acting wholly within tradition-specific expectations and understandings, make their own decisions as to whether a medium of depiction is appropriate. This should not be seen as undermining the authority of the Virpur custodians; rather it appears to be indicative of the autonomy accorded to individual temple communities.

I would like to suggest, therefore, that this contest over the legal rights to portray Jalaram Bapa is the culmination of all the elements that have formed the chain of memory for devotees. Those wishing to make such films would point to the already existing catalogues of widely available material on Jalaram. Furthermore, *mandir* communities exemplify the diverse range of representations of Jalaram, artistically, textually, visually and orally. Moreover, devotees play the character of the saint in plays, sing devotional songs about him, extol his virtues and tell of his miracles in religious recitations and performances, post his image online and print his story in widely available books in English and Gujarati. Much of this appears to have no recourse to the authorities who maintain the Virpur shrine and who are related to the saint through adoption. What does seem clear, however, is that if such a representation is presented by a non-devotee, in this case in commercial cinematic form, members of the community will react with solidarity and in some cases actively contest such proposals on legal and religious/ethical grounds.

The official view of the tradition's authoritative spokespersons is that Jalaram Bapa was not, and is not considered, divine; Jalaram himself left no spiritual heir, there is no central hierarchy and whilst his memory has been preserved and transmitted in a number of ways there are tradition-determined restrictions when it comes to the nature of that transmission. Throughout India and the diaspora, locally-formed autonomous temple organizations are run by local community leaders, temple committees and the *pandits* employed by those committees. Reflecting the diverse nature of memory transmission spoken of in this chapter, this loose-knit structure allows the Jalaram tradition to constantly incorporate and communicate fresh events and narratives within and throughout its religious framework. The narrative of the saint, whilst deriving from a central source, is not slave to any one authoritative expression or method of transmission; it is fluid, dynamic and interpreted and expanded in a number of contexts.

What is also important here is the nature of the devotees' experiences, which are central in the formation of these new narratives because they are beyond official, authoritative sanction, although in this respect the individual experience forms part of the collective memory and consequently the collective experience. Furthermore, any well-rehearsed debate concerning the historical value of such narratives and hagiographies is of little importance to the devotees themselves. As with many such narrative traditions, Jalaram devotees are not seeking any clear distinction between history and hagiography.

What is more important to Jalaram devotees is the way in which the hagiographical tradition has remained fluid and that these contemporary narratives continue to be communicated in a variety of ways forming a dynamic narrative tradition. As Gavin Flood (1996: 104) suggests, 'Hindu traditions have been communicated through the generations in these narrative genres, which still play a vital role in contemporary Hindu life … [having and continuing] to have, immense impact on Hinduism at all levels'.

Furthermore, as we have seen, the ways in which the saint is represented can also create tensions and contestation when it comes to the question of ownership and tradition. Whilst it seems that devotees are comfortable to see Jalaram represented in a number of ways through a variety of media, those who could be considered as the central authority refuse to allow the saint to presented in a manner that they would consider inappropriate, namely in a commercial film made by non-devotees and designed to generate revenue. This also calls into question the role of the divine in the world of Indian cinema and highlights the pressures of market considerations that Derné discusses when it comes to the divine on the big screen. It could be suggested that the contestation over the film of Jalaram arose from an uneasy tension between the need to facilitate the transmission of the narrative of Jalaram and the rejection of secular values that are reflected in what many Hindus see as a 'denigrated medium' (Babb and Wadley 1995: 212), a medium that might promote inappropriate innovations when it comes to the narrative of Jalaram Bapa.

## Notes

1. This shortened account is taken from the first abridged and translated edition of *Bhakta Shree Jalaram* published by Rajdev in 1966.
2. Later it has been specified that he was a rich Muslim (Soni 1984: 15).
3. For more detailed accounts of the Gujarati Hindu diaspora migration from Gujarat to the UK via east Africa see Mattausch 1998 and Wood 2010.
4. For a full account see Wood 2010.
5. Endogamous Gujarati caste (*jati*) traditionally involved in business (Jackson and Nesbitt 1993: 213).
6. I have left the central characters in this event anonymous.

7   The Puranas are a body of Hindu sacred literature from the early centuries of the common era that were transmitted in manuscript form and orally (see Cush, Robinson and York 2008: 634).
8   With reference to Khojas, they should be understood to be Ismaili Muslims who share the same Lohana heritage as their Hindu counterparts.

## References

Assmann, Jan. 2006 [2000]. *Religion and Cultural Memory: Ten Studies*, translated by Rodney Livingstone. Palo Alto, CA: Stanford University Press.
Babb, Lawrence A., and Susan S. Wadley. 1995. *Media and the Transformation of Religion in South Asia*. Philadelphia: University of Pennsylvania Press.
Chakrabarty, Dipesh. 2000. *Provincializing Europe: Postcolonial Thought and Historical Difference*. Princeton, NJ: Princeton University Press.
Cush, Denise, Catherine A. Robinson and Michael York, eds. 2008. *Encyclopaedia of Hinduism*. London: Routledge.
Doniger, Wendy. 2015. *The Norton Anthology of World Religions: Hinduism*. New York: Norton & Co.
Flood, Gavin. 1996. *An Introduction to Hinduism*. Cambridge: Cambridge University Press.
Halbwachs, Maurice. 1992 [1925]. *On Collective Memory*, edited and translated by Lewis A. Coser. Chicago: Chicago University Press.
    https://doi.org/10.7208/chicago/9780226774497.001.0001
Hegarty, James M. 2012. 'Hagiography and the Historical Imagination in Eighteenth Century Punjab'. In *Time, History and the Religious Imaginary in South Asia*, edited by Anne Murphy, 133–150. Abingdon: Routledge.
Jackson, Robert, and Eleanor Nesbitt. 1993. *Hindu Children in Britain*. Stoke-on-Trent: Trentham Books.
*Jalaram Jyoti*. n.d. http://jalaramjyot.net/ (accessed May 19, 2021).
*Jalaram parcha*. n.d. http://jalaramjyot.net/parcha.php (accessed May 19, 2021).
Johnson, Richard, Gregor McLennan and David Sutton, eds. 1982. *Making Histories: Studies in History-Writing and Politics*. London: Hutchinson.
Mattausch, John. 1998. 'From Subjects to Citizens: British "East African Asians"'. *Journal of Ethnic and Migration Studies* 24 (1): 121–141.
    https://doi.org/10.1080/1369183X.1998.9976621
Monge, Rico G., Kerry P. C. San Chirico and Rachel J. Smith, eds. 2016. *Hagiography and Religious Truth: Case Studies in the Abrahamic and Dharmic Traditions*. London: Bloomsbury.
Narayan, Kirin. 1989. *Storytellers, Saints, and Scoundrels: Folk Narrative in Hindu Religious Teaching*. Philadelphia: University of Pennsylvania Press.
    https://doi.org/10.9783/9780812205831
Novetzke, Christian Lee. 2007. *Studying Hinduism: Key Concepts and Methods*, edited by Sushil Mittal and Gene Thursby, 230–251. New York: Routledge.
Pauwels, Heidi. 2010. 'Hagiography and Community Formation: The Case of a Lost Community of Sixteenth Century Vrindāvan'. *Journal of Hindu Studies* 3 (1): 53–90.
    https://doi.org/10.1093/jhs/hiq007

Rajani, Amrit. 2015. *Shree Jalaram Mandir Greenford 15th Anniversary Souvenir Magazine*. Alperton: Printing Eye Ltd.

Rajdev, Saubhagyachand M., ed. 1966. *Bhakta Shree Jalaram*. Rajkot: Jai Hind Printing Press.

Rajdev, Saubhagyachand M., ed. 2010 [1958]. *Bhakta Shree Jalaram*. Rajkot: Kanakari.

Rampley, Matthew. 2000. *Remembrance of Things Past: On Aby M. Warburg and Walter Benjamin*. Wiesbaden: Harrassowitz Verlag.

Rinehart, Robin. 1999. *One Lifetime, Many Lives: The Experience of Modern Hindu Hagiography*. New York: Oxford University Press.

Rinehart, Robin. 2004. 'Hearing and Remembering: Oral and Written Texts in Hinduism'. In *Contemporary Hinduism: Ritual, Culture and Practice*, edited by Robin Rinehart, 67–98. Oxford: ABC Clio.

Shah, Mukeshkumar Rakshik. 2010. *Kirtibhai vs Raghuram on 20 January, 2010*. https://indiankanoon.org/doc/1515842/ (accessed August 20, 2019).

Shah, Rekhaben. 2000. *Shri Jalaram Vandana*. Surat: Sahitya Sangam.

Sharma, Arvind. 2003. 'Did the Hindus Lack a Sense of History?' *Numen: International Review for the History of Religions* 50 (2): 190–227. https://doi.org/10.1163/156852703321506169

Soni, Ramanlal. 1984. *Jalaram Bapa*. Ahmedabad: Enka Prakashan Kendra.

Stier, Oren Baruch. 2015. 'Memory'. In *Key Terms in Material Religion*, edited by S. Brent Plate, 145–151. London: Bloomsbury. https://doi.org/10.5040/9781474280709.ch-019

Thapar, Romila. 1990. *A History of India*, vol. 1. Delhi: Penguin.

Trivedi, R. K., C. C. Doctor and R. M. Vankani. 1965. *Census of India, 1961*, vol. 5. *Gujarat VII-B: Fairs and Festivals*. Delhi: Manager of Publications.

Wood, Martin. 2010. 'Jalarām Bāpā: The Public Expression of Regional, Vernacular Traditions among Gujarātī Hindus in the UK'. *Journal of Hindu Studies* 3 (2): 238–257. https://doi.org/10.1093/jhs/hiq017

Wood, Martin. 2015. 'Jalarām Bāpā: Miracles and Meaning in Nineteenth Century Gujarāt'. In *Religious Transformation in Modern Asia: A Transnational Movement*, edited by David W. Kim, 115–139. Leiden: Brill.

Wood, Martin. 2017. 'Blessed Food from Jalarām's Kitchen: Narrative, Continuity and Service among Jalarām Bāpā Devotees in London'. In *Materiality and the Study of Religion: The Stuff of the Sacred*, edited by Tim Hutchings and Joanne McKenzie, 52–66. Abingdon: Routledge.

## Chapter 5

# Truth, Variation and the Legendry: The Case of Saint Madhavadeva's Birthplace in Assam

*Ülo Valk**

## Introduction

In the year 2000, when I made my first journey to Assam, my knowledge about the country was scarce, to say the least. When travelling in India I was fascinated by the expressions of religious life that could be experienced at every step—colourful, loud, compelling and often incomprehensible. I lacked a research focus and was open to study the culture as it unfolded in my daily experiences. Historical sites, old temples and people whom I met in Assam revealed lively heritage and various strands of Hinduism, including goddess worship, sacrifice, tantric traditions and Bihu festivals, intertwined with the beliefs and religious practices of the local tribal peoples. However, I soon learned that Assamese cultural identity was particularly linked to the legacy of one man, a cultural reformer who had reshaped the religious landscape of the country during the fifteenth and sixteenth centuries and preached the doctrine that is today known as neo-Vaishnavism. This man was Shankaradeva, a scholar, poet, writer, visionary and a charismatic leader of the bhakti movement. He was a strict monotheist who preached total obedience to Krishna—the

---

* **Ülo Valk** is Professor of Estonian and Comparative Folklore at the University of Tartu. His publications include the monograph *The Black Gentleman: Manifestations of the Devil in Estonian Folk Religion* (Academia Scientiarum Fennica, 2001), *Vernacular Religion in Everyday Life: Expressions of Belief* (co-edited with Marion Bowman; Equinox, 2012), and *Storied and Supernatural Places: Studies in Spatial and Social Dimensions of Folklore and Sagas* (co-edited with Daniel Sävborg; Finnish Literature Society, 2018). He is the editor of *Numen: International Review for the History of Religions* (Brill).

only God and Supreme Being—and worshipped him through chanting his different names (Neog 2008 [1965]: 348). Shankaradeva contested the authority of the dominant Brahmanic religion, goddess worship and the esoteric magic of tantra, and welcomed people from the lowest castes, tribal peoples and Muslims among his followers. He introduced the institution of *nāmghar*s, which can today be found all over Assam—village prayer halls where people gather for religious worship, cultural performances and meetings. Shankaradeva also laid the foundation for the tradition of monastic *sattra*s as centres of learning and the arts.[1] His achievements as the cultural hero of Assam are so extraordinary that his advent has been regarded as 'the single most important event in the history of the Assamese society' (Datta 2012: 131). Indeed, a single lifetime seems insufficient to accomplish everything that has been connected with his name. Perhaps it should not surprise us that, according to academic books of Assamese history, Shankaradeva was born in 1449 and breathed his last in 1569. His unimaginably long lifespan seems to indicate that there is something miraculous in the lives of saints. It also shows that history and belief narratives cannot be separated, but coexist and depend on each other, which is also the underlying idea of the current article. I want to show how vernacular and institutional discourses about the past co-produce lived realities.

In February 2011 I visited the historical birthplace of Shankaradeva in Bordowa, Nagaon district in central Assam, one of the most popular religious destinations in northeastern India. In 1493 Shankaradeva had returned home from a 12-year pilgrimage, started to preach, and established a prayer hall, which grew in time to become a famous *sattra*. Here visitors can feel the continuous presence of the great saint in many ways, as their imagination is awakened through fine art and relics that remind them of him. I remember a moment in a dark room when a monk displayed a stone slab with Shankaradeva's footprints. They were of an extraordinary size, perhaps 40–50 centimetres long and had been miraculously imprinted in stone. Obviously, from such evidence, Shankaradeva could not have been an ordinary man of average height; rather, his stature was gigantic. My companion, a PhD student from Gauhati University, seemed less surprised and commented that indeed Shankaradeva had been a tall and athletic man, so strong that he could hold a wild buffalo by his horns, and already as a child used to swim back and forth across the mighty Brahmaputra River. Both accomplishments sounded like mythic feats. The powerful cold currents of the Brahmaputra are deadly and dangerous and the banks of the flooded river can be nearly ten kilometres apart. There are many folk narratives about extraordinary episodes in Shankaradeva's life, which is also well reflected in several biographies (*carit-puthi*) that appeared soon after his death. One of the crucial events in his life was his encounter with another Assamese cultural hero, Madhavadeva, whose lifespan also appears to have been exceptionally long (1489–1596) and is reflected in many sources. Madhavadeva had an excellent education but his mindset was different from Shankaradeva because he was devoted to the Goddess and her ritual worship. Dramatic days in Madhavadeva's life came in 1522 when his mother fell seriously ill. Hearing the sad news, he vowed to offer a pair of white goats to the goddess Durga and he asked his brother-in-law to bring him goats for the sacrifice (Deka Hazarika 2006: 29). To Madhavadeva's dismay the brother-in-law refused, because he had accepted the faith of Shankaradeva, who was preaching the supremacy of Vishnu and who had condemned blood sacrifices. Hearing about this teaching, Madhavadeva was enraged and wanted to confront Shankaradeva, who happened to be nearby. The two men met and had a religious debate about the Supreme in which both quoted scriptures as arguments of faith. The verbal duel lasted for four and half hours and finally Madhavadeva surrendered. He bowed down in front of Shankaradeva and became his devoted disciple, dedicating his whole life to the service of his new master and his mission (Neog 2008 [1965]: 110). Madhavadeva was a talented poet and composed the popular neo-Vaishnava hymnal *Nāmaghoshā*, which is widely known and used in Assam today (see Pathak 2005). In 1569, when Shankaradeva passed away, he appointed Madhavadeva as his successor and the next guru of the order, which had grown considerably and become socially influential.

Madhavadeva died in 1596. When his end was near, his followers asked him to nominate a new leader for the order but Madhavadeva refused. Instead, he referred to the hymnal *Nāmaghoshā* as his substitute, saying that all his energy and intelligence can be found in the book (Deka Hazarika 2006: 52; Neog 2008 [1965]: 319). This choice seems crucial, because it probably hastened the disintegration of the centralized movement, which had been led by one guru. The power to direct and control the organization was transferred from a human agency to a textual tradition. Without an authoritative leader the movement became divided into four sub-sects (Neog 2008 [1965]: 153–155). Madhavadeva's decision implied the supremacy of a literary source; not a book of rules, regulations and statutes but a collection of mystical devotional poetry that is open to manifold interpretations. The movement and the doctrine started to take divergent paths, which led to disagreements among the followers and to further divisions. Neo-Vaishnavism became a book religion, as its holy scripts, composed by Shankaradeva and Madhavadeva, acquired a central position in worship and started to stand for their authors (ibid.: 319). These two men are singled out by their followers as the only gurus and the greatest souls—*Mahāpurusha*s ('supreme being', also an epithet of Vishnu) (ibid.: 349–350). Both have very high status in Assam and there are many historical places that are connected with their life stories.

## Madhavadeva's Birthplace in Letekupukhuri

There is not enough historical evidence to locate Madhavadeva's birthplace and childhood home geographically. The place must have been somewhere near Narayanpur in present-day Lakhimpur district in upper Assam. The exact village is often identified as Letekupukhuri. The first half of the compound refers to the Burmese grape tree (*leteku*), which grows widely in Assam, and the second, *pukhuri*, means a tank, usually a man-made pond. Such ponds can be found all over Assam in residential areas and can be of different sizes from grand royal lakes to small pools in people's back gardens. Hence, the toponym is not very helpful in identifying the exact place where the future saint took his first steps. The site, which had fallen into oblivion, was revealed in the twentieth century through signs such as meaningful dreams, omens and miracles.

In February 2009 I visited the birthplace of Madhavadeva in Letekupukhuri for the first time. I had taken part in a workshop in North Lakhimpur and when it was over, my Assamese colleagues arranged a sightseeing tour in the district with a stop in Letekupukhuri. It was a rural place, surrounded by fields and small groves; the shrine was peaceful and uncrowded, and hence quite different from many other pilgrimage destinations in India. We saw a large pond, and age-old banyan and mango trees as the last survivals of the jungle which had once surrounded the place but had been cut to allow space for agriculture. The large prayer hall could house hundreds of pilgrims, although at the time only a few people were present apart from our group (see Figure 5.1). Our local guide was Jogendra Borah Bayan, an elderly monk from the famous Uttar Kamalabari *sattra* on Majuli island. He had lived in Letekupukhuri since 1955, when he was nine or ten years old. He told us a brief history of the place:

**Figure 5.1.** Prayer hall (*nāmghar*) in Letekupukhuri. Photograph by Ülo Valk, 2009

This place Letekupukhuri was a dense forest. There were a lot of wild animals and no people here. As time passed, people slowly began to settle around the place. Somewhere in the middle of the jungle the earthen lamp of a guru was seen burning. People who came to hunt for deer saw this burning lamp; the area was lit. The old folks started to talk about the matter. They thought that as the earthen lamp was burning, it must mean that a great soul had been born in the jungle. Then the local old men from this place went to meet Kamalakanta Deva Goswami[2] to tell him about the matter. They told him that a great man must have been born here. They also asked him to visit the place and he came. As people showed him the place, he lit two earthen lamps in the name of the two gurus Shankaradeva and Madhavadeva. The earthen lamp, which was lit in the name of Shankaradeva, went out, but the other one, lit in the name of Madhavadeva, burned day and night. The people came the next day and saw that the earthen lamp was still burning. They sent word to the *sattrādhikār* in Tipling. Then the *sattrādhikār* came and started *pāl nām*[3] for three days, day and night. Until that time, nobody knew about the birthplace of Madhavadeva in Assam. People who came to know about that continuous prayer, came to join. They stayed, singing the songs day and night. Then a dream was revealed by God to a man in Kochuwagaon village of Dholpur area. He was about 60 years old. He was told in the dream to go to the place where people were praying, to find the birthplace of Madhavadeva and show it to the people. He learned in the dream that the birthplace of the saint was an earthen altar on the southern side, covered by a creeper. So, he informed his family and came walking to the place where the continuous prayer was going on. There he kneeled down and told the devotees about his dream. He asked them to clear the jungle and to look for the holy place. Then all of them started to clear the jungle, chanting the name of God. Finally, they found the place in the southern direction. It was a place covered by a creeper. Then they started to sing devotional songs, and this lasted day and night. They also lit an earthen lamp in the name of the guru. In this way, the birthplace of Madhavadeva became known. The place is being developed and has become more famous every day. After Kamalakanta Deva Goswami died, Janardan Deva Goswami became the *sattrādhikār* [of Uttar Kamalabari *sattra*]. Celibate devotees serve under the *sattrādhikār* and there is also a committee to look after the institution.

Every temple and shrine in Assam has at least one story that reflects upon its history and explains why the place is special and how it came into being. Many of these stories are mythical, referring to deities and episodes in their lives; others include Assamese kings as heroes. If there is anything unusual in the story above, it is the historical proximity of the events described. The discovery of Madhavadeva's birthplace does not take us to the mythical past but to a more recent time, to the middle of the twentieth century. Historical reality dominates, although the supernatural elements, such as the mysterious light in the jungle and the auspicious dream, are also included. The narrative recounts the main events that led to the discovery and to the establishment of the shrine; it also confirms that the place is well maintained and looked after. There is no conflict in the story; the only obstacle is the wild forest that has to be cut to clear the place. This was the first story about Letekupukhuri that I had heard and it drew a complete and balanced picture. I had no idea that a complex web of stories would start to unfold from this preliminary visit to Madhavadeva's birthplace, consisting of personal memories, oral histories and legends that revealed a contested landscape. Later I heard that only a kilometre away in Ronga-jan there was another shrine, also purporting to mark the birthplace of the same saint. It appears that there are two lively narrative traditions that aim to identify the real birthplace, and there is strong confrontation between the two religious institutions that maintain rival shrines. The stories of the devotees of each site function as counter-narratives challenging evidence produced by the opposite party.

In February 2011 I visited Letekupukhuri again and met Jitu Saikia, a young monk from Uttar Kamalabari *sattra*. His rendering of the origin of the shrine was quite similar to the first story. He said that the original inhabitants of these places were the Khamti people,[4] who saw the earthen lamp in the jungle and heard the sound of a *doba*, a big drum that is the musical instrument of the prayer halls. From the Khamtis neo-Vaishnava Hindus heard about these mysterious signs and reported to the head of Uttar Kamalabari *sattra*, which was in Tipling during these years. The head of the *sattra* came to visit the place. Then people found the first plinth (*bheti*) in the jungle, probably the foundation of a former house. They relied on Lakshminath Bezbaruah's book of Madhavadeva's life story.[5] They were singing devotional hymns for three days and three nights. On the last day of singing a person in Uttar Kāthani (near Dholpur) had a dream about people who were singing hymns and looking for the birthplace of a saint. He had dreamed of a plinth covered by the branches of a *bamunibar* tree.[6] According to information from Bezbaruah's book and from the dream, the place of the other plinth in the jungle was found, and identified as the birthplace of Madhavadeva. Obviously, Jitu Saikia was talking about historical events, although he had not witnessed them. Orally transmitted stories displayed variation and folkloric patterns. According to one version, recorded by Karuna K. Kakati at the very beginning of the twenty-first century, Madhavadeva's birthplace was revealed to a monk from Uttar Kamalabari *sattra*. The supernatural creature *burha dangoria*[7] appeared to him in a dream and showed him the plinth of the saint's birthplace in the jungle near Narayanpur. Next morning the monk travelled to Narayanpur, met some villagers and together they started to look for the place. They were cutting the jungle and discovered the plinth of a house near a tank, which was identical to the dream. The tank was known as Letekupukhuri. The men cleaned the plinth and then invited Kamalakanta Deva Goswami, the head of Uttar Kamalabari *sattra* as the expert to examine the place and compare it with the description in a book about Madhavadeva's life. The head of the *sattra* visited the place and confirmed the discovery. The story continues:

> To convince the common people he decided to light two earthen lamps in that very plinth, one in the name of Shankaradeva and another in the name of Madhavadeva. Then he said to the villagers to come again the next morning to that place to see if the lamps would still be burning. The villagers did so and saw that only the lamp which was lighted in the name of Madhavadeva was burning. Then they were convinced that this was the place where Madhavadeva had been born. After the recognition of the plinth of the house, the villagers collectively performed a *nāmkīrtan* ('chanting the names of God') for three days. (Kakati 2000/2001: 29–30)

The test with the two burning lamps that appeared in different stories seemed to be a folkloric motif. However, there was no reason to doubt that the visit of the head of Uttar Kamalabari *sattra* and his participation in establishing the shrine was a historical fact, as with the discovery of the pond and the foundation of a house in the forest. The narrated events in the middle of the twentieth century were not too distant in time and it seemed likely that some of the witnesses were still there, living in the neighbourhood. In January 2014 I met one of them, Mohan Hazarika, who was 86 years old and had played an active role in establishing the shrine. He was a former army officer and fighter for Indian independence. Together with an Assamese folklorist, Neelakshi Goswami, we were sitting in his home drinking tea and listening to his rendering of the events, as he remembered them.

Mohan Hazarika told us that the region was once forested and inhabited by tribal peoples, such as the Mising, Koch and Khamti. In the 1930s around thirty or forty Assamese families had bought the land and settled there. The place was known as Letekupukhuri and there was a big pond in the forest. Some stories were circulating that Madhavadeva had been born somewhere nearby. Then people found a plinth in the forest and thought that this might be the birthplace of a guru. In order to find out the truth, they made an experiment with two oil lamps in which Mr Hazarika had an important role to play. That is what he said:

> They decided to light two lamps [*bonti*]. They said that we won't light the lamp with mustard oil. In my house there was ghee and I said, 'well, you clean the plinth, and I'll go to get some ghee'. They decided that we won't light earthen lamps but we'll cut a papaya into two halves and put ghee inside and light it. They prepared the papaya lamps. The lamp on the right was lit in the name of Shankarguru [i.e. Shankaradeva] and the lamp on the left was meant for Mahapurusha Madhavadeva. Whoever is the great soul to whom the shrine belongs, that lamp will be burning till the next morning. Ten people prayed this. They lit the lamps at three o'clock in the afternoon and came back at eight o'clock the next morning. Of the lamp on the left only half of the oil had burned, the rest was still there. The lamp on the right had burnt out. They were very much surprised that although both lamps were lit at the same time, one of them was out and the second was still half-intact. How can it be? This is strange. This is the great evidence. They decided to call for a big general meeting and organize *pāl nām* for three days.

The traditional story suddenly appeared as a personal narrative with much attention to detail. There was no doubt that Mr Hazarika was talking about events in which he had participated. Moreover, he then confirmed the veracity of other episodes that belonged to oral tradition. Indeed, there had been a man from a distant village near Dholpur who had come and pointed out Madhavadeva's exact birthplace. The name of the man who had had the miraculous dream was Dattram Borah. He followed the guidance that he had received in his dream, left home and reached a village nearby. People there knew about the ongoing events in Letekupukhuri and gave the man the contact details of Mohan Hazarika's father. Thus, Mr Hazarika had personal memories of Dattram Borah. He said that in his dream he had seen the ongoing ritual chanting (*pāl nām*) and a big and healthy *bamunibar* tree with a large branch that had withered. Somebody revealed in the dream that the branch had died because it had grown on the birthplace of the saint. Dattram Borah's description of the plinth helped to identify the place in the jungle, then the trees around it were felled and the surrounding was cleared. These events happened in 1942 and during the same year the committee of the shrine was formed.

A comparison of Mr Hazarika's story with the narratives of the two monks from Uttar Kamalabari *sattra* reveals some differences. Whereas the monks underlined the role that the head of their *sattra* had played in these events, Mr Hazarika did not mention him at all. Perhaps there was no need to refer to an institutional authority because his own authority as witness was beyond doubt. Mr Hazarika's rendering of the events relied on his own memory, not on the web of stories that were circulating around the place—and there were many of these stories, often with supernatural overtones. The historical pond was said to be mysterious because many people had seen a golden boat in the bottom of the water. The huge banyan tree next to the pond was considered a historical memorial from Madhavadeva's time. Jitu Saikia said that in 1988 a ceremony was held at which *Bhāgavata purāna* was recited for many days. There was a small boy who saw on top of the tree the image of Ganesha, the popular elephant-headed Hindu deity. Later, other people saw Ganesha too and the image remained there for four days until it disappeared. In addition, Jitu Saikia saw it but could not explain what it was. As he said,

> nobody dared to climb up to check. There was an old man there who had said something bad about the Ganesha image—that it was fake. Mysteriously he was slapped three times so badly that he had to be hospitalized.

Another majestic tree, a mango tree, grew next to the prayer hall, which had been constructed on top of the plinth and was the onetime birthplace. The tree was considered a witness from Madhavadeva's lifetime. The third witness, the *bamunibar* tree growing next to the birthplace had withered and had been cut down. Stories about the place in the jungle before it was linked to Madhavadeva and turned into a shrine were also spread. People talked about seeing mysterious light in the dark jungle and about hearing the sounds of a big drum and cymbals. As there was something supernatural about the place in the jungle, people were afraid of it and kept it intact. It was also implied that there had been a historical shrine at the site but because of wars and devastation it had fallen into oblivion and the area had become forested, until the Assamese people returned. Even today there is something mysterious and scary about the prayer hall on top of the birthplace. Mohan Hazarika said that if something goes wrong during the rituals, or otherwise, Bhagvan ('the supreme lord') himself comes and people can hear the sound of a big drum (*khol*) and cymbals (*tal*). The sound of drumming from the shrine can be so loud that it even reaches Mohan Hazarika's house, although it is nearly two kilometres away. Mr Hazarika said, 'when we hear it, we lay down and pray. No one knows where the sound is coming from'.

## Madhavadeva's Birthplace in Ronga-jan

People in Letekupukhuri were well aware of the existence of the competing shrine, the alternative birthplace of Madhavadeva nearby (see Figures 5.2 and 5.3). Jitu Saikia did not talk much about it but mentioned the controversy briefly:

> People in Ronga-jan later claimed that the place of their shrine is the birthplace of Madhavadeva. Then political leaders appointed a committee to investigate the matter. The committee invited people from both shrines and declared that Letekupukhuri is the birthplace of Madhavadeva. The shrine of Ronga-jan was not allowed to write that Madhavadeva had been born there until, in 1989, there was a meeting of the *Srimanta Shankaradeva Sangha* and they changed the word shrine [*thān*] to birthplace [*janmasthān*].

**Figure 5.2.** Main gate of the birthplace of Madhavadeva in Ronga-jan. Photograph by Ülo Valk, 2014

**Figure 5.3.** Offering food to pilgrims in Ronga-jan. Photograph by Ülo Valk, 2014

The *Srimanta Shankaradeva Sangha* is a society which was formed in the 1920s with the purpose of spreading Shankaradeva's doctrine and challenging the dominant position of Brahmins. From these early years the society preached monotheism, the abandonment of ritual impurity,[8] the abolition of untouchability, the creation of equal rights for men of all castes, and fostering good relations between ethnic communities (Cantlie 1984: 275). Today the society has grown into an extremely popular and powerful organization consisting of more than 650,000 people.[9] While propagating Shankaradeva's and Madhavadeva's doctrine, the society emphasizes egalitarianism and resistance to caste hierarchies. The society rejects Brahmanic rituals and worship of deities other than Vishnu and Krishna. Thus, the controversy about Madhavadeva's two birthplaces also reveals disagreements about doctrine and ritual practice between different schools within Assamese neo-Vaishnavism.

I visited the birthplace in Ronga-jan for the first time in February 2011. The place was far more crowded than the Letekupukhuri shrine, and therefore it reminded me of other popular pilgrimage destinations in Assam. At such places it is not difficult to find people who know the stories of the place and are eager to share their knowledge with visitors. Seventy-eight-year-old Padmadhar Saikia, who works as a helper at the shrine, remembered its history well. His grandfather had told him that it was established in 1926. At that time people were settling in the forested region. They found a plinth in the jungle, which was surrounded by four ponds. The place was very clean and people witnessed how a wild elephant brought bananas there and how monkeys ate them. People realized that the place must have some significance, so they constructed a tent on the plinth and started religious worship there. They cleared the jungle and constructed a prayer hall, which was made from straw. The prayer hall derived its name from the nickname of a local man, Moniram Borah, who caught wild elephants, and had had an accident which made him lame (*lengera*). He was called Lengera Burah and the prayer hall was called *Lengera nāmghar*. Local people spread the word about the shrine in the vicinity, trying to find the history of the place. Then a man from Nagaon came, Keshabananda Vaishnav, who had dreamed about a place near Narayanpur where Madhavadeva had been born. He started to look for it, and while staying in Sakrahi *sattra* he heard about the *Lengera nāmghar*. Then he reached Ronga-jan and identified the shrine as Madhavadeva's birthplace. He settled there and continued to develop the prayer hall. As Padmadhar Saikia said, Keshabananda Vaishnav informed all the *sattras* of Assam about the place and all of them acknowledged it as the birthplace of Madhavadeva. However, others later claimed that they had found the birthplace of Madhavadeva nearby in Letekupukhuri. As Padmadhar Saikia said, Madhavadeva was born in Ronga-jan and was brought up there until the age of seven. Then his family moved to the place of the Letekupukhuri shrine. As he was brought up there from the age of seven, this place is very holy too. Padmadhar Saikia also commented on the history of the competing birthplaces:

> In 1954 some people from [Uttar] Kamalabari *sattra* came to establish a *sattra* in Letekupukhuri. However, this *sattra* did not persist and has become a shrine. There are still monks there who are running the shrine. When Keshabananda Vaishnav saw that a new shrine was established at Letekupukhuri and it was slowly becoming powerful, he started to worry about the existence of this shrine [in Ronga-jan]. So he gave this place to Shankaradeva's society [*Srimanta Shankaradeva Sangha*]. Influence of the devotees and their offerings are greater here. Whatever offerings and visits of devotees we have in a day, the other shrine has in a month. People have no faith there … Many people have dreamed that Madhavadeva was born here. The first one who saw the dream was Lengera Burah. There is also a teacher who has claimed that he had dreamed that Madhavadeva had been born in this place.

This story by Padmadhar Saikia is a concise summary of events and processes behind the shrine in Ronga-jan and its controversial relationship with the shrine in Letekupukhuri. Dates, names, historical data and supernatural episodes are intertwined but next to narrated evidence we were also shown tangible proof to verify the shrine's connection with Madhavadeva. Devotees had found some historical objects in the ponds and nearby that have been attributed to the saint. These relics include a *shankha* ('conch shell'), manuscripts of Shiva worship, a golden idol (*mūrti*) of Garuda, and a bell. These precious things were demonstrated to us in the prayer hall by another devotee, Liladhar Borah. Obviously, some of these objects cannot be directly connected with the neo-Vaishnava movement but rather to the worship of deities that had been condemned by Shankaradeva. Liladhar Borah said that Madhavadeva had used these things earlier, when he still worshipped the Goddess. When he met his guru Shankaradeva, he was converted and did not need the objects so he threw them away. Liladhar Borah also showed me a black stone with Madhavadeva's footprint (*pada-silā*) as evidence of the saint (see Figure 5.4). (True, it needed good imagination from me to recognize a human footprint in this stone.) Liladhar Borah said that the people who had found these objects had no idea that their original owner had been

Madhavadeva. Because they did not handle the things respectfully, they fell ill. Later they realized that this was the birthplace of Madhavadeva and that the objects had belonged to the saint. They recognized the greatness of Madhavadeva, became neo-Vaishnava devotees and recovered.

**Figure 5.4.** Liladhar Borah with Madhavadeva's footprint in stone in the prayer hall of Ronga-jan. Photograph by Ülo Valk, 2011

After this preliminary visit to Ronga-jan I returned to the place in 2014 together with Neelakshi Goswami. We interviewed several people, from Jiban Bhuyan, the secretary of *Srimanta Shankaradeva Sangha* in Narayanpur and other members of the committee, to the people who serve in the shrine and the village people living nearby. We also interviewed Padmadhar Saikia and Liladhar Borah again. We collected quantities of evidence about the history of the shrine and proofs about its connection with Madhavadeva. It seemed that word was spreading about a foreign scholar who wanted to find the historical truth, so some people came to find me at the guest house while others addressed me in the streets of Narayanpur, the small town nearby, to tell me what they knew. And they all knew the truth, although they were also aware of the misinformation that had been spread by the other party and therefore tried to enlighten me. Some people talked about the meetings of some powerful committees that had made decisions about the real birthplace of Madhavadeva. They recounted lists of names of politicians and other important people who had taken sides in the matter or were somehow involved in the history of shrines. Indeed, hundreds of names appeared in the interviews and in written sources—far too many for me to understand who was who and why these particular people were named. The consistent tendency to include names shows to what extent the discourse was imbued with social reality and touched the lives of real people. Other interviewees were more interested in early history and interpreted the old stories of the life of Madhavadeva and connected them with the micro-geography of the area around the two shrines, where the local rivers formed natural boundaries of the contested territory. Evidence for the historical truth appeared even in the place names. Chandra Nath Saikia, one of the volunteer assistants at the Ronga-jan shrine, said that according to the belief of the local people even the toponym Ronga-jan reveals the birthplace of Madhavadeva. Ronga-jan ('red stream') refers to a small river that flows beside the shrine. People say that after giving birth, Madhavadeva's mother had washed her clothes in this river and its water turned red with blood.

Bhadreshwar Borah's (b. 1947) memories about the establishment of Ronga-jan shrine were of particular importance. It turned out that his father Phanidhar Borah was the brother of Moniram Borah, the legendary Lengera Burah who was called the founder of the shrine by many people. Phanidhar had come to this place from Jorhat. According to the words of his son, Phanidhar had once fallen seriously ill and had a dream. A man in a turban, somebody like a devotee (*bhakat*), appeared to him and said, 'don't worry, you will be cured, come with me'. He took Phanidhar to the dense forest on the back of an elephant. Moniram Borah was riding the same elephant. They reached a huge plinth and the man in the turban told him that in order to be cured, he had to arrange a certain ritual there, a *pūjā*. After this meaningful dream Phanidhar Borah identified this place in the jungle and after a couple of weeks performed the ritual. That night the same person reappeared in his dream and said that the *pūjā* had failed because the clothes of the ritual specialist had been torn. Phanidhar told the others about his dream, and as the same person had appeared in the dream twice, people began to believe in the dream. Then Phanidhar arranged the ritual again and corrected the mistake. Every week he walked one and a half kilometres to the place in the jungle to light a lamp there. He could not go alone because there were too many elephants, boars and tigers in the jungle, so at least two other men accompanied him. Bhadreshwar Borah's story about the early years of the shrine is rich in detail, including the following episode:

132   *Vernacular Knowledge*

> then a big thing happened. An elephant came, his leg was so big ... He brought ripe bananas, completely perfect bananas. The elephant left the bananas, bowed down and went away. They found signs of it later. So the next morning when they came to light the lamp and found the footprints of an elephant and the bananas, everybody was informed and they all shared the bananas. An old person, who died recently, would keep talking about that as he also got a share of the bananas. It was before 1924 or 1925. Ever since everybody ate from this bunch of bananas the fame of this place increased.

Worship at the shrine became more regular. In 1935 the shrine committee was established and a man was appointed to take care of the shrine and light the lamp. Bhadreshwar Borah said,

> this place was considered a divine [*devottor*] place. At that time nobody knew it was Madhavadeva's birthplace. In 1940 when [Keshabananda] Vaishnav came and from that time on the fame of this place as Madhavadeva's birthplace started to spread.

## Evoking Truth through Variation in the Legendry

It is not difficult to notice common elements and parallel developments in the narrative cycles about the two shrines. Everything starts from the late fifteenth century when Madhavadeva was born—somewhere near Narayanpur, as his historical life stories claim. Temporal distance to the original events is vast, almost mythically long. Wars and other calamities have broken the historical continuity of settlement in the region, former villages have disappeared, and the jungle has taken over. Both Letekupukhuri and Ronga-jan as holy places rise from wilderness—the domain of wild animals and non-Hindu tribal peoples. Oral histories reveal the Assamization of the landscape: clearing the jungle, building homes for newcomers, re-introducing agriculture, marking out the holy sites of the Assamese Hindus and constructing the shrines. Stories do not only tell of finding Madhavadeva's birthplace, they also tell of the revival of the Assamese culture. Both birthplaces, Letekupukhuri and Ronga-jan, have been identified through supernatural signs, for example seeing mysterious lights, hearing drumming or witnessing pious elephants that pay homage to the sacred place in the jungle. Devotees bring extra-textual material evidence of the honourable history of both sites in connection to Madhavadeva's life, such as ancient trees in Letekupukhuri and relics in Ronga-jan. Vivid miraculous dreams help to identify both places, and some important historical people have a role to play in their early years.

History, personal memories and the storyworld entangle and merge into one realm of endless variation, sometimes recycling the same basic facts, traditional narrative motifs and supernatural episodes, but sometimes presenting major deviations and inconsistencies in the names and social positions of some main characters, the years mentioned and the events described. However, the whole discourse is carried by one goal, that of sharing and reconfirming the historical truth. Georgina Smith (1983), who has studied both legends and oral history, has made a distinction between literal truth and social truth in storytelling and shown that if people believe in the veracity of their stories, they prefer the social truth. My fieldwork revealed the same: belief in the truth of stories did not depend on the inclusion of factual data or its accuracy. Rather, it depended on personal involvement in the discourse, and on which side of the dispute the person belonged.

On January 13, 2015 Neelakshi Goswami, Pallavi Dutta and I were visiting the island of Majuli in the Brahmaputra River, the heart of Assamese culture and place of many historical *sattras*. We met Janardan Deva Goswami, the head of Uttar Kamalabari *sattra* (see Figure 5.5)—one of the most powerful *sattras* and the institution that administers Madhavadeva's birthplace in Letekupukhuri. Janardan Deva Goswami is the twentieth *sattrādhikār* in the historical order of succession; his predecessor was Kamalakanta Deva Goswami, who figured in the narratives of monks at the Letekupukhuri shrine. Janardan Deva Goswami said that the conflict between the two shrines has a long history and has become a political issue. Local government and political parties support both shrines and the confrontation helps them to get votes. The head of the *sattra* said that recently a discussion has started about finding a compromise so that the whole Letekupukhuri area, including both shrines, could be declared the birthplace of Madhavadeva. 'Let the two lamps keep burning', the *sattrādhikār* said, referring to the continuous worship at the two shrines. However, he also confirmed that Letekupukhuri was the original shrine and the true birthplace, and that the Shrimanta Shankaradeva Sangha people made their claims much later, connecting the birthplace with an existing prayer hall. When I asked him how the holy place was discovered in Letekupukhuri, he responded:

> The local people of that area went into the jungle because of their cattle. There were tigers too at that time. Even the *sattrādhikār*, who was my predecessor, told me that when he used to go there in 1951 he could see tigers. When those local people said that there is the pond and plinth of a house then the Supreme Lord [*prabhuishwar*][10] took a tour in that area

on his elephant to check it. Three lamps were lit there after discovering this place to prove that it was the real birthplace of Madhavadeva. If these three lamps did not go out but gave light for the whole night, then it would be Madhavadeva's true birthplace. And those lamps gave light for the whole night, so people consider that it was the true birthplace of Madhavadeva.

**Figure 5.5.** The head of Uttar Kamalabari *sattra* Janardan Deva Goswami. In the background: portraits of Shankaradeva and Madhavadeva. Photograph by Ülo Valk, 2015

This was another version of this experiment with burning lamps used to reveal the truth. Was it the same event that Mohan Hazarika had participated in but which he described differently? Was it some other occasion? Or was it only a traditional narrative motif? It was impossible to find out. In addition to the oral tradition of storytelling, the controversy has also been discussed in print, as both shrines have published small booklets about their past. The booklets do present historical data, although sometimes they also refer to the arguments of the competing party. Thus, a publication prepared by the shrine in Ronga-jan sheds some light on the shrine in Letekupukhuri (Borā 2006). The publication claims that the Uttar Kamalabari *sattra* was shifted to Letekupukhuri in December 1952, following the dream of the *sattrādhikār*. He saw Madhavadeva, who showed him the birthplace in Letekupukhuri. The *sattrādhikār* related his dream to the village people, who claimed the birthplace on the basis of this dream (ibid.: 18). As the author notes, Ronga-jan was identified as Madhavadeva's birthplace as early as 1926. This undermines the claims of the *sattrādhikār*, making his dream questionable. However, in the current context we can see something else: the story is a new version of identifying the place through a meaningful dream. Who was the man who first dreamed about Madhavadeva's birthplace? Was he the man from the Dhalpur area, a man from the Nagaon region, the *sattrādhikār*, or a monk? They all appear in different versions of the story.

It makes no sense to expect consistency in arguments presented in legends, a genre that is prone to variation (cf. Siikala 1990: 36–89; Tangherlini 1994: 123–135). However, I have to admit that I became interested in the historical truth of the two shrines, trying at least to find out the simple fact of which place was the first to be identified as the birthplace of Madhavadeva. The further I went searching for the answer, the more puzzled I became. The number of interviewees during my fieldwork trips grew and was finally around 20 or 25, among them five to ten major informants, a more or less equal number on both sides. Thus, thousands of people were neglected in this investigation and I do not have their versions, although I can imagine that most of them have taken sides in the dilemma, meaning that they might visit only one shrine, depending on their religious belonging. Adherents of the strict *Srimanta Shankaradeva Sangha* go to Ronga-jan and avoid Letekupukhuri; others might prefer Letekupukhuri but also visit Ronga-jan.

The fieldwork around the two shrines was one of the most intense experiences for me of being surrounded and imbued by the vernacular legendry and its 'rhetoric of truth' (Oring 2008). Truth was reported to me systematically and convincingly—I was its elicitor and target. However, my confusion only grew, and at a certain moment I realized that the accumulated information had become so overwhelming that I simply could not process it, although it was nothing more than an assemblage of fragments. I could imagine the range of the discourse and its strands, and its overpowering expressivity, but its horizons remained beyond my field of vision.

The case study revealed the generative power of folklore expressions of high frequency, the 'natural variation of traditions in social life' that was called organic variation by Lauri Honko (2000: 16–17). The historical fact that Madhavadeva had not nominated his successor but had given authority to a textual body of a hymnal seems meaningful.[11] Authorizing the transmission of mystical poetry, letting the powerful tradition flow in its own right, seems irreversible. Religious institutions can try to use the power of folklore for their own benefit, to support their institutional authority, but they cannot control or standardize it. As the flow of arguments that I encountered in the field was forceful, I was sometimes carried along, almost taking sides in a contested truth that was so obvious to the local people. Far from being equal to Shankaradeva, who could safely swim over the Brahmaputra and watch its flow from the other side, I was deeply immersed in the flow of arguments, and my bewilderment only grew because it was difficult to distance myself from the ardent discourse and observe it from outside. The dispute could not be reduced to the conflict between two religious institutions whose authority was challenged by the counter-discourse. The issue of truth was far more complex because both traditions were closely intertwined and displayed internal controversies, such as the dates, names and historical facts, which often did not match in different versions. I found myself in a multi-dimensional and expanding discursive realm of oral histories, personal memories, legends and historical facts, all in animate variation. Stories received their truth value within the particular context of social enactment (Mills 2007: 72), while in other conversational contexts—challenged by the arguments and evidence of the rival party—the same stories became untrue. The truth that was produced in interaction was far from univocal. Rather, the communication process led to epistemological uncertainty—similar to a state of perplexity between factuality and fictionality that evokes a sense of the supernatural in experience narratives about magic and about otherworldly encounters (Valk 2015). Discussions about the supernatural touch upon existential matters—ontological reality—and therefore stand out from the mundane communications of everyday life. In the case of Madhavadeva's birthplace the truth that is negotiated is not only supernatural or historical; the discourse is about expressing local and religious identity through claims that a significant place is the 'location of an eruption of the sacred' into the everyday world (Mills 2007: 64). The truth that is discussed and debated becomes an instrument 'through which important social work gets done' (Duranti 1993: 218)—the work of defining one's belonging, reassuring the discursive foundation of a selected shrine and thus supporting its future growth.

The two shrines in Letekupukhuri and Ronga-jan exist as material proof of discursive powers, as controversial, inconsistent and uncertain as they are. The epistemological uncertainty, which is brought to life by arguments and counter-arguments in narratives, and evidence from personal memories, has powerful effects in producing tangible and intangible reality. It generates vernacular knowledge for individuals, groups and factions as well as creating emotional attachments. As sceptical and perplexed as I was in the field, it seemed impossible to ignore the call for truth and remain neutral in this quest, and I did develop a clear feeling of a favourite birthplace for Madhavadeva. It also seemed to me that there was more evidence to prove that the same shrine had been the first to be identified as the birthplace. However, I do not know if it was only because of my emotional attachment or for some other mysterious reason that the matter started to seem clear and certain, even though there was no way out from the storyworld. The birthplace of the saint, which was once surrounded by the jungle, is now hidden again, and this jungle of stories can never be clear cut.

## Acknowledgements

I am thankful to Kailash Dutta, Palash Dutta, Pallavi Dutta, Meenaxi Barkataki-Ruscheweyh, Neelakshi Goswami and Baburam Saikia who have helped me in fieldwork and with translations. As they are all experts and carriers of Assamese culture, discussions with them have been valuable for me to understand the religious life and the related storytelling traditions of Assam. I also thank Kishore Bhattacharjee for his constant support in my endeavours to understand northeastern India in its ethnic and cultural diversity and for his friendship. My special gratitude goes to interviewees in Letekupukhuri, Ronga-jan and the neighbouring areas—those whose names are listed below, and to others whose names I missed during the fieldwork. I have fond memories of the hospitality and friendliness of these people, of their willingness to share with me their knowledge without remaining anonymous but allowing me to include their names in the publication. Last but not least, I acknowledge the role of the Estonian Research Council (projects IUT02-43 and PRG670) and the EEA Financial Mechanism Baltic Research Program in Estonia (EMP340) in supporting my work.

## Fieldwork

February 7, 2009: interview with Jogendra Borah Bayan.

February 11, 2011: interviews with Padmadhar Saikia, Liladhar Borah and Jitu Saikia.

January 27–29, 2014: interviews with Jiban Bhuyan, Durna Dutta, Benudhar Baruah, Niran Saikia, Chandra Nath Saikia, Rajen Borah, Jitu Saikia, Khogen Neog, Sarbeshwari Neog, Lakheshwari Neog, Meenu Kakati, Mohan Hazarika, Puspalata Borah Saikia, Indreshwar Bhuyan, Liladhar Borah, Puna Saikia, Bhadeshwar Borah, Padmadhar Saikia.

January 13, 2015: interview with Janardan Deva Goswami.

## Notes

1. As an introduction to neo-Vaishnavism and the *sattra* culture see Saikia 2018.
2. Kamalakanta Deva Goswami was the head (*sattrādhikār*) of Uttar Kamalabari *sattra*. Madhavadeva's birthplace in Letekupukhuri is administered and maintained by this *sattra*.
3. *Pāl nām* is continuous congregational prayer chanting God's name.
4. The Khamti are a Tai people who migrated to Assam from Burma in the eighteenth century. Their religion is Theravāda Buddhism (Baruah 2002).
5. Lakshminath Bezbaruah (1868–1938) is a well-known Assamese writer who published biographies (*carit-puthi*) of Shankaradeva and Madhavadeva.
6. As Jogendra Borah Bayan later explained, *bamunibar* is a rare and special tree; its leaves are similar to the leaves of the banyan tree.
7. According to the classical study on Assamese demonology by Benudhar Rajkhowa (1972 [1905]: 129), *burha dangoria* is a religiously disposed spirit who attends religious assemblies among men. He appears as a tall, strong and elderly Assamese gentleman wearing a magnificent turban, a wrapper, and a dhoti. His clothes are white as marble. *Burha dangoria* resides in trees.
8. The Brahmin families have traditionally observed ten days of ritual impurity after a death in the family but the period of impurity has lasted for one month for the others. This distinction was challenged by non-Brahmins who refused to follow the old customs (Cantlie 1984: 273).
9. About the society see https://sssangha.org/ (accessed June 15, 2021).
10. Traditionally the *sattrādhikār* is identified as the Supreme God.
11. There is a remarkable parallel in Sikhism, where the sacred scripture, the Guru Granth Sahib, is taken as the eternal Guru (see Dusenbery 1992). I thank Marion Bowman for pointing this out to me.

## References

Baruah, Geetanjali. 2002. 'Khamti'. In *Assam*, edited by B. K. Bardoloi, R. P. Athaparia and K. S. Singh, 406–411. Calcutta: Seagull Books.

Borā, Padma. 2006. 'Mahāpuruh Mādhavdevor Janmasthān Xomporkot Duākhār'. [A few lines about Madhavadeva's birthplace]. In *Mahāpurush Shrī Shrī Mādhavdevor Janmasthān*, edited by Prabin Saikia, 17–19. Nārāyanpur, Uttar Lakhimpur: Shrī Shrī Mādhavdevor Janmasthān Porisalona Homiti Uziror Tul, Rongajān.

Cantlie, Audrey. 1984. *The Assamese: Religion, Caste and Sect in an Indian Village*. London; Dublin: Curzon Press.
Datta, Birendranath. 2012. 'Sankaradeva and Tribals of North-east India'. In *Cultural Contours of North-East India*, edited by Birendranath Datta, 130–133. New Delhi: Oxford University Press.
Deka Hazarika, Karabi. 2006. *Mādhavadeva: His Life, Art and Thought*. Dibrugarh; Guwahati; Tezpur: Bani Mandir.
Duranti, Alessandro. 1993. 'Truth and Intentionality: An Ethnographic Critique'. *Cultural Anthropology* 8 (2): 214–245. https://doi.org/10.1525/can.1993.8.2.02a00050
Dusenbery, Verne A. 1992. 'The Word as Guru: Sikh Scripture and the Translation Controversy'. *History of Religions* 31 (4): 385–402. https://doi.org/10.1086/463294
Honko, Lauri. 2000. 'Thick Corpus and Organic Variation: An Introduction'. In *Thick Corpus, Organic Variation and Textuality in Oral Tradition*, edited by Lauri Honko, 3–28. Helsinki: Finnish Literature Society.
Kakati, Karuna Kanta. 2000/2001. 'A Study of the Temple Legends of the Hindu Religious Centres of Lakhimpur District'. Master's diss., Gauhati University. Manuscript at the Department of Folklore Research, Gauhati University in Guwahati.
Mills, Margaret. 2007. 'On the Problem of Truth in Ethnographic Texts and Entextualisation Processes'. In *Research Ethics in Studies of Culture and Social Life*, edited by Bente Gullveig Alver, Tove Ingebjørg Fjell and Ørjan Øyen, 56–75. Helsinki: Academia Scientiarum Fennica.
Neog, Maheswar. 2008 [1965]. *Early History of the Vaiṣṇava Faith and Movement in Assam: Śaṅkaradeva and His Times*. Guwahati; New Delhi: LBS Publications.
Oring, Elliott. 2008. 'Legendry and the Rhetoric of Truth'. *Journal of American Folklore* 121 (480): 127–166.
Pathak, Pranabananda, trans. 2005. *Naam Ghosa: Hymns to the Blessed Lord as It Is by Mahapurush Shree Shree Madhabdeva*. Translated from the original Assamese by Pranabananda Pathak. New Delhi; Chicago: Promilla & Co. in association with Bibliophile South Asia.
Rajkhowa, Benudhar. 1972 [1905]. *Assamese Popular Superstitions and Assamese Demonology*. Guwahati: Gauhati University Press.
Saikia, Baburam. 2018. 'An Introduction to the Sattra Culture of Assam: Belief, Change in Tradition and Current Entanglement'. *Journal of Ethnology and Folkloristics* 12 (2): 21–47. https://doi.org/10.2478/jef-2018-0009
Siikala, Anna-Leena. 1990. *Interpreting Oral Narrative*. Helsinki: Academia Scientiarum Fennica.
Smith, Georgina. 1983. 'Urban Legend, Personal Experience Narrative and Oral History: Literal and Social Truth in Performance'. In *ARV. Scandinavian Yearbook of Folklore 1981*, vol. 37, 167–173. Uppsala: The Royal Gustavus Adolphus Academy.
Tangherlini, Timothy R. 1994. *Interpreting Legend: Danish Storytellers and Their Repertoires*. New York; London: Garland Publishing.
Valk, Ülo. 2015. 'Conceiving the Supernatural through Variation in Experience Stories: Assistant Spirits and Were-Tigers in the Belief Narratives of Assam'. *Shaman: Journal of the International Society for Shamanistic Research* 23: 141–164.

Chapter 6

# Unearthing the Narratives of the Róngkups of Sikkim: From Vernacular Alternatives to Institutionalized Beliefs

*Reep Pandi Lepcha**

My interest in oral narratives goes back to my childhood when exposure to folklore and legends about my people caught my imagination. What began as a simple exercise of listening to the oral retelling of tales and personal exchanges, over a period of time developed into a fascination linked to the intricacies within narratives that are left in the care of the narrator. Although considered a means of entertainment, for ages oral tradition has played an important role in the transmission of knowledge, especially among indigenous communities. A tendency to undermine such sources of knowledge exists, usually due to the precedence that is given to rigid forms like written records. The functional importance of oral narrative is, however, tremendous. It is a carrier of the culture, tradition and thought processes of a community. These can be defined as 'alternative spaces' where one embeds one's deepest thoughts and opinions without hesitation. In this chapter, I plan to explore the oral narratives of one of the indigenous communities of the eastern Himalayas.

* **Reep Pandi Lepcha** was awarded a SYLFF (Ryoichi Sasakawa Young Leaders Fellowship Fund) doctoral fellowship at Jadavpur University, India, in 2014. Reep has carried out archival work at the Kern Institute (Leiden University) and was a visiting fellow at the University of Tartu, Estonia in 2016. She secured the Dora Plus fellowship from the Department of Estonian and Comparative Folklore, University of Tartu, in 2017. Reep's doctoral dissertation focuses on examining the narratives of the Róngkups/Lepchas who are indigenous to Sikkim. She applies a self-reflexive approach to understanding indigenous knowledge systems while exploring their vernacular context. Currently, Reep is a faculty member at the Department of English, Nar Bahadur Bhandari Government College, Sikkim.

Although Sikkim is one of the smaller states of India, this landlocked state has been politically significant due to its geographical location. It shares no less than three international borders, cradled between Nepal in the west and Bhutan in the east, with the Tibetan Autonomous Region of today's China in the north. In 1642 Sikkim became a kingdom ruled by the Namgyal Dynasty, who trace their ancestry to Tibet. During the late nineteenth century Sikkim became a protectorate of the British Empire, although the Namgyal Dynasty's rule continued until 1975, when the country was annexed by India. The history of the region is etched with various momentous turning points, although here I concentrate on narratives that are circulated among the indigenous people of the region, the Róngkups. Mutanchi Rumkup Róngkup or simply Róngkup/Róngs, they are more widely identified as 'Lepchas' but I will refrain from using the latter nomenclature as historically it has derogatory connotations—mentioned as early as 1894 in *The Gazetteer of Sikhim* (Risley 1894: 39)—that have shadowed the ethnonym Lepcha to date. By using the term indigenous, I am subscribing to the popular belief that the Róngkups are endemic to the region. Currently, other communities such as the Bhutia and few ethnicities belonging to the Nepalese also fall under the indigenous heading, owing to the dilution of the meaning associated with the term, especially in the Indian context (Karlsson and Subba 2006). However, here I will be using the term exclusively for the Róngkups to avoid any confusion.

The junctures that proved to be pivotal in the history of the region were also the crossroads for cross-border cultural exchanges for centuries, and today this is reflected in the ethnic diversity present within the state. Sikkim now has three main ethnic communities: the Róngkups (who are a minority in terms of population compared to the other two communities), the Bhutia and the Nepalese (Planning Commission 2008: 191). The Lhopo, more commonly known as Bhutia, are Tibeto-Sikkimese (Mullard 2011: 2) and trace their origin to Tibet; they have been residing in Sikkim ever since it was established as a Buddhist kingdom. The Nepalese, who mainly follow Hinduism, were previously not allowed to enter or settle freely when Sikkim was still a kingdom, but things changed when Sikkim became a protectorate of the British, who encouraged Nepalese settlement intentionally to change the demography of the region, what Pranab Kumar Jha calls 'de-Tibetanizing' (1985: vii). This perhaps gives us an idea about the stronghold that the Tibetan monarchs had in the region, enough to make the British act on it, as Jha writes:

> The Lepchas soon came under the control of the Bhotias and those Lepchas who proved themselves trustworthy were appointed in the household establishment of the Raja while those who failed to gain the chief's confidence or favor were employed for outdoor job. Besides, they had to contribute summer Nazzars [form of taxation] in the shape of gathered crops, grains and fruits and had to carry grains etc. to any market for trade or barter. (Jha 1985: 52)

This leads one to believe that the relationship established between the two communities, namely the Lepcha/Róngkup and Bhutia, was far from ideal.

With this in mind, I will be concentrating on three sets of folk narratives still widely circulated among the Róngkups. Some narratives have even found their way into the print medium, the texts ranging from religious manuscripts composed by Lhatsun Chenpo in the form of *nesol*[1] texts, as pointed out by Scheid (2014: 71), books, and even website databases. I understand that it was the endorsement of the narratives by the Namgyal Dynasty monarchs and later by the state-sponsored celebrations which contributed to the circulation of the narratives. By considering the 'institutionalization' of the narratives, I am implying that the dominant versions have garnered the support of the state authority, thus overshadowing the indigenous variations of the narratives discussed. This institutionalization serves two purposes: the first concerns affixing roles to communities that are distinct in character and function, the second introduces a mirage of stability between them. Both contribute towards maintaining preferred power dynamics, thus lending support to the propagation of one strain of narrative, specifically the institutionalized state-preferred version.

Drawing on interviews conducted during fieldwork over the past few years, I will illustrate these points with the help of three sets of narratives. Although it is difficult to assign a chronological timeline for the transmission of the folk narratives, the narrative body itself suggests various points in history and can superficially be arranged chronologically for coherency purposes. The common factor governing them is that these narratives deal with cultural contacts and connections either implicitly or explicitly, and they provide interesting grounds for observing the influence of one ethnicity over another.

## Brief Overview of Indigenous Beliefs and Myths

The regions the indigenous people have resided in are Sikkim, Darjeeling, Kalimpong, Ilam district of Nepal and a few regions bordering Bhutan (Mainwaring 1876; Risley 1894; Gorer 1987). Basically, these are the places from where the third highest peak in the Himalayas, Mt. Kanchendzonga (Kangchenjunga)—referred to as Kongchenchyu in *róngaring* (the vernacular language of the Róngkups)—is visible. Alternatively, the peak is also referred to as Kingchumdzongbu, which when translated means 'the fortunate and honest', perhaps referring to the duties of protection given to the mountain or hinting at the preconditions required to experience the magnanimity of the deified mountain. Hence, this peak is significant for the Róngkups and in all likelihood they are familiarized with the lore about the mountain from childhood, as was true in my case. Kongchenchyu is considered the protector, erected with the responsibility of safeguarding the region and its people by It-bu-deburuum or It-bu-mu, who is the creator figure among the Róngkups. She is also referred to as a mother creator, which is reflected by the suffix *mu*. One version of the origin myth explains that a fistful of snow in each hand was taken from this peak by It-bu-mu and the mounds were shaped into the ancestors of the Róngkups: Nuzong-Nyu, a woman, and Fudong-Thing, a man. They were meant to live as siblings and were instructed by It-bu-mu to follow two different paths, which both led to one destination, Mayal Lyang. The term Mayal Lyang for the Róngkups embodies the idea of perfect harmonious existence, free from suffering of any kind. Although often compared to 'utopia' (Scheid 2014: 72), it is not simply a conceptual ideal, because the narratives and the religious beliefs of the community repeatedly try to determine its actual geographical presence around the region of Kongchenchyu (Foning 1987: 2), and it is also defined as a *kyong* or village (Tamsang 2008: 18–22), further emphasizing its image as a physical presence. Interviewee Phuchung[2] who lives in the north district of Sikkim narrated the above-mentioned creation myth to me in October 2013; he holds a special interest in Róngkup culture and tradition and is an ardent propagator of indigenous ritualistic practice. However, he endorsed another version of the myth, which speaks of the ancestors being moulded from the earth itself and Kongchenchyu being erected only at the very end to act as the overseer and protector to all creations. Stressing the fact that everything originated from the soil, Phuchung commented that it was no different when it came to humans, thus justifying the notion that the Róngkups have a close association with nature because It-bu-mu gave her people the responsibility of looking after the world she had created. Both versions are insightful as they represent the indigenous beliefs that uphold their relationship with the environment and landscapes surrounding them.

The *chyu* or mountain is revered by the Róngkups and a ritual specially dedicated to worshipping mountains, called *Chyu-Ruum-Faat*, is conducted periodically to appease the mountain deity. This ritual is performed by offering *chi* or millet beer, which is an important component in the form of a libation. The Róngkups also pray to their ancestors, who are believed to be residing on the lap of Kongchenchyu in Mayal Lyang, offering gratitude and prayers seeking protection in times to come. Blessings are sought from the mountain and different deities before any important function or occasion, and this can be conducted either within the walls of a household or even at a larger community gathering. The significance of the Kongchenchyu can be gauged through its symbolic representation on the *sungkyo* or wooden bowl filled with the offering of *chi*, for the vessel is smeared with tiny amounts of butter around the brim, imitative of the mountain's snowy peaks.

It is unanimously believed by the Róngkups that Mayal Lyang, and even the Tibetan Buddhist concept of Beyul Dremojong or 'The Sacred Hidden Land', consists of a much larger geographical region than Sikkim of today. Sikkim is known among the Buddhists there as Beyul Dremojong, because they believe that Guru Padmasambhava, founder of the Vajrayana form of Buddhism in the Himalayan belt, incorporating tantric practices, meditated in the four corners of the region. This activity of Guru Padmasambhava apparently fortified Sikkim against evil. Padmasambhava visited Sikkim during the eighth century, leaving his teachings hidden in different places (Acharya 1995: 20). Although the Róngkups are familiar with the Buddhist concept of Beyul Dremojong, at this point it should be noted that the concept of Mayal Lyang has an element of exclusivity attached to the place according to the Róngkups (Scheid 2014). There exists a strong belief among the Róngkups that only those who know their language *róngaring* will be allowed to enter Mayal Lyang. Additionally, Mayal Lyang also features prominently in the death rituals of the tribe, who believe that the souls of the Róngkups are led to this location by the *muns*,[3] a term used for shamans from the community. The Buddhists also practise a certain degree of exclusivity when it comes to the question of entering Beyul Dremojong, but this is connected more to maintaining the moral tenets of Buddhism than exclusivity based on community identity.

Dzongu, an area comprising a group of villages in the northern district of Sikkim, is considered the land of origin of the Róngkup and this notion perhaps fuels the concentration of myths and legends around this location, owing to its close proximity to the mountain. The area has been under the protection of the modern state system against encroaching settlers belonging to other ethnic communities since the time of the Namgyal Dynasty (Gorer 1987: 37), which leads us to believe that the monarchs were aware of the vulnerability of the tribe. A portion of the area currently falls under the buffer and transition zone between man and animal, the Kanchendzonga Biosphere Reserve, established in 1977 as a National Park and high-altitude biodiversity hotspot (UNESCO 2016).

If one chooses to delve deeper into the historical past of Sikkim, it is mandatory to engage with the history recorded in the oral traditions of the Róngkups. It is hard to resist being swept away by the implications of narrated encounters, especially when such narratives are considered to contain prophecies, which the Róngkup believe to stand fulfilled. The establishment of the Namgyal Dynasty in Sikkim is foreshadowed in such prophecies, as is the introduction of the new faith of Buddhism, both occurring simultaneously and having an impact on the lives of the indigenous people. The monarchs of Sikkim were given the Buddhist title *Chogyal* or *Dharma Raja* ('righteous king'). They acted not just as administrative heads, but as the title suggests, were also endowed with the responsibility to propagate the faith that they had brought from Tibet (Acharya 1995: 22). The Róngkups, prior to the advent of this faith in the region, were mainly nature and ancestor worshippers; there is no definite term assigned to this faith because it appears to be a co-mixture of animism, institutionalized Bon, ancestor and nature worship. Although people refer to it as 'Bon' for lack of a better definition, the term has a confining effect and does not accurately reflect a much larger body of vernacular beliefs.

**Narratives Featuring Contest**

In the light of these beliefs the first narrative that I want to discuss reflects on the meeting of the two faiths, Buddhism and the indigenous religion practised by the Róngkups. According to the legendary narratives, it all began with a chance meeting of Thekung Aadik and Guru Padmasambhava, who was apparently heading for Tibet to preach Vajrayana Buddhism. Thekung Aadik is a legendary character, a powerful shaman (*bongthing*), and although the following narrative seems to be the only one to which his name is linked, he is considered on a par with the other most significant Róngkup heroes. Many Róngkups in Dzongu and Chungthang (both in the northern district of Sikkim) told me about Thekung Aadik and stressed the location Numzhet Partam-sa-longklyok in Chungthang, which is a religious site today. The story is as follows:

*Spiritual Contest between Thekung Aadik and Guru Padmasambhava*
Guru Padmasambhava, also known by the name Guru Ugyen, wanted to preach Buddhism in Mayal Lyang. He happened to pass through a settlement which was under the protection of Thekung Aadik, the chief and a powerful *bongthing*, steeped in the ways of magic and spirituality, and who was unconvinced about the abilities of Guru Ugyen. Thekung Aadik believed that he had already achieved immense knowledge in terms of spiritual power, an understanding that could not be taught by any wayfarer. Hence, these two individuals, who wanted to prove their knowledge, agreed to test their powers and meet at Numzhet Partam-sa-longklyok for a test of spiritual strength. A series of tasks were proposed, with both managing to complete several difficult tasks, each matching the wit and strength of the other. Guru Ugyen tried to explain to Thekung Aadik that he was the lotus-born and a practitioner of the pure path of living, who had acquired the ability to walk on water and pass through fire unscathed. Hearing this, by way of a challenge Thekung Aadik flew and alighted upon a blade of grass[4] without stirring it. Guru Ugyen, trying to mirror his opponent's move, flew and tried to alight on a blade of grass, but unfortunately the grass swayed a little, indicating that the power of the Guru was less effective than Thekung Aadik's. The Róngkups who were witnessing the spiritual duel were jubilant and began to jeer at Guru Ugyen, reminding him of his defeat. Soon a celebration feast ensued, where the Guru was given hospitality and offered puffed rice and boiled wild tubers along with the revellers. When a girl named Numchermit[5] came to offer water to the Guru, he told her about the precepts of the knowledge that he had discovered, and that since the people did not recognize his powers he would proceed towards Tibet according to plan, and a great misfortune would soon befall the people. Alarmed, the girl went and reported this to Thekung Aadik, who [apparently] realized his arrogance, and went to the Guru repenting and asking for forgiveness. [Some narrators of this story believed that Thekung Aadik never pleaded for forgiveness, but just called upon the Guru to reconsider his unbecoming wrath.] Before leaving, the Guru displayed his spiritual powers through soothsaying. He threw the puffed rice on the ground and saw it growing in the place that he had strewn it, so he predicted that people from the north of the region would come and rule the land of the Róngkup. Then Guru Ugyen threw the cooked wild tubers on the ground and said that if the

vines of the tuber plant grew and encompassed the paddy choking it in the process, then people from other regions would come and spread in the land of the Róngkup even surpassing the tribe's numbers, and eventually the tribe would perish. Legend specifies, however, that Guru Ugyen did not allow the vines of the tuber plant to cover the paddy completely; he tore at it and threw them away, hence changing his prediction into a blessing. Guru Ugyen added that these tuber vines and their fruit would be of great use to the tribe in future; this is one reason why the Róngkups are still considered knowledgeable when it comes to identifying edible fruit and tubers found in the jungle.

This narrative is a reflection of the earliest contact between the indigenous culture exposed to an alien religion, expressing the later conflicts and complicated power relations between the ethnic communities and their faiths. There are a few surviving variations with minor differences in detail,[6] but the overall content of the tale remains unchanged. My interviewees kept stressing that the spiritual understanding of the Róngkups was considered quite phenomenal, and that they attributed this to their close affiliation with nature-worshipping practices. The symbolic representation of their respect for nature can perhaps be linked to the portrayal of Thekung Aadik, who mounted a blade of grass without disturbing it. Moreover, the apprehension towards change and the introduction of a new religion by a foreigner is quite understandable and well embodied in the character of Thekung Aadik and addressed in the narrative as a whole. The legend further points to an interesting juncture, where people who have been following a particular mode of cultural and religious belief are introduced to other possibilities. However, one must also observe that it is ultimately the foreigner who is given the upper hand, all the while hinting at the subjugation of Thekung Aadik by the end of the narrative, a curious twist which throws open speculation about the origin of this narrative. I was further informed that due to Numchermit's role in the story, the Róngkups believe that the ultimate deliverer of the indigenous community during times of trouble will be a woman. Numchermit is undoubtedly a pivotal character in the narrative; until her arrival on the scene Thekung Aadik is seen as the successful defender of the indigenous faith, but that soon changes and he is reduced to a fumbling, pleading chief. I cannot help but speculate whether the sharp shift in the power play was perhaps a later addition to the legend, especially as it involves giving one faith importance over the other. The details of the augury and predictions seem indisputable for the people in the region, as the legend foretells the new faith of Buddhism triumphing while indigenous belief fades, effects that are clearly visible today. It is quite apparent that through the 'prediction', by way of a powerful curse, Guru Padmasambhava predestines the fate of the Róngkups and projects Buddhism in a new aggressive light, quite unlike its usual characteristic tenets. This is not the first time that Guru Padmasambhava has been portrayed in an aggressive light, for he is famed for subduing demons and deities throughout his travels, with even the Kongchenchyu deity figuring as among the deities subdued by him (Balikci 2008: 89; Scheid 2014: 70). It might be that the quality of aggression was introduced later by practitioners of Buddhism rather than the guru himself as conveyed through the narrative.

People living near Numzhet Partam-sa-longklyok, now more popularly known as 'Ney-doh' or sacred rocks, continue the tradition of sowing paddy in the midst of the cacophonic modern development that has engulfed the locality. The astounding factor is that paddy would not normally grow at such cold altitudes, as the region falls within the snow belt; the people there believe that the grain grows only in that patch of land where Guru Ugyen threw the puffed rice for his augury. Now only a small area enclosed within cement walls remains of what was once a larger plot of land. People from all ethnic communities try to participate in the yearly sowing of paddy, which has acquired a religious sanctity for the residents there. A huge stone, which was once said to be a cave, stands a few metres away from the paddy patch, the only reminder of the place where two spiritual men once tested each other's strength. The fact that the residents carry out such rituals can be considered a supreme example of a culture trying to sustain itself in the face of unabated development because of the belief instilled by the ancient legend.

Interestingly, I encountered a variation of the narrative which hardly made historical or even ritualistic sense, although a handful of people, mainly from mainland India, strongly believed in it. The difference in this variant is that the 'Guru' shape-shifts and is associated with Guru Nanak, the founder of Sikhism, so much so that the Sikh regiment of the Indian army built a *gurudwara*[7] a few metres away from the walls of Ney-doh. Though Guru Nanak is said to have travelled widely (Singha 1984), there are hardly any means of determining whether he visited Sikkim in particular. His appearance in the historical legends of Sikkim is a recent phenomenon and arises when any place associated with the word 'guru' is automatically linked to Guru Nanak. Similarly, a lake called Gurudongmar, which is considered sacred by the Buddhists due to its associations with Guru Padmasambhava, has of late also gained popularity among Sikhs, who consider that Guru Nanak blessed the lake. The local populace remains unfazed by this new development; they are united in their belief that it was Guru Padmasambhava and not Guru Nanak who is portrayed in the narrative connected to the location, mainly because they believe Buddhist religious scriptures chronicle the travels and feats of Guru Padmasambhava (Mullard 2011), as well as having faith in their version of the legend.

The above folk narratives highlight jarring conflicts in their versions, and close consideration of such narratives gives one an opportunity to observe how varied cultures and religions react on contact. Such observation may help gauging some of the factors that determine the mass acceptance of a particular strain of narrative and its subsequent effects on the indigenous culture and religion. As of now, the indigenous people continue to refute the Guru Nanak version, although it has gained popularity. However, it remains to be seen whether, and how, such narratives play a part in charting the socio-cultural and religious structures of the region. If one takes into account the experiences of indigenous people worldwide, it can safely be assumed that the homogenizing tendency of cultural and religious assimilation has directly affected the vernacular beliefs of the people. It has been no different for the Róngkups, who have had their vernacular beliefs marginalized and their only surviving form of history, oral narrative, consigned to the shadow of canonical or institutionalized narrative. Under such circumstances, a figure like Thekung Aadik, kept alive in the oral narratives of the tribe, gives them a reason to believe that they had a formidable ancestor in the past who exhibited grit to combat new challenges. In all likelihood, however, the various disputed facts revolving around the lore at the same time provides soil for sowing discontent, especially because it deals with sensitive issues of religious beliefs.

The other narrative cycle that I want to draw upon deals with the legend of Thekung Mensalong. There are many legends revolving around this powerful individual who is considered on a par with other legendary figures like Thekung Aadik or even Gebu Aachok, who fought against the Bhutanese army. Reputedly living for centuries, Thekung Mensalong's name is mentioned in the chantings of *muns* and *bongthings* in their state of trance. The frequency of this legendary figure in the narratives of the indigenous people is comparatively greater than any other figure (such as Thekung Aadik). It appears that the Róngkups have a penchant for narratives involving trials or duels; such narratives, apart from recording conflicts, also have a tendency of tying the indigenous community to a geographical locale. For example, Lee-sung, a cave located in south Sikkim, has a narrative involving Thekung Mensalong. When directly translated from *róngaring*, *lee* is a term for 'house' while *sung* roughly translates into 'stories/narrations', the implied meaning with respect to the narrative account being 'stories pertaining to a particular area'. I recorded the first narrative in North Sikkim and the other at Lingee-Payoung in South Sikkim during my field visits. The first one highlights why Thekung Mensalong acted as a guide, and the second concentrates on a particular place in the southern district of Sikkim. The *ters*, *terma* or *gter-ma* in the stories below are hidden spiritual treasures which can be anything ranging from texts, idols or any other element with religious value and are prominent in the Buddhist belief system (Mullard 2011: 29).

*The Legends of Thekung Mensalong*
As narrated by Phuchung, Thekung Mensalong is once said to have met Guru Padmasambhava. After an initial test of strength, Thekung Mensalong acknowledged that they were equals when it came to spiritual prowess. Guru Padmasambhava became aware that Thekung Mensalong held the power of prolonging his life if he wished it, and this also meant that Mensalong could end his immortal quality whenever he wanted. Owing to such powers Guru Padmasambhava bid Thekung Mensalong fulfil a task, as Guru Padmasambhava expressed his inability to carry it out himself, owing to his responsibilities of subduing the evil entities in the region. Guru Padmasambhava showed Thekung Mensalong the places where he had hidden spiritual treasures or *ters*, which the Guru felt would be useful to the people living in the region in due course, basically when there would be a need to control evil forces. The Guru therefore left Thekung Mensalong in charge of the *ters*, with the instructions that another tantric *lama* or monk, equal in calibre, would arrive in the region and it would be Thekung Mensalong's duty to show him the places, as instructed. Thekung Mensalong reportedly waited until the sixteenth century, when Lhatsun Chenpo, one of the three *lama*s responsible for the consecration of Phuntsog Namgyal, the first *Dharma Raja* or *Chogyal*, arrived in the region. Thekung Mensalong tested the strength of Lhatsun Chenpo's tantric powers and once he was convinced that Lhatsun Chenpo was the individual he had been anticipating, Mensalong took him to the various holy sites where the Guru had hidden the *ters*. One by one, the *lama* prayed at the sites, while Thekung Mensalong acted as his guide.

The second legend is about a particular cave called Lee-sung at Lingee. It is a translation of a passage from a longer interview, conducted on March 1, 2015 in *róngaring*, in Nepali and English. In the following narrative account of Tekung Mensalong the comments within square brackets are those of interviewee Byekbu:

> Thekung Mensalong and Lhatsun Chenpo agreed to a wager; the challenge was to reach the hill where the first rays of the sun fell. Thekung Mensalong reached the place early and while he waited for Lhatsun Chenpo to arrive, he started a fire and toasted a cob of corn. Lhatsun Chenpo, travelling on the rays of light themselves, saw on his approach that Mensalong had already reached the agreed place and was busy roasting corn. When he arrived, Mensalong exclaimed 'Oh! You have arrived? Please sit'. Lhatsun Chenpo felt guilty and thought to himself, 'I should have reached here first, but Mensalong has already arrived earlier than me'. Although defeated, he accepted it and sat down. Meanwhile Mensalong broke the corncob into two equal halves as there was just one. The top portion of the cob he presented to Lhatsun Chenpo. Lhatsun Chenpo observed that the portion that Mensalong kept for himself appeared bigger [the bottom half is always bigger and broader] and though he did not protest out loud he thought to himself, 'He gave me the smaller portion, but he has kept the better portion for himself'. Mensalong had thought out his actions well, 'He is a *lama* [monk], so I have to give him the tip portion, I am the host [*zhinda*] so I will eat the bottom portion'. Mensalong's intentions were good, but Lhatsun Chenpo took the gesture otherwise...[8]

I think it is important to mention that Byekbu had recently converted to Christianity, despite his religious affiliation he narrates the legend to people who are interested in understanding the community and in keeping the oral narrations of the tribe alive. At the same time, he clearly expressed discomfort when it came to Buddhism. Here the square brackets are my comments:

> I sometimes wonder if Buddhism had not come to Sikkim, what would it be like today? ... Buddhism according to my observation ... I cannot comment on other places, but in Lingee, a lot has been 'damaged'; the reason why it has caused damage is because our younger generations, nobody could 'come out' [implying the inability to achieve changes in terms of social mobility] due to monastic studies. Look here, even our legend degrades us, isn't it? We Róngkups are dull; we blindly follow wholeheartedly, dedicatedly without questioning anything. According to my experience, children of school-going age, instead of getting admission into schools, are taken to monasteries to become monks. Now these children become 'victims' because they lose their language ... and parents take them there ... and after studying in the monastery what else can they do? Only become a monk. I don't think one can lead a sustainable life, isn't it? I do not think it is a sustainable way of leading life ... what if everyone turns into monks in the future? Is that possible? But times are changing, we cannot rely on old ways of living. Even if you want to follow Dharma, it is not necessary to turn into a monk to do so. At the time of getting education and studying, if one goes into monastic

studies ... then we Róngkups have become victims. Then we will never progress, we will remain in the lower tiers of society. (Interviewee 1, Byekbu)

The discussions which followed each interview opened up a vista of life experiences that consisted of direct commentaries on the conditions faced by the indigenous community. These were influential in understanding the layered depths of each narrative recounted.

I was also fortunate to witness a portion of the story enacted as a skit at Lingthem (Dzongu, north Sikkim) monastery, during the harvest festival, called Namsoong/Nambun, when the Kagyed Cham (a monastic mask dance) is usually conducted annually on the 28th or 29th day of the Tibetan calendar, which falls in the month of January or December. The skit, however, was premiering in this particular monastery and was organized by Phuchung and Kaymit,[9] who felt that the version highlighting the alternative narrative thread should also be emphasized. This particular section of the narrative contributes to continuity in the tapestry of possible historical legend when juxtaposed with the first narrative discussed. It exemplifies preliminary differences in cultural practices and beliefs, which develop into misunderstandings between individuals, or for that matter communities. When folkloric structures are considered, one notices a trend of repetition where a narrative plot is concerned. It is also fascinating that Thekung Mensalong lived for many centuries. The Róngkup have attributed his immortal qualities to the fact that he knew the way to Mayal Lyang and consider that he is still alive and residing in the region of Mayal Lyang. After fulfilling his task, he is said to have offered prayers to Kongchenchyu from a seat at Lingthem before proceeding to Mayal Lyang. The people of Lingthem hold prayers in his honour from time to time. Phuchung, who arranged the skit at Lingthem monastery, is an ardent propagator of Róng *lungten sung* or mythologies. He believes that Thekung Mensalong was not happy with how things unfolded after the visit of Lhatsun Chenpo, giving this as one of the reasons why he returned to Mayal Lyang. The moot point is that Thekung Mensalong actually fulfilled his task, which included staying alive for centuries awaiting the fruition of the Guru's prophecy, when in retrospect it was not absolutely mandatory for him to do so; making one weigh the contribution of the narrative towards building the legendary figure vis-à-vis the proselytizing quality of Buddhism. Since this is a lesser-known appendix to the narrative, it leaves room for speculation concerning the integration of heroic indigenous figures into mainstream religious beliefs, in this case Vajrayana Buddhism, and the possible purpose of its incorporation. The cave at Lingee is not visited by Buddhist devotees, unlike other holy sites. Byekbu went on to remark that this happened owing to Thekung Mensalong's noble gesture: 'for wanting nothing more than to show respect to the monk'. It appears this Janus-headed narrative divulges more about the socio-cultural milieu both then and now than meets the eye.

This assumption is fuelled further in another version of the narrative which was also recorded in Lingee. There were suggestions that Thekung Mensalong deliberately did not take Lhatsun Chenpo to the Lingee cave as he wanted to hide it from the monk, hoping that the Róngkups would have a place exclusively for their own worship, but since only a few people from the community had any knowledge of such a place, it soon fell into neglect. This adds a new dimension to the narrative, and the intentional secrecy triggered by the legendary figure Thekung Mensalong can be read as a hint, mainly foregrounding the unease of an individual about the new religion that would soon occupy the collective psyche of his community, leaving the old religion forgotten. If the inclusion of this supplementary narrative is possibly a development over time, it would mean a retrospective projection of insecurities concerning religion with the help of a legendary figure, and this exemplifies the use of legend to bolster an opinion. However, an alternative possibility also remains, that of purposely leaving out this section of the narrative in order to maintain the communal harmony that the state promotes. One factor governing such narratives is the audience, their receptivity level, and the acceptability level of the narrative. I have reasons to believe that my identity as a tribe member also determined the direction of the narrative, gauging the content of the discussions that followed the narration, which clearly voiced the apprehensions of the narrator regarding identity-related issues.

There is now a Hindu temple dedicated to Shiva adjoining the cave. There has always been a tendency to link caves to Shiva.[10] While interviewing Byekbu and other villagers, I was told that the temple was built around the 1950s, and although the permission was given only for temple construction, the landowner (who is a Róngkup) was robbed of a few acres of land and now the temple and its surrounding areas have been registered under the trustees of the temple. A politico-economic trend of land grabbing emerged from the discussion that followed, highlighting one of the major troubles that the Róngkup have faced in their own land. Owing to the various ethnic communities in Sikkim, the intermingling of people from different faiths invariably occurs and this leads to the tendency of establishing ownership over certain worship sites. This in turn encourages narratives justifying such ownership, especially when they tie identity to a particular geographical locale, for doing so establishes a strong sense of belonging, as with any narrative catering to identity formation. From what I could gather from the discussions concerning Leesung, Byekbu repeatedly used the English word 'capture' to indicate that the establishment of the Shiva temple led to encroachment of the cave of significance to the indigenous people and was in a way an imposition of an alien belief system on vernacular religion. The latter was bound to crumble under pressure from a well-established religion like Hinduism.

**Narrative Engaging Harmony**

I come to the final narrative, which contributes to the chronological culmination of the narratives I have discussed: this narrative recounts the visit of Khye-Bumsa, the Tibetan nomad chief, to Thekung-Thek and Nikung-Ngal, who are considered the ancestors of the Róngkups.[11] While this narrative is well known among the general populace, here I am using the version narrated by Phuchung, who drew my attention to sections of the narrative that are generally left out from the popularly reiterated version.

> *The Blood-Treaty*
> A long time ago, Khye-Bumsa, a powerful Tibetan nomad chief, travelled to Mayal Lyang or Sikkim seeking out the blessings of Thekung-Thek and Nikung-Ngal. He was instructed by his tribesman to visit the couple, of whom they had heard. The couple were endowed with supernatural powers, and Khye-Bumsa, who was childless, would benefit from their blessings. Thekung-Thek and Nikung-Ngal, acknowledging the perseverance of Khye-Bumsa who had travelled the difficult terrain to search them out, not only blessed Khye-Bumsa but also agreed to sign a blood treaty at Kaavi-Lyong-Chok at his request, and *Kongchenchyu* was called to bear witness to the oath.

It is believed that the stones erected at Kaavi[12] now stand as silent testimony to the blood treaty, an act meant to instil feelings of brotherhood between the Róngkup and Bhutia communities and still largely cited by individuals from the region to celebrate unity. The festival of *Pang Labsol*[13] marks the worshipping of Kongchenchyu and the signing of the blood treaty, which gained prominence since the rule of Chagdor Namgyal, the third king of the Namgyal Dynasty. This ruler officially institutionalized the occasion by initiating special religious ceremonies to commemorate the blood treaty. According to scholars like Tanka Bahadur Subba (Karlsson and Subba 2006: 147) and Saul Mullard (2011: 140), the agreement is also referred to as *Lhomentsongsum*,[14] and was originally signed between three communities and not two. The third community was the Limbu or Subba community who had a large population in the western parts of Sikkim close to the border with Nepal, but who lost their stronghold after 1641 with the establishment of the Namgyal Dynasty (Karlsson and Subba 2006: 146). The state currently endorses the festival, although recognizing only the Róngkup and Bhutia as the two parties involved in the treaty, from the time of the Namgyal Dynasty. It has now become a narrative that is supposed to endorse a heightened sense of brotherhood, but in the process it has quietly done away with the third community, something that is still the subject of debate within the state.

What really sparked my interest, however, directly concerns the Róngkups, namely the appearance of a rarely mentioned prologue and epilogue to the Thekung-Thek and Nikung-Ngal story:

> When Khye-Bumsa was searching for Thekung-Thek, he came across a man working in the fields and asked him for directions to the house of the renowned couple. The man, on seeing a large retinue accompanying Khye-Bumsa, denied knowledge of any such couple living in the vicinity. Khye-Bumsa was not convinced, but proceeded to depart from the place and a little further off instructed his retinue to remain there while he returned to keep an eye on the man. Khye-Bumsa followed the man to his house and continued to eavesdrop on the conversation the man had with his wife. It turned out that the couple was none other than Thekung-Thek and Nikung-Ngal. Khye-Bumsa came out from his hiding place and approached them; he presented his problem of being issueless and pleaded for their blessing. Thekung-Thek and Nikung-Ngal reluctantly agreed. (Interviewee 2, Phuchung)

> Khye-Bumsa, after returning to his land, was indeed blessed with a male heir.[15] He sought the blessings of the old couple once again, this time accompanied by his wife and son. According to the legend, when Nikung-Ngal lifted the child to play with him, the child kicked the forehead of the old woman [while some say it was Thekung-Thek's forehead that the child kicked], displacing the cloth that is usually worn by the women of the region to cover their head. Nikung-Ngal was immediately worried, and taking Thekung-Thek into her confidence spoke with the foreboding that something terrible was at hand. The couple tried their best to protect the future of their community by making Khye-Bumsa promise that no harm would come to the generations of Róngkup that would follow. Khye-Bumsa gave his word, but the couple knew that it was too late to make amends. (Interviewee 3, Kaymit)

It is common knowledge in Sikkim that the *Chogyals* are descendants of Khye-Bumsa, and that after a few decades of what transpired in the narrative, Lhatsun Chenpo came to Sikkim to consecrate the first *Chogyal* and established the Namgyal Dynasty, which ruled for twelve generations (Mullard 2011: 204). The events are considered the fulfilled prophecies of Guru Padmasambhava about Sikkim, recollected from the story of Thekung Aadik. The blood treaty is considered a major historical event which has had a considerable effect on the fate of the Róngkups, according to the interviewees. In retrospect, the folkloric historical narrative which is circulated without the prologue or epilogue in its entirety, does tend towards avoiding any conflict between communities, and is usually the version which is promoted by the state;[16] this is the version in which two communities came together and signed the treaty without hesitation, while leaving the third (Limbu) completely out of the picture. This to my understanding has resulted in the smooth assimilation of cultures, but it has come at the cost of undermining a narrative which projects the apprehensions of the indigenous community, not readily divulged in the version promoted by the state. The three narratives discussed are exemplary in that respect.

Time and again the Bhutia (once rulers) and the Róngkup (once subjects) have stood together, citing the blood treaty when they saw a common cause.[17] In 1997 a statue portraying the visit of Khye-Bumsa to the Róngkup couple (Thekung-Thek and Nikung-Ngal) was installed in the heart of the capital, Gangtok. The statue was dubbed the Statue of Unity[18] and during the festival of Pang Lhabsol, people from all ethnic communities congregate at the site to celebrate the institutionalization of blood brotherhood. Another 'Statue of Unity' was installed at Kaavi, the site where the blood treaty took place, apparently with the intention of developing it into a tourist spot. There were further construction plans for the site but there was a strong outcry from the local populace against any 'beautification' drives spearheaded by the government. The local populace around the area and the Sikkim Bhutia Lepcha Apex Committee (SIBLAC), a non-governmental organization, formed the Save Kabi Longtsok Committee and argued that such actions would lead to the desanctification of the sacred grove[19] and end up making it another tourist spot encroaching upon nature, ecology and the beliefs tied to the place.

## Conclusion

The three sets of narratives discussed highlight the shifting functional aspects that any narrative can assume, under changing circumstances over a period of time. Folk narratives have been a stronghold of vernacular belief systems for communities the world over. It is no different for the Róngkups, as narratives are more than a receptacle for vernacular beliefs, they are potent mediums of instruction for every passing generation. A narrative legend provides a window into the historical past, and hence its importance cannot be undermined for generations who treat it with a sense of nostalgia. However, one must also bear in mind that narratives serve as tools for indigenous communities to voice insecurities, while state authorities use them as vehicles for imposition of an institutionalized understanding of situations in order to quell ethnic differences. Although such undertakings may appear inconsequential, they have successfully contributed to the silencing of marginalized communities by undermining indigenous knowledge systems. Any narrative version working tangentially to the version propagated by the state or the larger populace is considered a threat to the fragile status quo maintained by the state.

As the state prioritizes harmony, versions of narratives, or for that matter portions of narratives, that harbour conflict are consciously left out in the process of the institutionalization of narratives by the state. If narrated at all it comes after much hesitation. Hence the sets of narratives discussed are clearly narratives of contact that reveal encounters between differing faiths and socio-cultural groups. Furthermore, with the help of these lesser-known epilogues and prologues one can sense the thoughts of the indigene on the matter. From the discussions that followed the interviews with the resource persons, one could gather the prevailing sense of discrimination experienced by the indigenous people of Sikkim through varied lenses of the historical past. If transformation is indeed the governing principle of any narrative, it should be a fruitful exercise to gauge the implications of these epilogues or prologues. One must be wary, however, that these alternative narratives may not necessarily be early survivals, and may have been generated over a period of time.

Sikkim, as mentioned earlier, currently acknowledges three ethnic communities, namely the Róngkup, Bhutia and Nepali; each come with their traditional and cultural frames of reference. Although considered one of the most peaceful states in India, an image which the state authorities try hard to maintain, the narratives endorsed by the state, especially in the case of the blood treaty narrative,[20] not only silences one of the communities (Limbu), but also straitjackets any voices of discontent as displayed by the indigenous people through the epilogues and prologues. The narratives are enmeshed in the cultural-political milieu, divulging social commentaries as deemed fit by the state.

What I tried to demonstrate repeatedly through this chapter is that certain versions of narratives gain prominence over others, while some versions find space only in the repertoire of certain narrators, or in the context of certain audiences. In my case, for example, it would not be far-fetched to assume that the most influential factor in uncovering these narratives has been my own Róngkup identity.[21] As an individual belonging to the indigenous community, I was aware of and also exposed to certain pre-conditions that other scholars might find advantageous or even disadvantageous. It is difficult to overcome the biases and circumstances that one is exposed to in the course of fieldwork; nevertheless, in this case it has proved insightful and beneficial to have my Róngkup identity acknowledged as this gave access to these alternative narratives, scenarios and lifeworlds.

Sometimes the endorsement of narratives by institutions as politically inclined as the state, or for that matter the preoccupations of a proselytizing religion of the region, can regulate the trajectory of folk narratives. The purpose behind such undertaking can be as disparate as instilling an illusion of harmony among a populace of diverse ethnic affiliations, or to affirm the distinctive character of an ethnic community. However, in the midst of these conditions, I have tried to unearth the version that the indigenous people repeatedly engage with, and in doing so, I have hopefully provided a space for these alternative narratives, which have been marginalized through the undue pressures exerted by institutions like the state or religion.

These examples show how vernacular narrative can both subvert and be subverted.

## Fieldwork Details

The interviews were conducted over a span of several years and the indigenous resource persons were from different regions in Sikkim. The sound files of the interviews are slated for submission to an archive. As mentioned in endnote 2, most of my interviewees chose to remain anonymous owing to the possibility of ethnic tension emerging from their narratives. In the order of occurrence, some of the details of the interviews are as follows:

Interviewee 1 Byeku: the interviews spanned several days and the particular interaction cited in the text occurred at Lingee, on March 1, 2015. Sound file no. 150301_008WAV.

Interviewee 2 Phuchung: the resource person in question is a folk music practitioner steeped in knowledge of indigenous folk narratives, rites and rituals. This person was interviewed on several occasions spanning my research years. This particular interview took place at Thingvong on December 20, 2015, where the resource person was engaged in a discussion with me. Sound file no. 150120_002WAV.

Interviewee 3 Kaymit: during this interview my primary resource person accompanied me and the input was provided by interviewee 3 while they were engaged in collectively recounting the narrative in question. Lingthem, January 20, 2015. Sound file no. 150122_010WAV.

## Notes

1. The concept of *nesol* is also described by scholars like Anna Balikci (2008: 89) in her book *Lamas, Shamans and Ancestors* as a ritual celebrating Sikkim as the hidden land, or *beyul*, where offerings are made to the Kongchenchyu deity along with all the deities of the region.
2. I have changed the names of my interviewees in order to protect their identities, as some information recorded deals with the sensitive issues of the region.
3. While interviewing a *mun* from Mirik, I was informed of the various procedures for guiding a soul to Mayal Lyang. It is also widely believed that *muns* are of a higher order than the *bongthings*, they are gifted shamans and one of their duties is to guide the souls of the Róngkup to Mayal Lyang after death. *Bongthings* are basically trained shamans who carry out various rituals and rites in the indigenous community. Every clan has their own *bongthing* and it is said that even their rebirth takes place within the lineage of the family clan.
4. The grass is specifically named *mungshyel* in *róngaring* and is used by *bongthings* and *muns* when conducting special prayers or rituals to ward off evil spirits. Byekbu from south Sikkim and Achong from north Sikkim both named the grass on different occasions and stressed its usage during rituals in their interviews.
5. In some versions the girl is shown offering food or even *chi*. It is intriguing that the name Numchermit does not crop up anywhere else in the various Róngkup narratives, although there are occurrences of a few strong female characters.
6. A version of the narrative is in the article by Jenny Bentley (2009-2010: 139-140).

160    *Vernacular Knowledge*

7   A *gurudwara* is a Sikh place of worship. The *gurudwara* in question has sparked religious controversies between Buddhist stakeholders on the one hand and Sikhs on the other, owing to claims based on the identity of the said 'Guru' in question (see Banerjee 2018; Eyben 2018).
8   Byekbu went on to describe the various sites blessed by Lhatsun Chenpo and also the *pomphet* or competitions that the two legendary figures engaged in, but since that would lead to digression from the discussion at hand, I have not incorporated it in the text.
9   Phuchung is a resident of Passingdang, the northern district of Sikkim, and Kaymit of Lingthem. The short skit was performed on January 9, 2015 alongside the monastic mask dance. It chronicled the meeting of Thekung Mensalong with Guru Padmasambhava, and Lhatsun Chenpo. It also dealt with the visit paid by Khye-Bumsa to the patriarch Thekung-Thek, eventually leading to the consecration of the first *Chogyal* by Lhatsun Chenpo.
10  In Hindu mythology Shiva is an ascetic who would meditate in caves.
11  Whereas Nuzong-Nyu and Fudong-Thing are considered the first humans and hence ancestors to the Róngkup, even though Thekung-Thek and Nikung-Ngal come after them chronologically they are still called upon as ancestors of the Róngkup regardless of the clan affiliations. They were reputedly well known for their supernatural powers, a notion exemplified by the narrative.
12  There are monoliths erected at the spot, which is moss-ridden and supposed to symbolize Kongchenchyu, who was called to bear witness to the blood treaty. Róngkups who had gathered there on the occasion of Pang Labsol believed it was erected by Thekung-Thek himself and have been worshipping at the spot since time immemorial. The nomenclature is a shortened form of the phrase *kaayu-savi*, which translates as 'our blood', referring to the blood brotherhood. The place is alternatively spelt Kabi. As *bi* in *róngaring* means 'vegetable' and Kabi is a word that has been misspelt overtime, I will stick to Kaavi.
13  See Government of Sikkim 2009.
14  *Lhomentsongsum*, or as Mullard (2011: 140) breaks it down, the 'Lho Mon Gtsong gsum agreement' (where 'Lho' or 'Lhopo' is an alternative term for the Bhutia; 'Men' or 'Mon' is used for the Róngkup; 'Tsong/Gtsong' or 'Chong' is the term used for the Limbu; and '*sum/gsum*' is the numeral three and signifies the three communities who came together for the treaty).
15  Some versions also state that the blessings from the couple resulted in not one, but three male heirs, which I understand as a way of emphasizing the supernatural powers of the couple (Tamsang 2008: 22).
16  The official website of the ministry of Cultural Affairs and Heritage Department, Government of Sikkim, cites the festival as one of the most important festivals of Sikkim (see Government of Sikkim 2009).
17  The Sikkim Bhutia Lepcha Apex Committee has worked together to fight against hydropower projects, which threatened to run the sacred rivers of the region dry (SIBLAC 2008a).
18  A dome was slated to be constructed over the 'Statue of Unity' and was partially funded by the state government of Sikkim, thereby establishing the endorsement of the narrative by the governing institution (*Sikkim Now* 2014).
19  An appeal was sent out to the people, and uploaded to the website, that emphasizes that the sanctity of the place should be maintained. The appeal uses the

phrase 'sacred grove' as leverage to discuss the issue, well aware of its implications (see SKLC 2013).
20 The version provided by SIBLAC in 'History of Sikkim' (SIBLAC 2008b) is widely accepted in the state, although it clearly focuses on a Buddhist proselytization narrative which overshadows the narratives of the Róngkups.
21 I have leaned heavily on Leanne Betasamosake Simpson's *Dancing on Our Turtle's Back* (2014) to help understand and practically apply the position of an insider and gain further insight into the indigenous beliefs. I have adopted the empathetic approach encouraged by Simpson, herself an indigenous scholar, who clearly increases awareness of such approaches through her work.

## References

Acharya, Chewang. 1995. 'Guru Padamasambhava's Contribution: The Genesis of Buddhism in Sikkim'. *Bulletin of Tibetology* 31 (1): 19–24.
Balikci, Anna. 2008. *Lamas, Shamans and Ancestors: Village Religion in Sikkim*. Leiden: Brill. https://doi.org/10.1163/ej.9789004167063.i-406
Banerjee, Rabi. 2018. 'Nanak Lama Ignored'. *The Week*, April 22, 2018. https://www.theweek.in/theweek/cover/2018/04/14/gurudongmar-gurdwara-in-sikkim-converted-into-a-buddhist-shrine.html (accessed July 5, 2021).
Bentley, Jenny. 2009–2010. 'Narrations of Contest: Competition among Representatives of Local Lepcha Belief and Guru Rimpoche in Sikkim'. *Bulletin of Tibetology* 45 (2) & 46 (1): 135–159.
Eyben, Vivian. 2018. 'Religious Tensions Escalate in North Sikkim over the Demolition of the Gurdwara'. *News Click*, January 9, 2018. https://www.newsclick.in/religious-tensions-escalate-north-sikkim-over-demolition-gurdwara (accessed July 5, 2021).
Foning, Arthur Rapgay. 1987. *Lepcha, My Vanishing Tribe*. New Delhi: Sterling.
Gorer, Geoffrey. 1987. *The Lepchas of Sikkim*. New Delhi: Gian Publishing House.
Government of Sikkim. 2009. 'Pang Lhabsol'. *Tourism and Civil Aviation Department, Government of Sikkim*. https://www.sikkimtourism.gov.in/Public/ExperienceSikkim/FairsAndFestivalDetails/FF20A071?type=Festival (accessed July 2, 2020).
Jha, Pranab Kumar. 1985. *History of Sikkim (1817–1904): Analysis of British Policy and Activities*. Calcutta: S.N. Printing Works.
Karlsson, Bengt G., and Tanka Bahadur Subba, eds. 2006. *Indigeneity in India*. London: Kegan Paul.
Mainwaring, George Byres. 1876. *Grammar of the Róng (Lepcha) Language: As It Exists in the Dorjeling and Sikim Hills*. Calcutta: Baptist Mission Press.
Mullard, Saul. 2011. *Opening the Hidden Land: State Formation and Construction of Sikkimese History*. Leiden: Brill. https://doi.org/10.1163/9789004208964
Planning Commission [Government of India]. 2008. *Sikkim Development Report*. New Delhi: Academic Foundation.
Risley, Herbert Hope. 1894. *The Gazetteer of Sikhim*. Calcutta: Bengal Secretariat Press.
Scheid, Claire S. 2014. 'Hidden Land and Changing Landscape: Narratives about Mount Khangchendzonga among the Lepcha and the Lhopo'. *Journal of the Irish Society for the Academic Study of Religions* 1 (1): 66–89.

SIBLAC. 2008a. 'Welcome to SIBLAC'. *Sikkim Bhutia Lepcha Apex Committee*. http://www.siblac.org/index.html (accessed June 15, 2016).

SIBLAC. 2008b. 'History of Sikkim'. *Sikkim Bhutia Lepcha Apex Committee*. http://www.siblac.org/history.html (accessed June 15, 2016).

*Sikkim Now*. 2014. 'Dome to Be Constructed over Statue of Unity'. *Sikkim Now*, July 25, 2014. http://sikkimnow.blogspot.nl/2014/07/dome-to-be-constructed-over-statue-of.html (accessed June 27, 2016).

Simpson, Leanne Betasamosake. 2014. *Dancing on Our Turtle's Back: Stories of Nishnaabeg Re-Creation, Resurgence and a New Emergence*. Kolkata: Adivaani.

Singha, Karatāra. 1984. *Biography of Guru Nanak*. New Delhi: Hemkunt Press.

SKLC. 2013. 'An Appeal for Saving Kabi-Longtsok'. Kabi: Save Kabi Longtsok Committee. http://www.siblac.org/doc/Appeal_Kabi_Longtsok.pdf (accessed June 8, 2021).

Tamsang, Lyangsong. 2008. *Lepcha Folklore and Folk Songs*. New Delhi: Sahitya Akademi.

UNESCO. 2016. 'Khangchendzonga National Park'. *United Nations Educational, Scientific and Cultural Organisation*. http://whc.unesco.org/en/list/1513/ (accessed July 18, 2016).

# Part 3

# Renegotiating Tradition and Authority

Chapter 7

# When a Cosmic Shift Fails: The Power of Vernacular Authority in a New Age Internet Forum

*Robert Glenn Howard**

## Introduction: Prophecy without End

The *2012Forum* forum (see Figure 7.1) was part of a large and diffuse popular discourse about an impending 'shift' or global transformation of consciousness. On YouTube channels, personal blogs, internet forums, and every other sort of internet network location, people are sharing their New Age spiritual beliefs in ongoing online discussions. In these discussions, individuals have forwarded the idea that global energies connect our personal dispositions to the material world; they have offered prophecies based on specific interpretations of the ancient Mayan calendar; they have shared tips and techniques for surviving a coming interstellar collision with a dark planetary mass called Nibiru—and these are just some of the spiritual discussions that form a diffuse and wildly variant discourse. Despite its variety, this tradition functions as a vernacular religious tradition—a tradition that primarily exists at online network locations where like-minded people gather to participate.

---

\* **Robert Glenn Howard** is Director of Digital Studies, Director of DesignLab, and Professor in the Department of Communication Arts at the University of Wisconsin-Madison. Most broadly, his research seeks to uncover the possibilities and limits of empowerment through everyday expression on the internet by focusing on the intersection of individual human agency and participatory performance. His publications include *Digital Jesus: The Making of New Christian Fundamentalist Community on the Internet* (New York University Press, 2011) and *Network Apocalypse: Visions of the End in an Age of Internet Media* (Sheffield Phoenix Press, 2011).

At these network locations, individuals engage in what appears to be deliberation, and this deliberation is so valuable to these users that they seem willing to keep it going even when the most basic question it seems to be seeking to answer is unequivocally answered. On January 31, 2013, Rob, the founder of the internet forum called *2012Forum*, informed his users that he was shutting down the site because the belief that he had founded the site for people to discuss had proven unquestionably wrong: that a 'cosmic shift' would occur on December 21, 2012 as predicted by the ancient Mayans. When that date passed without event, Rob posted: 'Lots of bad things happening around the world, but that's just business as usual' (Rob 2013).

While Rob might have been ready to accept the failure of the prophecy, some *2012Forum* users were not. One user responded by suggesting that maybe the shift had happened but it just wasn't that obvious yet: 'I think 2012 started off things-but it may take several years before it all comes to fruition'. Another user agreed, castigating Rob for being so quick to assume that the end of time had not already occurred:

> The irony of this site and it closing down wouldn't happen if it were renamed 2013 Forum, or rather, should have been that in the first place. For %$#@'s sake, it's ALL happening THIS year, is as clear as a bell. However, if matters worsen, we all here shall be in the dark, i.e. no Web, no electricity and no people. Perhaps Rob knows, deep down, that the game is up.[1] (Rob 2013)

Then another user offered a different, though not contradictory theory: 'AND, it could be, we were just a year or two off on the catacylisms? But the begining time was Dec 21?' But another disagrees: 'Imo the aware Mayans had exlent maths and harmonic convergence then venus transit plus last 21 st dec were perfectly numbered by them'. Rob finally shut down the entire forum (Rob 2013), but only after 14 more posts deliberating the date (by then past) as bringing the end of time.

Why are these forum users so intent on maintaining the idea that a past date may have been the end of time? In this chapter, I will use this specific case to throw into sharp relief how digital network communication is positioning everyday people as the primary sources of expertise. As this occurs, we find that digital networks can amplify the authority that everyday communication holds through a technologically enabled form of what I term 'aggregate volition'. Aggregate volition is emergent from shared communication. This has perhaps always been true, but in the online environment individuals can choose to go to specific network locations where their specific ideas are already shared and re-enact the communal sharing of those ideas. This ability to find like-minded others magnifies the perception of aggregate volition even when the ideas being shared at one of these locations are very obscure, such as the case of the imagined 2012 Mayan prophecy about a cosmic shift.

Figure 7.1. *2012Forum*, 2013

## Prepping after the Harmonic Convergence

A common folk belief in this community was that December 21, 2012, the winter solstice, was a date the ancient Mayans predicted would mark a massive shift in consciousness. The interest in the winter solstice in 2012 is thought to originate in another New Age event, the Harmonic Convergence that occurred on August 16–17, 1987. On these dates, eight planets were aligned in an unusual configuration called a 'grand trine'. That configuration was thought by many to mark a very rare moment in the Mayan calendric system. This moment marked the beginning of the 26-year final period in the 5,200-year Great Cycle of the calendar, at the end of which the Mayan God of peace Quetzalcoatl would return (Ivakhiv 2005).

Leading New Age thinkers at that time such as actress and author Shirley MacLaine and philosopher and theologian José Argüelles suggested that this planetary configuration would correspond with what came to be termed a cosmic 'shift' of global consciousness. This shift would usher in a new age of peace. An example of what Daniel Wojcik (2011) has termed an 'avertive apocalypse', Argüelles stated that if at least 144,000 people assembled, meditated, prayed, chanted and visualized at places thought to be spiritual power centres such as Mount Shasta, the Great Pyramids, Glastonbury and New York City's Central Park then a 'negative cycle' would be averted. If the cycle were averted, a new global consciousness in which human beings would live in peace with each other would be set to begin 26 years later: at the supposed end of the Mayan 5,200-year 'long count' cycle on December 21, 2012 (Argüelles 1987: 170; Wojcik 2011). For most, the meditation event occurred, nothing obvious changed, and so they moved on. However, for some at least as early as 1996, the internet became a means to locate each other and discuss the Mayan calendar as predicting a global 'rise to another level of consciousness' (Howard 1998: 69).

Probably the most influential New Age thinker about this cosmic shift in consciousness, Argüelles held a PhD in Art History from the University of Chicago and was the author of ten books. As early as 1975, he began to suggest that the 2012 date would be significant (Argüelles 1975). In 1987, the year of the convergence, he published *The Mayan Factor: Path Beyond Technology* in which he articulates a complicated numerological system that combines an interpretation of the Mayan calendar with other esoteric and contemporary scientific ideas to make the argument that 1987 would be 26 years before the 'major galactic synchronization' in which humans had the chance to shift themselves into the greater galactic intelligence with which the Mayans had been connected. As the convergence approached, he claimed that, if enough humans brought their spiritual power to bear, it would begin a final 25-year countdown to the end of the Mayan Long Count calendar in 2012. The winter solstice of 2012 could mark the end of history and usher in a new cycle in which war, materialism, violence, abuses, injustice and oppression would end. His admonishment in the *Mayan Factor*—'Either we shift gears right now or we miss our opportunity' (Argüelles 1987: 21)—was powerful enough to be featured on the front page of the *Wall Street Journal* (Sullivan 1987).

After the Harmonic Convergence was deemed a success and the galactic shift was set to arrive in 2012, vernacular religious beliefs about Mayan prophecy proliferated. The material basis for these beliefs was focused on an inscription on a monument found at the Mayan site in Tortuguero in southern Mexico. The monument contains a series of inscriptions dating from the seventh century AD that chronicle the achievements of the local leader. One inscription, known as Tortuguero Monument 6, is the only inscription known to refer to the end of thirteenth *b'ak'tun* as a significant date. The inscription has been defaced, but archaeologists have translated it as: 'It will be completed the 13th *b'ak'tun*. It is 4 *Ajaw* 3 *K'ank'in* and it will happen a "seeing" [partially defaced]. It is the display of *B'olon-Yokte'* in a great "investiture"'. The *baktun* and *ajaw* refer to the Mayan Long Count calendar, which was used to track historical dates. Bolon-Yokte is a deity that was, it is thought, periodically brought out and 'invested' or ritually dressed. Based on work in the early twentieth century, Mayan archaeologists synchronized the Long Count calendar to the Gregorian calendar yielding the end of the longest of the Mayan long counts at December 21, 2012 (Gronemeyer and MacLeod 2010). Reading the archaeological discussion of this text, the translated term 'seeing' in the inscription seems to have caught Argüelles's interest and served to spark a whole vernacular religious movement after 1987.

By December 2012, this movement had grown and was involved in a wide range of beliefs from the need to 'hide guns and weapons' in anticipation of a 2012 disaster (Murphy 2009) to the need to find a 'safe area in case of pole shift' of the earth (HeavenSent 2012) to the belief that the 'point of hugging is to connect positive energy fields' (randomdude 2009) or the idea that:

> If you multiply 1111 by 1111 you get 1234321, representing a pyramid, and number 11 is a sacred number of the pyramid with the proportions of the great pyramid being of the ratio 7:11. Eleven is also a number harmonious with Pi. Therefore, it seems that number eleven is of central importance in understanding the mathematical infrastructure of the universe. (binskiboys 2007)

## Vernacular Authority and Aggregate Volition

To begin to understand the powerful appeal of these kinds of online discussion, we must understand that they are both a product of and the producer of vernacular authority and this authority emerges from the aggregation of volition. This aggregation occurs through the repeated expression of shared beliefs by different members in a community. In this case, those beliefs are about an impending cosmic shift predicted by the ancient Mayans for December 21, 2012.

Vernacular authority is a sort of authority similar to what Erika Brady (2001: 7) has termed 'relational authority', Sabina Magliocco (2012) has called 'participatory consciousness', or what I have documented extensively among online fundamentalist Christians as 'aggregate authority' (Howard 2011: 20–21). Alternate to institutional authority, vernacular authority emerges when an individual makes appeals that rely on trust specifically because they are *not* institutional, in the sense that they do not rely on any authority arising from formally instituted social formations like a church, newspaper company or academic journal. Based in its classical definitions, 'vernacular' can best be defined dialectically as that which is opposed to its alternate term 'institutional' (ibid.: 7–10). An appeal to vernacular authority is an appeal to trust in either tradition or individual knowledge (Howard 2013: 76). Tradition is what is imagined as handed down outside of any formally instituted social formation. Individual knowledge could come from, for example, an individual's personal revelation from God or individual discovery of a pattern in the Mayan calendar system.

While people must have had a sense of vernacular authority since the first institutions emerged, global communication technologies have changed the dynamics between institutional and vernacular authority because they magnify the aggregation of volition. At the dawn of the age of print, the control of the capability to manufacture inexpensive books destabilized the manuscript-based authority of the priest class in Europe and, ultimately, contributed to the Protestant Reformation (Eisenstein 1980: 336ff). However, the rise of both public and private institutions that could provide the means to distribute physically large numbers of books across vast geographic spaces engendered a publishing industry that created a unidirectional means to assert institutional authority. When broadcast media arose to displace publishing, there still seemed to be a bright and easily discerned distinction between individual or traditional expressions and the institutional mechanisms that made the movie *Star Wars* or the news program *60 Minutes* (Howard 2015).

However, internet media (particularly 'participatory media' like Facebook, Twitter, or any WordPress blog) blurs the more physical distinctions between mass media and traditional or individual communication that characterized earlier eras (Howard 2008b: 490–491). When the *New York Times* allows its readers to comment on their institutional articles in a text-box just below the published piece, the vernacular and the institutional stand side by side in the same medium. Both are marked, of course: one as an institutional product and one as the vernacular commentary. Unlike a book or television broadcast (that has not been placed online anyway), however, there is the opportunity for vernacular voices to informally comment in a way that accesses the same audience as the institutional communication. This is a significant shift because traditional or individual voices now have access to the same size and scope of audience on which broadcast and publishing institutions used to have a monopoly.

While mass media locates the decision-making involved in the creation of global communication in the hands of institutionally empowered actors like writers, producers and editors, participatory media offers everyday individuals more choice both in the media they consume and in the globally accessible communication they enact. The increased freedom of choice, combined with more opportunities to consume vernacular expression more quickly, increases vernacular authority because individuals can choose to consume ideas based on their already accepted values. When they do this, perceived continuities and consistencies in the communication of others give rise to aggregate volition.

Aggregate volition occurs when individuals perceive themselves to be acting together. By locating a particular internet location and sharing beliefs with others who seem to share those beliefs, individuals aggregate their volition by enacting continuities and consistencies in their expression. As a result, perceived vernacular authority is increased because the individuals are consuming media premised on their already-held values thus aggregating more action into the same volitional expression of beliefs. When individuals frequent specific online locations that are linked by a shared value or interest, they enact what I have previously termed 'vernacular webs' (Howard 2008a; 2008b). Though webs of informal communication have always existed, the ability for individuals to access and enact very specific webs with more people than they could hope to find face-to-face is the mechanism through which network communication technologies are increasing the aggregating effect of communication and thus increasing the perception of vernacular authority.

As optimistic media researchers like Yochai Benkler (2008) and Henry Jenkins (2006) have demonstrated, this increased choice in volitional aggregation can be very empowering because individuals can seek out, compare and assess large amounts of information before they make decisions. Similarly, it can create new opportunities for transformation as individuals access and are influenced by ideas with which they might not have otherwise come into contact (Howard 1997). On the other hand, there are less optimistic researchers, such as Administrator of the White House Office of Information and Regulatory Affairs, Cass Sunstein (2007: 138), who has demonstrated how this aggregation can be disempowering if individuals allow it to reify into communication enclaves that 'filter' out ideas which might give them access to useful information or challenge them to think in new ways (Howard 2011).

## Ritual Deliberation as Epideictic

In previous research, I found online fundamentalist Christian communities did 'filter' out alternate ideas much as Sunstein described. In that community, individuals debated the relative merits of particular biblical interpretations even while they accepted that no human could know the divine will (Howard 2011: 58–59). Users were banned, ignored or otherwise excluded if they attempted to express ideas that challenged the basic idea that it was worthwhile to deliberate about these different unresolvable possible interpretations. As a result, this 'ritual deliberation' functioned as what communication theory terms 'epideictic' discourse. Epideictic discourse was first defined by Aristotle as the form of oratory that attributed 'praise or blame' to individuals or things based on shared values most often made at ceremonial events (Aristotle 1991: 48). Twentieth-century communication scholars associated this non-controversial kind of discourse not with persuasion or deliberation, but with educational communication 'promoting values shared by the community' (Perelman and Olbrechts-Tyteca 1991 [1969]: 52).

Deliberation is the process of weighing options prior to a decision. Deliberative discourse, as opposed to epideictic discourse, seeks to persuade an audience to take or not take a particular action based on the weight of different options. Deliberative discourse is the public performance of this process of deliberation, and it seeks to come to a decision about something not already agreed upon. Unlike epideictic discourse, it very much seeks to persuade and thus is associated with controversy, reason giving and compromise. 'Ritual' deliberation among fundamentalist Christians online, however, is the process of weighing options without seeking to make a decision or persuade others to action because fundamental to this group's belief system is the idea that humans cannot know God's will (Howard 2011: 58–66). In this sense, the sharing of different interpretations of the Bible served to enact the shared belief in both the inerrancy of the Bible but also in the unknowability of the divine plan it describes in its prophetic passages. In this sense, ritual deliberation appears to be seeking a decision about the correct interpretation of prophecy but its observable function is to enact the shared values associated with epideictic discourse. Thus, ritual deliberation can be thought of as a form of epideictic discourse.

To call this sort of communication behaviour epideictic, however, is a contradiction in terms because epideictic describes a process of deliberation that seeks to express shared values instead of trying to come to some decision. Unlike other deliberative processes, there is no natural end to these epideictic discursive behaviours. In ritual deliberation, the point is not decision making but instead the shared action itself: the ritual performance of the shared beliefs held by the online community. This deliberation is meant to aggregate the volition of the believers. It is a vernacular practice that aggregates volition through repeated performances of shared beliefs or values.

For fundamentalist Christians awaiting an imminent return of Christ, the lack of any clear ending or end date is not a problem. They can (and do) continue to ritually deliberate about Christ's return because no human can rightly know God's divine plan and thus no human can set the date of His return. The users of the *2012Forum*, however, present a very different case. Their epideictic deliberation was about if a cosmic shift would occur in December 2012. It *did* have a specific end date: December 21, 2012. On that day, something that would constitute a cosmic shift would or would not happen. As it turns out, nothing happened. Even though confronted with a direct challenge to the forum's very reason for being, some users could not understand or accept that observable fact that their many predictions for dramatic and undeniable events on the 2012 winter solstice simply did not occur. As the creator and moderator of the *2012Forum* stated that the shift had not occurred and announced the forum's imminent closure, some users became angry. For them, the forum was not about what would or would not happen on December 21, 2012—it was not about regular deliberation. It was about enacting the shared values of an online community that focused on a hopeful spiritual vision of the future. It was about epideictic deliberation.

## Methods: Graphing Vernacular Authority

The *2012Forum* was open from early 2006 to July 1, 2013. During that time, it had approximately 11,000 users who posted 491,283 posts in 27,443 threads. Spending one minute on each of those posts, it would take a researcher 341 days reading continuously 24 hours per day without any breaks to read all the posts in this forum. Since that is not practical, I used a computational method to create what Timothy Tangherlini (2013) has famously termed a 'folklore macroscope'. Using computers to download and process all the nearly half a million forum posts, I can create visual representations of who was speaking to whom about what on the forum. Doing so reveals interesting or key actors in the network. Then I can access the posts made by those key actors to see what they were doing on the forum.

To do this, I created a series of PERL computer language scripts with software coders. The first sets of scripts used the HTML tags on the website site pages in the forum to download specific information and load that information into an SQL database. Once loaded into the database, that data can be queried. Using several different sorts of queries, different datasets can be generated. The most useful for this chapter is the User by Co-Thread matrix. This is a network data table that takes the form of comma-delimited rows of user pairs followed by a number representing the number of times they posted in the same thread on the forum. Loading that dataset into network visualization software, we can see a graph in which each dot or node is attached to other nodes via coloured lines or links (see Figure 7.2). The nodes represent each user and the links between them represent the number of times they appeared in the same thread. The more threads they both appear in, the thicker and redder the line becomes. Looking at all 11,000 users was really not possible, so I reduced them to those with the highest co-occurrences.

In addition to seeing which users are appearing in the same threads, various calculations of mathematical 'centrality' can be made. There is a wide range of ways of calculating the centrality of a node in a network. In this work, I have focused on two most common and basic ways of imagining centrality: 'total degree centrality' and 'betweenness centrality'. When graphing the nodes, the nodes get bigger the greater their total degree centrality. Total degree centrality is the overall number of links a node has to other nodes. In addition to graphing the nodes with an increased size to represent more links, the nodes appear redder the higher their betweenness centrality score. The betweenness centrality

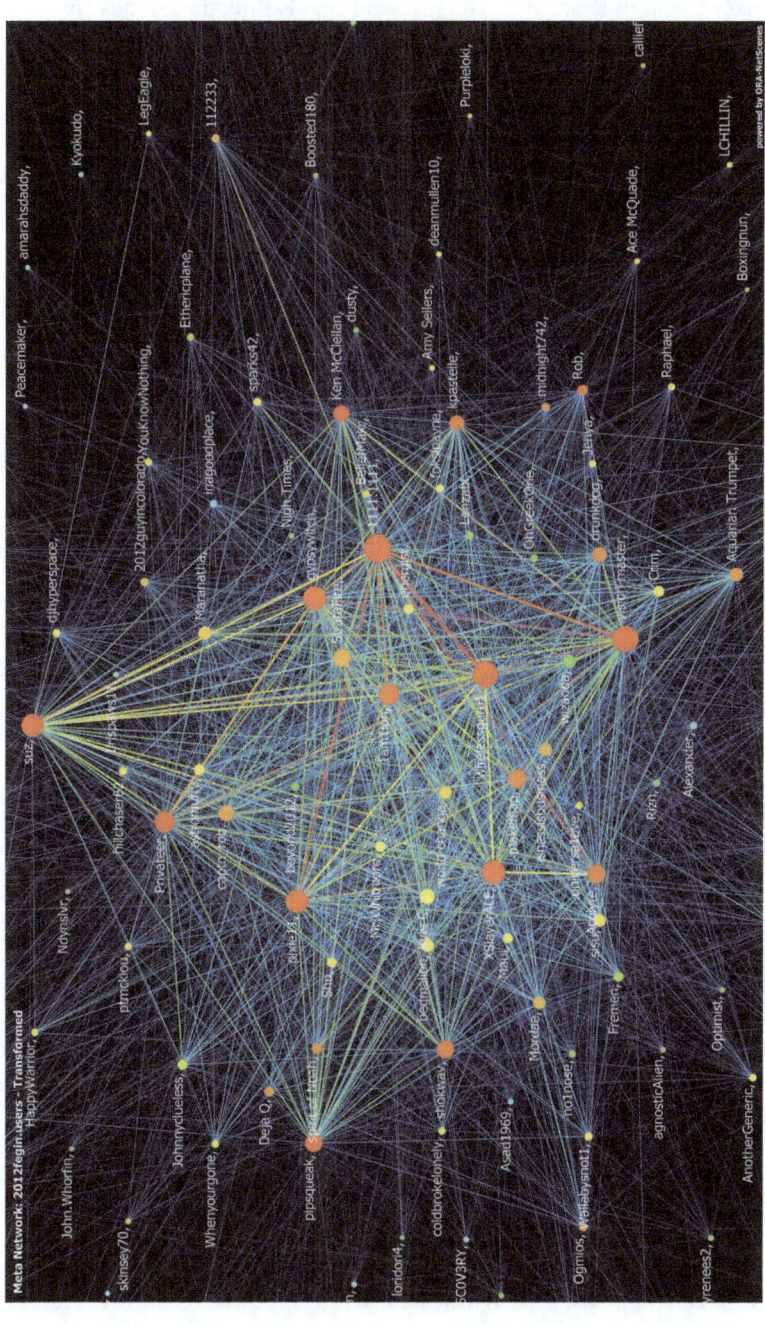

**Figure 7.2.** Network graph: *2012Forum*, 2014

score of a node is the number of shortest paths from all nodes to all others that pass through that node; the more a node is linked to nodes that are linked to a lot of other nodes, the more 'between' they are. In essence, the measurement is the same as the total degree centrality score except it is weighted so that a node gets a higher score if it is connected to other nodes that are also connected to a lot of other nodes. Looking at a graph of this network, people who post a lot get bigger nodes because they are in more threads. People who post a lot to threads with other people who post a lot to threads with a lot of other people get redder nodes. People with redder instead of bluer lines between them post in more of the same threads and are thus more linked.

Looking at this network graph, the researcher can easily identify individuals inhabiting influential or otherwise interesting positions in the discourse on the forum. People of interest, for example, are those who appear to be very small and very red on the graph. That would suggest that they do not post to a lot of different threads, but when they do post to threads those threads contain the most connected individuals in the network. Rob, the founder and main moderator of the forum, appears very small and very red on the graph because while he was not a heavy user of the forum, when he posted to a thread many other users posted in to that same thread. He was very well known, as the forum creator, and an influential author on 2012 beliefs. As a result, he didn't post much, but when he did many people participated in that thread. While the graph pointed to his unique position in the community, the researcher still has to look at the actual content of the posts Rob was making and place that in the context of his larger role of the community in order to understand what that unique position really was.

## Deliberating before the Shift

The most obvious content to look at in this forum is the content from users who appear big and red on the graph. That is to say, the researcher should look at the individual users with a high total degree centrality and a high betweenness centrality. Not surprisingly, there are many big and red users who also have heavy red lines between them because those users who are central on the network have become so precisely because they interact a lot with others who are central on the network. Based on these calculations, Suz, WirelessGuru1, Vision-Master and 1111:1111 were among some of the most prominent leaders on this forum because they have a lot of connections between them, which results in high centrality scores. There is a clear second-tier of highly active and highly connected individuals who show up in the graph with higher than average centrality scores.

Users like Privateer tended to swing into a thread, make a couple of snarky comments, and then move on. This user added a sceptical voice to the discourse (which was itself not that common on the forum), but despite higher than average centrality, it is unclear if this user really contributed or if the user simply tended to comment on threads that were large and thus had many of the most central users in them. Acolyte is another relatively central figure who seems to have been well liked for long and comprehensive posts engaging complex issues like how the great pyramids in Egypt could have been built. XSlayerALE was a well-known user who tended to be quite focused on prepping supplies for an impending 2012 global natural disaster. Pixie11 was another fairly central leader who was also more focused on prepping. Formerly a member of the military, Pixie11 tended to be particularly interested in weapons, and is perhaps the best-connected prepper in the forum. Pixie11 gets a lot of that centrality in the graph because this individual was very closely linked to 1111:1111, who is one of the top four forum leaders. Pixie11 is interesting in this sense as a sort of representative that linked the less central group on the forum primarily interested in prepping to the core forum leaders—a kind of minority leader for the preppers. Gypsywitch was a sort of opposite to Pixie11: a popular pagan hippie type not interested in weapons at all. Quite outside of the prepper and weapons discourse was Pipsqueak, a well-loved and almost always upbeat poster. Though having a high betweenness centrality score, Pipsqueak did not post that much and seldom expressed any strong opinion.

While each of these figures increased the overall diversity of this inherently wildly diverse community of belief in fascinating ways (as did many, many others), focusing on the most central forum users gives us a way to gain a sense of how the vernacular leadership in this community operated and what communication practices led to these individuals taking on the informal leadership positions they fulfilled in this network. Based on the top 10 users with the highest total degree centrality and the highest betweenness centrality, the next section will analyse the posts from four very different top forum leaders in this community: Suz, WirelessGuru1, Vision-Master and 1111:1111.

178  Vernacular Knowledge

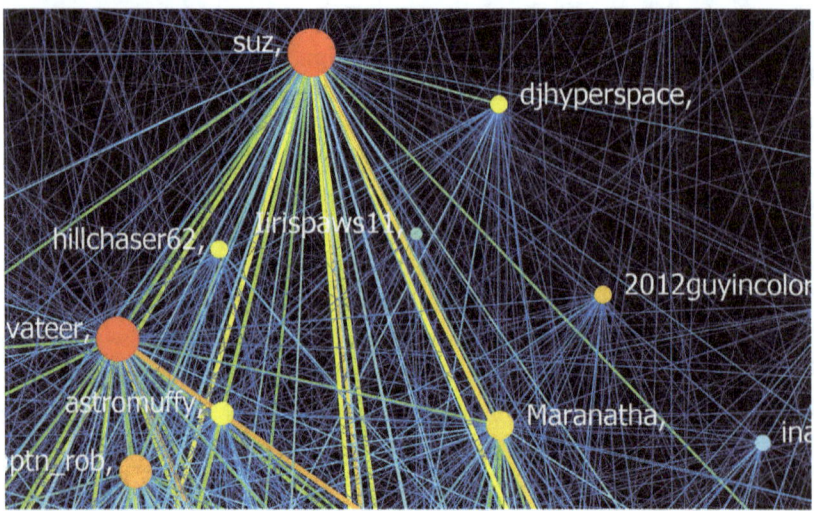

**Figure 7.3.** Network graph: *2012Forum*, 2014: Suz detail

In a way, Suz generated the least vernacular authority despite holding one of the most central positions of any user on the forum. Suz is an older British woman who was one of the most loved individuals on the forum, if not the best loved. Mathematically, she has the highest betweenness score but a relatively low total degree centrality score for such a prominent forum leader. While she was well known because she posted in large threads with other very prominent users, she falls in the lower portion of the top ten users in terms of total degree centrality: for a top ten forum leader, not that many people saw her posts but her betweenness was still very high. This makes her interesting and unique because she posted mostly in threads that a lot of heavy users posted to, but she (among the top forum leaders anyway) did not really post all that much.

Part of her unique network position is a result of her role as an official forum moderator. As the most active official moderator, she tended to ask people to be polite and otherwise moderate in the more lively threads, and those threads typically also contained many of the most central users. As a moderator, she seldom made assertive claims about the actual ideas being expressed. On the rare occasions I found where she posted outside of her moderator role and actually participated in the deliberation, she typically added cues like 'just my opinion' to indicate she was not interested in engaging in strongly assertive deliberative exchanges. The topics she did engage more fully tended to be non-confrontational and not part of the 2012 belief tradition such as when she started a thread on nice places to visit on her vacation to Peru (Suz 2009) or her generous offering of advice to other forum members travelling to the United States (MagicalBlack 2012). In one case, she responded to a post with a link to a YouTube video of a popular song, writing: 'Music is a great way to express yourself', while others rapidly delved into a heated debate about the meaning of the song relative to the 2012 belief system (WhiteWolf 2008).

Based on her content, Suz seemed to generate the least vernacular authority of the most central forum users because, despite commenting and even using the forum technologies to moderate the discussion, she seldom engaged in active deliberation about the 2012 beliefs, and when she did, she did so without asserting authority. In short, she did not engage in deliberation about the nature of the coming 2012 cosmic shift and so she really didn't afford herself the opportunity to be authoritative about any of the ideas others were exchanging. As moderator, she had a sort of institutional authority to shut down a thread and probably ban and unban users, but she did not seem to assert vernacular authority at all.

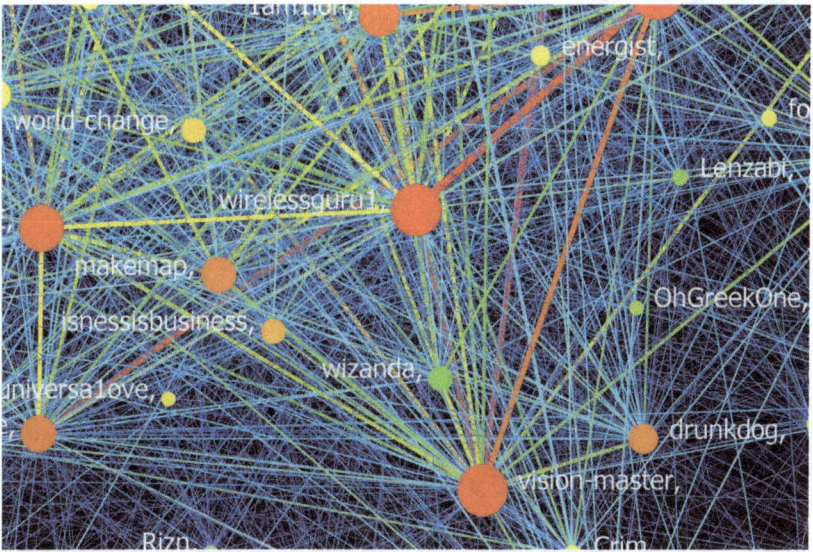

**Figure 7.4.** Network graph: *2012Forum*, 2014: WirelessGuru1 detail

WirelessGuru1 is, in a sense, the opposite of Suz—at least in terms of being well loved. Looking at the threads in which WirelessGuru1 posts, it seems he was tolerated, but disliked because of his failure to 'explain' his theories adequately and his tendencies to use 'abuse sentences aimed

180    *Vernacular Knowledge*

at others'. Some members even called for banning him, saying 'even among this august crowd ... he has a wire loose' (Acolyte 2011; McClellan 2011). Generally, his posts always seemed to emphasize his overall theory about the nature of being and he tended to be very aggressive in tone, using phrases like: 'Speak for yourself fool!' (WirelessGuru1 2010a) and 'Rubbish' in reference to those who disagreed with him (2010b). His self-presentation was as a mystic with special knowledge about what he termed a 'binary' or 'digital point of view', which seems to be a very complex and idiosyncratic theory that 'reality' is 'just "code" in execution' (WirelessGuru1 2009).

Based on the content of his posts, WirelessGuru1 can be seen as leading from an extreme sense of individual authority. Although not generating significant vernacular authority by aggregating his expression of similar beliefs with those of others on the forum, he generated a less strong form of vernacular authority by asserting a uniquely mystical nature that has given him access to special knowledge outside of any institution. Not relying on expertise in a tradition or even a community that seems to like him, he instead became central in the network by repeatedly enacting his own individual authority in communications so often and to the most central other users that he became one of the most prominent and thus most pervasively known individuals on the forum. While he is linked to many including the major leaders, he is, notably, not very between. He has the second highest total degree count, but his betweenness is seventh and it is far below both of the two top forum leaders: Vision-Master and 1111:1111.

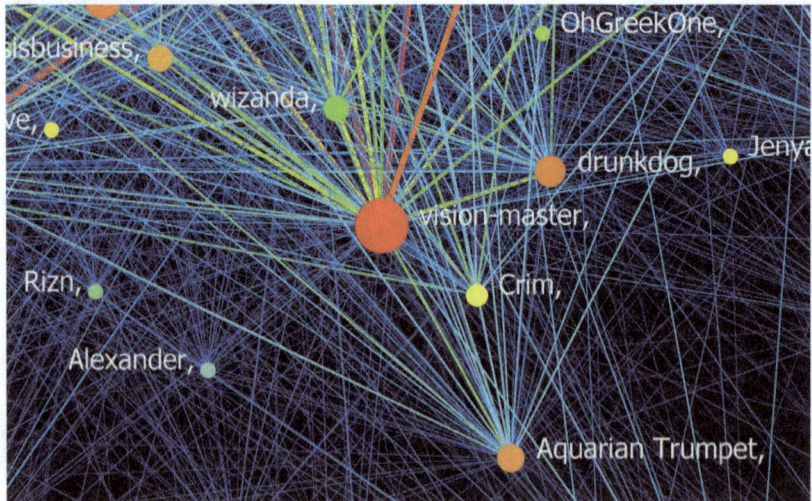

**Figure 7.5**. Network graph: *2012Forum*, 2014: Vision-Master detail

Vision-Master was in many ways very much like WirelessGuru1, but he was even more like 1111:1111. In this sense, he was, arguably, the second most influential forum leader. In total degree centrality, he is just slightly behind WirelessGuru1 and significantly behind 1111:1111. He differs from WirelessGuru1, however, in his betweenness: ranking the third most between while WirelessGuru1 is seventh. This makes Vision-Master a more overall central discourse leader because he has both high total degree and high betweenness centrality. Being very central in both calculations suggests that Vision-Master participated a lot and did so in sustained and repeated engagements with others instead of the more one-off engagements that seem to characterize WirelessGuru1's abrupt and often harsh interjections into the discourse. To sustain this kind of longer engaged deliberation, Vision-Master was less hostile in his posts and thus seemingly better liked by other forum users. In these engaged deliberations, it is easy to see how Vision-Master generated vernacular authority by aggregating his volitional claims to belief with those of many others on the forum.

While Vision-Master often did make very assertive claims, his posts were conciliatory and did not seem to engage in terse insults, like WirelessGuru1. Vision-Master spoke very openly about the community that would end when the forum shut down. He posted a simple diagram with the words: 'We will all go our own way after 2012................This 4um will have no value..............' (Vision-Master 2012). In response to hearing the forum would shut down, he clearly expressed his valuing of the human connections that his online deliberation was making. His style of communication on the forum also suggested that valuing of connections. Instead of focusing on stating and defending his own theories, he engaged many topics that are part of the vernacular religious tradition surrounding the 2012 cosmic shift and some even outside the discourse. From conspiracy theory to the best hi-fi audio equipment to his support for gun rights and ownership, his diversity of engagement made him much more central—and these qualities make him a slightly less central version of the overall forum leader: 1111:1111.

Based on the mathematics of this network, 1111:1111 was one of the top leaders, if not the top leader of the forum, in the sense that he was the most central. He had far and away the top total degree score and was the fifth most between user of the forum. Two of the users that were more between than him were very non-confrontational: Pipsqueak and Suz. The only other individual more between than 1111:1111 was Ken. While Ken was clearly an important user, we have little data on him because he pulled down as many posts as he could after the final winter solstice passed and the many predictions for 2012 had failed.

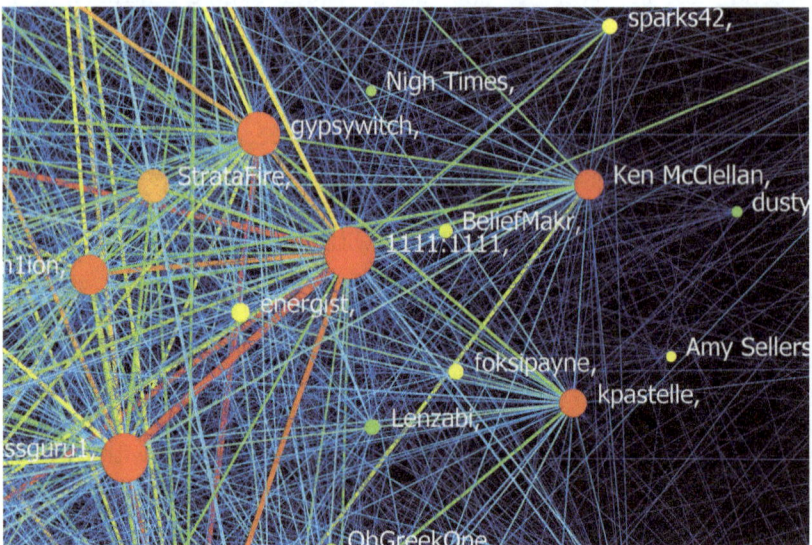

**Figure 7.6.** Network graph: *2012Forum*, 2014: 1111:1111 detail

Looking at 1111:1111's posts, his ability to generate vernacular authority becomes clearer. That authority is reflected in his high betweenness but more so in his total degree centrality. His total degree centrality is high because he engaged individuals, often in some detail, in deliberation about all the main topics the forum regularly brought up. He could be aggressive and he stated, seriously I think, that he talked to aliens daily and thus had access to special knowledge (1111:1111 2010). That claim gave him individual vernacular authority, like WirelessGuru1 above, but his tireless engagement with the community in deliberation about the shared beliefs of the 2012 shift also gave him the aggregation effect of vernacular authority magnified by epideictic deliberation.

Even his name, 1111:1111, was an affirmation of a shared belief common on the forum. The number referred to the common belief that the Mayan calendar ends on December 21, 2012, 11:11 PM; this belief then spawned the '1111:1111 Phenomenon' which dominated 1111:1111's thoughts. Many on the forum would report randomly seeing the number 1111 (on clocks, receipts, etc.). These reports served as evidence of a connection between that individual and cosmic energies coming to a head in December 2012 (binskiboys 2007). 1111:1111 was clearly a leader if not the leader of this sub-discourse on the forum and since that discourse was actually quite popular and common, 1111:1111's authority on this widely shared belief generated a significant amount of deliberation and thus a significant amount of aggregated vernacular authority for him.

## Generating Individual Authority Together

1111:1111's case demonstrates an important aspect of how internet discourse generates vernacular authority. On the one hand, 1111:1111 garnered authority because he individually experienced more '1111:1111' experiences than others. While this made him special and gave him a sort of individual vernacular authority, lots of people were having the 1111:1111 experience as well, though maybe to a lesser degree. In a clear difference, WirelessGuru1's claim to special knowledge was *not* shared by others, and he did not effectively connect it to the beliefs of others through epideictic deliberation. So even though they were similar in many ways, 1111:1111 generated more vernacular authority because he engaged with others about the already shared belief surrounding 1111:1111 and thus aggregated more volition. This made him the most central user and, arguably, the user with the most vernacular authority on the forum.

Not only did 1111:1111's ability to deliberate allow him to aggregate his ideas with others generally, he also aggregated his ideas with those who were most connected themselves. In networks, this sort of behaviour magnifies the centrality of individuals as they gain more exposure every time they appear close to others who are also getting a lot of exposure. In fact, 1111:1111 was highly connected to the arguably second most central individual on the forum: WirelessGuru1. 1111:1111 and WirelessGuru1 appeared in more of the same threads than any other pair in the entire eight years the forum was active. Looking at their exchanges, it is clear that 1111:1111 got along with and even defended WirelessGuru1, who was not well liked. When some forum members suggested that WirelessGuru1 should be banned, 1111:1111 reminded them:

> You must understand that even though wg1 like comes off the way he does......we must still respect that he has a unique point of view ... This goes for anyone and everyone who shares a point of view or perspective on this forum. (1111:1111 2011a)

This statement is typical of 1111:1111's leadership role: he often stepped in with affirmative posts about other mystical ideas even when they seem to not be terribly congruous with his own. While WirelessGuru1 and 1111:1111 have very different views of the world, they seem to respect each other's spirituality. 1111:1111 is also heavily connected to Vision-Master—and fully willing to engage in the discussions about conspiracy theory in which Vision-Master was most interested. The reason 1111:1111 generated the most vernacular authority on the forum is because he bridged between many different other leaders by engaging their very diverse ideas in deliberation. In particular, he deliberated a lot about the ideas the other very central forum users wanted to deliberate about: such as Vision-Master's posts about conspiracy theory and WirelessGuru1's extremely idiosyncratic mysticism.

WirelessGuru1, however, generated less vernacular authority because he engaged in far less of this epideictic deliberation. He seemed not to be able to engage others on topics that didn't relate to his own mystical worldview—a worldview that was not shared by others on the forum. 1111:1111's main topic of deliberation, on the other hand, was the widely shared 1111:1111 phenomenon belief. Repeatedly engaging in deliberation about this belief allowed him to engage in more deliberation with more people and thus he could aggregate more of the shared volition of the community into his own communication, meaning, ultimately, he could generate more vernacular authority.

## Epideictic Deliberation

1111:1111's centrality in the forum rested, in the end, in his ability to facilitate what I am calling epideictic deliberation and his posts serve as an excellent example of how this deliberation works in online belief communities. 1111:1111 facilitates this deliberation because his style of communication encourages the continued exchange of ideas that are part of the vernacular religious tradition that emerged between 1987 and 2012. While WirelessGuru1 generated a significant amount of individual vernacular authority by repeatedly asserting his idiosyncratic beliefs, 1111:1111 encouraged and supported the interactive expression of different views of mysticism by anyone willing to take up the discussion. As a result, 1111:1111 aggregated more individual expressions of shared belief together into his own communication and thus increased his perceived connection to the continuities and consistencies of belief about the 2012 shift.

In the end, 1111:1111 garnered more vernacular authority because he associated himself with the volition of others instead of his own. His authority emerged from a willingness to allow his expressions to be seen as aggregations of the expressions of others. Take for example his deliberative exchange with a relatively unknown user. Upagainstit wrote a 616-word rambling post about the nature of perception, of which—after several reads—I honestly could not develop a clear understanding. After no one responded, Upagainstit posted to his own thread requesting a response in order to 'bump' the thread back up the list of threads with recent activity—hoping others would take notice of it and respond. Another user, responding more or less as I did, noted that nobody was responding because, 'it's so god damn cryptic' (Equinox 2011).

Despite its unintelligibility, 1111:1111 chimes in with an affirmative statement, saying:

> Upagainstit is saying your world leaders want you to depend on them and 'god' rather than your self because yourself is powerful and they want ... to be controlled for their selfish wants and fears. He saying look within which is what the[y] don't want. (1111:1111 2011b)

He concluded with his characteristic personal affirmation: 'Upagainstit keep living brother your one of a kind ... Ever need someone to talk to outside yourself pm me. But great post' (1111:1111 2011b). Despite espousing some sort of musical theory that had nothing to do with 1111:1111's aliens or 1111:1111 numerology, Upagainsit's post became a resource for 1111:1111 to aggregate more continuities and consistence of expression to himself by encouraging another user, Mr.Whitmore, to affirm Upagainstit as well. Mr.Whitmore (2011): 'Bingo...the self is powerful...and 2012 is about peace and unification...with other "selfs" and maybe they don't want folks knowing this...'. While all three of these forum users, undoubtedly, held quite different mystical views and while Mr.Whitmore could only muster a 'maybe' in agreement with Upagainstit, the deliberation is kept going precisely because they agree on the idea that '2012 is about peace and unification' (Mr.Whitmore 2011).

In the end, peaceful unification is what the *2012Forum* seems to have been about. Creating the opportunity for individuals to share in a sense of community around the obscure but powerfully hopeful idea that a cosmic shift would usher in a new age of peace in 2012, the forum was not easily given up by its users. Many of its topics veered into paranoid claims and many users were driven by fear to see threats around them and even collect and train with firearms. However, the most avid users were not driven away from the forum when they encountered differing ideas about what 2012 might bring. Instead, they seemed energized by the wild diversity of this belief community. That makes sense when we realize that the reason so many users did not want to accept that nothing had happened on December 21, 2012, that there had been no cosmic shift, was not because they wanted to be right. It was because they wanted to continue to deliberate about what *might* be right.

The reason these individuals are so slow to give up on the 2012 date for the end of time is not that the date is particularly important to them in and of itself. Instead, it is that the date had been the nexus around which they gathered, deliberated, and through that deliberation enacted the aggregate volition that was their community. The community is what they valued, not sorting out who is right or wrong about the prophecy. In this case, it becomes clear that the aggregate volition of vernacular authority seeks not so much to be authoritative but instead it seeks simply to be. Vision-Master may have put it best when he lamented not the fact that there was no shift but that without the potential for a shift to generate epideictic deliberation, the forum users no longer shared a reason to use the forum to enact their shared hope for a new age of peace. Vision-Master put it more simply: 'This 4um will have no value' (Vision-Master 2012).

## Acknowledgements

I would like to thank Sanish Mahadik, Ashish Maurya, the Hamel Family, the Vilas Associate Award Committee, and the University of Wisconsin Office of the Vice Chancellor for Research and Graduate Education for the expertise and funding that have made this ongoing project possible.

## Notes

1 In order to preserve the original form of this online vernacular expression, all quotations in this article have preserved nonstandard spelling, grammar and formatting as much as possible.

## References

1111:1111. 2010. 'Re: 2,012. Nibiru,etc. A fuller picture'. *2012 Forum*. http://2012forum.com/forum/viewtopic.php?f=53&p=326850 (accessed May 21, 2015).

1111:1111. 2011a. 'Re: WG1 banned ?' *2012 Forum*. http://2012forum.com/forum/viewtopic.php?f=6&t=22189&start=15 (accessed May 21, 2015).

1111:1111. 2011b. 'Re: Are we in the midst of anything?' *2012 Forum*. http://2012forum.com/forum/viewtopic.php?f=8&t=22358&view=next (accessed May 21, 2015).

Acolyte. 2011. 'Re: WG1 banned'. *2012 Forum*. http://2012forum.com/forum/viewtopic.php?f=6&t=22189&start=30 (accessed May 21, 2015).

Argüelles, José. 1975. *The Transformative Vision: Reflections on the Nature and History of Human Expression*. Boston, MA: Shambhala.

Argüelles, José. 1987. *The Mayan Factor: Path Beyond Technology*. Santa Fe, NM: Bear and Co.

Aristotle. 1991. *On Rhetoric: A Theory of Civic Discourse*, translated by George A. Kennedy. New York: Oxford University Press.

Benkler, Yochai. 2008. *The Wealth of Networks: How Social Production Transforms Markets and Freedom*. New Haven, CT: Yale University Press. http://yupnet.org/benkler/archives/8 (accessed August 21, 2019).

binskiboys. 2007. 'The 11:11 phenomenon'. *2012 Forum*. http://2012forum.com/forum/viewtopic.php?f=60&t=10195 (accessed May 21, 2015).

Brady, Erika. 2001. 'Introduction'. In *Healing Logics: Culture and Medicine in Modern Health Belief Systems*, edited by Erika Brady, 3-12. Logan: Utah State University Press. https://doi.org/10.2307/j.ctt46nwrq.4

Equinox. 2011. 'Re: Are we in the midst of anything?' *2012 Forum*. http://2012forum.com/forum/viewtopic.php?f=8&t=22358&view=next (accessed May 21, 2015).

Eisenstein, Elizabeth L. 1980. *The Printing Press as an Agent of Change*, vols. 1 and 2. Cambridge: Cambridge University Press. https://doi.org/10.1017/CBO9781107049963

Gronemeyer, Sven, and Barbara MacLeod. 2010. 'What Could Happen in 2012: A Re-Analysis of the 13-Bak'tun Prophecy on Tortuguero Monument 6'. *Wayeb Notes* 34: 1-68.

HeavenSent. 2012. 'Re: anyone know of a safe area in case of pole shift'. *2012 Forum*. http://2012forum.com/forum/viewtopic.php?t=27737 (accessed May 21, 2015).

Howard, Robert Glenn. 1997. 'Apocalypse in Your In-box: End-Times Communication on the Internet'. *Western Folklore* 56 (3-4): 295-315. https://doi.org/10.2307/1500281

Howard, Robert Glenn. 1998. 'Researching Folk Rhetoric: The Case of Apocalyptic Techno-Gaianism on the World-Wide Web'. *Folklore Forum* 29 (2): 53-73.

Howard, Robert Glenn. 2008a. 'Electronic Hybridity: The Persistent Processes of the Vernacular Web'. *Journal of American Folklore* 121 (480): 192-218. https://doi.org/10.1353/jaf.0.0012

Howard, Robert Glenn. 2008b. 'The Vernacular Web of Participatory Media'. *Critical Studies in Media Communication* 25 (5): 490-513. https://doi.org/10.1080/15295030802468065

Howard, Robert Glenn. 2011. *Digital Jesus: The Making of a New Christian Fundamentalist Community on the Internet*. New York: New York University Press.

Howard, Robert Glenn. 2013. 'Vernacular Authority: Critically Engaging "Tradition"'. In *Tradition in the Twenty-First Century: Locating the Role of the Past in the Present*, edited by Trevor J. Blank and Robert Glenn Howard, 72-99. Logan: Utah State University Press. https://doi.org/10.7330/9780874218992.c03

Howard, Robert Glenn. 2015. 'Why Digital Network Hybridity is the New Normal (Hey! Check This Stuff Out)'. *Journal of American Folklore* 128 (509): 247-259. https://doi.org/10.5406/jamerfolk.128.509.0247

Ivakhiv, Adrian. 2005. 'Harmonic Convergence'. In *Encyclopedia of Religion and Nature*, edited by Bron Taylor, 738. New York: Continuum.

Jenkins, Henry. 2006. *Convergence Culture: Where Old and New Media Collide*. New York: New York University Press.

McClellan, K. 2011. 'Re: WG1 banned ?' *2012 Forum*. http://2012forum.com/forum/viewtopic.php?f=6&t=22189&start=45 (accessed May 21, 2015).

MagicalBlack. 2012. 'In need of some travel advice'. *2012 Forum*. http://www.2012forum.com/forum/viewtopic.php?t=27124&p=454383 (accessed May 21, 2015).

Magliocco, Sabina. 2012. 'Beyond Belief: Context, Rationality and Participatory Consciousness'. *Western Folklore* 71 (1): 5–24.

Mr.Whitmore. 2011. 'Re: Are we in the midst of anything?' *2012 Forum*. http://2012forum.com/forum/viewtopic.php?f=8&t=22358&view=next (accessed May 21, 2015).

Murphy, E. 2009. 'Re: How to hide Guns & Weapons in case of Gun Sweeps Obama tryin'. *2012 Forum*. http://2012forum.com/forum/viewtopic.php?f=63&t=10642 (accessed May 21, 2015).

Perelman, Chaim, and Lucie Olbrechts-Tyteca. 1991 [1969]. *The New Rhetoric: A Treatise on Argumentation*. Notre Dame, IN: University of Notre Dame Press.

randomdude. 2009. 'Are you front-hugging people? You're going to hell'. *2012 Forum*. http://2012forum.com/forum/viewtopic.php?f=8&t=15604 (accessed May 21, 2015).

Rob. 2013. 'Re: Dec 21 and Beyond - Please Read!' *2012 Forum*. http://2012forum.com/forum/viewtopic.php?f=32&t=29084&start=75 (accessed May 21, 2015).

Sullivan, Meg. 1987. 'New Age Will Dawn in August, Seers Say, and Malibu Is Ready'. *Wall Street Journal*, 23 June 1987: 1.

Sunstein, Cass R. 2007. *Republic.com 2.0*. Princeton, NJ: Princeton University Press.

Suz. 2009. 'Trip to Peru'. *2012 Forum*. http://www.2012forum.com/forum/viewtopic.php?f=8&t=14501&start=0 (accessed May 21, 2015).

Tangherlini, Timothy. 2013. 'The Folklore Macroscope: Challenges for a Computational Folkloristics'. *Western Folklore* 72 (1): 7–27.

Vision-Master. 2012. 'Re: 2012 - the time to say goodbye....'. *2012 Forum*. http://www.2012forum.com/forum/viewtopic.php?t=28198&p=476693 (accessed May 21, 2015).

WhiteWolf. 2008. 'A song dedicated to our world's Youth'. *2012 Forum*. http://www.2012forum.com/forum/viewtopic.php?f=8&t=6625 (accessed May 21, 2015).

WirelessGuru1. 2009. 'Re: Theory of Everything Part 2: Creating a kink'. *2012 Forum*. http://2012forum.com/forum/viewtopic.php?f=15&t=12677&start=153 (accessed May 21, 2015).

WirelessGuru1. 2010a. 'Re: Time is like, dissapearing...' *2012 Forum*. http://2012forum.com/forum/viewtopic.php?f=8&t=19104&p=282073 (accessed May 21, 2015).

WirelessGuru1. 2010b. 'Re: I've figured out the 2012 Enigma – the (9) nine directions'. *2012 Forum*. http://2012forum.com/forum/viewtopic.php?f=16&t=17843&start=165 (accessed May 21, 2015).

Wojcik, Daniel. 2011. 'Avertive Apocalypticism'. In *Oxford Handbook of Millennialism*, edited by Catherine Wessinger, 66–88. Oxford; New York: Oxford University Press. https://doi.org/10.1093/oxfordhb/9780195301052.003.0004

## Chapter 8

# Making Sense: The Body as a Medium to Supernatural Reality

*Kristel Kivari*[*]

In this chapter, my aim is to bring the non-verbal part of contemporary vernacular thinking into focus, joining it to the web of stories and practices, for folklore goes beyond verbal expressions; 'the text' includes the senses, impulses and environments. The focus on the bodily aspect comes naturally from the research material discussed here: feeling and *sensing* places are essential parts of dowsing practice. Assigning authority to bodily impulses makes the human body the instrument for clairvoyance, affording the possibility of apprehending supernatural reality intuitively as instant cognition, which is the foundation for further action. Considering the various uses of the body in the web of practices and stories around dowsing reminds us that vernacular religion and knowledge emerge through practice. Belief is not presented here as coherent ideology, but is echoed and articulated in actions, decisions and the web of verbal hints and accounts; it occurs on the holistic continuum of the interaction between different human subjects with the living sphere, negotiated with particular local and transnational traditions, and drawing authority from these and personal experience.

---

[*] **Kristel Kivari** is a Research Fellow at the Department of Estonian and Comparative Folklore, University of Tartu, Estonia. Her work discusses experiences of the supernatural, place-lore, vernacular practices of healing, and contemporary vernacular theories of nature, energies, and the human body. She has carried out fieldwork in Estonia, documenting the practices of dowsing and other energy-related concepts.

## Dowsing: Detecting Unseen Reality

The body is the first filter when taking and making meaning from the outer world; it is a vehicle for various feelings, sensations and movements. Dowsing, a practice that could be described as 'bodily clairvoyance', works with knowledge that is often an expression of negotiation between subjective perception and traditional interpretation. The practice itself, using a forked twig, metal rods or a pendulum to find the unseen, such as underground water, streams, pipes, cables, and special points, lines and nodes of energy, is the subject of different usage as well as vernacular, scientific and sceptical debates. Although dowsing is a practice far older than the cultural trend labelled as New Age, contemporary concepts of energy have inevitably created new interest in and attention to it. Adrian Ivakhiv notes important lineages within the contemporary usage of the idea:

> The ambiguous notion of energies plays a crucial function within New Age discourse, serving as a kind of conceptual glue that binds alternative and non-Western physico–medical theories, ideas inherited from late nineteenth and early twentieth century Spiritualism and metaphysical religion, the post-1960s vocabulary of humanistic and consciousness psychology, and an imagined future in which advanced technology is reconciled with earthly and cosmic ecology. (Ivakhiv 2007: 277)

In addition to the widespread distribution of dowsing practice in all Western countries, its popularization through literature, courses and individual use, there are societies of dowsers, organizations that investigate and promote the use of dowsing in various situations. The dowsing method usually serves to complement other forms of knowledge, although the role and status of the authority, such as an experienced or professional dowser or psychic, might be significant. Despite the official purposes as stated in the agendas or statutes, the meetings of these groups are vivid environments for discussion, storytelling and other social interaction.

Historically, dowsing has been more widely known as a practice with a definite purpose, such as finding ore seams or underground water. Despite the establishment of the natural sciences, which underpin Enlightenment ideals and rhetoric, the practice has continued in 'occult science', serving various inquiries. In this dichotomy of separation from and unity with the scientific, materialist understanding of the natural world, the senses and individual perception have been crucial.[1]

Dowsing practice often functions as a supporting argument in various interpretations linked to the vernacular web of stories where contemporary discussion of the supernatural so often takes place (see Kivari 2018). The concept of an unknown power described as energy, with 'power points' or channels, relates the category of the supernatural with mundane natural objects and places deemed to be the source of the signal which is as yet undescribed and not fully understood. Despite its possibly natural origin, the 'x-factor' in nature is associated with various supernatural accounts (particular somatic impulses both in the body and the senses, loss of orientation, feelings of otherness and sacrality).

This chapter provides insight into the dowsing practices performed within the wide field of vernacular debate relating to supernatural experiences during recent years in Estonia. As a contemporary phenomenon, dowsing is considered part of the New Age scene, although here it has developed in a way that is not typical of the 'cultic milieu' framed by the schools of various bodily and spiritual practices. The article uses original fieldwork material that focuses on a particular segment in the activity of dowsing enthusiasts, sometimes involving only a couple of practitioners, sometimes engaging a bigger group of interested people. The aim of this collection of research material is to show the generative chain of dowsing tradition that is embraced by the wider legendry about supernatural contacts, where bodily feelings function as key sources of authority and knowledge about supernatural presence in the everyday environment. Elliott Oring (2008) has used the term legendry to mark various activities and cultural expressions addressing a central plot (a legend) about encounter with the supernatural. Thus, the legendry marks the 'gravitational field' of a central story which consists of the voices of support and rejection, various practices, techniques and web discussions.

I will first present material about the 'well-catching' practice from the end of the nineteenth and first half of the twentieth century in Estonia, a tradition that is not usually regarded as an 'occult' practice, but which reflects the dissemination of ideas about super-sensitivity. The next part of the chapter follows the lineage of authorities: it shows the role of the sensuous 'turn' in the formation of certain people who are influential in the larger dowsing and paranormal scene. Although there are many competing authorities practising as trainers, consultants and detectors of various supernatural influences, mainly described as energies, the people introduced here are engaged in research of the paranormal. As such, they create new knowledge within larger traditions that are based on the interpretation of bodily impulses. They also produce knowledge of the environment, which they see as having an enchanted sensuous layer, making the supernatural possible to apprehend. The material for the current chapter was recorded during fieldwork carried out in the period 2013–2015. As a lay member of the group, I also use my own reflections on fieldwork situations. The environment for observing the larger dowsing scene is the Estonian Geopathic Association, a local club for dowsers and others interested in various alternative views.

David Cave and Rebecca Sachs Norris (2012: 2) claim in their introduction to the book *Religion and the Body* that 'there *is* no study of religion without a study of the body. Religious experience is irreducibly an experience of the body'. Decision-making and the larger area of accepting, rejecting and negotiating authority/authorities are based on subjective bodily experiences that connect situations with the larger whole of enchanted reality: 'Efficacy and experience are builders, consolidators and maintainers of belief, however and wherever expressed' (Bowman and Valk 2012: 10). Following this line of thought raises two important questions: how does understanding of the environment include bodily-attained knowledge, and how is it experienced and transmitted in real-life situations?

## Well-Catchers and the Dissemination of Dowsing Practices

Despite the fact that many dowsing practitioners suggest the method as an easy way to make practical decisions, dowsing has been linked with the pre-existing tradition of psychics since the field of well sitings began. The currents of esoteric lore from the early modern period in Central Europe allow us to assume that various uses of divining rods were made by famous 'detectives' whose abilities were at the same time used and contested.[2] Thus, while employed for locating ore seams and underground water, the rods were used for other divination purposes as well. Early physico–medical theories about vapours, pneuma and ether (Vermeir 2004; 2005) attempted rationalization of such techniques, positing concealed qualities in nature or the human body that could be responsible for foretelling the future and dowsing, at the same time making connections with the moral qualities of man (Vermeir 2005: 3). In the occultist revival of the nineteenth century, research into psychic phenomena was central to the Theosophical movement, searching for the third way between Christianity and positivist science, because of the appeal to individual experience (Asprem 2008; 2013). During the twentieth century, use of as well as research into dowsing and dowsers (both in relation to detecting abilities as well as an overall increase in sensory ability) became a hidden part of the technological research of authoritarian regimes in Germany and the Soviet Union.[3] Concurrent with these broader currents, meanwhile, the practice has been used and debated at the vernacular level.

The period of systematic collection of folklore in Estonia, beginning in the 1880s, coincided with rapid changes in culture, education and the economy. The records of techniques for deciding where to place wells before the mechanization and complete professionalization of the field, give a picture of dowsing and 'well-catching' as essential vernacular practices in which the source of the expertise might lie in several different areas that both complemented and competed at the same time.

Although the purpose of collecting knowledge about how to site wells was inevitably not to reflect theories of the fabric of the groundwater, the keyword 'water vein' reveals some ideas about it (compared to simply a silty or damp spot). The most common indicator was to observe natural signs, such as plants, and the temperature and humidity of the surface, whereas 'hearing' the underground water or references to the veins echo the idea that water flows underground like blood in the human body, which flows through veins that twist and cross.

The test for locating underground water with a pot and a wool fleece appears in Estonian printed, manuscript and oral sources.[4] Three examples give a flavour of this technique.

### How to find a water vein

A sheep's skin, fleece upwards should be placed upon even ground where the grass has been cut off. In the middle of the skin an egg should be placed which will be covered with a new clay pot. It should be done in the evening, when the ground and the weather are still dry. In the morning the pot will be taken away and if the fleece and the egg are covered with dew, there is a vein of an underground spring near. If the egg is dry and the fleece is moist, the vein is deeper in the ground. If both are dry, there is no water. (*Isamaa kalender* 1891: 188)

The place for the well is decided by lines in the morning dew, as though a mouse or a mole has run through it. There are veins of water which show themselves off like this. (ERA II 166, 61 (47) < Jõhvi parish, Tarakuse village (1937))[5]

In olden times there were the well-catchers [*kajuvõtja*]. But well-catching wasn't like that just if you wanted to, it came sometimes upon you wherever you were, and you had to catch the well. Seljamää Otsa Juhan, who lived 40 years back, was a well-catcher. Sometimes Juhan went along the road, and suddenly the well-catching came upon him. He sat on the wayside and looked straight into the ground. After some time he stood up and said if it is a good place for the well or it is not. Then it was possible to move on until the well-catching affliction [*kajuvõtmise haigus*] again hit him and he had to do it again. (ERA II 276, 421 (75) < Karja parish, Pärsamaa (1940))

Locating a well was thus semi-professional work, consisting of the 'feel' of various locations accompanied by the lore surrounding the professional's skills and practices. In several accounts hearing the water is mentioned, and fine hearing was among the skills of a good well-catcher. 'Catching the wells' is a conditional translation of various vernacular terms that include references to verbs such as to 'bring', 'touch', 'see', 'feel' or 'understand' the wells or veins (*kaevuvõtja, soonevõtja, soonetundja, kaevukatsuja*). Although the use of rods appears among the methods, the expertise of the well-catcher also seemed to involve several bodily senses. Refined or heightened senses might be inherent or discovered by chance. The sensing of the spot is described as a special feeling, often as a disease-like pressure or pricking in certain parts of the body, unlike normal senses. Sensing the place while sleeping appears in the old records of well-planning, and also in modern lore about the influence of water veins on human wellbeing.

> In the olden times there were special people, the well-catchers, who explored the land by smelling and hearing it (putting their ear against the ground) to see where and how deep the good water lay. (ERA II 139, 308 (22) < Hanila parish, Massu (1937))

> If a well was going to be planned, there were special people who knew the signs in the sky that told them how near water was. He [the well-catcher] lay on the sledge and looked up, the others were pulling the sledge. If there were signs in the sky, he let the sledge stop and dug the well, because the water was supposed to be near then. Sometimes he said that there are two stones on the well, one you can get out, the other not; and so it happened. Nowadays wells are done without [this method], the water comes out indeed. Some also observed herbs, where the water herbs grow. (H II 74, 826 (12) < Torma parish, Avinurme (1906))[6]

> There were *kaevumõistjad*[7] who heard like this, and did their tricks, lying on the ground and praying. There are green spots in the grass during the time of drought, under this must be a vein of water. One man jumped up: here you cannot sleep, it will drown the land. They have the great ability to hear. (ERA II 62, 82/3 (98) < Lääne-Nigula parish, Oru < Martna parish—R. Põldmäe (1933))

There are also records from the 1930s that describe the contradictory opinions of users on well-catching practices. Usually there are no references to wells that remain dry; rather the reservation is about the specialists' esoteric methods or possible fraud.

Some conclusions can be drawn from the historical material analysed. While the archive has collected records since the end of the 1880s there are some notable changes in ideas about the presence and influence of underground water. As my interest in the historical material is framed by contemporary concepts, I have also looked into the practices around choosing the right place to live and siting the house generally.

In older records, the proximity of the house to water (and a water vein) might bring tears and weeping, also poor health. The linking concepts, however, are notable: the water was supposed to bring 'water-illness', boils and lacerations, whereas choosing a well was done using herbs, hearing and looking for signs in the sky. The particular senses that refer to the inner connection between the human body and an underground vein, or references to sleeping, are absent.

While texts refer to the dissemination of general knowledge of the esoteric practice of well-catching, the divining rod appears in few records. Building a new house and choosing the right place for the well were done using various signs such as the movements of animals and bugs, topography and the compass. There are many suggestions which aim to minimize the main risks for the wooden constructions, such as humidity and fire, but this knowledge belongs to the separate sphere of practical knowledge. Ideas about the influence of underground water on general living conditions belongs to the modern knowledge of the second half of the twentieth century. Records about the well-catchers reflect the spread of esoteric practices of 'water witching' during the twentieth century, whereas making inner connections between underground water, health and wellbeing would be considered a modern trend. Nevertheless, the contemporary beliefs and praxis surrounding dowsing in Estonia have their roots not simply in the local traditions of Estonian parishes, but in the wider context of Western esoteric traditions.

## Continuation of Occult Practices in Research into the Paranormal

The siting of wells is an essential practice but it carries the skills and underlying ideas of supernatural contact between the human body and the earth, particularly the underground sphere. Esoteric practices disseminated in the first half of the twentieth century into healing practices involved ideas of magnetism[8] and the vitalizing of bodily fluids (Kõiva 2014a: 7). Some healers also claimed the ability to find lost people or animals (Kõiva 2014b: 88). In addition to periodicals on the theme of occultism, mysticism and spiritualism, the Estonian Metaphysical Society carried out experiments with dowsing methods, clairvoyance and psychic mediums (Abiline 2013: 55–56).

In the course of my fieldwork interviews (hereafter FM 1–5) with dowsing experts and enthusiasts in Estonia, the interwar period of parapsychology and scientific occultism is traced through some charismatic leaders who continued their interests partly through private gatherings of small groups during the Soviet period. Another influential current was the covert inquiry and research carried out in connection with the military of the Soviet Union (the specialized departments at engineering, communication and military institutes in Leningrad and Moscow and the Factory of Radio and Electronics in Tallinn, RET), which became intermingled both in personal and professional relationships. The decade from approximately the mid-1980s until the mid-1990s saw developments in both political thought and scientific ideas that touched the border zone between hard science and secret research into problematic/esoteric areas such as anomalous phenomena in nature (various sightings of light phenomena, UFOs, poltergeists, yetis) and concepts such as biofields and uses of bioenergy. These areas of interest had been pursued at the upper echelons of the Soviet regime, such as the special institutes mainly controlled by the army, although the discourse became slightly more open towards the mainstream academy with some reservations. According to one interviewee, interest in super/supranatural phenomena was supported by shared enthusiasm and dissidence when formulating scientific policy: 'You were warmly welcomed any time be in [research institutions in] Alma-Ata, Tomsk or Krasnodar' (FM 2). Thus like-minded researchers and engineers formed a sort of web across the Soviet Union that did not directly depend on their institutional affiliation. The best example of such research was presented at a series of 'school-seminars' under the title *Non-periodic Rapid-Flowing Phenomena in the Environment*[9] at the Polytechnic Institute in the Siberian city of Tomsk with the organizers inviting the elite from the Academy of Science, intelligence officers from the army and personnel from special institutes for research into and training of cosmonauts.

The enthusiasm for this research has cooled since the mid-1990s, partly due to the lack of both theoretical advancement and scientific and infrastructural support. Two of the interviewees had been in touch with those currents through personal relationships that were based on the circulation of ideas, reading materials and shared enthusiasms in which they saw the technical and spiritual potential of alternative research.

The Estonian Geopathic Association was founded as a uniting body for researchers and other specialists interested in unorthodox methods and information about natural anomalies, as the different geological and atmospheric sightings were called. Now the Association is mainly influenced by New Age ideas, and its regular activity consists of lectures and some fieldwork. Many active members also practise as entrepreneurs, acting as consultants on questions of bioenergy and earth radiation. The Association's interests are still mainly focused on dowsing phenomena, although smaller groups tackle independent activities. The two men introduced in the following section have a common background in the practical side of paranormal research. They no longer operate as independent practitioners, but their authority lies in decades-long experience and in the fact that they are not 'corrupted' by the need to meet the demand of the market.

## Authorities: Heikki

Heikki (FM 3) described himself as being interested in physical exercise and experiments since his adolescence: he was actively engaged with sports and experimented with different diets and fasting. During his army service he spent his spare time in the troop's library, reading literature on medicine and physiology. Through his family he got to know Johannes Aamissepp, publisher of the interwar magazine *Vaimsuse ideoloogia* ('The Ideology of Spirituality'), a healer and member of the Estonian Metaphysical Society. With his mentor's help, he continuously educated himself in alternative healing and medicine, and developed as an influential healer during the 1980s, seeing up to 30 or 40 patients a day at the peak of his activity. In this aspect he represents the tradition of psychics manipulating inner bioenergy. Despite his own continuous interests and self-education, and the input of his mentor, he describes the turning point for him as a sudden opening of the senses.

> We were at Heino's place, there were Vigala Sass[10] and other people. They were asking 'How do you, Sass, see things?' He answered that he

> also could not understand it. And then ... suddenly, I felt like the windows were opening. I started to see auras and other things, as if a blind person can see, a deaf person can hear, or you get pitch perfect musical hearing. And your thinking changes, everything changes around you, your sense of touch, perception and values. It goes very quickly, like—click—over about one day. It is just seeing things differently, when the world around you changes. I have the opinion that every person has these abilities, only you have to find a teacher who enables you to see things differently. It is thought of as a miracle, I say there is nothing miraculous ... For me there is no such thing as clairvoyance, it is more like a high perception, you do not use your eyes. It is more connected with the use of certain functions of your brain. Then you will see quite interesting things. (FM 3)

Despite Heikki explaining his healing process with the standard medical diagnoses and recoveries, his practice involved the handling of bioenergy, a fluid concept of a vitalizing force. The reason he quit the practice was his own exhaustion, which resulted in serious health problems. Although he uses the phrase 'mental activity' (*mentaalne tegevus*), the healing involved various bodily and spiritual efforts.

> Healing is a terribly hard thing. 15 minutes of bioenergetic operation with one's hands decreases 0.1 units of haemoglobin. I have only read this, I never measured my own rates when I was practising during the peak times. There were so many people during the day whom I bioenergetically induced, that I got my own gunshot. Also after the operation I had serious problems with blood. It is connected with the mental activity when the person radiates active energy. Only you have to know what you are doing, be it the stimulation of the blood, leucocytes, lymphocytes, the separate components of the blood, it was extremely important. These people are still alive to this day. (FM 3)

The circle of shared interests brought him into contact with geologists interested in dowsing, and evidence and techniques in the search for the unusual connection between certain places and the human body.

> It is such a weird story. One afternoon, it was probably in 1981, I looked at my garden and saw a yellowish column of light, a bit transparent, standing on the slope. And my students, those doctors, they also saw it and later went there and fixed the location. They got very bad sensations, and one of them even fainted a little there. Once, we took a common friend and put him in the centre of the location. He started to rise up into the air, though the feet were on the ground. But when I looked at him from the front, his face was completely changed, he wasn't himself, the likeness was changed. People are positive and negative according to the character of their natural base field. It does not

mean that they are bad or good. Those who are negative felt bad, those who are positive felt weightless there. Later V. measured the place with his gravimetric equipment and insisted he had never seen a place like this, as there was a natural anomaly with a diameter of 5 metres and 40 centimetres. (FM 3)

In 1988, Heikki, together with an interested group of geologists, set up a 'research polygon' on the slope of his back garden. The group started the measuring work using various methods, both from the technical and alternative sides (e.g. dowsing and observing various bodily reactions). Unfortunately, the sudden death of the leader, the leading geologist, interrupted the work. People from his circle have claimed that his materials got lost soon after his passing, as his notes and reports included valuable and sensitive information. Since the worsening of his physical condition, Heikki no longer practises healing, instead focusing on herbalist medicine.

## Authorities: Erkki

Erkki, Heikki's colleague by virtue of the shared experience of belonging to the same circle of interested people, was a founding member of the Estonian Geopathic Association, a research group on dowsing methods and so-called natural anomalies, which was formed on the basis of academic geology. Being professionally involved with research on agriculture and soils, he combined his interests in the experimental fields of his institute and other places while moving around in different natural environments. The beginning of his interests was not sudden, although it was marked by remarkable physical experiences.

> About 1984 I came to feel strangely uneasy. I felt hot all the time and had a small fever. So I went to the doctor, I had a friend working at the central hospital to ask what the matter was. He had all sorts of equipment. So the nurse gave me two sticks to hold and measured my electroconductivity. The nurse was so astonished—I had a rate of conductivity so many times higher than normal people. After that I talked to my neighbour who then introduced me to Enn Parve.[11]

> And then I was on duty in Finland, but the ship was only to leave on Monday. Then a girl told me that there was to be a *maasäteily*-men [dowsers] gathering on Sunday. I went there, seeing all the men wandering around the school gym, the twigs moving in their hands. So I tried, no, nothing [happened]. Then an older man put an arm on my shoulder, kept it there for a while and—it started to work! It works on

the basis of induction. So I was so active there, that afterwards I was completely exhausted. Later I asked Parve what this was, and was there any literature on it; he said, yes, but it is too early for you to deal with it. A year will pass, and then it will be the right time. I was thinking, 'he's talking nonsense', but a year went on, and everything started to roll. ...

It was 1987, 27th August, I do not know what happened to me. I have no explanation for this but something important changed. I was completely surprised because I know myself well and my condition was good at this time. I passed a mirror and felt that somebody pushed me, and after that I heard a low hum, like mmmmmm, and started to rise up about half a metre. I was only afraid that I would hit my head against the ceiling and at this moment it was like 'stop!' and I came down slowly. It was completely physical. After this, all such things started. (FM 1)

In addition to the expertise Erkki gained from his education, professional experience and access to laboratory resources, he was involved in research as a dowser. The sites of research were mainly so-called natural anomalies that were connected with UFO sightings, the sites of poltergeists or grass circles. In addition to supernatural accounts, one project was connected with the training centre for sportsmen from the University of Tartu, where they mapped the living and sleeping quarters on the basis of positive and negative locations, together with sports medicine researchers at the University of Tartu. The task mainly involved the quality of sleep and rest time of the sportsmen, and the possible influence of earth fields or other unknown disturbances to the person's physical condition. On both occasions a dowser was consulted due to his heightened senses. Having been actively engaged in research into dowsing phenomena, like other researchers from the alternative stream, Erkki withdrew his enthusiasm in the second half of the 1990s or even earlier. The reason for his reduction in interest was, in his words, the exhaustion of the dowsing model, and the lack of both theoretical and technological advancement and support. Despite this, he remained in contact with the leader of the small group interested in UFOs and other supernatural encounters and gave his opinion when they went out to expand on or investigate particular stories.

When asked about his bodily sensations at 'active spots' he describes how nettles would burn his feet, as well as experiencing pressure, itching or unspecified feelings of disturbance. For example, while driving along the road, he often grabs his neck or otherwise mentions that we have passed a zone or spot. During a drive he also directs my attention to the series of cracks in the asphalt, which according to his experience coincide with lines or zones of earth energy. Cracks in the asphalt are regarded within the wider dowsing lore as a sign of water veins or networks of radiation. Natural peculiarities, such as remarkable or unhealthy shapes of trees, or changes in plant cover, could indicate the anomalous quality of the spot.

From my various fieldwork trips with the aim of investigating places connected with supernatural contact, I have observed three types of principles in Erkki's dowsing practice. These are different concepts for the anomalous or unknown signal in the environment that he proves by his bodily reactions, and makes them visible for other people with the dowsing twig or pendulum.

1. The wavy shape of the signal in the air is proved with the dowsing twig. The twig reacts at the different points at different heights from the ground as though drawing a sinusoidal wave in the air. This is connected with the recommendation sometimes to move the bed lower or higher in order to avoid health problems that could occur when sleeping long-term under the influence of this disturbing unknown radiation. He says that the amplitude of the wave is not fixed, it changes by location and time. The idea of the dynamics of 'the something'—the unknown signal that makes the dowsing twig bend or vibrate—is confirmed by other practitioners as well; it is said to lock itself on the contours of the landscape. However, the dowser may be able to manipulate the signal with his own inner power, emerging in a state of contemplation.

2. The active spot is most forceful at the centre and then about six points at the radius of two or three metres stem upwards into a whirling vortex of radiation. The vortex is not static but is influenced by the moving of the sun or other unknown forces. As with the smaller spots, the nature of these activities is not fixed, although supernatural accounts of what happened nearby highlight the activity of the particular place. These active spots can be felt from a distance, by meditating upon the map of a particular area. The active centre can be united with other such points along lines and thus form a direction which would be the basis of further associations. In his regular state, Erkki is a balanced and sanguine type of personality; however, his movements and emotional state of attentiveness change at the investigation sites. If he finds a location, he looks for corresponding spots or other natural markers with focused excitement that is expressed in rapid movements.

3. The lines, zones and circles of anomalous quality or environment are visible in the landscape, as cracks in the asphalt, or changes in the construction of the buildings, the different colour or shape of the vegetation. Grass circles are a distinctive type of possible anomaly as the locations of these circles are associated with different bodily sensations and supernatural accounts. These circles are given special attention in dowsing lore, as they can reveal the place of possible future contact with the supernatural.

A diverse and dynamic system of different waves, energies and impulses describes the natural environment as rich in concealed forms of life, networks and correlations. Despite the fact that Erkki's physiology lets him detect these signals and locations, he is much more tongue-tied in giving the explanations of the origin of these anomalies and possible links with supernatural phenomena. He says he does not know how to associate the active spots with an elusive network or system within nature that could explain the sightings of different lights, UFOs or other visions. His methods and role in this kind of investigative work are to give his original interpretation of the places. The interpretation is exclusively bound to his bodily experience, forming the voice of authority into the further formation of knowledge about the supernatural places and the broader understanding of delicate sensory environments. The bodily approach, supported by wider dowsing lore and principles, addresses the issue of serious hazard: the risk to health (for example, staying too long sleeping or working under the influence of intense earth energy). In such investigations of the supernatural the risk is in stepping over the natural limits and over the border of legitimate knowledge. Crossing this border may not only retard the works but more seriously may have damaging health implications. Having enhanced sensuous abilities, the *sensitiiv* (a person like Heikki or Erkki, with enhanced senses) is a possible crosser of the border between visible everyday reality and the concealed world of supernatural reality.

## Investigating the Paranormal: Fieldwork Notes I

Over the last couple of years I have had a dual identity in the Estonian Geopathic Association, that of folklorist, writing on the theme of earth energies, and that of active member. Although modest in my ability to dowse, I have got to know the language of that particular field of interest, so in the cause of autoethnography, I can add my experiences to other reflections as a lay member of the group.

From this position, I will describe one episode in early June 2014 in the Estonian countryside, on a fieldwork trip with the dowsing enthusiasts from the Estonian Geopathic Society from Tallinn (FM 4). Although I have participated in several such trips more oriented towards fieldwork, this one was organized as a broader, partly social event, an annual trip with an educational and investigative purpose.

One reason for our visit was to meet a woman who is a practitioner of neoshamanistic healing and to get to know her practices, although primarily we went to investigate some of her stories using dowsing methods. Prior to our visit she had sent descriptions of her inexplicable experiences to one of our group members, and the fact that she was actively involved with healing using the pyramid in her back garden was a bonus. We had a nice time together both with our group and with her: it was a happy mixture of being outdoors together in early summer, with discussion of our common interest and the shaman's way to guide us to the themes of inner reflection and spirituality.

Though the shaman had had several supernatural experiences, the one that we were interested in concerned the busy road nearby. While driving home late at night she encountered a bright light coming from above as though from a huge projector. She put on the brakes and got out. She was looking up and felt paralysed; she could not tell for how long. As quickly as it appeared the light went out and she was able to drive again as if nothing had happened.

We had a map with us. It was a printout from the cartography server of the Estonian Land Board (*Maa-amet*), a database that offers different layers for the base map of the aerial photography of the locality. There were pencil marks on the map, drawn by Erkki. His method involves the intuitive recognition of 'active' or 'anomalous' regions and spots on maps, being among those who claim the ability to dowse on maps. His hand or intuition recognizes the active spots that could be a diameter from a couple of metres, to wider lines and zones that are accompanied by spots of lesser activity. In his maps he relates the stories to different landscape conditions and objects in nature. By doing this, we are conceptually linking earth energies or active spots to give relevant meaning and network mapping to the supernatural experiences.

Erkki had found a negative spot on the map situated near the place where the shaman's experiences took place. It turned out to be the yard of an abandoned farmhouse, a property our guide explained had belonged to distant relatives. The last inhabitants had been two single brothers of 'partly insane mental state' who had not taken care of the house for a long time, and now some of the buildings were near to collapsing. We drove there by car, jumped into the wasteland overgrown with high grass, thorns and nettles and slowly approached the location, the partly collapsed farmhouses.

As only some of our group knew exactly what we were looking for, or who had given us the instructions, or how they might relate to experiences on the road, most of the people just followed with trust and curiosity to assess the place with their rods and bodies. One of the first trailblazers into the high grass was the shaman herself, who, approaching in silence and possible meditation, lit smoking herbs in front of the doors of the buildings. As the landscape was really hard to pass through, I was somewhere in the middle of the group, which, one after another on the narrow trail, had reached the garden and come back. The emotional mood was attentive and excited. I assume that to a greater or lesser extent we were all preparing to encounter a reality that would be completely different from our own, while still being part of our natural early summer environment. A group of vernacular concepts were all at hand: parallel worlds, shadow worlds, conduits, portals or energy spots; here or there some of them popped up while people were attentively interpreting their bodily and emotional perceptions. I was moved by the scene: the situation could easily have been comical yet we shared an intimate moment of intense inner contemplation and readiness to encounter the unknown.

When I was halfway to the buildings and entered the perimeter of the spot, marked in the landscape, I myself began to feel strange. I felt pressure on the back side of my jawbones, the same feeling in my chest and weird dizziness in front of my eyes. I recognized that it must be the magic of the special spot, which consisted of the layers just described: people who strive for the unknown through several linking stories and a negative energy spot. In both respects the bodily feelings constitute an essential part of the language with the other reality and within the group, they mark the presence of the supernatural and serve as the key into the experience-stories.

How this place may be connected to the episodes on the road, it is hard to say. Usually, this kind of investigation stays in a raw state in which the stories from the place or other similar experiences give some means to interpret them in a broader context. However, at the spot, the logical analysis has only remote meaning for the people measuring the active point, where the senses (in the form of the feeling of stress in my case) are one possible way to have access to the supernatural. That is why the strange bodily feelings I got from there mark this event for me as special among many similar fieldtrips.

This episode is a distillation of contemporary vernacular ideas which could be labelled emerging contemporary place-lore and have some features of 'legend-tripping'; it has roots in the investigation of psychic phenomena, in experiments in clairvoyance and geomancy.

## Fieldwork Notes II

Another similar story started from two supernatural encounters that were recounted by Aivar (FM 5), a middle-aged farmer from south-west Estonia living near the coastline of the Baltic Sea. I visited him twice with a small group, in summer and winter 2014, when he repeated his experiences for the record:

> I came from the town; it was on 22nd of November 2003 or 2004 in the evening at 22.30. I entered the yard and saw a column of light standing in front of the house. I went there and put my hands on the column. I stood closer and saw an upright figure of a man. The light streamed from his head. It was a body of a man, not of a woman. If I looked up, his hands were doing this [waving]. I went to take the camera from the house and made some snaps, which went wrong when I later wanted to print them out. I was strangely calm; afterwards I went to the house and had a meal, like forgot about it. About half past midnight I went to see it again, if it was there, by then it had disappeared. It might have been a warning of a storm perhaps, because I have always had some kind of way that has saved me from the worst.

The great storm at the beginning of January 2005 continues to be central to the local time calculation. For a couple of days, because of the unlucky direction of the wind in a winter cyclone, the coastal area of west and south-west Estonia was flooded. Like many people in the region, Aivar had to start from the beginning with his household and fields. Another experience of a similar kind led us to investigate the area more widely and to engage the dowsing methods.

> I stood at the same place [where the previous sighting took place] and the stream of light ran over the garden, curving a bit, not straight. It was a soft, warm light. I would not have seen it, but the dog woke me up in the middle of the night, barking. I woke up, put clothes on; it was a cold night. I could not understand where the light came from. It was a

completely weird light, thuja trees in front were like not touched by the light, but the spruces at the back were like skeletons in an x-ray image. It was three weeks before the storm. (FM 5)

These two stories, told to the leader of our group, brought us to the place. The initial idea to engage Erkki on the trip was to let him check the invisible profile of the anomalous place and possible active zones associated with such sightings. Erkki had looked at the map and pointed out a series of points in the vicinity of the household using his method of distant dowsing. We decided to follow the direction of the tunnel of light and see what was in the landscape. At the end of the summer, the landscape in some places was hard to pass, and Aivar absolutely insisted that we not go into the bushes because of the poisonous plants that were growing on the path. Despite his warnings, and with Erkki in the lead, we examined the surroundings; Erkki was clearly excited and moved quickly, sensing the environment and searching for places that he had marked on the map. Despite refusing to build up theories or fixed explanations for such sightings, and the correlations with the sensory profile of the landscape, he was searching for a distinctive spot of intense sensory activity on the coastal meadow. The meadow is flat and open, overgrown with some reeds and high grass. Finally, we reached the place of two circles that were a bit higher than the rest of the surface. The circles were covered with lush bindweed, which stood out brightly from the background of faded brownish fallow. We looked at the circles, completely astonished by the find. Erkki confirmed that this was the spot, but he later changed his mind and said that we did not get the right point. Despite this, the impression was that what we were looking for and what we found almost supernaturally coincided. The spot was distinctive indeed. As a junior and female member of the group, I was told to stay aside as the hazardous border of supernaturality was so close. Having cautiously familiarized ourselves with the place, later we all examined our feelings at the circles in order to make sense of the trip, the connection between the stories, the landscape and possible contact with the unknown.

We continued our examinations in winter, when it was easier to pass through a grove of bushes on the possible line of the light. The bushes hid a loose circle or a pile of big ironstones, and a couple of tall black alders and some rowans were growing in between the stones. Neither Aivar nor his neighbour could give an explanation about the origin of the pile. Instead, the fact that alders and also the rowan had been hit by lightning made us more attentive. The electrical solutions in the environment and their connection with geology and landscape were among the check questions about the possible anomalous character of the place that could give correlations with the results of dowsing. Aivar confirmed that the area draws the thunderstorms; he had to cut a tall tree nearby the house which attracted the lightning. Also, after a couple of power cuts to his electrical system, he has learned to know how to protect himself.

Thus the story of Aivar, the landscape and our two fieldwork trips give an example of research into anomalous phenomena merging the natural and supernatural, where the sources of knowledge come from the environment, supernatural experience and sensory examination. Apart from the intimate experience of the participants in such fieldwork, this kind of examination provides new information and inspiration for the wider audience in dowsing circles.

## Discussion: Story as the Tip of an Iceberg

These stories, which would better be the subject of a film than a black and white written description, present how people make sense of the supernatural, through experiences, practice and stories. Borrowing the model from Linda Dégh (2001: 200) for comparison, the narrated, printed or aired story presents only the tip of the iceberg, the expressive result of a multitude of networks of meaning within a group or society. In folklore studies, such a cultural flow is characterized by the legend genre in which each story is part of a bigger whole, and in which the plots merge into and dissolve from one to another. These stories do not have a distinct storyteller, except the researcher whose position in a discursive field enables her or him to consider such practices to be the subject of folklore research, and vice versa, to face the questions put by participants who strive for meanings and answers in such situations. People participate in cultural and environmental dialogue, acting as both protagonists and audience at the same time. Each participant has a lineage or legacy of legends behind her/him, be it healing or research into the paranormal, influenced by personal, political or local meanings. The legends are, in Terry Gunnell's words, a map of behaviour, underlining moral and social values and offering examples to follow or avoid. Simultaneously, they reminded people of the temporal and physical borders of their existence, questions of life and death, periods of liminality, insiders and outsiders, and the continuous physical and spiritual division between the cultural and the wild (Gunnell 2008: 15). As several researchers have pointed out, the function of a legend is to open up the question of the truth of a particular situation, understanding or concept (Oring 2008). In supernatural experiences everyday order becomes subverted and hierarchies and relations disturbed or disrupted.

At the same time, though, legends also build up truths supporting alternative explanations and challenging conventional understandings. Much of the activity of dowsers or researchers into the paranormal is guided by the opinion that what folklorists call legends are simply the artefacts of a different kind of system and reality, forces or relationships other than those presented in the mainstream policies of society. The experimental method of examining places is an attempt to go into the situations and experiences of the witnesses, where experience is the link for expressing the underlying systems of particular streams of culture.

One reason for the popularity of dowsing practice could be its ability to experience the supernatural, and to make various experiences communicative on both sides: within the community of people and towards the transcendent force or signal itself. By their disturbing but transcendent character, legends 'make people honest and humble, and express their true feelings, concerns, fears, weaknesses and failures' (Dégh 2001: 313). Dowsing as a practice of making sense of nature or landscape is a bit more optimistic as it builds up a new, subjective truth in which experience creates authority among people who share the knowledge of a particular way of thinking, a tradition, a viewpoint. However subjective, the perceived truth unites the community of a tradition, where people who share particular stories carry out fieldwork to examine the supernatural.

Robert Glenn Howard (2013: 81) has approached the *vernacular* as one side of the field of social power where certain clusters serve the legitimate institutional authority, whereas the *vernacular* emerges from a different type of trust that does not consciously rely on any of those institutions. Howard's approach has engaged Erika Brady's (2001: 7) point that there are different settings of trust in institutional credentials on one side, but 'relational authority' from the side of the vernacular where the tradition, different stories and experiences build up the community: 'These expressive forms derive strength not only from the ways in which they fulfil the immediate needs of community members, but also from the ways in which they embody larger patterns of shared beliefs and values'.

Despite the fact that folk beliefs also serve as a kind of a battlefield where the ideas of tradition-bound communities are hardly recognizable, the immediate situation of legend telling or the places where the dowsing twigs flex, allow us to recognize how relationships are built between witnesses to the situation. This is why analysis that purely employs different systems of thought cannot serve to critique such situations. Thus the sceptic's words fall on deaf ears, as the principles of weaving together the source, meaning and effect are built on different relationships.

## Making Sense of a Sensuous Landscape

The 'well-catching disease', the sensuous turn in the lives of two dowsers, and the employment of dowsing methods in wider circles of interested people bring forth the essential character of particular legends. These situations are evoked in the process of investigation of the paranormal, where the participants try to re-create the situation in feeling the stories not only by emotional contact with witness when making interviews, but also entering into the landscape touched by the supernatural. In the processes of circulation of these plots, the senses and feelings are among the builders of understandings about these experiences. A single experience transcends into the wider conception of supernatural presence in the natural environment.

The questions that are most often asked about situations like that are, what happens to these people, and how and under what influences are their conditions changed? I have no expertise to answer such questions except to note that these problems bring up the paradigmatic gap between two orientations in decision-making. These often-contradictory orientations see the world from one point as an objective, natural system of units, and from the other perspective as stemming from subjective, relational and sensuous modes of operation (Tambiah 1990: 86; Greenwood 2009: 29). The body, at the same time vehicle and object of analytical categories, creates a sort of a blind spot where the socially informed body is, according to Pierre Bourdieu, determined by different sets of relations by the metaphor of the senses. According to Bourdieu, in addition to the five senses, the sense of necessity and the sense of duty, the sense of direction and the sense of reality, the sense of balance and the sense of beauty, common sense and the sense of the sacred, tactical sense and the sense of responsibility, business sense and the sense of propriety, the sense of humour and the sense of absurdity function as the thermometers of human morality (Bourdieu 1977: 124). Thus the senses, as a concealed realm within the individual body, are the site of refinement of the existential relations within society and beyond. The ambiguous position of the well-catchers or contemporary dowsers includes the fear of being fooled, or being made to look foolish. The antithesis of fear is in the morality present in the process of refining and enlarging the sensuous scope through practising and testing the ability to perceive the supernatural signals from the environment in the courses and clubs of dowsers. Despite the hazardous border of the supernatural posing a risk to health, borders challenge us to find ways to step over and to have access to the other side, along with an enhanced understanding of it.

As in numerous themes in culture, vernacular practices emerge in the border areas or in the conflicting orientations in society. The philosophical gap in understanding between perception, consciousness and culturally transformed principles are the themes of negotiation over authority that are expressed in the situation of making decisions. How should I trust my feelings, be they physical or inner impressions? What role do they actually play and how are they formed in the question of locations or moreover making sense of supernatural experiences?

A set of relations to the natural world, and among the practitioners of the tradition, are shared in the moment of dowsing, which weaves together the different fabrics of the supernatural. Shared tradition involves the shared conditions of situations, be they the temperature of emotions or the weather.

## Acknowledgements

This work was supported by the Estonian Research Council grant (PRG670) 'Vernacular Interpretations of the Incomprehensible: Folkloristic Perspectives Towards Uncertainty'.

## Fieldwork

FM 1: Two interviews with Erkki on October 2, 2013 and October 8, 2013.

FM 2: Interview with Heldur Haldre on May 9, 2014.

FM 3: Interview with Heikki on May 24, 2014.

FM 4: Fieldwork to Veriora parish with Geopathic Association on June 1, 2014.

FM 5: Fieldworks to Tahkuranna parish in south-west of Estonia on August 9, 2014 and December 6, 2014.

## Notes

1. Much has been written about dowsing in the context of epistemological and cultural conflict since the Renaissance, most notably Warren Dym's monograph *Divining Science: Treasure Hunting and Earth Science in Early Modern Germany* (2011), a detailed analysis of relationships between mining lore (particularily dowsing) and early geology in Saxony.
2. In discussion of morality and imagination and its embeddedness in human physiology, between soul and body, during the seventeenth–eighteenth centuries in France, Koen Vermeir has referred to the stories of Jacques Aymar, a famous dowser, who was the subject of various publications of the period. While seeking for water one day in 1688 Aymar's rod was dipping at the place of a buried woman, who had been murdered some months earlier. With the help of his rod he soon found the culprit, who confessed his crime (Vermeir 2005: 2). Jacques Aymar's fame spread for his ability to solve crimes, to find the murderers, and locate plunder, weapons and other belongings (Lynn 2001: 35).
3. The references to this information are from the interview material conducted for my PhD research 'Dowsing as a Link between Natural and Supernatural: Folkloristic Reflections on Water Veins, Earth Radiation and Dowsing Practice' (2016). Some of the experiments with dowsing practice are referred to in Watson 1973.
4. This method has been recorded in various sources throughout history, one of the earliest being by Roman architect and engineer Marcus Vitruvius Pollio (Kölbl-Ebert 2009: 213).
5. The reference is to the collection of the Estonian Folklore Archives (ERA). The sign < marks the place where the record has been written up; the year of the collecting of the record is in brackets.
6. The record refers to the Jakob Hurt's (H) collection in the Estonian Folklore Archives.
7. The word *kaevumõistja* could be understood in a broad sense: the person who can 'seize' water or see where and how to build a good well.
8. Ernst Gottlob Jesche (the priest of Häädemeeste church 1909–1932) among other methods magnetized water for his healing practice. He brought two buckets of water into the room, held one hand above one bucket and the other above another bucket, moving them round for some minutes and shaking his fingertips towards the water. Doing this, one bucket got a positive charge and the other got a negative charge (Haava 2013: 73).
9. Original title: *Mezhdistsiplinarnaya nauchno-tekhnicheskaya shkola-seminar 'Neperiodicheskiye bystroprotekayushchiye yavleniya v okruzhayushchey srede'*. The title is taken from the cover of the programme of the Conference in 1992.
10. Aleksander Heintalu, known as Vigala Sass (1941–2015), was a popular shamanistic healer. Starting from the 1990s he published several books on health, healing, and spirituality.
11. An engineer at the factory of Radio Electronics in Tallinn (RET), also the key person to the alternative research and techniques. His influence was based on his well-informed status, access to and involvement with similar research on a much larger scale at the closed institutions in Moscow and Leningrad.

## References

Abiline, Toomas. 2013. 'Uue vaimsuse eelkäijad: antroposoofia, teosoofia, vabamüürlus ja parapsühholoogia Eestis 1918–1940'. In *Mitut usku Eesti* III, edited by Marko Uibu, 37–78. Tartu: Tartu Ülikooli Kirjastus.

Asprem, Egil. 2008. 'Magic Naturalized? Negotiating Science and Occult Experience in Aleister Crowley's Scientific Illuminism'. *Aries* 8: 139–165. https://doi.org/10.1163/156798908X327311

Asprem, Egil. 2013. 'The Problem of Disenchantment: Scientific Naturalism and Esoteric Discourse 1900–1939'. PhD diss., University of Amsterdam, Faculty of Humanities. (The thesis is published in a revised version in Asprem, Egil. 2014. *The Problem of Disenchantment: Scientific Naturalism and Esoteric Discourse 1900–1939*. Leiden: Brill.)

Bourdieu, Pierre. 1977. *Outline of a Theory of Practice*. Cambridge: Cambridge University Press. https://doi.org/10.1017/CBO9780511812507

Bowman, Marion, and Ülo Valk. 2012. 'Introduction: Vernacular Religion, Generic Expressions and the Dynamics of Belief'. In *Vernacular Religion in Everyday Life: Expressions of Belief*, edited by Marion Bowman and Ülo Valk, 1–19. Sheffield; Bristol, CT: Equinox Publishing.

Brady, Erika. 2001. 'Introduction'. In *Healing Logics. Culture and Medicine in Modern Health Belief Systems*, edited by Erika Brady, 3–12. Logan: Utah State University Press. https://doi.org/10.2307/j.ctt46nwrq.4

Cave, David, and Rebecca Sachs Norris. 2012. 'Introduction'. In *Religion and the Body: Modern Science and the Construction of Religious Meaning*, edited by David Cave and Rebecca Sachs Norris, 1–15. Leiden; Boston: Brill.

Dégh, Linda. 2001. *Legend and Belief: Dialectics of a Folklore Genre*. Bloomington; Indianapolis: Indiana University Press.

Dym, Warren A. 2011. *Divining Science: Treasure Hunting and Earth Science in Early Modern Germany*. Leiden; Boston: Brill. https://doi.org/10.1163/ej.9789004186422.i-218

Greenwood, Susan. 2009. *The Anthropology of Magic*. Oxford; New York: Berg.

Gunnell, Terry. 2008. 'Introduction'. In *Legends and Landscape: Articles Based on Plenary Papers Presented at the 5th Celtic-Nordic-Baltic Folklore Symposium, Reykjavík, 2005*, edited by Terry Gunnell, 13–24. Reykjavik: University of Iceland Press.

Haava, Ursula. 2013. 'Ernst Gottlob Jaesche—imearst Häädemeeste pastoraadis'. In *Õpetatud Eesti Seltsi aastaraamat/Annales Litterarum Societatis Esthonicae*, edited by Kadi Kass, Pille-Riin Larm, Marten Seppel, Tõnu Tannberg and Heiki Valk, 57–80. Tartu: Õpetatud Eesti Selts.

Howard, Robert Glenn. 2013. 'Vernacular Authority: Critically Engaging "Tradition"'. In *Tradition in the Twenty-First Century: Locating the Role of the Past in the Present*, edited by Trevor J. Blank and Robert Glenn Howard, 72–99. Logan: Utah State University Press. https://doi.org/10.7330/9780874218992.c03

*Isamaa kalender*. 1891. Tartu: Schnakenburg.

Ivakhiv, Adrian. 2007. 'Power Trips: Making Sacred Space through New Age Pilgrimage'. In *Handbook of New Age*, edited by Daren Kemp and James R. Lewis, 263–286. Leiden; Boston: Brill. https://doi.org/10.1163/ej.9789004153554.i-484.91

Kivari, Kristel. 2016. *Dowsing as a Link between Natural and Supernatural: Folkloristic Reflections on Water Veins, Earth Radiation and Dowsing Practice*. Dissertationes Folkloristicae Universitatis Tartuensis 24. Tartu: University of Tartu Press.

Kivari, Kristel. 2018. 'Webs of Lines and Webs of Stories in the Making of Supernatural Places'. In *Storied and Supernatural Places: Studies in Spatial and Social Dimensions of Folklore and Sagas*, edited by Ülo Valk and Daniel Sävborg, 114–133. Helsinki: Finnish Literature Society. http://library.oapen.org/handle/20.500.12657/29738

Kõiva, Mare. 2014a. 'Loomulik ravi 20. sajandi alguse arstimispraktikas'. In *Medica IX: Tervis, linn ja loodus*, edited by Mare Kõiva and Marko Uibu, 7. Tartu: EKM Teaduskirjastus.

Kõiva, Mare. 2014b. 'Äksi nõid: nõukogude aja selgeltnägija'. *Mäetagused, Electronical Journal* 58: 85–106. https://doi.org/10.7592/MT2014.58.koiva

Kölbl-Ebert, Martina. 2009. 'How to Find Water: The State of the Art in Early Seventeenth Century, Deduced from Writings of Martine de Bertereau (1632 and 1640)'. *Earth Sciences History* 28 (2): 204–218.
https://doi.org/10.17704/eshi.28.2.3675823j24h9uv9r

Lynn, Michael R. 2001. 'Divining the Enlightenment: Public Opinion and Popular Science in Old Regime France'. *Isis* 92 (1): 34–54. https://doi.org/10.1086/385039

Oring, Elliott. 2008. 'Legendry and the Rhetoric of Truth'. *Journal of American Folklore* 121 (480): 127–166. https://doi.org/10.1353/jaf.0.0008

Tambiah, Stanley J. 1990. *Magic, Science, Religion, and the Scope of Rationality*. Cambridge; New York: Cambridge University Press.

Vermeir, Koen. 2004. 'The "Physical Prophet" and the Powers of the Imagination. Part I: A Case-Study on Prophecy, Vapours and the Imagination (1685–1710)'. *Studies in History and Philosophy of Science Part C: Studies in History and Philosophy of Biological and Biomedical Sciences* 35 (4): 561–591. https://doi.org/10.1016/j.shpsc.2004.09.001

Vermeir, Koen. 2005. 'The "Physical Prophet" and the Powers of the Imagination. Part II: A Case-Study on Dowsing and the Naturalisation of the Moral, 1685–1710'. *Studies in History and Philosophy of Science Part C: Studies in History and Philosophy of Biological and Biomedical Sciences* 36 (1): 1–24. https://doi.org/10.1016/j.shpsc.2004.12.008

Watson, Lyall. 1973. *Supernature*. London: Hodder & Stoughton.

# Chapter 9

# Seeking as a Late Modern Tradition: Three Vernacular Biographies

*Steven J. Sutcliffe*[*]

### The Trope of Seeking in Folklore and Anthropology

> The gods did not reveal, from the beginning,
> All things to us; but in the course of time,
> Through seeking, men find that which is the better.
> (Xenophanes [c. 570–478 BCE] cited in Torrance 1994: 276)

I want to argue in this chapter that, despite preconceptions of superficial content and low salience, the role of 'seekership' in and beyond the 'cultic milieu' (Campbell 1982; 2002 [1972]) constitutes a late modern tradition with substantial historical and cultural roots. Rather than a sign of idiosyncrasy, eccentricity or even pathology, 'seeking' is a social role adapted to the demands on the subject posed by exposure to the radical pluralization of authorities, both religious and secular, in late modernity. I approach seeking as a routinized mode of thinking and acting which is transposable across numerous fields of activity; not only in the 'religious' field—for example, in New Spiritualities where arguably we see its most concentrated expressions—but also in 'secular' fields where the accumulation of experiences and accreditations has become a central feature of the ubiquitous 'journey' to which late modern subjects are increasingly subscribed in the fields of education, work, well-being and leisure.

---

[*] **Steven J. Sutcliffe** is Senior Lecturer in the Study of Religion at the University of Edinburgh. He is author of *Children of the New Age: A History of Spiritual Practices* (Routledge, 2003) and co-editor of *Beyond New Age: Exploring Alternative Spirituality* (with Marion Bowman; Edinburgh University Press, 2000), *New Age Spirituality: Rethinking Religion* (with Ingvild Sælid Gilhus; Routledge, 2013) and *The Problem of Invented Religions* (with Carole Cusack; Routledge, 2016).

As evidence I discuss three vernacular biographies of 'seekers' published between 2001 and 2011 in different regions of the UK. By vernacular, I refer to 'the power of the individual and communities of individuals to create their own religion' (Primiano 2012: 383), with 'people becoming the focus of study and not "religion" or "belief" as abstractions' (ibid.: 384), although I prefer the term 'subject' over individual to highlight the social and collective formation of biography. To understand the practical logic of seeking, I draw on a theoretical framework based in the work of Vladimir Propp and Walter Burkert. Despite differences in voice and content I argue that each biography is structured by means of a narrative search, through which the author evaluates the numerous symbolic goods (theologies) made available by the multiple authorities of late-modern religion.[1]

In this first section I sketch a prototype to think with when we read the biographies. In *Creation of the Sacred: Tracks of Biology in Early Religions*, Burkert (1996) argues that recurring tropes of 'quest', 'journey' and 'search' structure classic Greek and Sumerian epics such as the labours of Heracles (or Hercules) or the descent of Inanna into the underworld. Burkert argues that these tropes have the capacity to excite their listeners/readers at both narratological and biological levels, and that the resulting confluence between 'cultural' and 'natural' levels of arousal can explain more compellingly than a solely hermeneutic account how and why 'the tale is the form through which complex experience becomes communicable' (Burkert 1996: 56). The chapter in which Burkert develops this idea, 'The Core of a Tale', especially the sections 'Caught up in Tales' and 'From Biological Programs to Semantic Chains' (ibid.: 56–67), is based on his engagement with the analysis of Russian fairytales (*skazki*) by Vladimir Propp.

In *Morphology of the Folktale*, Propp (1998 [1968]) identifies 31 basic functions of the prototypical folktale, using for his source a collection first published in Russian in the mid-nineteenth century. Each of these 'functions' constitutes a unit of the underlying narrative structure and represents 'an act of a character, defined from the point of view of its significance for the course of the action' (Propp 1998 [1968]: 21). Propp is thus interested less in enumerating the qualities of the (multiple) *dramatis personae* of the tales than in delineating their (rather limited) range of functions within a (fairly predictable) sequence of actions (plot), since 'the number of functions is extremely small, whereas the number of personages is extremely large' (ibid.: 20). This combination of granular detail yet limited functionality yields what Propp calls 'the two-fold quality of a tale: its amazing multiformity, picturesqueness, and color, and on the other hand, its no less striking uniformity, its repetition' (ibid.: 21). Not all 31 functions need to be present in any one narrative, which means that tales can be more or less complex depending on how many functions can be detected. As we shall see, the number of functions in seeker biographies is relatively small, although no less potent structurally for that. As we shall see, Propp's function #9 is particularly relevant, defined in this way: 'misfortune or lack is made known; the hero is approached with a request or command; he [sic] is allowed to go or he is dispatched' (ibid.: 36). Identification of a basic 'lack', and the start of a search to rectify this, enables functional differentiation between the hero as a 'seeker' (if proactive in the search) and as a 'victimized hero' (if reactive to another's search; ibid.). This is immediately followed by function #10 in which the seeker-hero 'decides upon counteraction' (ibid.: 38) and by function #11 in which s/he 'leaves home' (ibid.: 39). The quest is further delineated through functions which designate encounters, trials and deceptions to test the hero's stamina and discernment. Eventually the hero is 'led to the whereabouts of [the] object of search' (function #15, ibid.: 50) and in function #19 the 'initial misfortune or lack is liquidated' as s/he obtains the object of search (ibid.: 53–55) before embarking on the return journey.

Extrapolating from Propp's synchronous model, Burkert argues that the quest is one of the earliest known historical plot types. Gilgamesh's search for immortality on the death of his companion, Enkidu, is illustrative. As translated by Nancy K. Sandars (1972 [1960]: 97):

> [I]n his bitterness [Gilgamesh] cried, 'How can I rest, how can I be at peace? Despair is in my heart. What my brother is now, that shall I be when I am dead. Because I am afraid of death I will go as best I can to find Utnapishtim whom they call the Faraway, for he has entered the assembly of the gods'. So Gilgamesh travelled over the wilderness, he wandered over the grasslands, a long journey, in search of Utnapishtim, whom the gods took after the deluge ... and to him alone of men they gave everlasting life.

On the basis of Gilgamesh's search for this rare symbolic object (immortality) and similar Greek and Sumerian epic plots, Burkert (1996: 62, 63) concludes that Propp has identified 'a general and transcultural form of organising experience' which is both 'repetitive and fascinating' and 'surprisingly persistent'. The key to a successful tale is that 'we can easily memorize it, reproduce it, even reconstruct it from incomplete records'; in the most memorable examples 'whether by instinct or by routine, we seem to know what should happen next' (ibid.: 62).

Since Propp has identified the narratological support for the search, Burkert turns to ethology, or the study of animal behaviour, for biological clues to its persistence. By analogy with the search for food as basic material sustenance, Burkert argues that 'practically the whole of the Propp sequence is prefigured in [a] series of biological necessities' (ibid.: 63). He finds a 'biological equivalent of the quest' (that is, in its narratological functions of encounter, trial and deception) in 'the search for food, which includes the struggle against others who are in quest for the same resources, and the possibility of tricks, fight and flight' (ibid.: 63–64). Burkert (ibid.: 64) further reduces the quest plot to a series of linguistic formulae in which 'actions are represented by verbs'. Arguing from multiple examples (including Latin, Greek, Semitic and Turkish) that the verbal imperative form is the most basic form of communication, Burkert concludes that 'the deepest deep structure of a tale would, then, be a series of imperatives: "get", that is "go out, ask, find out, fight for it, take and run"' (ibid.). In this way he argues not only that the quest as a 'means for problem-solving' is 'represented and communicated through the tale' but that 'the soul of the plot' must operate 'at the level of biology' (ibid.: 65). By reduction to the imperative to 'go out, ask, find out, fight for it, take and run' (ibid.: 64), Burkert maps Propp's narratological quest onto a behavioural and ethological level.[2]

So far I have described search as a hybrid on both 'cultural' and 'natural' levels based in the models of Propp and Burkert, with an emphasis on identification of a problem and its solution. In *The Spiritual Quest: Transcendence in Myth, Religion, and Science*, Robert M. Torrance draws attention to the missing middle stage in this equation by means of which the problem has to be resolved. Torrance calls this stage the 'spiritual quest', which he represents as a property of 'the indeterminate self-transcendence of living things as open systems' (1994: 53). Like Burkert, he also turns to Propp, this time via the work of folklorist Alan Dundes who further reduces Propp's 31 functions to the two *ur*-functions of 'Lack' and 'Lack Liquidated' (ibid.: 290).[3] In Dundes' view, as paraphrased by Torrance, the quest structure serves to narrate the 'transcendence of initial insufficiency through attainment of a new, though always provisional, equilibrium' (ibid.). But Torrance argues that Dundes underplays the qualitative experience of the middle stage of the search which is precisely 'the *movement* by means of which the hero either overcomes lack or fails' (ibid.; emphasis original). Rather than being subordinate to the dialectic between lack and lack liquidated, the period of substantive search is the 'necessary liminal passage' through which lack is resolved by identifying and sifting potential solutions (ibid.: 291). This 'liminal passage' corresponds to what Burkert (1996: 65) calls the 'soul of the plot'.

In this way Torrance helps us to understand that, in his words, the quest is 'not a binary but a ternary model' (1994: 290) in that only the middle stage of searching itself can uncover the appropriate symbolic object to liquidate the felt lack and restore the lost equilibrium.[4] Seekers' biographies may reveal transparent or disguised motives, they may encounter various distractions and tests, they will probably find villains as well as helpers amongst the authorities they engage, the aims of each stage of their search may come in and out of focus, and the final destination itself may change or may not be reached. However, my argument suggests that seekers' behaviour is not idiosyncratic but follows a plot with recognizable functions.

## A Tradition Re-emerges

The above proposes a hybrid model of seeking as a disposition with cultural and biological supports. This is not a Jungian interpretation (cf. Campbell 1964 [1949]) but an empirical model that can be tested and falsified. Nor can it be normatively dismissed as 'floundering about among religions' (Lofland and Stark 1965: 869), as seeking is described in an earlier phase of the sociology of new religions. Rather, seeking in its late modern iteration represents a logical response to the 'pluralization of life-worlds' (Berger, Berger and Kellner 1974: 62), a phrase which describes a heightened awareness of the religious field as manifold and heterogenous. This is not to say that the experience of a plurality of religions is a unique feature of the contemporary world, but it is to suggest that late modernity can be characterized by an accelerated exposure to pluralized authorities. As a result the 'life-world', understood as the everyday experience of a 'reality that is ordered and that gives sense to the business of living', is increasingly felt as a *'plurality of life-worlds'* (ibid.; original emphasis). In such circumstances seeking describes a rational form of thinking and acting on the part of subjects sensitized to multiple life-worlds, some of whom begin to search amongst available authorities for the means to 'liquidate' their 'lack'.

In his essay 'The Cult, the Cultic Milieu and Secularization', first published in 1972, Colin Campbell identified seekership as a core practice within a cultural environment which he dubbed the 'cultic milieu'. He described this milieu as 'the sum of unorthodox and deviant belief-systems together with their practices, institutions and personnel' which, he argued, 'constitutes a unity by virtue of a common consciousness' (Campbell 2002 [1972]: 23). Following Campbell's emphasis on the social and collective functions of seeking, some commentators began to identify the 'seeker' as the principal subject of the 'conversion careers' amongst the new religions of the 1970s onwards (Sutcliffe 2003; 2017; Lewis 2016).

An important late modern medium for communicating seekership is the inexpensive paperback book. This can be published on a small print run by a local press or as a trade edition by conglomerates. Good examples include David Spangler's *Pilgrim in Aquarius* (1996) and Timothy Tattersall's *Journey: An Adventure of Love and Healing* (1996), both published by the Findhorn community in Scotland. Also published by Findhorn Press is Judith Boice's *At One with All Life: A Personal Journey in Gaian Communities* (1990), an autobiographical account of the author's sojourns in a series of New Age communities including the Bear Tribe in the US and Auroville in India. In contrast, Marie Herbert's *Healing Quest: A Journey of Transformation* (1996) was issued under the Rider imprint, previously a niche publisher of occult titles but now published by Penguin/Random House.

These examples are only the latest wave of an emergent genre. If we retroject the concept of the cultic milieu into the first half of the twentieth century, we find subjects who already identify as seekers. A good example is Rom Landau's *God is My Adventure: A Book on Modern Mystics, Masters and Teachers*. This enquiry into various 'mystics, masters and teachers' included encounters with Jiddu Krishnamurti, Frank Buchman, G. I. Gurdjieff and Rudolf Steiner amongst others. First published in 1935 it was immensely popular and was reprinted for the eleventh time in 1945, this time by the influential London publisher, Faber and Faber. In the original preface Landau describes himself as someone who has 'always been attracted by those regions of truth that the official religions and sciences are shy of exploring' although 'my aim has never been to identify myself with any one teacher' (Landau 1945 [1935]: 5). In the preface to the new edition, he goes further, attributing its success to the fact that 'people are always eager to learn from the spiritual experiences of a fellow seeker' (ibid.: 7). Many readers were 'only too willing to delve into the ways and methods of unorthodox schools of thought' although they would refuse 'to accept this or that method as the only valid one' because 'in spiritual research the utmost personal freedom is a *sine qua non*' (ibid.). Landau's self-identification as a 'fellow seeker' is akin to breaking the fourth wall in film or theatre, inviting readers to step into his 'adventure' as a collective experience.

A fresh iteration of seekership emerged in and after the 'long 1960s' (Marwick 1998) in the 'do-it-yourself' sub-genre of countercultural guides and directories. For example, *Alternative England and Wales* (Saunders 1975) included 'Mystical' and 'Therapy' entries in its listings of tools and techniques alongside 'Drugs', 'Sex', 'Community Action', 'The Left' and 'Technology' (ibid.: 2–3). Other directories soon emerged which specialized entirely in 'personal growth' and 'spirituality', such as *The Many Ways of Being: A Guide to Spiritual Groups and Growth Centres in Britain* (Annett 1976) and *The New Times Network: Groups and Centres for Personal Growth* (Adams 1982). The seekership function is explicit in trade titles such as *The Seeker's Handbook: The Complete Guide to Spiritual Pathfinding* (Lash 1990), *The Seeker's Guide: A New Age Resource Book* (Button and Bloom 1992) and *The Seeker's Guide: Making Your Life a Spiritual Adventure* (Lesser 1999). Each invites the reader to engage with multiple 'paths', 'resources' and 'adventures'.

Although seeking became associated with post-Christian identities around this time, there is a substantial Christian literature which can be read as vying for the same symbolic capital. For example, reflections by Christian campus activists in the US were published as *Search for the Sacred: The New Spiritual Quest*, including chapters called 'Seeking Truth' and 'The Search for Community' (Bloy 1972: vii–viii). In the UK, *Priestland's Progress: One Man's Search for Christianity Now* by the BBC correspondent Gerald Priestland (1981) described his exploration of Christianity which led him, finally, to join the Religious Society of Friends. And the conversion to Greek Orthodoxy of another BBC journalist, Peter France, is described in *Journey: A Spiritual Odyssey* (France 1988).

All these sources (and many more could be cited) illustrate a substantial popular literature modelling the role of the seeker as a response to the accelerated plurality of life-worlds especially in and after the long 1960s. But since at least the interwar period, through searching amongst multiple authorities, readers have been invited to imagine themselves as 'fellow seekers' in a practical tradition: 'not as the scholar but as the ordinary man [sic] who tries to find God in daily life' (Landau 1945 [1935]: 5). The cumulative evidence suggests that seeking is a recognizable behaviour, that it is social and collective rather than idiosyncratic and charismatic, and that it is a sensible orientation to the symbolic bonanza of late modern religion/s.

**Three Vernacular Biographies**
A tale is not a series of words but a sequence of events and actions that make sense (Burkert 1996: 57–58)

I now test this model of seeking against three illustrative biographies by subjects who, like Landau (1945 [1935]: 5), are not scholars and do not belong to elites or institutions but identify as 'the ordinary man [sic]'. Each engages multiple authorities and through publication comes to function as an authority in their own right. Each biography is explicitly articulated in terms of a search or quest. Each was first published in paperback in the UK in the early 2000s: two by local publishing houses, one by a trade publisher. The authors come from different geographies: the rural south-west of England, metropolitan London, and the Isle of Skye. Each was born in the post-war period and thus serve as a UK sample of the 'generation of seekers' described in the US context by Wade Clark Roof (1993): that is, the so-called 'baby boom' cohort born between 1946 and 1962 following the privations of the 1939–1945 war. Each hails from a natal Christian background and each in various ways has 'lapsed': the first (Kathy Jones, Glastonbury) to form a new Pagan religion, the second (Isabel Losada, London) to explore an open or nonformative position, and the third (Myles Campbell, Skye) to return to a form of Presbyterianism. Two are women, one is a man, and all are white.

My first case study is an interview transcript edited by Alison Leonard from her collection *Living in Godless Times: Tales of Spiritual Travellers* (2001). An adult educator, Leonard stresses the exemplary function of her book: 'What the spiritual field lacks more than anything else … is a collection of role models, guides, companions on the way' (ibid.: 10). By role models she means exemplary seekers (ibid.):

> I longed for people whom I respected to say to me: 'Look, I followed my inner promptings and this is how it's turned out for me. It'll be different for you, no doubt. But maybe there's something in my story that will help and support you'.

Leonard recommends reading her interviews in a 'spirit of open enquiry' referring to her own search as a prototype: 'I had been brought up a Christian in the Anglican and Methodist churches, I had become a Quaker, and I was developing interests in Buddhist meditation, Ignatian-style visualization and Goddess stories' (ibid.). Notably she describes a 'sense of lack which propelled me out of the mainstream Christian faith and into a lifetime of seeking' (ibid.: 11).[5]

My example from Leonard's cast of 'spiritual travellers' is Kathy Jones whose biography is entitled 'Embodying the Goddess' (Jones 2001). Like all three case studies, this text is rich in content and circumstance, in this case of post-1960s countercultural and 'New Age' religion, to which I cannot do justice. At the same time key stages or functions in Jones's narrative illustrate the structure of the search described by Propp and Burkert.

Kathy Jones was born in 1947 in Gateshead on the River Tyne in northeast England. She grew up in a nominally Christian but functionally secular household. 'My parents were not religious at all', she recalls, 'but they sent me to Methodist Sunday school, I think to make me a good girl' (Jones 2001: 240). Around the age of 12, she tells us, 'I really fell in love with Jesus. It was a very passionate thing. I would go to church three times a Sunday. Sang a lot of hymns, loved it' (ibid.). She was baptized 'in front of everybody, getting sprinkled with water [and] went into quite mystical raptures' (ibid.). At the age of 16 or 17, however, 'sex came along ... it was the sixties, the sexual revolution, and I'm afraid Jesus lost out' (ibid.). After receiving a university degree in psychology and physiology, Jones worked as a researcher for the BBC documentary programme *Horizon*. Feeling unsettled—'the relationships I was having were always going wrong'—she visited friends in Morocco who were 'on a spiritual journey' (ibid.: 240–241):

> Something happened when I was there. I was looking at this mountain, and at the pilgrims walking up it, and I realized that there was more to life than what I'd known. There was this whole area of life that I knew nothing about. All these people, following so many traditions. There were books to read and things to explore.

Jones tells us that she 'began to meditate' and to read 'all sorts of spiritual books, east and west' (ibid.: 241). She left her job and moved to rural Wales, which from the early 1970s began to accommodate experiments in self-sufficiency and communal living as part of an 'alternative Wales'.[6] Jones lived there for several years, summarizing her experience as 'back to the earth, self-sufficiency. I dug the earth, planted vegetables, chopped wood' (ibid.). She began 'a spiritual practice' consisting in 'so many hours of reading, so many hours of meditation' which she followed for five years (ibid.: 242). In terms of legitimating her practice, she tells us that 'there was no one to ask, how do I do this, no one to query whether it was a good idea' and asserts that she was 'anti-guru' and 'driven to do it myself' (ibid.). However, we also know (because she tells us) that she had 'read Taoism, Buddhism, those sort of things' as well as books by Alice Bailey (ibid.; on Bailey as a 'New Age' authority, see Sutcliffe 2003: 45–54). Jones also mentions attending a conference at Findhorn in the early 1970s with 'hundreds' of participants, and practising full moon meditations in the Bailey tradition with her friends who had re-settled from Morocco to Glastonbury (Bowman 2005). Jones herself later moved to Glastonbury as part of a 'whole group' of 'spiritual explorers' (Jones 2001: 244). Here, she became involved in a women's group 'reading all the feminist books, Mary Daly in particular' and participated in the protest camp at the Greenham Common air base which stored US nuclear missiles from 1981 onwards (ibid.: 245).[7] Her encounters with the UK goddess movement stimulated her to create a 'sacred drama' based on Inanna's descent to the underworld (also discussed by Burkert 1996: 61–62) in which, as she writes, 'we experienced the Goddess energy. We experienced Her' (Jones 2001: 246–247). As she explains (ibid.: 247):

> I began to experience different goddesses ... For instance, Green Tara [who] is the Tibetan goddess of compassion. Someone had given me a poster, an image of Green Tara [which] I'd just bunged up on the wall. I had a desk underneath this picture, and it was like someone tapped me on the shoulder and said, 'Look at me'. I heard her say, in my head, 'I am Green Tara. Find out about me, write a play about me'.

Kathy Jones's narrative ends in the late 1990s, but the subsequent history of the Goddess Temple in Glastonbury, which she co-founded in 2000 on the authority of Inanna (Sumeria) and Green Tara (Tibet) amongst others, can be followed on relevant websites.[8]

Despite her disavowal of 'gurus' and assertion of the value of self-enquiry, as asserted in the sub-heading 'A Lone Development of Spirituality' (ibid.: 241), Kathy Jones's own evidence suggests that she is socialized throughout her search via her interactions with numerous texts, persons and groups. From this perspective, her avowedly personal story illustrates a generational narrative in which 'secular' countercultural exploration, including sex and drugs, mixes with 'spiritual' traditions, including rejection of natal Christianity for the allure of goddesses both 'other' and 'indigenous'. The process of her search from secularized Methodism to new Paganism illustrates the range of content available to 'fill' the gap between 'lack' and 'lack liquidated' in the pluralized 'lifeworld'. Establishing the Goddess Temple brings her search to a close.[9]

In contrast to Jones's resolution of her quest, my second case study, *The Battersea Park Road to Enlightenment* (Losada 2001), describes a process of apparently endless search. Isabel Losada's narrative is propelled via snow-balling contacts with multiple individuals and groups. The perpetual motion of her narrative is confirmed by the title of the epilogue, 'standing in the middle of the road', in which she ends the relationship with her newly-found romantic partner, the search for whom the book has largely been about. Losada's playful and self-deprecating voice also contrasts noticeably with Jones's earnestness. 'I am blessed with wanton curiosity. I want to find out how to be absurdly happy every day', she begins. She continues: 'You know those people who always radiate cheerful optimism whatever is going on in their lives? Nauseating, aren't they? I want to become one of those' (ibid.: 1).

We can compare this ironic tone with a similar enquiry into the biographical impact of the 'plurality of life-worlds'. In *Shopping for God: A Sceptic's Search for Value in Britain's Spiritual Market Place*, Roland Howard (2001: 1) announces:

> I am loath to explain the gritty little details that forced me onto the road of what Americans might call 'spiritual questing', because they are so banal. Describing these spurs is akin to exposing myself in a personal ad: 'Boring, neurotic 37-year-old male, NSOH, WLTM *Meaning of Life* for fun and spiritual fulfilment'.[10]

In the same way that Kathy Jones illustrates a wider counter-cultural sensibility, the self-deprecatory voices of Isabel Losada and Howard illustrate a more than personal story: in this case, the 'Human Potential' scene of the 1970s and 1980s, driven by psychotherapeutically-inflected goals of 'personal growth'.[11] Where Jones's narrative is characterized by a sincere tone of rural protest and renewal, Losada's voice is knowingly irreverent and playful. Metropolitan London is the location of most of her explorations and the consumption of a user-friendly 'spirituality' bundle is her goal. And where Jones is published by a local niche press (Floris, Edinburgh), Losada is published by a multinational conglomerate (Bloomsbury, London).[12]

Isabel Losada was born in the US to a Spanish father and English mother and raised largely by her grandmother in England from the age of six months (Losada 2001: 1–2). She worked as an actress before becoming, like her mother before her, a single parent. At the age of 26 she finds herself 'horribly stuck' (ibid.: 4) so a friend advises her to undergo the Insight seminar, a week-long human potential programme developed in the US and available in London from 1978.[13] Participation strongly affects Losada: she describes it as being 'converted' to the practice of 'self-awareness' which reminds her of 'the words of Christ, "The kingdom of God is within you"' (ibid.: 24).

Like Kathy Jones, Isabel Losada received a Christian upbringing. She describes her younger self as a 'good evangelical' who 'invited God into my life, admitting that I'd made a pretty hopeless job of it' and that 'this was where my Road had really begun' (ibid.: 41). But she discovers, like Jones, 'a catch':

> I had been converted in a church where they believed in following exactly what the Bible says—according to how they understand it. They understand it to say 'Don't have sex outside marriage'. I was puzzled. Nowhere could I find Christ saying, 'I have come in order to tell you not to have sex with your boyfriend'. (Ibid.: 41–42)

She decides that 'the evanglicals were too much' and moves to 'my local C of E [Church of England] with the traditional empty pews' (ibid.: 42). But despite the 'sweet elderly vicar and the good people of his flock', she finds that 'slowly and surely, like all good members of the Church of England, I ... finally stopped going at all' (ibid.). Losada now turns to the meat of her tale: her participation in numerous courses, events and techniques including an Anglican retreat, T'ai Chi, astrology, tantric sex, co-dependency, colonic irrigation, rebirthing, past lives, Rolfing, anger release therapy, hypnotism, and working with angelic guides (see her appendix for listings of teachers, ibid.: 239–246). The cumulative effect of her narrative depends upon the bathos between her exploration of these practices' capacity to offer 'Enlightenment' and her simultaneous search for 'Mister Right' as her ideal romantic partner. Thus the title of chapter 2, 'T'ai Chi and Optional Moral Decline' (ibid.: 25), links what she calls this 'rather magical' practice (ibid.: 29) with her attraction to her teacher, whom she describes as 'a gorgeously assured, lithe, beautiful and sensitive presence' (ibid.: 26). Similarly, the title of chapter 6—'Tantric Sex—Yes! Yes! Yes!'—celebrates (profane) orgasm as much as (sacred) Tantra through its reference to the famously faked orgasm by the heroine Sally in the romantic comedy *When Harry Met Sally* (1989) which has become a popular culture meme. Losada's irreverent juggling of sacred and profane continues in the final chapter which describes an angelic guide retreat led by William Bloom, an established New Age teacher, under the title 'Angels, Fairies and Bald Northerners' (Bloom n.d.). The last term teasingly references Losada's newly-found romantic partner, Mark, with whom she attends the retreat on the Isle of Man. Bloom teaches participants how to follow guided meditations, to attune to nature, and to 'play' with 'invisible energy' (Losada 2001: 220):

> I had to send invisible energy out of the top of my head, over in a circle and into his energy field, then down through what would have been his roots if he'd been a tree, then back into my roots, up through me and out of my head again towards him ... Then William asked us to reverse the loop so he was sending his energy to me and I swear I did feel a subtle energy, a something.

Despite her appreciation of the retreat, her relationship with her partner Mark vacillates. She concludes: 'I love the bald northerner ... but somehow there has always been a somehow' (ibid.: 236). But it is Mark who makes the decision to part since Isabel admits 'I didn't have the guts' (ibid.: 237). However, she is quick to add: 'I don't think I have a problem with commitment as long as I think it's to the right person. Damned elusive, the right people, aren't they?' (ibid.: 237–238). Where Kathy Jones's tone is serious and committed, Isabel Losada's is playful and ironic.[14] Despite these different tones and outcomes both accounts are structured as a search amongst multiple authorities.

My third and final example is the co-authored narrative by Myles and Margaret Campbell entitled *Island Conversion: The Transition of a Gaelic Poet from Sceptic to Believer* (Campbell and Campbell 2011).[15] Born in Staffin, Isle of Skye, in 1944, Myles Campbell's narrative is formed by his Free Church Presbyterian upbringing which is even further decentred from the UK ecclesiastical (state) power than Kathy Jones (as a secular Methodist) and Isabel Losada (as a US-born Londoner). Skye is a Gaelic-speaking landscape historically shaped by Catholicism but since the Reformation subject to Presbyterianism. Like Kathy Jones, Myles Campbell's narrative is published by a local press.[16] Unlike Jones, who settled in Glastonbury after her Tyneside upbringing, Campbell is indigenous to the Hebrides; he was born on Skye and completed *Island Conversion* in his natal township. His narrative therefore differs from both Jones and Losada in representing a return to an extant tradition rather than creating a new tradition (Jones) or oscillating between multiple traditions (Losada). His tale also differs in including his spouse as an integral actor, but whereas Isabel Losada's 'Mr Right' is contingent, Myles's relationship with his spouse Margaret is unconditional, as signalled by her co-authorship.

Myles Campbell worked as a seaman and a clerk before training to be a schoolteacher. His father was a Free Church of Scotland lay preacher, and devout Presbyterianism played a formative early role: 'I attended church twice on the Sabbath, plus Sunday School and a prayer meeting on Wednesday. There was also family worship in the morning and at night. The Bible was looked on as the inspired word of God' (Campbell and Campbell 2011: 11).

Campbell acknowledges the 'profound effect' of this upbringing but also notes the 'serious doubts' he began to entertain as a teenager. These were triggered by reading a children's encyclopaedia 'written from a contemporary Anglo-centric, secular point of view' which confronted him with 'two conflicting world views' in which the theory of evolution 'seemed in complete contradiction to the creation story in the Bible' (ibid.: 11). An 'intellectual rebellion' was the result (ibid.: ix) which led him to become 'an agnostic and rationalist' (ibid.: 12). Campbell's approach from the outset is manifestly earnest (ibid.: 106): 'I said to myself: "Before I die I want to find out the truth about the world"'.

The bulk of the book consists in a narrative 'search for the truth' (ibid.: 138). Campbell refers throughout to canonical writers on comparative religion such as Carl Jung, William James, Evelyn Underhill, Rudolph Otto and Mircea Eliade, as well as Hume, Nietzsche and other European sceptics and naturalists. Until the age of 50, he maintains his acquired naturalistic outlook. Then he mentions what he calls his 'first brush with the supernatural' which consists in a 'weird or uncanny' experience of hearing footsteps outside his front door. His cat also experiences this, and when the cat becomes ill and dies, Campbell interprets this as a *manadh*, a Gaelic word meaning 'a supernatural omen, apparition or warning' (ibid.: 45-47). Next, a brief encounter with a roadworker—the most apparently mundane of occupations and settings—in a Fort William public house inspires Campbell to complete his poem 'A' Càradh an Rathaid' ('Mending the Road') (1988). Its final sections hint at a mature turn away from scepticism (ibid.: 39):

> Don't believe, don't believe/
> that it goes nowhere
> (said the old man of the road) ...
> For now, fill the holes
> and go forward:
> everyone must travel/pass on—
> and be mending.

Otto's famous concept of the 'numinous' and, later, Eliade's idea of 'sacred space', provide further waystations for Campbell as he begins his theological homecoming. His personal relationship with Margaret plays the pivotal role in resolving his felt lack. As young adults Margaret and Myles had briefly been together. Now they resume contact, guided by dreams and supernatural events: 'pushed by powers ... beyond us to come together again, to write this book and to tell this story' (Campbell and Campbell 2011: 3). After her return as a widow to the family croft on the Isle of Lewis, Margaret dreams of a man standing at a gate into a field whom she recognizes as Myles (ibid.: 4). She telephones him, they cautiously renew contact, and eventually they marry. After Myles's retirement, and their resumption of Free Church worship, a series of supernatural events occurs. This involves a stick or pole for opening the loft hatch, which on five occasions falls from its secure hook on the wall with no rational explanation (ibid.: 85ff.). Each 'fall of the stick' is interpreted as a *manadh* by means of which '"someone" was trying to tell us something', which they link to milestones in their new life not least the completion of *Island Conversion* (ibid.: 85, 86). Upon the second fall of the stick, Myles is prompted to clear old books and papers from the loft (to which the stick, of course, is the means of access). One morning when Margaret awakes with the name 'John Bunyan' on her mind, the first book Myles happens to handle in the loft is his father's copy of Bunyan's *Pilgrim's Progress* in Gaelic. That same day their minister makes a surprise visit (ibid.: 88):

> After the fall of the stick, and the Bunyan incident in the morning, it was a notable event for ... a 'Man of God' ... to appear ... He explained that he had been looking in the phone book for another number and that our number kept cropping up, and that he was, as it were, prompted to visit us ... [I]t was rather strange that he had come on that precise day and was 'prompted' by the Spirit to come.

In other words, the fall of the stick which opens the loft prompts a clear-out of content in which Bunyan's Puritan allegory of life as a journey is rediscovered (notably his father's copy, in Gaelic) and the Free Church minister visits their house for the first time. No wonder that Myles Campbell comes to view the place where the stick falls as an Eliadean 'sacred place'; as he puts it, 'our stick is our *axis mundi*, the means by which the transcendent communicated to us' (ibid.: 115). To mark this sequence of events, he sets up a table on the spot in the hall where the stick first fell 'with a candle on it to represent the eternal presence of God, a copy of the illustration on the Turin Shroud to represent Christ and a white stone to represent the Holy Spirit' (ibid.). This 'shrine' (ibid.: 116) would be an unusual item to find in a Free Presbyterian household but it vividly demonstrates Campbell's vernacular integration of Gaelic *manadh*, comparative religion and Reformed theology.

The narrative must be understood in turn within a long tradition of supernatural discourse in the Scottish Highlands and Islands, especially 'second sight' (*dà-shealladh*) or the ability to 'see' the future.[17] There is also a more recent history of Christian home mission leading to personal conversion during local revivals and 'awakenings' such as on the Hebridean islands of Lewis in 1949–1952 and North Uist in 1957–1958.[18] However, whereas for Kathy Jones and Isabel Losada, personal experience and Christian tradition appear irreconcilable, there appears to be no such problem for Myles Campbell. His statement 'I have all along been guided by a power hugely greater than myself' (ibid.: 116) might be comprehensible to Kathy Jones if put in a different theological lexicon, but it appears to contrast markedly with the objects of human potential pursued by Isabel Losada. Thus Campbell can conclude confidently: 'I now have no doubts whatsoever that the supernatural is as real as anything can be, and that is because of what has happened in my own life' (ibid.: 117). This enables him finally to 'mend the road' (in the words of his poem above):

> I have come to the end of my search and I have discovered that the truth is stranger than I could ever have imagined. Some poets, philosophers, scholars and thinkers of various kinds have helped me along the way. But, looking back on my life ... I have all along been guided by a power hugely greater than myself. (Ibid.: 116)

To recap, I have described above key details in three vernacular biographies of seekers from different parts of the UK. Each has very different content—Pagan, Human Potential, Presbyterian—but all testify to a common practice of a search for symbolic resources to resolve lack or discontent. Across the three narratives lies a tension between a modernist representation of singular truth as the outcome, as in the case of Kathy Jones and Myles Campbell, and a more postmodern and irreverent play of signifiers in which closure is deferred, as for Isabel Losada.[19]

## Seeking as a Late Modern Tradition

> We like a tale to be retold. (Burkert 1996: 62)

Earlier I introduced Colin Campbell's theory of seekership as the key structural component of the cultic milieu. Echoing the problem of 'lack' identified by Propp and Dundes, Campbell defined seekers as expressing relative deprivation insofar as they adopt 'a problem-solving perspective while defining conventional religious institutions and beliefs as inadequate' (Campbell 2002 [1972]: 15). In other words, seekers feel worse off in respect of the quality of their 'spiritual' capital than others to whom they compare themselves. As a New Age informant told this author in 1997: 'the church dissatisfies me. I know all the things they teach. I want more, you know?' (Sutcliffe 2003: 195).

Because the cultic milieu is 'united and identified by the existence of an ideology of seekership and by seekership institutions' (Campbell 2002 [1972]: 19), seeking is as much an effect of the wider environment as its cause. Campbell later expanded the scope of his model to include a 'population of incipient seekers' who were 'sympathetically disposed towards some form of spirituality but not participating members of any particular church' (Campbell 1982: 236). This led him to propose a meta-shift in the late modern religious field 'not so much from belief to unbelief as from belief to seekership' (ibid.: 237).

If we read our three biographies through a model based in the work of Propp, Burkert and Campbell, we find a socialized and relatively predictable disposition whose divergent contents cannot disguise an underlying common functionality. Thinking about the detailed itineraries of Kathy Jones, Isabel Losada and Myles Campbell in terms of a more general model of seekership helps to explain how a longstanding vernacular tradition of search has been reconstituted, communicated and legitimated in late modernity. As Sutcliffe (2000: 22) puts it: 'as seekers become models for action ... they themselves come to function as "exemplary persons"'. Rather than expressing an idiosyncratic disposition, seeking has emerged as a rational practice with both 'cultural' and 'natural' supports.

In theoretical terms, seekership can be understood as a practical response to symbolic 'lack'. For Kathy Jones and Myles Campbell, their 'lack' appears eventually to be 'liquidated' at which point the search is formally complete. For Losada, the 'lack' remains open and alive: formally incomplete. In each case seekership is better understood as dynamic adaptation to a multipolar field of action formed by the 'pluralization of life-worlds' (Berger, Berger and Kellner 1974: 62) rather than a pathological expression of 'floundering about among religions' (Lofland and Stark 1965: 869). On this evidence seekership represents a late-modern tradition of practice which has re-emerged to equip practitioners to navigate a complex, heterogenous field characterized by the increasing multiplication of authorities (plural) with the concomitant relativization of authority (singular). Moreover, as signalled at the start, its transposability across different fields suggests that seekership is not confined to the cultic milieu nor even to the ostensibly 'religious'. As Campbell (2002 [1972]: 15) argues:

the basic seekership belief that truth (or enlightenment) is an esoteric commodity only to be attained after suitable preparation and a 'quest' exists outside the purely mystical religious tradition. It can apply equally well to the search for interpretations and explanations of non-religious phenomena and in situations where there is no expectation of 'revelatory experiences' and even in the context of the pursuit of worldly success, health or consolation.

When reading this quotation, episodes from all three biographies come to mind. On their basis I argue that subjects learn how to seek through socialization into a discourse and practice that is culturally and historically widely distributed. The searches described above should therefore be understood as a form of late modern tradition with deep roots in narrative and biology.

## Notes

1 This formulation is indebted to Matthew Wood's (2007: 70–74) model of tension between the 'formative' and 'nonformative' impact on subjects which results from exposure to multiple religious authorities.
2 For an earlier rehearsal of Burkert's argument, see Chapter 1, 'The Organisation of Myth', especially pp. 5–10 and 14–18, and Chapter 2, 'The Persistence of Ritual', especially 'The Biological Approach', pp. 35–39, in Burkert 1979.
3 Dundes presented this dialectic in his PhD thesis on the morphology of Native American folktales (Dundes 1962), describing it as 'a move from disequilibrium to equilibrium', where disequilibrium is 'a state of surplus or of lack' (ibid.: 113–114). He concludes that 'folktales can consist simply of relating how abundance was lost or how a lack was liquidated' in the sense that 'something in excess may be lost or something lost or stolen may be found' (ibid.: 114).
4 Torrance's focus on the 'necessary liminal passage' is helpful, but his totalizing claims are uncomfortably reminiscent of the 'monomyth' of the 'hero' as 'the destiny of Everyman' in *The Hero with a Thousand Faces* (Campbell 1964 [1949]: 36). I cannot agree with Torrance that 'the spiritual quest can include both the intellectual and scientific search for truth and the religious pursuit of salvation, which are fundamentally akin' (Torrance 1994: 55).
5 See the official web page of Manchester Writing School (n.d.).
6 For example, Tipi Valley n.d. and CAT official webpage n.d. See also Saunders 1975 and Preston 1982.
7 See Hipperson n.d. On goddess spirituality at Greenham see Welch 2010.
8 Glastonbury Goddess Temple n.d. and Jones n.d. On the UK goddess movement see Long 1994 and Feraro 2015.
9 Following the logic of the cultic milieu, Jones now serves as a formative authority for other seekers: see Bowman 2014: 260–267.

232  Vernacular Knowledge

10  Abbreviations widely used in digital text messaging: NSOH = 'No Sense of Humour' (an ironic variation on GSOH = 'Good Sense of Humour'); WLTM = 'Would Like to Meet'.
11  For rich US and UK descriptions, see Gustaitis 1969 and St. John 1977.
12  Compare Floris Books official website (n.d.) and Bloomsbury official website (n.d.)
13  See Insight Seminars UK official website (n.d.). The seminar is a well-established format for teaching and learning 'self religion': see Heelas 1982.
14  See Dumit 2001 for an interesting ethnography of 'playing truths' in US New Age. Losada's *The Battersea Park Road to Enlightenment* (2001) was followed by *For Tibet, with Love: A Beginner's Guide to Changing the World* (Losada 2004), *Men!* (Losada 2007)—described as 'the book that answers the question "where are the interesting and available men?"' (see Losada n.d.b)—and *The Battersea Park Road to Paradise* (Losada 2011). Non-committally subtitled 'five adventures in doing and being', *Paradise* confirms *Enlightenment*'s impression that the 'road' remains resolutely open. Losada subsequently published *Sensation: Adventures in Sex, Love and Laughter* (2017) and *The Joyful Environmentalist: How to Practise without Preaching* (2020) and her website carries the slogan 'Think Globally, Act Joyfully' (Losada n.d.a). In 2019 Losada was described in *The Bookseller* as 'the UK's sassiest spiritual author' and voted Mind Body Spirit Writer of the Year by the new spiritualities magazine *Kindred Spirit* (est. 1987) (Russell 2019). For a similar seeker narrative in the 'self help' field, see Power 2018.
15  Myles Campbell (in Gaelic: Maoilios Caimbeul) is a distinguished poet writing in Gaelic and English; a selection of his poems in both languages forms the second part of the book. See Campbell n.d. and Scottish Poetry Library n.d.
16  Islands Book Trust, Balallan, Isle of Lewis: see the official website at www.theislandsbooktrust.com.
17  The classic text is Robert Kirk's *The Secret Commonwealth*, a collection of folklore on second sight, fairies and fauns, gathered in 1691–1692 and published posthumously in 1815 by Walter Scott; see Hunter 2001 for a scholarly edition. See also the two volumes by John Gregorson Campbell, *Superstitions of the Highlands and Islands of Scotland* (1900) and *Witchcraft and Second Sight in the Highlands and Islands* (1902), republished with an informative introduction as *The Gaelic Otherworld* (Black 2005).
18  See the evangelical histories by Peckham 2004, Ferguson 2000 and Lennie 2009.
19  My model predicts a similar structure to atheist, humanist and Islamic biographies. Space precludes detailed discussion but see biologist Ted Schultz's account of his 'personal odyssey' from 'New Ager' to sceptic (1988), journalist Ziauddin Sardar's narrative of his 'journeys' within Islam as a 'sceptical Muslim' (Sardar 2004) and academic Robert Irwin's account of his Sufi search in the 1960s counterculture (Irwin 2011).

## References

Adams, Robert, ed. 1982. *The New Times Network: Groups and Centres for Personal Growth.* London: Routledge and Kegan Paul.

Annett, Stephen, ed. 1976. *The Many Ways of Being: A Guide to Spiritual Groups and Growth Centres in Britain.* London: Abacus/Turnstone Press.

Berger, Peter, Brigitte Berger and Hansfried Kellner. 1974. *The Homeless Mind: Modernization and Consciousness.* Harmondsworth: Penguin.

Black, Ronald, ed. 2005. *The Gaelic Otherworld.* Edinburgh: Birlinn.

Bloom, William. n.d. Official website. https://williambloom.com/ (accessed July 7, 2021).

Bloomsbury. n.d. Official website. http://www.bloomsbury.com (accessed July 7, 2021).

Bloy, Myron, ed. 1972. *Search for the Sacred: The New Spiritual Quest.* New York: Seabury Press.

Boice, Judith. 1990. *At One with All Life: A Personal Journey in Gaian Communities.* Forres: Findhorn Press.

Bowman, Marion. 2005. 'Ancient Avalon, New Jerusalem, Heart Chakra of Planet Earth: The Local and the Global in Glastonbury'. *NUMEN* 52 (2): 157–190. https://doi.org/10.1163/1568527054024722

Bowman, Marion. 2014. 'Vernacular/Lived Religion'. In *Bloomsbury Companion to New Religious Movements*, edited by George D. Chryssides and Benjamin E. Zeller, 253-269. London: Bloomsbury. https://doi.org/10.5040/9781472594518.ch-023

Burkert, Walter. 1979. *Structure and History in Greek Mythology and Ritual.* Berkeley: University of California Press.

Burkert, Walter. 1996. *Creation of the Sacred: Tracks of Biology in Early Religions.* Cambridge, MA: Harvard University Press.

Button, John, and William Bloom, eds. 1992. *The Seeker's Guide: A New Age Resource Book.* London: Aquarian Press.

Campbell, Colin. 1982. 'Some Comments on the New Religious Movements, the New Spirituality and Post-industrial Society'. In *New Religious Movements: A Perspective for Understanding Society*, edited by Eileen Barker, 232-242. Lampeter: Edwin Mellen.

Campbell, Colin. 2002 [1972]. 'The Cult, the Cultic Milieu and Secularization'. In *The Cultic Milieu: Oppositional Subcultures in an Age of Globalization*, edited by Jeffrey Kaplan and Heléne Lööw, 12-25. Walnut Creek, CA: AltaMira Press.

Campbell, Joseph. 1964 [1949]. *The Hero with a Thousand Faces.* Cleveland; New York: World Publishing Company; Meridian Books.

Campbell, Myles. n.d. Official website. http://www.maoilioscaimbeul.co.uk/ (accessed July 7, 2021).

Campbell, Myles, and Margaret Campbell. 2011. *Island Conversion: The Transition of a Gaelic Poet from Sceptic to Believer.* South Lochs: Islands Book Trust.

CAT. n.d. 'History'. *Centre for Alternative Technology.* https://cat.org.uk/history/ (accessed July 11, 2021).

Dumit, Joseph. 2001. 'Playing Truths: Logics of Seeking and the Persistence of the New Age'. *Focaal* 37: 63–75.

Dundes, Alan. 1962. 'The Morphology of North American Indian Folktales'. PhD diss., Indiana University.

Feraro, Shai. 2015. 'Connecting British Wicca with Radical Feminism and Goddess Spirituality during the 1970s and 1980s: The Case Study of Monica Sjöö'. *Journal of Contemporary Religion* 30 (2): 307–321. https://doi.org/10.1080/13537903.2015.1025560

Ferguson, John. 2000. *When God Came Down: An Account of the North Uist Revival 1957-58.* Inverness: Lewis Recordings.

Floris Books. n.d. Official website. http://www.florisbooks.co.uk (accessed July 7, 2021).

France, Peter. 1988. *Journey: A Spiritual Odyssey.* London: Chatto and Windus.

Glastonbury Goddess Temple. n.d. https://goddesstemple.co.uk/ (accessed July 12, 2021).

Gustaitis, Rasa. 1969. *Turning On: One Woman's Trip through Consciousness-Expansion without the Use of Drugs.* London: Weidenfeld and Nicolson.

Heelas, Paul. 1982. 'Californian Self-religions and Socializing the Subjective'. In *New Religious Movements: A Perspective for Understanding Society*, edited by Eileen Barker, 69–85. Lampeter: Edwin Mellen Press.

Herbert, Marie. 1996. *Healing Quest: A Journey of Transformation.* London: Rider; Penguin Random House.

Hipperson, Sarah. n.d. *Greenham Common Women's Peace Camp 1981-2000.* http://www.greenhamwpc.org.uk/ (accessed July 7, 2021).

Howard, Roland. 2001. *Shopping for God: A Sceptic's Search for Value in Britain's Spiritual Market Place.* London: HarperCollins.

Hunter, Michael, ed. 2001. *The Occult Laboratory: Magic, Science and Second Sight in Late Seventeenth Century Scotland.* Woodbridge: Boydell Press.

Insight Seminars UK. n.d. https://www.insightseminarsuk.com/about-insight/ (accessed July 7, 2021).

Irwin, Robert. 2011. *Memoirs of a Dervish: Sufis, Mystics and the Sixties.* London: Profile Books.

Islands Book Trust. n.d. Official website. https://islandsbooktrust.org/ (accessed July 7, 2021).

Jones, Kathy. n.d. *In the Heart of the Goddess.* The website of Kathy Jones. https://kathyjones.co.uk/ (accessed July 7, 2021).

Jones, Kathy. 2001. 'Embodying the Goddess'. In *Living in Godless Times: Tales of Spiritual Travelers*, edited by Alison Leonard, 238–252. Edinburgh: Floris Books.

Landau, Rom. 1945 [1935]. *God is My Adventure: A Book on Modern Mystics, Masters and Teachers.* London: Faber.

Lash, John. 1990. *The Seeker's Handbook: The Complete Guide to Spiritual Pathfinding.* New York: Harmony Books.

Lennie, Tom. 2009. *Glory in the Glen: A History of Evangelical Revivals in Scotland, 1880-1940.* Fearn: Christian Focus.

Leonard, Alison. 2001. 'Introduction: The Decline of Religion and the Rise of Spirituality'. In *Living in Godless Times: Tales of Spiritual Travelers*, edited by Alison Leonard, 7–18. Edinburgh: Floris Books.

Lesser, Elizabeth. 1999. *The Seeker's Guide: Making Your Life a Spiritual Adventure.* New York: Villard Books; Random House. (First published as *The New American Spirituality: A Seeker's Guide*.)

Lewis, James R. 2016. 'Seekers and Subcultures'. In *The Oxford Handbook of New Religious Movements*, vol. 2, edited by James R. Lewis and Inga Tøllefsen, 62–71. New York: Oxford University Press.
https://doi.org/10.1093/oxfordhb/9780190466176.001.0001

Lofland, John, and Rodney Stark. 1965. 'Becoming a World-Saver: A Theory of Conversion to a Deviant Perspective'. *American Sociological Review* 30 (6): 862–875. https://doi.org/10.2307/2090965

Long, Asphodel. 1994. 'The Goddess Movement in Britain Today'. *Feminist Theology* 2 (5): 11–39. https://doi.org/10.1177/096673509400000502

Losada, Isabel. n.d.a. Official website. http://www.isabellosada.com (accessed July 7, 2021).

Losada, Isabel. n.d.b. Books: 'Men!' Official website. https://www.isabellosada.com/men (accessed July 12, 2021).

Losada, Isabel. 2001. *The Battersea Park Road to Enlightenment*. London: Bloomsbury.

Losada, Isabel. 2004. *For Tibet, with Love: A Beginner's Guide to Changing the World*. London: Bloomsbury.

Losada, Isabel. 2007. *Men!* London: Virgin.

Losada, Isabel. 2011. *The Battersea Park Road to Paradise*. London: Watkins.

Losada, Isabel. 2017. *Sensation: Adventures in Sex, Love and Laughter*. London: Watkins.

Losada, Isabel. 2020. *The Joyful Environmentalist: How to Practise without Preaching*. London: Watkins.

Manchester Writing School. n.d. 'Alison Leonard'. https://www.manchesterwritingschool.co.uk/published-students/alison-leonard.html (accessed April 4, 2022).

Marwick, Arthur. 1998. *The Sixties: Cultural Revolution in Britain, France, Italy and the United States, 1958-1974*. Oxford: Oxford University Press.

Peckham, Colin N. 2004. *Sounds from Heaven: The Revival on the Isle of Lewis, Scotland, 1949–1952*. Fearn: Christian Focus.

Power, Marianne. 2018. *Help Me! One Woman's Quest to Find out if Self-help Really Can Change Her Life*. London: Macmillan.

Preston, Jon, ed. 1982. *Alternative Wales*. Llandeilo; Newport: Orkid Books; Cilgwyn Publications.

Priestland, Gerald. 1981. *Priestland's Progress: One Man's Search for Christianity Now*. London: Ariel Books; BBC.

Primiano, Leonard Norman. 2012. 'Manifestations of the Religious Vernacular: Ambiguity, Power and Creativity'. In *Vernacular Religion in Everyday Life: Expressions of Belief*, edited by Marion Bowman and Ülo Valk, 382–394. Sheffield; Bristol, CT: Equinox Publishing.

Propp, Vladimir. 1998 [1968]. *Morphology of the Folktale*. Austin: University of Texas Press.

Roof, Wade Clark. 1993. *A Generation of Seekers: The Spiritual Journeys of the Baby Boom Generation*. San Francisco: HarperSanFrancisco.

Russell, Leah. 2019. 'Kindred Spirit Award Winners'. *Kindred Spirit*. https://kindredspirit.co.uk/2019/08/30/kindred-spirit-award-winners-19/ (accessed July 7, 2021).

Sandars, Nancy K. 1972 [1960]. *The Epic of Gilgamesh*. Harmondsworth: Penguin.

Sardar, Ziauddin. 2004. *Desperately Seeking Paradise: Journeys of a Sceptical Muslim*. London: Granta.

Saunders, Nicholas. 1975. *Alternative England and Wales*. London: The Author.

Schultz, Ted. 1988. 'A Personal Odyssey through the New Age'. In *Not Necessarily the New Age: Critical Essays*, edited by Robert Basil, 337–358. New York: Prometheus Books.

Scottish Poetry Library. n.d. 'Maoilios Caimbeul'. https://www.scottishpoetrylibrary.org.uk/poet/maoilios-caimbeul/ (accessed July 28, 2021).
Spangler, David. 1996. *Pilgrim in Aquarius*. Forres: Findhorn Press.
St. John, John Richard. 1977. *Travels in Inner Space: One Man's Exploration of Encounter Groups, Meditation and Altered States of Consciousness*. London: Gollancz.
Sutcliffe, Steven. 2000. 'Seekers and Gurus in the Modern World'. In *Beyond New Age: Exploring Alternative Spirituality*, edited by Steven Sutcliffe and Marion Bowman, 17-36. Edinburgh: Edinburgh University Press.
Sutcliffe, Steven. 2003. *Children of the New Age: A History of Spiritual Practices*. London: Routledge.
Sutcliffe, Steven. 2017. 'Seekership Revisited: Explaining Traffic in and out of New Religions'. In *Visioning New and Minority Religions: Projecting the Future*, edited by Eugene V. Gallagher, 33-46. Abingdon; New York: Routledge.
Tattersall, Timothy T. 1996. *Journey: An Adventure of Love and Healing*. Forres: Findhorn Press.
Tipi Valley. n.d. *Diggers and Dreamers*. https://www.diggersanddreamers.org.uk/community/tipi-valley/ (accessed July 11, 2021).
Torrance, Robert M. 1994. *The Spiritual Quest: Transcendence in Myth, Religion, and Science*. Berkeley: University of California Press. https://doi.org/10.1525/9780520920163
Welch, Christina. 2010. 'The Spirituality of, and at, Greenham Common Peace Camp'. *Feminist Theology* 18 (2): 230–248. https://doi.org/10.1177/0966735009348668
Wood, Matthew. 2007. *Possession, Power and the New Age: Ambiguities of Authority in Neo-Liberal Societies*. Aldershot: Ashgate.

Chapter 10

# Practices of *Niggunim*: Contemporary Jewish Song in a Vernacular Religion Perspective*

*Ruth Illman***

## Introduction

As the traditional Hasidic way of life was extinguished during the nineteenth century, the last phase of 'authentic' Jewish mysticism came to a close. Thus argued the prominent researcher of Jewish mysticism, Gershom Scholem, who stated that Jewish mysticism 'has become again what it was in the beginning: the esoteric wisdom of small groups of men out of touch with life and without any influence in it' (1961 [1941]: 34). To be sure, Kabbalah and other mystical practices were gaining ground and

---

\* This chapter is based on a specific theme addressed as part of a larger research project, previously published in my book *Music and Religious Change among Progressive Jews in London: Being Liberal and Doing Traditional* (Lanham, MD: Lexington Books, 2018).

** **Ruth Illman** is the Director of the Donner Institute for Research in Religion and Culture in Åbo/Turku, Finland. She holds the title of Docent in the study of religions at Åbo Akademi University and in the history of religions at Uppsala University, as well as doctoral degrees in both the study of religions (2004) and Jewish studies (2018). Her main research interests include contemporary Judaism, interreligious dialogue, religion and the arts (especially music) as well as ethnographic research methodologies. Among her latest publications are the article 'Knowing, Being, and Doing Religion: Introducing an Analytical Model for Researching Vernacular Religion', in *Temenos: Nordic Journal of Comparative Religion* 56.2 (2020) and the books *Music and Religious Change among Progressive Jews in London: Being Liberal and Doing Traditional* (Lexington, 2018) and *Theology and the Arts: Engaging Faith* (Routledge, 2013/2016) co-authored with W. Alan Smith. Since 2016 she has been the editor of the scholarly journal *Nordisk judaistik / Scandinavian Jewish Studies*. She is also the director of the *Boundaries of Jewish Identities in Contemporary Finland* research project.

attracting new practitioners already during Scholem's time as the countercultural movement popularized esotericism in society at large (Myers 2011: 177). But Scholem did not regard this as an authentic continuation of the age-old Jewish tradition he was dedicated to studying, claiming that there was no genuine mysticism left in his time (Huss, Pasi and von Stuckrad 2010: 1).

Nevertheless, practices stemming from Kabbalah and Jewish mystical sources have since the turn of the millennium become more popular than ever inside as well as outside Jewish communities in Israel, Europe and North America, relocating and reframing traditional practices for a late-modern, urban, liberal and inclusive spiritual milieu (Cohen 2016: 492–494; Huss 2007b: 107; Weissler 2011: 41). Novel perspectives and methods are therefore introduced, such as ethnography and critical methodologies adapted from psychology and social sciences, in order to broaden the understanding of what Jewish mysticism can be and who can be involved in it (Wexler 2012: 123). Among scholars it remains debated whether such contemporary practices are to be seen as 'authentic' continuations of the tradition or merely as vulgar popularizations, superficially motivated by the prospect of making money by commodifying the heritage for the contemporary spiritual market (Huss 2011: 357–362; Scholem, Garb and Idel 2007 [1972]: 685).

This chapter's point of departure is the controversy over 'authenticity' in research on Jewish mysticism. A vernacular religion perspective is applied as a means of untying the knot that has formed through the unfruitful juxtaposing of classic and contemporary Jewish mysticism. Discourses of authenticity are exemplified by a case study dealing with contemporary practices of *niggunim*[1] singing: (mostly) wordless melodies sung as a means of elevating the soul to God, repairing the world and strengthening the divine presence in the world, *Shekinah* (Weissler 2011: 74). *Niggunim* is a practice with roots in Hasidic Judaism, which is currently experiencing a renaissance within contemporary Jewish spirituality (Huss 2007b: 108; Kahn-Harris and Moberg 2012: 101–102). Ethnographic material has been gathered among Jews from progressive milieus in London to shed light on the practice at large, and this chapter analyses how the practitioners reflect upon authenticity (Illman 2018).

## Ambiguity, Power and Creativity

Vernacular religion is defined as 'religion as it is lived: as human beings encounter, understand, interpret, and practice it' (Primiano 1995: 44). In this perspective, a nuanced view of religiosity is introduced in which private and public, historical and cultural context, belief and practice, materiality, embodiment, social class and power are interlaced into a comprehensive image of the religious landscape (Bowman and Valk 2012: 5). Leonard Primiano first introduced the concept as a tool for researching religion as a part of everyday life in a theoretically and methodologically rigorous way but without being restrained by the troublesome dichotomy between 'official' and 'folk' religion (Primiano 1995: 52). This juxtaposition automatically seemed to imply the inferiority of the latter, equating it with the 'distorted', 'popular' (in a negative sense) and 'superficial', simultaneously implying the existence of a category of 'pure', 'undistorted' and 'genuine' religion untainted by ordinary people's thoughts, interpretations and practices (Bowman 2014: 102; Howard 2011: 6).

The objective of vernacular religion research can be described as studying religion in practice without the pejorative burden implied by approaches that regard religion as a neatly compartmentalized phenomenon (Bowman 2014: 102; Primiano 2012: 383). Thus, the problems involved in studying religion from a platform based on dichotomies are acknowledged and the black-and-white opposition of different forms of religious knowledge is seen as unable to render ethnographic accounts meaningful and to illuminate contemporary religiosity: 'Vernacular religious theory understands religion as the continuous art of individual interpretation and negotiation of any number of influential sources' (Primiano 2012: 384).

Not only has the binary differentiation between official and personal crumbled in contemporary, ethnographically driven research on religion—so too has the idea of religious and secular as mutually exclusive categories (Nynäs, Illman and Martikainen 2015: 219–220). The diversified process through which human beings form religious knowledge and practice often includes elements from several different traditions as well as from secular sources such as popular culture. This development appears paradoxical only against the background of a narrow, theoretical apprehension of religion as a downright intellectual search for a plausible claim to truth. One finds increasing interest in how theologically unsystematic life-views are formed through everyday religious conversations and practices—and how these relate to institutional religion

(Goldstein 2015: 126; Whitehead 2013: 15). Therefore, it is important to maintain the dialectic between institutional and everyday practice, official and personal, included in the original linguistic notion of vernacular while leaving the binary perspective behind (Goldstein 2015: 138; Howard 2011: 5–6).

Flexibility, fluidity and change become keywords in research on vernacular religion, focusing on the dialogue between self-reflexivity and external conditions such as physical and mental dispositions, environment, family, political and economic conditions, education, media and so on (Bowman and Valk 2012: 5). Furthermore, human religiosity always includes a measure of artistry, innovation and adaption. Therefore, the vernacular approach is especially well suited to studying creative forms of religiosity (Primiano 1995: 43). Indeed, the notion of vernacular is often associated with expressive forms of culture, paying attention to local detail (Bowman and Valk 2012: 16; Howard 2011: 5). That is the case also in this chapter. Through speech, music and song, dance, ritual and drama as well as foodways, dress and routines, performed religion offers the researcher an insight into the versatile world of vernacular religion (Bowman and Valk 2012: 7–8; Primiano 1995: 45; 2012: 385). Religion as it is acted out bears personal imprints: 'There is always some passive accommodation, some intriguing survival, some active creation, some dissenting impulse, some reflection and lived experience that influences how … individuals direct their religious lives' (Primiano 1995: 46).

Primiano (2012: 387) highlights three concepts that have become central to the vernacular approach: ambiguity, power and creativity. Vernacular religion carries the potential to legitimize existing hegemonies but it can also offer resistance against cultural and social forms of power—sometimes subtle, sometimes dramatically outspoken (ibid.: 388). It facilitates a process through which various dimensions of religious faith and practice are formed into a living, dynamic totality in individual lives. The individual learns and adopts, accepts and rejects, changes or denies, values or devalues the religious elements provided by her or his surroundings. Through this process, both ambiguity and power as aspects of vernacular religion are at play. Creativity, finally, is an especially central aspect of vernacular religion as it is often associated with expressive practices (Illman 2018: 2–4). These three concepts—ambiguity, power and creativity—are central to the analysis of *niggunim* practices presented in this article. Questions arise, however: Does this continuous adjustment to time, place and context—the never-ending creativity and reflexivity or the deeply felt impulse to rebel against norms and follow one's heart—imply a falsification of a genuine, original religiosity? If so, who has the right to determine what constitutes a rightful continuation of a given tradition? At this point, the central concept of authenticity enters the stage.

## Essential or Existential Authenticity

'Be Thyself': today, this maxim of the Romantics seems to have grown stronger than ever, Charles Lindholm argues. In his view, the need to create and express personal authenticity has taken hold of the human mind in a decisive way, stirring an ever fierier debate on what can be regarded as 'authentic' in cultural heritages and religious traditions in today's globalized, diverse societies (Lindholm 2008: 10). In a world apprehended as increasingly corrupt and commercial, the question arises as to what the consequences may be for the individual—emotionally, culturally and religiously. Why is it so important to find and hold on to the 'authentic' and, in so doing, condemning the counterfeit and false? (Vannini and Williams 2009: 1).

The term authentic is mainly associated with positive traits such as honest, truthful, essential, genuine, natural, legitimate and rightful (Lindholm 2008: 1). It does, however, imply a more serious claim than its synonyms, carrying an extraordinary moral weight built on historical lineage and authority, implying that practices are 'correct' and harmonize with historically formed patterns (Lindholm 2013: 362–363). Asserting authenticity as an individual, on the other hand, involves claiming an identity that is 'true' to one's own, innermost self, to one's roots and the lineage one is part of (Charmé 2000: 134). The authentic is the opposite of the pseudo-, quasi-, neo- or semi-, terms carrying negative associations. It is serious, a contrast to what has been adapted, reformulated and merged and thus has become superficial and insincere (Lindholm 2008: 2–3).

Authenticity can be claimed both individually and collectively in social, cultural and religious contexts. Hence, the notion builds on the problematic assumption that there is a world of empirical facts against which practices can be checked for congruence and fidelity. Furthermore, it implies the equally problematic assumption that researchers and practitioners can assess these facts from a perspective unaffected by personal, emotional and contextual anchorage (Vannini and Williams 2009: 2). Even if authenticity as such neither can nor should be defined within the humanities, it is nevertheless clear that *apprehensions* of authenticity, faith in the authentic, plays a crucial role in scholarly and personal efforts to separate the true from the false in contemporary religious practice (Charmé 2000: 133–134). Authenticity is a value-laden, ideological notion revealing what ideals are cherished and desired. It is also a forcible means by which social and religious control can be exercised. Due to its constructed character, authenticity is always a moving target for research—transforming over time and in different spaces (Vannini and Williams 2009: 3).

It is safe to say, hence, that a vernacular religion approach to authenticity cannot strive to assert what practices and traditions in fact *are* authentic, but to investigate what is apprehended as authentic and why (Ochs 2007: 28). The point is not to dismiss all claims of authenticity as illusory or unsophisticated but to try to grasp the lure of the discourse (Lindholm 2008: 141). How are ideas of authenticity put into practice? Why do some practices merit the definition rather than others? How do discourses of authenticity create meaning for individuals and groups? (Lindholm 2008: 144; Vannini and Williams 2009: 14). To understand the attraction of the perceived authentic is relevant because this attraction persists strongly irrespective of the plausibility of such perceptions:

> Demonstrating the contingency of faith in authenticity does not alter the power of that faith over the hearts and minds of men and women today. Whether we like it or not, authenticity, as a motivating force in the modern world, is here to stay. (Lindholm 2013: 390)

These value-laden and emotional aspects of the authenticity debate are interesting in relation to the vernacular religion perspective. In the encounter between official and everyday religion, the theologically correct and the practically applied, authenticity is often a core issue. Indeed, the binary mode of argumentation, criticized by the vernacular approach, can be understood as struggles over the power to define the authentic—a struggle that has emotional, economic, religious and strategic dimensions. Similar interpretations are presented by researchers taking an interest in issues of authenticity in contemporary practices of Jewish mysticism (Lindholm 2008: 112–124). Many progressive Jewish communities today seek to legitimize their existence by relating to aspects of the tradition that are generally regarded as authentic, Stuart Z. Charmé notes, posing the question of why the quest for authenticity has become so important for Jews now:

> As feminist, progressive, gay/lesbian, environmentalist, secular, and many other kinds of Jews lay claim to parts of traditional Judaism that offer recognition and respect to the previously marginalized parts of their identities, they also seek elements that they consider to be 'authentically Jewish'. (Charmé 2000: 133)

A key issue is, according to Charmé, whether this authenticity is seen to exist on the essential or the existential level: whether the true and genuine is sought for in a given normative form of historical Judaism or whether it is regarded as a quality of the individual self and the personal faith. It is obvious that Jews of different inclination and worldview choose to assert authenticity on rather different grounds. This can form a breeding ground for heated controversies that are also reflected in the research on Jewish mysticism (Charmé 2000: 150–151). Chava Weissler suggests that researchers should abandon the hunt for genuinely authentic mysticism as an illusory quest and instead engage in studying 'vernacular Kabbalah' on a practical level, posing questions such as: How is mysticism enacted in practice? Who takes part, what rituals are formed, in what context, where and why? (Weissler 2011: 39–40). To assess what is authentic in Jewish mysticism is complicated, Matt Goldish (2005: 67) agrees, as authenticity can be claimed on vastly different premises: what one regards as a continuation and deepening of the tradition is seen by the other as a mendacious distortion. Searching in history for a gauge of the authentic is a nostalgic project, where authenticity arises from a feeling of timelessness and familiarity rather than rational reconstruction, Vanessa Ochs (2007: 29, 31) writes. Nevertheless, controversies over the 'authentic' are deeply rooted in the research on Jewish mysticism—a historical development that deeply affects the research of today.

## Controversies over Authenticity in the Research on Jewish Mysticism

Jewish mysticism and Kabbalah[2] were for a long time disregarded areas of research: those who took an interest in them were often rejected as practising proselytizers or romantic idealists without scholarly repute or influence. At the end of the nineteenth century, however, an academic interest in esoteric religion at large emerged and also the curiosity in Jewish mysticism grew among non-Jewish as well as Jewish researchers—Zionistic motives often being a notable spur for the latter (Huss, Pasi and von Stuckrad 2010: 2; Scholem, Garb and Idel 2007 [1972]: 674). The study of Jewish mysticism was established as an academic discipline by Scholem, who began his pioneering work in the 1920s and whose text-centred, historical approach dominated the field for several decades (Garb and Wexler 2012: 1; Huss, Pasi and von Stuckrad 2010: 2; Huss 2011: 362–363; Idel 1988: 1, 11; Lachter 2011: 14–16). Critical approaches and novel methodologies were introduced to the field from the 1980s onward, and, eventually, as the popular interest in Kabbalah exploded at the turn of the new millennium, a more comprehensive reorganization of the research field was brought about (Huss 2007b: 109–110; Myers 2011: 175, 187). Many scholars today criticize previous research for being essentializing and one-sided, simultaneously introducing novel perspectives and methods to the study of Jewish mysticism, such as fieldwork and methodologies from the social sciences (Cohen 2016: 487; Swartz 2011: 37; Wexler 2012: 123).

Mainly on the basis of Scholem's work, Jewish mysticism has been divided into a chronology of historical and geographic eras, which ends with the Hasidic dynasties in eighteenth and nineteenth-century Eastern Europe (Myers 2011: 175). Scholem devoted his career to defining categories and methods for researching Jewish mysticism, the goal of which, in his opinion, was to find its essence, its inner core and distinctive character, its historical origin and influence on Jewish culture (Huss 2007a: 85–86; Lachter 2011: 17). From this perspective, he found it feasible to distinguish between authentic and inauthentic mysticism—modern practices falling into the latter category. Thus, he claimed that genuine mysticism had come to an end in his time and that the revival that took place during his lifetime could not lay claim to authenticity (Huss 2007a: 87; Lachter 2011: 22–23; Meir 2010: 199). The idea of Hasidism as the 'last authentic form of Jewish mysticism' has reappeared in much of the research following the path cleared by Scholem. Moshe Idel, to give an example, was critical of Scholem's strictly text-centred methodology and advocated a multi-method approach including comparative endeavours (Garb and Wexler 2012: 1, 5). Nevertheless, he too assessed Hasidism as the last authentic form of Jewish mysticism, writing about it in the past tense as 'the last major Jewish school of mysticism' (Idel 1988: xvii, 260).

Today, however, these views—which have formed a self-evident starting point for decades—are increasingly met with critique (Garb and Wexler 2012: 1). The historical time axis is challenged by researchers, who neither accept the neatness of the hegemonic structure nor the idea that Jewish mysticism came to a close with the decline of Hasidism (Meir 2010: 199, 215–217; Swartz 2011: 37, 43). As a consequence, the entire methodology underpinning classical research into Jewish mysticism is called into question, namely, the search for an authentic Jewish mysticism with certain definable, recurring criteria (Lachter 2011: 21). Since the turn of the millennium, research on mysticism has been significantly diversified, a prominent reason being extra-academic: the considerably growing interest in Kabbalah among secular and orthodox Jews as well as spiritual seekers from various backgrounds (Huss, Pasi and von Stuckrad 2010: 1). New forms of Kabbalah are continuously created, and mystical themes frequently appear in popular culture and on the internet (Huss 2011: 357). The Hasidic movement is also flourishing again, proving the verdict that it was a closed chapter in history utterly untenable (Ariel 2011: 17–18).

This development has caught the interest of the academic community and, thus, the research into Jewish mysticism has grown significantly during the twenty-first century (Myers 2011: 184). Today, the historically oriented perspective introduced above is no longer the only legitimate approach and writing about Hasidism and Kabbalah as phenomena only of the past is increasingly difficult (Huss 2011: 367). Through participant observation and interviews, new fields in which to research Jewish mysticism are created, fields where mystical texts are accompanied by amulets, pop songs, videos, chants, personal rituals and so on (Huss 2011: 366). Mysticism, hence, becomes an aspect not only of texts but also of images, experiences, emotions and social engagement (Ochs 2007: x). This in turn highlights mysticism as a complex, contextually situated phenomenon with theological as well as social, economic and political implications (Wexler 2012: 123).

The quest for an authentic essence in Jewish mysticism thus appears to be an out-dated endeavour (Huss 2011: 366). Today, most researchers have abandoned the idea of an 'organic' mythical heritage where all branches develop according to the same template. Instead, the complex and even contradictory nature of Jewish mystical heritage is highlighted. Contemporary forms of Jewish mysticism do not always seem to fit into the moulds created in the past: characteristics that were regarded as central in previous times have lost their influence while new practices and themes are added to the mystical palette (Ariel 2011: 36–37). Neither can the Kabbalah of today be described as unequivocally Jewish—many contemporary practitioners view it as a universal wisdom that can and should be shared with non-Jews as well (Huss, Pasi and von Stuckrad 2010: 7). Kabbalistic practices are to an increasing degree combined with elements from, for example, Buddhism, Hinduism or Christian mysticism

(Garb and Wexler 2012: 3). Contemporary researchers therefore tend to focus on phenomena, groups and practices within the mystical context, rather than trying to define grand schemes or distinguishing authentic forms from inauthentic ones (Lachter 2011: 23). There is no single template that fits all forms of Jewish mysticism or all of Kabbalah; there are always texts and contexts that overthrow the structures and go against the flow (Tirosh-Samuelson 2011: 222).

Against this background, it is easy to see why the question of authenticity in contemporary Jewish mysticism is so complicated. Goldish points to the forceful marketing and commercialism that often accompanies neo-Hasidic[3] practices as an aspect from which many Jews want to distance themselves. The strikingly spiritual and openly expressed—even 'anti-rational'—sides of these practices are also rejected (Goldish 2005: 63). Boaz Huss (2011: 372) underlines the fact that contemporary mysticism goes against many of the central theoretical and methodological tenets of academic research. This should not be a reason for dismissing contemporary mysticism altogether, he claims, but rather an incitement to rethink and reformulate the research tradition (Huss 2007a: 101; Huss 2007b: 111). By combining different kinds of expertise, an understanding of Jewish mysticism can emerge that is embedded in—but not locked into—an historical and cultural context. This understanding is still sensitive to the globalized context that surrounds Jewish mysticism today (Garb and Wexler 2012: 3). Thus, Kabbalah and mysticism are viewed as 'cultural constructs defined only by changing contingent historical and social factors' (Huss 2011: 371). In my opinion, this view can be supported by the vernacular religion approach and further illuminated by an analysis of authenticity as it is formulated in the ethnographic material focusing on contemporary *niggunim* practices in London.

## Singing Wordless *Niggunim*

What kinds of views on authenticity are found among Jews, who are personally involved in contemporary spiritual practices with roots in the Jewish mystical heritage? This theme was touched upon as part of a comprehensive ethnographic study of contemporary *niggunim* practices among progressive Jews in London (Illman 2018).[4] The material is comprised of participant observation and in-depth interviews with 26 persons (born between 1940 and 1990) involved in the progressive Jewish milieu in London and with a special interest in music and song, liturgical renewal and Jewish spirituality.[5]

*Niggunim* (sg. *niggun*) are religious melodies with roots in the Hasidic tradition[6] that have experienced a renaissance in contemporary Jewish communities around the world (Illman 2018: 16–19). The rekindling of the *niggunim* tradition commenced during the 1960s in the USA as part of the so-called Jewish Renewal movement, which was in turn part of the larger countercultural movement of that time (Ochs 2007: 37). In Modern Hebrew the word *niggun* (נגן) refers to the playing of instruments, but in the Hasidic context it is translated more widely into 'tune', denoting a genre or a musical entity that can entail singing—with or without words—as well as instruments (Gartner et al. 2007 [1971]: 429). In a religious context, a *niggun* is associated with spirituality and holiness, especially the repetitive performance of syllables or words as a form of melodic prayers (HaCohen 2011: 439; Summit 2000: 163–164; Weissler 2011: 44). A *niggun* is thus characteristically a wordless vocal melody 'used as an extension of the existing liturgy, and serves as a prelude or postlude to the traditional prayers' (Avenary 2009: 48). Ochs (2007: 37) offers the following definition: 'The *nigun* is a Jewish spiritual melody often sung with universal sounds, rather than words. Initially used among Hasidim to warm up for prayer and also as a prayer in and of itself'.

As mentioned above, *niggunim* can be sung with words but are often performed using only syllables such as *ya-ba-bam* or *lay-lay*. This brings out the central fact that it is the melody, not the words, that forms the nexus of *niggunim* (Gartner et al. 2007 [1971]: 429; Idelsohn 1992 [1929]: 411). Today, *niggunim* are practised not only in Hasidic and neo-Hasidic communities, but have become an important part of contemporary, embodied and un-dogmatic, Jewish spirituality (Huss 2007b: 109; Levine 2009: 4–5). This development sits alongside a decreasing interest in institutionally bound, intellectually anchored forms of Judaism and reliance on professional religious authorities (Ochs 2007: 17; Summit 2000: 95). In this situation, the wordless melodies—with roots in tradition but adapted to the spiritual context of the twenty-first century—offers an attractive alternative to many Jews, who seek intensified and meaningful spiritual experiences through music (Cohen 2016: 491; Kahn-Harris and Moberg 2012: 101). This process within Judaism has interesting connections to the patterns of religious change observed on a global level—what researchers of religion have called the post-secular turn. A central aspect of this renewal is the primary orientation towards expressive rather than cognitive aspects of religiosity (Nynäs, Illman and Martikainen 2015: 17–22).

248 *Vernacular Knowledge*

The quest for embodied forms of religiosity is thus a recurring phenomenon, occurring not just in contemporary Jewish spirituality but also on a more global scale. Consequently, it becomes interesting to try to understand how mystical elements such as *niggunim* are interpreted and implemented as part of Jewish liturgies, art and music today (Weissler 2011: 40, 42). The interest in reviving the *niggunim* practice is often referred to as *neo-niggunim* (Levine 2009: 4–5). Many practices that are formed today have discernible connections to mystical practices of the past but are consciously being reframed in relation to the contemporary religious landscape and the requirements set by it: the demand for liberal, egalitarian and democratic forms of religiosity, for embodied forms of religious practice and the neo-capitalist market logics that orchestrates it all (Huss 2007b: 108–109, 117, 120). In addition, academic research has functioned as an important source of information and inspiration (Myers 2011: 175, 178–179). The revival today is seldom regarded as an exact re-enactment of practices of the past, but rather reflects the yearning to find religiously and culturally significant models from the past to transform into highly eclectic forms of practice that agree with contemporary spiritual crossover aesthetics: collage, montage, bricolage, pastiche (Huss 2007b: 118). Against this background, it is interesting to analyse how the informants relate to the Hasidic heritage and the question of authenticity: is it relevant to them, and if so, how do they interpret it against the background of the opposition between historical, authentic practices and contemporary inauthentic ones?

### 'A Musical Tradition that I Can Inhabit Somehow'

In discussing *niggunim*, the interviewees often refer to their Hasidic background as well as the American countercultural movement, Jewish Renewal and the leading figures within these movements. In fact, Daniel declares, the Renewal movement chose to draw on the Hasidic tradition 'because it offered the music'. Most interviewees agree that *niggunim*, in addition to the Hasidic influence, also have a strong 'hippie kind of flavour' (Dinah) to them including guitars and song leaders, repetitions and changes of pitch. In this way, the cultural process behind contemporary *niggunim* is described. Micah describes the allure of *niggunim* by saying:

> I think part of the beauty of *niggunin*, especially the wordless *niggunim*, is the whole idea, [that is,] the spiritual theological approach within Hasidism which exhausts the wordless melody—the wordless

meditation as a way of getting even closer to God than any words can achieve.

*Niggunim* are generally experienced as meaningful and 'Jewish', even if one may not have grown up with the tradition. 'I'm completely outside of this tradition, I never experienced it first hand', Adam admits, but still declares affinity for it: 'I have a sense of it, maybe a sense of some kind of ownership, however authentic that sense might be, of it as a musical tradition that I can inhabit somehow'. When *niggunim* are revived outside the Jewish context, Adam says his first reaction is that 'there is something inauthentic about that'. On the other hand, he continues, 'my second reaction is, well, I sing Bach ...' Thus, Adam problematizes the notion of authenticity and acknowledges that people can engage meaningfully in music that has no ties to their 'own' religious background—Bach for him and *niggunim* for non-Jews. Still, on an emotional level, he may react negatively:

> It's just that it's mine, you know, the Jewish stuff is mine, so I feel a sense of ... 'what are you doing taking my things'. [But] I'm just, I'm far from any kind of real developed sense, I'm only having emotional reactions to this at this point, and I'm not sure that they're good reactions, to tell you the truth.

Similarly, Daniel says he rarely encountered *niggunim* in his childhood Orthodox synagogue in London. When he did, however, he was worried:

> They didn't sound very real to me. They sounded a bit cheerful and, you know, invented and improvised. But I wasn't interested in improvised things, I wanted *serious stuff* [laughing] ... I wanted stuff that was ancient; that had some sort of authenticity. And now I know that it isn't authentic ...

Micah, on the other hand, is closely familiar with the Hasidic *niggunim* tradition due to his past as a member of the Chabad movement,[7] including several years at a *yeshiva* (traditional Jewish education institution) in Jerusalem. Today, he has left Chabad and become a Liberal rabbi, but still treasures his *niggunim*:

> I never had a problem with that, except occasionally I had the thought or the feeling that I was maybe using something that wasn't really mine. You know, taking something that is part of a very different ideological tradition, ripping it out of its context and using it ... Just occasionally I felt, you know, is this authentic, is this real?

*Niggunim* are, of their very essence, a mystical practice, Micah continues, even if they are seldom used that way today: 'I think of it as an inherently mystical practice, singing *niggunim*, but for most people in progressive contexts it's done in a fairly non-mystical way'. Bringing in musical elements from the Hasidic tradition is experienced as a largely positive thing by the informants: 'I would say that there's a conscious attempt to really claim some kind of Jewish traditional mode of prayer with some more contemporary melodies for some of these prayers, and it nearly works', Dinah notes. As a critical comment, however, David thinks that most Jews who engage in *niggunim* probably have minimal knowledge of their background. Micah airs the same suspicion:

> We often introduce [*niggunim*] by saying: This is a Hasidic tradition, it's part of Jewish spirituality and this is the reason: to liberate yourself from words and from rational thought and climb to a higher level, but whether ... Well, people listen with interest and politely but whether it actually works for them that way or whether it's just an exercise in exoticism is a question mark.

To sing *niggunim* is, however, often perceived as 'spiritual', Dinah and Daniel note. *Niggunim* are relevant for many Jews today, but perhaps for other reasons and in other ways than for the Hasids two centuries ago, Miriam contends. The classical Hasids wanted to elevate their souls, restore the creation, unite with the divine and hasten the coming of the Messiah by singing *niggunim* (Jacobs 1993 [1972]: 68)—contemporary Jews seek meaningful ways of expressing their faith, relating to their heritage and creating community. The differentiation between classical and contemporary motifs for singing *niggunim* is not watertight, however. As Dinah points out, many Jews, who do not self-define as Hasids or mystics, still have a colourful Jewish background:

> In the Jewish community, I think it's very likely that most people have a number of different kinds of Jewish experiences, and therefore, when I sing the *niggun* in my Reform synagogue, am I really thinking about bringing the Messiah? Maybe not, but that would be to discount the likelihood that a lot of people might well know that information from some other part of their Jewish life experience.

Against this background, Sarah, who works as a cantor, notes that *niggunim* seem to 'spark something' in many Jews who, after some initial hesitation, 'grab on to' them quickly and intensely. Perhaps they have childhood memories of wordless singing hidden somewhere in their souls, she ponders. Above the historical and theological anchorage, the melodies are experienced as meaningful for personal reasons, and many informants mention that certain melodies are dear to them because they are associated with beloved parents and grandparents. Dinah comments that there is 'very little in way of aesthetics that isn't very personal': shaped by culture, upbringing, experiences, and so on. The growing interest in *niggunim* is therefore not just seen as a romantic longing for one's own family roots, but as a result of a much more complex mix of personal, social and religious sentiments and needs, including an explicit fascination for Jewish traditions with which one did *not* grow up.

Despite the desire to engage with the tradition, the term 'authenticity' is experienced as deeply problematic. 'Well, what does that really mean?' Sarah asks sceptically, and adds: 'I think we get into real trouble' if we start claiming this or that tune to be authentic. Having moved to London a year ago, originating in North America, Sarah has been involved in many, rather frustrating, discussions on how 'things have *always* been done' and 'what's traditional and what's authentic: I bump up against this all the time!' Nevertheless, she concludes: 'You have to be sensitive to that because people attach emotion and memory to it. So you have to be able to introduce [the] new without getting rid of the old and that's the challenge'.

Daniel laughingly responds to the question of authenticity by adapting a Yiddish phrase: 'What kind of animal is that?' He continues on a more serious note, however, recognizing that all religions, including Judaism, have 'that side to them' and that authenticity can be a real danger:

> I wish more people were aware that their religions were *not* authentic. We see ghastly things being done all over the world because people think that they have to do what they're doing because the ancestors always did it. Well they don't! They really don't.

'I would be careful with the word authentic', Miriam states in a similar vein: anything can be claimed to be authentic, regardless of your knowledge about the background and connotations of a melody you use. 'A very tricky word', Dinah agrees, saying that she is 'very conscious that most Jewish music is derivative in some way or another'.

Thus, for the informants, authenticity is not a feature to be ensured through rightful historical heritage. While the Hasidic background of *niggunim* is often highlighted, this is really not such a big deal, most informants agree. Hannah, who is an academic expert on Hasidic music, says she is not too worried about where a melody comes from: 'I don't differentiate so much, Hasidic *niggun* or not Hasidic *niggun* ... it doesn't matter to me, music is music to me ... It's labels that for me get in the way. If the melody is good, it's good!' she contends with a laugh. Miriam makes a similar argument about the tunes she uses as a prayer leader: 'I don't know who created the melodies, they're just there!' Rebecca, who is a cantor, agrees: she assumes that most Jews find it interesting and relevant to know that *niggunim* have a Hasidic origin, but that one should not 'intellectualize' too much:

> I often give talks about roots of stuff and people say it's interesting, but that doesn't mean a thing! Because they're involved in it, you know, and they're *doing* it. They don't care where it comes from! It's what's going on here [points to her heart] and what's left in the silence of the moment that's hanging in there for them, so that they come out ... [exhales relieved] ... like that.

As a consequence, both Hannah and Rebecca are open to bringing in melodies from other religious traditions as well: 'I can use a Sufi chant as a *niggun*, and I do sometimes, why not?' (Rebecca). Daniel describes his experience of introducing Buddhist prayer techniques into the Jewish morning prayer (*shaharit*) as 'quite fun', but nevertheless thinks of it as superfluous: 'It *can* be done, but isn't necessary. We actually have these words, Hebrew words and Hebrew sounds, music, within which we can grow'.

The Hasidic heritage is thus important, but not vital and definitely not a guarantee of undisputed legitimacy in the informants' relationship to *niggunim*. Thus, they are reluctant to talk about contemporary *niggunim* practices as a revival of previous Hasidic ones. Daniel describes the relationship to the Hasidic past by saying: 'It's a resource, which is available'. Sarah opts for the same description—the revival happened back in the 1960s with the Jewish Renewal movement, she contends:

> So I wouldn't say that I'm doing anything in terms of revival or even reframing, I just think it's a tool that we have that widens the breadth of what we can do, of how we can express our Judaism.

Rebecca, too, sees the Hasidic heritage as a resource, but regards *niggunim* in a broader perspective as a universal asset: 'I mean: we know it's there [the Hasidic heritage] but I don't for one minute believe that it wasn't there with everybody forever'.

Authenticity, then, is used hesitantly by the informants to denote a shared search for meaning and community, rather than a historically essential or purely individual existential striving. In Dinah's words: 'I would say, using that terrible word authenticity again, it's about trying to feel authentically Jewish by doing Jewish'. An aspect that is highlighted as crucial is that using *niggunim* in liturgy and prayer creates community.

Within classical Hasidism, song and dance functioned as important markers of attachment within the group (Avenary 2009: 48–49). Similarly, Miriam and Daniel speak of *niggunim* as a form of social singing that creates a feeling of togetherness, 'a frontier zone between liturgy and society', as Daniel says. According to David, the wordless melodies can be 'vital in terms of creating community'. In Jewish communities where theological, political and ethical issues divide people, 'it's the idea of community that is based on shared practice rather than shared belief'. Thereby, we move into the domains charted by the analytical approach of vernacular religion.

According to Miriam, creating community is a linchpin in Jewish liturgy: one takes part not as an individual but as a member of a group. Through the wordless singing, a '*niggun* atmosphere' is created, which strengthens and embodies this affinity. It would hardly occur to anyone to sing *niggunim* alone, she contends; that is incomprehensible. The longing for authenticity, thus, can perhaps be understood best as a social and historical sense of meaning, Sarah concludes: 'It's an expression of ... so again I really struggle with the word authentic ... It's an expression of a form of connection'.

## Conclusions—Expressive Authenticity

As shown above, the traditional framework that has dictated the conditions of research into Jewish mysticism is today the target of critique and reformulation. This chapter has suggested that vernacular religion offers a way of reconciling the cemented dichotomies that have restrained the research field, such as the sharp, ideologically coloured division into 'authentic' versus 'inauthentic' Jewish mysticism. By applying the perspective of vernacular religion, a way of researching religion in practice is facilitated, focusing on the ways in which religiosity is expressed by and in the lives of individuals, and how these expressions are embedded in and conditioned by historical and social contexts. Thus, the depreciatory division into authentic and inauthentic can be left aside and a new way of assessing the research field theoretically and methodologically is facilitated. A relevant step in this direction is the integration of ethnographic research material into the analysis, as done in this chapter. By questioning the basic dichotomy between authentic and inauthentic and taking seriously the thoughts and practices of people active in the field today, the vernacular perspective breaks with established forms of knowledge creation.

I also want to return to the three notions proposed by Primiano as decisive for research on vernacular religion: ambiguity, power and creativity. According to him, these notions facilitate the understanding of vernacular religion as a challenge to prevailing norms. In my opinion, the research history of Jewish mysticism mirrors the interplay between these three dimensions and their capacity to provide a platform on which critique of current interpretations can be built. By questioning the structured systematization of Jewish mysticism as a rational process that has come to an end, ambiguity is introduced as a feature to take into account, an enriching resource rather than an anomaly. By pointing to the untenable character of the neat structures, furthermore, the hierarchies and structures of power that define research are questioned. In so doing, however, one must refrain from simply substituting one oppressive dichotomy for another and maintain a view of vernacular religiosity as a constant dialogue between personal, everyday creativity and historical, social and theological structures. These insights are especially valuable in relation to such creative practices as *niggunim* singing.

Returning to the case study on *niggunim*, I conclude that the informants paint a picture of a practice that resembles the historical counterpart but also differs from it. The informants do not strive to recreate the tradition as faithfully as possible. Rather, they regard their heritage as a well to draw inspiration from. In my interpretation, the fact that the Hasidic tradition is described as a resource highlights the reflective, open and interpretative attitude expressed by the interviewees in relation to the Jewish heritage. The tradition is available to them to explore and to preserve, but also to develop according to their needs and the prevailing context.

This conclusion parallels Ochs's findings in her study on innovative Jewish rituals. She notes that inspiration is often found in a variety of different Jewish sources. Practices that previously have been open only to restricted groups—be it on the basis of ethnicity, social class or gender—are introduced to larger audiences, and practices that have fallen into oblivion are rekindled. By emphasizing the Jewish origin an aura of familiarity is created—generating the feeling that the new practice is in fact already part of one's own, well-known way of being Jewish—even as you partake for the first time: 'Turning to the past evokes certainty, security, and imagined community' (Ochs 2007: 6). Thus, the mystical heritage functions as a resource employed in the building of a personal religious identity and the perceived link to tradition gives meaning and legitimacy to new practices, even though they may have been fundamentally altered in the process (Myers 2011: 175).

The division into authentic and inauthentic practices of Jewish mysticism appears irrelevant in the ethnographic material. Thus, I believe the sharp ideological discussion on true and false in the research on Jewish mysticism can be re-evaluated. For the informants, authenticity is a question to follow up on, but not along the paths paved by previous research (Illman 2018: 137–140). At this point, I recall Charmé's distinction between essential and existential authenticity, that is, the opinion that a true and genuine religiosity can be found within and based upon a normative form of historical Judaism as opposed to the view that such qualities can be found within the personal self and expressed through an individually formed religious practice. It is clear that the informants dismiss essential authenticity and the existence of a 'true' Jewish mystical practice or a 'correct' way of practising *niggunim* unaffected by individual interpretations and context. Existential authenticity, as described by Charmé, is more relevant as a description of the images arising from the interviews but nevertheless it is not totally satisfactory. The quest to form a practice that is experienced as true and meaningful in one's own life is indeed important, but even more so is the social aspect: being part of a community that shares the individual's views and sentiments. Indeed, *niggunim* are explicitly described as pointless if practised alone.

Therefore, I wish to complement Charmé's two-part model of essential and existential authenticity with a third option: *expressive authenticity*, a term that was initially introduced by Lindholm to denote the wish not just to 'search for depths of the soul hidden beneath surface convention and appearance' but to express this conviction together with others, to live so that you truly 'feel life' (2013: 371, 378). In my opinion, this term captures the reflections on authenticity provided by the informants in an apt way: as an effort to find a way to express one's faith that is experienced as historically relevant, liturgically defensible, individually meaningful and socially cohesive. In addition, the distinct embodied dimension actualized by the *niggunim* practice needs attention as it further underscores the importance of the expressive: authenticity is a feeling and the body becomes a tool for creating meaning (Ochs 2007: 17). Weissler (2011: 74) stresses that the quest for authenticity in contemporary Jewish mystical practice is not an intellectual question, but rather a quest to find religious experiences that feel real: '[They] seek meaning through the body.

Embodiment is the key to achieving the influx of spirit, which can come through singing, chanting, dancing, and other sorts of ritual movement'.

In singing *niggunim*, the body can be regarded as a source of authenticity from which knowledge and conviction are mediated to mind and heart. In my opinion, this description captures expressive authenticity as it is reflected in the ethnographic material. *Niggunim* can be seen to move partly in the 'frontier zone between liturgy and society', to use Daniel's words. But even more importantly, I regard *niggunim* as a practice that reveals the inadequacy of mapping such border zones at all, as the dichotomous differentiation between official and everyday practice, institutional and popular as such is untenable.

## Fieldwork Details

Twenty-six people were interviewed in North London between July 2014 and November 2016 by the author. All interviews were recorded in mp3 format and later transcribed into text documents. These recordings and transcripts are stored at the Cultura Archive at Åbo Akademi University, Turku, Finland.

## Notes

1. In English, you can find the alternative ways of spelling the Hebrew word: *nigun/ niggun* as well as *nigunim/niggunim*. In this article, I have chosen to follow the spelling used in *Encyclopaedia Judaica*, which is *niggun/niggunim*, unless I refer to direct quotes where an alternative spelling has been used.
2. Generally speaking, the term Jewish mysticism is used in scholarly works to denote a broad spectrum of doctrines, practices and movements relating to mystical interpretations of Judaism, while the Hebrew term *Kabbalah* (קבלה), denoting 'received tradition', has a more theoretical, intellectual ring connected to esoteric religious beliefs, especially the *sephirot* system (Lachter 2011: 5). In more common use, however, Kabbalah is used to denote Jewish mysticism and esotericism at large, in all forms from Biblical times to date. Thus, the terminology often overlaps.
3. The term neo-Hasidic denotes new forms of Jewish spirituality that are formed on the basis of the Hasidic heritage, often combined with influences from other religious traditions such as Buddhism, Sufism and yoga (Weissler 2011: 41).
4. The material was collected during four visits to London between July 2014 and November 2016. The informants were all tied to the progressive, urban and international Jewish milieu centred around Leo Baeck College (LBC), where rabbis for the Reform and Liberal movements in the UK are educated. The LBC website is found at http://www.lbc.ac.uk/ (accessed June 13, 2021). During my stays, I

participated in services and meetings where *niggunim* were sung, and conducted 21 in-depth interviews with 26 people (individually and in groups) involved in the practice. Thus, the research material is qualitative by nature and its creation has been guided by the striving to understand the points of view of the informants. As a self-reflexive note I want to add that the selection of the research question naturally reflects my interest in and sympathies for the practices under study but that I am not myself involved in this practice. See Illman 2018: 30-32 for details on the ethnographic material.
5   For details please see the Fieldwork section. The interviewees have been given aliases—common Jewish names—in order to protect their anonymity.
6   For comprehensive presentations of the Hasidic tradition, see, for example, Gartner et al. 2007 [1971]; Jacobs 1993 [1972].
7   Chabad-Lubavitch is an Orthodox Jewish Hasidic movement which has spread all over the Jewish world, and is well-known for its outreach work among secular and non-Orthodox Jews. For detailed presentations, see Rubinstein and Lior 2007 [1971].

## References

Ariel, Yaakov. 2011. 'From Neo-Hasidism to Outreach Yeshivot: The Origins of the Movement of Renewal and Return to Tradition'. In *Kabbalah and Contemporary Spiritual Revival*, edited by Boaz Huss, 17-37. Negev: Ben Gurion University of the Negev Press.

Avenary, Hanoch. 2009. 'The Hasidic Niggun: Ethos and Melos of a Folk Liturgy'. *Journal of Synagogue Music* 34: 48-54.

Bowman, Marion. 2014. 'Vernacular Religion, Contemporary Spirituality and Emergent Identities: Lessons from Lauri Honko'. *Approaching Religion* 4 (1): 101-113. https://doi.org/10.30664/ar.67542

Bowman, Marion, and Ülo Valk. 2012. 'Introduction: Vernacular Religion, Generic Expressions and the Dynamics of Belief'. In *Vernacular Religion in Everyday Life: Expressions of Belief*, edited by Marion Bowman and Ülo Valk, 1-19. Sheffield; Bristol, CT: Equinox Publishing.

Charmé, Stuart. 2000. 'Varieties of Authenticity in Contemporary Jewish Identity'. *Jewish Social Studies* 6 (2): 133-155. https://doi.org/10.2979/JSS.2000.6.2.133

Cohen, Judah M. 2016. 'A Holy Brother's Liberal Legacy: Shlomo Carlebach, Reform Judaism, and Hasidic Pluralism'. *American Jewish History* 100 (4): 485-509. https://doi.org/10.1353/ajh.2016.0057

Garb, Jonathan, and Philip Wexler. 2012. 'After Spirituality: Introducing the Volume and the Series'. In *After Spirituality: Studies in Mystical Traditions*, edited by Jonathan Garb and Philip Wexler, 1-15. New York: Peter Lang.

Gartner, Lloyd P., Avraham Rubinstein, Judith R. Baskin, Bonnie J. Morris, Louis Jacobs and Rivka Schatz-Uffenheimer. 2007 [1971]. 'Hasidism'. In *Encyclopaedia Judaica*, vol. 8, edited by Michael Berenbaum and Fred Skolnik, 393-434. Detroit: Macmillan Reference.

Goldish, Matt. 2005. 'Kabbalah, Academia, and Authenticity'. *Tikkun* 20 (5): 63-68. https://doi.org/10.1215/08879982-2005-5024

Goldstein, Diane. 2015. 'Narrative, Local Knowledge, and the Changed Context of Folklore'. *Journal of American Folklore* 128 (508): 125–145. https://doi.org/10.5406/jamerfolk.128.508.0125

HaCohen, Ruth. 2011. *The Music Libel against the Jews*. New Haven, CT: Yale University Press.

Howard, Robert Glenn. 2011. *Digital Jesus: The Making of a New Christian Fundamentalist Community on the Internet*. New York: New York University Press. https://doi.org/10.18574/nyu/9780814773086.001.0001

Huss, Boaz. 2007a. '"Authorized Guardians": The Polemics of Academic Scholars of Jewish Mysticism against Kabbalah Practitioners'. In *Polemical Encounters: Esoteric Discourses and Its Others*, edited by Olav Hammer and Kocku von Stuckrad, 81–103. Leiden: Brill. https://doi.org/10.1163/ej.9789004162570.i-326.27

Huss, Boaz. 2007b. 'The New Age of Kabbalah: Contemporary Kabbalah, the New Age and Postmodern Spirituality'. *Journal of Modern Jewish Studies* 6 (2): 107–125. https://doi.org/10.1080/14725880701423014

Huss, Boaz. 2011. 'Contemporary Kabbalah and Its Challenge to the Academic Study of Jewish Mysticism'. In *Kabbalah and Contemporary Spiritual Revival*, edited by Boaz Huss, 357–373. Negev: Ben Gurion University of the Negev Press.

Huss, Boaz, Marco Pasi and Kocku von Stuckrad. 2010. 'Introduction: Kabbalah and Modernity'. In *Kabbalah and Modernity: Interpretations, Transformations, Adaptations*, edited by Boaz Huss, Marco Pasi and Kocku von Stuckrad, 1–10. Leiden: Brill. https://doi.org/10.1163/ej.9789004182844.i-436.4

Idel, Moshe. 1988. *Kabbalah: New Perspectives*. New Haven, CT: Yale University Press.

Idelsohn, Abraham Z. 1992 [1929]. *Jewish Music in Its Historical Development*. New York: Dover Publications.

Illman, Ruth. 2018. *Music and Religious Change among Progressive Jews in London: Being Liberal and Doing Traditional*. Lanham, MD: Lexington Books.

Jacobs, Louis. 1993 [1972]. *Hasidic Prayer*. London: Littman Library of Jewish Civilization.

Kahn-Harris, Keith, and Marcus Moberg. 2012. 'Religious Popular Music: Between the Instrumental, Transcendent and Transgressive'. *Temenos: Nordic Journal of Comparative Religion* 48 (1): 87–106. https://doi.org/10.33356/temenos.6948

Lachter, Hartley. 2011. 'Reading Mysteries: The Origins of Scholarship on Jewish Mysticism'. In *Jewish Mysticism and Kabbalah: New Insights and Scholarship*, edited by Frederick E. Greenspahn, 1–29. New York: New York University Press.

Levine, Joseph A. 2009. 'The Issue of Niggunim in Worship: Too Much of a Good Thing?' *Journal of Synagogue Music* 43: 4–7.

Lindholm, Charles. 2008. *Culture and Authenticity*. Malden, MA: Blackwell.

Lindholm, Charles. 2013. 'The Rise of Expressive Authenticity'. *Anthropological Quarterly* 86 (2): 361–396. https://doi.org/10.1353/anq.2013.0020

Meir, Jonatan. 2010. 'The Imagined Decline of Kabbalah: The Kabbalistic Yeshiva Sha'ar Ha-Shamayim and Kabbalah in Jerusalem in the Beginning of the Twentieth Century'. In *Kabbalah and Modernity: Interpretations, Transformations, Adaptations*, edited by Boaz Huss, Marco Pasi and Kocku von Stuckrad, 197–220. Leiden: Brill.

Myers, Jody. 2011. 'Kabbalah at the Turn of the 21st Century'. In *Jewish Mysticism and Kabbalah: New Insights and Scholarship*, edited by Frederick E. Greenspahn, 175–190. New York: New York University Press.

Nynäs, Peter, Ruth Illman and Tuomas Martikainen, eds. 2015. *On the Outskirts of 'the Church': Diversities, Fluidities and New Spaces of Religion in Finland*. Zürich: LIT Verlag.

Ochs, Vanessa L. 2007. *Inventing Jewish Ritual*. Philadelphia: Jewish Publication Society.

Primiano, Leonard Norman. 1995. 'Vernacular Religion and the Search for Method in Religious Folklife'. *Western Folklore* (Special Issue: *Reflexivity and the Study of Belief*) 54 (1): 37–56. https://doi.org/10.2307/1499910

Primiano, Leonard Norman. 2012. 'Afterword: Manifestations of the Religious Vernacular: Ambiguity, Power and Creativity'. In *Vernacular Religion in Everyday Life: Expressions of Belief*, edited by Marion Bowman and Ülo Valk, 382–394. Sheffield; Bristol, CT: Equinox Publishing.

Rubinstein, Aryeh, and Rachel Lior. 2007 [1971]. 'Chabad'. In *Encyclopaedia Judaica*, vol. 8, edited by Michael Berenbaum and Fred Skolnik, 553–555. Detroit: Macmillan Reference.

Scholem, Gershom. 1961 [1941]. *Major Trends in Jewish Mysticism*. New York: Schocken Books.

Scholem, Gershom, Jonathan Garb and Moshe Idel. 2007 [1972]. 'Kabbalah'. In *Encyclopaedia Judaica*, vol. 11, edited by Michael Berenbaum and Fred Skolnik, 586–692. Detroit: Macmillan Reference.

Summit, Jeffrey A. 2000. *The Lord's Song in a Strange Land: Music and Identity in Contemporary Jewish Worship*. Oxford: Oxford University Press.

Swartz, Michael Dov. 2011. 'Ancient Jewish Mysticism'. In *Jewish Mysticism and Kabbalah: New Insights and Scholarship*, edited by Frederick E. Greenspahn, 33–48. New York: New York University Press.

Tirosh-Samuelson, Hava. 2011. 'Gender in Jewish Mysticism'. In *Jewish Mysticism and Kabbalah: New Insights and Scholarship*, edited by Frederick E. Greenspahn, 191–230. New York: New York University Press.

Vannini, Phillip, and J. Patrick Williams. 2009. 'Authenticity in Culture, Self, and Society'. In *Authenticity in Culture, Self, and Society*, edited by Phillip Vannini and J. Patrick Williams, 1–18. Farnham: Ashgate.

Weissler, Chava. 2011. 'Performing Kabbalah in the Jewish Renewal Movement'. In *Kabbalah and Contemporary Spiritual Revival*, edited by Boaz Huss, 39–74. Negev: Ben Gurion University of the Negev Press.

Wexler, Philip. 2012. 'Society and Mysticism'. In *After Spirituality: Studies in Mystical Traditions*, edited by Philip Wexler and Jonathan Garb, 107–125. New York: Peter Lang.

Whitehead, Amy. 2013. *Religious Statues and Personhood: Testing the Role of Materiality*. London: Bloomsbury.

Part 4

# Vernacular Knowledge and Christianity

## Chapter 11

# Feminist Folk, Christian Folk and Black Madonnas

*Melanie Landman**

**Introduction**

Black Madonnas are found in some of the most famous Christian shrines in Europe. For example, the Christian shrines of Montserrat in Spain, Loreto in Italy, Le Puy in France and Częstochowa in Poland are all home to black Madonnas. They are often associated with natural phenomena, such as forests, caves, mountains and springs. These are also miracle-working figures resuscitating dead babies, helping women conceive or freeing prisoners. Precisely what constitutes a black Madonna is not straightforward. In his gazetteer of black Madonnas across the world, Ean Begg (1996 [1985]: 3) estimated that there were at least 450 images of the Virgin Mary across the world, even without including those in Africa, that are either black, dark brown or grey in colour. However, as Sarah Jane Boss points out, some statues that are no longer black are still labelled as 'black Madonnas' by the people who worship at that particular shrine, such as Our Lady of Orcival. Boss therefore defines the black Madonna as: 'an image of the Virgin Mary whose devotees commonly refer to her as "black"' (Boss 2007: 461).

The difficulties with trying to define what actually is a black Madonna are coupled with difficulties in trying to uncover why these images exist at all. Who created these images and when are also difficult to ascertain. It is the lack of information regarding the origins of the black Madonnas and what their blackness might signify that has led to these images being

* **Melanie Landman** received her PhD on the phenomenon of the Black Madonna from Roehampton University, where she worked as a visiting lecturer. She is currently enjoying raising her daughter, researching her interests as an independent scholar and being a trustee of the Centre for Marian Studies.

the subject of much speculation. Because there is no definitive explanation for the blackness of black Madonnas this has created an air of mystery and intrigue around them, allowing much creative conjecture and interpretation. Even a cursory glance at the literature available demonstrates the volume of work on offer. Attempts to uncover these mysteries and provide explanations have led to a wide range of literature on the subject, from both within and outside academia. These include the works of Begg (1996 [1985]); Anne Baring and Jules Cashford (1993); Margaret Starbird (1993); Lucia Chiavola Birnbaum (2000 [1993]; 2001); Lynn Picknett (2003) and Malgorzata Oleszkiewicz-Peralba (2007). Although some works such as Begg are more influenced by Jungian psychology and others such as Oleszkiewicz-Peralba by anthropology, these works are often multi-disciplinary and very much challenge a more traditional, discipline discrete approach to research.

This chapter examines the phenomenon of the black Madonna in relation to the methodological concept of 'lived' or vernacular religion and considers two issues. Firstly, it suggests that the literature on black Madonnas that has emerged from feminist spiritualities can be seen as a type of feminist vernacular religious knowledge. The term 'feminist spiritualities' is used here rather than other descriptive terms such as 'goddess spiritualities' or 'New Age' or 'alternative spiritualities'. This is partly because these terms have their own problems with regards to definition and applicability and there is not space to discuss all those issues here. It is also because there is a political dimension to the interest in black Madonnas shown by the authors discussed in this chapter. 'Spiritualities' is used in the plural to acknowledge the variety within the field. The chapter will trace some of the origins of the field and how a particular understanding and interpretation of the black Madonna coming from a European and North American perspective have developed. Secondly, it considers some of the criticisms of white feminists' use of the black Madonna. This section includes a brief look at the work of researchers who have challenged the domination of white, European and North American feminists in this area, examining the black Madonna in wider cultural and global contexts.

What is of interest here is when the religious knowledge and experiences of feminist spiritualities and the figure of the black Madonna are considered in relation to other sorts of vernacular experiences or understandings. This chapter considers how different forms of authority are created and challenged within these experiences with regard to empirical work conducted at a black Madonna shrine located in an Anglican church in London. As the chapter will show, this particular shrine challenged some of the existing assumptions regarding these figures and their place in both Christianity and feminist spiritualities.

The use of the term 'vernacular' to describe the types of knowledge and experience illustrated in this chapter draws on Leonard Primiano's use of the word vernacular when talking about everyday religious lives. For Primiano, the vernacular 'is a way of communicating, thinking, behaving within and conforming to a particular cultural circumstance' (1995: 42). Anna Fedele, whose own anthropological work on alternative spiritualities includes fieldwork at various black Madonna shrines, advocates a similar approach. She points out that:

> a universal and therefore transhistorical definition of ritual, religion, and in this case also of spirituality is not viable because religions, rituals and spirituality are deeply embedded in the societies producing them. The elements that constitute them are historically specific; they tend to change over time in a constant relationship with social and cultural changes. (Fedele 2013: 6)

With regards to the feminist and Christian 'folk' discussed in this chapter, both of these groups have their own particular set of cultural circumstances in which they connect to the figure of the black Madonna. Feminist vernacular knowledge and understanding of the black Madonna comes out of a wider alternative spiritual and political milieu. The group of Anglican Christians who share their parish church with a black Madonna shrine not only relate to this figure within a local network of historical and religious narratives about their church, but their experiences are also situated against wider concerns about the place of the Virgin Mary in the Anglican Church. Primiano argues for a concept that does justice 'to the experiential component' of those everyday religious lives, and that 'equally significant is the relationship of the vernacular to the "arts" manifested in the creativity and artistry expressed by the human drive to interpret religious experience' (1995: 43). For Primiano (1995: 44), 'vernacular religion is, by definition, religion as it is lived: as human beings encounter, understand, interpret, and practice it. Since religion inherently involves interpretation, it is impossible for the religion of an individual not to be vernacular'.

The interpretive, experiential and creative aspects of vernacular religion are central to examining the relationships both feminists and Anglican Christians have with the figure of the black Madonna. As this chapter will show, vernacular religion as it pertains to black Madonnas manifests in diverse ways. These include pilgrimage, devotions and ritual (both private and public) as well as the production of written texts, art and media platforms such as websites. These forms of expression are drawn from multiple sites, experiences and traditions.

## Black Madonnas: Creating Feminist Vernacular Knowledge

How might we account for this growth in interest in black Madonnas, and in particular the situating of this figure as an alternative one? I would suggest that in part this lies in a wider growth of interest in the rise of what Gordon Lynch has described as 'progressive spirituality'. Lynch defines this as: 'A particular form of religious ideology that has been refined over the past thirty or so years by a range of "organic intellectuals" within the progressive milieu of western religion' (2007: 10). Progressive spirituality is closely linked with the rise of second-wave feminism and the growth of 'green' or ecological concerns. Lynch identifies feminist spirituality and a renewed interest in goddess worship as important aspects of these new movements.

This revival of interest in goddess worship, and the associated theories of matriarchy and the Great Goddess, found a receptive audience amongst some sections of the feminist movement in the late 1960s—a popularity that continues up to the present. In her book *Living in the Lap of the Goddess: The Feminist Spirituality Movement in America*, Cynthia Eller describes how those theories have been important in the development of the feminist spirituality movement, politically as much as spiritually:

> However varied the specifics, feminist spirituality always relies on an interest in the feminine, or at least gender, to sustain its system of symbols, beliefs, and practices. Finally, much of the feminist spiritual imagination is given over to speculation about how gender relations have been structured over the history of the human race. This 'sacred history' is an on-going reconstruction of Western history according to which prehistoric societies worshiped goddesses, and were possibly matriarchal as well, until they were replaced by patriarchal societies, which are today the status quo worldwide. (Eller 1995: 3–4)

Much of the literature on black Madonnas that has grown out of feminist spiritualities draws on several ideas and sources. In particular, the idea that the many female deities found across the ancient world were different manifestations of a 'Great Goddess' figure is explored in works such as Stone (1976); Sjöo and Mor (1987) and Gimbutas (1982; 1989). Although not specifically concerned with black Madonnas, theories of pre-historical matriarchies and worship of the goddesses have nevertheless been instrumental in the creation of feminist vernacular knowledge of black Madonnas.

Anthropological-based theories that established specific connections between black Madonnas and pagan goddesses, whilst not overtly feminist in themselves, have also contributed to a feminist vernacular understanding of the phenomenon. Some of the earliest studies came from France in the 1930s and 1940s. Marie Durand-Lefèbvre's work, *Étude Sur L'Origine des Vierges Noires*, was published in 1937 and Emile Saillens's work *Nos Vierges Noires, Leurs Origines* in 1945. Both Durand-Lefèbvre and Saillens suggested there was a direct connection between pagan goddesses and black Madonnas, with many ancient pagan sites of worship now being occupied by a black Madonna shrine (Begg 1996 [1985]; Markale 2004).

Following on from the French studies, the work of anthropologists Leonard Moss and Stephen Cappannari was some of the earliest research on black Madonnas written in English and extended the study of the phenomenon to Italy. In 1953, their original paper 'The Black Madonna: An Example of Culture Borrowing' was published in *The Scientific Monthly*. Their work suggested that black Madonnas fall into three categories. The first category Moss and Cappannari identify are those Madonnas that reflect the colour of the indigenous population of worshippers. This included statues such as Our Lady of Guadalupe and other black Madonnas found in South America and Africa. Secondly, there are some images that may become dark due to physical factors, such as ageing of wood, paints, etc. Or they may have suffered environmental damage such as fire. The third category, into which the majority of black Madonnas in Western Europe seem to fall, are those for which there appears no obvious explanation for their blackness.

It is this third category on which the majority of literature on black Madonnas concentrates. Moss and Cappannari suggested that these black Madonnas were an example of cultural borrowing. By this they meant that black Madonnas were a Christianized version of earlier deities worshipped throughout Europe. These deities included Isis, Demeter and Cybele, all of whom were represented as black in colour:

> The adoption of new beliefs is facilitated when the beliefs can be equated in some fashion with the older and compatible experiences. It is in this light that we offer our hypothesis that these Madonnas exemplify a reinterpretation of pagan customs, that they have functioned as aids in the preservation of continuity in the transition from pagan beliefs to Roman Catholicism. (Moss and Cappanari 1953: 324)

In a later paper, Moss and Cappannari describe what happened when they tried to present their original findings at a conference of the American Association for the Advancement of Science. The paper received a hostile reaction and every nun and priest in the audience walked out:

> We were confused by the hostile reaction of the religious members of our original audience. The confusion was clarified immediately after publication: the chaplain of the Newman Club at Wayne State University gave a sermon in which he fulminated against the campus atheists who would defile the name of the Blessed Virgin. (Moss and Cappannari 1982: 55)

The work of Moss and Cappannari has been central to the development of theories as to both the origins and meanings of the black Madonna, not only in their theorizing of possible pagan or pre-Christian sources for these figures, but equally important for those interested in goddess or feminist spiritualities, the potential for black Madonnas to challenge the religious status quo. Moss's own tale as to how he became interested in the subject is oft-repeated in the work of those who see the alternative potential in the black Madonna. Moss discovered his first black Madonna whilst stationed in Italy during World War II. Surprised at this colourful representation of the Virgin Mary, he asked the priest why she was depicted in this way and received the enigmatic reply, 'My son, she is black because she is black' (Moss and Cappannari 1982: 53). The reluctance of the priest to discuss the subject matter and the subsequent reactions to Moss and Cappannari's work had given much credence to the idea that black Madonnas might represent something more than the Christian figure of the Virgin Mary and that this is problematic for the Catholic Church. These ideas have become the focus of the feminist writings on this subject.

The other important strand that has contributed to feminist understanding of the black Madonna has grown out of a much more interpretive approach, focusing on the deeper symbolism of the black Madonna, drawing, in part, on Jungian concepts of the unconscious, anima and mother archetype. Most notable in this approach is Begg's *The Cult of the Black Virgin* (1996), first published in 1985, which was influenced by Moss and Cappannari and has, in turn, influenced other works.

Begg applies psychoanalytic theories to a wide range of traditions and assumes they have all had some influence over the symbolic meaning of the black Madonna. This would appear to be regardless of any archaeological and historical evidence. Begg's work is detailed and wide-ranging in tracing the pre-Christian origins of black Madonnas. He examines possible influences from several pre-Christian traditions—the classical tradition of ancient Greece and Rome, the Celtic and Teutonic traditions and the ancient Near East, including Egypt. He cites the influence of deities such as Isis, Diana, Cybele and Demeter, all of whom were portrayed as black.

Begg's work relies heavily on his interpretations of myths from these different cultures. Influenced by Jungian concepts of the collective unconscious and the archetype, he moves beyond seeing direct links from pre-Christian to Christian in the location of black Madonna shrines, and examines more closely the symbolic aspects of black Madonnas. Emphasis is placed on the difference between the more orthodox white Madonna and what the black Madonna represents:

> The return of the Black Virgin to the forefront of collective consciousness has coincided with the profound psychological need to reconcile sexuality and religion. She has always helped her supplicants to circumvent the rigidities of patriarchal legislation and is traditionally on the side of physical processes. (Begg 1996 [1985]: 28)

Begg argues that black Madonnas are not only pre-Christian in origin but their cult is part of a heretical tradition within Christianity itself and it is this, as much as their pre-Christian origins, which helps to explain the Church's rather negative attitude to a phenomenon that includes some of its most famous and popular shrines.

The influence of both Moss and Cappannari and Begg over subsequent works on the black Madonna cannot be overestimated; this interweaving of the anthropological and the symbolic has permeated so much of the writing on black Madonnas. The black Madonna is seen as another manifestation of the mother archetype, in the tradition of the Great Goddess of the ancient world. In this respect, the black Madonna, like the Mother Archetype, is a universal figure. Fred Gustafson, for example, describes the black Madonna as 'archetypal and her power thus exists in every person and every culture' (1990: 118). The black Madonna is therefore a 'touchstone in our understanding of the archetypal dark feminine' (ibid.: xiv).

The black Madonna is also positioned as a sexually, politically and spiritually liberating alternative, something beyond the 'usual submissive mother image of the Virgin Mary' (Baring and Cashford 1993: 588). For writers such as Baring and Cashford, Chiavola Birnbaum (2000 [1993]; 2001) and Picknett (2003), the white image of the Virgin Mary represents Church hierarchy, obedience and passivity, the repression of the feminine. Their writings suggest the black Madonna symbolizes the power of female sexuality and the cycle of birth, death and rebirth in such a way that a white Madonna simply cannot. Perceived Church hostility to black Madonnas is cited as proof of this symbolism:

> Differing from white Madonnas, who may be said to embody Church doctrine of obedience and patience, and differing in shades of dark, what all black Madonnas have in common is location on or near archaeological evidence of the pre-Christian woman divinity, and the popular perception that they are black. Elusive, they are frequently removed from religious and political implication by art historians, who call them 'Byzantine' and by the church hierarchy, which has 'retouched' several of them white. (Chiavola Birnbaum 2000 [1993]: 3)

In her work on black Madonnas in Italy, Chiavola Birnbaum describes how certain practices associated with black Madonna shrines were prohibited by church authorities for being too pagan and unseemly. On the pilgrimage to the Madonna dell'Arco she notes:

> The bishop 'recommended' that pilgrims not dance and not carry the image of the Madonna when soliciting alms. Pilgrims were admonished to behave with dignity, propriety, and discipline lest the popular pilgrimage become 'nothing more than an expression of resurgent paganism'. (Chiavola Birnbaum 2000 [1993]: 128)

Church authority and doctrine are shown in stark contrast to what researchers such as Chiavola Birnbaum consider to be the more authentic, vernacular beliefs and practices of ordinary worshippers.

It is important to point out that although many of these works are highly speculative regarding the possible origins, purposes and symbolic meanings of the figure of the black Madonna, this is not just theoretical knowledge. Amongst the substantial body of work, in the form of books, articles and websites dedicated to the exploration of the phenomenon, there is also a strong experiential element to this knowledge. It is this experiential aspect that makes Primiano's definition of vernacular religion so pertinent here. Whilst exploring the origins and meanings of the black Madonna, some authors, such as China Galland (1990) and Starbird (1993) for example, describe being on personal quests or journeys. These journeys led them from mainstream patriarchal Christian traditions to embracing an alternative, feminine-centred way of experiencing faith.

Such experiences are not just limited to authors who write books and articles, but to anyone who has the means by which to participate. There are courses and workshops built around exploring the symbolic meanings of the black Madonna and even organized holiday tours in Europe where participants visit various sites associated with this figure. The work of Deana Weibel (2002a; 2002b) and Fedele (2013) shows how this experiential knowledge is so vital for participants in these tours. Weibel describes how at the black Madonna shrine of Rocamadour in France members of this group spoke of the 'intense spiritual experiences they had had while in the chapel itself':

> The youngest woman on the pilgrimage claimed to have made contact with her deceased mother through the intercession of the death goddess, Sulevia, and had left the shrine feeling reassured that her mother was proud of her. One of the group's leaders had a different experience. She said that the energy inside the chapel was so strong that it had 'blown up' her head, expanding her crown chakra. This was a positive experience, she told me, indicative of her advanced spiritual status. (Weibel 2002a: 82)

Fedele observed the experiences were equally powerful for the participants in the groups:

> The dark divinities of the pilgrimage helped men as well as women to come to terms with passages of their life and aspects of their personality left unaddressed by the sociocultural and religious system they grew up in. If men who had been socialized to be strong and assertive could acknowledge and voice their vulnerability, women could come to terms with their anger and the other emotions and states they had learned to consider as inappropriate for a good girl. (Fedele 2013: 241)

It is clear these pilgrims found sources of empowerment, healing and comfort from their encounters with black Madonnas, and the liberating potential of the black Madonna for so many is unmistakably demonstrated in the passionate writings on these figures.

However, it should be noted that feminist interest in black Madonnas has not gone unchallenged. Eller's critique, for example, has largely concentrated on the use of dark goddesses by white women in the feminist spirituality movement. Eller (1995) acknowledges that the intentions of scholars are non-racist and these intentions have sometimes been accepted as such, citing the work of Chiavola Birnbaum as an example. But she is sceptical of the use of dark goddesses by white women as a solution to racism and suggests that white feminists' use of the 'Dark Mother' could function as a means of reasserting white privilege. Charting the use of the dark goddesses by the feminist spirituality movement, Eller shows how the early days of the movement saw an embracing of a range of goddess figures, of all colours and from many different traditions. However, there was a backlash against these appropriations from women of colour:

> women of colour told white spiritual feminists that their worship of black goddesses was an unacceptable appropriation of religious resources not their own, and furthermore, that racial identities were not just so many delightfully different flavours skimming the surface of underlying femaleness. (Eller 2000: 368)

Eller notes another shift in relation to the 'discovery' of the European black Madonnas by the feminist spirituality movement, a 'discovery on their own cultural turf' (Eller 2000: 368). She suggests that initially, early spiritual feminists were not particularly interested in black Madonnas as they were representations of the Virgin Mary, a problematic figure for many feminists. However, despite these initial reservations, as demonstrated clearly in the examples given previously in this chapter, the figure of the black Madonna has increasingly become a powerful symbol for many women in the feminist movement.

Eller's points were certainly illustrated by the women interviewed in Weibel's research who centred their spirituality on the concept of an all-pervading feminine deity that crossed boundaries and traditions, both national and religious. This included Catholic saints and the Virgin Mary. At the black Madonna shrine of Le Puy-en-Velay:

> The replacement statue was said to have come from the Sudan. Because of this story, the group's meditation focused on the 'Primordial Mother of Africa', and because of Le Puy's volcanic geography, Louise also led a prayer to the Hawaiian goddess Pele. (Weibel 2002a: 82)

I would concur with Eller that a critical examination of the feminist spirituality movement's use of black Madonnas is necessary. In particular, the attempt to find explanations as to the origins and meanings of the black Madonna has led to an over reliance on the same theories and a construction of what one might describe as a 'grand narrative' approach to the phenomenon. However, although the literature is largely dominated by white, European and American writers, the vernacular, as Primiano has demonstrated, can take many forms. Other writings and research on the black Madonna show an interest in this figure that go beyond the concerns raised in Eller's article.

## Beyond the Feminist Vernacular

Oleszkiewicz-Peralba's detailed look at the black Madonna and 'her role in a time of global culture and hybridization' includes an examination of the 'blending of African, European and Amerindian cultures of the highly African-influenced areas of northeastern Brazil and the Caribbean' (2007: 2). For Oleszkiewicz-Peralba, the black Madonna functions not only as a symbol of matriarchal beliefs and religious practices, but also as a symbol of national identity. In Mexico for example, Our Lady of Guadalupe 'carries complex layers of meaning': 'As an icon born on the soil of the Americas that bears characteristics of two main cultural and ethnic groups inhabiting Mexico, the Indian and the European, she is transformed into an important national and patriotic symbol' (ibid.: 79).

Oleszkiewicz-Peralba is also interested in the 'appropriation and use of the Madonna in various unexpected forms as an example of cultural transformations and hybridity in postmodern times' (ibid.: 9). She examines the ways in which the image of Guadalupe has been reinvented in cultural forms such as street murals, tattoos, t-shirts and by artists who have 'liberated' Guadalupe: 'from her static pose, she is transformed into a truly active woman who works, walks, dances, jogs, even practices martial arts' (ibid.: 154).

The work of African American scholars Danita Redd (1987) and Eloise McKinney Johnson (1987) highlights the possible relationships between the Egyptian goddess Isis, Byzantine art and black Madonnas. Redd and McKinney Johnson suggest that the presence of Isis in Europe is a positive connection between Europe and Africa, reflecting a history of an African presence in Europe that is often ignored or marginalized. The black Madonna by extension becomes part of that presence. The difficulty here is that the artists of these images leave no records so we cannot be sure such connections can be definitively established. Despite this criticism, however, Redd and McKinney Johnson's research are thoughtful contributions to a field often dominated by white scholars and suggests that interest in the black Madonna could function as a means of addressing areas of history that do not otherwise get attention.

Others who have written about the black Madonna give moving accounts of this image that reflect wider issues of race on a more personal level. For example, Necia Harkless recounts how during World War I, her father was stationed in France:

> Since Paris was off limits for all African American soldiers, my father had to find a place to worship south of Paris. Dad worshipped in the

> Great Marian Sanctuary of Notre-Dame De Myans. On the back of the postcard my father wrote 'My Love, This is the Black Madonna as she stands on the altar of the old church today. Everything is pure gold only her face is black'. I myself made a pilgrimage to Myans in 1994. The message over the entrance read: 'Then saith He to the disciple: Behold Thy Mother'. (Harkless 2005: 262)

Harkless explains that the black Madonna has always been a part of her life. She explains that as a child she thought her mother 'was a Black Madonna and I would grow up to be one' (ibid.). The black Madonna was significant not only as a personal source of comfort and inspiration but also as a means of educating others about black cultural history.

Jeanette Rodriguez's study, *Our Lady of Guadalupe: Faith and Empowerment among Mexican-American Women* (1994) considers the importance of race, culture and faith in relation to a black Madonna figure. Rodriguez describes the purpose of her research as follows:

> Struck by the prominence of the feminine image of Our Lady of Guadalupe in Mexican-American culture and concerned with the ways in which Mexican-American women might relate to and identify with this image, I set out to study its effect on their lives and identities. I chose to do an exploratory study that would identify these women's perception of Our Lady of Guadalupe and describe the nature of the relationship between them—the first step in understanding how Our Lady of Guadalupe influences the daily existence of Mexican-American women. (Rodriguez 1994: xxvii)

Rodriguez uses primary data she collected from questionnaires, written reflections and interviews to provide a picture of individual women and their religious lives. She not only puts the image of Guadalupe in its political and historical context, but also considers the cultural and political forces that may have shaped the experiences of the women who take part in her study. This gives her research a deeper layer of understanding of the responses of her interviewees, showing the benefits of conducting research on how individuals use this particular religious image, and the relationships between the image and wider cultural concerns.

The experiences related by Harkless and by the women interviewed by Rodriguez, and the practices and uses of the black Madonna identified by Oleszkiewicz-Peralba, are powerful demonstrations of the importance of including the many and varied voices of those who have found themselves connecting with a black Madonna. The figure of the black Madonna remains equally as powerful and liberating as in the literature that comes from the largely white, feminist standpoint.

**Figure 11.1**. Black Madonna statue by Catharni Stern, St Mary's Anglican Church, Willesden, North London. Photograph by Melanie Landman

## Vernacular Religion at an Anglican Shrine

The next part of this chapter concentrates on research conducted at a black Madonna shrine based at St Mary's Church in Willesden, North London. The research was very much influenced by the work of Rodriguez, Weibel and Oleszkiewicz-Peralba discussed above, as these researchers demonstrated the importance of considering the black Madonna in specific cultural contexts, and in the cases of Weibel and Rodriguez, how individuals related to these figures.

The research at St Mary's was situated within a framework that adopted a vernacular or 'lived religion' approach. Robert Orsi suggests that implementing this type of method 'situates all religious creativity within culture and approaches all religion as lived experience, theology no less than lighting a candle for a troubled loved one' (2002 [1985]: xix). For Orsi, the study of lived religion 'directs attention to institutions and persons, texts and rituals, practice and theology, things and ideas' (ibid.) and takes account of the relationship between religious practice and the history and culture in which that practice takes place. In this approach, people's relationships to the sacred are complex, dynamic ones. It also recognizes that religion can be rooted in materiality and embodied practice. As Meredith McGuire argues:

> If our conception of religion is too narrow, then we fail to comprehend how central people's material bodies are in the very practice and experience of religion. All religions engage individuals through concrete practices that involve bodies as well as minds and spirits. (McGuire 2008: 98)

For the individuals at St Mary's, such 'concrete practices that involve bodies as well as minds of spirits' would include walking the route of pilgrimage and, in some cases, singing—either in church or indeed at home. Other practices might include the physical relationship with the statue of the black Madonna, such as touching the statue, kneeling in front of it to pray, carrying an icon during pilgrimage, and lighting candles. For the worshippers at St Mary's, taking part in pilgrimage is also a link with the past. Such activities are physical expressions of this relationship with tradition. As McGuire points out, 'religious ritual is like a chain of such embodied practices, each link having the potential to activate deep emotions and a sense of social connectedness, as well as spiritual meanings' (2008: 100).

The St Mary's Willesden black Madonna statue itself was made in 1972 by artist Catharni Stern, carved in limewood and deliberately darkened. The statue was commissioned in order to replace the original image which was said to have been destroyed during the Reformation, although, as this chapter will show, the history of the shrine is a contested one. The initial reaction to the arrival of the black Madonna in the early 1970s was not universally positive. As the vicar writing in the parish magazine at the time comments:

> I am very pleased too that the younger members of our congregation like the statue so much. I think a number of our older members had expected something more simple and perhaps less challenging. Even so, a lot more of them have told me they like it better as they see it more.
> (*Willesden Parish Magazine* 1972)

Once I began to observe what went on in the church and by talking to individuals, a complex picture of religious life began to emerge. I was interested in the relationship the congregation have with this black Madonna, particularly in light of the assertions made about the conflicts between the official and the vernacular and black Madonnas in the existing literature. For the purposes of this chapter, I shall give two examples of the ways in which the networks of relationships between congregation and church operated. Firstly, there were contestations over histories, and whose knowledge was the 'real' story. This was particularly evident when considering the existence of the original black Madonna and the holy well. The story promoted by the church was that the original black Madonna and shrine had been a popular pilgrimage destination during the Middle Ages and that the statue was destroyed during the Reformation. However, local historians, whilst establishing the existence of the shrine, found no evidence that a black Madonna ever existed, and that any references to the statue were probably a Victorian hoax. Similarly, investigations into the holy well questioned the assumption that the water was coming from an underground spring.

Accounts of the church's history are given in local history books and pamphlets, guidebooks to shrines and by the church itself via its website. In the course of fieldwork at the church, particular connections relating to the church's history and its importance to the congregation began to emerge. There were clear relationships between narratives of the church's history and with its shrine as a special space. As Gary Waller observes, shrines can produce narratives 'with significant cultural meanings: the history of any community contains multiple, contradictory stories'. Such stories are ones of 'loss, abandonment and renewal' (Waller 2011: 8). The loss and abandonment that Waller speaks of relates to the destruction of Marian shrines during the Reformation and this is especially pertinent to the story of St Mary's. The stories relating to the destruction of the original shrine and its subsequent renewal provide a rich context in which worship currently takes place. Despite these challenges from local historians, members of the congregation (although by no means all) were happy to accept the church's presentation of its history. Their connection with the church's history was of great importance and the congregation took great pride and interest in the historical narratives that surrounded their church.

Secondly, rather than conflict between worshippers and church authorities there was a spectrum of opinion amongst the congregation regarding Marian devotions; how important Mary, and by extension the black Madonna, was; how comfortable people were with the Marian aspects of devotion and other aspects of worship that were deemed too 'high' church or too close to Roman Catholicism for comfort. But this did not manifest itself in any straightforward 'official' vs. 'folk' religion conflict. For example, a person might be happy to light a candle in front of the statue but this might be seen as an act of remembrance for a loved one, not as an explicit act of Marian devotion. Even for some members of the congregation who did not consider themselves particularly devoted to Mary, there was still a sense that the church would not be the same without the shrine or statue. Worshippers were engaged in creating their own ways of religious practice and expression that drew on different sources. People were actively interpreting scripture and engaged in debates about theology and church teachings.

There was also an emphasis on the importance of Mary as Mother: firstly in terms of her compassion and powers to heal, but also in a broader theological sense that being the Mother of God was central to her place in the Church. For one interviewee, the discussion of Mary's motherhood turned to its theological significance. This interviewee talked about how he accepted that Mary was the Mother of God and the image of the black Madonna was a physical manifestation of Mary and this gave the image its power. To this interviewee, Mary as Christ's human mother was central because it was she who gave him his humanity. Both the humanity of Mary and Christ was then connected directly to the humanity of the congregation.

Not all members were comfortable with an emphasis on Marian devotions. Parishioners made it clear that they were not worshipping Mary as Roman Catholics would. Mary was important as the Mother of God but was not divine in her own right. As one person put it, one prayed to Mary because what son could refuse his mother. For some, there had been a more gradual acceptance of Marian devotions. One parishioner who initially had some difficulties regarding these devotions explained they had reservations about certain aspects such as the Immaculate Conception and the Assumption—that these were not really Anglican beliefs. However, she suggested that it was possible for the way one practised one's faith to change, and recognized that the relationship between the Virgin Mary and Christ needed to be taken into consideration. It was possible for one's faith to grow and change and if Mary as Christ's mother was dear to him then we as worshippers should hold her in higher esteem.

Mary has been a point of division for Anglicans and Roman Catholics, and within the Anglican tradition itself, Paul Williams has argued, the place of Mary 'is assured' because of her place 'in the Gospel tradition, but the way in which that place is celebrated by Anglicans has varied greatly and it continues to do so' (2007: 315). Whilst other aspects of Marian devotion, such as the Assumption or Immaculate Conception or Mary as Co-Redemptrix, might cause difficulties, Mary as mother, given its scriptural basis, is perhaps the least difficult aspect of Mary to incorporate into the worship at an Anglican church. This was certainly reflected in some of the comments made by members of the congregation.

As to whether the black Madonna was important to the congregation, there was no straightforward answer. For some she was a central part of their worship and devotion; for others, they were not interested in any way. There was a sense from some people that the church would not be the same without her, but this was more because she was a familiar part of the fabric of the church, not because any great symbolic significance was attached to her. For at least some of the congregation, the black Madonna had no bearing on their reasons for attending the church. It was simply their local parish church. Even for those people who did take part in Marian devotions, there were more important reasons to attend: the style of liturgy or the musical aspects of the church, for example.

## Conclusion

What is so striking about the feminist and Christian 'folk' discussed in this chapter is the creativity demonstrated individually and collectively in the interpretations of and relationships with the figure of the black Madonna, all showing the potential to challenge what could be construed as 'official' institutions and narratives. At first this seems much more obvious with feminist understandings and their challenge to the mainstream presentation of the black Madonna in the Catholic Church. The merging of different sources such as Jungian psychology, feminist politics and goddess mythology provide potent, imaginative ways in which to relate to the black Madonna. As Fedele observes in her fieldwork with groups on alternative pilgrimages, close attention to their 'theories, practices, life stories and ritual narratives reveals not only an innovative approach to ritual and pilgrimage but also a critique of gender inequality, and more generally of the existing social and religious order' (2013: 275).

It could be suggested, however, that the congregation at St Mary's are equally creative and challenging in multiple ways. This was demonstrated in worshippers' attitudes towards local historians questioning the foundation story of the church and the historical importance of the shrine. Whilst the history of the church was identified as important, and indeed as one of the reasons for the church being a special place, this was not always connected to the existence of the black Madonna. On the one hand, the existence of an original black Madonna image was accepted by members of the congregation. On the other hand, the black

Madonna alone did not necessarily give the church its authenticity. It was the thought that the location had been a place of worship for over a millennium that gave it its atmosphere.

When the black Madonna was considered important, she was seen as a representation of the Virgin Mary, and not simply as a 'black Madonna'. Unlike the dualistic construction of the black Madonna and the Virgin Mary seen in some of the literature, at St Mary's the black Madonna was very much integrated with the Virgin Mary. Here is a black Madonna who is not necessarily a powerful, esoteric alternative. In this respect, the black Madonna at St Mary's brings into question some of the assumptions made in feminist vernacular understandings of the black Madonna.

The notion of a clash between church hierarchy and popular devotion to black Madonnas as highlighted by some scholars was not apparent at St Mary's. Although the extent of devotion to the black Madonna may have differed in practice and intensity between parishioners, such devotion was nonetheless an officially sanctioned element of worship at the church. Likewise, the use of the holy well, whether people chose to use the water at home or receive a blessing from the church itself, was also within the bounds of accepted practice. When there were challenges to these practices, they were either from outside the church, such as the local historians disputing the claims about the well, or else they came from members of the congregation who were not as comfortable with certain devotions but even here, this was not challenged in confrontational or censorial ways. People largely accepted that others may have a different tradition from themselves.

Examining the ways in which different groups and individuals approach their relationships with black Madonnas also encourages an examination of the terminology used when talking about the everyday religious lives of said groups and individuals. The examples discussed in this chapter reveal how the divisions between 'official', 'folk' and 'popular' religions are often so blurred that it is difficult to meaningfully keep these categories separate. Who are the 'folk' when it comes to looking at the ways in which the figure of the black Madonna is interpreted and incorporated into religious practices? For example, the presentation of the black Madonna as a liberating alternative is so ubiquitous in feminist writings on the subject that what began as a challenge to the mainstream Christian version has in its own way become the 'official' way of interpreting this figure for many. But as the research at St Mary's shows, not all black Madonnas can or indeed should be read in this way.

In the examples given in this chapter, what constitutes authority is sometimes more complicated than it first appears. There are more obvious examples: traditional forms of authority such as church authorities and hierarchies. These are represented in the form of priests and bishops and also in the practices sanctioned by these authorities. At St Mary's this would include pilgrimage and the use of the holy well. However, as demonstrated in this chapter, not all members of the congregation are willing to participate in such activities. At the same time, those members who do not participate would not necessarily see themselves as anything other than devout Anglicans. This brings us back to the notion of the vernacular as experiential and creative. Individuals are able to incorporate and act on their own understandings, knowledge and experiences of what it means to be an Anglican Christian, to act as their own religious authority yet at the same time being part of a wider congregation under the supervision of the Church of England. The fluidity of these categories underlines just how apposite the use of terms such as vernacular or lived religion can be. These terms help to break 'the distinction between high and low' whilst at the same time, do not 'displace the institutional or normative perspectives on practice' (Hall 1997: ix). By acknowledging this fluidity, employing a term like vernacular allows for a more holistic approach when trying to understand how groups and individuals relate to the figure of the black Madonna.

## Acknowledgements

Many thanks to Marion and Ülo for asking me to contribute to this volume; to Tina, Lynn and Marzia for all their support during my research; the congregation of St Mary's for all their help with my project; my friends at the Centre for Marian Studies, and last but not least, my family for their love and encouragement.

## References

Baring, Anne, and Jules Cashford. 1993. *The Myth of the Goddess: Evolution of an Image*. London; New York: Penguin Arkana.
Begg, Ean. 1996 [1985]. *The Cult of the Black Virgin*. London: Penguin Arkana.
Boss, Sarah Jane. 2007. 'Black Madonnas'. In *Mary: The Complete Resource*, edited by Sarah Jane Boss, 458–475. London; New York: Continuum.

Chiavola Birnbaum, Lucia. 2000 [1993]. *Black Madonnas: Feminism, Religion and Politics in Italy*. New York: Excel Publications.

Chiavola Birnbaum, Lucia. 2001. *Dark Mother: African Origins and Godmothers*. San José; New York: Authors Choice Press.

Durand-Lefèbvre, Marie. 1937. *Étude Sur L'Origine des Vierges Noires*. Paris.

Eller, Cynthia. 1995. *Living in the Lap of the Goddess: The Feminist Spirituality Movement in America*. Boston, MA: Beacon Press.

Eller, Cynthia. 2000. 'White Women and the Dark Mother'. *Religion* 30 (4): 367–378. https://doi.org/10.1006/reli.2000.0276

Fedele, Anna. 2013. *Looking for Mary Magdalene: Alternative Pilgrimage and Ritual Creativity at Catholic Shrines in France*. Oxford; New York: Oxford University Press. https://doi.org/10.1093/acprof:oso/9780199898404.001.0001

Galland, China. 1990. *Longing for Darkness: Tara and the Black Madonna*. New York: Viking.

Gimbutas, Marija. 1982. *The Goddesses and Gods of Old Europe 6500–3500 BC*. London: Thames and Hudson.

Gimbutas, Marija. 1989. *The Language of the Goddess: Unearthing the Hidden Symbols of Western Civilization*. London: Thames and Hudson.

Gustafson, Fred. 1990. *The Black Madonna*. Boston, MA: Sigo Press.

Hall, David D. 1997. 'Introduction'. In *Lived Religion in America: Towards a History of Practice*, edited by David D. Hall, vii–xiii. Princeton, NJ: Princeton University Press.

Harkless, Necia. 2005. 'The Black Madonnas in My Life'. In *She Is Everywhere: An Anthology of Writing in Womanist/Feminist Spirituality*, edited by Lucia Chiavola Birnbaum, 260–271. New York; Shanghai: iUniverse Inc.

Lynch, Gordon. 2007. *The New Spirituality: An Introduction to Progressive Belief in the Twenty-First Century*. London; New York: Taurus & Co. https://doi.org/10.5040/9780755626335

Markale, Jean. 2004. *Cathedral of the Black Madonna: The Druids and the Mysteries of Chartres*. Rochester, VT: Inner Traditions International.

McGuire, Meredith. 2008. *Lived Religion: Faith and Practice in Everyday Life*. Oxford; New York: Oxford University Press.

McKinney Johnson, Eloise. 1987. 'Egypt's Isis: The Original Black Madonna'. In *Black Women in Antiquity*, edited by Ivan Van Sertima, 64–71. New Brunswick; London: Transaction Publishing.

Moss, Leonard, and Stephen Cappannari. 1953. 'The Black Madonna: An Example of Culture Borrowing'. *The Scientific Monthly* 76 (6): 319–324.

Moss, Leonard, and Stephen Cappannari. 1982. 'In Quest of the Black Virgin: She Is Black Because She Is Black'. In *Mother Worship: Themes and Variations*, edited by James J. Preston, 53–74. Chapel Hill: University of North Carolina Press.

Oleszkiewicz-Peralba, Malgorzata. 2007. *The Black Madonna in Latin America and Europe: Tradition and Transformation*. Albuquerque: University of New Mexico Press.

Orsi, Robert. 2002 [1985]. *The Madonna of 115th Street: Faith and Community in Italian Harlem 1880–1959*. New Haven, CT; London: Yale University Press.

Picknett, Lynn. 2003. *Mary Magdalene: Christianity's Hidden Goddess*. London: Constable and Robinson.

Primiano, Leonard Norman. 1995. 'Vernacular Religion and the Search for in Religious Folklife'. *Western Folklore* (Special Issue: *Reflexivity and the Study of Belief*) 54 (1): 37–56. https://doi.org/10.2307/1499910

Redd, Danita. 1987. 'Black Madonnas of Europe: Diffusion of the African Isis'. In *Black Women in Antiquity*, edited by Ivan Van Sertima, 162-187. New Brunswick; London: Transaction Publishing.

Rodriguez, Jeanette. 1994. *Our Lady of Guadalupe: Faith and Empowerment among Mexican-American Women*. Austin: University of Texas Press.

Saillens, Emile. 1945. *Nos Vierges Noires, Leurs Origines*. Paris.

Sjöo, Monica, and Barbara Mor. 1987. *The Great Cosmic Mother: Rediscovering the Religion of the Earth*. San Francisco: Harper & Row.

Starbird, Margaret. 1993. *The Woman with the Alabaster Jar: Mary Magdalene and the Holy Grail*. Santa Fe, NM: Bear & Co.

Stone, Merlin. 1976. *When God Was a Woman*. (Originally published as *The Paradise Papers: The Suppression of Women's Rites*.) San Diego; New York; London: Harcourt Brace & Co.

Waller, Gary. 2011. *The Virgin Mary in Late Medieval and Early Modern English Literature and Popular Culture*. Cambridge; New York: Cambridge University Press.

Weibel, Deana. 2002a. 'The New Age and the Old World: The Interpretation and Use of European Shrines by "Religious Creatives"'. *Maria: A Journal of Marian Studies* 2 (2): 80-87.

Weibel, Deana. 2002b. 'This Energy We Call the Goddess'. *Maria: A Journal of Marian Studies* 2 (2): 88-94.

*Willesden Parish Magazine*. 1972. *Willesden Parish Magazine*, June 17, 1972.

Williams, Paul. 2007. 'The Virgin Mary in Anglican Tradition'. In *Mary: The Complete Resource*, edited by Sarah Jane Boss, 314-339. London; New York: Continuum.

Chapter 12

# Negotiating Vernacular Authority, Legitimacy and Power: Creativity, Ambiguity and Materiality in Devotion to Gauchito Gil

*Marion Bowman*[*]

### Introduction

Antonio 'de la Cruz' Gil Núñez (1847–1878), more commonly known as Gauchito Gil, is a historical but much mythologized figure who is the focus of considerable popular devotion in Argentina. Understanding the term vernacular religion to denote 'religion as it is lived: as human beings encounter, understand, interpret, and practice it' (Primiano 1995: 44), in this chapter I consider some of the strategies used in vernacular religion to establish, express and negotiate legitimacy, authority and power.

---

[*] **Marion Bowman** has been based in Religious Studies at The Open University UK since 2000. She has conducted long-term research in the town of Glastonbury, on which she has published extensively, and has also written on vernacular religion, pilgrimage, Celtic spirituality, material religion, spiritual economies, and religion in Newfoundland. She was Co-Investigator on the AHRC funded project Pilgrimage and England's Cathedrals, Past and Present (2014–2018), and a visiting Professor at the University of Oslo (2016–2018) and the University of Tartu (2014). She co-edited *Vernacular Religion in Everyday Life: Expressions of Belief* (Equinox, 2012) with Ülo Valk; a Thematic Issue on *Religion in Cathedrals: Pilgrimage, Place, Heritage, and the Politics of Replication* with Simon Coleman (*Religion* 49 (1), 2019); and a Special Issue on *Reframing Pilgrimage in Northern Europe* (*NUMEN* 67 (5–6), 2020) with Dirk Johannsen and Ane Ohrvik.

**Figure 12.1.** Gauchito Gil image painted on a wall beside a garage, San José de Feliciano, Entre Ríos Province, Argentina. Photograph by Marion Bowman

I first encountered devotion to Gauchito ('Little Gaucho') Gil through visiting my husband's relations, who are fourth- and fifth-generation Argentines of English and Scottish descent, some of whom live on an *estancia* (ranch) in rural Entre Ríos Province. I was first struck by a life-size depiction of Gauchito Gil on a wall (Figure 12.1) in the local city San José de Feliciano, and then noticed stickers of Gauchito Gil on the *gauchos*'[1] cars. On enquiring about this (to me) unfamiliar figure, I was told about how loved Gauchito Gil is, how effective he is considered to be, and how important it is to many *gauchos* to make an annual visit to the Mercedes shrine (220 km away) if at all possible, ideally on his 'feast day' January 8th.² His legend has a number of variants, but Gauchito Gil is primarily narrated as a Robin Hood-type figure who was unjustly executed. He is widely considered to be the common people's friend and protector, with considerable post-mortem powers.

Gil's complex imagery and the multivalent material culture connected with him became a source of fascination to me and a trip to Gauchito Gil's shrine in Mercedes crystallized some aspects of 'strategic' materiality in respect to devotion and relationality, something on which I have worked in different contexts over many years (e.g. Bowman 2016; 2017; 2021). By relationality here I mean the deeply personal and significant relationships people form with others (including, for example, both living people and the dead, and diverse non- or supra-human beings) and the praxis that expresses and sustains such close relationships.

Participant behaviour at the shrine of Gauchito Gil confirmed and conformed to that seen at shrines and special sites in myriad places and traditions, but of particular interest were the objects for sale at Mercedes. The range of such objects there, and particularly the visual and material messages they projected, were significant in understanding both the operationalizing and functioning of the cult. One devotional/decorative item on sale, for example, consisted of a red ribbon (30 cm long by 4 cm wide) with a hanging loop, on which had been stuck four small pieces of card, bearing from top to bottom images of Pope Francis then Gauchito Gil, the words *Protege Nuestra Hogar* ('Protect Our Home') and below that an image of San Pantaleon (see Figure 12.2). This configuration of Pope Francis (the Argentinian hierarchical head of the Catholic church), Gauchito Gil (a figure often described as a 'folk saint'), an exhortation for protection, and a popular and an institutionally 'legitimate' saint visually indicated some parity between the figures and highlighted the importance of materiality in vernacular authentication and legitimacy.

The study of vernacular religion, encompassing 'the process of religious belief, the verbal, behavioural, and material expressions of religious belief, and the ultimate object of religious belief' (Primiano 1995: 44) is naturally concerned with the worldviews and experiences that shape people's discourse, their actions, their relationships with others (both human and 'other than conventionally human' beings) and their engagement with the material world (Bowman and Valk 2012: 5–10).

In this context, vernacular authority, characterized as 'trust in what is handed down *outside* of any formally instituted social formation' (Howard 2013: 81; original emphasis), is a significant factor. For Catholics, Leonard Norman Primiano observes, 'the multitude of beliefs and practices represented within institutionalized and non-institutionalized Catholicism form a rich source of inspiration within the process of believing' (2001: 54).

**Figure 12.2.** Collection of items from Gauchito Gil shrine, Mercedes, Corrientes Province, Argentina. Photograph by Marion Bowman

The history of devotion to Gauchito Gil and praxis at his shrine spotlight complex interactions and negotiations around vernacular culture and religiosity in general, and vernacular Catholicism in particular. It draws out differing perspectives not only between Gil's devotees and some Catholic church personnel, but also *between* some Catholic figures of authority who are themselves 'believing and practicing vernacularly, even while representing the most institutionally normative aspects of their religious tradition' (Primiano 1995: 46).

Vernacular knowledge and authority are materialized and operationalized in interaction with institutional models and local lifeworlds in devotion to Gauchito Gil; the devotion is embedded in a rich repertoire of 'communicative resources and practices' (Bauman 2008: 32). Strategies of proximity, approximation and appropriation are used effectively as material means of bolstering Gil's legitimacy and power alongside and beyond institutional understandings and models. Primiano observes that the hallmarks of vernacular religion are ambiguity, power and creativity (2012: 382–394). This exploration of Gauchito Gil's cult helps to demonstrate how materiality functions in conferring and transferring power, both creatively and ambiguously, in relation to saints and significant, powerful dead people without 'institutional' recognition or status. It 'highlights the power of the individual and communities of individuals to create and re-create their own religion' (ibid.: 383).

## Contextualizing Gauchito Gil

There is considerable variety, ambiguity and creativity in the praxis and material culture relating to Gauchito Gil, who is the focus of considerable popular devotion, promissory prayer, ex votos and material culture at his shrine in Mercedes in Corrientes Province, Argentina, and beyond.

Details and versions of Gauchito Gil's life and death vary and have multiplied over the years.[3] Commonly described in academic literature and by some clergy as a 'folk saint', he is popularly portrayed as a simple *gaucho*, a man of the people. Born in Corrientes Province around 1847, Antonio Gil Núñez was said to have been pressganged into military service during one of the civil wars that characterized Argentine politics between 1814 and 1880. Having deserted, it is said, because he was unwilling to kill fellow gauchos in a conflict not of their making, he became an outlaw and popular hero known for his altruism, reputedly robbing from the rich to give to the poor. Gil was betrayed and arrested, and although he was supposed to be taken to Goya for trial, he was executed en route on the outskirts of Mercedes. In one version recorded by Frank Graziano, 'Gil was hung upside down from an espinillo tree and his head was cut off with his own knife, which he offered for this purpose' (2007: 113).

Having been unjustly executed, in the manner of a martyr, an immediate posthumous miracle gave rise to a popular and still burgeoning cult. It is said that Gauchito Gil told his executioner (or the official responsible for his execution) that when he got back home, he would discover both a letter of pardon for Gil, and he would find that his son was mortally ill. However, if the executioner prayed to Gauchito Gil, he would cure the child. (Another variant is that Gil told his executioner that if he took back a handkerchief soaked in Gil's blood, the child would be cured.) Although the executioner was sceptical of these predictions, this is allegedly what happened. The executioner subsequently set up a cross at the blood-stained site of Gauchito Gil's execution at Mercedes in thanksgiving for his son's cure, where the current shrine still stands. The message was clear from the start: Gauchito Gil *knows*, he is *compassionate*, and he *works*.

Graziano points out that Gauchito Gil is one of a number of 'gaucho folk saints' in Argentina, and that the 'typical story of gaucho sainthood is as political as it is religious' (2007: 114-117). Gauchito Gil became a popular hero, technically an outlaw, but with a lifestyle and morality popularly thought superior to that of the authority figures and institutions above him. Gil's contemporary iconography reflects his persona as a 'typical *gaucho*'. Gil tends to be depicted as a rather dashing figure with dark flowing hair and a moustache, usually wearing a blue or a white shirt, a red bandana around his head, a red scarf at his neck and a red textile sash (*faja*).[4] In some representations he also sports below the waist a dark garment called a *chiripa*, a sort of woollen cloth. Generally wearing the traditional horseman's baggy trousers (*bombachas*) and on his feet canvas shoes (*alpargatas*), Gil is usually depicted carrying in one hand *boleadoras* or bolas, the traditional hunting device of the *gaucho*: three stones, each wrapped in rawhide, at the end of rawhide ropes.[5]

A significant aspect of Gauchito Gil's identity is that he is portrayed as an 'ordinary' Catholic, devoted both to the nationally revered Virgin of Luján[6] and the locally popular Our Lady of Itati, but also to the locally significant 'San La Muerte'.[7] The San La Muerte cult is thought to have originated in Corrientes Province and there is a San La Muerte shrine very close to Mercedes. San La Muerte's legend varies and the devotion's history is complex and controversial (see Graziano 2007: 77-111), but we were told at the San La Muerte shrine in Corrientes Province that he was a monk or priest who ministered to lepers,[8] who annoyed the church and other authorities, who was incarcerated with the lepers to whom he was devoted, and died amongst them. (San La Muerte is frequently depicted as a skeleton in a monk's robe, often wielding a scythe.) That Gauchito Gil's Catholic credentials are confirmed by devotional preferences which include both the Virgin and San La Muerte underlines the practical lack of differentiation between 'institutionally' sanctioned and sanctified figures and others whose powers are common knowledge in local communities of practice.

As I have observed elsewhere (Bowman 2021) roadside crosses and memorials have recently attracted considerable academic attention, especially in countries where these have not been the norm. Argentine roadside crosses marking a death site, in common with similar crosses and markers internationally, can become regarded not simply as reminders of an untimely death and a prompt to pray for the victim, but as 'a link between this world and the next' (Graziano 2007: 118). However, the symbolism and significance of roadside crosses in Corrientes Province have particular local significance and longevity. A large cross erected by colonists during the founding of Corrientes city in 1588 withstood the attempt by local Guarani resisters to burn it down, thereafter becoming known as the *Cruz de Milagro* ('Cross of the Miracle'), an object of power and devotion in its own right, reproductions of which were 'enshrined on home altars' (ibid.: 117). The cross erected at the site of Gil's execution was the genesis of the contemporary shrine at Mercedes (originally referred to as *la Cruz de Gil, la Cruz Gil* or in Guarani *Curuzú Gil*) and became the locus for prayers not only for the soul of Gil, but eventually also to Gil.[9] Graziano notes that miracles were 'at first attributed to the cross, not to Gil' (ibid.: 119). In many images and statues, Gil is depicted standing in front of a large cross, generally understood to be *la Cruz Gil*, which tends to be either brown or red in colour.

In matters of vernacular religion, vernacular knowledge and vernacular authority, appreciating local, historical and political contexts can be significant in understanding the ways in which individuals, groups, practices, beliefs and what is regarded as 'common knowledge' fit and interact with specific landscapes. As Richard Bauman neatly put it, 'if you want to understand a culture, examine its texts, and if you want to comprehend a text, read it in relation to the culture to which it gives expression' (2008: 31). Regarding religious material culture as a species of text, Bauman's conceptualization of the vernacular as 'a communicative modality' is helpful. This communicative modality is characterized by: (1) communicative resources and practices that are acquired informally, in communities of practice, rather than by formal instruction; (2) communicative relations that are immediate, grounded in the interaction order and the lifeworld; and (3) horizons of distribution and circulation that are spatially bounded, by locality or region. (Ibid.: 32–33)

Contemporary transport infrastructure, communications media and growing popularity have expanded the 'reach' of the horizons of the distribution and circulation of Gauchito Gil's cult, with roadside and other shrines to him appearing throughout Argentina (see Figure 12.3) and beyond. Appreciating the loci and foci in which the devotion and material praxis has evolved and developed is nonetheless invaluable.

**Figure 12.3.** Gauchito Gil roadside shrine, Corrientes Province, Argentina. Photograph by Marion Bowman

## Ambiguity, Creativity and Negotiation in Vernacular Catholicism

Gauchito Gil is not officially recognized by the Catholic Church, but in that he is not alone. Not only in Argentina but around the globe people are praying to myriad 'unrecognized' saints, as that is a necessary part of the beatification and canonization process, a regular aspect of vernacular Catholicism. Between his death in 1914 and his beatification in 2013, for example, Jose Gabriel del Rosario Brochero (1840–1914) was an unrecognized saint for around a century. Better known now simply as Cura Brochero, described by Pope Francis (2016) as 'that gaucho priest who felt compassion for his beloved people in Serrana and fought for their dignity', he was beatified in 2013 and eventually canonized in 2016.

The practices and material culture of devotion to Gauchito Gil, as with other aspects of vernacular Catholicism, do not seek to divest Catholic priests and the church of their powers; rather they appropriate, re-version and redistribute them. Cura Brochero is now institutionally 'legitimate', despite years of being in an ambiguous situation vis-à-vis the Church; his status was initially established, communicated and negotiated among local people, not from above. That devotion to Gauchito Gil is neither technically legitimate in nor legitimated by the Catholic Church is in many respects irrelevant, 'the strategies of appropriation, sublimation and transference' (Kapaló 2013: 11) having been successful for some considerable time in establishing his credentials.

Communal and personal experiences and perceptions of efficacy have been and continue to be important in the creation and adaptation of 'communicative resources and practices' (Bauman 2008) which draw on devotional expressions and expectations familiar from vernacular Catholicism. While Gauchito Gil is generally referred to by scholars, Catholic clergy and commentators as a 'folk saint', on account of the ritual and devotional paraphernalia accruing to him, it seems that Gil is never given the honorific title of 'saint' by his devotees, nor depicted with a halo, though he is expected to operate in a similar manner. In the prayer printed on a votive candle (see Figure 12.2) for example, the wording carefully reflects that used as standard in relation to saints more generally, asking for help and thanking God, via the intermediary, in this case Gil:

> Oh! Gauchito Gil
> I humbly beg you to fulfill the miracle that I ask of you through God, and I promise you that I will fulfil my promise, offering you my faithful thanks and demonstration of Faith, in God and in you, Gauchito Gil. Amen.[10]

While there has been a contested history of condemnation by various Catholic church officials and commentators in relation to Gil's cult, as well as some 'turning a blind eye' to people's extra-institutional activity, there has been also empathetic engagement with it. One aspect of vernacular religion that possibly has not received as much attention as it deserves relates to Primiano's contention that priests can be 'believing and practicing vernacularly, even while representing the most institutionally normative aspects of their religious tradition' (Primiano 1995: 46). Father Julian Zini, parish priest at Mercedes for many years, was both heavily influenced by Vatican II and a member of the socially and politically active Movement of Priests for the Third World; he was persecuted during Argentina's brutal military regime in the 1970s and 1980s. A native of Corrientes Province, Zini was a collector, champion and practitioner of vernacular culture, particularly the distinctive *chamamé* musical form; he actually wrote *chamamé* lyrics celebrating Gil. By the time of Zini's death at the age of 80 in August 2020, he had become known not only as a '*chamamecero*' but a defender of Argentina's biodiversity; Pope Francis sent a handwritten note to the province of Corrientes, describing Zini as 'one of the great "Poets of the People", a creator of song, of life, of beauty' (San Martín 2020).

Graziano contends that the growth of Gil's cult is 'largely indebted' to Zini, whom he describes as a 'local hero' among many Catholics in Corrientes, by enabling his parishioners to feel that they could 'belong to the Church without abandoning their traditional beliefs and cultural identity' (Graziano 2007: 134). From conversations with the priest in the early 2000s, Graziano reports Zini as arguing that 'when intolerant priests discount the validity of local culture, prohibit folk expressions of faith, and impose Church dogma from above', they were simply repeating and perpetuating the mistakes of colonial missionaries (ibid.: 133). He believed that 'folk devotions are the expression of a profound faith integral to everyday life, and that they should be accepted, even celebrated, as they are gradually guided towards orthodox practices' (ibid.: 132).

Under Zini, a mass for Gauchito Gil's soul was celebrated at the parish church in Mercedes, Our Lady of Mercy, early on the morning of his annual fiesta, with the cross from Gil's shrine being brought to the church and blessed. The cross was then returned in a flamboyant procession to the shrine for the fiesta proper. Graziano notes that many priests disapproved of what they regarded as 'inappropriate encouragement of unauthorized devotions' (2007: 134). Nevertheless, in 2005 Zini persuaded Ricardo Faifer, Bishop of Goya, to attend the Gauchito Gil fiesta, in what Faifer saw as 'a gesture of peace and to demonstrate the Church's interest in "channelling the religious faith" of devotees toward approved devotions' (ibid.:

135). Unsurprisingly, whatever the nuanced intention or theological logic underlying such interventions, participation by church representatives has tended to be interpreted by devotees as a kind of endorsement. While Robert Glenn Howard rightly argues that trust in vernacular authority can and does arise *because* it 'does not rely on any authority arising from formally instituted social formations like a church' (2013: 81), it is nonetheless the case that vernacular authority can be bolstered when institutional authority is construed to support its case.

Primiano asserts that 'vernacular religiosity has the potential to manifest dimensions of both confirmation and contestation, of legitimation of the hegemonic as well as resistance to such societal and cultural manifestations of power' (Primiano 2012: 387). Devotion to Gauchito Gil has developed under circumstances where contestation of societal, cultural and religious power has not been the prerogative simply of 'the people' in opposition to the Church or the state. Individual lives and experiences, like religious and cultural milieux, are considerably more complex and 'messy'. Appropriate to this context, Primiano (ibid.) picks up on the phraseology used by Michael Candelaria in his work on South American liberation theology, to describe vernacular religion as 'stubbornly ambiguous' (Candelaria 1990: 2).

## Materializing Devotion to Gauchito Gil

David Morgan claims that

> material analysis consists of a series of inquiries that move from consideration of the concrete features of an individual object to comparison with other objects like it to its circulation and use and finally to what the object does and how it may be understood to perform different kinds of cultural work. (Morgan 2017: 15)

To appreciate the religious and cultural work performed by the material culture of Gauchito Gil, it is helpful to return to the idea of religious material culture as a species of text, and the observation that the 'nature and capacities of texts are closely tied to the communicative technology employed in their production, circulation, and reception' (Bauman 2008: 32). People act and interact with things; things act on and interact with people as they use them to 'build and maintain life-worlds' (Morgan 2008: 228). The meaning of religious objects therefore is 'embodied, felt, interactive, and cumulative' (ibid.: 228). Religious goods can be significant communicative media, frequently perceived to communicate something well beyond the simple representation of the person depicted. While statues and representations of holy figures are said to be aids to contemplation and accessories to devotion, consistently in vernacular Catholicism they have been related to, promoted and regarded in far more complex, power-oriented ways—as William Christian (1972), Robert A. Orsi (1985; 1996), Patricia Lysaght (1994), Amy Whitehead (2013), Bowman (2016) and many others have demonstrated.

Pilgrimage shrines, being 'the pre-eminent centres for dealings between human beings and the divine', operate as 'the stock exchanges of the religious economy' (Eade and Sallnow 1991: 24) in which myriad material items are regarded as valuable currency. The meanings of and significance invested in such objects and transactions are complex, and the desire to go to, leave something at and take something away from the site is strong (see Bowman and Jenkins 2020). In this respect Gil's shrine at Mercedes is unremarkable, featuring many of the usual material culture manifestations of a pilgrimage destination, with candles, a range of ex votos, and a flourishing 'spiritual economy' of devotional items and mementoes.

Many pilgrims, *gauchos* and their families, truck drivers, motorists and others come to publicly thank Gauchito Gil, to privately seek his help, to communicate with him, leave objects for him, and buy artefacts related to him. The shrine itself has grown considerably beyond the tree where Gil was reputedly executed and where the cross was erected (see Figure 12.4). The shanty town which grew up around the site, the many stalls and hawkers selling Gil related merchandise and the somewhat chaotic atmosphere at the shrine have attracted—and continue to attract—negative comments (Graziano 2007: 137–140).[11] At many sites of pilgrimage there are shrine keepers and figures of authority who attempt to control the site, behaviour at it, and the sale of appropriate goods; frequently such attempts are subverted by both pilgrims and determined vendors and others who benefit from the associated pilgrim economy that flourishes at such sites. With so many people coming to the shrine as day-trippers, sightseers and devotees, it is a significant boost to the peripheral local economy as well as being the pre-eminent point for purchase of Gil related goods. As the Mercedes shrine is not under institutional control, the goods for sale there reflect the 'available materiality' (Insoll 2015: 49) of what it is possible to produce and sell in relation to the devotion.

**Figure 12.4.** Streetside view of Gauchito Gil shrine, Mercedes, Corrientes Province, Argentina. Photograph by Marion Bowman

The materiality of Gauchito Gil devotion and the behaviours associated with and promoted by that materiality draw richly on the repertoire learned from vernacular Catholicism, which itself is enhanced and enriched by the relationality that materiality affords. The extent of the material flourishing of Gauchito Gil's cult at Mercedes, and the ways in which items on sale intertwine and interact with both 'traditional' Christian devotions to the Virgin Mary and institutionally recognized saints, and to other officially 'unrecognized' saints (such as San La Muerte) and vernacular praxis, clearly signal 'communicative resources and practices that are acquired informally' (Bauman 2008: 32). The shrine at Mercedes thus provides a rich concentration of Gauchito Gil material culture and is the site of intricate material transactions and praxis. As with any successful pilgrimage destination, it is instructive to consider what occurs on site, what is left there, what is seen there, what is for sale there and what is taken away.

**Figure 12.5.** Devotional and sales activity, Gauchito Gil shrine, Mercedes, Corrientes Province, Argentina. Photograph by Marion Bowman

One of the most visually striking aspects of the shrine is its 'redness'.[12] Numerous red candles are purchased, lit and left at the shrine; many of the items for sale there are predominantly red (Figure 12.5). People spend time in conversation with Gil, and a considerable degree of quite intimate contact with and affection for Gil is demonstrated through acts such as lighting a cigarette and leaving it burning for him or leaving red wine for him. Specialized, personal and personalized items are brought to the shrine by devotees, to be left in thanksgiving or 'activated' there. The efficacy of Gauchito Gil's interventions and granting of requests is materially expressed through the enormous quantity and range of ex votos, including photographs of longed-for children or the grateful healed, wedding dresses, guitars, football shirts, and innumerable plaques which sometimes detail the favour granted but more often simply give the names of grateful and successful petitioners. Statues of Gil of varying sizes have been left at different points on site. Particularly striking are the enormous numbers of real and replica licence plates, as Gauchito Gil is considered powerful both in aiding the acquisition of a car and looking after drivers and their passengers (see Figure 12.6). Red ribbons of various sizes with words of thanks to Gauchito Gil printed on them are bought to be left there, thanking him 'for giving me health and work' and 'for favours received'. Others beseech protection for the home and family, blessings on a car, and protection on journeys.

**Figure 12.6.** Number plates at Gauchito Gil shrine, Mercedes, Corrientes Province, Argentina. Photograph by Marion Bowman

However, in addition to the items purchased for use there, there is a huge array of material culture to take away, for as we know there is a long tradition of people wanting to take things away from shrines that establish a connection with that place and with the special person associated with it (see Bowman and Jenkins 2020). Over the centuries, technological developments (such as printing) and new materials (such as plastic) have given rise to a plethora of material options, though these have frequently attracted disparaging comments about the cheapness, shoddiness or poor taste of many mass-produced pilgrim souvenirs.[13] Understanding such items as identity markers, material signs that devotees have made a special journey, and 'as reminders and even as tangible channels of connection with the sacred experience' (Coleman and Elsner 1995: 100) explains why their value lies not in monetary or aesthetic considerations, but in their assumed status and power as having come from a pilgrimage centre.

The ubiquitous red candles and statues and pictures of various sizes are on sale to be taken for home use or for placing in other contexts; on the altar of the cemetery chapel in San José de Feliciano, for example, various statues of Gil appear alongside statues and prayer cards of Our Lady of Lujan, St Joseph, Sacred Heart of Jesus, St Expedite, St Cayetano[14] and others. There are items to be used in the construction of roadside shrines (see Figure 12.3)—large statues, candles, banners featuring Gauchito Gil—which function to further spread and make visible devotion to Gauchito Gil. Given the significance of cars in the devotional transactions at Mercedes, it is unsurprising to find many car stickers, some simply celebrating the trip to the shrine ('Gauchito Gil—Mercedes—Corrientes'), others petitioning 'Gauchito Gil Protect my Car', 'Gauchito Gil Protect my Family' or 'Gauchito Gil Guide my Way'. Thin red ribbons printed with the words Rdo del Gauchito Gil can be bought to tie around the wrist.

In his material analysis schema, Morgan characterizes 'remediation' as 'a reissuing of a product in a new medium or format', a process which can place 'the artefact in a new interpretive context' (Morgan 2017: 25). He gives the example of the dashboard statue as a remediation through which the car dashboard could become a place 'to practice a certain form of devotion that was different from the bedroom, sanctuary, pilgrimage shrine or workplace' (ibid.: 26). With prayer cards, medals, and car statues and stickers, holy or powerful figures are frequently on the move, often cast in protective roles (Bowman 2016).

In addition to statues and pictures of Gauchito Gil, there are numerous examples at Mercedes of what we might term 'domestic remediation', that is, items of everyday use that are enhanced—possibly empowered—by the presence of images of Gauchito Gil. These include trays, hot water flasks and receptacles for drinking maté,[15] wooden platters and cutlery sets of the type used on the move, knives in leather holders decorated by an image of Gauchito Gil, and so on. This signifies that Gauchito Gil is an obvious companion in multifarious contexts; the images might be decorative but they are also potentially expressive of relationality and presence.

At Mercedes, devotees can thus acquire statues, car stickers, banners, practical items and other memorabilia, for placing in the home and vehicles and other contexts where they may be felt to perform protective roles and confirm relationality in numerous significant situations. Timothy Insoll talks of objects and assemblages of objects as 'dynamic reflections of available materiality' (2015: 49), a phrase that rather neatly captures the atmosphere and material complexity of the shrine.

## Proximity, Approximation, Appropriation

To some extent, this range of material objects and the varied significances attributed to them at Mercedes might be said to apply to any shrine, its material culture and pilgrim economy. However, in relation to understanding how objects 'perform different kinds of cultural work' (Morgan 2017: 15), in the case of Gauchito Gil there are additional visual and material credential-confirming and authority-conferring elements to be taken into consideration. Material objects strategically employ proximity and approximation to appropriate and express status and legitimacy. Various images of Gil on artefacts are configured and juxtaposed with other figures to serve as communicative texts expressing and reaffirming Gil's status.

Items sold for the creation of shrines and home altars may feature Gauchito Gil alone, as in the case of statues of him and banners, candles and prayer cards solely bearing his image, but his depiction in relation to other saints and holy figures projects significant messages. Gauchito Gil's alleged devotion to San La Muerte is represented on items such as pictures and banners which feature them both. The repeated stress on Gauchito Gil being a good Catholic, with devotion to the Virgin and other saints, is expressed in a number of ways in relation to the artefacts at Mercedes. On one car sticker, a representation of Gauchito Gil appears encircled within the rosary, which both underlines his devotion to Mary and his practice as a good Catholic, and physically aligns both figures. Popular devotional items to be taken away from the shrine, designed to ask for protection in the car, and protection of the home, include red ribbon hangings (as described above) on which are stuck small cardboard or plastic pictures of Gauchito Gil *and* Our Lady of Itati or Gauchito Gil *and* Our Lady of Lucan, which again not only establishes a historical connection between the two but visually indicates that through having this item in your home or car, both are potentially equally present and powerful. As mentioned already, Gauchito Gil also appears on ribbon devotional hangings in the company of popular saints such as St Cayetano, St Pantaleon and St Expedite, and Pope Francis (Figure 12.2). There is the very practical example of a tray which is both useful, but also has great creative and ambiguous visual power: by depicting Gauchito Gil with the Sacred Heart of Jesus and St Cayetano, it physically and figuratively places him on the same level as them (see Figure 12.7).

**Figure 12.7.** Tray on shelf with other items such as Gauchito Gil, San La Muerte and St Expedite statues, stall at Gauchito Gil shrine, Mercedes, Corrientes Province, Argentina. Photograph by Marion Bowman

Artefacts in which Gil is presented alongside more established, institutionally recognized divine figures, and in conjunction with other vernacular saints, make important points about equality and efficacy. Such visual representations suggest a connection, conferring a sort of power sharing or even power transference dynamic. On devotional ribbon hangings which feature a picture of Gauchito Gil at the top and a picture of San Cayetano below, for example, or a picture of Gauchito Gil at the top and a picture of Our Lady of Itati below, the words printed in white beneath the images are nevertheless addressed solely to Gil: 'Revered Gauchito Antonio Gil. Bless my Journeys. Protect my Home and Family. Give health, love and work. Protect us always'.[16]

Just as proximity to other saints and powerful figures is suggestive of some sort of parity, there is also an element of visual approximation. Gauchito Gil in some of his iconography and narrative is strikingly Christlike. Here is an innocent man whose blood is shed, and who can help others from beyond the grave. There is the tree associated with his execution, which might easily approximate to the tree of the cross, but above all there is his depiction in front of a large cross. Though Graziano claims that in his fieldwork this parallel with Jesus was not specifically mentioned, the imagery is nevertheless redolent with ubiquitous crucifixion iconography.

While items sold at the Mercedes shrine with such combinations of images of Gauchito Gil, the Virgin and other saints establish parity through proximity, there are of course numerous instances of similarly meaningful assemblages elsewhere. An almost life-size statue of Gil in a case opposite an identically encased statue of San La Muerte at the entrance to the nearby San La Muerte shrine, and inside the shrine a large carved wooden Gil statue alongside the statue of San La Muerte, establish a similar visual conjunction.[17] As mentioned above, in the cemetery chapel in San José de Feliciano, the inclusion of Gauchito Gil statues alongside those of Our Lady of Lujan, St Expedite, St Cayetano and others indicates that they are all performing identical 'cultural work' in the lifeworlds of those who placed them there.

In a more secular context, in 2015 the controversial art display *Barbie: The Plastic Revolution* by Argentine artists Pool & Marianela (Marianela Perelli and Emiliano Paolini) opened as part of the Saints and Sinners exhibition at Popa Galeria, a gallery in Buenos Aires. Their exhibit featured 33 Ken and Barbie dolls, predominantly dressed as Catholic saints and figures, with some from other religious traditions such as Buddha and Kali. The artists claimed to have drawn 'inspiration from the rigorous detailing and perfectionism employed by artisans in the past to represent Mary and other saints in statue form' (Bell 2015). They have subsequently stated that they 'do not conceive art if it does not have rebellion ... We cry out by testing the limits of the nexus between religious mentality and consumerism' (Gallery 30 South n.d.). Despite its stormy reception in Argentina, with much conservative Catholic and right-wing opposition, Pope Francis owns one of their Virgin of Lujan dolls (presented by the artists) and the exhibition has enjoyed international critical acclaim. What is interesting in relation to this chapter is the fact that on the poster for the *Barbie: The Plastic Religion* exhibition in 2015, beside Barbie and Ken dolls dressed as Jesus, Mary and St Cayetano appeared Gauchito Gil! Even in a secular Argentine assemblage, Gil is featured alongside and on a par with the more conventional holy figures.[18]

For devotees Gauchito Gil is 'one of us', while simultaneously, in relation to other popular, revered and significant religious figures,

Gauchito Gil is commonly considered to be 'one of them'. In devotion to Gauchito Gil, material and visual proximity and approximation underline the successful vernacular appropriation of the power which the institutional church might seek to control and dispense, bypassing the legitimation bestowed by Catholic protocols of beatification and sanctification.

## Conclusion

In this chapter we examined how vernacular authority, legitimacy and power have been negotiated and established in relation to the cult of Gauchito Gil in Argentina. We have been confronted with the 'messiness' to be found in the study of vernacular religion, for vernacular religion defies easy compartmentalizing and has to take into account 'individual interpretation and negotiation of any number of influential sources' (Primiano 2012: 383–384).

Drawing on Bauman's work on the vernacular as communicative modality, I have contextualized some of the 'communicative resources' acquired informally and in practice that have informed the cult of Gauchito Gil, and the 'communicative relations' central to it as people negotiate and confer status in response to experiences and efficacy (Bauman 2008). This is a case study that exemplifies the modelling of vernacular religion as 'an interplay between three dimensions: "knowing"; "being"; and "doing" religion', modalities that are 'tied together by the dynamic forces of continuity, change, and context' (Illman and Czimbalmos 2020: 176–177).

In exploring some of the ways in which material religion operates in mediating, bolstering and establishing the power of Gauchito Gil, and in line with Primiano's contention that hallmarks of vernacular religion are ambiguity, creativity and power (Primiano 2012), I have suggested that proximity, approximation and appropriation are operational strategies in creative and ambiguous vernacular 'power grabs'. Showing how devotional items 'may be understood to perform different kinds of cultural work' (Morgan 2017: 15), some of the credential-confirming and authority-conferring aspects of the abundant 'available materiality' (Insoll 2015: 49) of the Mercedes shrine have been demonstrated.

**Figure 12.8.** Souvenir from Gauchito Gil shrine, Mercedes, Corrientes Province, Argentina. Photograph by Marion Bowman

My initial interest in Gauchito Gil was sparked by the wall painting of him in San José de Feliciano (Figure 12.1). The significance of relationality and materiality, and 'the power of creative contestation, the fluidity of religious negotiation, and the capacity of choice in religious lives' (Primiano 2012: 383) are for me summed up in my favourite purchase from Mercedes (Figure 12.8). On top of a small basket there is a little statue of Gauchito Gil alongside a slightly smaller picture of the Virgin of Lujan which is edged in gold-coloured beading. Both figures stand on a layer of varnished seeds, popularly symbolizing abundance. In front of the Virgin is an artificial fabric red rose, a perpetual offering and sign of devotion (in the colour primarily associated with Gil), while before Gauchito Gil is a garlic clove, known for warding off the evil eye. Around the top edge of the basket there is a thin red ribbon with the words Rdo del Gauchito Gil printed in white upon it. On the side of the basket is a smaller circular picture of St Expedite, edged in silver coloured beading, and a little rectangular card edged in gold coloured beading bearing the words '*Gauchito A. Gil Benedice mi hogar y familia*' (Bless my home and family) and below that 'Mercedes Ctes', establishing that the whole ensemble comes from the Mercedes shrine in Corrientes Province. We have here an encapsulation of the importance of material culture as an expression of relationality, the significance of the shrine, a visual hierarchy of operational power and the ever-present possibility of 'things working'. What better physical expression could there be of the experiential falsity of any abstract distinction between 'official' and 'folk' religion, of the absurdity of 'either/or' when you can have 'both/and', and of the pragmatism, creativity and complexity of vernacular religiosity?

## Acknowledgements

My sincere thanks to Jean and Sandra Morley for introducing me to Gauchito Gil, Cura Brochero, Ramoncito Muñoz and Difunta Correa; for answering my many questions; for stopping at roadside shrines; and for taking us to significant and fascinating places including the cemetery at San José de Feliciano (Entre Ríos Province), Villa Cura Brochero (Córdoba Province) and above all the Gauchito Gil shrine at Mercedes (Corrientes Province).

For innumerable conversations in relation to vernacular religion and for decades of friendship I am indebted to Leonard Norman Primiano. I am grateful also to Ülo Valk and Jessica Hughes for their helpful comments on this chapter and thank Ülo especially for our friendship and collaborations over many years.

## Notes

1 The term *gaucho* here is used as broadly descriptive of those people sometimes called Argentine cowboys, skilled horsemen, generally working with cattle on rural *estancia*s or ranches.

2. Having only rudimentary Spanish, in Argentina I have been reliant on the information given to me by and via my bilingual relations.
3. See, for example, the extensive accounts given in Graziano 2007; I received other information through oral sources.
4. The *faja* is a long piece of fabric wound around the waist, into which could be stuck the *facón*, the multipurpose knife typically carried and used by gauchos.
5. The *boleadoras* is used to bring down an animal by being thrown, spinning, to entangle its legs.
6. Pope Pius XI formally declared Our Lady of Luján the Patroness of Argentina, Paraguay and Uruguay in 1930.
7. This San La Muerte figure is different from, and should not be confused with, the better-known Mexican Santa Muerte (see Chesnut 2012).
8. He is said to have been a Jesuit in some versions, reflecting the huge influence of Jesuits in Argentina.
9. The sudden, unjust or early death is widely believed to create a penumbra of power for the person, who can then help those who relate to him/her. In the cemetery at San José de Feliciano, for example, the grave of the young Ramoncito Muñoz has become the focus of petitionary prayers and votive objects frequently left by children asking for success in exams.
10. The prayer as it appears on the candle: *Oh! Gauchito Gil. Te ruego humildemente se cumpla por intermedio ante Dios, el milagro que te pido, y te prometo que cumplire mi promesa, brindandote mi fiel agradecimiento y demonstracion de Fe, en Dios y en vos, Gauchito Gil. Amen.*
11. When we visited the nearby San La Muerte shrine, which was very clean and orderly with sales stalls discretely off to one side of the building, the shrine attendant with whom we spoke criticized the Mercedes shrine for being dirty and chaotic, lacking the respectful atmosphere of their shrine.
12. Graziano (2007: 128–130) elaborates on the possible political colour symbolism of red and its nineteenth-century associations with the Federales and the Automonistas, as opposed to the blue of Unitarios and Liberales. The colours (and political affiliation) associated with Gil may have changed over time. However, nowadays the perception of red as a 'lucky' colour, its power to avert the evil eye (see Molina 2016) and the association with Gil's innocent blood were all I heard about in person. The blue and white in relation to Gil's clothing can be seen as reflecting the Argentine flag, with its blue, white and blue triband, and a sun on the central white stripe.
13. This disdain for such items is nothing new: the English word 'tawdry' derives from 'St Audrey's lace', the ribbons sold on the feast of St Etheldreda at Ely Cathedral (Blanton 2007: 4).
14. St Cayetano (also known as St Cajetan), generally described as the patron saint of work/labour and bread, is extremely popular in Argentina.
15. Mate or maté is an immensely popular hot herbal tea, rich in caffeine, which has significant cultural significance and protocols. Traditionally it was served in a container made from a gourd and consumed through a metal straw, though now gourds are frequently replaced by plastic and other receptacles.
16. *Rdo del Gauchito Antonio Gil Bendice me viage Protégé mi Hogar y Familia Damos salud amor i trabajo Progete nos sempre.*

17 Graziano claims that there is some ambivalence in this relationship, claiming 'many Gaucho Gil devotees want nothing to do with San La Muerte' (2007: 82).
18 When I last checked online, like other Pool and Marianela artwork Barbie and Ken creations, a Gauchito Gil doll in a customized box could be purchased for $750.

## References

Bauman, Richard. 2008. 'The Philology of the Vernacular'. *Journal of Folklore Research* 45 (1): 29–36. https://doi.org/10.2979/JFR.2008.45.1.29

Bell, Vanessa. 2015. 'Controversial Religious Barbie Doll Exhibition Opens in Buenos Aires'. *The Guardian*, October 21, 2015. https://www.theguardian.com/travel/2015/oct/21/barbie-and-ken-religious-art-exhibition (accessed May 21, 2021).

Blanton, Virginia. 2007. *Signs of Devotion: The Cult of St Aethelthryth in Medieval England 695–1615*. University Park, PA: Pennsylvania State University Press.

Bowman, Marion. 2016. '"He's My Best Friend": Relationality, Materiality, and the Manipulation of Motherhood in Devotion to St Gerard Majella in Newfoundland'. In *Canadian Women Shaping Diasporic Religious Identities*, edited by Terry Woo and Becky Lee, 3–34. Waterloo, Ontario: Wilfrid Laurier University Press.

Bowman, Marion. 2017. 'From Production to Performance: Candles, Creativity and Connectivity'. In *Materiality and the Study of Religion: The Stuff of the Sacred*, edited by Tim Hutchings and Joanne McKenzie, 35–52. London; New York: Routledge.

Bowman, Marion. 2021. 'Trees, Benches and Contemporary Commemoration: When Ordinary Becomes Extraordinary'. *Journal for the Study of Religious Experience* 7 (3): 33–49.

Bowman, Marion, and John Jenkins. 2020. 'Leaving and Taking Away: Cathedrals and Material Culture'. In *Pilgrimage and England's Cathedrals: Past, Present, and Future*, edited by Dee Dyas and John Jenkins, 215–233. London: Palgrave Macmillan. https://doi.org/10.1007/978-3-030-48032-5_10

Bowman, Marion, and Ülo Valk, eds. 2012. *Vernacular Religion in Everyday Life: Expressions of Belief*. Sheffield; Bristol, CT: Equinox Publishing.

Candelaria, Michael R. 1990. *Popular Religion and Liberation: The Dilemma of Liberation Theology*. Albany: State University of New York Press.

Chesnut, R. Andrew. 2012. *Devoted to Death: Santa Muerte, the Skeleton Saint*. New York: Oxford University Press. https://doi.org/10.1093/acprof:oso/9780199764662.001.0001

Christian, William A., Jr. 1972. *Person and God in a Spanish Valley*. New York: Seminar Press.

Coleman, Simon, and John Elsner. 1995. *Pilgrimage Past and Present in the World Religions*. Cambridge, MA: Harvard University Press.

Eade, John, and Michael J. Sallnow. 1991. 'Introduction'. In *Contesting the Sacred: The Anthropology of Christian Pilgrimage*, edited by John Eade and Michael J. Sallnow, 1–29. Urbana; Chicago: University of Illinois Press.

Gallery 30 South. n.d. 'Pool & Marianela Barbie: The Plastic Religion Exhibition Publicity'. *Gallery 30 South*. https://gallery30south.com/plastic-religion/ (accessed May 21, 2021).

Graziano, Frank. 2007. *Cultures of Devotion: Folk Saints of Spanish America*. New York: Oxford University Press.

Howard, Robert Glenn. 2013. 'Vernacular Authority: Critically Engaging "Tradition"'. In *Tradition in the Twenty-First Century: Locating the Role of the Past in the Present*, edited by Trevor J. Blank and Robert Glenn Howard, 72–99. Logan: Utah State University Press. https://doi.org/10.7330/9780874218992.c03

Illman, Ruth, and Mercédesz Czimbalmos. 2020. 'Knowing, Being, and Doing Religion: Introducing an Analytical Model for Researching Vernacular Religion'. *Temenos: Nordic Journal of Comparative Religion* 56 (2): 171–199. https://doi.org/10.33356/temenos.97275

Insoll, Timothy. 2015. *Material Explorations in African Archaeology*. Oxford: Oxford University Press.

Kapaló, James. 2013. 'Folk Religion in Discourse and Practice'. *Journal of Ethnology and Folkloristics* 7 (1): 3–18.

Lysaght, Patricia. 1994. 'The Uses of Sacramentals in Nineteenth- and Twentieth-Century Ireland: With Special Reference to the Brown Scapular'. In *Religion in Everyday Life*, edited by Nils-Arvid Bringéus, 187–224. Stockholm: Konferenser-Kungliga Vitterhets Historie och Antikvitets Akademien.

Molina, Anatilde Idoyaga. 2016. 'The Evil Eye as a Folk Disease and Its Argentine and Ibero-American Historical Explanatory Frame'. *Western Folklore* 75 (1): 5–32.

Morgan, David. 2008. 'The Materiality of Cultural Construction'. *Material Religion* 4 (2): 228–229. https://doi.org/10.2752/175183408X328334

Morgan, David. 2017. 'Material Analysis and the Study of Religion'. In *Materiality and the Study of Religion: The Stuff of the Sacred*, edited by Tim Hutchings and Joanne McKenzie, 14–32. London; New York: Routledge.

Orsi, Robert A. 1985. *The Madonna of 115th Street: Faith and Community in Italian Harlem, 1880–1950*. New Haven, CT: Yale University Press.

Orsi, Robert A. 1996. *Thank You, St. Jude: Women's Devotion to the Patron Saint of Hopeless Causes*. New Haven, CT; London: Yale University Press.

Pope Francis. 2016. 'Message of His Holiness Pope Francis to the People of Argentina'. *The Holy See*, September 30, 2016. https://www.vatican.va/content/francesco/en/messages/pont-messages/2016/documents/papa-francesco_20160930_messaggio-popolo-argentino.html (accessed June 21, 2021).

Primiano, Leonard Norman. 1995. 'Vernacular Religion and the Search for Method in Religious Folklife'. *Western Folklore* (Special Issue: *Reflexivity and the Study of Belief*) 54 (1): 37–56. https://doi.org/10.2307/1499910

Primiano, Leonard Norman. 2001. 'What is Vernacular Catholicism? The "Dignity" Example'. *Acta Ethnographica Hungarica* 46 (1–2): 51–58. https://doi.org/10.1556/AEthn.46.2001.1-2.6

Primiano, Leonard Norman. 2012. 'Afterword—Manifestations of the Religious Vernacular: Ambiguity, Power and Creativity'. In *Vernacular Religion in Everyday Life: Expressions of Belief*, edited by Marion Bowman and Ülo Valk, 382–394. Sheffield; Bristol, CT: Equinox Publishing.

San Martín, Inés. 2020. 'Pope Praises Priest who Pioneered Argentine Form of Liberation Theology'. *The Tablet*, August 24, 2020. https://thetablet.org/pope-praises-priest-who-pioneered-argentine-form-of-liberation-theology/ (accessed May 10, 2021).

Whitehead, Amy. 2013. *Religious Statues and Personhood: Testing the Role of Materiality*. London; New York: Bloomsbury.

Chapter 13

# The Upper Room: Domestic Space, Vernacular Religion, and the Observant University Catholic

*Leonard Norman Primiano**

## Introduction

The title and theme of this book, *Vernacular Knowledge: Contesting Authority, Expressing Beliefs*, has prompted me to write about the vernacular religious knowledge of a devout individual Roman Catholic, who contests authority, but ostensibly not the authority of the institutional Church. He instead challenges the authority of the community of peers living around him in his collegiate dormitory—could I call them representatives of his collegiate habitus?—who in his eyes oppose the moral authority and standards of his Church through their libertine lifestyles of late-night parties, drug taking, alcohol consumption and sexual assignations as undergraduates in a Roman Catholic university. At the same time, he supplements what could be described as his 'traditionalist' Catholic beliefs and practices with notable spiritual contributions from his Italian American ethnic heritage. My chapter specifically concerns the vernacular religion of this university undergraduate as he expresses it materially. A case study of the phenomenology of creativity, belief and practice in

* **Leonard Norman Primiano** (11 January 1957–25 July 2021) was Professor at Cabrini College, Radnor, Pennsylvania. He was the author of the groundbreaking 1995 article 'Vernacular Religion and the Search for Method in Religious Folklife' (*Western Folklore* 54 (1): 37–56). Primiano's nuanced appreciation and analysis of vernacular Catholic images and praxis; his research on the 'Dignity' movement; his long-term study of Father Divine and the International Peace Mission; and his insatiable interest in religious material culture all contributed to a rich and varied body of work, some of which will be celebrated in a collection of his writings published under the title *Vernacular Religion: Collected Essays of Leonard Norman Primiano* (NYU Press, 2022).

consort, as well as material religion, my consultant exemplifies vernacular Catholicism, vernacular knowledge and vibrant 'spiritual practices' (Ammerman 2014) which I see as both a complement to how he has been formed and notably a contestation to the decision of his peers to live less than Godly lives. This chapter takes on several challenging themes associated with vernacular religion which some scholars find attractive and others troubling: 1) an emphasis on the lived religion of the individual; 2) vernacular religion as a hermeneutic for studying religious interpretation and negotiation within both individual and communal contexts; 3) the relevance of the study of privatized religious identity rooted in its own practical reason and artful everyday experience; 4) finally, the evocative reality of vernacular religion found within religious institutions.

## Vernacular Religion and the Individual

Vernacular religion (Primiano 1995; 2012; 2017), the ways in which people are religious in their everyday lives, is found everywhere. It is all around us in the same sense that 'folklore' as local individual and community organic knowledge and expressivity can be located in innumerable contexts and expressions throughout societies and cultures.

Folklore's central interest includes 'vernacular knowledge', art, aesthetics and traditional practices that exist alongside formal institutions in complex societies. Since the discipline's inception in the early nineteenth century, folklorists have made their primary concern the nuances of local and informal knowledge, whether of health, geography, climate, nutrition, agriculture, history, religion or the social order. They have documented and theorized how everyday knowledge is constructed and transmitted, the relationship of knowledge to practice and how knowledge is granted authority and codified into systems. Using ethnographic field methods such as participant observation and interviewing, they work to make explicit the understandings implicit in everyday social relations. Folklorists, therefore, make their central concern the study of the grounding of human creativity in social life. In addition, they study the rich relationship of vernacular cultures with formal institutions and professional practice, examining how social power interacts with cultural forms, and how vernacular processes reshape cultural institutions. While the 'lore' studied by folklorists was the object of suspicion from the discipline's early days to the mid-twentieth century, today that lore is perceived as wisdom, and a key to understanding human communities, as well as such significant issues as the potency of power and agency in the reality of inter-personal relationships. These issues are of scholarly concern to folklorists and their practical importance is widely recognized across a variety of other disciplines by educators and other professionals working to understand the complexities of the contemporary social world.

Vernacular religion finds expression in response to the way religion and religions have developed in societies, indeed as a dimension of its integration. As a folklorist, I certainly appreciate, for example, the colourful material displays of informal religion observed in settings such as the *edicole sacre* (or street shrines of the Madonna also known locally as *Madonnelle*) in Italian cities and towns as much as I do the exuberant public and private displays of Catholic material culture in an American metropolitan area such as New York City and its boroughs, represented by yard shrines, private chapels, Christmas light displays, and so on (Sciorra 2015). I also enjoy it when I discover examples of vernacular religion in 'popular' culture such as movies and television (Primiano 2009; 2011), or as kitsch (Primiano 2015), as well as in cultural works that members of Western society esteem as formally learned arts such as opera. Yes, staged grand operas can be filled with personal expressions of the religious imagination, and no one was better at evoking the vernacular religious negotiation of everyday life in characters than the Italian master Giacomo Puccini (1858–1924). Take, for instance, his famed verismo-style opera *Tosca* about the final hours in the life of a famed opera singer set in the turbulent era of Napoleonic Rome. In the famous second act soprano aria, 'Vissi d'Arte', when faced with the agony of betraying a trust or watching her lover be tortured and shot by firing squad, as well as giving in to the sexual advances of the torturer, she vocally asks God why her floral adoration at the altar and statue of the Madonna, her dutiful fulfilment of Marian devotions, has resulted in no positive outcomes or blessings in her everyday life and relationships:

> Ever in pure faith,
> my prayers rose
> in the holy chapels.
> Ever in pure faith,
> I brought flowers to the altars.
> In this hour of pain, why,
> why, oh Lord, why
> dost Thou repay me thus?
> Jewels I brought
> for the Madonna's mantle,

> and songs for the stars in heaven
> that they shone forth with greater radiance.
> In this hour of distress, why,
> why, oh Lord,
> why dost Thou repay me thus?

*Tosca* is in fact filled with characters negotiating their 'religion' or lack thereof. The treacherous villain Baron Scarpia during the 'Te Deum' that closes Act One highlights his own complex vernacular religious negotiations (for Puccini, perhaps, representative of the abuses of power of the institutional Church itself) by singing an aria during the service about his lustful desires for the heroine: 'Tosca, you make me forget God!'[1] These operatic examples aim specifically to stimulate readers to focus their attention on considerations of vernacular religion, especially within the context of the individual, which I have designated the study of religious uniculture (Primiano 1995: 49–50; 2012: 390).

The concept of vernacular religion engages with a broad range of classic social scientific and philosophical concepts such as the nature of the individual and collective society; free will and determinism; the power of social structure or agency in determining a human behavioural paradigm; the strength of the individual or the unconscious influence of structured community; the nature and ability of independent personal choice in religious decision making as markers of religiosity in the historical and post-modern eras; or the undoubted and continuous dynamic of local and community social structures in forming religious or spiritual choices. Many of these themes have been taken up in the last 30 years with an expanding scholarly attention to religious-spiritual beliefs, believing (see Gatling 2020), and practicing by individuals within and outside of institutional religions. In the discipline of American religious history, for example, such engagement has energized and widened the purview and diachronic analysis of belief and practice within communities and the religious institutions and adherents within their fabric.[2]

Within the sociology of religion, the movement to study 'lived' religion has challenged the quantitative standards of discerning religious orthodoxy and most certainly understanding the nature of religious institutions themselves (see Ammerman 2014: xiii; McGuire 2008: 3–17). Anthropologists have expanded how they view and study religion moving from a concentration on its presence integrated throughout a culture to post-modern forms of new translocal or world religions whose more centralized structures and characteristics develop local vernacular expressions (see Eller 2015 [2007]: 176–201). Of course, within the international field of folkloristics, the observation, preservation, study and analysis of the eclectic and diverse occasions, sites, materials and expressions of religion in everyday life both within and outside of religious institutions have been standard for many decades when these other disciplines had no interest in understanding religion via such expanded boundaries and categories or developing methods to study them (see Bowman and Valk 2012: 1–19).

I have written that vernacular religion as 'the folkloristic study of religious belief and believers should emphasize the integrated ideas and practices of all *individuals* living in human society' (Primiano 1995: 47; original emphasis). My emphasis on the individual as the starting point of interest in religious creativity has its foundation within folkloristics itself. In their discussion of the individual and tradition, Ray Cashman, Tom Mould and Pravina Shukla have noted—in this celebration of the work and method of folklorist Henry Glassie—how folklore scholarship, as they interpret it:

> necessarily begins with close attention to the words, actions, and creations of specific individuals. In order to interpret and to generalize—to earn conclusions—folklorists gather information from specific individuals because tradition is enacted only through an individual's acts of creative will ... This starting point—the study of tradition through attention to the individual—is not merely a methodological necessity (one must start somewhere), but more significantly a matter of philosophical conviction ... this formulation—the role of the individual in tradition—can too easily slide into misleading conceptions of tradition as mysteriously external, autonomous, and superorganic, and of individuals as merely bearers, carriers, and greater or lesser stewards and practitioners. The fieldwork experience in particular convinces us that there is no such thing as tradition without the individuals who enact it. (2011: 1–2)

I remain convinced there is no such thing as religious tradition 'without the individuals who enact it' (see recent studies by Mould 2011; Sciorra 2015; Cashman 2016). It is valuable, therefore, to continue a (post-Durkheimian and even post-Bourdieuan) consideration of the individual as essential to the genesis of religion even as we consider the interaction of the individual with influential social structures which can ostensibly influence strongly historical and contemporary religious behaviour (see Dillon 2001; McGuire 2008). If nothing more, it would be good to follow the complementary reservations of French sociologist François Dubet:

> The question of the social is not abolished, but problematized, as a space whose tensions are focused in individual action: ... the social subject is

neither the individual in the outside world who only realizes his individuality in ascetism, nor the social actor fully defined by his roles. He is the tension between these two elements. (1994: 22–23)

It is precisely such interstitial, bridging experiences that my scholarship explores. I am excited that my work on vernacular religion continues to be discussed in the expanding cross-disciplinary sub-fields of anthropology, religious studies (see Allen 2014; Eller 2015 [2007]; DeNapoli 2017; Illman and Czimbalmos 2020) and folkloristics (see Kapaló 2013; Fabbrini 2019; Lesiv forthcoming). Using ethnographic instances from Orthodox Christian and Roman Catholic Christian devotionalism, James Kapaló and Marco Fabbrini have been concentrating in fieldwork on examples of practice within non-urban settings which contest institutionalized religion designating them 'folk religion'. Kapaló explains (with his words quoted by Fabbrini 2019: 247) that he has made the decision to retain the term 'folk religion' instead of using 'vernacular religion' because it has:

> descriptive value in the sense that its 'chains of associations' can communicate something of the political nature and the political-knowledge relations that shape the religious field of practice ... Replacing the term 'folk religion' with an alternative, may inadvertently help to divorce the object of study from issues of national ideology, political and ecclesiastical power and the concerns of marginalized social, economic, or ethno-linguistic groups ... the deployment of new terminology and analytical categories may, in some cases ... mask the political nature of a field of practice thus defined. (2013: 8, 9, 10, 15)

Such a singular emphasis on the political/hegemonic definition of all 'folk' religion leaves out a major non-political component of the concept, at least as it was conceptualized by Don Yoder using sources from German, Swiss and Austrian *Volkskunde* (Yoder 2001b: 67–68). Yoder, the man who concluded his 1963 article defining American folklife studies with 'perhaps a flail can teach us more about a man than a Civil War sword' (2001a: 38) was certainly quite aware of the political nature of history, culture and religion in his life and scholarship. It was Yoder's point though that folk religion is not only 'apart from', but also 'alongside' the institutional religion (a point from Yoder reiterated and expanded upon by Robert Glenn Howard [2011: 4–7] in relation to the dialectical nature of vernacular religion), frequently complementing it with artistic self-expression with no ostensible connotation of power. To reword an apocryphal statement attributed to Sigmund Freud (see Elms 2005): in Yoder's folk religion hermeneutic, sometimes an ex-voto or retablo—examples of Catholic 'folk' art produced by untrained artists—are just expressions of religious folk belief and art, and not contestational pieces of creativity commenting on power, influence or leadership. Non-politically motivated religious creativity was a significant dimension of Yoder's explanation, sensibility and adaptation of traditional belief, experience and practice from spirituals to fraktur.

As I have noted previously, while I see 'folk religion' as a term with descriptive value in pedagogical contexts of folkloristics, the label remains too closely associated with a two-tiered approach or model for understanding religion as a bifurcation of 'unofficial' and 'official' to be useful (Primiano 2012). 'Lived religion' as employed by Meredith McGuire (see, for example, 2008: 6, 12, 16, 45, 75, 95–96, 152–154, 166–168) also unfortunately maintains such a dualistic legacy. The vernacular religious approach seeks to eliminate such a model of religion, by emphasizing that *all* terms such as 'folk', 'popular' and 'unofficial' when applied to the study of religion and belief are ultimately dividing practices that call attention to status differences between those individuals who practice religion *and* those individuals who administer religious institutions as well as practice it, and between those individuals who theologize or philosophize about it, *and* those individuals who study it. 'Vernacular' is hopefully to be seen as not a dividing, but as a leavening term; not a bifurcation but a concept that transforms the understanding of religion as a practiced reality for the better.

My colleague Sabina Magliocco, in personal communication (October 2019), has noted to me her understanding of the historical context in which my term 'vernacular religion' emerged in the United States, and within the politics of the anthropological and folkloristic study of religion in the West more broadly. In the American context, the shift in perspective from 'folk' to 'vernacular' became possible beginning in the 1980s; my first use of the term 'vernacular religion' can be found in a 1985 folklore journal (Primiano 1985) although it became widely known through the publication and circulation of my definition of vernacular religion in 1995. At this time, more practitioners from marginalized groups, such as women, people of colour, religious minorities, as well as lay representatives of religious majorities entered the academy, and working to balance scholarly objectivity with spiritual subjectivity began to study their own religious traditions—not as observers, but as practitioner-observers representative of a rich religious, ethnic and racial diversity. They began to study their religious selves and their religious communities as folk groups (see, for example, Fish 1982; Santino 1982). Vernacular religion developed as an evocation of the performance orientation of folkloristics crystallized in Alan Dundes's (1977: 34) explanation that we are all the folk. My development of vernacular religion synthesized this sensitivity to and appreciation of the religious creativity of self historically and in the present, and others in public and private, in isolation and in community.[3]

Furthermore, vernacular religion as a concept arose, not out of a masking of the political nature of the field of practice, but out of the recognition in my own fieldwork of the possibilities of power and contestation within personal and community religion (2012: 387–390). Indeed, evolving out of the study of what I describe as a 'community of individuals'—specifically my ethnography of the Philadelphia chapter of the gay and lesbian Roman Catholic organization known as Dignity (Primiano 1993a)—my concept of vernacular religion was inspired by my consultants' specific and passionate ideological, political and ecclesiastical struggle within and without the Roman Catholic Church as an American and international institution. The individual experiences of sexuality and religion and subsequently developed spiritual ontologies of the Dignity family that I characterized as vernacular religion, rather than isolating the membership as individuals, bound them together both as a local base community and a national representative body. Through liturgy, song, homiletics, prayer, individual occasions of group solidarity, even their handling of traditional religious material culture, they sought to apply positively and creatively to their individual life experiences a concept of Church necessitating a need to question, challenge, disrupt, re-create and create the broader historical tradition in which they were raised (Primiano 1993a; 1993b; 2001; 2004).

Finally, vernacular religion as the study of the religion of the individual inside and outside of religious institutions exemplifies both the notion of the individual's creative dialogue with tradition and the personal reflection of the self with feelings, beliefs and practices that take one beyond both self and nature. Accompanying Kapaló's power-oriented vision of 'folk religion', and Fabbrini's perspective on 'folkloric religion' as preferential paradigms for communal actors' expressions of agency, I detect a cautionary note that the concept 'vernacular religion' is a methodological conceit on my part to offer and extend to the international community of folkloristics a theorizing of the American trait of radical individualism. Within the sociology of religion, this recognition of religion as purely internal, a form of religious privatism, has in fact been labelled 'Sheilaism' after a nurse, one of the 200 white, middle-class consultants that sociologist Robert N. Bellah et al. used in the preparation for their well-known study titled *Habits of the Heart: Individualism and Commitment in American Life* (2008 [1985]). Sheila Larson noted in an interview that she called her own personal religion Sheilaism. Bellah, colleagues, and subsequent interpreters critiqued this stress on the personal experience of religion or 'spirituality' for having neither theological or historical roots nor community claim on a person. To be sure, sociologists within the study of the later 'lived religion' movement in that discipline have criticized Bellah's dismissal of Sheilaism as short-sighted, an excessive defence of the need for denominational affiliation, and in need of serious reconsideration. In an exceptional study of religious individualism among LGBT Christians, Melissa M. Wilcox provides the following rejoinder:

> the individualism evident in respondents' strategies exists despite the fact that most either have been or are currently involved in a religious community. Some attend weekly, others a few times a year; a few now find their spirituality in solitude. But by attending to this complexity rather than sorting religiosity into dichotomous categories we can see the role of individualism in the 'lived' or 'vernacular' religion of religious attendees and non-attendees alike. For those whose identities collide sharply with official religious doctrine, the increased flexibility of individual belief and practice, along with the growth of congregational, denominational, and religious shopping and switching, can be of critical importance—and from their experiences there is a great deal to be learned about contemporary forms of religiosity. (2002: 511)

I detect an avoidance of the term vernacular religion by some folklorists because its emphasis on the religiously personal is misunderstood as an evocation of American spiritual narcissism. Such personally created spirituality can, it follows, be interpreted as actually working to erode community traditions to the detriment of shared community values. It could be additionally interpreted as a challenge to and dismissal of the possibly important role of local instances of 'folk religion' in Europe (historical, contemporary, and most certainly post-Socialist) for understanding everything from the viability of Durkheimian social cohesion and Gramscian religious contestation for the support of community values against hegemonic institutions such as the Catholic Church, to a Bourdieuan practice theory, socially deterministic, and at times rather mechanical explanation for all of post-modern social life. Vernacular religion is as perfectly suited to community study as it is to the microanalysis of an individual within a religious community. My accentuating of individual religious creativity as an exemplar of agency complements and does not detract from the dynamics involved in collective acts of religiosity. Admittedly, I do not mind challenging the scholarly hegemony of a widely accepted social constructionist paradigm of conscious and unconscious formation and development of religious belief and practice; indeed, I leave the door open to future application of vernacular religion to cases of individual religion, future work interfacing psychology and folklore (see Mechling 2006), as well as community creative religious responses to contexts of power.[4]

Having reviewed recent responses to the study of religion as it is lived and especially to vernacular religious theory, it is time to turn to the case study at hand: the encounter of religion as it is lived by a university undergraduate whose contemporary dormitory room—the Upper Room—is a unique configuration of residential space which illustrates that the sacred in many forms and the secular in many forms are social realities that can potentially co-exist in the same space. Vernacular religious practice thus enervates everyday life as an amalgamation of the traditional and the new, ever asking the folklorist to listen and look carefully to note potentially robust examples of private and public creativity and knowledge.

**The Upper Room**

Dormitory rooms of American undergraduate students are often plainly appointed spaces equipped with functional furniture including a desk, chair and bunk beds. In rooms accommodating two or three individuals known as doubles or triples, an uneasy détente often needs to be achieved between excessive sloppiness and negotiated order. When occupied and decorated, however, they do possess their own unique physical charms as adorned statements about the influence of technology, family, athletics, collegiate drinking culture, popular media, and sometimes even actual learning in the life of the twenty-first-century teenager/post-teenager. Single student rooms are naturally prized because of an individual preference for privacy for study, sleep or sexual activity especially in the face of communally-shared bathroom facilities in more traditional dormitories. Such private rooms are often in short supply and, of course, they permit an occupant a completely free rein to create a lived environment suited to his or her individual taste. It is not surprising, then, to encounter collections of beer cans, alcohol bottles, sports equipment or piles of clothing in student rooms. Perhaps photographs of family, a girl or boyfriend, or a profusion of stuffed animals might be present to accompany a laptop computer or television.

Occasionally, for a Roman Catholic student, there can even be a string of rosary beads wrapped around a lamp or a holy card of a deceased loved one present, but a room remodelled as a sacred space is a somewhat startling discovery. My chapter concerns such a space.

**Figure 13.1**. The Upper Room's 'Holy Corner' including crucifix, relics, an opened Bible and lit sanctuary lamp[5]

Upon entering what has been named by a friend of my student consultant the Upper Room, an ironic homage to those holy spaces referenced in 1 Chronicles 28:11-12 and Acts 1:12-14 of the Bible, one's attention cannot help but be immediately drawn to the corner table (Figure 13.1) covered by a linen lace cloth. Adorned with a crucifix, an opened Bible, bronze candlesticks and reliquaries with relics, this space is a 'holy corner' creating a sacred environment complemented by other religious art. With a dressed statue of the Infant of Prague nearby (Figure 13.2), hung above the ornamented table is a sanctuary lamp with a lit candle inside its red glass casing. Is this space found in a chapel connected to a parish church or seminary or convent? Perhaps, the room of the university chaplain? No, this room is found in an American college dormitory at a Catholic university. Neither the residence of a chaplain or campus minister nor a publicly accessible prayer space in the dorm, it is the 20 by 20 feet single residential room of a male undergraduate student which also includes a bed along with a desk, chair, refrigerator and microwave oven.

**Figure 13.2.** An additional sacred space accompanies a personal safe adorned with a statue of a dressed Infant of Prague, holy water, and images of St. Frances Xavier Cabrini

I now draw your attention to the vernacular religion of a university undergraduate and the material expression of what I call his *vernacular religious uniculture*, the religious culture of an individual. A study of both the phenomenology of creativity and of belief, my consultant exemplifies a case of vernacular Catholicism which I see as both a complement to how he has been raised and now a contestation to the decision of his peers to live less than Godly lives.

My research has been stimulated by a variety of statistics about how contemporary American Catholics identify as religious people. The Pew Research Center[6] notes a rapidly changing American 'religious landscape'. In the period of the development as a Catholic by my informant, namely the first two decades of the twenty-first century, the percentage of citizens who self-identified as Christian fell (to 65%, a 12% drop). Religiously unaffiliated people—people who describe their religious identity as atheist, agnostic or 'nothing in particular'—rose (to 26%, up from 17% in 2009). The Roman Catholic population in 2019 was reported to have declined: 'one-in-five adults (20%) ... down from 23% in 2009'. The loss of Catholic population has been particularly felt in the north-eastern United States where my informant was reared and attended university (here 36% identified as Catholic in 2009, compared with 27% towards the end of the second decade). (See PRC 2019.)

Among his own peer group of individuals reaching adulthood in this period, 'Only half ... (49%) describe themselves as Christians' (ibid.). A 2014 Pew study noted that:

> Catholicism has experienced a greater net loss due to religious switching than has any other religious tradition in the U.S. Overall, 13% of all U.S. adults are former Catholics—people who say they were raised in the faith, but now identify as religious 'nones', as Protestants, or with another religion ... No other religious group analyzed in the 2014 Religious Landscape Study has experienced anything close to this ratio of losses to gains via religious switching. (Masci and Smith 2018)[7]

Certainly, these statistics on the individualization and subjectivity of religious tradition are an indication of a dynamic that folklore and ethnology scholars in Europe and America have been aware of for some time: that people make, create, re-create and negotiate their own religion, alongside similar patterns in the turn to alternative or complementary medicine seen among contemporary Americans. The role of this re-creation, or what John Nelson has called 'experimental religion' (2013; 2017), is beginning to be appreciated in the discipline of religious studies as a hallmark of religion of the Millennial generation. But at this moment in the twenty-first century, when the relative freedom to first interpret and then actively shape one's own identity and especially one's own religious identity is so clearly indicated in the USA, I decided to research the exact opposite: an individual who throughout his life has clearly identified with one religion, namely Roman Catholicism, in his church attendance, personal life choices, in his ritualistic expressions, and in his relationship to religious material culture.

## A 'Play Altar'

One of folkloristics' most ardently invoked patron saints, Henry Glassie, has written that tradition is 'the creation of the future out of the past' with history 'an artful assembly of materials from the past, designed for usefulness in the future' (1995: 395). I see my consultant expressing both those qualities in the way he intentionally engages with religious material culture in his life. His religious future is being built from a tradition of Catholic sacramental understanding and appreciation and use; and his life history will no doubt be invigorated by the consistent artful assemblage of material objects made useful by the potency and expectancy of their sacred usefulness in the past, present and future.

Let me take you a bit further into the world of this Catholic undergraduate student, who, since age ten, has built personal altars that I would term vernacular Catholic shrines in his bedrooms, first at his home in New Jersey, and eventually in his dorm room at college. A product of public schools in New Jersey, not Roman Catholic parochial or private education, he has been drawn to Catholic beliefs and practices since childhood.

In a revealing personal statement responding to some questions that I posed, my consultant explained to me the role of altars in his life:[8]

> ... since I was 10 years old. In my room, I would display a 'play Altar' where I would sometimes play priest with grape juice and a [potato] chip that is in a perfect circle, pretending to be the wine and host. Today, I continue this habit of mine but more serious. I have a bookshelf in my room where the top portion is my Altar and Sanctuary. My mom gave me a beautiful home altar set from Italy on Christmas. I have two real Altar candles on either side and a crucifix in the middle representing the old Latin Tradition Mass. I always use 51% or 100% beeswax candles and real flowers for my Altar, representing that all things are coming from the earth that God himself made from bees to nature. The liturgical seasons are a favorite part of my interest in the Catholic Tradition and I have all four colors of the seasons of the year as my Altar Cloths ... Every night and morning I say the Liturgy of the Hours which is what all seminarians and priests are instructed to say and be part of our lives. The Liturgy of the Hours is known as the 'official prayer of the Universal Church of Christ'.

I am especially taken with my consultant's understanding of the importance of using 'real' or 'authentic' material for his altar: the pure beeswax candles and the fresh flowers. And the care he takes to profess only 100 percent authentic Catholic beliefs complements his material expression of those beliefs including his placement of a Vatican flag by his desk and

Philadelphia Flyers ice-hockey memorabilia. But there are some other fascinating components to his room. In addition to the statues of saints such as stigmatic Padre Pio, reliquaries, candles and flowers, even a St. Benedict medal promulgated by Pope Benedict XVI to protect one against all forms of the devil—all representations of normative Catholicism for my informant—are expressions of his ethnic or should I say Mediterranean heritage: an Italian flag and an object of very traditional Italian occult belief, a red horn or *cornicello*, *cornetto* (Italian for 'little horn' or 'hornlet') or *corno* (Italian for 'horn'), an Italian amulet or talisman worn to protect against the evil eye (or *malocchio*) and bad luck in general, and, historically, to promote fertility and virility (see Figure 13.3).

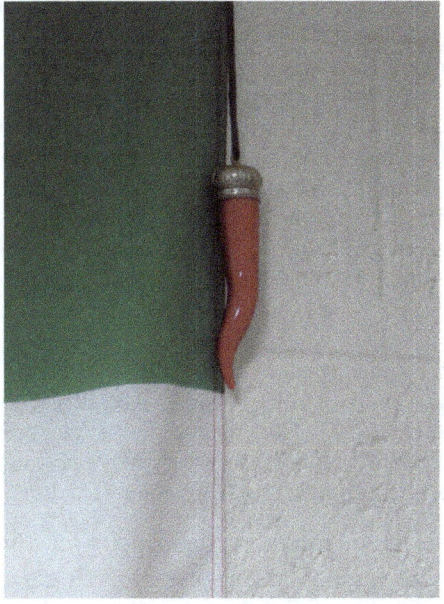

**Figure 13.3.** The red horn hanging to the right of an Italian flag on the cinder block wall of the dormitory

What is this student exemplar of 'real' Catholicism doing with this very traditional folk symbol? There was more fascinating vernacular religious material culture until a breakage occurred, for his room also included another talismanic device: the blue eye-like charms/symbols known as *nazars*, which are also used to repel the evil eye, a common sight across many countries in the Mediterranean and Middle East.

In a field trip to my informant's dorm room to absorb his Catholic aesthetic, he revealed an entire constellation of beliefs around the evil eye which he says were passed on to him through family, a tradition especially expressed by his Sicilian American grandfather and mother, and practiced on his grandmother. His explanation both underscores his connection to his ways of understanding the tradition and argues how its application in everyday life does not take him away from the normative Church, but rather draws him closer to it:

> My grandfather and my grandmother, (grandfather the most) believed heavily on the *malocchio* ... We believe in the 'overlooks', a set of prayers that a person says to ward off the evil eye ... My family believes this very deeply that when you have a headache that someone gave you the evil eye. In my family no one ever took aspirin or pain medication for headaches. What my grandmother got was headaches all the time and she told my Pop-Pop [grandfather], 'do the overlooks' ... The overlooks consist of Catholic Prayers and calling upon the Saints ... If you have a headache all day, I would ask you for your watch [a personal object of yours to hold] and I say prayers. I cannot tell you what they are. I am not allowed. If you want to learn the overlooks, I have to teach you in one hour at midnight on Christmas in order for you to learn the prayers because that is when Christ was born. That is the only time that I can teach you to do it ... My mom and I do it all of the time. She taught me when I was 13 years old how to do it. She taught me in church at like 11:59 PM, so it falls into midnight before the Mass starts ... So you keep saying these prayers and keep making the sign of the cross over the object and your left eye will start to tear; if your left eye starts to tear that means that someone gave you an overlooks, and when my grandfather did it he would also start yawning constantly ... My uncle, who I never talk to anymore, says it is witchcraft ... We don't believe that it is a form of witchcraft or anything because there are prayers within it that are connected to the Church. It is an old Italian tradition.

My consultant fits perfectly a description of the persistence of an Italian consciousness, or in this case fourth generation of Italian American consciousness, concerning magical practices and healing traditions described by folklorist Sabina Magliocco as occurring both historically as well as in contemporary perspective. She is quite careful to portray these practices as 'spiritual' (2004: 156), because people combine such traditional practices with more formal religion to form a network of belief, an 'entire context' (ibid.: 153) of vernacular religiosity. Magliocco notes 'the spiritual meaning of such practices', viewing them 'as an integral part of the individual experience of the numinous' (ibid.). Religious Studies scholar Kathleen Malone O'Connor adds:

> When scholarship strips religious culture, particularly religious folk culture, of these affective components by erasing magic or attempting

to devalue it by categorizing magical beliefs and practices as not 'real religion', our view of that religious culture becomes distorted and diminished. (2011: 819)

Here my consultant's statement of explanation allows us to observe an inter-penetration: of the power of one of the most solemn days of holy and joyous observation on the Roman Catholic calendar with what Magliocco calls 'the vernacular magic of Italy' (2004: 165). Christmas day, the birth of the Saviour, is a potent time for the sympathetic passing of powers of healing, knowing and feeling which are all connected to a vernacular understanding of the power of prayer. Whether these beliefs and practices represent the submission of the Italian magical tradition to the power of Catholic sacramentality or vice versa, there is nonetheless something especially significant in this example of religion as it is lived. It is not an occasion of religious/spiritual blending, one incident of 'folk religious' practice in a devoted Catholic's life, but a rather rich exemplification of the connected strands in the tapestry of the vernacular religious life. *Vernacular religion* as a term can certainly be used to describe such singular occasions encountered in the field, classroom, exhibition or museum, but importantly the idea of vernacular religion emphasizes not only 'beliefs and practices ... presented as fragmentary and incomplete', but 'as parts of the integrated belief systems of individuals and small communities' (ibid.: 154). Put differently, this is what Don Yoder was attempting to explain in the reference in his classic definition of 'folk religion' to 'a unified organic system of belief' (2001b: 80).

My consultant, for his part, portrays beautifully a dimension of hybridization possible in vernacular Catholicism by not seeing some aspect of his spiritual practice as incompatible to Catholicism, since it is for him 'part of a logical continuum of vernacular religiosity' (Magliocco 2004: 157). This fluid spiritual logic is a significant element that enables Catholic life to function as real, local, communal, familial, individual, and yet somehow also universal, and its associated religious practices quotidian, spiritually rational, useful, sensible, effective, open to artistry and certainly the expression of the beautiful. Did I not mention the equally powerful possibility of contestation to the power of hegemonic institutional and social forces? Such spiritual practices have been described by Nancy Ammerman as often lying 'at the creative tension between structuring patterns and individual agency' (2014: 57). Again, an emphasis on the individual does not eliminate the importance of social, learned, shared meaning and experiences influencing the individual (see McGuire 2008: 13), but each site needs careful understanding and unfolding.[9]

Joseph Sciorra's 2015 monograph *Built with Faith: Italian American Imagination and Catholic Material Culture in New York City* analyses the way Italian American Catholics in NYC have produced a unique expression of vernacular religious artistry in domestic, secular and religious contexts. Especially useful is Sciorra's discussion of 'men making altars':

> The domestic altar tradition and, in particular, the annually assembled festive altar, while historically considered the purview of women, is practiced by a number of men in New York City ... Altars socially coded as female, created by men, prompt consideration of social behaviors associated with women's familial practices such as the creation and maintenance of kin-centered networks and the work of relationships. (2015: 42)

Indeed, associated with my informant's formal holy corner is a space in his room reserved for a reverence for his family, especially his beloved grandparents mentioned in his narrative of the evil eye (Figure 13.4). Alyssa Maldonado-Estrada has also studied the place and enactment of creativity and masculine religiosity within New York Italian American community (2020).

**Figure 13.4.** On the room desk is a statue of Padre Pio (also known as Saint Pio of Pietrelcina) adorned with a rosary and images of grandparents, with photo from World War II military service and an American flag presented at the time of grandfather's death for that service

Because this undergraduate was raised in southern New Jersey, living away from metropolitan areas, I found that my research concerning him unexpectedly resonated with fieldwork that I had conducted in the region several decades ago. This return—across time and space—provides a useful reflection on the importance of critical distance in refining one's thinking. At that time, I was weighing the vernacular beliefs of Catholic practice against the normative dogmatic and doctrinal perspectives taught, if you will, from the pulpit and not viewing them all as one sustained context of belief. My current understanding of this young man's belief traditions is something that I approach now with a far more holistic and widened scope than the mindset with which I had been conducting and interpreting fieldwork in the late 1990s. My hypothesis theory at that time, proffered in a study titled: 'Catholics in the Countryside: Traditional Catholicism in Rural New Jersey' (funded by a Louisville Institute Summer Stipend) was that, like the theory that the 'pagans' in the first centuries of the development of Christianity knew less about normative Christian ideas because they lived furthest away from more urban centres, these more rural New Jersey communities of Catholics knew less about the reforms of the Second Vatican Council because its teachings had not spread from the adjacent urban centre of Philadelphia. Of course, I soon learned the complexities of such a transition of information also depended on the conservative positions of local urban prelates such as John Cardinal Krol (1910-1996) in Philadelphia who did not agree with or quickly apply Vatican II reforms, even in his own city. I found to my astonishment in 1999, in even modest research in a few southern New Jersey parishes, that there were some pastors and their parishioners still using Latin, maintaining paraliturgies, stagnating Eucharistic reforms, and acting as if the Council changes had not happened. While I met reform-minded priests and parishioners, I also encountered laity *and* recalcitrant parish priests who negotiated the Council's promulgations in both public and private religious settings as a form of religious resistance to change. I see my present consultant as possessing a similar Catholic double vision: he loves the normative Church, its dogmas and doctrines, and at the same time he is contesting them, especially as they relate to the reforming changes of the Second Vatican Council, and the progressive tendencies of Pope Francis. In true vernacular Catholic form, as one of the annual student migrants who bring the religion of their home parishes with them into the religious setting and practice of the Catholic university, my consultant is creating, re-creating and negotiating his religious beliefs and practices influenced by regional spiritual sensibilities, family ties, and his own understanding of what is right and wrong for and to him.

Finally, I see embedded in his bold reassessment of his collegiate space and place, accentuating traditional Catholicism of a past generation, a direct challenge to the culture of his own generation. The recent work of Donna Freitas (2009; 2013) and Jason King (2017) on the relationship of spirituality and sexuality in the lives of contemporary American undergraduates suggests a tension in the life of Catholic students, especially women, who resist, but do not often succeed in challenging, the culture of sexual 'hooking up' pervasive on American college campuses. I see the Upper Room as a direct challenge to that culture of hooking up, or using a dorm space for casual sexual activity, deemed sinful by this student. He has decided not to pollute his personal space, but to sacralize it through a use of religious material culture and a vernacular understanding and enactment of 'Catholic' space and place. This contemporary, conservatively religious Roman Catholic undergraduate student is contesting what he sees as the secularizing, non-devout, non-observant and irreligious lifestyles and personal choices of same-age peers residing in community around him by employing what he believes to be the most powerful cultural force he knows: the mediated material religion of Catholic sacramentality. In this sense, he is making a political argument out of his aesthetic material expression.

## Closing Reflection

I find in my hockey-loving, Mediterranean-influenced, altar-building college student a reminder of what surprises can emerge in relation to vernacular religion and material culture, and why such artful riches need to be identified and studied, especially when they are illuminated by the light found in the Upper Room. But I have one more point for reflection. Considering his interview comments, it should not surprise you that my consultant is interested in the priesthood and has entered a Roman Catholic seminary to become ordained as a priest. In this context, can he comfortably continue to express some version of his Catholic vernacular knowledge and live this interpretative diversity as a Catholic priest? In developing his own discernment as a minister of the Church, how open will he be to the diversity of his flock? What will he make in time of his own tradition of magical beliefs and practices? Will his own vernacular religious practices as described in this study become the root of Catholic diversity and religious openness or the path to a state of clerical hegemony over the laity?

Sociologist of religion Michele Dillon in her monograph, *Postsecular Catholicism*, asks a question which complements well this article's discussion of the vernacular religion of my consultant: 'Who and what speaks for Catholicism?' (2018: 11). She explains that in the years following the 1962–1965 Second Vatican Council, 'interpretive autonomy', the individual freedom to disagree with institutional Church teaching, has become a central element of Catholic identity. There are 'multiple doctrinal strands within the Catholic tradition', the structure holding within itself 'interpretive diversity'. One marker of 'postsecular society' is that believers largely rely on their own individual authority, 'the individualization of religious authority'—long a feature of Protestantism—rather than on institutional Church functionaries.

Wresting herself away from sociology's understanding of the homogeneity of its 'official' religion, she appreciates the flexibility of institutionalized religion and the functionaries/believers in it in a more ethnographically, dare I say, folkloristically, realistic way. She writes that the Catholic Church:

> is a hierarchical institution with a great deal of interpretive and legal authority vested in the Church hierarchy. The hierarchy, embodied by the pope and the bishops, is the Church's religiously grounded 'teaching authority'. At the same time, the Church is a community of discourse in which individual reason and lived experience hold sway. Catholicism is thus an interpretive community with multiple diverse voices in ongoing conversation over doctrinal and other matters that have an imposing relevance in the everyday lives of Catholics. This is a model of the Church that was itself confirmed by the bishops themselves at Vatican II. (Dillon 2018: 11–12)

Dillon argues that in postmodernity an interpretative diversity has developed within the tradition that is representative of all levels of its devout, from Pope and bishops in the hierarchy all the way through to the laity in the pews and homes. This dimension of interpretation and associated actions has become a central component within post-modern Catholic identity.

Of course, while Dillon would lay this interpretative diversity and authority at the feet of modernity and secularization, I would ask for a fuller examination of individualization and a root of religious authority as a historical fact of vernacular religiosity which makes up a part of the entire entity of the religious life and religion in general.[10]

It seems that the sociology of religion has caught up to an insight that folklorists and ethnologists who work with vernacular religion have long recognized: that the faithful have been quite busy creating, recreating and interpreting dimensions of their beliefs and practices even before modernity (a point that was also raised by a sociologist, McGuire, in her 2008 monograph, *Lived Religion*). And that the clergy who later become the hierarchy, themselves a part of the 'folk', are also natural communicators of vernacular belief and practice, some of which then becomes reified into the institutional Church (Primiano 1995: 46). What will be worth observing and considering is how my consultant, as an ordained Catholic priest, ostensibly a functionary of the institution, brings into the Church his vernacular religion and translates it into his pastoral work, his creation and supervision of future sanctuary altars, and the further clerical embellishment of his rectory Upper Rooms.

## Acknowledgements

Versions of the material in this chapter were presented at the 2016 meeting of the American Folklore Society, Miami, Florida; the 2018 meeting of the American Academy of Religion, Denver, Colorado; and the 2019 meeting of the International Society for Ethnology and Folklore (SIEF), Santiago de Compostela. I wish to thank John DiMucci, J. Gregory Garrity, Nicolas Le Bigre, E. Ann Matter, István Povedák, Lisa Ratmansky, Joseph Sciorra, Matthew Slutz, Nancy Watterson, Steve Wehmeyer, as well as Adam Altman and especially Anne Schwelm of Cabrini University's Holy Spirit Library for their assistance. I am grateful to Patti Stocker for her technical assistance. Ben Danner has been an indispensable sounding board for theoretical discussion and technical assistance. Nicholas Rademacher read final drafts with great dedication and care. Sabina Magliocco shared her invaluable scholarship. I am continuously grateful to Marion Bowman and Ülo Valk for their unfailing support.

## Notes

1 Read more about Puccini and religion in Moomjy 2020, Lyric n.d. and Digaetani 1984. Examples of individual religion can easily be found in Puccini's *Madama Butterfly* and *Suor Angelica* as well, and I must mention an American verismo opera, Gian Carlo Menotti's *The Saint of Bleeker Street* which with its representations of

visions, stigmata, and saint festivals and devotion make it a fascinating opera to see staged.
2   See as one prominent example in Religious Studies, the work of Robert A. Orsi (2016), as well as the debates presented by Thomas Tweed (2015) and Randall Balmer (2017).
3   See Magliocco's history of the study of 'vernacular magic' (2004: 154); also, her own historical discussion (2012: 143–148). For 'folk groups', see El-Shamy 2011.
4   I contributed an Introduction for a special issue on Experimental Dharmas in Hinduism, Buddhism and Sikhism for the *International Journal for Dharma Studies*. See DeNapoli 2017.
5   All photographs were taken and provided by my student consultant.
6   The Pew Research Center (https://www.pewresearch.org/) is a nonpartisan 'fact tank' sponsored since 1996 by the Pew Charitable Trusts and located in Washington, DC. Its empirically based social science research includes work on world religions. Its findings on Roman Catholics in the United States in the post-millennium have been most illuminating.
7   Additional facts from the Pew surveys fill in the demographic picture: While the approximately 51 million Catholic adults in the US represent only about one-fifth of the total US adult population, Catholicism is still the largest single religious institution in the country. These Catholics are sharply divided in terms of American political opinion, affiliation, and in their opinions of the politics of the Catholic Church (see Lipka and Smith 2019).
8   I wish to thank my consultant who shall go nameless, as will his institution of higher education, for his detailed explanation, excellent narratives, and for his permission to photograph his dormitory altars which changed seasonally, as mentioned. This information was gathered between 2016 and 2020. I have summarized/synthesized various significant points from numerous encounters: 1) in addition to his dorm room altar, he still kept an altar in his room at home; 2) I do recall asking him what his dorm mates thought of his religious door decorations and various altar displays when he left his room door open. He noted that they appeared to respect them and did not attempt to disturb them; 3) my consultant frequently remarked in casual conversation that he deplored the way his peers behaved in the dorms: drinking to excess, taking illegal drugs, and engaging in premarital sexual relations.
9   This method is demonstrated in Glassie and Shukla's artistic ethnography on Brazilian religion carvers and artists (2017); and in Cashman's (2016) rich delineation of the religious uniculture of regionally representative, yet distinctive, Packy Jim McGrath, a storyteller from the Irish border.
10  In terms of a series of contemporary events solidifying and empowering individuals to feel a greater freedom of discernment to create for themselves acceptable versions of Catholicism, one cannot remove the impact of the clerical sexual abuse scandals from the minds of the faithful (see Bowman 2016).

## References

Allen, William. 2014. 'A Nation Preferring Visions: Moving Statues, Apparitions, and Vernacular Religion in Contemporary Ireland'. PhD diss., National University of Ireland, Cork.

Ammerman, Nancy Tatom. 2014. *Sacred Stories, Spiritual Tribes: Finding Religion in Everyday Life*. New York: Oxford University Press. https://doi.org/10.1093/acprof:oso/9780199896448.001.0001

Balmer, Randall. 2017. 'Afterword'. In *Everyday Sacred: Religion in Contemporary Quebec*, edited by Hillary Kaell, 254–257. Montreal: McGill-Queen's University Press. https://doi.org/10.2307/j.ctt1vjqqhp.15

Bellah, Robert N., Richard Madsen, William M. Sullivan, Ann Swidler and Steven M. Tipton, eds. 2008 [1985]. *Habits of the Heart: Individualism and Commitment in American Life*. Berkeley: University of California Press.

Bowman, Marion. 2016. 'Crisis, Change and "the Continuous Art of Individual Interpretation and Negotiation": The Aftermath of Clerical Sexual Abuse in Newfoundland'. *Journal of the Irish Society for the Academic Study of Religions* 3: 140–170. https://jisasr.files.wordpress.com/2016/06/crisis-change-and-e28098the-continuous-art-of-individual-interpretation-and-negotiation_-the-aftermath-of-clerical-sexual-abuse-in-newfoundland-pdf1.pdf

Bowman, Marion, and Ülo Valk, eds. 2012. *Vernacular Religion in Everyday Life: Expressions of Belief*. Sheffield; Bristol, CT: Equinox Publishing.

Cashman, Ray. 2016. *Packy Jim: Folklore and Worldview on the Irish Border*. Madison: University of Wisconsin Press.

Cashman, Ray, Tom Mould and Pravina Shukla, eds. 2011. *The Individual and Tradition: Folkloristic Perspectives*. Bloomington: Indiana University Press.

DeNapoli, Antoinette. 2017. 'Experimental Religiosities and *Dharma* Traditions: New Directions in the Study of Vernacular Religion in Asia and the Diaspora'. *International Journal of Dharma Studies* (Special Issue: *Experimental Dharmas in Asia and the Diaspora*, edited by Antoinette DeNapoli) 5 (11). https://doi.org/10.1186/s40613-017-0054-z

Digaetani, John Louis. 1984. 'Puccini's *Tosca* and the Necessity of Agnosticism'. *The Opera Quarterly* 2 (1): 76–84. https://doi.org/10.1093/oq/2.1.76

Dillon, Michelle. 2001. 'Pierre Bourdieu, Religion, and Cultural Production'. *Cultural Studies* 1 (4): 411–429. https://doi.org/10.1177/153270860100100402

Dillon, Michelle. 2018. *Postsecular Catholicism: Relevance and Renewal*. New York: Oxford University Press.

Dubet, François. 1994. 'The System, the Actor, and the Social Subject'. *Thesis Eleven* 38 (1): 16–35. https://doi.org/10.1177/072551369403800103

Dundes, Alan. 1977. 'Who Are the Folk?' In *Frontiers of Folklore*. AAAS Selected Symposium 5, edited by William Bascom, 17–35. Boulder, CO: Westview Press. https://doi.org/10.4324/9780429050756-2

El-Shamy, Hasan. 2011. 'Folk Group'. In *Folklore: An Encyclopedia of Beliefs, Customs, Tales, Music, and Art*, Vol. II, 2nd revised edn, edited by Charlie T. McCormick and Kim Kennedy White, 518–522. Santa Barbara, CA: ABC-Clio.

Eller, Jack David. 2015 [2007]. *Introducing Anthropology of Religion*. London: Routledge. https://doi.org/10.4324/9781315740157

Elms, Alan. 2005. 'Apocryphal Freud: Sigmund Freud's Most Famous "Quotations" and Their Actual Sources'. *Luzifer-Amor: Zeitschrift zur Geschichte der Psychoanalyse* 18 (35): 82–108.
Fabbrini, Marco. 2019. 'Folkloric vs. Vernacular: Reconsidering Old and New Approaches to Ethnographic Study of Religion'. *Erreffe: La ricerca folklorica* 74: 245–256.
Fish, Lydia. 1982. 'Ethnicity and Catholicism'. *New York Folklore* 8 (3–4): 83–92.
Freitas, Donna. 2009. *Sex and the Soul: Juggling Sexuality, Spirituality, Romance, and Religion on America's College Campuses*. New York: Oxford University Press.
Freitas, Donna. 2013. *The End of Sex: How Hookup Culture is Leaving a Generation Unhappy, Sexually Unfulfilled, and Confused about Intimacy*. New York: Basic Books.
Gatling, Benjamin. 2020. 'There Isn't Belief, Just Believing: Rethinking *Belief* as a Keyword of Folklore Studies'. *Journal of American Folklore* 133 (529): 307–328. https://doi.org/10.5406/jamerfolk.133.529.0307
Glassie, Henry. 1995. 'Tradition'. *Journal of American Folklore* 108 (430): 395–412. https://doi.org/10.2307/541653
Glassie, Henry, and Pravina Shukla. 2017. *Sacred Art: Catholic Saints and Candomble Gods in Modern Brazil*. Bloomington: Indiana University Press. https://doi.org/10.2307/j.ctt1zxz1kw
Howard, Robert Glenn. 2011. *Digital Jesus: The Making of a New Christian Fundamentalist Community on the Internet*. New York: NYU Press. https://doi.org/10.18574/nyu/9780814773086.001.0001
Illman, Ruth, and Mercédesz Czimbalmos. 2020. 'Knowing, Being, and Doing Religion: Introducing an Analytical Model for Researching Vernacular Religion'. *Temenos: Nordic Journal of Comparative Religion* 56 (2): 171–199. https://doi.org/10.33356/temenos.97275
Kapaló, James Alexander. 2013. 'Folk Religion in Discourse and Practice'. *Journal of Ethnology and Folkloristics* 7 (1): 3–18.
King, Jason. 2017. *Faith with Benefits: Hookup Culture on Catholic Campuses*. New York: Oxford University Press. https://doi.org/10.1093/acprof:oso/9780190244804.001.0001
Lesiv, Mariya. Forthcoming. 'Folk Belief and Religion in Ukraine: Creating the Charisma of Place'. In *Oxford Handbook of Slavic and East European Folklore*, edited by Margaret Beissinger. New York: Oxford University Press.
Lipka, Michael, and Gregory A. Smith. 2019. 'Like Americans Overall, U.S. Catholics are Sharply Divided by Party'. *Pew Research Center*. https://www.pewresearch.org/fact-tank/2019/01/24/like-americans-overall-u-s-catholics-are-sharply-divided-by-party (accessed June 8, 2021).
Lyric. n.d. 'Puccini and Religion'. *Lyric Opera of Kansas City*. https://kcopera.org/tosca-15/puccini-religion/ (accessed June 8, 2021).
Magliocco, Sabina. 2004. 'Witchcraft, Healing and Vernacular Magic in Italy'. In *Witchcraft Continued: Popular Magic in Modern Europe*, edited by Willem de Blécourt and Owen Davies, 151–173. Manchester: Manchester University Press.
Magliocco, Sabina. 2012. 'Religious Practice'. In *A Companion to Folklore*, edited by Regina F. Bendix and Galit Hasan-Rokem, 136–153. Malden, MA: Wiley-Blackwell. https://doi.org/10.1002/9781118379936.ch7

Maldonado-Estrada, Alyssa. 2020. *Lifeblood of the Parish: Men and Catholic Devotion in Williamsburg, Brooklyn.* New York: New York University Press. https://doi.org/10.18574/nyu/9781479872244.001.0001

Masci, David, and Gregory A. Smith. 2018. '7 Facts about American Catholics'. *Pew Research Center.* https://www.pewresearch.org/fact-tank/2018/10/10/7-facts-about-american-catholics/ (accessed June 8, 2021).

McGuire, Meredith B. 2008. *Lived Religion: Faith and Practice in Everyday Life.* New York: Oxford University Press.

Mechling, Jay. 2006. 'Solo Folklore'. *Western Folklore* 65 (4): 435–453.

Moomjy, Gregory. 2020. 'Personal Faith and Manipulative Religion in Puccini's "Tosca"'. *The Font* (blog). https://www.patheos.com/blogs/thefont/2020/05/faith-and-religion-in-tosca/ (accessed June 8, 2021).

Mould, Tom. 2011. *Still, the Small Voice: Narrative, Personal Revelation, and the Mormon Folk Tradition.* Logan: Utah State University Press. https://doi.org/10.2307/j.ctt4cgjj5

Nelson, John K. 2013. *Experimental Buddhism: Innovation and Activism in Contemporary Japan.* Honolulu: University of Hawaii Press. https://doi.org/10.21313/hawaii/9780824838331.001.0001

Nelson, John K. 2017. 'An Experimental Approach to Buddhism and Religion'. *International Journal of Dharma Studies* (Special Issue: *Experimental Dharmas in Asia and the Diaspora*, edited by Antoinette DeNapoli) 5 (16). https://doi.org/10.1186/s40613-017-0052-1

O'Connor, Kathleen Malone. 2011. 'Magic'. In *Folklore: An Encyclopedia of Beliefs, Customs, Tales, Music, and Art*, Vol. III, 2nd revised edn, edited by Charlie T. McCormick and Kim Kennedy White, 811–821. Santa Barbara, CA: ABC-Clio.

Orsi, Robert A. 2016. *History and Presence.* Cambridge, MA: Harvard University Press.

PRC. 2019. 'In U.S., Decline of Christianity Continues at Rapid Pace'. *Pew Research Center.* https://www.pewforum.org/2019/10/17/in-u-s-decline-of-christianity-continues-at-rapid-pace/ (accessed June 8, 2021).

Primiano, Leonard Norman. 1985. 'Feminist Christian Songs: Occasions of Vernacular Religious Belief'. *New Jersey Folklore* 10: 38–43.

Primiano, Leonard Norman. 1993a. 'Intrinsically Catholic: Vernacular Religion and Philadelphia's "Dignity"'. PhD diss., University of Pennsylvania.

Primiano, Leonard Norman. 1993b. '"I would rather be fixated on the Lord": Women's Religion, Men's Power, and the "Dignity" Problem'. *New York Folklore* 19: 89–103.

Primiano, Leonard Norman. 1995. 'Vernacular Religion and the Search for Method in Religious Folklife'. *Western Folklore* (Special Issue: *Reflexivity and the Study of Belief*) 54 (1): 37–56. https://doi.org/10.2307/1499910

Primiano, Leonard Norman. 2001. 'What is Vernacular Catholicism? The "Dignity" Example'. *Acta Ethnographica Hungarica* 46: 51–58. https://doi.org/10.1556/AEthn.46.2001.1-2.6

Primiano, Leonard Norman. 2004. 'The Gay God of the City: The Emergence of the Gay and Lesbian Ethnic Parish'. In *Gay Religion: Innovation and Continuity in Spiritual Practice*, edited by Scott Thumma and Edward R. Gray, 7–30. Lanham, MD: Alta Mira Press.

Primiano, Leonard Norman. 2009. '"For what I have done and what I have failed to do": Vernacular Catholicism and *The West Wing*'. In *Small Screen, Big Picture: Television and Lived Religion*, edited by Diane Winston, 99–123. Waco, TX: Baylor University Press.

Primiano, Leonard Norman. 2011. '"I wanna do bad things with you": Fantasia on Themes of American Religion from the Title Sequence of HBO's *True Blood*'. In *God in the Details: American Religion in Popular Culture*, edited by Eric Michael Mazur and Kate McCarthy, 2nd edn, 41-61. New York: Routledge.

Primiano, Leonard Norman. 2012. 'Manifestations of the Religious Vernacular: Ambiguity, Power, and Creativity'. In *Vernacular Religion in Everyday Life: Expressions of Belief*, edited by Marion Bowman and Ülo Valk, 382-394. Sheffield; Bristol, CT: Equinox Publishing.

Primiano, Leonard Norman. 2015. 'Kitsch'. In *The Routledge Companion to Religion and Popular Culture*, edited by John C. Lyden and Eric Michael Mazur, 281-312. London: Routledge.

Primiano, Leonard Norman. 2017. 'Editorial Introduction'. *International Journal of Dharma Studies* (Special Issue: *Experimental Dharmas in Asia and the Diaspora*, edited by Antoinette DeNapoli) 5 (15). https://doi.org/10.1186/s40613-017-0055-y

Primiano, Leonard Norman. 2022. *Vernacular Religion: Collected Essays of Leonard Norman Primiano*. Ed. Deborah Dash Moore. Foreword by Judith Weisenfeld. New York: New York University Press.

Santino, Jack. 1982. 'Catholic Folklore and Folk Catholicism'. *New York Folklore* 8 (3-4): 93-106.

Sciorra, Joseph. 2015. *Built with Faith: Italian American Imagination and Catholic Material Culture in New York City*. Knoxville: University of Tennessee Press.

Tweed, Thomas A. 2015. 'After the Quotidian Turn: Interpretive Categories and Scholarly Trajectories in the Study of Religion since the 1960s'. *Journal of Religion* 95 (3): 361-385. https://doi.org/10.1086/681112

Wilcox, Melissa M. 2002. 'When Sheila's a Lesbian: Religious Individualism among Lesbian, Gay, Bisexual, and Transgender Christians'. *Sociology of Religion* 63 (4): 497-513. https://doi.org/10.2307/3712304

Yoder, Don. 2001a. 'The Folklife Studies Movement'. In Don Yoder, *Discovering American Folklife: Essays on Folk Culture and the Pennsylvania Dutch*, 25-42. Mechanicsburg, PA: Stackpole Books.

Yoder, Don. 2001b. 'Toward a Definition of Folk Religion'. In Don Yoder, *Discovering American Folklife: Essays on Folk Culture and the Pennsylvania Dutch*, 67-84. Mechanicsburg, PA: Stackpole Books.

# Part 5

# Afterlife and Afterdeath

Chapter 14

# Dealing with the Dead: Vernacular Belief Negotiations among the Khasi of Northeastern India

*Margaret Lyngdoh**

This article analyses narratives about death, dying and reanimation from an emic viewpoint. It will attempt to show how the Khasi reframe their articulated beliefs and practices using the primary tradition-trope of funerary customs from the Christian perspective and in the context of those who follow the indigenous religion. While death occupies a central position in the lifecycle of a Khasi, rituals relating to death are context-specific. The stereotyping and marginalization of specific groups of people on the basis of mortuary rites will be shown through empirical data derived from fieldwork.[1] In this article I do not target or malign specific clans or communities. Rather, I look at negotiations as expressed in narratives that discuss 'bad' deaths and the fulfilment of death rituals and how these narratives enforce the othering and marginalization of communities and groups among the Khasi. I use the concept of 'death' as a generic resource that spawns multiple articulations of belief. This article

---

\* **Margaret Lyngdoh**, University of Tartu, Faculty of Arts and Humanities, Institute of Cultural Research, received her PhD in 2016 from the University of Tartu, Estonia. She studied at Ohio State University, Columbus, USA; University College Cork, Ireland; and the University of Tartu, Estonia. She was awarded the position of Albert Lord Fellow 2016 at the Centre for Studies in Oral Tradition, University of Missouri. She received the Estonian Research Council Grant in 2017 for her post-doctoral research PUTJD746 on the topic Tradition and Vernacular Discourses in the Context of Local Christianities and Hinduisms in Northeastern India. She is also editor for the newsletter of the International Society for Folk Narrative Research (ISFNR). Her research interests include indigenous folklore, tradition, indigenous ontologies with theoretical focus on current 'turns' in anthropology, the study of religion, and indigenous religious research methods.

will show how notions of living and dying shape the Khasi cosmology, inclusive of societies of the human and non-human.

The Khasi as a community make up the major ethnic group living in Meghalaya, in the northeastern region of India. The conventional view of the origin of the Khasi is that they are a people of Austric origin speaking a Mon-Khmer/Mon-Annam linked language (Lyngdoh 1991: 19; Bareh 2001 [1997]: 15-16). The Khasi had no script of their own until the arrival of Welsh Calvinistic missionaries in about 1841-1842. Today, the majority of Khasi are Christian, the most popular denominations being Presbyterian and Catholic. With an approximate population of 1.3 million (Statistical Profile 2013: 167), the Khasi are matrilineal, key features of which are lineage and inheritance. The main communities include Khynriam, Pnar, Bhoi, War, Lyngngam, Maram, Muliang, Nongtrai, among others. While clans originate from a specific ancestress, communities are made up of groups of clans who speak a common language, inhabit a certain area, and who have a common endonym for their own group. Traditionally, the Khasi call themselves *Khun u Hyññiewtrep* or 'Children of the Seven Huts', effectively recalling the central Khasi myth of the fall of the seven families and the severing of the connection between man and God as a result of sin. I hypothesize that the word 'Khasi' is an imposed exonym that was utilized by the British to designate speakers of the Austroasiatic language group who lived in proximity to each other. Another example of such a phenomenon is the categorization of various communities who inhabit the present-day Nagaland and Manipur (in Northeast India) under the common umbrella term of 'Naga'.

## Khasi Indigenous Religion and the Role of Christianity

It was with the arrival of the first effective missionary, Thomas Jones of the Welsh Calvinistic Methodist Mission and his wife in 1841 that Christianity was formally introduced to the Khasi.[2] The Khasi language, which until then was oral, received a Roman script, primarily so that the missionaries could translate the Bible into Khasi. Further, mission schools were opened along with primary health facilities.[3] Writing in 1906, colonial officer Major Philip Richard Thorndagh Gurdon (1863-1942), in his important ethnography of the Khasi, anticipated the changes that Christianity would cause in religion and society: 'In a few years' time, if the progressive rate of conversions of Khasis to Christianity continues, probably the greater number of the Khasi social customs will have disappeared and others will have taken their place' (Gurdon 1907: 6). The colonial document, which is popularly known as 'Pemberton's Report', was published in 1835. In the third section of the report, Captain Robert Boileau Pemberton, who was the Joint Commissioner in what was then known as *Muneepoor* (contemporary Manipur) wrote about the struggle to subjugate the *Cossyahs* (Khasi) and the final victory of the British in the Khasi Hills. What stands out impressively in this account is that the colonial masters truly believed in their mission to 'civilize' the 'savage natives' and in the superiority of European culture (Pemberton 1979 [1835]: 221-261).

These examples from the early colonial writers are important in understanding the beginnings of the ideological differences between Khasis who are Christian converts and the small Khasi percentage who today still follow the traditional indigenous religion. They provide insights not only into the early spread of Christianity but also the governing mindset of Khasi Christians towards Khasi non-Christians.

Other names of Khasi religion, *Niam Tynrai* (lit. 'original religion' or 'root religion'), include *Niam tip briew tip blei* (lit. 'man-knowing, god-knowing rituals') and *Niam tip kur tip kha* (lit. 'clan knowing, kin-knowing'). In 1899, in the face of overwhelming conversions, 16 Khasi intellectuals set up the Seng Khasi, a socio-cultural organization that aimed to preserve and promote the interests of the Khasi religion. Transmission of basic Khasi tenets had previously been oral, although today an increasing number of Khasi writers publish pamphlets, essays, books and opinion pieces in vernacular and English language newspapers, along with other media as a means of commenting upon the Khasi religion. Orality is a key feature of Khasi cosmology and continues to maintain the indigenous worldview in the face of multiple conversions and the arrival of cosmopolitan culture. In Khasi language the word, *ktien*, represents the sacred aspect of the auditory component of a Khasi ritual that is also relevant for serious deliberations held during councils. Ritual language interspersed with colloquial expressions have authority and are generally expressed through linguistic parallelisms, reduplication and repetition thus articulating the 'mental text' (Honko 1996) that accounts for memory markers in long oral narratives recounted during any religious event. The place of kinship in the Khasi understanding of their ontology, by which I mean the entirety of existences inclusive of human and non-human, is central.

The significant principles of the Khasi religion are linked with its clan structure and associated rituals. The Khasi are matrilineal, which means that lineage and inheritance follow from the mother's line and that clans trace their origin to the first ancestress. An example may be given from the Talang clan. In oral narrative, Iawtalang had nine daughters who were very industrious and hard working. They were so diligent that when the youngest sister was in childbirth, the sisters still went to the fields. The husband of the youngest daughter was from the Dhar clan. He was so furious that he cooked the afterbirth and fed it to the elder sisters. Afterwards, he taunted them saying that they were the devourers of their own kith and kin. In shame at committing a taboo sin, the sisters fled and each founded their own clan. One of them fled to Chyrmang and retained the original name of Talang. It is taboo for someone from the Talang clan or the related clans (who descended from the other sisters) to have dealings with someone from the Dhar clan.

Khasi clans are strictly exogamous. A person is born into the world in order to live righteously through the orally transmitted codes of conducts that elders teach. The first duty of a person is towards their clan. A good example would be the absence of beggars in Khasi society. In the event of a person becoming an orphan or having misfortune befall them the clan steps in to help, otherwise it would be a matter of great shame. Therefore the greatest misfortune to occur in the life of a Khasi is their clan extinction. Rituals in this way are connected to the prosperity of the clan. Clan ancestors are also responsible for the upkeep and continuation of the clan and thus there are many rituals to venerate them. Clan ancestors are venerated notably through the erection of megaliths (see Figure 14.1), many of which dot the Khasi and Jaintia Hills.

**Figure 14.1.** Cluster megaliths by a village road in West Khasi Hills. Photograph by Margaret Lyngdoh.

Khasi philosophy is centred around the idea of cause and effect. This means that any kind of misfortune, illness or death has a cause that can be divined. Purifying or correcting the cause would remove the affliction. Divination rituals are carried out by ritual performers who are called Lyngdoh. (Thus Lyngdoh has more of a functionary connotation than a clan name.)

## Dying, Death and the Afterlife

A peaceful afterlife for the Khasi individual is dependent on many factors: the manner of death, proper performance of the funerary rites and whether the departed spirit has any unfulfilled wishes. There is no concept of hell in the Khasi religion as understood in the Christian worldview. Therefore, according to Khasi writer H. Onderson Mawrie (2000 [1971]), when a person who has lived an honourable life dies, he or she rejoins the clan members who have died before, along with the clan ancestress (*iawbei*) and the first maternal uncle (*suitñia*). The restless dead among the Khasi are placed by Mawrie into three classes: firstly, those who have committed unforgivable sins, such as breaking a taboo, become highly malicious and harmful to human beings; secondly, those whose funerary rites were not complete also become restless, although they seek lonely places and shun any contact with human beings; thirdly, the most notorious of spirits is created when a person dies because of an accident, or murder or suicide. Such spirits are malevolent and always seek to harm humankind (ibid.: 18–21). For the Khasi, suffering for one's sins after death is conceived as denial of a reunion with one's clan and family members.

In the contemporary worldview of the Khasi, the status of restless dead is conferred upon the spirit of the dead person when explicit signs are witnessed. Thus, one confirmation of this is when, during the cremation ceremony, the dead body does not burn, even after a few hours.

Mario Sunn belongs to the Seng Khasi. In an interview carried out at my request by my research assistant at the time, Damang Syngkon, on May 4, 2013, in Mawkhar, Shillong, Mario said:

> My father told me this story—this happened about 35 years ago. Earlier, if somebody died within a community, all the people in the village would participate and help with the funeral preparations ... But this is not so anymore. The family just gives responsibility to the Seng Khasi to carry out the funeral procedures; we from the Lum Jingthang Committee, we

> carry out the cremation rituals. But earlier on, the community took responsibility. So my father told me about an event which happened during a funeral where the pyre burned until 11:30 PM but the body did not burn. The flesh was intact. The elders were then called in order to divine the cause of such an ominous sign. According to the divination that was carried out, it was found that the deceased person used to dance during the *Shad Suk Mynsiem*.[4] The spirit desired that the members of his family would dance around the funeral pyre in ceremonial dress. This was done and after that the cremation passed off peacefully.

This narrative is explicit in its reference to traditional Khasi religion. The dead person is dissatisfied and provides signs through which it became possible to divine the cause of the unhappiness of the departed spirit. But more significantly, this narrative illustrates the provisions that are made by the traditional religion for such occurrences. Social mechanisms accommodate the restless dead and provide ways in which the dead can be dealt with.

Another narrative was collected from a family belonging to the Khasi traditional religion, who had to cope with the death of their mother in September 2012. The son of the deceased gave this account in a telephone interview in November 2012:

> My mother died after a prolonged illness in a hospital in Shillong. After they had brought the body back home and they had given the ritual bath to the corpse, they laid it out in the formal sitting room of the family home. One of her daughters noticed after a while that there were many lice swarming on the face of the corpse. She cleaned it up immediately. After a while, the same thing happened and there were more lice swarming over the face of the corpse. The daughter cleaned it up again. But soon, the lice were back again. This continued for some time. The family then understood that something was wrong and that the spirit of the dead person was unhappy. They spoke to the corpse saying, 'Why do you want to embarrass us in front of the community? If there has been a mistake on our part, then forgive us and forget it'. After they had spoken, the lice stopped coming.

This narrative is expressive of Khasi belief in the preservation of clan and family honour. The signs of an unfulfilled death and a dissatisfied spirit compromise and threaten the family's status and respect in the community. This forces the restless spirit to quiet down and conform to societal values. Even the dead do not transgress the prescribed norms laid down by the Khasi religion (*tip kur tip kha* or 'know your clansmen and kinsmen').

Other instances illustrate Khasi experiences with death and the afterlife from a Christian perspective. The following example was collected from a Presbyterian Church Elder, Ridor Donn, in Shillong in an interview in the winter of 2012. His narrative is reproduced here:

> My father had a heart attack while he was in the office at the District Council. By the time we got him to the hospital ... he was unable to recognize me, his son, and not even my mother. Soon afterwards he died. At the funeral, years later my mother told me she felt a kiss on her forehead during the funeral and suddenly she was happy and realized that everything was going to be all right.

This narrative is significant because it does not involve the community or a ritual healer. The private experience of grief and coming to terms with it become central. The dead still communicate with the living. This is also the purpose of satisfying and calming the restless dead in the traditional religion, but the mechanisms through which this is achieved differ according to the context.

The differences between the narratives of the families belonging to the Christian and traditional Khasi religion are pronounced. The *Niam Tynrai* accommodates the possible occurrence of restless spirits after death within the religious beliefs and the community. This is because, within the Khasi worldview, death is not the end of existence but the beginning of an ideal state of being close to God and the clan ancestress, and other family members. Within the various Khasi sub-communities the dead are not perceived as inert, ambivalent entities but active agents promoting the prosperity of the clan they belonged to while alive as members of society, and sometimes, in certain circumstances, harming the clan through misfortune, illness and death.

In the Khasi Christian ontology, the dead wait for the final judgement, when Christ will come again. I have not come across any instances among the Khasi Christians of the possibility of a soul becoming restless being discussed inside the Church. The only pitfalls are temptation by the devil and the seduction of the Christian mind by various aspects of modern life. The dead are not conferred any status. They remain marginal entities and if there is a manifestation of the spirit of a loved one, within the official discourse of the Church, they are demonized. But in everyday vernacular life spirits exist, interfere with human life, and exposure to them causes illness, misfortune and bad luck.

According to the Khasi worldview, the afterlife is not limited to a bounded 'heaven' that represents, in a way, the end of action or participation in life. In reality, different Khasi sub-communities have differing conceptions of what happens to a person after death. In Ri Bhoi district in the northern Khasi Hills, Dising Marin, now deceased and an erstwhile resident of Pahamskhen village, told me that certain individuals who are invested with the ability to shape-shift into the form of a tiger, also have the unique ability to be ritual performers in the community. If such people live according to the specific code (not to be confused with living a sinless life) laid down by the Tiger Deities and the clan ancestors, then the *rngiew* or soul-essence of such people will go on to become a *syrngi* or ancestor spirit. The *syrngi* is a significant entity for the Bhoi community of Khasi because it is the *syrngi* who is invested with responsibility for the upkeep, procreation and welfare of a given clan.

### The Lyngngam and Nongtrai Khasi Communities

**Figure 14.2.** West Khasi Hills District outlined on a map provided by © OpenStreetMap contributors

The communities inhabiting areas beyond Nongstoiñ, which is the headquarters of West Khasi Hills district, comprise the Nongtrai, Lyngngam and Muliang. The term Lyngngam has been used as an umbrella term to designate all three communities (see Figure 14.2). However, I try to distinguish them from each other because they are different communities despite residing in the West Khasi Hills District. Gurdon dedicates a subchapter to the Lyngngam in his ethnography on the Khasi (1907).

The generally accepted view is that the Khasi migrated from Myanmar and other nearby areas. However, the Nongtrai claim an alternative origin. About them, P. S. Ñianglang (2000: 18), a Khasi scholar and government official, writes that the word Nongtrai:

in a singular form is derived from two Khasi words, 'shnong' which means village, and 'trai' means 'owner' or 'possessor'. Thus 'Nongtrais' means 'the indigenous possessor of the native villages or native settlers of the soil who inhabit the north-West of the Khasi Hills'.

Thus, people belonging to the Nongtrai community believe that they are the original inhabitants of the area. In the lifecycle of the people living in the Lyngngam and Nongtrai areas, death seems to be a resource for differing interactive concepts. In the traditional worldview of the people, seasons, the environment, and other-than-human beings all participate in the death process. For example, west of Langdongdai, footmarks of the ancestors are imprinted upon a sizeable stone, *mawdienjat*, which marks the path the spirits should take to the land of the dead. The relatives and family of a dead person would have to wait for the autumn harvest in order to acquire the new paddy to make the rice beer which is specially required during a funeral. The *sangkhini* is a human-animal who is variously visualized as having the head of a cat and the body of a lizard, or the head of a bull and the body of a snake, and is the only entity (apart from the natural phenomenon of lightning) that can destroy a person who has come back from the dead (Kharbani 2004: 45–54). These examples make up the vernacular religious landscape through the usage of narratives, belief, practice, and special geography. Hence, the epistemology of the Lyngngam and Nongtrai is inclusive without divisions made between the human, the environment and the perceived afterlife. Various components then seem to come together to make up an elaborate, multivalent culture, especially of death rhetorics and belief. A disconnection in the worldview of a community then takes place when a foreign religion interferes with, and roots itself in, its cultural constructs.

About the Lyngngams, Gurdon writes 'they do not have any special birth customs' (1907: 198). In contrast, my informant, Karland Langrin of Seiñduli village, claimed: 'The most significant ritual in the life of the Nongtrai is the death ritual. This is because people from Lyngngam respect the death of a person the most' (Interview, September 4, 2014). The intricacy and engagement of the rituals and transformation beliefs associated with death among the Lyngngam and Nongtrai might explain why birth is not given as much prominence. As mentioned earlier, death comprises a tradition-trope that becomes a generic resource and thus the lifecycles of the Nongtrai, Lyngngam and Muliang are organized around it. Life is conceived as fluid, moving from habitation in one realm to habitation in another, with the ritual process becoming significant because it ensures the success or failure of a crossing over. Movement from one state of being to another is not linear because a person may die and come back to life; and a person can die and still retain animation; or a person can die and cross over successfully into the land of the dead.

## Death Ritual: Vernacular Description and Enactment

Before the advent of Christianity in Nongtrai, Lyngngam and Muliang, when a death occurred in the family it was very important that all the clan members should be present. Owing to the terrain and the poor road infrastructure between villages, it took some time before all the clan members were notified. For instance, if the death occurred during the monsoon, then rivers would be swollen, and it would be impossible to cross because the bridges were submerged. This would usually lead to delay. In addition, if the person died before the harvest, then people would have to wait until the harvest was done so as to have rice to brew alcohol, which is one of the necessary components of any funeral. The brewing of rice beer generally takes three weeks.

In the meantime, the body was kept inside the household at a specially designated place close to the hearth, with the closest kin sitting near the body until all the funeral arrangements were made. The practice differs in that in some villages the body is wrapped in a bamboo mat and kept on a makeshift platform on the top of a tree. In the fieldwork that I carried out in the village of Nongmyndo, Nongtrai, Theocratis Riangtem gave the following example of his father:

> When my father died, I came across this practice. Even when my other relatives died, this was performed in this way. I was very young at the time, it could be 1960 or 1962. Our house was not like it is now. It was made of bamboo and thatch and it stood on stilts ... so I remember my father grew more and more swollen, more and more stinky. We were not allowed to cremate him; we kept him for more than a month. Our father's body was laid out next to the hearth and we had to cook and eat next to it with the stench and the flies. But we had no choice, we had to eat there. And my mother, according to tradition and custom, she had to sit by the corpse. Until the cremation she had to sit beside it day and night: sit, eat, sleep there next to the corpse ... as children we were afraid to go near the corpse, but my poor mother had to be next to it. But what was very strange was that, regardless of the stench and the flies, not one of us got sick. (Interview, January 22, 2012)

Pollution associated with post-mortem bodily effluents are not of concern; ritual purity is what matters. The dignity afforded to the essence of the dead is of foremost importance. This 'forced' engagement with human remains forces the dead to 'live' among the living during this interim liminality. On certain death occasions, more elaborate ceremonies are carried out. One of the most important death rituals, the *Phor Sorat*, practised by the Lyngngam, comes from vernacular concepts derived from the root word *Phor* (in Umshyrkon village), *Bor* (in Umdang village) and *Phur* (among the Khynriam Khasis), terms which in their variation show the narrative origin of funerary rites among the Khasi. *Phur* among the Khasi in general means a ceremonial dance on the occasion of the post-mortem ceremony of a person of social significance. It is not practised among Christian Khasis. The last recorded *Phor Sorat* took place in the late 1990s in Nongshyrkon village in the Nongtrai inhabited area. The Lyngngam (inclusive of Muliang and Nongtrai) came to the notice of the general Khasi populace in 1997 when the documentary film *Ka Phor Sorat*, by Khasi filmmaker Raphael Warjri, was released. This went a long way to popularizing the death rituals of the Lyngngam among the greater Khasi population in Shillong and elsewhere.

*Bor*, as it is called in Umdang village in Lyngngam territory, refers to a funerary dance. Among the Khynriam, the *Phur* dance is held during the bone deposition ceremony of the paternal grandparents. But the *Phor Sorat* practised in West Khasi Hills is a long-drawn-out festival that takes a lot of time and money. The funeral festival may take place anywhere between six months and two years after the death of the person. *Phor* or *Phur* means to dance with the accompaniment of traditional drums and musical instruments on the occasion of someone's death. It is the last 'party' that is thrown symbolically by the dead for the living. Even though Christian Khasis no longer practise *Phur*, one year from the death of a person, a major commemorative party is thrown complete with a Holy Mass or prayer service for the departed, along with food and drink. This completes the period of mourning for the dead.

According to the origin narrative of how the *Phur* dance began, a boy named Synring and his mother lived peacefully in the Khasi Hills until one day she suddenly died. Synring thus became very lonely. One day when he was working in the fields he saw a sow. Thinking that the sow would destroy the crops, Synring shot at it with his arrow. But he wanted this arrow back and so he followed the injured sow and reached the land of the dead. The sow turned out to be his mother who had come to help him. Thus he lived happily with her for a while. But his mother told him that it was not his time to live in that world, and so she told him to go back to the human world. She gave him some drums and musical instruments and told him to collect her bones and place them in the clan ossuary. She further asked him to hold a feast and a ceremonial dance which then came to be called *Ka Phur Ka Siang* (lit. *ka* is the denominative of the feminine gender; 'dance and veneration of the dead').

In the indigenous religion of the Khasi, funerary rituals are elaborate and performed in great detail. Generally today, funerals among those who belong to the Khasi religion can be described briefly so as to show how some elements of the indigenous tradition have been adopted in Khasi Christian funerals. The village or local community, clan members, friends and family of the deceased come to the home to mourn. All the time, food and drinks are offered to the mourners. Sometimes, the number of people exceeds one thousand. It is important to note that all doors and windows in the home are kept open as long as the body of the deceased is in the house. This is to enable the spirit to visit the home as and when it likes. Then, following more rites, the body is usually kept in the house for three nights. On the third day, a bamboo bier (*krong*) is prepared and the body is kept inside it. The *krong* is covered with rich silk cloths, usually Khasi ceremonial women's attire called *dhara* or *muka*. Then a procession of mourners moves to the *Lum Jingthang* (place of cremation). During the cremation, three arrows are shot into the air (except in the westerly direction) and betel nut is thrown into the funeral pyre continually throughout by all those present. After the body is completely burned, the bones are collected and then deposited in the clan ossuary with more elaborate rituals. Such praxis articulates the experience and participation of the entire village in the event of a death.

A significant statement, made by Gurdon (1907: 105) about the afterlife convictions of the Khasi, expresses a misrepresentation of belief:

> It is believed that the spirits of the dead, whose funeral ceremonies have been duly performed, go to the house or garden of God, where there are groves of betel-nut trees; hence the expression for the departed, *uba bam kwai ha iing u blei* (he who is eating betel-nut in God's house), the idea of supreme happiness to the Khasi being to eat betel-nut uninterruptedly.

I would like to clarify that the meaning of the term *uba bam kwai ha iing u blei* actually expresses the idea of reunion with one's clan members and ancestors. To eat betel-nut with the supreme God symbolizes a time of peace and contentment for the departed.

Among the Khasi Christians, the dead body is kept for three days. On the third day it is buried. It is bathed by the family members and dressed and kept in a coffin in the house. As mentioned above, the huge feast is also part of the continuation of traditional death rituals or *Ka Phur Ka Siang*. The participation of the community and the number of mourners remain the same in the traditional Khasi or Christian funeral.

Two informants who are Christian, Witing Mawsor and Karland Langrin from Umdang and Seiñduli villages, West Khasi Hills, confirmed the contention that post-mortem rites are so significant in the life of a person from Lyngngam and Nongtrai communities because they enable the continuation of the existence of the person's *rngiew* (counterpart of the soul, which enables a person to succeed or fail in life endeavours) in another world. Among the Lyngngam and Nongtrai communities, death is not a final end to existence but a negotiated process between life and the desired afterlife.

According to Karland Langrin, in an interview carried out on September 3, 2014 in Seiñduli village, when a person dies, his or her soul crosses the Um Bylleiñ River (beyond the village of Umshynrut, in the Lyngngam area) and only then is able to let go of earthly attachments and living relatives.[5] In the case that a soul is unable to cross this river, the person comes back to life. Langrin recounted to me incidents in which such events have occurred. After the soul crosses the Um Bylleiñ River it goes to the *Lum Ngunrei*, the abode of the spirits. This is a physical place located west of Umsohpieng village. I have been told by my informant that at dusk, in *Lum Ngunrei*, mysterious sounds of merrymaking, singing and drums can be heard. Another version of this is recorded in the documentary film *Ka Phor Sorat* made by Raphael Warjri in which a soul on its journey to the *Krang Raid* or the land of the dead, goes to the Um Bylleiñ in order to cast off earthly longing and attachments. For the people of Umdang village, the name of the land of the dead is *Lum Pyndeiñr*.

Death rituals, then, are of great consequence in the context of the culture and belief of the Lyngngam and Nongtrai. It is necessary now to expand upon the Rashir, a clan whose death rites are rather different from other Khasi communities. The following passages refer to the ritual narratives associated with the death of those Rashir people who followed the indigenous religion. The Rashir clan mainly live in the Nongtrai and Lyngngam region of the West Khasi Hills. Today most of them are Christianized and do not practise the traditional death ritual. According to K. S. Riangtem, my informant, they originally belong to the Garo ethnic community and their name used to be Richel. After their migration to the Lyngngam region of the Khasi Hills, they adopted the name 'Rashir'. *U Rongna Bad Ka Shir* (lit. Rongna [male] and Shir [female]), published in 1995, is a narrative about the origin of the Rashir clan as told by Sijun Nongbri (who lived in Umsohpi Nongirai) to Sterian Shampliang. According to this narrative, the ancestors of the Rashir clan were Rongna and Shir and originally came from present-day Bangladesh. The significant element in all these versions is that the Rashir are originally foreigners and therefore not indigenous Khasi.

The death rites of the Rashir clan were mentioned in the narratives collected from all the villages in Nongtrai. For the purposes of this article, I will quote three versions translated from Khasi and transcribed verbatim from interviews, and a fourth collected from a published work.

The descriptions of spirit propitiation are transmitted through the oral tradition and are so significant because these are the only narratives that detail the existence of ritual 'head hunting' among the Khasi.[6] Earlier works stress the absence of headhunting practices among the Khasi. The term headhunting is primarily a colonial term which was attributed mainly to the various tribes of the Naga and the Mizo ethnic community. In the first ethnography on the Khasi, Gurdon (1907: 97) states that, 'the Khasis, unlike the Nagas, the Garos, the wild Was of Burma, the Dayaks of Borneo, and other head-hunting tribes, cannot be said to have indulged in head-hunting in ancient times'. Gurdon further seems to acknowledge, however, that in some narratives there are accounts of propitiating the war deity of the Khasi, Synkai Bamon, by offering an enemy's head (ibid.). *The Encyclopaedia Britannica* mentions the Khasi as a headhunting tribe (Britannica 2013 [1998]).

I have collected oral accounts of human sacrifice by beheading from the Northern Khasi Hills, while Lamare in his account on the Jaintias mentions that human sacrifice occurred historically in Nartiang to propitiate the Goddess Jainteswari. Human sacrifice was also carried out to venerate the Goddess Kopili (Lamare 2013: 89–99). In the Western Khasi Hills the secret, supernatural practice of offering human heads to propitiate the dead is mentioned in print both by G. Badaiasuklang L. Nonglait, although this topic is not detailed or extensively researched (Nonglait 2012: 297), and in Hamlet Bareh's publication (2001 [1997]: 299) which gives a casual and sketchy description of the practice. Shampliang (1995) also details this practice, which is largely the origin story of the Rashir collected from Sijun Nongbri.

The first version was collected from K. S. Riangtem from Shillong City (originally from Nongmyndo village in the West Khasi Hills) in an interview carried out on January 14, 2012:

K. S. R.: In earlier times, when a Rashir died ... after he or she has died, ok? It was told to us that after three days and three nights the dead person will come back to life. So after the dead person sits up, according to their [Rashir] belief, the dead person requires human heads before the cremation can take place. Before the dead body is burnt, this is required. So, when the dead body sits up—I'll tell you more clearly—the relatives and clan members who are present there are shown [informant gestures with his finger] one; and if the number of human heads required is one, then the corpse falls back. So the dead person communicates the number of heads he/she wants. So until the human heads are acquired ... they kill people to get these human heads, they are not permitted to cremate the dead body.

M. L.: So what happens to the body in the interim?

K. S. R.: They rot, madam, they rot. The dead person remains dead thereafter.

The second version was collected from Theocritus Riangtem, Nongmyndo village on January 21, 2013:

The Rashir clan now mainly exist in the Lyngngam area. Most of them are Christian converts, but we hear that some of them still exist [meaning that they still practise the traditional customs] in different places ... when we were younger, in winter time, we were afraid to wander around because of the Rashir ... My mother told me that when she was young, it was well known that the Rashir hired people to bring human heads. They had so much power that they would carry the human heads through the villages, and they didn't care about anyone. We got the smell of decomposing corpse when they went by, but they didn't care. But now, madam, they just take a finger, an ear, the nose, etc., in order to sacrifice to their dead. Yes, we have heard that they do it this way now.

Now, these Rashir, what they do if one of their clan or family have died, after three days ... they do not cremate the corpses ... When someone from the Rashir clan dies, they do not like or allow anyone else from another clan or an outsider to look at the dead body. Why this is, or what there is, I don't know ... Rashir keep the death a secret and we have a suspicion that the feeding of the corpse takes place in the presence of other human heads that are procured...

So, say for instance, an old Rashir woman has died. After three days and three nights she sits up, she does not talk to anyone but she sits up. Then the ritual performer of the clan, the clan members and the elder of the family are present there, they make a ritual, you know, like a prayer and then they ask, 'how many do you want? How many heads do you want?' Then the ritual performer [*nong kñia*] gestures with his fingers showing one, two, three, etc. If it is three she wants the corpse falls back. Until the specific number that the corpse wants is gestured, it continues to sit up. There have been cases where even 12 heads have been demanded. Then the ritual performer informs the clan that it is so and so number and the clan gathers in great secrecy to confer, saying, 'she has asked for so many heads, what shall we do?'

The third version is collected from Karland Langrin from Seiñduli village in an interview on September 4, 2014.

The Rashir ... have to cremate their dead quickly. Because if the body is left for a long time, then it comes back to life. Once he/she comes back to life, he/she begins to kill and eat people. There was an incident in the area of Tynghor about 50 or 60 years ago, not recently ... they call it *khie nawang*.[7] So there was a man from the Rashir clan, because his children failed to cremate him on time, he came back to life. Then he came back to life and the only one present there was his son in law ... that man he woke from the dead, slowly, like that, he sat up slow. The son in law knew that if the dead man wakes up then he will kill him [the son in law]. So he fled then. The dead man chased his son in law into the forest until he almost caught up with him. The son in law ran into the forest. And at that time lightning struck and destroyed the dead man, or he would have killed his son in law. So he died. After he had died once, then he came back to life, then lightning struck him and he died some more.

The fourth narration of secret Rashir funerary practices can be found in Nonglait 2012. In the last chapter on films and folklore, Nonglait mentions the Rashir clan and states that,

during the period of waiting for the time to celebrate *Ka Phor* they have to perform certain rituals by the priest called Nongkhiat Byllei to conclude if the death was peaceful or not. The priest falls into a trance during the process and he begins to speak with the relatives of the dead person with words that are unintelligible. These words have to be translated by another priest who is the assistant of the main priest. Thus if the person has died peacefully, the spirit will ask for no other rituals ... But, if the person dies an unfulfilled, unsatisfied death, he would ask his relatives to kill somebody and offer the head to his spirit while the rest of his body would either be consumed or buried. Sometimes the spirit of the dead person would demand only one head, while sometimes, more than one was demanded. (Nonglait 2012: 236)

Nonglait goes on to say that on some occasions, up to ten human heads were demanded. The source of Nonglait's material is mentioned as field interviews, although the place of collection is not stated. The difference between the last narrative and the other three narratives is marked. There is no mention of corpse reanimation in this version. The person who performs the ritual is not a Rashir clan member, but a *nongkhiat byllei* or *nongbyllei* who is not the equivalent of a Khasi *nongknia* (usually, ritual performers belong to the Lyngdoh clan) or priest. A *nongkhiat byllei* is the most powerful sorcerer among the Lyngngam and he or she can perform all manner of deeds. In the variants drawn from my fieldwork, the issue of secrecy and ritual separation from the village community is pivotal in the performance of the rituals. However, the printed account tells of how widespread and diverse the narratives about the Rashir can be.

Lostin Lawrence Kharbani is a Khasi writer and author of the book *U Sangkhini* (2004). I was fortunate to interview him on the topic of Rashir clan death rituals on February 6, 2013, and I quote him here:

> The Rashir were very well-established headhunters and my great uncle (who was the brother of my paternal grandmother) married into the Rashir clan. My great uncle became very adept at headhunting. He died in 1976 or 1977. He was from Nongrathaw village. In his time he was the clan leader of the Rashir and very famous.

When I asked my informants when active headhunting in the Rashir clan declined, I was told that the prevalence of these headhunting practices was officially stopped in 1984–1985 when an individual by the name of Leibiskot, from the Ñianglang clan of Mawbru, was pursued by the Rashir headhunters. Leibiskot spent the entire night hidden underneath a plant with big leaves and in the morning was discovered in a near-dead condition. Community rage against the Rashir clan was thus roused and the matter was taken to the district administration. Since then, the Rashir and their headhunting activities were curtailed.

## Negotiating the Reframing of Beliefs through Post-mortem Practices

Rituals associated with death are negotiated in the vernacular discourse of the people. I had an emphatic conversation with a member belonging to the Rashir clan, from Nongdambur village, West Khasi Hills on June 10, 2016. Nathuram Rashir talked about the extent to which his family was stereotyped and subjected to discrimination as a result of the discussion, and proliferation, of negative sentiments against his clan. Death practices ascribed to the Rashir present a challenge because these narratives are transmitted only with the in-group, in this case the Lyngngam and Nongtrai, and not among other Khasi communities.

The beliefs and practices associated with corpse reanimation and spirit propitiation that have been mentioned in the previous section do not fit into the categories assigned by the Church—Catholic or Presbyterian—or the Seng Khasi. The categories sanctioned by the Khasi Christian Church include the internment of the physical body, the placement of the soul in heaven or hell, or a soul's wait for Judgement Day. The Seng Khasi, on the other hand, has no fixed procedure in order to cope with the unquiet dead, or even the consequent fate of the soul after death. The apparent silence of these institutions on the subject of beliefs connected with how to deal with the restless dead does not mean that such beliefs have become obsolete or non-functional. Rather they exist outside the norm of acceptance, contesting such institutionally authoritative discourses through the vernacular discourse. Leftovers of older practices, spilling out of the sanctioned prism of Khasi beliefs, beliefs about death and the narratives about clan death rituals are narrated by my informants as obsolete, or not, as various interpretations differ. In the everyday life of the Khasi, they continue in everyday places describing the acts of the Rashir clan—their now extinct village, Nongmatsaw; the places where stones sacred to the Rashir are gathered, with each stone symbolizing a human head; a small cave where the abundant money of the Rashir is hidden, or in the places of commemorative megalithic structures.

In another interview with Karland Langrin, on April 25, 2015, in Seiñduli village, I collected another significant narrative in which the death of a father was announced to his son at the exact moment of his death:

> K. L.: In my understanding I believe that because parents love their children very much they make a manifestation to them, or talk to them through signs or by other means. So this pastor's father's spirit made a visitation because he [the father] loved his son so much ... This incident is much more closely related to the Khasi traditional religion. It has no relationship with Christianity because Christians don't believe in this. They believe that after death the soul goes to heaven or hell. Because [in the Khasi religion] after the soul has left the body and begins its journey to the land of the dead, it will first make a manifestation to its living relatives.
>
> M. L.: Was the father of the Pastor Christian or did he belong to the Khasi religion?
>
> K. L.: He was Christian.

Why do such beliefs and the fear associated with the dead and rituals such as these persist in the stories that are circulated, especially in a

Christian context? These beliefs and rituals are theorized to be outside the boundary occupied by the two factions of Khasi Christianity and the formalized institution of Seng Khasi because neither of these institutions accommodates or is able to make sense of or create meaning for these beliefs. The narrative above makes a clear distinction about the contestation that exists between the old and the new religion in which both participants, the Pastor and his dead father, belong to the Christian religion and yet have supernatural experiences that belong to the Khasi religion. Karland Langrin also seems to suggest by his reference to the manifestation being part of the soul's journey to the afterlife, that the soul of the pastor's father is going back to *Lum Ngunrei*, or the land of the dead. The awareness of the discontinuity of the beliefs associated with the dead and the ways of mediating or understanding an encounter with the otherworld is present in the ways in which people understand and practise belief.

The diversity of afterlife beliefs, combined with multivalent attitudes to death, renders any notion of a monolithic Christian construction redundant. The extreme deviations from what some perceive as 'civilized' or accepted afterlife beliefs, then, stand outside the purview of Christian demonizing discourse, into which all other traditional supernatural phenomena are pushed. Most of the narratives about Rashir death rituals discussed above were collected from pastors, church elders and Christian informants. In the interviews, there was no condemnation or demonization of the Rashir. These accounts were narrated as a matter of fact and without opinion. The only emotion that I could ascertain about the way that my informants feel about this topic is fear. But this also is relegated to the past.

## Conclusion

Folklorist Leonard Norman Primiano (1995) introduced the concept of vernacular religion as a new way to approach religious folklife. Focusing on religion as individuals encounter it and experience it, this method allowed for the everyday, lived senses of religion according to which the personal interpretation of religious tenets is accommodated, acknowledged, and as is plentifully illustrated in this article, exemplified. Contesting narratives that are derived from centrally located traditions such as death in a primarily oral culture become part of a vernacular discourse. Variations of death ritual, as discussed, may be seen as highly 'folklorized' and contradictory. But they also indicate how norms are contested, undermined and re-presented. These narratives communicate worldview and state beliefs, creating contested, dialogic responses that challenge, subvert or suppress the authorial religious discourse of the Church. Narratives that push boundaries of knowledge and thought, existent within a system that refuses to acknowledge the implications of such practices, become powerful as items of folklore that are sustained by the community that disowns and/or suppresses them. Beliefs about the dead and the restless dead continue to exist alongside accepted Christian afterlife doctrines in the vernacular discourse of the community.

Bearing this in mind, while the community, led by devout pastors and priests, adhere to Christian beliefs about the dead and the resurrection of the dead, pre-Christian narratives persist within culture and consciousness. The monolithic authority that the Khasi Christian Church attempts to impose through conversion and serious missionary work upon the Khasi community is keenly felt in all aspects of the daily life of the Khasi people.

Within the realm of individual vernacular experience of religion, there is no systematic way in which belief about the afterlife can be organized into a clear coherent whole. Thus it is useful to look at vernacular religious theory as it understands religion to be 'the continuous art of individual interpretation and negotiation of any number of influential sources' (Primiano 2012: 384). Death beliefs, which are so disturbingly fascinating that they fall outside the realm of the demonizing discourse of the Church or the othering tendencies of Seng Khasi, manifest themselves in narratives and the quiet circulation of these narratives. The Khasi community, then, is in a state of transition where the impact of westernization and its concomitant Christianity replaces and assimilates the beliefs that existed prior to colonialism and Christianization. The upheaval in the social organization and the epistemology and consequent strategies that the community has to employ in order to make new sense of the world, create a new identity based on religion rather than clan or kinship affinities, resulting in contradictions and conflicts, and expressing itself in folklore.

## Acknowledgements

I am grateful to all my research participants mentioned in this article for sharing their knowledge with me. I am indebted to Ülo Valk and Marion

Bowman for their comments and questions, Helen Kästik for technical editing the final proof, and Daniel Allen for language editing. This research project was carried out with funding from project PUTJD746.

## Notes

1 Fieldwork on this topic was carried out in West Khasi Hills District in the villages of Nongmyndo, Langdongdai, Riangdo and Nongporla. Additional interviews were carried out with tradition bearers from the West Khasi Hills in the State Capital of Meghalaya, Shillong. Dates of specific interviews are noted after each fieldwork reference. Where an interlocutor is named, it is at the person's request; where the initials only are given, along with the clan name, that also is according to my interlocutor's wish.
2 Alexander Burgh Lish (of the Serampore Baptist Mission active from 1832–1837 in the Khasi Hills); William Carey (who published a version of the New Testament in 1824 in the Bengali script) and Krishna Chandra Pal also belonging to the Serampore Baptist Mission (who converted the first two Khasis to Christianity in 1813) were the predecessors to Jones. See May 2020.
3 In an informal conversation with an anonymous informant who is a practitioner of the Khasi ethnic religion.
4 Dance of Contentment, annual three-day festival and dance.
5 The word *byllieñ*, in the Lyngngam language, means 'to forget'.
6 Human sacrifice was more common among Khasi and was practised in Iapngar, Northern Khasi Hills, and in the Jaintia Hills.
7 To wake up from the dead, or to wake up possessed by the malignant spirit, Nawang.

## References

Bareh, Hamlet. 2001 [1997]. *An Encyclopaedia of North-East India: Meghalaya*. New Delhi: Mittal Publications.
Britannica. 2013 [1998]. 'Headhunting'. In *The Encyclopaedia Britannica*. http://www.britannica.com/EBchecked/topic/258121/headhunting/ (accessed June 11, 2021).
Gurdon, Philip Richard Thorndagh. 1907. *The Khasis*. http://www.gutenberg.org/files/12786/12786.txt (accessed June 9, 2021).
Honko, Lauri. 1996. 'Epics along the Silk Roads: Mental Text, Performance, and Written Codification'. *Oral Tradition* 11 (1): 1–17. https://journal.oraltradition.org/wp-content/uploads/files/articles/11i/5_Introduction_11_1.pdf (accessed July 27, 2021).
Kharbani, Lostin Lawrence. 2004. *U Sangkhini*. Shillong: Bluebell Printers.
Lamare, Shobhan N. 2013. *The Jaintias: Studies in Society and Change*. New Delhi: Regency Publications.
Lyngdoh, Mary Pristilla. 1991. *The Festivals in the History and Culture of the Khasi*. New Delhi: Visas Publishing House.

Mawrie, H. Onderson. 2000 [1971]. *Ka Pyrkhat U Khasi*. Shillong: Tmissilda Soh.
May, Andrew J. 2020. 'How Should We Remember Thomas Jones'. *Raiot Webzine*, June 22. https://raiot.in/how-should-we-remember-thomas-jones/ (accessed July 21, 2021).
Ñianglang, P. S. 2000. 'Settlement Pattern and Traditional House of the Nongtrais'. In *Heritage of Meghalaya*, 18. Shillong: Directorate of Arts and Culture, Government of Meghalaya.
Nonglait, G. Badaiasuklang L. 2012. *Khasi Folklorismus: A Study of Khasi Phawar, Media and Films*. New Delhi: Academic Excellence.
Pemberton, Robert Boileau. 1979 [1835]. *Report on the Eastern Frontier of India*. Delhi: Mittal.
Primiano, Leonard Norman. 1995. 'Vernacular Religion and the Search for Method in Religious Folklife'. *Western Folklore* (Special Issue: *Reflexivity and the Study of Belief*) 54 (1): 37–56. https://doi.org/10.2307/1499910
Primiano, Leonard Norman. 2012. 'Afterword: Manifestations of the Religious Vernacular: Ambiguity, Power, and Creativity'. In *Vernacular Religion in Everyday Life: Expressions of Belief*, edited by Marion Bowman and Ülo Valk, 382–394. Sheffield; Bristol, CT: Equinox Publishing.
Shampliang, U. Sterian. 1995. *U Rongna Bad Ka Shir*. Shillong: Ibani Printing Press.
Statistical Profile. 2013. *Statistical Profile of Scheduled Tribes in India 2013*. Government of India, Ministry of Tribal Affairs, Statistics Division. https://www.brlf.in/wp-content/uploads/2018/05/Statistical-Profile-of-STs_2013.pdf (accessed July 7, 2021).

Chapter 15

# An Immured Soul: Contested Ritual Traditions and Demonological Narratives in Contemporary Mongolia

*Alevtina Solovyeva**

## Introduction

The subject of this chapter is the contestation of authority in Mongolia. It is based on fieldwork material collected by the author during annual expeditions to various parts of Mongolia (2007–2017).

Modern Mongolian society provides a distinctive, rich case study of regional development in a complex East Asian cultural context. Mongolian culture has been influenced by regional religion systems like Zoroastrianism and Tengrism,[1] by indigenous shamanic traditions, by different schools of Tibetan Buddhism, by the historical traditions of nomadic societies and complicated relations with Mongolia's two nearest neighbours, China and Russia, all of which contribute to the cultural particularity of this region.

During the last century Mongolia, a descendant of the Great Mongolian Empire, was part of the Chinese Empire, went through a leapfrog of revolutions (starting from 1911), had a period of theocratic rule (headed by Bogd Khaan), experienced the trials of cultural change, the persecutions

* **Alevtina Solovyeva** is a Research Fellow at the Institute of Cultural Research, University of Tartu (Estonia); Research Fellow at the Centre of Typology and Semiotics of Folklore, Russian State University for the Humanities; Leading Research Fellow at the Institute for Oriental and Classical Studies, National Research University Higher School of Economics (Moscow, Russia). She has studied oriental studies, historical anthropology and folkloristics at the Russian State University for the Humanities (Moscow), the National University of Mongolia (Ulaanbaatar), the University of Bonn and the University of Tartu. In 2007 she started annual fieldwork in Mongolia and China, focusing on mythology, rural and urban folk traditions, and vernacular religion.

of religion and the fight against 'superstition' during the period of the socialist republic (as the Mongolian People's Republic from 1921 to 1992), as well as the challenge of democratic reform alongside intriguing processes of globalization.

Simultaneously to the collapse of the socialist regime, new processes started in Mongolia which strongly affected various realms of society. Among them are ideological delimitation with the past and the construction of new identities (both national and local), movements encouraging a return to 'traditional roots', alongside processes of retraditionalization and reinvention of tradition, the revival and renovation of religious life, and movements encouraging westernization.

Mongolia's exposure to and involvement in the modern global, social, economic, political and cultural milieu brought to Mongolian society new challenges and standards that have complicated interactions with some traditional elements of culture—which in spite of the changes are still strong in Mongolia. Mongolian society has some distinctive characteristics that provide favourable circumstances for the conservation of traditional lifestyles, including traditional customs and beliefs. Among them are nomadic cattle breeding, which is still one of the foundations of the economy, and a relatively young urban culture.[2]

From the research point of view, the contemporary situation in Mongolian society could be described as one of very intensive transformation in various realms of life, and conflicts between different elements of culture—the traditional, the socialist past, and the modern mainstream. Demonology as one of the most sensitive and adaptive parts of folklore reflects these complicated and conflicting social situations using its own rules, images and forms to make a statement—'ghosts are in fact "social figures" who often address public issues, such as the tension between cultural conservatism and rapid change' (Valk 2006: 35).

This article is dedicated to one such case from contemporary Mongolian society, a case of contesting authority and conflict between different ritual traditions reflected in social life, vernacular beliefs and demonological narratives.

## Restless Places

Contemporary Mongolian demonology is represented by a wide range of supernatural creatures and topics connected both to Mongolian traditional beliefs and influences from other cultures. An important aspect of this concerns different kinds of supernatural locus. These include natural objects (stones, rocks, springs, single trees, haunted areas), abandoned houses and roads, cemeteries, and so on. Among the most popular topics in the contemporary rural tradition is *güideltei gazar*, which might be loosely described as 'restless places', places with permanent supernatural activity.³ These are usually small areas located in the steppe or on mountain slopes, marked in local traditions as having bad reputations. According to interviews they are regarded as the loci of demonic possession or they act as independent supernatural entities.⁴ Narratives about them are a part of local landscape mythology and could be taken as an example of place-lore. Usually, local people and drivers know about such places: where they are situated, what has happened there before and what goes on now. In spite of the popularity of the character, beliefs, narratives and even ritual practice connected to such places, *güideltei gazar* have not yet been properly observed and discussed in previous sources and works devoted to Mongolian and folklore studies.

But what are these mysterious loci? 'There are places where a horse stumbles, a car fails, even the instruments on a plane flying above such places become crazy' (G. H., 1975, Khalkha, 2009).⁵ This passage, a kind of verbalized belief, might be taken as an extract of the basic topic connected with such places in Mongolian tradition—at the 'restless places', where something supernatural restlessly runs back and forth, while humans in contrast lose their ability to move and get hopelessly stuck. If a horse suddenly stops or falls down, does not want to or cannot move, as if somebody hobbled it, if a car or a motorcycle gets stuck, the wheels stop rolling and no repair helps to restart it, also if compasses and watches (any 'running' devices) suddenly and without any visible reasons stop, then it is *güideltei gazar*.⁶ Below is a typical narrative about restless places:

> Not far from here, on the way to Tsetserleg sum [settlement], there is such a place, a bad place. Once I was passing there, with my friend. It was already twilight. When we came to that place our car stopped. We tried to restart it several times, everything was all right, but it just did not want to move. Then we tried to push it, but even this was hopeless. We decided to sleep in the car and wait till the morning. But when we lay inside, much stranger things started: first we heard a feeble moan, repeated several times, then something began to walk around the car, but when we tried to look out, there was nothing. We were very scared and were going to leave the car and run away. At that moment my friend remembered a method that old people talked about a lot. So we two 'made water' straight onto the four wheels of our car, and then

everything became alright and normal again. That is the method. (H. B., 1974, Khalkha, 2011)

This motif, a human stuck in a supernatural locus, losing the ability to move (or as a related motif, losing his/her way), is widespread. It appears in Slavic, Finno-Ugric and Altaic traditions (Doronin 2016), and among the Buryats and Kalmyks, whose traditions are related to Mongolian culture. Local beliefs contain a rich variety of details describing additional forms of supernatural phenomena (*güidel*) at such places. In Mongolian traditions, such additional forms often include acoustic manifestations. Among the most popular demonic sounds we can find some common sounds for haunted places in general, such as (kids') crying, human voices calling the witness by name, sounds of movement, and some specific ones (more probably connected to certain regional motifs or beliefs) like a camel screaming and a female voice asking the witness to return her comb.[7] According to some narratives there also might be visual manifestations of the supernatural presence. Among the most popular images are a white camel (alone or with a rider), a horse, a child, different female images, which the witness sees either while awake or in dreams. Most people though are agreed that *güidel* (used separately) is *hii üzegdel* (this term might be translated as 'an empty appearance') and cannot be seen by ordinary people.[8] On rare occasions tactile manifestations can be found in descriptions. These additional descriptions, which might be found in some narratives about *güideltei gazar* in Mongolian tradition, are more common for haunted places, *chötgörtei gazar* ('place with a ghost/demon'), *sünstei baishin* ('house/building with a soul'), and are given as relative characteristics for a whole class of bad places.

In comparison with other traditions (Doronin 2016: 28–30) *güideltei gazar* very seldom have any special marks (rarely it might be a lonely, dry, crooked tree or a dry bush) and usually do not stand out from the surrounding landscape. The same with the location, although special placements are sometimes mentioned (such as a mountain promontory or the space between two ancient Kurgans). *Güideltei gazar* can be everywhere in the steppe, which dramatically increases the chances of becoming stuck. In addition, Mongolian 'restless places' keep their powerful influence at any time of day and night (although the period from twilight to sunrise is regarded as the most dangerous).

There is a complex of beliefs concerning the methods to be safe on a trip. This complex includes some preventive rites, such as the widespread practice of sprinkling milk on the hoofs of a horse or on the wheels of a car before a trip (usually the oldest female of the household performs this). There are also a number of prescriptions for those who are already stuck at the 'restless place', among the most popular of which is to wave with a knife between the legs of the stopped horse (this action breaks the invisible demonic shackles), or to turn the whip-handle down to the ground (it is believed that spirits and demons are scared of being caught by the noose which is usually on the handles of whips), or to urinate[9] on the hoofs of the horse or on the wheels of the car. Better still is to do all of these together with a prayer:

> My son was trying to catch a horse with his friend. They rode out to that bad place and their stirrups suddenly broke and they fell down. They turned their whips upside down so that the loops pointed downwards. They also started to say prayers. Only in this way they could get away from that *güideltei gazar*. (B. H., 1935, Khalkha, 2009)

When at such places, animals, especially dogs, feel uncomfortable and alarmed; they bark and try to catch something invisible. Children cry, adult people feel bad or can even die at such places. Even in the case of successful escape the results of passing 'restless places' usually include problems with business or health and might cause an early death. According to interviews, people who were so unlucky as to come across the 'restless places' should visit religious specialists, shamans or lamas.[10] This should be done with the purpose of self-cleaning in a ritual sense[11] and of getting rid of the negative and dangerous influences that are binding even after escaping from such areas. They should at least 'read *tarni* [Buddhist prayers] and go to a hospital' (Ch. M., 1962, Khalkha, 2014). Lamas have the ability and professional competence to deal with such places and demolish them:

> Before there were many *güideltei gazar* around, but then lamas started to come and to read *tarni* several years in a row, to clean the area, then *güidel* disappeared. If a lama comes and makes his rituals regularly in such places, then he can remove *güidel*, then *güidel* goes away. (M. O., 1956, Khalkha, 2016)

In different traditions, this motif has a wide range of interpretative models, explaining this mysterious 'stuckness' according to local beliefs. Often these models concern certain situations. For example, it happens when a human comes to a special area possessed by a supernatural being,[12] or comes across a gathering of supernatural beings (Doronin 2016); or it also happens when a human path accidentally crosses the road of spirits and demons.[13] Thus, this stuckness is also connected to certain supernatural characters who prevent the human from moving (forest, water or house spirits, the devil, demons, souls of deceased, etc.).

Mongolian folklore also includes these situations, but they are embodied in a range of separate motifs, associated with other characters and are not connected to 'restless places'. In addition, the motif of supernatural stuckness is not linked directly to any particular character and often the restless place is a character itself. At the same time interpretative models explaining why such places exist and what the cause of their influence is have multiple variations related to supernatural beliefs as well as to pseudoscientific notions. 'Supernatural versions' include references to such characters as *chötgör* (demon, spirit, soul of deceased which did not get another birth and stayed on the earth), *muu süns* ('a bad soul', the soul of the deceased which has remained on earth), *lus-savdag* (nature spirits), *muu yum* ('all bad'—referring to an uncertain demonic and malevolent influence). The names of these characters are often used in descriptions given by interviewees to explain what *güideltei gazar* are and how they are related to other, more common, supernatural notions. Later in the chapter I shall discuss some of these relations. Pseudoscientific versions include such concepts as magnetic fields, magnetic radiation, strong energetic field, bad energy. It is interesting to note that the power of rites to be performed in restless places is explained by both interpretative models. For example, it was said that waving with a knife between the stuck horse's hoofs 'cuts the invisible shackles and scares away all the bad, because demons are frightened of everything sharp' (L. A., 1975, Khalkha, 2012), but I also documented the following statement, 'a knife, you know, it's metal, you wave with it and it demolishes that magnetic field' (G.B., 1967, Khalkha, 2016). Different interpretative models also concern urinating and other rites.

One of the most popular folkloric explanations of the origin of such places today, correlating with various supernatural and pseudoscientific models, is connected to a group of vernacular beliefs about the soul and its post-mortem existence. According to these beliefs, the cause of the emergence of restless places is the bones and remains of deceased people buried in those places: 'A soul immured under the earth cannot find the next birth, the form of reincarnation, and is doomed to stay on the earth as a shelterless evil demon, disturbing living people' (H. D., 1941, Khalkha, 2011).

In one of the written versions of the story published in a popular Mongolian newspaper (*Bolson Yavdal* 2012), this interpretation is embodied in a more literary plot (incidentally typical for Chinese literature).

The story is about a young man who spent a night in such a place because his car broke down. During the night, he saw in a dream a woman whose life was tragically ended by a car crash. He woke up feeling that somebody was touching his hand; he looked around but nobody was there. But at this moment he found out that he was sleeping with his head on a gravestone. After this discovery, he left his car where it was and ran away from that place. When he came home, he became ill and dreamed about that dead woman for a long time.

The materials collected allow us to assume that the popular interpretative model which uses this notion of 'the immured soul', linked to the traditional motif of supernatural stuckness,[14] evokes new meanings, functions and in particular contexts gives a voice to opinions around current problematic issues. One goal of this research was to discover the background and roots of the 'restless places' topic. A further step was to analyse the key image of the interpretative model in contemporary Mongolian folk traditions—the immured soul—which leads to various groups of Mongolian beliefs and ritual practices.

## Confronting Ritual Traditions

The basic idea of the immured soul is that bones buried in the ground keep the soul on the earth, preventing the next reincarnation. It is interesting to point out that, according to vernacular belief, options for the post-mortem existence of the soul are often connected to many different, sometimes very practical and material, things rather than to the concept of karma. (Or there is an inverse connection to the concept.) Some of these beliefs are associated with the idea of the soul as a character from Mongolian folklore, which I shall discuss a little later. Other beliefs are connected to the idea of the importance of ritual and the specific folk perceptions of it.

Now we come to the conflict in contemporary Mongolian society surrounding different funeral traditions. In the past, Mongolian funerals had different forms depending on the historical period, the tribe, the social status of the dead person and so on (Zhukovskaya 1977; Galdanova 1987; Gerasimova 1992; Drobyshev 2005). The most widespread form of traditional funeral was leaving in the steppe,[15] in which the body of the deceased was left in the steppe at a place prescribed by a lama through divination.

> Then it's the turn of the wild animals and birds to take care of the body, to do their job. A few days after the family comes back, if there is nothing left, then everything is good; if the body is still there, it's a bad sign. The family calls the lama to perform special rituals, to show the way to the soul, the *luizhinch*. Soon afterwards the family comes again. If the body has disappeared, then all is good, the soul has left to be reborn. (M. Ch., 1934, Khalkha, 2011)

According to interviews the vanishing of the body, which is part of the funeral, is the sign of the soul leaving this world, and the way it happens shows how the process is going, that is, if the soul will be reborn or if there is a problem and that requires help from a religious specialist. At the same time the funeral also says something about the 'quality' of the soul—is it the soul of a good person, or someone bad and sinful:

> If the body of the deceased vanishes, then it was a good person, nothing kept it on the earth, leaving was easy. My grandfather's body disappeared the next day already, it was remarkable; it means he was a very good person. But sometimes the body might stay for a very long time, even after the lama's prayers. This is very bad for the whole family; this means the soul doesn't want to leave, there were too many sins—it is hard for a bad person's soul to leave. (Ch. M., 1942, Khalkha, 2012)

Thus, at the same time the ritual gives signs about the past of the soul and about its present and future (is it already on the way to rebirth or still on earth), which also affects the family of the deceased.

In addition, it is important to point out a difference between perceptions of burial places (graves and cemeteries), which are usually described as *chötgörtei*, haunted areas, and places where someone accidentally can see human remains left in the steppe, which does not have any negative connotations and sometimes is even regarded as a good omen. These beliefs obviously reflect attitudes towards different ritual traditions.

Attempts to institute inhumation as the official form of funeral were undertaken in Mongolia several times, with the greatest effort to impose this coming during the socialist period after the revolution of 1921 (*Obychai* 2006). (Here, probably, the influence of China and Russia should be mentioned, as their general funeral tradition is inhumation.) Among the common people this ritual practice consistently met with very strong opposition. During the socialist period, in spite of possible persecution, traditional funeral rituals were performed secretly for the older and more highly respected members of local communities (D. X., 1931, Khalkha, 2015). The collapse of the socialist regime alongside the movement advocating the return to traditional Mongolian roots, among others, contributed to the development of a ritual pluralism that became an important issue in the identity construction of local communities.[16] In this context, the role of the funeral, and ancestor worship rituals, as a frame within which to establish a relationship with a family's deceased is remarkable. For the majority the traditional ritual of leaving in the steppe was found to be more convenient and preferable, so with the easing of official control and sanctions more and more families today support and perform this ritual. At the same time the 'modern' official form of funeral in Mongolia is inhumation, which conforms to international norms and, although by softer methods, is still imposed on society and local communities. Thus, the conflict continues, taking new forms in the realms of social life, justice and folklore.

The roots of this long resistance, the survival of the traditional ritual and its preferred status among local communities in spite of potential trouble stem from certain vernacular beliefs and images that are still nurtured within a fruitful environment in contemporary Mongolian society.

Above, I briefly discussed a few reasons for the importance of the traditional funeral ritual in Mongolia: the ritual indicates the 'quality' and status of the soul of the deceased and its current 'position', providing the right way to leave the earth and be reborn in the future (aspects that also concern the wellbeing of the family of the deceased). Below I shall discuss some Mongolian traditional beliefs connected to the images of souls and bones, the status of the deceased, the importance of the earth and nature spirits and some other concepts that seem to underpin the traditional understandings relevant for the research case.

## Souls, Demons and Bones

A reasonable starting point here might be why the bones buried under the ground keep the soul on earth and prevent it from reincarnating. According to the data collected, Mongolian folklore's attitude to the conditions of the soul's post-mortem existence, as well as the path to rebirth, are a complicated challenge to understand.

Let's start from the vernacular beliefs concerning the soul itself. Those souls who, after death, disappear quickly and do not bother relatives or scare random people are regarded as good souls, capable of finding their way to rebirth. Those souls who are unable to find the way to reincarnation by themselves (*muu süns, chötgör*) often have to stay on earth until religious specialists can help them.[17] According to belief, there can be many reasons why souls remain on earth in this new embarrassing status. One of them, connected with the concept of karma and remaining on earth as a demon, is regarded as a negative form of reincarnation, a post-mortem punishment: 'If a person did good things in his or her life, one will become a human again. But if they did bad things, their soul will become a worm or an insect, or *chötgör*' (V. D., 1939, Khalkha, 2012).

Another, more popular, reason for the soul to remain is some kind of emotional attachment the soul keeps after death. According to narratives, it might be worries about the family, anger or an insult that the person received during his or her life; or it might also be greed or attachment to material objects; or one of many other factors.

Popular reasons include a wide-ranging complex of motifs connected to 'the wrong death', i.e. a tragic or early death, or death before marriage, and so on.

> As many dark hairs as the person had when he or she died, so many years he or she should have lived and will live on the earth as a ghost (*chötgör*), after that only the soul will be able to be reborn again. (N. T., 1978, Khalkha, 2011)

According to some other versions each soul has to spend three years as a ghost after death before reincarnation (T. B., 1967, Khalkha, 2014).

However, despite a person's good behaviour in the previous life, a 'good' death does not guarantee an easy journey to rebirth. According to some beliefs, souls have a very timid, diffident, easily frightened character. That is why some souls, like those of small children, feel confused and lost and stay on earth, unable to find a way to the other world, or cannot understand that they have already finished their previous existence.[18] Such lost and confused souls often hide in different objects, in some cases belonging to them during life, or they simply hide in appropriate things in their surroundings.[19] My informant explained it this way:

> A soul that has got lost, which cannot find the next reincarnation, and begins to harm people, they call it a *chötgör*. A soul that is not reborn wanders around on the earth and can occasionally find shelter within certain objects, in furniture for example. Sometimes people can even see it. They then call a lama to exorcise it. These souls want to return home but their relatives are afraid of them. (S. V., 1936, Khalkha, 2009)

In addition, there are beliefs about the multiplicity of souls which emphasize connections between the soul and the body: 'Each human being has three souls—a flesh soul [*mahny suns*], a bone soul [*yasny suns*] and a mental soul [*setgeliin suns*]. When a person dies, the bone soul stays with the corpse' (D. Z., 1918, Buryat, 2008).

As we saw above, the traditional funeral ritual and its emic interpretations reveal the certain dependence the soul has on the body—as soon as the body disappears the soul also leaves the earth.

Digging deeper into traditional beliefs reveals more reasons for such dependence, and some of these reasons are hidden in the specific meaning that bones have in the folk traditions. In Mongolian cattle-breeding culture, bones are very meaningful and represented in different realms of traditional culture: in verbal genres (including charms), rituals (giving birth, wedding, healing, divination), games, and everyday customs (Lovor 2002; Birtalan 2003; Skorodumova and Solovyeva 2014). They have positive semantic connotations (fertility, healing abilities, etc.) but also negative, including demonic, connotations (Skorodumova and Solovyeva 2014: 102-114). This demonic range of meaning concerning bones is important for comprehending another aspect of the contemporary conflict around the different ritual practices of funerals.

Certain bones, such as skulls and pelvic bones, are supposed to have the strongest demonic propensities in Mongolian tradition. Beliefs about these bones are reflected in narratives and everyday customs, for example a prohibition common to all Mongolian people against leaving a pelvic bone without meat inside the pelvic aperture and a skull with empty eye sockets in any dwelling overnight:

> After preparing meat, there are three things that should not be left at home overnight—a skull without eyes, a hollow bone without marrow and a pelvic bone without meat in the pelvic aperture. This is because 'something bad' [*muu yum*], demon [*chötgör*], can enter and settle in the holes, in the empty spaces (H. N., 1952, Khalkha, 2009)

Alternatively, a demon may immanently live in such spaces. One of my informants explained it: 'If someone leaves a pelvic bone without meat for a night, a *chötgör* will look at the family through the hole' (G. G., 1949, Khalkha, 2009). Usually after eating, people break these bones so that there are no empty spaces within them. So *chötgör* might also be considered a corporeal soul associated with a body or particular body parts.

Beliefs about pelvic bones are reflected in popular narratives where they are represented as independent demonic creatures with their own will. The following is a typical narrative about the pelvic bone, telling us about a lonely night traveller who was attacked by this demonic creature:

Suddenly the traveller felt that something had caught him and embraced him from behind. He tried to drop it but nothing helped, then he bound it tightly to himself by the belt and continued on his way. Something behind his back began to cry and beg him to set it free. With the first rays of the sun the traveller came to one village and asked a man passing by to look what was behind his back. The answer was: 'You have a pelvic bone bound to your back'. (G. H., 1968, Khalkha, 2012)

As another interviewee said: 'I say this: when a person dies and their soul becomes a *chötgör*, it looks like an old pelvic bone' (C. D., 1949, Khalkha, 2008).

Another topic relating to bones relates to a character called demonic light(s) (*chötgöriin gal*).[20] This is light, usually blue or white in colour, and moves around open areas in the steppe and mountains. Such lights are occasionally visible to travellers at night, and can follow people although they do not allow them to come close. According to such belief, 'the large demonic light, that is from a skull bone, and the smaller one is from a pelvic bone' (C. D., 1949, Khalkha, 2008). Usually they do not harm people, only 'confuse, fool them' (ibid.); 'if a person is not scared of them, there will be no harm, no illness, nothing bad, just let it pass, that is all' (D. V., 1978, Khalkha, 2014).

Obviously, these topics represent ideas of the autonomous, free movement of demonic objects, bones, which connect to the real practice of dealing with bodily remains. Older narratives appear to be slowly giving way in popularity in contemporary folklore to other ideas of demonic activity as being fixed to certain places, such as haunted houses and restless places with buried remains.

Summarizing the different beliefs, we can conclude that remains that are undestroyed, preserved under the ground and fixed at a certain location give additional strong reasons for the soul to get 'stuck' on earth in an ambiguous state.

## If Not People, Then Who Is Supposed to Be Buried in the Ground?

Another interesting point in this research might be who, or what, in Mongolian folklore traditions is supposed to be buried in the earth? The majority of motifs in this respect are connected to different kinds of supernatural being, both from epic stories and actual beliefs. A particular kind of inhumation is widespread in epic stories about duels between different personages, heroes and evil monsters. In these stories, burial in the earth is regarded as a method of suppressing an enemy (temporarily or finally), with a number of variations on this theme. For example, a popular method of such burial is putting the enemy in a pit (or a cave, crack or hole) and pressing upon the enemy with a piece of mountain or rock (Potanin 1883). In the southern Mongolian *Epic of Kalpa* (Dulam 1982: 168) the hideous *mangus* (a multi-headed monster from epics and fairy tales), suppressed by the hero, is pushed into a hole where the Ocean of Blood was located; one of the gods, *Sam Burkhan*, stood by the hole to guard the entrance. The same motif is very popular in local legends that relate to natural objects:

> This rock is very famous. In old times Galzu Baatar, a very strong hero, lived here. And one day an enormous snake came to our place and began to harm people. The hero decided to put an end to this. He and the snake began to struggle. They struggled day and night, and another day, and another night. In the end the huge snake started to lose its strength. Galzu Baatar overcame and killed the snake and put a very large stone on its head. That is it! This rock is that very stone, lying on the snake's head. Look at that very large and long bump over there. This is the body of that snake. (S. T., 1963, Khalkha, 2012)

The second special kind of inhumation relates to beliefs about the supernatural and obviously has the same meaning—to suppress (in visible form) demonic creatures and evil spirits. For example, this method is regarded as one of the most effective to use against a demonic creature called *oroolon*, which is widely represented among Buryat-Mongolian tribes:

> *Oroolon* is a name for that who was a human. It is the soul of a bad deceased person. Nothing and nobody can stop it. It brings harm and evil. Only a very strong shaman or lama can stop it. The shaman suppresses it. He makes a deep hole in the earth, rolls the demon in a goat skin, puts it between two large pots (one below, the other on top) and buries it. After this, it cannot harm people anymore. (B. H., 1956, Buryat, 2008)

The same practice in Mongolian tradition is used against local nature spirits, when they start to harm people. The following description is a fragment of a narrative collected during fieldwork in Mongolia:

> The shaman suppressed those enraged evil spirits [*lus-savdag*—nature spirits] and buried them on the riverside, pressing each of them under a stone to make them calm. When he came to the river a year later and checked the stones, there was a spirit in the shape of part of the human

body [hand, leg] under each of them, and under the last one he found a child. He made all these demons his helper spirits and started to raise that child as his own son. (R. L., 1958, Darkhad, 2007)

According to the data collected, catching *chötgör* and burying them in the earth is regarded among lay Mongolians as a normal (and real) practice performed by skilful and powerful lamas and shamans:[21] 'When lamas suppress something bad, or demons, they trap it in a vessel and bury it in the earth, then it can't harm people anymore' (Ts. J., 1927, Khalkha, 2009). Despite clearly malevolent supernatural creatures being buried there, such places are not regarded in the tradition as dangerous for people because the negative influence of the evil demonic beings has already been destroyed by this special inhumation.

It is interesting that this method of suppressing spirits, also performed by shamans, is at the same time one of the traditional forms of funeral ritual for strong and famous shamans among the Mongolian tribes and is regarded as part of the worship of a particular shaman after death (Batoyeva et al. 2002). In the context of the Mongolian tradition this point seems to be very logical. Mongolian shamans have strong ties with the earth through their helper spirits, who are usually local nature spirits, and the souls of previously deceased shamans. According to traditional beliefs, a shaman, especially a good and very strong one, becomes a nature spirit after death and thus embodies the range of nature spirits. So, burial in this context could be regarded as a form of moving the soul nearer to its post-mortem destination, where it is supposed to stay in a new state 'forever'. In addition, it should be mentioned that in Mongolian tradition a shaman is regarded as half human, half demonic:

> The shaman was placed in the most respected seat, begged to smoke and drink, and given deep bows even by the oldest people. 'Why? If you want to deal with devils, you must be a super-devil!' Urgunge said. 'Beautiful Buddha is not going to scare a devil away—he is just merciful to everybody, even to devils. A shaman has to be more powerful than any spirit. It is the best species of human being'. (Humphrey 1996: 28)

Some examples reflect important elements in the perception and meaning of burial in the earth for the common people. One story, transcribed by Caroline Humphrey from Daur Mongols (Inner Mongolian) tradition, concerns a Mongolian man, Tulga, who led the Red Guards and destroyed many local sacred places (including *oboo*, a sacred object of worship devoted to local nature spirits). Afterwards he felt guilty and offered a horse as compensation.[22]

Upon its dedication, the horse was set free and ran away into the mountains. Tulga, however, found the animal and sold it—a sinful action [which could provoke the anger of the local spirits towards the whole community]. Shortly thereafter he was beaten by local people and died from his injuries. (Evans and Humphrey 2003: 198)

After this behaviour, which went against Mongol customs, Tulga was buried. People reported seeing 13 snakes crawl from his grave—one for each of the ruined structures of *oboo*. In this situation, burial represents a form of punishment for someone who has broken traditional ritual rules (the regulatory relationships between the community and local supernatural beings) putting not just himself but the whole community in potential danger. The punishment in this story has two meanings. It can be regarded as a form of human sacrifice to the local spirits to calm them, while at the same time being a special form of punishment that extends the guilty person's suffering even to the other world (because a ritually incorrect funeral prevents a soul from reincarnating).

We can see from this range of traditional images of burials relating to epic monsters, demons, evil spirits, special religious specialists and guilty humans that a burial in the earth would not be perceived as appropriate for ordinary people. An inhumation in this traditional worldview can be seen as a violation because the deceased member of the family is being treated as if they were a bad or sinful person, or a demon.

## The Earth and Nature Spirits

In Mongolian folklore, the earth is one of the most important and worshipped characters. A popular traditional formula is eternal/silver blue sky and wide golden earth: paired with the sky, the earth is regarded as the most respected part of the universe and is widely represented as such in mythology, epic traditions, charms and other folk genres. In mythology and in everyday life the earth is represented through countless personifications, one of which is nature spirits, who are regarded as owners of all natural objects. 'Everything has a landlord. Every rock, every stone, every river or spring or wood, everything has its landlord and he cares about his property' (T. B., 1940, Darkhad, 2012). Vernacular beliefs concerning the earth and nature spirits are embodied in a rich variety of narratives and ritual practices, establishing and regulating relations between humans and nature. Basically, narratives illustrate the rules, prescriptions and taboos appreciated in Mongolian traditions and describe the relations between humans and nature spirits from this perspective. The most popular plots include the motifs of humans violating rules, the revenge of disturbed nature spirit(s), the destroying power of the nature spirits' anger and its frightening consequences (including natural disasters, epidemics, human and livestock deaths).[23] There are also many stories about religious specialists (lamas or shamans) calming down raging nature spirits.

According to beliefs, nature spirits, being principally ambivalent towards humans, do not need much provocation to get angry and to start their horrible revenge. They are also very sensitive both to physical (any interference with their property, the earth, natural objects, wild animals, etc.) and ritual abuse (wrongly performed rituals, inappropriate offerings, even the 'wrong' religious specialist as mediator, etc.). Every activity connected with the earth (from building a house to a simple action like driving a stake into the ground) and with natural objects should be accompanied by certain rituals. The purpose of these rituals (whether simple or elaborate) is to ask permission to disturb nature, warn nature spirits about possible danger in a particular area, and propose offerings as compensation. But even this system of rules and customs does not absolutely prevent a person from performing the wrong action and suffering an angry response.

One interesting aspect specific to the Mongolian tradition is the bodily metaphor of nature, when certain spots of earth and natural objects often turn out to be pieces of the body of nature spirits. This dramatically heightens the chances for unintended conflict between humans and local spirits. For example, there is a widespread motif that tells of the danger of putting something sharp into the earth as it might hurt a nature spirit who happens to be exactly at that place at that moment.[24] If this happens, of course the spirit becomes upset and angry and looks for revenge.

The problem comes when nobody knows where the nature spirits are at any one moment, so that even touching or moving random natural objects might be dangerous, as in the following story:

> Some years ago, one Chinese trader lived here. Once he was travelling around and saw a very pretty stone. It was white and smooth and in the shape of a woman's breast. That man could not go by. He was very surprised. He stopped and started touching and stroking that stone. Then he continued on his way and completely forgot about it. Soon after he returned home and became very ill. No doctors could help him. He had a strange nightmare, the same every night: a pretty, but very angry, woman with beautiful white skin came and tormented him. Later

one lama said that his illness was the revenge of *lus-savdag*, a nature spirit whose body he inadvertently touched. The lama said that he should return to that place to make offerings and ask for forgiveness. He returned to that place, but could not find the stone; it was no longer there. He died in a few months. Humans should think about what they touch and be very careful. (G. H., 1976, Khalkha, 2010)

The notion of the nature spirits' rage (*lusyn horlol*) is widespread throughout Mongolian tribes and has a variety of pragmatic applications in different kinds of discourse. The nature spirits' rage is one of the most popular terms in consultations with religious specialists and a universal explanatory model at both the individual and collective level. When people are reflecting on why things such as health, studies, business, personal relationships or whatever have gone badly, or not as well as they might have wished, their misfortune is often attributed to the rage of spirits over a possible accidental misdeed.[25] This notion is also reflected in a collective public discourse about the misfortunes of the Mongolian people in the past and in the present. This adds some particular overtones to discussions about ecological problems in contemporary Mongolia. One of the most important issues concerns extraction industries, which for economic and historical reasons are generally controlled by foreign companies (including a large number of Chinese firms). Discussions among ordinary people (and also some public figures) about these problems contain ideas of 'causing suffering to and exhausting the earth', 'sucking out the strength and good luck from Mongolian earth', 'heaping the Mongolian nation in misfortune and sorrows' (Delaplace 2012: 131-144) in a metaphorical and literal sense.

The notion of the nature of spirits' rage is connected to an important question of individual and collective (the latter being more traditional) responsibility towards nature spirits. In contemporary Mongolian culture, both cases are reflected in folklore and everyday belief. In this sense it is particularly interesting that some motifs concern modern interpretations of collective responsibility and a search for a guilty party. One popular contemporary example (which also shows a way of transforming the traditional motif of collective responsibility) endows nature spirits with blindness as a way of explaining how the nature spirits' rage might descend suddenly on an innocent person (J. B., 1963, Khalkha, 2010; D. H., 1947, Khalkha, 2015; M. G., 1975, Khalkha, 2016). On the other hand, it is also possible to pass responsibility on from the wrongdoer to someone else. This motif is also reflected in different ritual practices. According to one of these practices, before starting excavation work the digger should draw around the area with a boar's fang,[26] 'so that the nature spirits think that a boar did it, not a human: a boar is such kind of an animal who is always digging the earth, then nature spirits won't get angry at you' (G. H., 1941, Khalkha, 2017). Or there is another, more 'bureaucratic', method:

> Before starting the work you have to do, you should say the name and surname, position, and address of your boss, so as to say 'I'm doing it not by my own will, I'm just a worker, this man, his name, ordered me to do it'. (G. H., 1941, Khalkha, 2017)

Thus, there are some chances to avoid individual responsibility, although there is still a danger that the whole community will suffer because of these inappropriate deeds.

In the context of these beliefs, inhumation seems to present a greater danger as the situation included possible double abuse of the nature spirits, both material and ritual, and so was regarded as a grave sin and a serious crime. Examples of such situations, and even of diplomatic conflict, are known from history. Russian diplomat, historian and publicist Ivan Mayskiy wrote down a few such cases. In the 1880s, Nemchinov, a cossack whose duty was to escort the Russian post mission to Peking, died on the way from Urga to Kalgain. His body was immediately buried by the mission in the local area (the Belgih valley). However, this caused dissatisfaction among the local people and administration and the Russian consul in Urga was ordered to remove the corpse and bury it in a special area, the Russian cemetery in Urga. The consul saw no reason to do this, and a diplomatic conflict ensued. Finally, the government of Urga wrote a special note, which included the following passage:

> Burying the corpse in this area is very unpleasant to the *genii loci*, the patron of this area. Therefore, this district will be destroyed by drought: there will be permanent strong winds, the grass won't grow, *people passing that area will inevitably fall off their horses and die at that place, spreading infection.* (Mayskiy 1959: 80; emphasis added)

This accident helps us penetrate Mongolian traditional beliefs and their meanings a little more deeply. Actually, in the last fragment (marked by me with italics) we can recognize nothing other than our *güideltei gazar*, the 'restless place' which is predicted to appear as a result of a wrongly performed ritual performed in a wrong place, coming together with drought as the consequence of the nature spirits' rage. Following the notes written by Mayskiy, by a fateful coincidence the next year a horrible drought occurred in the Belgih valley and cattle died in an epizootic event. This was taken by the local people and administration as retribution for the sinful burial. 'Lamas had been performing rituals at that desecration place for a month, only after that disasters stopped' (Mayskiy 1959: 81).

Mayskiy witnessed another similar case when, during his winter stay near the river Hangeltsik, a 10-month-old child, the son of the Russian trader living there, died. At first the family of the child thought to bury him near the household, but local Mongolian people found out about this and were very worried. They declared that they could not allow this kind of desecration of their area, and if the family would not bury the corpse in the Russian cemetery they would have 'to exhume it and give it to animals and birds to eat'[27] (Mayskiy 1959: 81). So, in winter the family had to go 200 km from where they lived to conduct the funeral.[28]

The detail that is worth pointing out here is that according to the data, *güideltei gazar* are connected with nature spirits, and that their main cause of appearance, inhumation, is a kind of material and ritual abuse of the earth and those who represent it. But at the same time *güideltei gazar* are not the result of the nature spirits' rage (as are drought or disease). *Güideltei gazar*, as a result of the 'wrong ritual', are believed to cause harm not only to people but also to the earth and its patrons. A contemporary text transcribed during fieldwork emphasizes this perception. Answering the question 'what are the *güideltei gazar*?' one of our interlocutors told us the following story:

> Once a man was riding back home from his relatives. There was a small valley and a trace of a riverbed. When he tried to ride up the opposite bank, the man's horse stopped and he couldn't make it continue. He got off the horse to look around and saw two female creatures standing there with their breasts hanging down to their knees. They were naked and covered with hair.[29] He was very scared and ran away. When he came home he got very ill. One lama told him that those females were *savdag*, nature spirits, their breasts were hanging down to their knees and *they couldn't move, they were stuck there, as if hobbled*. He should have helped them put their breasts over their shoulders, then they would be free and could leave the place, but he got scared and didn't do that and ran away, that is why he got sick. The lama read many different prayers and using prayer put the breasts of the nature spirits over their shoulders setting these nature spirits free, and after that everything went well. (M. U., 1987, Khalkha, 2017; emphasis added)

As we can see from this story, according to some interpretations *güideltei gazar* influence and harm nature spirits the same way they do people—helpless demonic immobility overtakes even supernatural patrons.

Thus, the perception of specific Mongolian traditions and relations with the earth and its patrons adds another point to the tension between different ritual practices and the authorities behind them. Wrong deeds, materials and rituals committed against and abusing the earth and the nature spirits are regarded as very sinful and dangerous acts that might bring serious troubles to the whole community. The image of the earth in Mongolian tradition is connected to a rich variety of beliefs and ritual practices, giving considerable potential for tension and conflict in relation to outsiders and others unsympathetic to or dismissive of this worldview.

## Conclusion

This long-term conflict between two ritual traditions is rooted in important vernacular beliefs concerning the worship of the earth and appropriate behaviour towards its personifications (nature spirits), collective responsibility, the importance of rituals, the demonic abilities of remains and bones, the nature of souls and their potentially problematic post-mortem existence, as well as to some other concepts.

In the light of these traditional beliefs, modern 'official' funeral ritual practice could be interpreted as an enforced violation of the status of deceased family members, jeopardizing the future existence of their souls as well as relationships between community and nature. Thus, the norms of two different kinds of authority, the traditional and modern official, are deeply contradictory in this case.

Today, Mongolian society is going through a period of intensive change accompanied by complicated interactions between various processes (re-traditionalization, westernization, rethinking of the Socialist past and previous historical periods, globalization) and complex cultural negotiations (official culture, traditional culture, post-Soviet cultural conditioning, foreign economic and cultural influences, etc.). This interaction in various spheres of life can be represented by a wide range of situations reflecting examples of syncretic coexistence as well as cases of the glaring contrast between different traditions.

This chapter has concentrated on one of the great number of situations that are emblematic of conflict and tension between different elements of the Mongolian culture, especially between modern official and traditional ritual practice in the form of funeral traditions. This situation is reflected in social practice, belief and the rich ongoing repertoire of demonological narratives, revising the old motif of 'demonic stuckness' into the new statement of 'the immured soul', and in doing so giving a specifically folkloric voice to one of the sides in this ongoing ritual battle.

## Acknowledgements

This work has been supported by the Estonian Research Council (project PRG670).

## Notes

1. Tengrism is a complicated term which today includes different meanings. The first meaning (as used here) is the scholarly concept describing different beliefs and cults connected to the sky in ancient Turkic and Mongolian traditions. The second meaning refers to the modern New Age religious and national movements that have spread in a number of regions populated by Turkic and Mongolian peoples.
2. The majority of permanent Mongolian cities were founded as administrative or commercial centres, generally by Chinese and Russian settlers. The urban Mongolian population at the beginning of the twentieth century was only about 5% (Mayskiy 1959). Today Mongolia has a range of cities, some of them quite large, representing modern urban culture, while others are more like villages (in comparison with modern cities); there is only one real megalopolis with an intensive modern urban culture, Ulaanbaatar, the capital.
3. *Güideltei gazar* (also *gazrin güits*)—in Mongolian *güidel* means 'to run', 'running', 'circulation'; *gazar* 'earth', 'ground' (Pyurbeyev 2001 vol. 1: 9).
4. The same way as, for example, a spirit of the mountain is equated with the mountain.
5. G. H., 1975, Khalkha, 2009: here and further, 'G. H'. refers to the initial letters of the interviewee's name, '1975' the year of birth of the interviewee, 'Khalkha' the name of the Mongolian tribe the interviewee belongs to, '2009' the year when the interview was conducted.
6. Usually in descriptions of 'restless places' we find human transport (horses, cars, even planes) stuck, and people not walking. One explanation might be that these places tend to be quite distant from living areas.
7. In one such narrative the witness found an old hair comb under the wheel of his car. This detail was found only in the west of Mongolia, in Khovd province.
8. According to Mongolian folk beliefs, supernatural and demonic entities might be seen by certain observers, among them religious specialists, children under three years of age, dogs with 'four eyes' (a spot above each eye), ordinary people in special states, i.e. ill, weak, close to death.
9. Urinating as a universal ritual defilement, which is believed to neutralize a demonic influence, is found in many different traditions.

10 In the vernacular religion of contemporary Mongolia it is mainly the task for a special category of lamas who perform ritual *luizhin*.
11 To remove the *buzar*—ritual dirt, desecration.
12 In the Slavic traditions it is regarded as the influence of the forest spirit, *leshiy*, the house spirit, *domovoy*, the water spirit, *rusalka*, or the witch/wizard (Zinov'yev 1985); in Finno-Ugric traditions such loci are often connected to the spirits of the deceased (Jauhiainen 1998). In the Buryat tradition (related to Mongolian) this influence is connected to the spirits of the deceased, *boholdoi* (author's working diary from the 2010 expedition to Buryatia, the Mythological and Ritual Traditions of Contemporary Mongolia), in Kalmyk folklore such places are usually associated with demons, *shulmas* (Basangova and Burykin 2014: 55–56). The Altaic *tunrgak* are the supernatural loci, according to descriptions and motifs, that are closest to Mongolian 'restless places'; *tunrgak* are also often regarded in the tradition as an independent character (Doronin 2016).
13 In the Slavic traditions it might be a path used by the forest or house spirit, their wedding procession, or the devils' road (Zinov'yev 1985); Finno-Ugric traditions also include the path of the forest spirit, the procession of deceased spirits, and the wedding procession of trolls (Simonsuuri 2006 [1950]; Doronin 2016).
14 The former existence of this motif in Mongolian folklore historically is probable, as similar motifs are known in related traditions of the region, such as Buryat, Kalmyk and Altaic.
15 This type of funeral is related to the Tibetan sky burial, when the corpse was given to the wild birds. For practical reasons, such as the large area, scarce population and dry climate, the traditional type of funeral was convenient for Mongolia.
16 For specific regional funeral traditions see, for example, Delaplace 2008 on the anthropology of contemporary funerals and ancestor worship among the Dörvöd Mongolians of western Mongolia.
17 It is believed that, on the contrary, in the case of children's funerals this kind of ritual should not be performed because it might confuse the soul of the child who would then not find the path to the next birth (B. H., 1939, Khalkha, 2008). These beliefs are an example of the peculiarity of funeral rituals for children in traditional cultures.
18 The possibility of the soul becoming lost is found within a variety of shamanic beliefs (the soul can get lost even if the human is still alive, then such a person becomes ill and faces misfortunes, until a shaman finds the lost soul and calls it back using special rituals).
19 In Mongolian tradition, this kind of demonic soul, which stays in this world and hides in things, has the name *büg*.
20 There is also variation in the contemporary folklore motifs connected with the demonic lights, such as the lights of demonic invisible cars or motorcycles.
21 This practice is a very popular motif included in Asian narrative traditions of Mongolia, China and Japan and has connections with a variety of Buddhistic, Daoist and other monks.
22 A special type of offering in which an animal is set free in honour of a certain deity, or in honour of the spirits.

23 There are special expressions in Mongolian traditions for the harm caused by the revenge of nature spirits responding to careless human deeds against nature: *lusyn horlol* or *gazrin buzarsan* ('harm from the nature spirit' and 'desecration from the earth').
24 This belief about the sensitivity of incorporeal spirits towards material sharpness is widespread with many representations in Mongolian folklore: there is a similar prohibition against using sharp objects when dealing with a fireplace in the house, while at the same time different sharp objects (saw, hedgehog or plant spines, fish teeth) are very popular in apotropaic rites, being regarded as affective tools with which to scare away malevolent spirits and demons.
25 In this use, the concept of *lusyn horlol*, 'harm from the nature spirit', is very similar to the concept of Slavic *porcha* (curse, evil eye) and other concepts of harm accidentally coming from outside.
26 Similar actions are supposed to be performed before leaving the corpse as part of the traditional funeral.
27 This might be recognized as a description of the traditional funeral.
28 These cemeteries, located in a few large cities, were at that time for foreign populations, predominantly Chinese and Russian (Mayskiy 1959). Chinese people (mainly state administrative personnel and merchants) had the same tradition of inhumation as Russians, although they spent lots of time and money on long trips from the temporary cemetery in Urga (where corpses were kept in coffins) to China to take the deceased back to his/her homeland for burial (ibid.: 81). This practice is based on ideas common to East Asia, rooted in traditional beliefs about souls and local spirits. The soul of a person who has died on foreign soil will not be able to reincarnate and will be doomed to stay on the earth as a shelterless spirit.
29 The appearance of female nature spirits described in this narrative is very similar to the appearance of other Mongolian demonesses, such as *almas*, *shulmas*, *mam*.

# References

Basangova, Tamara Goryaevna and A. A. Burykin. 2014. *Tipologiya kalmytskogo fol'klora*. Dzhangar: Elista.
Batoyeva, Darima Batorovna, Galina Rinchinovna Galdanova, Darima Anatol'yevna Nikolayeva and Tat'yana Dmitriyevna Skrynnikova. 2002. *Obryady v traditsionnoy kul'ture buryat*. Moskva: Vostochnaya literatura.
Birtalan, Ágnes. 2003. 'Ritualistic Use of Livestock Bones in the Mongolian Belief System and Customs'. In *Altaica Budapestinensia MMII: Proceedings of the 45th Permanent International Conference, Budapest, Hungary, June 23–28, 2002*, edited by Alice Sárközi and Attila Rákos, 34–62. Budapest: Eötvös Loránd University.
*Bolson Yavdal*. 2012. 'Shulmas busguitei uchirsan zaluu'. *Bolson Yavdal*, December 8, 2012: 6.
Delaplace, Grégory. 2008. *L'invention des morts: Sépultures, fantômes et photographie en Mongolie contemporaine*. Paris: Centre d'Études Mongoles & Sibériennes—École Pratique des Hautes Études.

Delaplace, Grégory. 2012. 'Parasitic Chinese, Vengeful Russians: Ghosts, Strangers, and Reciprocity in Mongolia'. *Journal of the Royal Anthropological Institute* 18 (1): 131–144. https://doi.org/10.1111/j.1467-9655.2012.01768.x

Doronin, Dmitriy. 2016. 'Turgak: demony puti v altayskoy mifologii'. In *Demonologiya kak semioticheskaya sistema: Tezisy dokladov IV Mezhdunarodnoy nauchnoy konferentsii*, edited by Dmitry Antonov and Olga Khristoforova, 27–39. Moscow: RGGU.

Drobyshev, Yuliy Ivanovich. 2005. 'Pokhoronno-pominal'naya obryadnost' srednevekovykh mongolov i eye mirovozrencheskiye osnovy'. *Etnograficheskoye obozreniye* 1: 119–140.

Dulam, Sendenjav. 1982. 'Obraztsy mongol'skoy mifologii i literaturnaya traditsiya'. PhD diss., Institute of Language and Literature of the Russian Academy of Sciences.

Evans, Christopher, and Caroline Humphrey. 2003. 'History, Timelessness and the Monumental: The Oboos of the Mergen Environs, Inner Mongolia'. *Cambridge Archaeological Journal* 13 (2): 195–211. https://doi.org/10.1017/S095977430300012X

Galdanova, Galina R. 1987. *Dolamaistskiye verovaniya buryat*. Novosibirsk: Nauka.

Gerasimova, Kseniya Maksimovna. 1992. *Traditsionnaya obryadnost' mongol'skikh narodov*. Novosibirsk: Nauka.

Humphrey, Caroline. 1996. *Shamans and Elders: Experience, Knowledge, and Power among the Daur Mongols*. Oxford: Clarendon Press.

Jauhiainen, Marjatta. 1998. *The Type and Motif Index of Finnish Belief Legends and Memorates: Revised and Enlarged Edition of Lauri Simonsuuri's Typen- und Motivverzeichnis der finnischen mythischen Sagen*. Helsinki: Academia Scientiarum Fennica.

Lovor, Gavaagiin. 2002. *Uchir medehgüi hünd uuts bitgii tavi*. Ulaanbaatar.

Mayskiy, Ivan Mikhaylovich. 1959. *Mongoliya nakanune revolyutsii*. Moskva: IVL.

*Obychai*. 2006. *Obychai mongol'skogo naroda*. Ulaanbaatar: Montsame.

Potanin, Grigoriy Nikolayevich. 1883. *Ocherki Severo-Zapadnoy Mongolii*, vol. 4. St. Petersburg.

Pyurbeyev, Grigoriy T., ed. 2001. *Bol'shoy akademicheskiy mongol'sko-russkiy slovar'*, 4 vols. [Large academic Mongolian-Russian dictionary]. Moscow: Academia.

Simonsuuri, Lauri. 2006 [1950]. *Kansa tarinoi: Tutkielmia kansantarinoiden salaperäisestä maailmasta*. Helsinki: Suomalaisen Kirjallisuuden Seura.

Skorodumova, Lidiya Grigor'yevna and Alevtina A. Solovyeva. 2014. 'Kosti v mongol'skikh obryadakh i pover'yakh: predvaritel'nyye materialy'. *Mongolica* 13: 102–114.

Valk, Ülo. 2006. 'Ghostly Possession and Real Estate: The Dead in Contemporary Estonian Folklore'. *Journal of Folklore Research* 43 (1): 31–51. https://doi.org/10.2979/JFR.2006.43.1.31

Zhukovskaya, Nataliya L. 1977. *Lamaizm i ranniye formy religii*. Moscow: Nauka.

Zinov'yev, Valerij Petrovich. 1985. *Ukazatel' sibirskih bylichek i byval'shchin. Lokal'nye osobennosti russkogo fol'klora Sibiri: Issledovaniya i publikatsii*. Novosibirsk. https://www.ruthenia.ru/folklore/zinoviev2.htm

## Chapter 16

# Ghosts in Belief, Practice and Metaphor

*Paul Cowdell*\*

### Introduction

The relationship between belief and practice is complex. A written doctrine in institutional denominational groups, for example, may not provide as direct a map for the actual manifestation of belief in practice as one might expect. Leonard Primiano sought to address this in lived religious practice and experience by refocusing our studies on 'vernacular religion' as 'the continuous art of individual interpretation and negotiation of any number of influential sources' (2012: 384). This is salutary in a research context where there exist institutional bodies of a certain historical weight, influence and authority. In England, the Church of England has an 'official' status that can skew attention away from, or encourage misreadings of, vernacular practices within it. Robert Glenn Howard's negotiation of the 'empirical' and 'authorizing' in vernacular tradition allows us to better place such practices within what might elsewhere or otherwise be presented erroneously as 'official' in an authoritative sense.

Howard moves to define '"vernacular" ... dialectically as that which is opposed to its alternate term "institutional"' (2013: 81). This is not only invaluable for moving us further from the obstacles identified by Primiano; it also points towards understanding vernacular religious interactions across a wide variety and spectrum of institutional settings. Howard's identification of 'vernacular authority' seeks to place the participation of

---

\* **Paul Cowdell** is a Visiting Research Fellow at the University of Hertfordshire, UK, where he conducted his doctoral research on contemporary belief in ghosts. He is currently a serving Council member of the Folklore Society and a member of the editorial board of the *Folk Music Journal*.

> noninstitutional processes ... in the emergence of conditions that support current beliefs, values, or practices. In this sense, 'institutions' are ... social formations that have been founded through a formal speech act, usually in the form of a written document. (Howard 2013: 77)

While recognizing the hegemony specific institutions may have in particular contexts, and the apparently 'official' authority of their canonical texts and documents, this also points to its effects across a much broader spectrum of practices. Newer religious forms may take a more explicitly adaptive and incorporative attitude to a wider range of Primiano's 'influential sources' (2012: 384)—an attitude and practice that becomes syncretic in effect—that is by definition fluid, while still creating a less hegemonic, perhaps less stable institutional form.

The balance between consistency and contradiction, orthodoxy and heterodoxy, stern formality and imaginative leaps, is negotiated by believers/practitioners with remarkable adaptation, flexibility and grace, but scholars describing the same processes have managed less well. Good ethnographic work on neo-pagan festivals, for example, has focused on practice in order to draw out their eclectic adaptiveness, but may thereby have marginalized how practitioners consider and negotiate their belief, its development, and its interaction with their practice (Ezzy 2014, discussed below). Some scholars seem reluctant to acknowledge how far they are struggling to articulate (often, but not always, in a different linguistic register) the same theoretical conundrums their ethnographic subjects live through, leaving their developing academic language at risk of abandoning the actual lived belief practices of subjects who share their terminology. This is particularly the case with some metaphorical usages, where academic use depends upon removing words from any ethnographic context by denying vernacular usages.

These large questions should concern any scholar of religious practice, in both institutionally defined and more idiosyncratic observances, as they probe what is believed and how that is enacted. Ghost belief is a useful case study for exploring this interplay of belief and practice as belief in ghosts, itself a variable factor open to negotiation and reflection, is widespread even across denominational groups where doctrinal creed should exclude it. As one informant told researcher on ghosts Vivienne Rae-Ellis, 'We are practising Anglicans and do not believe in ghosts' (Rae-Ellis 1990: 80).

Ghost belief, in part because of its tension with more orthodox institutional codifications of belief, also involves verbal reflections bearing comparison with academic terminology. 'Ghost' is an awkward but inevitable entry point for discussions, but it cannot and should not therefore be removed from them. Equally it should not be abstracted for academic meanings that exclude wider popular usage, as some academic metaphors do.[1] A 'specific metamorphosis ... of ghosts and haunting from possible actual entities, plot devices, and clichés of common parlance ... into influential conceptual metaphors permeating global (popular) culture and academia alike' (del Pilar Blanco and Peeren 2013: 1) has taken place.

We shall return to academic language, but this terminology is already problematized in vernacular speech. (Every technical term here—ghost, religion, myth—is complicated, and I offer relevant caveats along the way.) Eve, the secretary of a Spiritualists' National Union (SNU) church in London, explained her conception of spirit or 'what you call "ghosts"', a word she never uses. Other informants expressed greater dislike of the word. Comments from Andy were prompted by my dissertation's title ('Belief in Ghosts in Post-War England'). He actively 'objects' to 'ghost' on similar grounds to Eve (preferring 'spirit' because 'we're all spirit') although without sharing her level of thought-out articulation and explanation.[2] These informants demonstrate that this is not just a question of terminology.

## Negotiating Belief, Praxis and Terminology in Spiritualism

Eve's administrative role in the church involved covering the many potential contradictions to be negotiated in the SNU's guiding eclectic '7 Principles' which posit a divine Creative Force, and an unspecific ministry of angels. The Principles, based on work by Emma Hardinge Britten (1823–1899), are regularly updated, allowing for constant adjustment and incorporation. Until recently the First Principle stated Spiritualism's 'core belief' as 'the acceptance of a Divine Energy. This force, whatever name given to it, has created all there is and sustains all its creation' (SNU n.d.b).[3] This is rather vague, allowing Spiritualism to appeal across institutional backgrounds, incorporating a wide variety of beliefs, however heterodox, under one umbrella church (for want of a better word, as by no means all are comfortable with it). Spiritualism's many strands, from the Christian-inflected to the more universalist, frequently with strong female leadership and demotic participation, have resulted in vigorous local autonomy, with disputes between churches, and churches clashing with the SNU. The process reflects well Howard's notion of vernacular authority in an institutional setting, played out against an institutional 'negotiation of any number of influential sources' (Primiano 2012: 384).

The SNU says its Principles 'are not intended to be binding rules or the basis of a dogma but to provide each individual, particularly those who are new to Spiritualism, a foundation for developing a personal philosophy'. Spiritualism has been called 'a religion that embodies the main ideas of all religions' and thus 'a universal religion' (SNU n.d.a).[4] These 'main ideas' are identified as 'a life after death, immortality and the existence of a God'. The latest iteration of the Principles goes further, stating that 'God, the Creative Force, manifests directly or indirectly in all things. We know this power as God and, as we are a part of the life created by God, we acknowledge God as our Father' (SNU n.d.c). While the first two 'main ideas' are open enough to accommodate many variations, even the seemingly less complicated third may be trickier than expected. 'The Religious and Other Beliefs of Americans' reported only 92 per cent of Catholics and 95 per cent of Protestants believing in God, while for self-identified 'Born-Again Christians' (where the highest level of orthodoxy on this point might be predicted) the figure was still only 97 per cent (Taylor 2007). A 2013 poll suggested a slight decline in belief in God (Shannon-Missal 2013). A somewhat different 2019 poll of Western European religious beliefs showed possibly similar trends, with 79 per cent of all self-identified Christians across the continent professing belief in God, indicating that this is an area requiring proper systematic study and investigation (Pew Research Centre 2018: 99).

To promote accessibility across religious backgrounds, the SNU has historically limited the use of traditionally Christian imagery in its churches. I was surprised therefore at the portraits of Jesus in Eve's church. Eve defended their use to support the very eclecticism that led the SNU to reject them. She added a further layer of idiosyncrasy of practice, stressing her church's independence within the independent SNU: 'the church may belong to the SNU, but I'm the president'. Eve told me of another '*very* SNU' (her emphasis) local church with no religious trappings at all: their representative came 'to check up on' her church, where some services begin with the Lord's Prayer.

Other researchers have expressed surprise at this apparent disjuncture between the SNU's stated religious and philosophical openness and local use of Christian imagery. Jack Hunter (2009) reported 'a surprising amount of Christian imagery' at a Bristol SNU church. The Lord's Prayer opened that service, while the following week's service began with what Hunter thought were 'fairly traditional Christian songs'. Noting that he 'wouldn't really have expected [this] from a "non-Christian organisation"', he indicated 'one of the fundamental dichotomies in the Spiritualist religion—whether they are Christians or not'.

Inevitably, within such a broad church, Spiritualism manifests these tensions itself. In a series of articles in *Psychic News*, then still the pre-eminent publication of British Spiritualism—the SNU acquired the paper shortly afterwards—medium Craig Hamilton-Parker (1993–1994) criticized the use of (Christian) denominational imagery, insisting from Bible reading that 'Spiritualism and Christianity are totally incompatible'. He encouraged purging SNU churches of 'Christian imagery put there by uncommitted Spiritualists who still can't let go of their ignorance'. He reasserted the Principles on 'personal responsibility', where 'Nothing should stand between us and our direct experience of God', noting 'We don't worship the ghost of an Essene Jew'.[5] His hostility to Christian imagery is again driven by a defence of Spiritualism's openness, pointing to conflicting approaches within the shared overarching Principles. When a church president defended displaying a cross because 'New visitors may have just left a Christian church ... It reassures them that we believe in God', Hamilton-Parker protested that it was *insufficiently* open: 'are we only looking to attract former Christians?'

The former advertising copywriter was exercising both his professional expertise and his own particular strand of Spiritualism, which he came to via Hinduism and Buddhism. He stressed the eastern influences in Spiritualism's development, showing his influences in his rewrites of the Principles (1993–1994).[6] He renders the sixth Principle, 'Compensation and Retribution Hereafter for all the Good and Evil Deeds done on Earth', as 'Karma' (1993–1994; SNU n.d.b).[7] He justified his attack on the 'Victorian language' of the 'far from memorable' Principles on the basis of opening up the incorporative flexibility of Spiritualist belief and practice ('Spirit can communicate the essence but it's the medium's mind that converts the concepts into language'). This is again a struggle for Howard's vernacular authority, performed in ongoing interaction within the institution over the foundational 'formal speech act', codified in written form as the Principles (Howard 2013: 77).

Spiritualism's emergence is well known, covering both sides of the Atlantic, and with different strengths (Barrow 1986; McGarry 2008). Its syncretism and heterodoxy have been central throughout, and the deliberately broad Principles codify its inclusivity. (The broad characterization of neo-paganism is based on a similar inclusivity but without a similar central codification, although the catch-all 'Nature Religion' is often cited.) Contemplation and disagreement, distinctions and idiosyncrasies are built into Spiritualism's positioning as a unifying religion, counter to any residual academic tendency to see adherents or congregants of a religion as simply 'orthodox'. Molly McGarry's account (2008: 3) suggests Spiritualism's failure to become a 'national religion' owes much to failures to appreciate fully the variations across a spectrum of religious institutions. Such a reductive view of orthodoxy dissolves at a fieldwork level.

Ghost belief consistently reveals heterodoxies contained within the institution without erupting into heresy. Historical surveys bring out the fluctuating relationship of this perpetually fringe belief within a developing mainstream orthodox religious body (Bennett 1987: 149–209). Spiritualism codifies belief to some extent, like other religious institutions, but explicitly allowing for a broader spectrum of potential belief and praxis. The SNU calls the Seven Principles the 'basis of SNU Spiritualism', which 'help Spiritualists to navigate and combine their spiritual and human journeys' (SNU n.d.c). The institutional development accommodates a negotiation of the doctrinally awkward, but that negotiation is not exclusive to religious institutions or affiliations specifically tailored to it. It is, demonstrably, how people negotiate their beliefs within broader belief contexts. Belief bodies built around the possibility of syncretic negotiation simply show this more clearly.

## Myth and Contesting Textual Authority

Judy was articulate and informed about her thinking and candid about the ongoing elaboration of her beliefs. She had chosen her undergraduate History degree because the university specialized in the history of witchcraft, an interest that intersected with her family traditions. Judy said she was still working out her religious beliefs. Her mother is a committed Anglican with, it seems, an appropriate denominational hostility to ghosts, but Judy's chief spiritual influence was her maternal grandmother, who regards herself as a Christian, although hardly conventional: one vicar in an Anglican church where she played the organ reacted angrily when she said a church ghost had moved her sheet music. Judy's grandmother's account of Heaven, surrounding us all the time and populated by spirits enjoying the activities they enjoyed in life, seems closer to Spiritualism's Summerland (see, for example, Barrow 1986: 246–249) than an Anglican afterlife. Judy said she had fallen out with organized religion but continued to work on a belief system: she still believed in God, she said, and an afterlife, 'I think'. Although it might conflict with her childhood religion, she was negotiating it.

Where Christianity predominates it can be easy to think of all prevailing religious mythologies as similarly fixed by authoritative textual tradition. This throws up another terminological issue, as 'myth' is widely used and abused in and out of academia, its problematic pejorative usage being compounded by the tendency for prevailing myths to be (or appear) relatively textually fixed. I use it here solely as a narrative type, implying no judgement on narratives in the process. Axel Olrik's summary, written in 1921, is my starting point: 'Myths about gods are not a special category of narrative ... "Myth", therefore, designates not form but content. It is a narrative that concerns supernatural situations, and whose main character possesses superhuman abilities' (Olrik 1992: 5). John Holmes McDowell's study of personalization within the apparently impersonal genre of myth, and the opening up of 'incidental ... accidental ... personal' spaces under conditions of 'the tendency in mythic narrative towards fixed and stable narrative armatures', is highly suggestive for looking at religious traditions with long-established and apparently more firmly codified textual accounts of their myths (2011: 325). My limited fieldwork exposure to other religions of firm textual foundation (Judaism and Islam) suggests that their traditions of theological discourse enable the creation of such spaces without undermining textual authority, whereas Christianity, which lacks such a discursive pedagogical character, accommodates negotiation less comfortably without quite eliminating it. Three experiences may stand as examples. Riz spoke of his implicit religious belief in ghosts because the Qur'an speaks of ghosts and jinn, although scholarship suggests the latter reading is not universal (e.g., El-Zein 2009; Al-Rawi 2009). A United Synagogue rabbi invited me to his weekly discussion group to talk about ghosts. Having prefaced the meeting with an authoritative statement on the Torah's doctrine, he left the discussion open: positions ranged from acceptance to extreme scepticism, including about the rabbi's own comments. A Catholic priest declined a request to circulate my research locally as it did not meet his criteria for 'what is relevant to the parish'. Some of his parishioners did complete my questionnaire, however, suggesting they differed as to its relevance. Like Primiano's investigation of gay Catholics (2001), this is another reflection of the contestation of vernacular authority *within* an institution.

As Judy's comments show, interaction with institutional religious bodies involves positioning the individual in relation to the church.

Edward, in his twenties, said he was 'no longer practising' his earlier Anglicanism but still believed in an 'Anglican-style Christianity, including an afterlife/heaven etc.'. Charis, recently retired, described herself as 'agnostic' and a 'disbeliever' in the Anglicanism of her upbringing. Given the dominant textual authority of these religious myths it is important to note that this negotiation of beliefs *does not* remove the believer from the tradition but involves reworking the textual tradition through a consideration of the personal belief system and its structure.

Mary was explicit about the doctrinal bricolage that could result, writing: 'I am a practising Christian but I do not have an affiliation to any of the religious bodies'. She outlined what was encompassed:

> I believe in the Holy Trinity; in the life, death and resurrection of Jesus Christ and in the day of Final Judgement. However, I also believe in the teachings of the Prophet Mohammed and in the words of the prophets in the Old Testament. I also think that souls are reborn as many times as necessary for them to fulfil God's purpose for them.

She worshipped privately, having 'no interest in organized religions', although she had 'worshipped as an Anglican' from the age of seven into her twenties, when she 'became disenchanted with the rules being put in place'. Some years later she was 'accepted into the Roman Catholic Church' but 'found that my idea of God didn't match theirs in some important areas' and left. Her partner Christie had followed a similar trajectory: christened in the Church of England, although not a practising congregant, she joined the Catholic Church but broke over its stance on homosexuality before she 'decided to follow my heart and embrace the Pagan/Wiccan religion'. It is unclear from her questionnaire how far 'follow my heart' was intended metonymically.

Above, I described ghost belief as 'perpetually fringe' to mainstream orthodoxies, but Mary's comments suggest ways we could renegotiate our appraisal of those orthodoxies. Notwithstanding her consideration of various textual orthodoxies and authorities, Mary's reply to the question 'Have your beliefs [on the afterlife] changed over time?' was 'No. I have always believed in ghosts and the supernatural'. My caution about Christie's possible metonymy stems from her using a similar formulation in another context ('I have always believed in spirits, ghosts and sprites'). The weight of textual authority of mainstream religions may be misleading, and rather than seeing ghost beliefs as fringe to a mainstream orthodoxy we should see the purported orthodoxy as unrepresentative of some persistent and widely accepted core beliefs. The heterodoxy is the mainstream, because that (privately, at least) is how informants themselves describe it. Even Charis, self-proclaimed 'agnostic' and 'disbeliever' in her former Anglicanism, made her comments while discussing pacts for the first to die to appear after death to the survivor and the character of the evidence required to prove this had happened. Such pacts have a long historical record, in part as a way of assessing or validating doctrinal positions (e.g. Joynes 2001: 9–10; Dick 1962: 350–351; Haynes 1982: 60–75). Because of caution over reporting (and the likelihood that pacts without results are less reported) it is difficult to assess their frequency, but their persistent resurfacing suggests a more common practice than is often acknowledged. Vernacular estimation of ghosts is an integral part of the active consideration of the afterlife. It involves a reappraisal of religious orthodoxies and is an active process. Active consideration *is* vernacular belief in action.

This is clearer in the more obviously adaptive groupings broadly identified as neo-pagan, but the appreciation of the relationship between their practice and their belief is easily overlooked because of the wide range of theoretical influences embraced. Neo-paganism covers many groups with specific and different textual bases, and none, and its deliberate definitional flexibility may reflect a greater tolerance of groups working in roughly the same area rather than their incorporation into one body. Understandably this has led to a tendency to view religious observation primarily as a practice rather than in relation to the elaborated thinking behind that practice.

Ezzy's discussion of a contemporary Australian pagan festival, anonymized as Faunalia, reveals the argument's strengths as well as its risk of inadvertently short-changing practitioners. The argument borrows from Graham Harvey's critique of ideas of religion as being, in Ezzy's words, 'defined as belief in God, or some variation of this that retains an emphasis on cognition and otherworldly transcendence' (Ezzy 2014: 22); these ideas are inevitably an overstatement if spiritual beliefs are less articulated around ideas of a deity. Several of my informants discussed numinousness in the natural world. Willow, for example, describing herself as 'spiritual' rather than 'religious', inclined towards a form of nature worship shaped by her mother's beliefs. As a child Willow had often said 'I've seen a ghost' but her mother disagreed as this did not accord with her more general view that all natural phenomena have their own spirits. Willow later embraced her mother's spiritual thinking wholesale, endorsing the rejection of 'religion' as a deity-specific (or -centred) belief system.

In this regard, the attempt to refocus our understanding of religion away from monotheistically derived models (with textually relatively stabilized mythologies) is a positive step towards understanding complex observational practices. For Ezzy it is an attempt to discard 'religion', because of its associations, without losing the word. There is no easy way out of this bind: observers/practitioners, like the scholars attempting to describe and understand them, must still work with received vocabularies. 'Religion', like 'ghost', may not be how informants describe the organization of their belief practice—any more than 'institution', in truth—but may still offer them a way into discussing the nuances and intricacies of their heterodox observation.

This may be what is missing from some attempts at redefinition. For Ezzy, 'rituals and practices are not only expressions of belief and ideas ... [but] beliefs and ideas can also be outworkings of rituals and practices' (2014: 22). The inversion is useful, but the engagement of the practitioners is elided in a circular moment of philosophical sleight of hand: participants at Faunalia are 'not overly concerned' with beliefs in a god so 'do not think of themselves as engaged in religion', which becomes '"Religion" as practiced at Faunalia is primarily about rituals and relationships, *not belief*' (ibid., my emphasis). It is not quite that this is wrong, but this attempt to codify vernacular understandings of 'religion'—associated with institutions—fails to give due weight to the active process of vernacular, extra-institutional thought about belief. There is a danger of diminishing the intellectual investment made by practitioners, the interaction between belief and practice, and the level of contestation actually being made.

Morgan, for example, was raised a Methodist, practising actively until she was 18. She had been 'happy for many years to attend occasional services in a wide variety of Christian churches' before turning to Druidry. Her brother is a Methodist preacher who, in Morgan's words, 'believes ... the Bible is all true'. That formulation and her own doctrinal fluidity over many years point to the inadequacies of appraising religious belief outside of practice, suggesting that the rigidity of doctrinal or institutional absolutism may be an exoteric construct of those outside or on the fringes of an institutional congregation. Morgan's self-description as 'spiritual' rather than 'religious' is consistent with one aspect of Ezzy's argument, but her practice does not stand outside of an active consideration and negotiation of belief. Morgan's beliefs resembled Willow's (she believes in 'the nature based religions', and 'commemorate[s] the seasonal festivals') but placed her definitely as an active contributor to and assessor of the process of syncretic development, even where she had ceased observational practice. Her church attendance had ended years earlier, but her turn to Druidry and membership of the Order of Bards, Ovates and Druids was connected to her continued deep thought on these matters: her introduction to the Order was seemingly accidental (reading 'a book which fell of[f] a shelf in a bookshop') but it 'seemed to be what I had been looking for and matched my interests in Arthurian literature and legend'. She followed a seven-year correspondence course before becoming a tutor herself. This is not an avoidance of beliefs, even as she describes her supportive but non-practising husband as being of 'no fixed religion'. Religious beliefs are negotiable and, more importantly, *are* negotiated.

Morgan participates regularly in an organized coven, so might be seen as having replaced one institutional body with one of a different character, but such patterns of negotiation and discussion emerged broadly around self-definition. Pearl, a 25-year-old pagan, wrote that she grew up believing in the Christian god 'because that is all my school taught me and I didn't know any better'. She described her mother as a spiritualist who believed in ghosts and angels. Increasingly uncomfortable with the Christian god (in line with Ezzy's model), Pearl broke from some elements of her mother's beliefs (angels, explicitly) and said she was an 'atheist' until she was about 20, when she met some pagans whose beliefs 'made more sense to me'. Since then she has identified as pagan. She does not participate regularly in a coven, but sometimes meets with 'like-minded people', a phrase redolent of the practice patterns described by Ezzy. Her negotiation of identification, belief and practice clearly also covers non-belief. Pearl identified her brother as an atheist, too, but where he 'thinks all this sort of thing [spiritual and ghost belief] is absolute rubbish', she said, 'I think I have always believed in ghosts', even when self-describing as an atheist. We inadvertently strip our informants of the serious thought they apply to their own beliefs at our own risk.

The problem comes into sharper relief if we look at 'religion' through the prism of 'myth'. Earlier scholars of mythology made some now familiar points about the relationship between belief and practice: 'Our modern habit is to look at religion from the side of belief rather than of practice' may sound like Ezzy but comes from William Robertson Smith's 1889 *Lectures on the Religion of the Semites* (1998: 27). Robertson Smith saw this habit stemming from a familiarity with Christianity that caused researchers to look for a doctrine to explain rituals. However, 'the antique religions had for the most part no creed; they consisted entirely of institutions and practices', so 'It may be affirmed with confidence that in almost every case the myth was derived from the ritual, and not the ritual from the myth; for the ritual was fixed and the myth was variable' (ibid.: 28).

Researchers and informants wrestle with the same words in trying to understand or describe the same questions around belief. This deliberate and informed process often also involves the same texts, and researchers should never underestimate the reading available to and used by informants: Ronald Hutton has noted the 'total lack of a dividing line between popular and learned magic' (1999: 13). Judy's choice of a degree programme reflecting her belief interests and Morgan linking her antiquarian literary tastes with her spiritual practices may be distinctive but not isolated examples. The rising number of scholars who identify as practitioners (more so even than practitioners who do not identify as scholars) are simultaneously explaining the basis of their belief practices and incorporating the practice into their theorizing with direct recourse to earlier theoretical works.

This throws up odd echoes. In the last edition of her book on American neo-Paganism, Margot Adler (2006 [1979]: ix–x) noted that these new old religions 'were based on the celebration of the seasonal cycles of nature. They were based on what people did, not what people believed'. Like Ezzy later, Adler argued from this that the religions 'had few creeds or dogmas. There were no prophets. There were myths and legends, but no scriptures to be taken literally' and they were ultimately all pagan (ibid.). This last point only appeared in the final revision, along with a developed caution about creedal doctrine. An earlier edition noted that 'If you go far enough back, all our ancestors practiced religions that had neither creeds nor dogmas, neither prophets nor holy books' (1986 [1979]: ix). The later caution brings her closer to Robertson Smith, while contemporary appeals to 'lost wisdom', particularly but not exclusively at the popular end of the theoretical spectrum, may also be a form of mythopoesis consistent with and based upon earlier conceptions and discussions of myth.[8] Seeing more clearly the relationship between myth and religion, as Robertson Smith indicated, does help clarify what we are discussing, whatever our consequent disagreements.

These are contested areas of discussion that carry an expectation of disbelief, dispute and argument. The language of legend involves a continued assessment of the legend's content, a point that is usefully carried into belief narratives more widely. If scholars are prepared to allow academic disputes over terminology, and sometimes happy to debate and contest meanings of vocabulary, it is not always clear that they recognize the processes as related. The same terminologies and linguistic techniques are involved. An ethnographic focus on what is actually believed and practised may lead us to overlook or downplay the rhetorical devices that do find vernacular use. Two factors may shape this tendency. Any serious discussion of belief and practice will inevitably concentrate on the meanings and implications of the language used because that is the purpose of the discourse. Inviting informants to discuss what they think and understand about a subject directs their reflections, although it does not preclude rhetorical elegance: my admiration remains undimmed for Eamonn's verbal felicity: 'There's nothing on earth would make me believe in god, but I'm an agnostic where ghosts are concerned'[9] (Cowdell 2006 [2010]: 71).

However, the relative infrequency of *purely* rhetorical vernacular usages of the terminologies of belief, metaphors above all, does not mean they are excluded. Leo, one of the few informants with an articulated philosophical atheism, was unusual in using 'ghosts' purely metaphorically for the memories and experiences of his youth. That it had no other available meaning for him may have shaped this use, although he discussed other people's beliefs and experiences with serious engagement. This was also true of Gerry, whose description of a long-past sleep paralysis experience was the more remarkable for being so infrequently recounted; an atheist by philosophical consideration, Gerry had no comfortable natural language for it but, like other informants who did not believe in ghosts, he related this and another anomalous experience he did not consider supernatural solely to aid my research.

In the absence of dedicated research into vernacular rhetorical usages, rather than considering terms as collateral to an investigation of belief narratives, we cannot generalize confidently about the possible concentration of such uses among non-believers or the circumstances under which believers might employ them. It would be reductive and implausible to expect a direct correlation between belief and rhetorical facility. Even in my research the capacity for self-deprecatory humour among ghost believers and religious practitioners secure within their own emic groups was evident. There was amusement at an SNU church that *Psychic News* had given the wrong date for a clairvoyance service: laughed one congregant, 'If they were psychic they'd have known'.

This is not always acknowledged in academic writing. Rather than proceeding from meaning to metaphor, some cultural commentators move to detach metaphors of ghosts and haunting from all but literary grounds.

Such metaphors became 'fashionable in academic discourse' primarily through Derrida's appeal to Marx's witty 1867 comparison of the supernatural and material (Motz 1998: 339; Marx 1990 [1967]: 163–164). Post-Derridean commentators, however, have not always felt the need to deal, like Marx, with both metaphorical and literal usages. Ethnographic traditions of discussion have been relegated and empirical data disregarded, and a textual focus has led to a proliferation of academic neologisms.

The key text, Avery F. Gordon's often elegant disquisition on postmodernism and sociology, has been described as 'possibly more influential than Derrida's' (Lincoln and Lincoln 2015: 194). Although it does speak to scholars of ghost belief, *Ghostly Matters* is an extended search for metaphors at the expense of their possible ethnographic meanings: the chapter on the Argentinian *desaparecidos* determinedly never considers them ethnographically (Gordon 2008 [1997]: 63–135). This is frustrating, and highlights what is missed: excellent folklore work on ghost narratives generated by local tragedies and the interrelationship between legend and belief could have fruitfully opened further research and restrained the speculative rhetoric.[10] Ghost belief and narratives may in fact *decline* proportionate to the scale of catastrophe. When my informant Ray summarized his reasons for disbelief in ghosts as being that 'there are no ghosts at Auschwitz' he was encapsulating a question that folklorists have been exploring around individual and group catastrophes, where different narrative genres may be employed to reflect differing scales of loss. Ilana Harlow's persuasive argument that 'while large-scale catastrophe can be affiliated with the genre of myth, local or personal tragedy can be affiliated with the legend' itself indicates a contributory factor in emic conceptualizations of ghosts and haunting (1993: 178).

Not all scholars interested in literary metaphors are oblivious to vernacular usages, but they often seem ignorant of, or lack interest in, studying the relationship between the two, and do not notice that vernacular discussions of belief invariably involve some self-scrutiny. Julian Holloway and James Kneale, for example, recognize that not all usages are metaphors, but get no further. They suggest that 'those interested in haunting and spectrality might look in one of the places where these manifestations tend to be quite common: the ghost story' (2008: 299, 301–302). Having looked to fictionalized textual sources, the authors do not see that discussion and measurement are also involved in the way real people talk about beliefs and stories.

At worst, scholars of metaphor display more than confusion and ignorance: they actively dismiss other usages and discount in advance any ethnographic consideration that might destabilize such literary appropriation. Sociologist Michael Mayerfeld Bell's 'The Ghosts of Place' (1997), referencing Avery Gordon, is an appropriately extreme example. Bell looks to expropriate 'ghost' from literal usages for his own nebulous metaphors: his 'ghost' starts as a version of memory attached to place and becomes a reading of a *relative* reality. This depends on a partial reading of Sigmund Freud, whom he accuses of failing to see that 'The ghosts of place may seem uncanny at times, but they are nevertheless a familiar and often homey part of our lives' (ibid.: 816, 834 n.14). Freud's (1985: 342–345) discussion of the contradictory and interrelated meanings of *heimlich/unheimlich* addresses that very point.

Bell's attempt to construct a rhetoric remains interesting to folklorists because vernacular usages nevertheless persist, forcing him to deliberately exclude ethnography. He moves instead to replace a wider consideration of vernacular usages by calling a focus on his own experience reflexive: 'Much of the evidence I use is reflexive, that is, drawn from my own experience of place' (Bell 1997: 816). In fact, his use of personal experience directly rules out reflexivity because Bell refuses to place himself and his experience in any broader context. Leo's remark to me is a reminder that such rhetorical constructions cannot be excluded as a vernacular device, but Bell's specific usage would invalidate all other levels of discussion, summarized by his disdainful 'I don't believe in *that* kind of ghost'. Shortly after discussing with me her serious thinking about ghost experiences and their meanings, one informant, Elisabeth, posted on social media the comment 'Ghosts ... the air is full of them in Whitechapel, all chattering at once. I've heard them'. This was metaphorical (not directly related to experience and practice) but interacted with her wider theoretical reflections. Bell's approach would deny her this. In doing so he also appears to miss, perhaps purposively, moments when legend nexuses arise, and the opportunities they provide for considering the content and meaning of vernacular speech about belief and experience (Bell 1997: 826–827).

These problems are increasingly being recognized: 'Initiatives in the new hauntology ... typically base themselves on a scant and idiosyncratic evidentiary foundation, developing the trope of haunting without considering how ghosts are theorized by those who take them as something other than metaphor' (Lincoln and Lincoln 2015: 196). Academic metaphors have led to disregarding the very people whose beliefs and practices we should be considering. María del Pilar Blanco and Esther Peeren (2013) recognize the tension between academic metaphorical usage and vernacular belief, but at the latter's expense. They claim, questionably, that 'the inclination to take the ghost literally largely abated over the course of the twentieth century, turning believing in actual ghosts (as the dead returned to life or able to communicate with the living) into something of a fringe eccentricity' but only to argue that scholars have suffered: 'its lingering association with such notions seems to have rendered the ghostly somewhat toxic for scholars seeking to be taken seriously'. Their complaint is that literal usages and beliefs, and their vernacular consideration, restrict academic metaphors: 'the widespread obsession with proving or disproving the reality of spiritualist feats and related phenomena ... prevented the ghost's figurative potential from fully emancipating itself' (del Pilar Blanco and Peeren 2013: 3).

Sociologist Martyn Hudson (2017: xi–xii) has written that 'Ghostly experiences are fabulated, fictionalised, and re-narrated', noting that 'In a sense it matters not what the original experience was so much as why it is re-told, what does it perform, and what happens socially around that retelling', but he then excludes any vernacular consideration of this, calling the experiences only 'the product of mistake, hallucination and delusion'. In a patrician tone worthy of Bell he declares he has 'little interest whether those experiences were delusional or pathological ... the most enigmatic question is really why those social delusions and pathologies remain so compelling in so many different social formations and historical epochs'. Treating them in this way makes impossible any serious treatment of negotiations of belief synchronically, much less diachronically (ibid.).[11]

I am not advocating uncritical agreement with informants. That is not how they deal with these questions, and my criticism of Bell's version of reflexivity also applies to scholars who manoeuvre on reflexivity to legitimize their own beliefs. The history of parapsychological research is torn fruitlessly and unnecessarily between these extremes, but informants carry on assessing, debating and disputing their beliefs in narrative forms. Rather than isolating this process from its attendant practices and inventing an ugly and unnecessary rhetoric that overlooks it altogether, would it be too much to ask that scholars actually look at it in context?

## Acknowledgements

When I was initially invited to contribute to this book, I was extremely unwell and unable to participate. I am extremely grateful to the editors for keeping open their invitation until I had recovered sufficiently to contribute, and I must acknowledge the late Leonard Primiano's solicitousness during my recovery. I bear full responsibility for the results, but I remain overwhelmed by and indebted to their kindnesses.

## Notes

1. My background argument is in Cowdell 2013: 161–162. I remain indebted to Bennett 1987: 26.
2. I had collected some ghost narratives in previous fieldwork, but the 2008–2010 research mentioned here was conducted during work at the University of Hertfordshire towards a PhD on contemporary belief in ghosts. I conducted research by interview, participant observation, questionnaire and email, seeking to investigate how informants understood ghosts, the details of their experiences and beliefs, and the relationship of these beliefs to broader, more congregational beliefs. For a summary of this fieldwork, see Cowdell 2013: 159–160. The doctoral fieldwork documented material from 227 informants. For details of the methodologies, see Cowdell 2011: 25–30. All informants were anonymized in accordance with University of Hertfordshire Faculty of Humanities, Law and Education Ethics Committee protocol 07.08.17. Cowdell 2006 [2010], submitted before that fieldwork began, covers the earlier collectanea, and the names used there have been changed to conform with the wider body of work. Subsequent fieldwork conducted since completion of the PhD has also been anonymized correspondingly. I have used throughout single forenames to indicate each anonymized informant.
3. My original observations on this were made on a prior version of the website, originally accessed September 14, 2010 (Cowdell 2011: 121). The whole site has been regularly and comprehensively rewritten during the drafting of this chapter, but this page is archived at https://web.archive.org/web/20170826140545/http://www.snu.org.uk/spiritualism/principles (accessed June 14, 2021).
4. This page has since been deleted from the website, but is archived at https://web.archive.org/web/20170912120052/http://www.snu.org.uk/spiritualism/religion (accessed June 14, 2021).
5. 'Is It Time Spiritualism Cut All Ties with Christianity?', first published December 17, 1993, in *Psychic News*. The blog page 'Spiritualism: Are You Dying from Democracy?' (Hamilton-Parker 1993–1994) brings together his *Psychic News* articles, but does not give all original publication dates.
6. From 'Cut All Ties' and 'Spiritualists are Urged to Listen to the East', first published 1994, now on Hamilton-Parker 1993–1994.
7. Hamilton-Parker's comments from 'The Magnificent Seven', first published 1994, now on Hamilton-Parker 1993–1994.

8 Some of these ideas were stimulated by Alan Phillips's talk 'Making Sense of Mythology', Quay Arts, Newport, Isle of Wight, October 5, 2017, although he may not recognize my use of them.
9 The question of narrative genres, with some reflection on artistry within legends, is considered further at Cowdell 2006 [2010]: 72–75. That article also acknowledges the breadth of scholarly meanings of 'legend' (ibid.: 71), leaning particularly on the work of Juha Pentikäinen (1973). To clarify the dating of Cowdell 2006 [2010]: the journal issue was dated 2006 for the purposes of journal continuity, but was published in 2010, the paper on which the article was based being given in April 2008.
10 Work has been done on exactly this aspect of Argentinian ghostlore by María Inés Palleiro (2012).
11 I am grateful to Jesse Fivecoate for pointing this out, and our subsequent discussion of it.

## References

Adler, Margot. 1986 [1979]. *Drawing Down the Moon: Witches, Druids, Goddess-Worshippers, and Other Pagans in America Today*. Revised edn. Boston, MA: Beacon.

Adler, Margot. 2006 [1979]. *Drawing Down the Moon: Witches, Druids, Goddess-Worshippers, and Other Pagans in America Today*. Revised edn. New York: Penguin.

Al-Rawi, Ahmed. 2009. 'The Mythical Ghoul in Arabic Culture'. *Cultural Analysis* 8: 45–69.

Barrow, Logie. 1986. *Independent Spirits: Spiritualism and English Plebeians, 1850–1910*. London: Routledge & Kegan Paul.

Bell, Michael Mayerfeld. 1997. 'The Ghosts of Place'. *Theory and Society* 26 (6): 813–836. https://doi.org/10.1023/A:1006888230610

Bennett, Gillian. 1987. *Traditions of Belief: Women and the Supernatural*. London; Harmondsworth: Penguin.

Cowdell, Paul. 2006 [2010]. '"You saw the ghost, didn't you? There's someone wants to ask you about it": Occupational Ghostlore, Narrative, and Belief'. *Contemporary Legend*, new series 9: 69–82.

Cowdell, Paul. 2011. 'Belief in Ghosts in Post-War England'. PhD diss, University of Hertfordshire. https://uhra.herts.ac.uk/handle/2299/7184 (accessed March 23, 2022).

Cowdell, Paul. 2013. '"A giant bedsheet with the holes cut out": Expectations and Discussions of the Appearance of Ghosts'. In *The Ashgate Research Companion to Paranormal Cultures*, edited by Olu Jenzen and Sally R. Munt, 159–169. Farnham: Ashgate.

Dick, Oliver Lawson, ed. 1962. *John Aubrey's Brief Lives*. Harmondsworth: Penguin.

El-Zein, Amira. 2009. 'Doctrinal Islam and Folk Islam'. *Cultural Analysis* 8: 67–69.

Ezzy, Douglas. 2014. *Sex, Death and Witchcraft: A Contemporary Pagan Festival*. London: Bloomsbury.

Freud, Sigmund. 1985. *Art and Literature*, translated by James Strachey, edited by Albert Dickson. London: Penguin.

Gordon, Avery. 2008 [1997]. *Ghostly Matters: Haunting and the Sociological Imagination*. Minneapolis: University of Minnesota Press.

Hamilton-Parker, Craig. 1993–1994. 'Spiritualism: Are You Dying from Democracy?' *Craig & Jane Hamilton-Parker*. http://psychics.co.uk/blog/spiritualism/ (accessed March 23, 2022).

Harlow, Ilana. 1993. 'Unravelling Stories: Exploring the Juncture of Ghost Story and Local Tragedy'. *Journal of Folklore Research* 30 (2–3): 177–200.

Haynes, Renée. 1982. *The Society for Psychical Research, 1882-1982: A History*. London: Macdonald.

Holloway, Julian, and James Kneale. 2008. 'Locating Haunting: A Ghost-Hunter's Guide'. *Cultural Geographies* 15 (3): 297–312. https://doi.org/10.1177/1474474008091329

Howard, Robert Glenn. 2013. 'Vernacular Authority: Critically Engaging "Tradition"'. In *Tradition in the Twenty-First Century: Locating the Role of the Past in the Present*, edited by Trevor J. Blank and Robert Glenn Howard, 72–99. Logan: Utah State University Press. https://doi.org/10.7330/9780874218992.c03

Hudson, Martyn. 2017. *Ghosts, Landscapes and Social Memory*. Abingdon; New York: Routledge. https://doi.org/10.4324/9781315306674

Hunter, Jack. 2009. 'Experiencing SNU Spiritualism'. *Paranthropology*. http://paranthropology.weebly.com/snu-spiritualism.html (accessed June 3, 2022).

Hutton, Ronald. 1999. 'Modern Pagan Witchcraft'. In *The Athlone History of Witchcraft and Magic in Europe*, vol. 6: *The Twentieth Century*, edited by Bengt Ankarloo and Stuart Clark, 1–79. London: The Athlone Press.

Joynes, Andrew, ed. 2001. *Medieval Ghost Stories: An Anthology of Miracles, Marvels, and Prodigies*. Woodbridge: The Boydell Press.

Lincoln, Martha, and Bruce Lincoln. 2015. 'Toward a Critical Hauntology: Bare Afterlife and the Ghosts of Ba Chúc'. *Comparative Studies in Society and History* 57 (1): 191–220. https://doi.org/10.1017/S0010417514000644

Marx, Karl. 1990 [1867]. *Capital: A Critique of Political Economy*, vol. 1, translated by Ben Fowkes. London: Penguin.

McDowell, John Holmes. 2011. 'Customizing Myth: The Personal in the Public'. In *The Individual and Tradition: Folkloristic Perspectives*, edited by Ray Cashman, Tom Mould and Pravina Shukla, 323–342. Bloomington; Indianapolis: Indiana University Press.

McGarry, Molly. 2008. *Ghosts of Futures Past: Spiritualism and the Cultural Politics of Nineteenth-Century America*. Berkeley: University of California Press. https://doi.org/10.1525/9780520934061

Motz, Marilyn. 1998. 'The Practice of Belief'. *Journal of American Folklore* 111 (441): 339–355. https://doi.org/10.2307/541314

Olrik, Axel. 1992. *Principles for Oral Narrative Research*, translated by Kirsten Wolf and Jody Jensen. Bloomington; Indianapolis: Indiana University Press.

Palleiro, María Inés. 2012. 'Haunted Houses and Haunting Girls: Life and Death in Contemporary Argentinian Folk Narrative'. In *Vernacular Religion in Everyday Life*, edited by Marion Bowman and Ülo Valk, 211–229. Sheffield; Bristol, CT: Equinox Publishing.

Pentikäinen, Juha. 1973. 'Belief, Memorate, and Legend'. Translated by Josephine Lombardo and William Kinneth McNeil. *Folklore Forum* 6 (4): 217–241.

Pew Research Center. 2018. 'Being Christian in Western Europe'. Pew Research Center, May 29, 2018. https://www.pewresearch.org/religion/wp-content/uploads/sites/7/2018/05/Being-Christian-in-Western-Europe-FOR-WEB1.pdf (accessed June 2, 2022).

del Pilar Blanco, Maria, and Esther Peeren. 2013. 'Introduction: Conceptualizing Spectralities'. In *The Spectralities Reader: Ghosts and Haunting in Contemporary Cultural Theory*, edited by Maria del Pilar Blanco and Esther Peeren, 1–27. New York; London: Bloomsbury Academic.

Primiano, Leonard Norman. 2001. 'What is Vernacular Catholicism? The "Dignity" Example'. *Acta Ethnographica Hungarica* 46 (1): 51–58.
https://doi.org/10.1556/AEthn.46.2001.1-2.6

Primiano, Leonard Norman. 2012. 'Afterword: Manifestations of the Religious Vernacular: Ambiguity, Power, and Creativity'. In *Vernacular Religion in Everyday Life: Expressions of Belief*, edited by Marion Bowman and Ülo Valk, 382–394. Sheffield; Bristol, CT: Equinox Publishing.

Rae-Ellis, Vivienne. 1990. *True Ghost Stories of Our Own Time*. London: Faber and Faber.

Robertson Smith, William. 1998. 'Lectures on the Religion of the Semites: Lecture I'. In *The Myth and Ritual Theory: An Anthology*, edited by Robert A. Segal, 17–34. Malden, MA; Oxford: Blackwell.

Shannon-Missal, Larry. 2013. 'Americans' Belief in God, Miracles and Heaven Declines'. *The Harris Poll*, #97, December 16, 2013. https://theharrispoll.com/new-york-n-y-december-16-2013-a-new-harris-poll-finds-that-while-a-strong-majority-74-of-u-s-adults-do-believe-in-god-this-belief-is-in-decline-when-compared-to-previous-years-as-just-over/ (accessed March 23, 2022).

SNU. n.d.a. 'The Religion of Spiritualism'. *Spiritualists' National Union*. https://web.archive.org/web/20170912120052/http:/www.snu.org.uk/spiritualism/religion (accessed June 14, 2021).

SNU. n.d.b. 'The 7 Principles'. *Spiritualists' National Union*. https://web.archive.org/web/20170826140545/http:/www.snu.org.uk/spiritualism/principles (accessed June 14, 2021).

SNU. n.d.c. '7 Principles'. *Spiritualists' National Union*. https://www.snu.org.uk/7-principles (accessed August 2, 2021).

Taylor, Humphrey. 2007. 'The Religious and Other Beliefs of Americans'. *The Harris Poll*, November 29, 2007. https://theharrispoll.com/wp-content/uploads/2017/12/Harris-Interactive-Poll-Research-Religious-Beliefs-2007-11.pdf (accessed June 14, 2021).

# Afterword: 25 Years of Vernacular Religion Scholarship

*Marion Bowman*\*

In this volume we have presented vernacular knowledge as a realm of discourses and beliefs, challenging institutional authorities and official truths, and bestowing upon groups and individuals distinctive forms of vernacular authority. Our case studies have demonstrated the conceptual and methodological complexities surrounding how people negotiate, narrate and contest authority in a variety of contexts. They highlight people's use of traditional forms of expression as means of acquiring and enacting agency in their daily interaction and discourses in relation to institutionalized, political, religious and other formal manifestations of authority and power. The examples have dealt not only with religious virtuosi but with 'ordinary' people as they articulate, create and maintain lifeworlds in their everyday lives. In this afterword, I briefly highlight some significant themes and issues to have emerged in relation to vernacular knowledge, vernacular authority and vernacular religion in

---

\* **Marion Bowman** has been based in Religious Studies at The Open University UK since 2000. She has conducted long-term research in the town of Glastonbury, on which she has published extensively, and has also written on vernacular religion, pilgrimage, Celtic spirituality, material religion, spiritual economies, and religion in Newfoundland. She was Co-Investigator on the AHRC funded project Pilgrimage and England's Cathedrals, Past and Present (2014–2018), and a visiting Professor at the University of Oslo (2016–2018) and the University of Tartu (2014). She co-edited *Vernacular Religion in Everyday Life: Expressions of Belief* (Equinox, 2012) with Ülo Valk; a Thematic Issue on *Religion in Cathedrals: Pilgrimage, Place, Heritage, and the Politics of Replication* with Simon Coleman (*Religion* 49 (1), 2019); and a Special Issue on *Reframing Pilgrimage in Northern Europe* (*NUMEN* 67 (5–6), 2020) with Dirk Johannsen and Ane Ohrvik.

the foregoing chapters. I then focus on vernacular religion specifically, and the significance of the scholarship and legacy of Leonard Norman Primiano, to whom this volume is dedicated.

Narratives naturally emerge in this volume as powerful strategic tools for expressing vernacular beliefs and 'mythtories', a useful phrase used by some in Glastonbury to express the impossibility of disentangling 'conventional' history from myth in certain contexts (Bowman 2003–2004). From legend to memorate, narratives can be sometimes conflicting, sometimes empowering, frequently with real world social, political, economic and power ramifications—as we see in the chapters presented by Martin Wood, Ülo Valk and Reep Pandi Lepcha. The contestation of authority and expression of beliefs tend to be multivocal enterprises; while they may be shared and shaped communally, they are nevertheless individually articulated and actualized. Vernacular knowledge and vernacular religion are invariably embedded in particular lifeworlds, and repeatedly demonstrate the resilience of certain ideas, beliefs and praxis, as exemplified here in relation to the persistence, manoeuvring and re-negotiations of traditions in changed and changing circumstances in the studies by Margaret Lyngdoh on the afterlife beliefs and related death customs of different Khasi clans, and Alevtina Solovyeva in her exploration of demonological beliefs, narratives and ritual praxis in rural Mongolia.

Not only serious narratives, but jokes, parodies and other traditional humorous verbal strategies can become significant modes of articulating, testing and contesting authority. In Irina Sadovina's article on the counter-cultural Anastasia movement, for example, we are shown communities of people who to some extent have put themselves beyond the pale of 'conventional' institutions and knowledge using these humorous forms to challenge and renegotiate Vladimir Megre's authority in their own construction of spiritual lifeworlds. Moreover, different vehicles of expression (online, face to face, social media, forums, networks, etc.) have provided new arenas for contestation, the articulation of beliefs, the construction of vernacular knowledge, and community building, as demonstrated by Robert Glenn Howard in the context of a New Age internet forum. People 'communicating, thinking, behaving within, and conforming to, particular cultural circumstances' (Primiano 1995: 42) are nonetheless able as individuals to creatively interpret, adapt and negotiate 'any number of influential sources' (Primiano 2012: 384) as well as means of expression and communication.

As the authors have shown here, vernacular knowledge tends to be fluid, ambivalent, pragmatic, multivalent. Vernacular religion and vernacular knowledge can challenge the apparent (though often illusory) homogeneity of dominant discourses and the hegemony of institutionalized authorities, to creatively utilize or subvert tradition in myriad contexts and forms. That inter-relationship is complex and interwoven. The Inochentists described by James Kapaló, for example, in their creative use of photomontage techniques and mass-produced photo icons, were simultaneously drawing on and challenging traditional orthodox Christian forms in their particular manifestation of religiosity. Ruth Illman's study of contemporary practices of *niggunim* demonstrates the assumption of individual authority in relation to vernacular understandings of authenticity and appropriate praxis, through the creative re-articulation and re-negotiation of one aspect of Jewish tradition. These exemplify Primiano's insistence on 'the power of the individual and communities of individuals to create and re-create their own religion' (Primiano 2012: 383).

While some manifestations of vernacular knowledge and religion may appear to be 'under the radar', there is an argument for recognizing the 'ambience' of vernacular forms as one aspect of their potency. Hillary Kaell, in her article on wayside crosses in rural Québec, explains that for anthropologists of religion, 'ambience refers to forces that are backgrounded but ubiquitous, filtering in and out of our sensory space' (2017: 139). She therefore characterizes the wayside crosses in terms of 'ambient Catholicism' in a notionally secular setting. This characterization of the concept of ambience can be usefully applied in relation to vernacular religion and vernacular knowledge, and by extension to vernacular authority. In devotion to Gauchito Gil, for instance, the ubiquity of visual reminders of Gil and the variety of ways in which he might be encountered among those who don't actively engage with him or go to his Mercedes shrine—the flash of red at a roadside shrine, the bumper stickers, the statue of him alongside more conventional saints, and so on—constantly reinforce his presence and legitimacy through ambience as opposed to proselytization. In Anastasiya Astapova's examples of political folklore in contemporary Belarus, by being entangled with official discourses despite their ambivalence towards them, the legends become 'forces that are backgrounded but ubiquitous' (Kaell 2017: 139).

Contesting authority might simultaneously involve assuming, expressing and exercising authority. Steven Sutcliffe's vernacular biographies of seekership underline the persistence of 'the quest' for meaning-making and the construction of lifeworlds in culturally fluid contexts with broad and flexible repertoires of potential resources, with vernacular knowledge and authority individually articulated and actualized in personal beliefs and praxis. In some cases, however, such as that of Kathy Jones, the seeker (perhaps ironically) becomes an authority figure for others. Among Paul Cowdell's respondents, too, some have been serial seekers, crafting mixes of received family or local wisdom, popular contemporary paganisms, individual experiences and their understanding of both Christianity and Spiritualism in their own formulations of knowledge about ghosts. Focusing on black Madonnas, Melanie Landman draws attention to two broad sets of knowledge and strategies in negotiations of authority—widespread feminist vernacular knowledge, which has become an authoritative source for many, and the locally negotiated and contested, experientially-verified vernacular Anglicanism of a London parish. Kristel Kivari's work on dowsing in the context of the Estonian Geopathic Association highlights the importance not only of articulated vernacular knowledge but also the non-verbal and sensory in the experience and acquisition of certain forms of knowledge and authority. Vernacular knowledge, vernacular authority and vernacular religion emerge repeatedly as experientially based, internally and externally contested, responsive, fluid and creative.

A common theme in relation to some of the chapters has been that of *our* experiences as researchers, and how we are positioned in relation to the experiences, vernacular knowledge and authority of our informants, consultants, interlocutors or however we prefer to term them. These are the people on whom we rely to share generously with us their beliefs, knowledge, stories, praxis, experienced realities and lifeworlds. Valk reflects upon the disconcerting position into which a researcher can be put when confronted by conflicting claims, each 'verified' by narratives and authoritatively stated 'proofs'. Kivari reflects upon the 'philosophical gap in understanding between perception, consciousness and culturally transformed principles' and asks concerning her own experiences in relation to dowsing 'How should I trust my feelings, be they physical or inner impressions?' (this volume, p. 210). The need for scholarly reflexivity has long been recognized, at both individual and disciplinary levels; when we interpose our academic baggage and personal perceptions in the manifestations of others' lifeworlds we bear a heavy responsibility. Liana Chua rightly cautions against presuming that '"knowledge" and "knowing" work for "others" as they do for ethnographers' (2009: 344), and Primiano contends that 'Vernacular religion challenges all of folklore to extend ethnographic reflexivity into the interdisciplinary domain of methodological reflexivity' (1995: 56). It is our job to take seriously and convey as accurately as possible the lifeworlds of others, as far as possible analysing without imposing inappropriate frameworks or ignoring aspects that do not fall neatly into *our* categories. The failure to appropriately engage with the manifestations of vernacular knowledge, the sources and processes inherent in vernacular authority, and the nuanced and complex creativity of vernacular religion, can diminish our apprehension of vital aspects of human behaviour. As Cowdell observes in this volume, 'The balance between consistency and contradiction, orthodoxy and heterodoxy, stern formality and imaginative leaps, is negotiated by believers/practitioners with remarkable adaptation, flexibility and grace, but scholars describing the same processes have managed less well' (this volume, p. 386).

Our chapters, then, have highlighted the importance of vernacular processes and means of expression, and what happens to beliefs, traditions, narratives and praxis when they are challenged *in situ* by changed religious, cultural or political power structures, or removed from their original context and re-used, recycled or re-positioned in different contexts. They have exemplified the creative role of individuals in making choices, activating, reinterpreting or bypassing tradition, and constructing complex identities and lifeworlds by drawing on different and (in some contexts) ever proliferating sources or 'pools' (Honko 2000) of tradition. And they have reminded us of the necessity of scholarly reflexivity and the extent to which we too are involved in complex (re)negotiations and (re)positionings in relation to personal experience, academic traditions and societal assumptions when we engage with the lifeworlds of others.

## The Study of Vernacular Religion and the Contribution of Leonard Norman Primiano (1957–2021)[1]

For many of us, engagement with concepts such as vernacular knowledge and vernacular authority developed as a result of first embracing Leonard Primiano's concept of vernacular religion. Having first used the terminology in a 1985 article ('Feminist Christian Songs: Occasions of Vernacular Religious Belief'), it was Leonard Primiano's 'Vernacular Religion and the Search for Method in Religious Folklife' published in 1995 that increasingly attracted attention and influenced subsequent scholarship. That article brought about significant refocusing in both Folklore Studies/Ethnology and Religious Studies in relation to how we might study, conceptualize, engage with and treat respectfully the messy, complex and creative reality of the ways in which people are religious and 'do religion' in their everyday lives.

Leonard's academic sure-footedness in this field was in great part due to his solid background in both Religious Studies and Folklore and Folklife Studies, with a BA in Religious Studies from the University of Pennsylvania (1978), a Master of Theological Studies from Harvard Divinity School (1980), then a Master's degree in Folklore and Folklife (1982) followed by a dual doctorate in Religious Studies *and* Folklore and Folklife Studies from the University of Pennsylvania (1993). Leonard's influential mentor at the University of Pennsylvania was folk religion scholar Don Yoder, with whom he was to develop a lifelong friendship. As we have commented elsewhere (Sutcliffe and Bowman 2000; Bowman and Valk 2012a), Religious Studies has been accused of being somewhat 'Protestant' in its focus on texts and statements of beliefs, downplaying or dismissing ritual activities, embodied praxis and material culture, and largely ignoring non- or extra-institutional manifestations of religiosity and individual creativity in relation to it. Within folklore studies, Yoder had promoted the study of religious folklife ('the folk-cultural dimensions of religion, or the religious dimension of folk culture') and deftly described folk religion as 'the totality of all those views and practices of religion that exist among the people apart from and alongside the strictly theological and liturgical forms of the official religion' (Yoder 1974: 13). Leonard recognized that 'one of the hallmarks of the study of religion by folklorists has been their attempt to do justice to belief and lived experience' (1995: 41). Nevertheless, over time Leonard increasingly felt that while the folkloristic study of religion was rich and textured, he was concerned with two big issues: the problems inherent in the binary model of official *and* folk religion or official *versus* folk religion, and the overlooking and underrating of the role of individuals in specific contexts including the ways in which they creatively negotiate their religiosity. These were highlighted in the 1995 article.

For Leonard, vernacular religion was religion *per se*, 'religion as it is lived: as human beings encounter, understand, interpret, and practice it' (1995: 44). It is emphatically *not* merely a synonym for folk religion! He insisted that terms such as 'folk', 'popular' and 'unofficial' when applied to the study of religion and belief were divisive and inappropriate, perpetuating status differences and false dichotomies. As 'an interdisciplinary approach to the study of the religious lives of individuals with special attention to the process of religious belief, the verbal, behavioral, and material expressions of religious belief, and the ultimate object of religious belief' (1995: 44), vernacular religion was envisaged as a means of seriously, respectfully and realistically engaging with how people live religion, and recognizing its all-embracing nature. He was passionately interested in material culture and its role in the creation and expression of people's beliefs and lifeworlds, and the role of individual agency and creativity within religion, themes emphatically reiterated in his 2012 afterword to *Vernacular Religion in Everyday Life: Expressions of Belief*, 'Manifestations of the Religious Vernacular: Ambiguity, Power and Creativity'.

A prolific author and authority in a number of fields, Leonard's conceptualization and articulation of vernacular religion as both subject and methodology were developed and refined in the quarter of a century following the publication of the ground-breaking 1995 article as he applied it in a variety of contexts. For his 1993 PhD dissertation Leonard had written about the Philadelphia chapter of the gay and lesbian Roman Catholic organization Dignity during the AIDS crisis (1993a; 1993b), and he continued to reflect upon the deep insights that experience had fostered (e.g. Primiano 2001; this volume). Passionately interested in and entranced by material culture, he studied it *inter alia* in relation to vernacular Catholicism (e.g. Primiano 1999; 2007; 2012; 2016), the hooked rugs of independent evangelical Sister Ann Ameen (Primiano 2002), and religious kitsch (Primiano 2015). He also curated numerous exhibitions, including Graces Received: Painted and Metal Ex-Votos from Italy which was based on his personal collection of Italian ex-votos (see Briscese and Sciorra 2012). Having curated Cabrini's Religious Folk, Popular, Liturgical Arts Collection from its inception in 2002, to his great satisfaction, he coordinated in 2006 its acquisition of the Don Yoder Collection of Religious Folk Art. For decades Leonard worked sensitively and respectfully with the racially mixed, Philadelphia-based community of Father Divine's International Peace Mission movement, and wrote about diverse aspects of the community, their beliefs, material culture and praxis (e.g. Primiano 2004; 2009; 2014; 2017). That is why Leonard invariably prefaced any communication with 'Peace!', the standard greeting within the movement.

A great communicator and international networker, Leonard was a significant participant in the conferences of the American Folklore Society (from 2002 co-chairing with Margaret Kruesi its Folk Belief and Religious Folklife section); the American Academy of Religion (where he co-chaired the Folklore and Religion Seminar from 2015); and SIEF (International

Society for Ethnology and Folklore), at whose Ethnology of Religion working group events he became a regular from 1996–2019. These examples merely scratch the surface of a rich and varied body of work and spheres of activity, but it is important to give a flavour of Leonard's considerable output and endeavour *beyond* 'Vernacular Religion and the Search for Method in Religious Folklife'. Even among those who espouse vernacular religion, some of his work after the seminal 1995 article remains comparatively neglected, which means that almost a quarter of a century of his reflections on, and refinement and application of, vernacular religious theory and methodology to a broad range of topics and contexts remain relatively underexplored. Other topics he worked on include American television, popular culture, shops, and African-based religions.[2]

It is fair to say that both Ülo Valk and I have been instrumental advocates of vernacular religion (Bowman and Valk 2012b). In addition to Ülo Valk's own wide-ranging scholarship (e.g. Valk 2018; 2019a; 2019b; 2021), the impressive international reach of the graduate programme of the Department of Estonian and Comparative Folklore, University of Tartu, Estonia has disseminated knowledge of it, and produced several dissertations on vernacular religion and beliefs (e.g. Sepp 2014; Kivari 2016; Lyngdoh 2016; Sadovina 2020; Solovyeva 2021; Bhutia 2022; Saikia 2022). In the UK, where the academic study of folklore is not well established, from 1991 I had been arguing from within the Study of Religion that we needed a more rounded and realistic view of what religion entailed in order to fully apprehend it; I had proposed a fluid, interactive model involving folk religion, official or institutional religion and individual religion, comprising both the individual's 'received' religious tradition (that is, what a person learns from family, cultural context and others in addition to institutional sources) and personal belief system, based on experience and efficacy (Bowman 2004 [1992]). Having met Leonard in 1995, I became an enthusiastic embracer of vernacular religion, drawing attention to it in Britain and elsewhere through my own work (e.g. Bowman 2000; 2004 [1992]; 2009; 2014; 2016; 2017). My institution, The Open University, has embedded vernacular religion in many of its religious studies modules, and there too our PhD students have made creative scholarly use of it (e.g. Lassander 2012; Whitehead 2013; Wanless 2021).

In some contexts, vernacular religion had almost immediate resonance and traction, not only in North America but in some Nordic countries where study of religion scholars have been used to working cooperatively with colleagues in folklore studies; examples of this fruitful interaction would include Åbo Akademi and the University of Turku in Finland and the University of Bergen, Norway. For some scholars, however, the term 'vernacular' has proved puzzling, inappropriate or problematic—and to Leonard's immense annoyance, some do use vernacular religion as a synonym for folk religion! The concept and methodology of vernacular religion nevertheless have been theoretically finessed and creatively developed in new ways and in a range of contexts (recently, for example, Kapaló and Povedák 2021; Illman and Czimbalmos 2020; Chryssides and Gregg 2019; Nygaard 2019; Magliocco 2018; Hiiemäe 2017; Goldstein 2015) and work on refining and developing them further continues.

It became increasingly clear as we were preparing this volume that Leonard's health was deteriorating alarmingly, and it is a tribute to Leonard's resilience and determination that his chapter was completed. He knew that this volume would be dedicated to him. In 'The Upper Room: Domestic Space, Vernacular Religion, and the Observant University Catholic', before proceeding to his case study, Leonard addresses criticisms that vernacular religion underplays the political and power nuances of religion, and his emphasis on the religiously personal as overly individualistic. Leonard's passion for orchestral music and opera are manifested in the example of the ubiquity of vernacular religion he gives, pointing out vernacular religious aspects of Puccini's opera *Tosca*. The detailed case study of the materiality of the 'Upper Room' and what that said about both his consultant's positioning in relation to his college context as well as the significance of individual objects in relation to family, tradition and religion; the highly personal and creative ways in which his consultant was negotiating and weaving together a number of diverse 'influential sources'; and the implications of this 'interpretative diversity' for his future as a Catholic priest where he might be a communicator of vernacular belief and practice *within* the institutional Church all reinforced for Leonard 'what surprises can emerge in relation to vernacular religion and material culture, and why such artful riches need to be identified and studied'.

Primiano noted that just as 'vernacular religion can be a process of contestation—of coming to a new understanding of religion—so vernacular religious "studies" can be a contestatory process in the midst of the study of religion' (2012: 390). Leonard Primiano's scholarship on vernacular religion and the myriad studies it has inspired or influenced have, as he desired, contributed to 'new approaches to the study of religion' (ibid.).

We have explored in this volume the value, nuances, importance, ubiquity, ambivalence and ambience of vernacular knowledge, vernacular authority and vernacular religion and their roles in contesting authority and expressing beliefs. Our hope would be that this work too will contribute to greater appreciation of, and further research and innovation in, these fields.

## Notes

1 Numerous tributes were paid to Leonard following his death, and his work, legacy and huge personality have been celebrated in online media, at conferences, and in obituaries for publications including *Folklore* (Bowman 2022) and *Journal of American Folklore* (Magliocco 2022).
2 As a tribute to his significant contributions to religious and folklore studies, a group of American Religion scholars have brought together 14 of Leonard's previously published pieces in *Vernacular Religion: Collected Essays of Leonard Norman Primiano* (2022). Future studies in vernacular Catholicism and vernacular religion will be promoted by awards established in Leonard's memory to be administered by the American Folklore Society Folk Belief and Religious Folklife Section, while other articles and publications in progress at the time of his death are being taken forward by friends and colleagues in Europe and America—so there is more to come!

## References

Bhutia, Kikee Doma. 2022. *Mythic History, Belief Narratives and Vernacular Buddhism among the Lhopos of Sikkim*. Dissertationes folkloristicae Universitatis Tartuensis 32. Tartu: University of Tartu Press.

Bowman, Marion. 2000. 'More of the Same?: Christianity, Vernacular Religion and Alternative Spirituality in Glastonbury'. In *Beyond New Age: Exploring Alternative Spirituality*, edited by Steven Sutcliffe and Marion Bowman, 83–104. Edinburgh: Edinburgh University Press.

Bowman, Marion. 2003-2004. 'Taking Stories Seriously: Vernacular Religion, Contemporary Spirituality and the Myth of Jesus in Glastonbury'. *Temenos: Nordic Journal of Comparative Religion* 39–40: 125–142.

Bowman, Marion. 2004 [1992]. 'Phenomenology, Fieldwork and Folk Religion'. In *Religion: Empirical Studies*. Reprinted with newly written Afterword, edited by Steven Sutcliffe, 3–18. Aldershot: Ashgate.

Bowman, Marion. 2009. 'From Glastonbury to Hungary: Contemporary Integrative Spirituality and Vernacular Religion in Context'. In *Passageways. From Hungarian Ethnography to European Ethnology and Sociocultural Anthropology*, edited by Gábor Vargyas, 195–221. Budapest: L'Harmattan Publishing House.

Bowman, Marion. 2014. 'Vernacular Religion, Contemporary Spirituality and Emergent Identities: Lessons from Lauri Honko'. *Approaching Religion* (Special Issue: *The*

*Legacy of Lauri Honko: Contemporary Conversations*) 4 (1): 101–113. https://www.doria.fi/bitstream/handle/10024/134724/AR_Bowman.pdf?sequence=2&isAllowed=y (accessed November 25, 2021). https://doi.org/10.30664/ar.67542

Bowman, Marion. 2016. 'Crisis, Change and "the Continuous Art of Individual Interpretation and Negotiation": The Aftermath of Clerical Sexual Abuse in Newfoundland'. *Journal of the Irish Society for the Academic Study of Religions* 3: 140–167. https://jisasr.files.wordpress.com/2016/06/crisis-change-and-e28098the-continuous-art-of-individual-interpretation-and-negotiation_-the-aftermath-of-clerical-sexual-abuse-in-newfoundland-pdf1.pdf (accessed November 25, 2021).

Bowman, Marion. 2017. 'From Production to Performance: Candles, Creativity and Connectivity'. In *Materiality and the Study of Religion: The Stuff of the Sacred*, edited by Tim Hutchings and Joanne McKenzie, 35–52. London; New York: Routledge.

Bowman, Marion. 2022. 'IN MEMORIAM: Leonard Norman Primiano (1957–2021)'. *Folklore* 133 (1): 96–100. https://doi.org/10.1080/0015587X.2021.2008143

Bowman, Marion, and Ülo Valk. 2012a. 'Vernacular Religion, Generic Expressions and the Dynamics of Belief: Introduction'. In *Vernacular Religion in Everyday Life: Expressions of Belief*, edited by Marion Bowman and Ülo Valk, 1–19. Sheffield; Bristol, CT: Equinox Publishing.

Bowman, Marion, and Ülo Valk, eds. 2012b. *Vernacular Religion in Everyday Life: Expressions of Belief*. Sheffield; Bristol, CT: Equinox Publishing.

Briscese, Rosangela, and Joseph Sciorra, eds. 2012. *Graces Received: Painted and Metal Ex-Votos from Italy. The Collection of Leonard Norman Primiano*. New York: John D. Calandra Italian American Institute.

Chryssides, George D., and Stephen E. Gregg. 2019. 'Vernacular Christianity'. In *The Bloomsbury Handbook to Studying Christians*, edited by George D. Chryssides and Stephen E. Gregg, 5–16. London: Bloomsbury Academic. https://doi.org/10.5040/9781350043411.ch-002

Chua, Liana. 2009. 'To Know or Not to Know? Practices of Knowledge and Ignorance among Bidayuhs in an "Impurely" Christian World'. *Journal of the Royal Anthropological Institute* 15 (2): 332–348. https://doi.org/10.1111/j.1467-9655.2009.01556.x

Goldstein, Diane E. 2015. 'Vernacular Turns: Narrative, Local Knowledge, and the Changed Context of Folklore'. *Journal of American Folklore* 128 (508): 125–145. https://doi.org/10.5406/jamerfolk.128.508.0125

Hiiemäe, Reet. 2017. 'Destiny, Miracle Healers and Magical Intervention: Vernacular Beliefs on Involuntary Childlessness in Estonia'. *Journal of Ethnology and Folkloristics* 11 (2): 25–50. https://doi.org/10.1515/jef-2017-0012

Honko, Lauri. 2000. 'Text as Process and Practice: The Textualization of Oral Epics'. In *Textualization of Oral Epics*, edited by Lauri Honko, 3–54. Berlin: Mouton de Gruyter. https://doi.org/10.1515/9783110825848

Illman, Ruth, and Mercédesz Czimbalmos. 2020. 'Knowing, Being, and Doing Religion: Introducing an Analytical Model for Researching Vernacular Religion'. *Temenos: Nordic Journal of Comparative Religion* 56 (2): 171–199. https://doi.org/10.33356/temenos.97275

Kaell, Hillary. 2017. 'Seeing the Invisible: Ambient Catholicism on the Side of the Road'. *Journal of the American Academy of Religion* 85 (1): 136–167.

Kapaló, James A., and Kinga Povedák, eds. 2021. *The Secret Police and the Religious Underground*. London; New York: Routledge.

Kivari, Kristel. 2016. *Dowsing as a Link between Natural and Supernatural: Folkloristic Reflections on Water Veins, Earth Radiation and Dowsing Practice*. Dissertationes folkloristicae Universitatis Tartuensis 24. Tartu: University of Tartu Press.

Lassander, Mika T. 2012. 'Grappling with Liquid Modernity: Investigating Post-Secular Religion'. In *Post-Secular Society*, edited by Peter Nynäs, Mika T. Lassander and Terhi Utriainen, 239–267. New Brunswick, NJ: Transaction Publishers. https://doi.org/10.4324/9781315127095-10

Lyngdoh, Margaret. 2016. *Transformation, Tradition, and Lived Realities: Vernacular Belief Worlds of the Khasis of Northeastern India*. Dissertationes folkloristicae Universitatis Tartuensis 23. Tartu: University of Tartu Press.

Magliocco, Sabina. 2018. 'Beyond the Rainbow Bridge: Vernacular Ontologies of Animal Afterlives'. *Journal of Folklore Research: An International Journal of Folklore and Ethnomusicology* 55 (2): 39–67. https://doi.org/10.2979/jfolkrese.55.2.03

Magliocco, Sabina. 2022. 'Leonard Norman Primiano (1957–2021)'. *Journal of American Folklore* 135 (536): 250–251.

Nygaard, Mathias Ephraim. 2019. 'Tomte Stories in Swedish Hälsingland: Place and Vernacular Religion'. *Folklore* 130 (2): 153–74.
https://doi.org/10.1080/0015587X.2018.1556980

Primiano, Leonard Norman. 1985. 'Feminist Christian Songs: Occasions of Vernacular Religious Belief'. *New Jersey Folklore* X: 38–43.

Primiano, Leonard Norman. 1993a. 'Intrinsically Catholic: Vernacular Religion and Philadelphia's "Dignity"'. PhD diss., University of Pennsylvania, Departments of Folklore and Folklife and Religious Studies.

Primiano, Leonard Norman. 1993b. '"I would rather be fixated on the Lord": Women's Religion, Men's Power, and the "Dignity" Problem'. *New York Folklore* XIX: 89–103.

Primiano, Leonard Norman. 1995. 'Vernacular Religion and the Search for Method in Religious Folklife'. *Western Folklore* (Special Issue: *Reflexivity and the Study of Belief*) 54 (1): 37–56. https://doi.org/10.2307/1499910

Primiano, Leonard Norman. 1999. 'Postmodern Sites of Catholic Sacred Materiality'. In *Perspectives on American Religion and Culture*, edited by Peter W. Williams, 187–202. Malden, MA: Blackwell.

Primiano, Leonard Norman. 2001. 'What is Vernacular Catholicism? The "Dignity" Example'. *Acta Ethnographica Hungarica* 46 (1–2): 51–58.
https://doi.org/10.1556/AEthn.46.2001.1-2.6

Primiano, Leonard Norman. 2002. 'Textures of a Religious Life: The Vernacular Religious Art of Sister Ann Ameen'. In *Art and the Religious Impulse*, edited by Eric Michael Mazur, 62–83. Lewisberg, PA: Bucknell University Press.

Primiano, Leonard Norman. 2004. 'Bringing Perfection in These Different Places: Father Divine's Vernacular Architecture of Intention'. *Folklore* 115: 13–26.

Primiano, Leonard Norman. 2007. 'The Vow as Visual Feast: Honoring St. Joseph in Sicilian American Homes'. *Traditiones* 36 (1): 113–125.
https://doi.org/10.3986/Traditio2007360108

Primiano, Leonard Norman. 2009. '"The consciousness of God's presence will keep you well, healthy, happy, and singing": The Tradition of Innovation in the Music of Father Divine's Peace Mission Movement'. In *The New Black Gods: Arthur Huff*

*Fauset and the Study of African American Religions*, edited by Edward E. Curtis IV and Danielle Brune Sigler, 91–115. Indiana: Indiana University Press.

Primiano, Leonard Norman. 2012. 'Afterword—Manifestations of the Religious Vernacular: Ambiguity, Power and Creativity'. In *Vernacular Religion in Everyday Life: Expressions of Belief*, edited by Marion Bowman and Ülo Valk, 382–394. Sheffield; Bristol, CT: Equinox Publishing.

Primiano, Leonard Norman. 2014. '"And as we dine, we sing and praise God": Mother Divine's Theology of Food'. In *Religion, Food, and Eating in North America*, edited by Ben Zeller, Marie Dallam and Nora Rubel, 42–67. New York: Columbia University Press. https://doi.org/10.7312/zell16030-005

Primiano, Leonard Norman. 2015. 'Kitsch'. In *The Routledge Companion to Religion and Popular Culture*, edited by John C. Lyden and Eric Michael Mazur, 281–312. London: Routledge.

Primiano, Leonard Norman. 2016. 'Artifacts of Belief: Holy Cards in Roman Catholic Culture'. In *Experiencing Religion: New Approaches to Personal Religiosity*, edited by Clara Saraiva, Peter Jan Margry, Lionel Obadia, Kinga Povedák and José Mapril, 119–142. Berlin: Lit Verlag.

Primiano, Leonard Norman. 2017. 'Encountering the Female Divine…Literally: Ethnographic Writing about Mother Divine and Father Divine's Peace Mission Movement'. *Antropologicheskiy forum/Forum for Anthropology and Culture* 13: 84–94.

Primiano, Leonard Norman. 2022. *Vernacular Religion: Collected Essays of Leonard Norman Primiano*, edited by Deborah Dash Moore. Foreword by Judith Weisenfeld. New York: New York University Press.

Sadovina, Irina. 2020. *In Search of Vedic Wisdom: Forms of Alternative Spirituality in Contemporary Russia*. Dissertationes folkloristicae Universitatis Tartuensis 28. Tartu: University of Tartu Press.

Saikia, Baburam. 2022. *Contradictions In(side) the Tradition: Lived Religion, Ritual and Change with Reference to Majuli Sattras*. Dissertationes folkloristicae Universitatis Tartuensis 33. Tartu: University of Tartu Press.

Sepp, Tiina. 2014. *Pilgrims' Reflections on the Camino de Santiago and Glastonbury as Expressions of Vernacular Religion: Fieldworker's Perspective*. Dissertationes folkloristicae Universitatis Tartuensis 21. Tartu: University of Tartu Press.

Solovyeva, Alevtina. 2021. *Reawakening Spirits in Post-Socialist Mongolia: Vernacular Theories and Practices*. Dissertationes folkloristicae Universitatis Tartuensis 30. Tartu: University of Tartu Press.

Sutcliffe, Steven, and Marion Bowman. 2000. 'Introduction'. In *Beyond New Age: Exploring Alternative Spirituality*, edited by Steven Sutcliffe and Marion Bowman, 1–13. Edinburgh: Edinburgh University Press.

Valk, Ülo. 2018. 'The Devil and the Spirit World in Nineteenth-Century Estonia: From Christianization to Folklorization'. In *Fairies, Demons, and Nature Spirits: 'Small Gods' at the Margins of Christendom*, edited by Michael Ostling, 213–232. London: Palgrave Macmillan. https://doi.org/10.1057/978-1-137-58520-2_9

Valk, Ülo. 2019a. 'Folk Narrative Genres, Liminality and Epistemological Uncertainty'. In *Contexts of Folklore: Festschrift for Dan Ben-Amos on His Eighty-Fifth Birthday*, edited by Simon J. Bronner and Wolfgang Mieder, 299–308. New York: Peter Lang.

Valk, Ülo. 2019b. 'Shrines, Stones, and Memories: The Entangled Storyworld of a Goddess Temple in Assam'. In *South Asian Folklore in Transition: Crafting New Horizons*, edited by Frank J. Korom and Leah K. Lowthorp, 105–119. London; New York: Routledge; Taylor & Francis Group.

Valk, Ülo. 2021. 'What Are Belief Narratives? An Introduction'. *Narrative Culture* 8 (2): 175–186. https://doi.org/10.13110/narrcult.8.2.0175

Wanless, Claire. 2021. *Individualized Religion: Practitioners and their Communities*. London: Bloomsbury Academic Press. https://doi.org/10.5040/9781350182530

Whitehead, Amy. 2013. *Religious Statues and Personhood: Testing the Role of Materiality*. London; New York: Bloomsbury.

Yoder, Don. 1974. 'Toward a Definition of Folk Religion'. *Western Folklore: Symposium on Folk Religion* 33 (1): 2–15. https://doi.org/10.2307/1498248

# Index

Adler, Margot 396
afterlife 11, 14, 358, 390-3, 406
   in Khasi worldview 343, 345, 347, 350-1, 357-8
agency 1, 119, 311-12, 316-17, 325, 405, 411
altar 84, 121, 274, 290, 299, 300, 311, 322, 326, 328, 330, 331n
ambiguity 2, 4, 9, 33, 49, 65, 190, 209, 239-40, 254, 284, 288, 291, 294, 300, 303, 372, 411
Anastasia movement 11, 47-66
angels 16, 387, 395
   angelic guides 225
Anglicanism, Anglican Church 265, 392-3
   vernacular Anglicanism 408
anthropology, anthropologists 4-5, 56, 214, 264-5, 267, 312, 314-15, 382n, 407
Archangelism 11, 72, 74, 89-90, 92-3
Argüelles, José 168-9
artefact 2, 13, 208, 295, 299-301
Astapova, Anastasiya 10, 407
atheism 91, 397
   atheists 92, 268, 321, 395, 397
authenticity 12-13, 107, 111, 237-8, 242-6, 248-9, 251-3, 270, 280, 286, 322, 407
   individual authenticity 241
   existential authenticity 241, 255
   expressive authenticity 253-6
   national authenticity 39
authority 1-2, 4, 7-8, 13, 15-17, 47-8, 54-8, 62-3, 65-6, 75, 84, 96n, 112-14, 118, 135, 142, 189, 190-2, 197, 202, 208, 210, 221, 230, 231n, 241, 264, 281, 289-90, 309-10, 341, 361-2, 380, 405-9
   aggregate authority 170, 183
   individual authority 180, 183, 329
   institutional authority 10, 125, 136, 386
   relational authority 170, 208
   religious/church authority 13, 270, 288, 329, 358
   textual authority 390-92
   vernacular authority 8, 12, 165, 169-71, 178-86, 208, 284, 287, 294, 303, 385, 389, 391, 405
autoethnography 203

Bailey, Alice 223
Bapa, Jalaram (saint) 11, 101-5, 110, 113-14
Baring, Anne 264, 269
Bauman, Richard 15, 290, 303
beatification 292, 303
Begg, Ean 263-4, 268-9
belief narratives 11, 16, 39, 43, 118, 396-7
belief system 150, 154, 157, 173, 179, 218, 325, 390, 392-3, 412
Bell, Michael Mayerfeld 399-400
Bellah, Robert N. 316-17
bewitchment 16
Bezbaruah, Lakshminath 123, 138n
Bible 86, 108, 173, 225, 227, 319, 340, 389, 394
blessings 103-5, 107-9, 144, 147, 154-5, 160n, 280, 298, 311
blood treaty 154-6, 158, 160n
Bloom, William 225
Boss, Sarah Jane 263
Bourdieu, Pierre 209, 317
Bowman, Marion 13, 295

420  Vernacular Knowledge

Brady, Erika 170, 208
Buddhism 7, 12, 144–8, 151–2, 160n,
  161n, 222, 245, 256n, 331n, 389
  Theravada Buddhism 138n
  Tibetan Buddhism 361
  Vajrayana Buddhism 144–5, 152
Bunyan, John 228
burial
  places 368 (*see also* cemeteries,
    graveyards)
  practices 373–5, 379, 383 (*see also*
    funerals)
  Tibetan sky burial 382
Burkert, Walter 215–18, 222–3, 230, 231n

Campbell, Colin 218–19, 229–30
Campbell, Myles 221, 226–30, 232n
Cappannari, Stephen 267–9
Cashford, Jules 264, 269
Cashman, Ray 35, 313
Catholicism, Catholic Church 35, 226,
  267–8, 277, 279, 286–8, 291–2, 316–17,
  321, 323, 325, 328–9, 331n, 340, 356,
  392
  'ambient Catholicism' 407
  vernacular Catholicism 13, 288, 291–2,
    295–6, 310, 320, 325, 411, 414n
cemetery, cemeteries 299, 302, 305, 306n,
  363, 368, 378–9, 383n (*see also* burial
  places, graveyards)
Charmé, Stuart Z. 242–3, 255
Chiavola Birnbaum, Lucia 264, 269–71
Chichagov, Serafim (= Bishop Serafim)
  75–6, 78
Christianity 5, 7, 14, 51, 72, 151, 192,
  220–1, 223, 265, 269, 327, 340–1, 345,
  348, 356–9n, 389, 391–2, 395, 408
  Khasi Christian Church 356, 358
  vernacular Christianity 13
Church of England 13, 225, 281, 385, 392
commemoration practices 37, 154, 349,
  394
conflict 3, 5, 10, 39, 43, 55, 57, 93, 133,
  136, 147, 149, 156–7, 210, 227, 276–7,
  288, 358, 362, 367, 369, 376, 378, 380
conspiracy theory 7, 9, 34, 55, 181, 184
Cowdell, Paul 14, 408–9
Culeac brothers (Alexandru, Grigore and
  Ion) 89–92

cultic milieu 191, 214, 218–19, 229–30,
  231n
curses 16, 88, 148, 383n

death customs 14, 406
death rituals 144, 339, 349, 351, 355–7
deities 4, 112, 122, 125, 128–9, 144, 148,
  159n, 169, 266–7, 269, 272, 346, 352,
  382n, 393
demonization 357–8
demonology 71, 138n, 362
  demonological narratives 14, 362, 381
  demonological beliefs 14, 406
demons 148, 364–6, 369–71, 373–5,
  379–81, 381n, 382n, 383n
  demonic powers/characteristics 16,
    363–4, 372, 379–81, 381n, 382n
Derné, Steve 112, 114
devils 323, 345, 366, 374, 382n
Dillon, Michele 329
divination 2, 16, 192, 343–4, 367, 371
divinity 70–1, 94–5, 270
Droogers, André 6
Druidry 394–5
Dundes, Alan 217, 229, 231n, 316
Durand-Lefèbvre, Marie 267

ecological spirituality 11, 48, 50
Eliade, Mircea 227–8
Eller, Cynthia 266, 271–2
Enlightenment 2, 5, 190
ethnography 55, 232n, 238–9, 246, 310,
  316, 329, 331n, 340, 346, 352, 386,
  397–9, 408
ethnology, ethnologists 321, 330, 409, 412
evil eye 305, 306n, 323–4, 383

Fabbrini, Marco 314, 316
Faifer, Ricardo 293
Fedele, Anna 265, 271, 279
feminism, feminists 13, 223, 243, 264–8,
  271–4, 279–80, 408
folk beliefs 1, 12, 167, 208, 315, 381n
folk religion 1–2, 13, 239, 277, 280, 305,
  314–17, 325, 410, 412–13
folklore (as a concept) 2–4, 57, 135, 189,
  310, 362
folklore studies, folkloristics, folklorists
  2, 8, 27, 56, 124, 202, 207–8, 214, 217,

310–11, 313–18, 321–2, 324, 329–30, 357, 363, 398–9, 409–10, 412, 414*n*
Foucault, Michel 7
Freud, Sigmund 314, 399
funerals (*see also* burial)
   among Khasi 343–5, 347–51
   Mongolian 367–9, 371, 374–5, 379–80, 382*n*, 383*n*

genres 9–10, 15, 26, 33, 114, 135, 207, 219–20, 247, 371, 375, 391, 398, 402*n*
ghosts 10, 14, 362, 364, 370, 386–7, 389–95, 397–401*n*, 408
Gil Núñez, Antonio (= Gauchito Gil) 13, 284–307*n*
Glassie, Henry 313, 322, 331*n*
goddess worship 117–19, 129, 266
   UK goddess movement 223, 231*n*
Goldish, Matt 243, 246
Goswami, Neelakshi 124, 130, 133
grand narrative 38, 272
graves 36, 301, 306*n*, 368, 375
graveyards 35, 37, 42 (*see also* burial places, cemeteries)
Graziano, Frank 289–90, 293, 302, 306*n*, 307*n*
Green, Martin 51
Gurdon, Philip Richard Thorndagh 340, 346–7, 350, 352

hagiography 11, 73, 81, 102–4, 107–8, 110, 114
Hamilton-Parker, Craig 389
Harkless, Necia 273–4
Hasidism 244–5, 247–8, 253
   Hasidic Judaism 238
haunted places 363–4, 368, 372
hauntology 49, 399
healing 11, 16, 49, 78, 81, 92, 101, 103–4, 111, 196–8, 203, 207, 211*n*, 271, 278, 324–5, 345, 371
Heelas, Paul 47, 50
Hegarty, James 102–3
Hinduism 7, 101–2, 106, 114, 117, 141, 154, 245, 331*n*, 389
   vernacular Hinduism 102
Holy Spirit 70, 78–80, 82, 90, 93–4, 228
Honko, Lauri 135
Howard, Robert Glenn 8, 12, 208, 294, 314, 385, 387, 389, 406

Howard, Roland 224
Hoyningen-Huene, Paul 6, 17
humour studies 56–8
Humphrey, Caroline 41, 374
Hunter, Jack 388

icons 11, 70–1, 74, 79–80, 84–7, 90–2, 95, 276, 407
   iconography, iconographic tradition 73, 80, 82, 86, 95, 289, 301–2
identity 3, 6, 34–5, 41–2, 56, 76, 79, 86, 89, 117, 144, 153–4, 202, 241, 243, 274, 289, 293, 358, 362, 369, 409
   national/ethnic identity 10, 12, 28–9, 31–2, 37, 43, 158, 273
   racial identity 272
   religious identity 84, 103, 136, 220, 255, 298, 310, 317, 321, 329
Illman, Ruth 12–13, 407
Inochentism 11, 71–2, 74, 82–4, 89, 94
Islam 7, 103, 232*n*, 391

Jewish Renewal movement 247–8, 252
Jha, Pranab Kumar 141
Jones, Kathy 221–6, 229–31*n*
Judaism 7, 78, 243, 247, 251–2, 255–6*n*, 391
   Hasidic Judaism 238 (*see also* Hasidism)
Jung, Carl Gustav 218, 227, 264, 268–9, 279

Kabbalah 237–8, 243–6, 256*n*
   vernacular Kabbalah 243
Kalinowski, Kastuś 26, 32
Kapaló, James 11, 314, 316, 407
Karatkevich, Uladzimir 10, 26–28, 30–33, 39–43
Kivari, Kristel 12, 408
Kuprin, Alexander 52

*lamas* 150, 365, 367–8, 370, 373–4, 376–7, 369, 382*n*
Landau, Rom 219, 221
Landman, Melanie 13, 408
Latour, Bruno 1, 4
legends 9–11, 15, 30, 33, 39–43, 122, 133, 135–6, 140, 145, 147–53, 155, 157, 191, 205, 207–9, 286, 289, 373, 395–6, 398–9, 402*n*, 406–7
   Missing Book legend 28–35, 38–40, 42

## 422   Vernacular Knowledge

Leonard, Alison 221–2
Lepcha, Reep Pandi 12, 406
Levitzki, Feodosie 71
Levizor, Ioan (= Inochentie of Balta) 71–82, 84–9, 93–6, 96n, 97n
lightning 82, 206–7, 347, 354
Lindholm, Charles 241, 255
liturgy 75, 84–5, 247–8, 252–3, 256, 279, 316, 322
lived religion 239, 264–5, 275, 281, 284, 310, 312, 315, 317–18, 325, 357, 385, 410 (*see also* vernacular religion)
Losada, Isabel 221, 223–6, 229–30, 232n
loss of enchantment 51
Lukashenka, Alyaksandr 29–30, 32, 34–5, 40–3
Lynch, Gordon 266
Lyngdoh, Margaret 14, 406

Madhavadeva 11, 119–26, 128–37, 138n
magic 2, 9–10, 118, 136, 146, 204, 324–5, 328, 331n, 396
Magliocco, Sabina 170, 315, 324–5, 331n
Maldzis, Adam 28, 30, 36
Martsinovich, Dzyanis 31
material culture 13–14, 74, 84, 286, 288, 290, 292, 295–6, 298, 300, 305, 311, 316, 321–3, 328, 410–11, 413
Mawrie, H. Onderson 343
Mayan calendar 12, 165, 167–70, 182
Mayskiy, Ivan 378–9
McGuire, Meredith 276, 315, 330
McKinney Johnson, Eloise 273
Megre, Vladimir 11, 48–9, 52, 55, 60, 62, 64, 67n, 406
memorates 101, 406
miracles 11, 81, 101, 103–11, 113, 120, 198, 289–90, 292
missions, missionaries 53, 229, 293
    Baptist missions 359n
    Inochentist missions 78–9, 85
    Khasi Christian Church missions 358
    Orthodox missions 74, 77, 80
    Welsh Calvinistic missions 340
Morgan, David 294, 299
Morreall, John 56–7
Moss, Leonard 267–9
Mullard, Saul 155, 160n
mysticism 184, 196, 238, 245–6

Christian mysticism 245
Jewish mysticism 237–8, 242–6, 253–5, 256n
Russian mysticism 94
mythology 14, 152, 160, 279, 363, 375, 391, 394–5
myths 25, 35, 39, 143, 145, 269, 340, 387, 390–2, 395–6, 398, 406

nature spirits 366, 369, 373–80, 383n
neo-Vaishnavism 117, 120, 128, 138
New Age 47, 50–1, 53, 66, 190, 222, 232n, 264
Nonglait, G. Badaiasuklang L. 352, 354
Novetzke, Christian Lee 102, 107

Ochs, Vanessa 243, 247, 254
Oleszkiewicz-Peralba, Malgorzata 264, 273–5
oral history 11, 122, 132–3, 136
Oring, Elliott 56, 67n, 191
Orsi, Robert A. 275, 295, 331n
Orthodoxy, Orthodox Church 11, 55, 71–4, 77, 79, 83–6, 94
    Greek Orthodoxy 220
    Romanian Orthodox Church 80, 83–4
    Russian Orthodox Church 53–4, 75, 94
Otto, Rudolph 227
Oushakine, Serguei 38–41

paranormal 48, 191, 195, 197, 202, 207–9
parody 11, 47–8, 59, 63, 65, 406
Partridge, Christopher 50
Pauwels, Heidi 102–3
Pazniak, Zianon 29, 35–6
Peck, Andrew 8
personal experience narrative 9, 15
Picknett, Lynn 264, 269
pilgrimage 13, 35, 83, 96n, 118, 120, 128, 265, 270–1, 274, 276–7, 279, 281, 295–6, 298–300
place-lore 205, 363
poltergeists 196, 200
Pope Francis 286, 292–3, 300, 302, 327
Popovschi, Nicolae 74, 78–80
post-secular turn 247
Presbyterianism, Presbyterian Church 221, 226, 345, 356

Primiano, Leonard Norman 2, 13, 16–17, 51, 53, 239–40, 254, 265, 270, 272, 287–8, 293–4, 303, 357, 385–6, 391, 406–13, 414n
prophecy 12, 35, 71, 78, 145, 152, 156, 165–7, 169, 173, 186
Propp, Vladimir 12, 215–17, 222, 229–30
Puccini, Giacomo 311–12, 330n, 413

Qur'an 108, 391

Rajdev, Saubhagyachand 104, 107–8, 110–12, 114n
Raval, Kirtibhai Mansukhbhai 110, 112
Redd, Danita 273
Reformation 170, 226, 276–7
reincarnation 94, 366–7, 369–70, 375, 383n
relics 10, 36, 71, 103, 118, 129, 132, 319
religious studies, study of religions 4–5, 8, 314–15, 318, 321, 324, 331n, 409–10, 412–13
Ries, Nancy 33–4
Rinehart, Robin 102, 106
rites 159n, 339, 343, 349, 351–2, 364, 366, 383n
Robertson Smith, William 395–6
Rodriguez, Jeanette 274–5

sacrifice 87, 117, 119, 353
  human sacrifice 352, 359n, 375
Sadovina, Irina 10, 406
Saillens, Emile 267
sanctuaries 274, 299, 320, 322, 330
Scholem, Gershom 237–8, 244
Sciorra, Joseph 326
Scott, James 34, 56, 72
seekership 12, 214, 218–20, 229–31, 407
  spiritual seeking and seekers 11–12, 63, 66, 214–16, 218–21, 229–32n, 245, 247, 255, 408
shamans 144, 159n, 203–4, 365, 373–4, 376, 382n
  *bongthings* 146, 149, 159n
  *muns* 144, 149, 159n
Shampliang, U. Sterian 352
Shankaradeva 117–21, 123–4, 128–9, 136, 138n
Shukla, Pravina 313, 331n

Simpson, Leanne Betasamosake 161n
sin 71, 96n, 340, 342, 378
sociology of religion 218, 312, 316–17, 329–30
Solovyeva, Alevtina 14, 406
souls (of the deceased) 144, 159n, 290, 293, 345–6, 351, 356–7, 366–75, 380–1, 382n, 383n, 392
Spiritualism 190, 196, 387–90, 408
Stalin, Joseph 26, 33, 41
Starbird, Margaret 264, 270
storyrealm 9–10
Sunstein, Cass 172
superstitions 1–2, 7, 362
Sutcliffe, Steven 12, 230, 407

taboo 342–3, 375
threshold 103–4
Tolstoy, Leo 51–2
Torrance, Robert M. 217–18, 231n
truth 5–7, 9–11, 15, 43, 47, 62, 66, 73–4, 80, 88, 102, 117, 124, 130–6, 207–8, 219, 227, 229, 231, 232n, 239, 394, 405

Valk, Ülo 11, 406, 412
variation/variants 9, 12, 80, 85, 117, 123, 132–3, 135–6, 142, 148, 165, 286, 289, 349, 357, 366, 373, 382n, 386, 388, 390, 393, 396
vernacular belief 2, 7, 10, 51, 53, 145, 149, 157, 270, 327, 330, 362, 366–7, 369, 375, 380, 393, 400, 406, 413
vernacular religion (as a concept and methodology) 2, 13, 16, 189, 238–40, 242, 246, 253–4, 264–5, 270, 284, 286, 288, 290, 293–4, 303, 310–18, 325, 330, 357, 385, 405–14 (*see also* lived religion)

Waller, Gary 277
Weibel, Deana 271–2, 275
Weissler, Chava 243, 255
Wood, Martin 11, 406

Yoder, Don 1, 314–15, 325, 410
Yurchak, Alexei 33, 65

Zini, Julian 293

www.ingramcontent.com/pod-product-compliance
Lightning Source LLC
Chambersburg PA
CBHW071435300426
44114CB00013B/1445